I0763233

The Orphan of Zhao
AND OTHER Yuan Plays

TRANSLATIONS FROM THE ASIAN CLASSICS

The Orphan of Zhao

AND OTHER Yuan Plays

THE
EARLIEST
KNOWN
VERSIONS

TRANSLATED & INTRODUCED BY

STEPHEN H. WEST
AND WILT L. IDEMA

COLUMBIA UNIVERSITY PRESS NEW YORK

Columbia University Press
Publishers Since 1893
New York Chichester, West Sussex
cup.columbia.edu

Columbia University Press wishes to express its appreciation for assistance given by the Pushkin Fund toward the cost of publishing this book.

♾

Library of Congress Cataloging-in-Publication Data
The orphan of Zhao and other Yuan plays : the earliest known versions / translated and introduced by Stephen H. West and Wilt L. Idema.
pages cm
Includes bibliographical references.
ISBN 978-0-231-16854-0 (cloth)—ISBN 978-0-231-53810-7 (electronic)
1. Chinese drama—Yuan dynasty, 1260-1368—Translations into English. I. West, Stephen H. editor of compilation. II. Idema, W. L. (Wilt L.) editor of compilation.
PL2658.E5O77 2014
895.12'4408—dc23
2013048900

Cover image: *The Captivity of Cai Wenji*, 14th–15th century. Freer Gallery of Art, Smithsonian Institution, USA. Gift of Charles Lang Freer. Bridgeman Art Library.
Cover and book design: Lisa Hamm

CONTENTS

ACKNOWLEDGMENTS

We would particularly like to acknowledge David Rolston's careful and thorough reading of the manuscript. His suggestions have made this a far better book. We would like to thank the following for their help in preparing the manuscript for publication: Chang Wenbo, Kimberly Harui, and Lucas Wolf; and the following for their help in the production: Jennifer Crewe and Kathryn Schell of Columbia University Press. A fellowship sponsored by the School of Historical Studies, Institute of Advanced Study, Princeton, and the National Endowment for the Humanities allowed Stephen West to work on completing the manuscript.

Stephen H. West, Tempe, Arizona, USA
Wilt L. Idema, Leiden, The Netherlands

A NOTE TO THE READER

We present in this volume seven Yuan *zaju* plays based on the earliest editions available. These printed versions date from the period 1250–1400 when these plays were performed in the fashionable urban theaters of the time. We have selected dramas that have a high level of literary value and represent a typical range of themes found in early urban theater such as revenge, career success and failure, domestic comedy, filial piety, religious conversion, usurpation, and negotiations between the human and spirit worlds, particularly the powerful deities of Mount Tai. Not all these scripts remained in the repertoire when *zaju* was adopted as court theater by the Ming dynasty (1368–1644), the main source of surviving *zaju* of the preceding Mongol Yuan dynasty (1260–1368), and not all the plays that were performed at the imperial palace were printed by literati editors in the last decades of the Ming when plays were edited for reading. These early scripts therefore are different in provenance, presentation, and audience from the later recensions of *zaju* texts of the last decades of the Ming. These later recensions, being prepared for educated readers and being more complete in their presentation, offer a fuller read because they have complete dialogue and may incorporate virtuoso texts of other genres into their written body; these later editions also tend to use a language that has been edited to be reminiscent of the high literature of China. As we explain below, it is these later editions that have been considered the canon of early drama from the seventeenth century onward. As such, they have served as the main source of Western-language translations of early Chinese drama until today.

But we would like to take the reader into a different realm, where drama is more closely related to its actual performance and to the pressures of a viewing audience, who must find in those plays reflections (hyperbolic as they may be) of their own lives. We do not claim that the plays we present here are "better reads" or of higher literary quality than the later literati editions, but we hold firm to the belief that literary texts are first and foremost documents that are subsumed by the society and culture from which they stem and which they represent. And the urban and popular world of the early theater differs dramatically from that of the imperial palace or the literati studio of one, two, or even three centuries later.

This work is presented with the goal of bringing a portion of that early theatrical world to life, valid in its own right. Part of the impulse is to provide a corrective for and a comparison with the overwhelming weight of the high tradition, but we are primarily concerned with trying to represent the qualities that made these dramas popular enough in their own day to be committed to print for mass circulation. In cases where it is possible, we have also provided later editions of these texts from the imperial court or the scholar's studio to allow the reader to assess not only the differences as literature but also the differences in the mental and social worlds they represent.

Some background will be helpful to first-time readers of early Chinese drama, and we point the reader to the preface of our prior work, *Monks, Bandits, Lovers, and Immortals*, where we have discussed the historical background, staging, acting troupes, and formal features of early northern and southern drama.

TABLE OF DYNASTIES

SHANG	ca. 1460–1045 BC
ZHOU	1045–256 BC
Western Zhou	1111–771 BC
Eastern Zhou	770–256 BC
Spring and Autumn	722–421 BC
Warring States	480–221 BC
QIN	221–207 BC
HAN	202 BC–AD 220
Western Han	202 BC–AD 9
Eastern Han	25–220
THREE KINGDOMS	
Wei	220–265
Wu	220–280
Shu-Han	221–263
WESTERN JIN	266–316
EASTERN JIN	317–420
NORTHERN AND SOUTHERN DYNASTIES	386–589
Northern	386–581
Northern Wei	386–534
Eastern Wei	534–550
Northern Qi	550–577
Western Wei	535–557
Northern Zhou	557–581
Southern	420–589

Song	420–479
Qi	479–502
Liang	502–557
Chen	557–589
SUI	581–618
TANG	618–907
FIVE DYNASTIES	907–960
Later Liang	907–923
Later Tang	923–936
Later Jin	936–947
Later Han	947–950
Later Zhou	951–960
SONG	960–1279
Northern Song	960–1127
Southern Song	1127–1279
LIAO	916–1125
JIN	1115–1234
YUAN	1260–1368
MING	1368–1644
QING	1644–1911

The Orphan of Zhao
AND OTHER Yuan Plays

Introduction

As a mode of performance, drama has a history of at least two millennia in China, but it first emerges as a literary art in the second part of the thirteenth century with the rise of miscellaneous comedy (*zaju* 雜劇) or northern drama (*beiqu* 北曲) as a new genre.[1] This was a form of musical drama that required one actor, playing the lead male or female character, to sing four suites (one per act) of eight to twenty songs. In some cases the metrical complexities of these songs might have been beyond the power of improvisation of the average actor or actress and required the intervention of an author who conceived of the play as a whole and drafted the text of the songs in the context of each linked scene. While thirty early *zaju* have been preserved in editions from the fourteenth century, the large majority of the plays from this period has been preserved in manuscript or printed editions from two or more centuries later. These later manuscripts derived first of all from Ming-dynasty (1368–1644) court agencies in charge of dramatic performances and often have been heavily edited to make them suitable for performance in front of the emperor. With a few notable exceptions, later printed versions were based primarily on these palace manuscripts but were once again edited in order to make them suitable reading matter for highly educated literati. The most popular of these printed anthologies was *A Selection of Yuan Plays* (*Yuanqu xuan* 元曲選), published in 1615–1616, which provided beautifully illustrated and nicely printed versions of one hundred *zaju*; in his two prefaces to the anthology the editor, Zang Maoxun 臧懋循 (d. 1621), prided himself on the frequent and extensive changes he had introduced in each of these plays. Zang's anthology represents a culmination of the printing of *zaju* anthologies, a canonization of format that provided full stage directions and dialogues for all roles. Educated in drama by reading this anthology, many modern scholars have failed to comprehend that the shape of the earlier fourteenth-century editions was determined by their use as role texts[2] and therefore do not demonstrate the same fully articulated format as later editions. As a result these scholars describe the fourteenth-century editions as incomplete or defective, and the conclusions they reach in their research on "Yuan drama"—based on what are clearly Ming texts—are often anachronistic. It should be obvious that if we want to study the earliest phase of Chinese dramatic literature and its subsequent development, we must begin with the earliest preserved texts. If we indeed base our research on these fourteenth-century editions, we encounter a world of raw power and vitality, high passion and bloody revenge. If we then compare the plays in these earliest editions with the manuscript and printed versions of the late Ming, we find that these elements have been considerably toned down in these later editions if not covered completely by a thick veneer of conventional Confucianism.[3]

In this volume we provide translations of seven plays in their fourteenth-century editions. In four of the seven cases we accompany that translation with a rendition of the same play in either a Ming palace manuscript or a late Ming printed edition. While in some cases the differences between versions are seemingly minor, in others they are extensive; but in each of these four cases these differences are substantial enough to speak of the later editions as completely new plays. Our first criterion in selection of these seven Yuan editions has been their intrinsic quality. We have also taken into account to what extent they would make good reading despite their nature as a role text (some texts, not translated here, make for very difficult reading because we do not understand the story they dramatize very well). We have made every effort to provide a representative selection that does justice to the thematic variety within the genre but have not included translations of Yuan editions that we have published earlier.[4] The seven Yuan dramas and the four Ming rewrites we include are meant to provide a comparative body of texts through which students and scholars of drama can trace the changes in plot, characterization, style, and meaning that a single story can go through in a process of change and adaptation over a period of three hundred years. As we have mentioned elsewhere,[5] this is a necessary step in understanding the social and cultural world from which each stratum of these texts derives and to whom they were addressed.

The seven plays in fourteenth-century editions and the later Ming rewrites we have selected are as follows:

1. Yuan edition: *The Orphan of Zhao* 趙氏孤兒
   Ming edition: *The Orphan of Zhao Greatly Wreaks Revenge* 趙氏孤兒大報仇 (*A Selection of Yuan Plays* version)
2. *Huo Guang Remonstrates as a Ghost* 霍光鬼諫
3. Yuan edition: *Xue Rengui Returns Home Clad in Brocade* 薛仁貴衣錦還鄉
   Ming edition: *Xue Rengui Returns Home in Glory* 薛仁貴榮歸故里 (*A Selection of Yuan Plays* version)
4. *Chen Jiqing Is Enlightened to the Way on a Bamboo-Leaf Boat* 陳季卿悟道竹葉舟
   Ming edition: *Chen Jiqing Mistakenly Boards a Bamboo-Leaf Boat* 陳季卿誤竹葉舟 (*A Selection of Yuan Plays* version)

5. *Tippler Zhao Yuan Encounters the Prior Emperor* 好酒趙元遇上皇
   Ming edition: *Tippler Zhao Yuan Encounters the Prior Emperor* (Yu Xiaogu manuscript)
6. *The Affair of the Eastern Window Exposed* 東窗事犯
7. *Little Butcher Zhang Immolates the Child to Save the Mother* 焚兒救母

The seven texts, which we here designate as the "Yuan printings" or "Yuan texts," are all four-act music dramas in which each act has as its core a suite of arias (*taoshu* 套數) sung to one of nine musical modes (*gongdiao* 宮調) and utilizing a single rhyme throughout one act. Within a single play, each of the four suites utilizes a separate mode, a more or less standard arrangement of arias for that mode, and all songs are assigned to a single performer, either a male or female lead. The majority of these Yuan printings provide only the texts of the arias and minimal stage directions (*guanmu* 關目) that may include some summary dialogue for the male or female lead; stage directions for other actors in the play—if given at all—tend to be limited to prompts to tell the male or female lead when to act, speak, or sing. Only plays printed from the early fifteenth century onward include fully written-out stage directions, rhymed poems, and dialogue (*binbai* 賓白) for every actor.

THE *THIRTY MISCELLANEOUS COMEDIES PRINTED IN THE YUAN* AND THEIR TRANSMISSION

Zaju, performed by a small troupe of actors, is part of a large body of oral performance genres that gained popularity in the Song and Yuan eras. Several of these narrative forms, including the performance ballads in all keys and modes (*zhugongdiao* 諸宮調), were a form of prosimetric literature (*shuochang wenxue* 說唱文學 or *jiangchang wenxue* 講唱文學) that used almost the same song forms as later drama (the *qu* 曲) and were sung by a single narrator.[6] Usually only one actor or actress sings onstage in *zaju*, which may be a borrowing from this type of oral narrative. Twenty-seven of the Yuan printings are clearly recognizable from their stage directions as role scripts for the male or female lead of a performing troupe,[7] while three editions provide us with only the texts of the songs.

The woodblocks from which these plays were printed appear to have been produced during the middle to late fourteenth century (that is, from the second part of the Yuan dynasty to the first decades of the Ming). We have no way of identifying the printing date of the editions, nor do we have any supporting historical evidence of the existence of such scripts before this time. A few of the thirty texts appear to have been printed in Dadu 大都 (modern Beijing),[8] the capital of the Yuan, but most were produced in Hangzhou, the Yuan administrative center for the conquered former territory of the Southern Song dynasty. While some texts can be grouped together because of shared features of layout, each of the thirty plays appears to have been printed individually.

These thirty independent editions of Yuan northern drama are now known collectively as *Thirty Miscellaneous Comedies Printed in the Yuan* (*Yuankan zaju sanshi zhong* 元刊雜劇三十種), a name given them by the pioneering modern drama scholar Wang Guowei 王國維 (1877–1927) in his preface to the 1924 Shanghai reproduction of a recutting and reprinting of the plays by Kyoto University in 1914. Before this, they were known as *New and Old Miscellaneous Comedies Printed in the Yuan* (*Yuankan gujin zaju* 元刊古今雜劇), a name bestowed on them by the renowned book collector Huang Pilie 黃丕烈 (1763–1825), who at one time owned these texts. In a postscript he wrote to the collection he remarked that he purchased these texts, along with many other rare editions, from the Dipping In for a First Taste Studio (Shiyintang 試飲堂) of Gu Tingyu 顧聽玉 (ca. 1800) located in Suzhou.[9] Huang acquired the plays in two different sets. The first was a group of twenty-five plays, for which he compiled the following list of contents, separating the publication information from the title of the play:

Fascicle 1: Five Plays (五種共一冊)

Newly Printed in Old Hangzhou, a Full Text with Plot Prompts 古杭新刊關目的本
Li Taibai Is Banished to Yelang 李太白貶夜郎
Newly Printed with Plot Prompts 新刊關目
Yan Ziling Drops His Hook at Seven-Mile Rapids 嚴子陵垂釣七里灘
Newly Compiled in Dadu 大都新編
King Zhao of Chu: The Most Distant Relative Goes Overboard 楚昭王疏者下船
Newly Printed in Old Hangzhou, a Full Text 古杭新刊的本
Yuchi Gong Wrests the Spear Away Three Times 尉遲恭三奪槊
Newly Printed in Old Hangzhou, a Full Text with Plot Prompts 古杭新刊的本關目
In Wind and Moon in the Courtyard of Purple Clouds 風月紫雲亭

Fascicle 2: Six Plays (六種共一冊)

Newly Compiled in Dadu 大都新編
In a Dream Guan and Zhang, a Pair, Rush to Western Shu 關張雙赴西蜀夢
Newly Printed with Plot Prompts 新刊關目
A Clever Wench Sports in the Wind and Moonlight 詐妮子調風月
Newly Printed, a Full Text 新刊的本
On Taihua Mountain Chen Tuan Rests with Easy Mind 太華山陳摶高臥
○○○○
The Orphan of Zhao 趙氏孤兒
Newly Printed, a Full Text [Plot Prompts Complete] 新刊的本[關目全]
Xue Rengui Returns Home Clad in Brocade 薛仁貴衣錦還鄉
Newly Printed in Old Hangzhou with Plot Prompts 古杭新刊關目
Aiding King Cheng the Duke of Zhou Acts as Regent 輔成王周公攝政

Fascicle 3: Three Plays (三種共一冊)

Newly Printed in Dadu with Plot Prompts, a Complete Edition 大都新栞關目的本
The Affair of the Eastern Window Exposed 東窗事犯
Newly Printed in Old Hangzhou, a Full Text 古杭新刊的本
Huo Guang Remonstrates as a Ghost 霍光鬼諫
Newly Printed with Plot Prompts 新刊關目
Zhang Ding Cleverly Investigates the Moheluo Doll 張鼎智勘磨合羅

Fascicle 4: Four Plays (四種共一冊)

Newly Printed in Old Hangzhou with Plot Prompts, a Full Text 古杭新刊關目的本
Great King Guan and the Single Sword Meeting 關大王單刀會
Newly Compiled with Plot Prompts 新編關目
Duke Wen of Jin Immolates Jie Zi Tui 晉文公火燒介子推
Newly Printed with Plot Prompts 新刊關目
Ma Danyang Thrice Converts Crazy Ren 馬丹陽三度任風子
Newly Printed with Plot Prompts 新刊關目
A Beauty Pining in Her Boudoir: Praying to the Moon 閨怨佳人拜月亭

Fascicle 5: Four Plays (四種共一冊)

Newly Printed with Plot Prompts Complete 新刊關目全
Xiao He Pursues Han Xin 蕭何追韓信
Newly Compiled in Dadu with Plot Prompts 大都新編關目
A Noble's Grandson: Story of the Undershirt 公孫汗衫記
Newly Printed with Plot Prompts 新刊關目
A Slave to Money Buys a Creditor as His Enemy 看錢奴買冤家債主
Newly Printed with Plot Prompts 新刊關目
The Exalted Emperor of Han Washes His Feet to Anger Ying Bu 漢高皇濯足氣英布

Fascicle 6: Three Plays (三種共一冊)

Newly Printed with Plot Prompts 新刊關目
*Tippler Zhao Yuan Encounters the Prior Emperor*好酒趙元遇上皇
Newly Printed with Plot Prompts 新刊關目
*Chen Jiqing Is Enlightened to the Way on a Bamboo-Leaf Boat*陳季卿悟道竹葉舟
Newly Printed with Plot Prompts 新刊關目
Zhuge Liang Burns the Stores at Bowang 諸葛亮博望燒屯

The above twenty-five specimens were originally bound in three fascicles; I rebound them in six fascicles.[10]

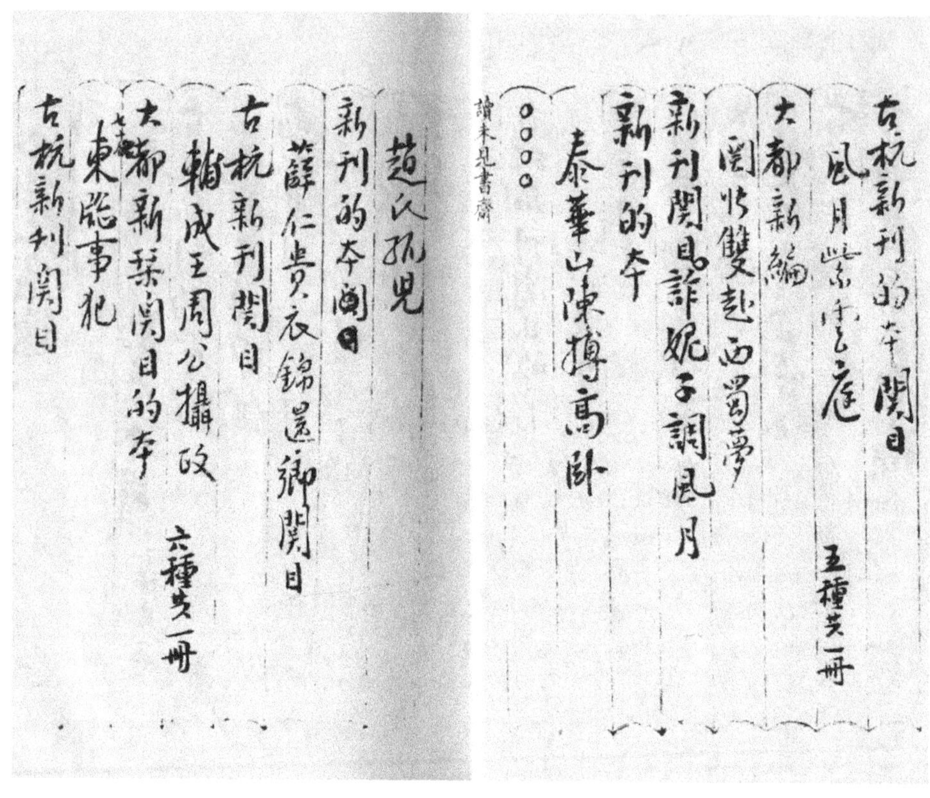
古杭新刊的本關目
風月紫雲庭
五種共一冊
大都新編
關張雙赴西蜀夢
新刊關目詐妮子調風月
新刊的本
泰華山陳摶高臥
讀未見書齋
趙氏孤兒
新刊的本關目
薛仁貴衣錦還鄉
古杭新刊關目
輔成王周公攝政
六種共一冊
大都新栞關目的本
東窗事犯
古杭新刊關目

FIGURE 1 Pages 1b–2a of Huang Pilie's list of twenty-five *Yuankan* editions

Huang Pilie acquired a second batch of five plays, which he lists in a different format. For the first twenty-five, he separated the title of the play from the advertising blurb, replicated in the translation above by the indented lines (see fig. 1). The second group of five is arranged differently. The list is broken into two sections: the first four titles are listed under the enigmatic rubric "Tenth Row of Yuan Print Editions" (Yuankan Shihang 元刊十行), and the fifth title is listed under the heading "Sixteenth Row of Yuan Print Editions" (Yuankan Shiliu Hang 元刊十六行). These may indicate the place the texts held within his total collection of all Yuan printed editions, of which he had many. Furthermore, instead of separating the advertising blurb from the main title (see fig. 2), he wrote them all in the same line:

Tenth Row of Yuan Print Editions

Fascicle 1: Two Plays (二種一冊)

Newly Printed: *Friends in Life and Death: Fan, Zhang, Chicken, and Millet* 新刊死生交范張雞黍

Newly Compiled: *Clerk Yue Avails Himself of Iron Crutch Li to Return from the Dead* 新編岳孔目借鐵拐李還魂

Fascicle 2: Three Plays (三種共一冊)

Newly Compiled, a Complete Edition with Plot Prompts: *Zhang Qian Kills the Wife Instead* 新編足本關目張千替殺妻

Newly Printed in Old Hangzhou: *Little Butcher Zhang Immolates His Child to Save His Mother* 古杭新刊小張屠焚兒救母

Newly Printed True Edition: *Dispersing Family Wealth Heaven Grants a Son Born in Old Age* 新刊的本散家財天賜老生兒

The above were originally bound in one fascicle; I rebound them in two fascicles.[11]

We have no way of determining how these two lists were constituted. It is clear that Huang acquired these five plays at the same time, bound in two fascicles.[12] It is unclear whether he then rebound them in the same order as in their original binding or if he changed that order. They might have been rebound in thinner volumes for easier reading. Or, since the texts were stored in wooden boxes to be kept on shelves, they may have been rebound to make storage easier. One thing seems clear: the order of the plays is completely random.

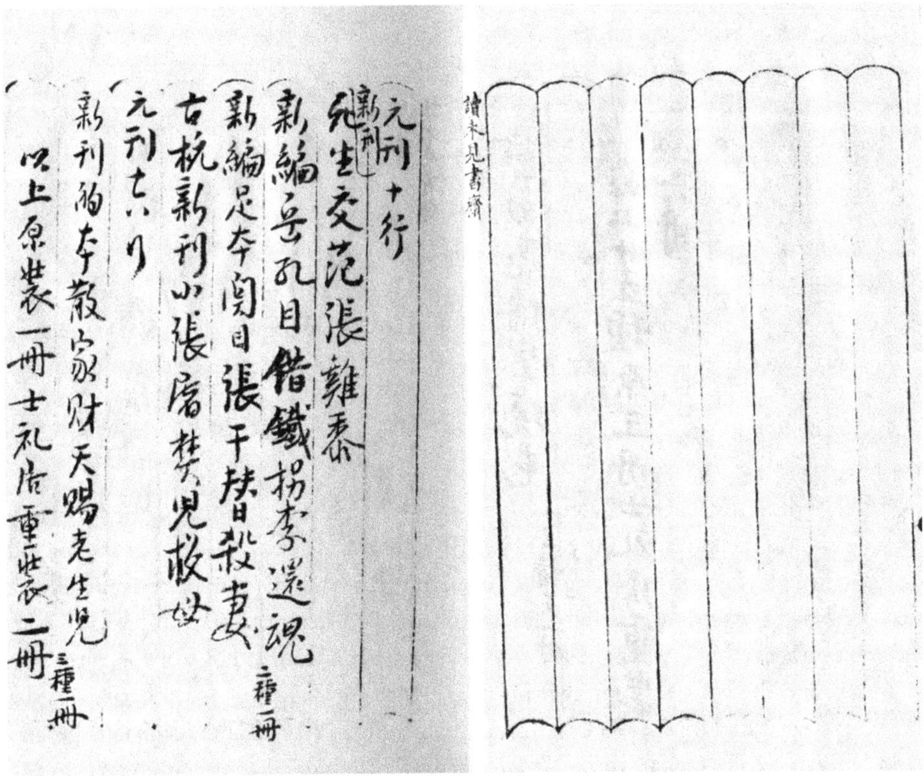

FIGURE 2 Huang Pilie's list of five *Yuankan* editions

While this is the earliest historical reference to the texts we now possess, we have information on their earlier existence based on their use in the eighteenth century to collate later Ming-dynasty print and manuscript editions. Since Iwaki Hideo published his article on the textual history of the *Yuankan zaju sanshi zhong* in 1961, it has been accepted that these thirty plays were once in the library of Li Kaixian 李開先 (1502–1568), a mid-Ming bibliophile, dramatist, poet, and critic.[13] Iwaki reached his conclusion on the basis of the notes of He Huang 何煌 (ca. 1680–1740), who had collated several Yuan texts against later *zaju* editions, both printed and manuscript. In the four instances in which He Huang used a Yuan edition (not necessarily the ones we have today), he has left the following colophons:

1. *The Single Sword Meeting* [collation of a Yuan print edition and an early Ming manuscript]:[14] *Newly Printed in Old Hangzhou, a Complete Edition: The Great King Guan and the Single Sword Meeting.* "Used a Yuan print edition for collation on the fourteenth day of the eighth month, the *yisi* year of the Yongzheng reign [September 20, 1725]" 雍正乙巳八月十日用元刻本校.[15]
2. *Zhang Ding Cleverly Investigates the Moheluo Doll* [*Gu mingjia* ed.]. "I have finished collating a Yuan print edition formerly held by Li Zhonglu [Kaixian]. I have abandoned Qingchang's [that is, Zhao Qimei] collation because it is wrong. Zhongzi [that is, He Huang]. The twenty-first day of the eighth month, the *yisi* year of the Yongzheng reign [September 27, 1725]" 用李中麓所藏元槧本校訖了。清常一校為枉廢也。仲子。雍正乙巳八月二十一日.[16]
3. *A Slave to Money Buys a Creditor as His Enemy* 看錢奴買冤家債主 [*Xijizi* ed.]. "Used a Yuan print edition to collate and correct the text by lamplight on the twenty-sixth day of the eighth month, the *yisi* year of the Yongzheng reign [October 2, 1725], Zhongzi" 雍正乙巳八月廿六日燈下用元刻校勘 仲子.[17]
4. *Friends in Life and Death: Fan, Zhang, Chicken, and Millet* 死生交范張鷄黍. "One day after the seventh night of the seventh month of the *yiyou* year of the Yongzheng reign [August 2, 1729], while collating [this text] to a Yuan print edition, twelve songs were missing [in the Yuan text]. This allowed the [missing songs] to be restored. This might hit the mark" 雍正己酉秋七夕後一日，元槧本校，中缺十二調，容補錄。耐中.[18]

Three of these texts were collated within a two-week period; the fourth, *Friends in Life and Death*, was done nearly four years later. This fourth play was also part of the second batch of five plays noted in Huang Pilie's catalogue list, and this would seem to indicate that He Huang acquired these two batches of texts at different times and perhaps from different sources.[19] Now, while these four cases show a near concordance between the collated text and the Yuan printing that remains extant, only He Huang's collations in the *Moheluo* clearly identify the source of the Yuan printing as being from Li Kaixian's library. And while the collations in the *Moheluo* are nearly the same as those preserved in the thirty Yuan editions, there are enough minor discrepancies between the collation interpolations and the Yuan text of the *Moheluo* to keep us from claiming that the *Yuankan* text we have today and the one held by Li Kaixian and used by He Huang are the same. As Zhen Weini remarks,

> Although there are not many discrepancies, they do in fact exist. Therefore we cannot rely on this text [of the *Moheluo*] to absolutely affirm that the extant Yuan printings were those collected by Li Kaixian. But, from the fact that the text He Huang used and the extant Yuan printings are very similar, we can at least acknowledge that the extant Yuan printings and those that came from Li Kaixian's library stem from the same source and that they represent the original features of scripts that were created in the Yuan.
>
> Because the other three texts have no clear evidence from their contents that they were in Li Kaixian's library, and although what is copied in He Huang's collation is highly similar to the extant Yuan texts, we can still only confirm that the Yuan texts used by He Huang for collation are preserved in the current *Yuankan zaju sanshi zhong*, but we cannot use them as evidence to prove any relationship between them and those held by Li Kaixian.[20]

THE MULTIPLICITY OF YUAN TEXTS

In another case, He Huang has used a manuscript edition held by Li Kaixian to collate the play *Wang Can Ascends the Tower* (*Wang Can deng lou* 王粲登樓) (*Gu mingjia* ed.). In his colophon, he remarks,

> On the eighteenth day of the eighth month of the *yisi* year, the third of the Yongzheng reign [September 24, 1725], I used a manuscript copy of Li Kaixian's to collate and to correctly rewrite several hundred characters. This [*Gu mingjia* ed.] is missing twenty-two arias that have been dropped, and there are two arias switched in sequence, and I have corrected this and supplied the missing arias from a manuscript edition. The manuscript edition was missing the complete dialogues. The mistakes and ill-informed nature of the dialogues were unbearable, many times more so than the arias, but there was no source to correct it. I can only hope that there will be a curious and profound scholar who will be able to add the dialogues according to the stage directions. And even more that there is a truly knowledgeable and good person whose power is enough to have a famous actor perform this [that is, my recension]—that would be a wonderful thing. I have written this in anticipation of such a thing. Recorded by He Zhongzi of Xiaoshan. 雍正三年乙巳八月十八日，用李中麓抄本校，改正數百字。此又脫曲廿二，倒曲二，悉據抄本改正補錄。抄本不具全白。白之繆陋不堪，更倍於曲，無從勘正。冀世有好事通人，為之依科添白。更有真知真好之客，力足致名優演唱之，亦一快事。書以俟之。小山何仲子記。[21]

In the fourth act of the *Gu mingjia* edition, which is obviously truncated, He Huang has inserted eight songs from the manuscript edition, including five after the song *Shuixianzi*. In a short collation note, he also remarks, "Another edition has these five songs after the song *Tianshui ling*: *Dianqian huan*, *Qiao pai'er*, *Gua yugou*, *Gu meijiu*, and *Taiping ling*."[22] Thus, we know that He had at his disposal two different Yuan editions, one of which is noted as a "manuscript," each with a different sequence of songs in the fourth act:

Gu mingjia edition	Li Kaixian manuscript	So-called "Another edition"
【雙調 新水令】	[Same]	[Unknown]
[Same]	【駐馬聽】	[Unknown]
[Same]	【雁兒落】	[Unknown]
[Same]	【得勝令】	[Unknown]
[Same]	【甜水令】	[Unknown]
[Same]	【折桂令】	[Unknown]
【喬牌兒】	【喬牌兒】	[Unknown]
【水仙子】	【水仙子】	[Unknown]
【雁兒落】	【川撥棹】	【殿前歡】
【得勝令】	【七弟兄】	【喬牌兒】
【梅花酒】	【掛玉鉤】	
【收江南】	【沽美酒】	
【鴛鴦煞】	【太平令】	

This is an important point, because it demonstrates that there were multiple editions of scripts of the same drama printed or circulating as manuscripts during the Yuan. We are fortunate that we can compare the changes He Huang made to the aria *Yingxian ke* (迎仙客) in the third act of *Wang Can Ascends the Tower* with a citation of the same song in the music formulary and rhyme book known as *The Rhymes of the Central Plain* (*Zhongyuan yinyun* 中原音韻), written by Zhou Deqing 周德清 (1277–1365) in 1324.[23] In *The Rhymes of the Central Plain* we find the aria cited as

雕簷紅日低,	Carved eaves, red sun lowering,
畫棟彩雲飛;	Painted rafters, colored clouds flying;
十二玉欄天外依。	Twelve jade balustrades recline beyond heaven.
望中原,	Gaze at the Central Plain,
思故國。	Think on my old state,
感慨傷悲,	Painful recollections, broken by sorrow—
一片鄉心碎。	A strip of homebound heart sunders.[24]

In Zhou's work this is presented as a song stripped of its extrametrical syllables ("padding words," *chenzi* 襯字) and titled simply "Ascending the Tower" (Deng lou 登樓). Whether this was intentionally done so that it could be read as an independent poem or whether "Ascending the Tower" was supposed to bring to mind the drama *Wang Can Ascends the Tower* is unclear. Later, when He Huang used a Yuan edition for his collation, he left the so-called padding words intact, which suggests that the text He Huang used was a script:

調簷外紅日低，
畫棟畔彩雲飛；
十二欄杆在天外依。
我這裡望中原，
思故里。
不由我感歎傷悲，
越鬧得一片鄉心碎。

Beyond Carved eaves, red sun lowering,
Beside Painted rafters, colored clouds flying;
Twelve **balustrades** recline *there* beyond heaven.
Here I Gaze at the Central Plain,
Think on my old state,
Unconsciously I **Painfully sigh**, broken by sorrow—
Vexed even more until A strip of homebound heart sunders.[25]

In these two renditions of the song, both presumably dating from the mid to late Yuan period, we also see two small lexical changes (underlined above): 十二玉欄 → 十二欄杆 and 感慨 → 感歎. These are small changes, but particularly in the second instance it changes the mood from a single subject who is silently struggling with painful recollections to a visible act of communicating those strong feelings externally to a second actor. In the drama of course, this is necessary because Wang Can is talking with Xu Da (see fig. 3). In *The Rhymes of the Central Plain*, the first reading is preferable because the poem is contextualized within the cliché scene of a lone subject climbing the tower to meditate on the view. These two readings point to the possibility of songs circulating in two different ways: both as independent lyrics and as dramatic verse.

There are other cases in which it is Zhou Deqing himself who points out variants to dramatic songs that were circulating at the same time when he wrote his book in 1324. For instance, he transcribes a song from the first act of Ma Zhiyuan's (?1254–?1320) *Lü Dongbin Thrice Drunk at Yueyang Tower* (*Lü Dongbin sanzui Yueyang lou* 呂洞賓三醉岳陽樓) as

據胡床，
對瀟湘。
黃鶴送酒仙人唱，
主人無量醉何妨？
若捲簾邀明月，

I sit upon this folding chair,
And face the Xiao and the Xiang.
A yellow crane urges on wine, a transcendent sings,
The host has no limits, what problem is there to getting drunk?
If you furl the curtain and welcome the bright moon,

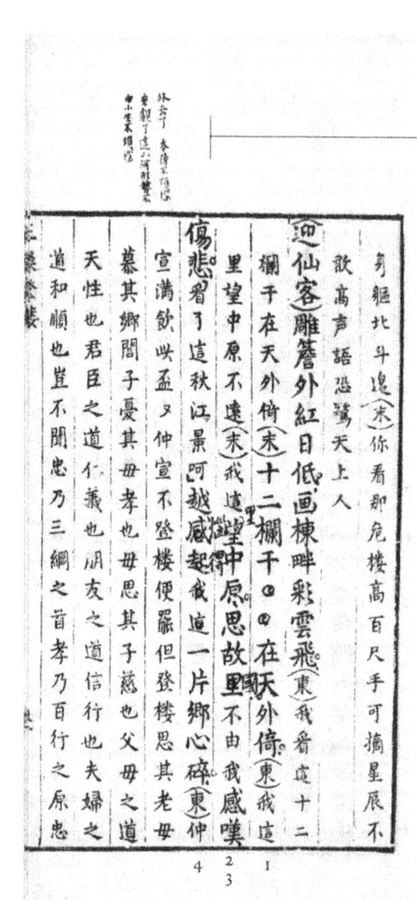
身軀北斗邊(末)你看那危樓高百尺手可摘星辰不
敢高声語恐驚天上人
(迎仙客)雕簷外紅日低画棟畔彩雲飛(東)我看這十二
欄干在天外倚(末)十二欄干〇〇在天外倚(東)我這
里望中原不遠(末)我這望中原思故里不由我感嘆
傷悲(末)看了這秋江景阿越感起我這一片鄉心碎(東)仲
宣满飲此盃ㄡ仲宣不登楼便罷但登楼思其老母
慕其鄉閭子憂其毋孝也母思其子慈也父母之道
天性也君臣之道仁義也朋友之道信行也夫婦之
道和順也豈不聞忠乃三綱之首孝乃百行之原忠

4 2 3 1

Changes made to text:

1. cross out repetition of balustrade (〈〈→ ◎◎)
2. add final 里 to "here" (這→這里)
3. change "old home" to "old state" (故里→故國)
4. change three character sung line (rhyming on 起) and compresses it with following to make it a padding phrase for the following line of song (越感起→越惱得)

Reconstructed text from He Huang's Collation

After the extra *has seen. — After acting out climbing the tower. —* extra *holds cup. — Speak:* What a high tower! [(*Sing:*)]

Ying xianke
Outside of the carved eaves the red sun falls low,
Beside the painted rafters the colored clouds fly,
Twelve balustrades
Lean beyond heaven.
Here I gaze at the Central Plain,
Think of my old state.
Unconsciously I sigh, broken in sorrow,
And it vexes so much until this strip of homebound heart
sunders.

After the extra *speaks. — Speak:* I did not want to be vexed, but after looking at the configurations of this landscape, I was unconsciously moved to vexation.

Original Text from *Guming jia* ed.

. . .my body beside the Northern Dipper. (MALE LEAD:) Look at that precarious tower, a hundred feet high. A hand can pluck the very stars! We dare not speak loudly, lest we startle the one up in the heavens.

Ying xianke
Outside of the carved eaves the red sun falls low,
Beside the painted rafters the colored clouds fly,

(HOST:) Look how those twelve balustrades lean beyond heaven! (MALE LEAD:)

Twelve balustrades, balustrades
Lean beyond heaven.

(HOST:) I gaze out, and the Central Plain does not seem so far. (MALE LEAD:)

Here I
Gaze at the Central Plain,
Think of my old home.
Unconsciously
I sigh, broken in sorrow,
And after seeing this autumnal River scenery
The more I begin to feel
My
Strip of homebound heart sunder

(HOST:) Zhongxuan, drink this cup to the full. If you hadn't climbed that tower, then nothing would have happened. But once you climbed it you began to think about your old mother and yearn for your old home. A child being anxious about his mother is filial piety. A mother thinking about her child is compassion. The way of parents is the nature of heaven. The way of the lord and minister is benevolence and righteousness. The way of friends is trust and action. The way of husband and wife is harmony and compliance. Have you not heard that loyalty is the chief among the three mainstays? That filial piety is the source of the hundred actions? Loyalty....

FIGURE 3 Original page, *Wang Can Ascends the Tower*, *Guming jia* ed., with He Huang's emendations

勝開宴出紅妝。	It would be so much better than setting out a feast and sending out "those rouged and made up."[26]
但得一樽留墨客,	Just get one cup to detain the "ink guest"[27]
是兩處夢黃粱。	And in two places "dream of yellow millet."[28]

Zhou then goes on to remark on variant recensions of the play that were circulating at that time:

> This is a lyric from the opening act of *Yueyang lou*, and the exquisiteness of it lies in the seven characters "A yellow crane urges on wine, a transcendent sings." Superlative language! Moreover, "wine" is in the rising tone in order to change its pronunciation, and the crux of the line hinges on this. There are those who do not understand the meaning of the words, and take "send" to mean "physically bring over." They say, "How can a yellow crane bring wine?" And they change the [two words "sending wine"] to "dance as a pair." Now they really do not know the affair of the yellow crane: an immortal used a pomegranate shell as a place to draw a crane, in order to repay the wine tender. When the guest drinks and clasps it in his hands, then the crane seems to dance in order to press the drinker to drink the wine. There were never two cranes, so how could a pair dance? Moreover, it loses the whole point of drinking wine. "To send" means something like "the beauties of Wu press one to drink wine." How hard indeed, to cure the vulgar scholar. 此是《岳陽樓》頭摺中詞也。妙在七字『黃鶴送酒仙人唱』。俊語也。況『酒』字上聲以轉其韻,務頭在其上。有不識文義,以送為齎送之義,言『黃鶴豈能送酒乎』? 改為『對舞』,殊不知黃鶴事,仙人用榴皮畫鶴一隻,以報酒家,客飲,撫掌則所畫黃鶴舞以送酒。初無雙鶴,豈能對舞?且失飲酒之意。送者,如吳姬壓酒之謂.[29]

"Immortal cranes dance as a pair" is indeed the change that appears in the two late Ming versions of the play:

我這裡據胡床,	*Here I* sit on this folding chair
對瀟湘。	Facing the Xiao and the Xiang.
有黃鶴對舞仙童唱,	*There are* a pair of Yellow Cranes dancing, an immortal lad singing,
主人家寬洪海量?	The host has a capacity as full as the sea!
直吃得捲簾邀皓月,	*Just drink until* you furl the curtain to welcome the hoary moon
再誰想開宴出紅妝。	*No one will think again of* setting out a feast and sending out "those rouged and made up."
但得一樽留墨客,	Just get one cup to detain the "ink guest"
我困了也,	I am sleepy.
我可是兩處夢黃粱。	*I truly am* dreaming of yellow millet in two places.[30]

We are fortunate to have Zhou Deqing's note. Were we to possess the Yuan performance text that has the phrase "A yellow crane urges on wine, a transcendent sings" and compare it with the Ming editions, the natural assumption would be that later editors had made these changes. This is the common tendency in modern studies, which often use the collation of Yuan and Ming texts as a way to find a direct chronological link between a presumed antecedent and its presumably evolved recension. That such an assumption takes place, and for it to hold such a powerful position in the study of drama, seems related to the belief that one author produced each individual play and that all other variants are introduced by others, particularly by actors or editors.

PLAYWRIGHTS, ACTORS, MANUSCRIPT PLAYS, AND PRINTED SCRIPTS

Such modern editorial policy posits a single authorial voice. One of the stronger and more enduring theories of literature in China is that writing is both an expression of a refined ethical interiority—as expressed by the commonly cited phrase "poetry speaks of heart's direction" (*shi yan zhi* 詩言志)—and as such a direct reflection of the personality of the writer, as in the equally cliché phrase "see the writing and know the person" (*jian qi yan zhi qi ren* 見其言知其人). But these are elite values, and when they appear in traditional and modern studies on theater or drama, they are clearly a result of a retrospectively applied concept that derives from the literary and cultural training of the writer.

In point of fact, none of the early Yuan editions carry any signature of authorship. Attributions of these plays to writers were made later on the basis of the first bibliography of drama, *The Register of Ghosts* (*Lugui bu* 錄鬼簿), a bio-bibliographical study of early and middle Yuan *qu* writers written by Zhong Sicheng 鐘嗣成 (ca. 1270–1360) that lists titles of dramas under playwrights' names. On the basis of that list, and another in *A Formulary of Correct Sounds for an Era of Great Peace* (*Taihe zhengyin pu* 太和正音譜), a musical and prosodic study of *qu* lyrics written by the dramatist and critic Zhu Quan 朱權 (1378–1448), Wang Guowei rearranged the thirty plays and assigned each an author (some plays were classified as anonymous). This certainly seems a logical process, but there is a problem in that the titles of the plays in the Yuan edition and those in the bibliographies often differ. Moreover, there exists no direct and provable tie between any Yuan edition and the later bibliographies. This is why this anecdote about the dancing cranes in *The Rhymes of the Central Plain* is so important: it does list one play with a direct attribution to an author, and it also contains coevally variant lines of that play that are found in later editions.

Zhou Deqing's anecdote about contending contemporary versions is equally important because it demonstrates that these plays are not purely authorial creations but a corporate enterprise in which a professional scriptwriter, profoundly knowledgeable about the stage, worked—if not directly with an actor as in the case of Ma Zhiyuan's collaboration with another playwright and two actors in authoring *The Yellow Millet Dream*[31]—at least in the environment of cooperation between actors, writers, and troupes to produce scripts for performance. Those that were popular were then copied and spread to other troupes. During such a process changes could be freely introduced into the scripts. This may be why, in the earliest editions, we find no names attached to the scripts—there were too many hands involved in their production. The extant texts that we have from this early period should probably be called an accidental selection of scripts rather than a representative body of what was there at the inception of written *zaju*. While Li Kaixian, He Liangjun 何良俊 (1506–1573), and Zang Maoxun claim to have had hundreds or even a thousand scripts in their possession, the Chinese penchant for unspecific and exaggerated whole numbers simply to indicate "a large quantity" makes their claims unreliable in terms of a concrete number. Yet there were probably hundreds of scripts circulating during the Yuan and Ming transition.

A problem arises, though, when we consider that what we have are *printed* texts, not handwritten scripts. A simple hand copy would suffice for the act of passing performance scripts back and forth between acting troupes or adapting other writers' scripts for a particular performance;[32] this simple need cannot account for mass printed versions. The thirty texts we have, which come from different places and different times and demonstrate a variety of formats, reveal a considerable difference in quality of printing. But they all share one feature: they are short enough to be hand copied within a few hours. Commercial printing implies mass circulation and thus an audience of readers or listeners rather than performers. The most likely hypothesis would be that these texts were printed primarily for the benefit of those members of the audience who experienced difficulty understanding the texts of the arias when sung.[33] The fact that the majority of printed texts come from Hangzhou may well reflect the linguistic situation in that city. The twenty-seven role texts that are extant were probably simply performance scripts turned over to print houses. In several of these plays, stage directions[34] and plot prompts become fewer and fewer as one moves from the beginning to the end of the play. This begs a question: does the reduction indicate that fewer prompts were necessary at the end or did printers begin to drop them to save space? The latter is a logical process in which text nonessential for a reader would be eliminated. This may explain why there are three texts with no prompts at all—it may be that those prompts originally were there, but the printer, realizing that the majority of people were purchasing them to be able to understand the arias, simply dropped the plot prompts from the very beginning.

Since these role texts were printed for mass circulation, we must acknowledge that they simultaneously represent both a performance and a reading text. Although they were certainly not the closet editions (*antou ju* 案頭劇) of the later Ming, they were indeed meant to be read by a public. Bao Jianqiang is of the opinion that they were printed for entertainers and master teachers to use in training students.[35] Before we reject this notion, we should acknowledge that many entertainers were capable of reading and even producing some of the lyrics (and, one supposes, the musical notations entered by hand) in a script. The *Collection of the Green Bower* (*Qinglou ji* 青樓集) lists a number of entertainers who read and had prodigious memories, were superior calligraphers, and who exchanged written poems with literati of the day.[36] The women of *The Collection of the Green Bower* were the most talented of the empire, but it also appeared that itinerant performers and low-class hucksters could at least read the script. In the southern drama *A Playboy from a Noble House Opts for the Wrong Career* (*Huanmen zidi cuoli shen* 宦門子弟錯立身), a reworking of an earlier *zaju*, we find the following passage in one of the incorporated northern songs:

FEMALE *sings*:
Shanghua shi[37]
My face haggard and worn, all because of you,
And just which classics do you apply yourself to in your study every day?

YOUNG MALE *sings*:
Don't waste time on idle talk,
Bring out those popular musical plays!

FEMALE *sings*:
Look at the scripts,[38]
And rehearse them all for me from the very beginning![39]

And, when memory failed, the worst of the profession could run their grimy hands over the pocket scripts, as noted in Gao Andao's 高安道 (ca. 1250–1300) "Exposing an Insipid Troupe" (Sang dan hangyuan 嗓淡行院):

【三】 *Third from Coda*[40]

妝旦不抹彪,	The one dressed as female lead is not sexily made up,
蠢身軀似水牛,	Her gross body just like a water buffalo;
嗓暴如恰[41]啞了孤庄狗。	Her voice screeches until it turns as hoarse as a homestead dog.[42]
帶冠梳硬挺著粗脖項,	Carrying cap and comb, she stiffly sticks up her coarse neck,
恰掌記光舒著黑指頭。	Fishing out a script, she openly spreads out blackened fingertips.
肋額的相迤逗,	Those who put up the advertisements really led us on
寫著道翩躚舞態,	By writing, "A swirling, whirling posture in her dance,
宛轉歌喉。	A lovely, modulated voice in her song."

These passages, as enlightening as they are about audience, are about reading, not production. They shed no light on who actually produced the texts.

Thus, it remains difficult to make any conjecture about these plays as a group. We must remember that they are the scant remnants of what must have been hundreds of scripts circulating in the Yuan and early Ming periods.[43] We have no way of even knowing if the thirty extant plays are a representative group of what was in circulation. We can presume with some confidence, however, that the scripts that have come down to us were all produced within the space of entertainment, and that this space (as a site of a particular habitus) would be replicated within the text itself.

CONVENTIONS OF PRINTING, CONVENTIONS OF FORM

The plays as they are represented in the editions we have now at hand show they were intended for users who had a deep knowledge of the conventions of stagecraft. The printed texts have no divisions that physically separate the acts: one act runs together with another. Scenes, however, are meticulously divided: a line of text will be terminated at the end of one scene within an act, and the new scene will begin on the next line (see fig. 4).

Individual scenes that do not involve the lead actor are identified by the term *zhe* 折, which designates their speech acts or actions; these markers are meant to clarify the order in which subsidiary actors appear onstage and mark the relationship between them. We judge this to be a common practice in early theater, since Ming court manuscripts often do not mark the act divisions either, but they do not use the term *zhe* for marking scenes of subsidiary actors since these actors' speaking parts are produced in their entirety in the manuscripts, obviating the need to signify the sequence of their appearance onstage. Ming editors later adopted the term *zhe* to identify "act" divisions on the printed page. At one level, the term remains the same in usage: as a marker between discrete sections of the drama. That is, in the Yuan editions it marks separate scenes and in the Ming commercial printings it is meant to clearly break the text into reading units that order the narrative (not the performance) and make reading and commentary easier.[44] As Bao Jianqiang and Hu Chengxuan remark, "The *zhe* in the Ming printed editions reflects the actions of closet drama of the literati and the *zhe* in the Yuan texts reflects the performing actions of the entertainer" 明刊本的『折』反映出文人的案頭化行為,而元本的『折』反映了藝人的演出活動.[45]

In the Yuan texts, what later become separate acts are signified as a unit by the use of a single suite of arias, all written to the same rhyme and performed in the same mode. It is usually the case that the designation of mode, which is a common feature of later commercial editions, is missing. This causes little problem, since the suites generally have a set sequence of tunes (*taoshu*) that are recognizable as belonging to a certain mode by their first aria. There are, in fact, only six exceptions to this general rule in all the thirty plays:

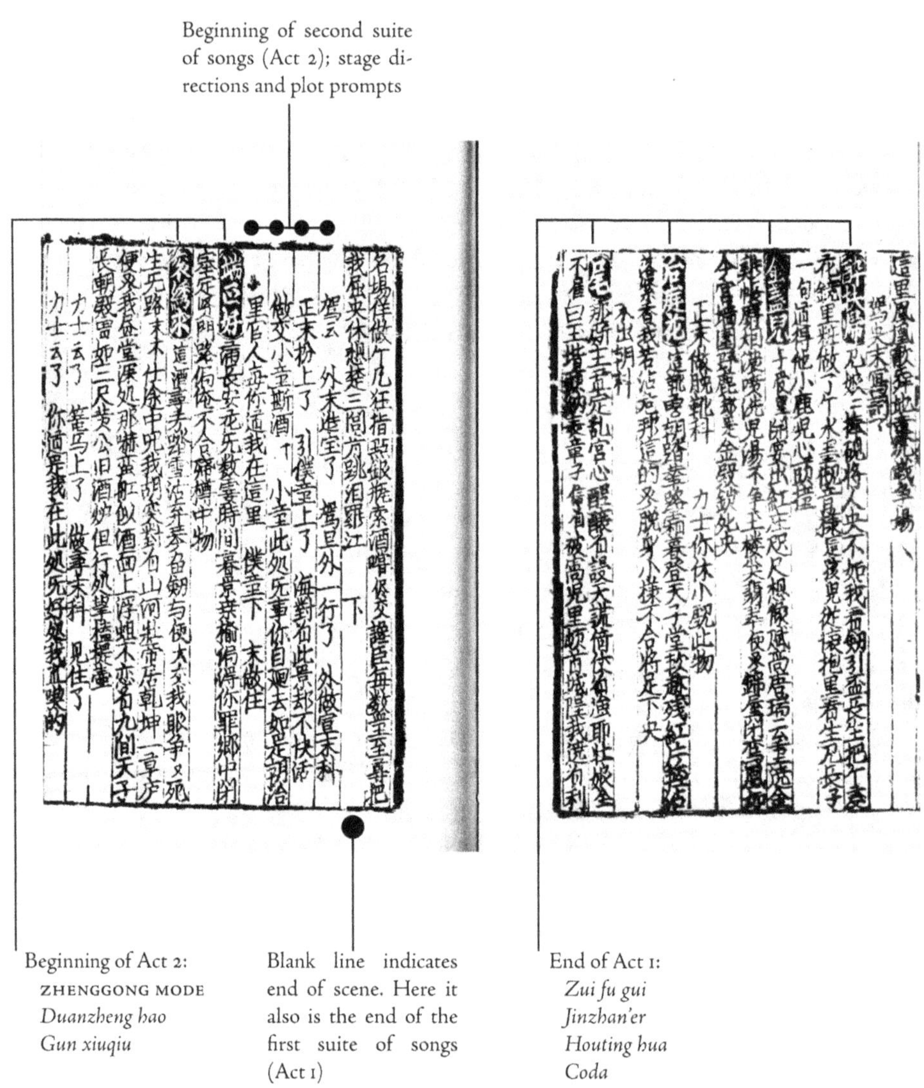

FIGURE 4 Acts 1 (end) and 2 (beginning) of *Banished to Yelang*

Name of mode is listed:	1. The eighteenth song of the play Newly Compiled: *Clerk Yue Avails Himself of Iron Crutch Li to Return from the Dead Xinshui ling* is marked *Shuangdiao*《新編岳孔目借鐵拐李還魂》第十八曲【新水令】標注『雙調』 2. The ninth song of Newly Compiled in Dadu with Plot Prompts: *A Noble Grandson: The Story of the Undershirt* is titled *Dou anchun* and is marked instead as *Yuediao*《大都新編關目公孫汗衫記》第九曲【斗鵪鶉】標注『越調』
Mode is listed, title of first song is missing:	1. The twenty-fourth song (first song of the third suite) of Newly Printed in Old Hangzhou with Plot Prompts: *Aiding King Cheng the Duke of Zhou Acts as Regent* is marked as *Yuediao* mode, but the title of the song, *Dou anchun*, is missing《古杭新刊關目輔成王周公攝政》第二十四曲標注『越調』而沒有曲牌【斗鵪鶉】 2. The thirty-sixth song (first song of the fourth suite) of Newly Printed in Old Hangzhou Complete Edition: *Yuchi Gong Wrests the Spear Away Three Times* is labeled as *Zhenggong* mode, but the title of the song, *Duanzheng hao*, is missing《古杭新刊的本尉遲恭三奪槊》第三十六曲標注『正宮』而沒有曲牌【端正好】
Modes are marked with unknown mode names:	1. The thirty-sixth song (first song of the fourth suite) of Newly Printed with Plot Prompts: *Zhang Ding Cleverly Investigates the Moheluo Doll* is marked as *Zimu diao Zui chunfeng*[46]《新刊關目張鼎智勘魔合羅》--第三十七取標注『子母調醉春風』 2. The twenty-sixth song of the play Newly Compiled: *Clerk Yue Avails Himself of Iron Crutch Li to Return from the Dead* is titled *Gudiao da qingge*《新編岳孔目借鐵拐李還魂》第二十六曲『古調大青哥』

Both performers and professional writers would know the modes and structural variations of each modal suite by heart, and there was no necessity to include well-known names of modes in a performance text as long as the name of the first song of the set was provided; conversely if the name of the mode was provided, the name of the first song could be omitted without any problem. The last two examples listed in the table are interesting because they present the possibility that these notations were introduced as ways to alert the singer to something that lies outside the ordinary: a method of performance in one case and, in the other, a reversion at that moment to an older mode, perhaps, to which the song *Da qingge* once belonged and to which the performer had to revert in this particular instance.

Any suite of songs may be preceded by "a wedge" (*xiezi* 楔子) of one or two songs. Because a very limited number of tunes can be used for a wedge, these songs are often not explicitly designated; if they are, the term "a wedge" follows the name of a tune. The songs of a wedge often conclude an independent scene, and so late Ming editions will designate a scene containing wedge songs as "a wedge," but that is not the practice in Yuan editions. Not all plays have wedges, and there is no play that has more than two. While modern editors have little problem in dealing with wedge songs preceding a suite, they have been more confused by the songs following at the end of a suite as later editions tended to do away with such "appendices." In Newly Printed with Plot Prompts: *Chen Jiqing Is Enlightened to the Way on a Bamboo-Leaf Boat* 新刊關目陳季卿悟道竹葉舟 at the end of the third suite (to the *Nanlü* mode), there are the following seven songs:

Jiejie gao	【節節高】
Yuanhe ling	【元和令】
Shangma jiao	【上馬嬌】
You simen	【遊四門】
Sheng hulu	【勝葫蘆】
Houting hua	【後庭花】
Liuye'er	【柳葉兒】[47]

Among the thirty Yuan plays, this is the only case of a third suite being followed by a set of songs in a different mode and a different rhyme. Rather than describing the world of spirits and the conversion of disciples as preceding arias had done, these intrusive songs shift the focus to a lyrical exposition of the ideal happiness of Chen's rustic life. While we do not find other examples in late Ming texts, there is at least one modest counterpart in an early fifteenth-century play by Zhu Youdun 朱有燉 (1398–1439), *A Leopard Monk Returns to the Laity of His Own Accord* (*Baozi heshang zi huansu* 豹子和尚自還俗). When at the end of the third suite of songs Lu Zhishen, a bandit turned monk, has convinced his mother that he will not return to a life of crime, he promises his mother he will provide her with a comfortable existence in the village of his patron, and the main suite of songs is then followed by two songs, separated by a long section in recited verse, that sing the joys of the countryside.[48] One is tempted to read these songs in praise of the simple country life as a parody of longer sets of songs on the life of immortals, such as the one found in *Zhuye zhou*.

It is more normal for the fourth set of songs to be followed by two songs, either *Houting hua* followed by *Liuye'er*, or *Gu meijiu* followed by *Taiping ling*. This phenomenon is found in the following three plays:

1. In *Newly Printed in Old Hangzhou with Plot Prompts, a Complete Text: Li Taibai Is Banished to Yelang*, there are two songs after the fourth suite (in *Shuangdiao* mode) that are written to the *Xianlü* mode: *Houting hua* 後庭花 and *Liuye'er* 柳葉兒.[49]

2. In *Newly Printed in Dadu with Complete Plot Prompts and Complete Edition: The Affair of the Eastern Window Exposed* there are two songs after the fourth suite (in *Yuediao* mode) that are written to the *Xianlü* mode: *Houting hua* and *Liuye'er*.[50]
3. In *Newly Printed in Old Hangzhou, a Complete Edition: The Great King Guan and the Single Sword Meeting* there are two songs at the end of the fourth suite (to the *Shuangdiao* mode), *Gu meijiu* 沽美酒 and *Taiping ling* 太平令.[51]

In modern editions, these "extra" songs are usually labeled "inserted songs" (*chaqu* 插曲) or "dispersal scenes" (*sanchang* 散場), however they are not labeled as such in the Yuan texts. These designations, all supplied by modern annotators, are essentially reintroduced into the text through the practice of reading backward from the idea of the "perfectly formatted" drama found in Zang Maoxun's *A Selection of Yuan Plays* and other late Ming editions. What these additional songs at the end of the fourth suite have in common is that they represent drastic breaks with the narrative story line of the dramas and serve as the core of separate scenes. The two songs at the end of *Banished to Yelang* are sung by Li Bai, but probably only after he has arrived in the dragon's palace; the two final songs in *The Affair of the Eastern Window Exposed* are sung by the ghost of Yue Fei, not the male lead, and the two songs in *The Single Sword Meeting* may well be sung by other players besides the main lead—or by Guan Yu in his divine manifestation.[52]

There are seven plays among the thirty Yuan printings that conclude with the legend *sanchang* (散場) or *chuchang* (出場), but these terms never refer specifically to any songs in the play. Coeval descriptions of theatrical performances strongly suggest that these terms refer to an independent performance routine (such as a dance routine) that might be put on as a bonus for the audience following the completion of the show. Only one of the thirty Yuan printings may have preserved the text of a *sanchang* song. This is Newly Printed in a Complete Edition with Plot Prompts: *In Wind and Moon in the Courtyard of Purple Clouds*, in which the main text of the play is followed by an independent "Partridge Heaven"[53] song (Zhegu tian 鷓鴣天). We know that the "Partridge Heaven" dance was a popular *sanchang* routine, and we even have the name of one actress who was famous for her performance of this item.[54]

The endings of these early plays are far less formal in structural terms than all the later editions, and they exhibit a variety of ways to end the fourth act (see fig. 5).

Later texts generally rationalize the endings, making them all conclude with a coda in the fourth suite of songs. But if we examine the endings of the thirty Yuan plays, we find the following:

1. Seventeen of the thirty plays use the mode *Shuangdiao* and begin the suite with the song *Xinshui ling*. Only one of these seventeen plays (number 8) has a suite that is formally concluded by a coda.
2. Seven of the plays are designated as having a dispersal section and an eighth (number 14, *Courtyard of Purple Clouds*) has an untitled final passage that we can confidently designate as a dispersal scene.

Name of Drama	*Dispersal Scene* 散場、出場	*Judgment or ritual* 斷出、祭出	*4th Suite* 雙調新水令	*4th Suite coda*	*4th suite Other mode, first song*
大都新編關張雙赴西蜀夢				●	正宮端正好
新刊關目閨怨佳人拜月亭	●		●		
新杭刊的本關大王單刀會			●		
新刊關目詐妮子調風月			●		
新刊關目好酒趙元遇上皇		●	●		
大都新編楚昭王疏者下船			●		
新刊關目看錢奴賣冤家債主				●	越調斗鵪鶉
新刊的本太華山陳摶高臥			●	●	
新刊關目馬丹陽三度任風子			●		
新刊的本散家財天賜老生兒			●		
古杭新刊的本尉遲恭三奪搠					
新刊的本漢高祖濯足氣布英	●	⊙		●	黃鍾醉花陰
趙氏孤兒				●	中呂粉蝶兒
古杭新刊的本關目風月紫雲亭	⊙		●		
大都新編公孫汗衫記	●		●		
新刊的本薛仁貴衣錦還鄉	●		●		
新刊關目張鼎智勘磨合羅				●	中呂粉蝶兒
古杭新刊關目的本李太白貶夜郎			●		
新編岳孔目竭力鐵拐還魂				●	中呂粉蝶兒
新編關目晉文公火燒介子推	●	⊙		●	越調斗鵪鶉
大都新刊關目的本東窗事犯		●		●	正宮端正好
古杭新刊關目霍光鬼諫	●		●		
新刊死生交范張雞黍					
新刊關目嚴子陵垂釣七里灘			●		
古杭新刊關目輔成王周公攝政		⊙	●		
新刊關目全蕭何追韓信		⊙		●	正宮端正好
新刊關目陳季卿悟道竹葉舟					
新刊關目諸葛亮博望燒屯	●	●			

⊙ Probable

● Certain

FIGURE 5 Endings of *Yuankan* texts

3. Three of the plays have a final section designated as a "judgment to send one from the stage" (*duanchu* 斷出) or "sent from the stage with a sacrifice" (*jichu* 祭出), and four more plays have stage directions that indicate such actions were carried out (numbers 12, 20, 25, 26). These are all scenes enacted by an "emperor role" (that is, in the context of Yuan plays, either an emperor or a feudal lord) or by the King of the Underworld. Since such characters were prohibited from appearing onstage after the beginning of the Ming dynasty, later editions relegate this function to an official deputy of the emperor.

We can conclude from this fragmentary evidence that it was not necessary to end a suite of songs with a coda, and that there was far more flexibility in form before the texts were rationalized for consumption by Ming readers. And, we can conclude that the overall structure of the texts represents a drama that would have the following constituents:

1. A short wedge that most often occurs at the beginning of the play, before the first suite of songs, but may also occur in other places where it might function as an interlude.
2. Four full-length suites of songs.
3. A separate demi-act at the end, in which some form of judgment occurs, and which usually comprises two songs written to a different rhyme than the fourth act. These scenes are related to the action in the play but are clearly distinct from the action of the main plot, although they may be a result of that action.
4. The texts indicate that there is also a metatheatrical ending, a dispersal scene unaffiliated with the action of the play, which was likely used to send the players from the stage and the audience from their seats.

As Tanaka Issei and Komatsu Ken have demonstrated,[55] more than half the Yuan texts are concluded with some form of ritual. In three cases, *Duke Wen of Jin Immolates Jie Zi Tui*, *Huo Guang Remonstrates as a Ghost*, and *Aiding King Cheng the Duke of Zhou Acts as Regent*, the final acts are concluded by sacrifices. In the case of *Jie Zi Tui* and *Huo Guang*, these are scenes to carry out sacrifices to settle the souls of the two departed. In the first case the stage directions are quite short, but specific:

(收尾)
　　　不爭
　　你個晉文公烈火把功臣盡,
　　枉惹萬萬載朝廷論議。
　　常想趙盾捧車輪,
　　也不似你個當今帝王狠。
駕云了 祭出
散場

Coda

So now

You, Duke Wen of Jin, brought this meritorious minister to his end with fire so fierce,

And uselessly stirred up court debates for tens upon tens of thousands of years.

And thinking back on the one who bore the wheel for Zhao Dun,

Find no one as evil hearted as the emperors of this age!

After EMPEROR *speaks.—Send off the stage with a sacrifice.*

Dispersal Scene[56]

In *Huo Guang*, however, it is more detailed:

駕提天明了 拿二淨上了 駕斷了、安排祭出了

(落梅風)
滅九族誅戮了髫齔,
斬全家抄佑了事產。
可憐見二十年公干,
墓頂上灩灩土未乾。
這的是承明殿霍光鬼諫。
散場

After EMPEROR *has indicated that it is dawn—after* TWO COMICS *are apprehended and enter—After* EMPEROR *makes his judgment and after sending him off with sacrifice.*

(*Luomei feng*)

Nine branches of the clan exterminated, all the young slain,

The whole family decapitated, all the family wealth seized.

How pitiful: Twenty years of public service,

The moist, rich earth on his grave not yet dry—

This was

"In the Palace of Receiving Sages' Wisdom, Huo Guang Remonstrates as a Ghost."[57]

The conclusion of *Acts as Regent* is more a celebratory ritual carried out after the Duke of Zhou has stepped aside as regent and restored authority to the young emperor. At the conclusion, the Younger of Tang, King Cheng's younger brother, enters to present "auspicious rice sprouts" (rice plants from different areas that look exactly the same). Since the word "sprout" and "harmony" are perfect homophones, this symbolized the union of different areas, particularly the Zhou homeland and the newly conquered area in the east. When the sprouts were presented, King Cheng ordered his brother to escort the Duke of Zhou to the east. The stage directions again are quite spare: (唐輸獻加[嘉]禾上了 祭出):

After THE YOUNGER OF TANG *enters with auspicious sprouts—send off with a sacrifice.*[58]

Several other plays, including *In a Dream Guan and Zhang, a Pair, Rush to Western Shu, The Orphan of Zhao,* and *Burning the Child to Save the Mother,* all show rituals that were held at the conclusion of the plays. They are, as such, a part of a broader structure of denouement that restores characters to their proper ethical and social status as a way of confirming social harmony. Whether by marriage, reunion of parents and children, addressing the deeds of malefactors, or offering sacrifices to dead souls, these are specifically social acts. In this sense, the sacrifices carried out onstage are less about religious belief and more about using ritual to establish proper family, social, and state relationships.

LATER INCARNATIONS OF THE TEXTS

Since the evidence is strong that these thirty Yuan texts were part of a corporate process of text production, it is no accident that these plays have no author's names attached to them. The scholarly assumption has been that this is an accident that can be rectified by restoring the names through late fourteenth century catalogues. But this would hold true only if there were a single authorial edition that had never undergone any changes. It is much more likely that the stories on which the scripts are based were freely circulating, and it is also likely that once the scripts were in public circulation, they were changed at will by actors and writers throughout the Yuan; consequently, what we have today, even in the earliest editions, may in fact be considerably different from the first iteration of the drama.

As we include four Ming-dynasty rewrites, it is important to understand the relation between the Yuan editions and the later texts of *zaju*. Among these later texts of *zaju*, the thirty Yuan editions have their closest connection with a body of materials collected by Zhao Qimei 趙琦美 (1563–1624) in his Studio of the Transformed Bookworm (Maiwangguan 脈望館) called "*Zaju* Old and New Copied and Collated" (Chaojiao gujin zaju 抄校古今雜劇). His collection of 242 volumes includes both manuscript versions and printed editions of dramas.[59]

The manuscripts in Zhao Qimei's collection involve two kinds of texts: first, court editions (from the eunuch agency in charge of theatrical entertainments inside the palace, the Office of Bell and Drum), and second the Yu Xiaogu collection. The process of copying between these two kinds of texts and the resulting format of the page in Zhao's collations differ significantly. For the palace texts from the Office of Bell and Drum, Zhao's

Distribution of Editions in the Maiwangquan Collection

Manuscript editions (172)	Print editions (70)
95 manuscripts drawn from the court	Xijizi, *Zaju Selections* (ca. 1589) 息機子《雜劇選》
60 have collation notes by Zhao Qimei, giving date of collation	15 plays 8 by known Yuan authors 5 by unknown Yuan authors 2 by known Ming authors
13 clearly noted as palace editions (*neifu ben* 內府本) but undated	
(The above two categories have collation notes and lists of props and costumes [*chuanguan* 穿關] appended to them)	Xu family, *Zaju by Famous Writers New and Old*
22 have no clear record that they are palace editions but have lists of props and costumes, leading both Sun Kaidi and Zheng Zhenduo to assume they are palace editions; also no collation notes	55 plays 22 by known Yuan authors 12 by unknown Yuan authors 15 by known Ming authors 6 by unknown Ming authors
(14 of these have the note "random stories" [*zazhuan* 雜傳] appended and are works by unknown Yuan or known Ming playwrights)	
33 that have been collated against manuscript collections in the collection of Yu Xiaogu	
23 specify a date of collation; 10 do not	
14 are noted as "put together for performance in the Court Entertainment Bureau" (Jiaofang Bianyan 教坊編演)	
45 demonstrate no provenance but seem to be palace editions	

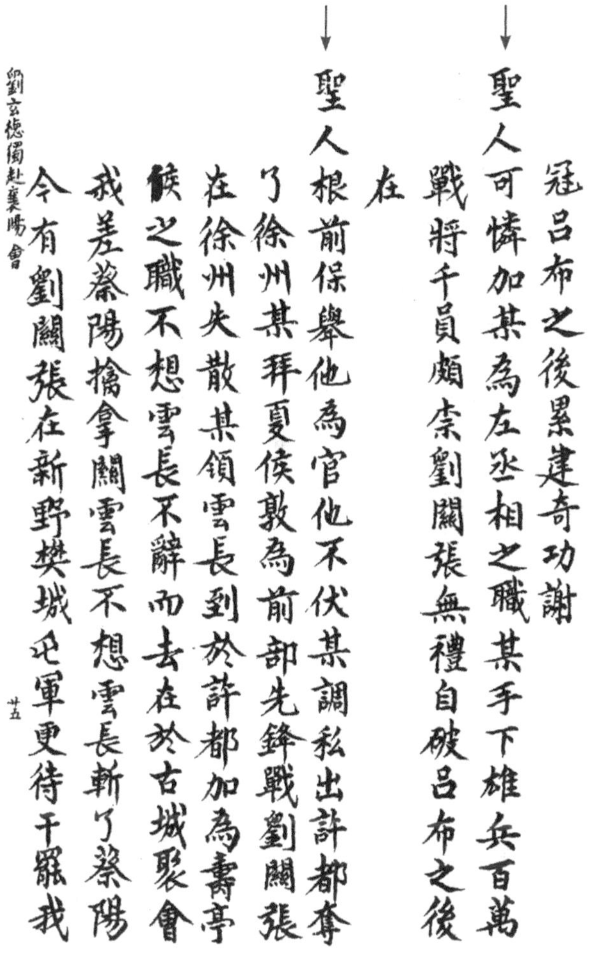

冠呂布之後累建奇功謝
聖人可憐加其為左丞相之職其手下雄兵百萬
戰將千員頗柰劉關張無禮自破呂布之後
在
聖人根前保舉他為官他不伏其調私出許都奪
了徐州其拜夏侯敦為前部先鋒戰劉關張
在徐州失散其領雲長到於許都加為壽亭
侯之職不想雲長不辭而去在於古城聚會
我差蔡陽擒拿關雲長不想雲長斬了蔡陽
今有劉關張在新野樊城屯軍更待干罷我

劉玄德獨赴襄陽會

廿五

FIGURE 6 Page 25 of *Liu Xuande Goes Alone to the Xiangyang Meeting*, from a palace edition showing raised characters for the term "the Sage," referring to Emperor Xiandi of the Han

copies are quite consistent. The format is regular, the characters are bright and clear, and there are normally ten lines of seventeen characters to each half page. The song titles are not in parentheses but are set in a single line two spaces below the normal upper level of text. "Entry" poems are set one space below. The size and boldness of the characters are uniform for both prose and arias, an empty space is left above and below stage directions, and there are few padding words in the arias. When an important person such as an emperor's name is encountered, the text stops and moves to a new line, elevating the new line two spaces above the text (see fig. 6).[60] The regularity of his copying suggests that Zhao was scrupulous about maintaining the format of the originals he transcribed, an important asset for understanding the original shape of the texts.

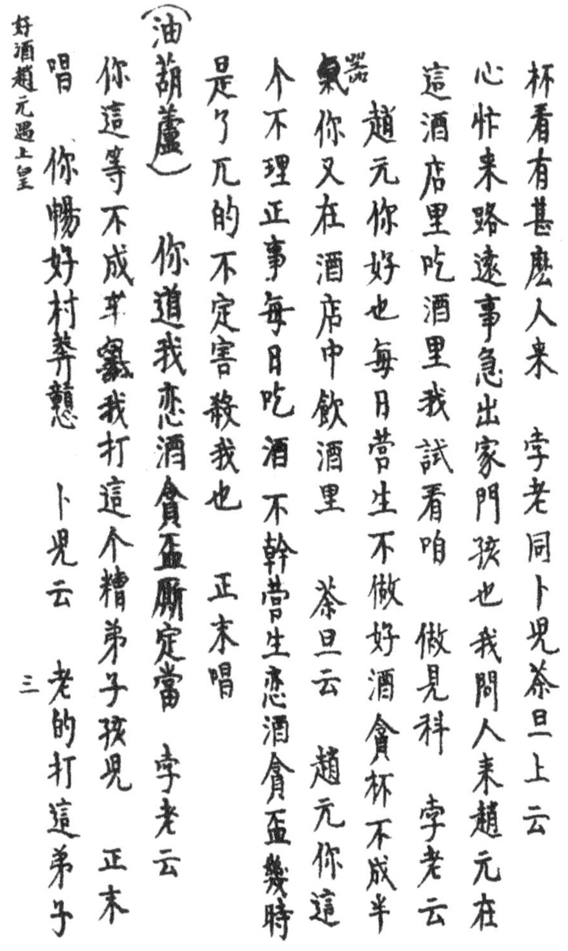

杯看有甚麼人来　孛老同卜兒茶旦上云
心忙来路遠事急出家門孩也我問人来趙元在
這酒店里吃酒里我試看咱　做見科　孛老云
趙元你好也每日营生不做好酒貪杯不成半
器氣你又在酒店中飲酒里　茶旦云　趙元你這
个不理正事每日吃酒不幹营生戀酒貪盃幾時
是了几的不定害殺我也　正末唱
（油葫蘆）　你道我戀酒貪盃厮定當　孛老云
你這等不成半器我打這个糟弟子孩兒　正末
唱　你暢好村莽憨　卜兒云　老的打這弟子
三
好酒趙元遇上皇

FIGURE 7 Page 3 of *Tippler Zhao Yuan Encounters the Prior Emperor*, a manuscript collated against a Yu Xiaogu edition

This holds true, as well, for Zhao Qimei's transcriptions from the Yu Xiaogu editions.[61] There is little consistency among the individual plays in Yu's texts in terms of number of lines and number of characters in each line, but Zhao's transcriptions again reflect the presumed format of the original: he did not separate the plays into acts but into scenes; he copied the arias in heavier characters to differentiate them from the prose, which was written in smaller and lighter characters; the titles of the songs were placed in parentheses; and he left the spacing between discrete scenes and stage directions—all conventions that we are accustomed to seeing in the *Yuankan* texts (see fig. 7). The Japanese scholar Komatsu Ken has convincingly argued that the manuscripts deriving from the Yu Xiaogu collection are based on plays as performed by the Court Entertainment Bureau in the

1460s, whereas the texts deriving from the Office of Bell and Drum would appear to reflect performances inside the imperial palace during the Jiajing period (1522–1566).

Both the texts emanating from the Court Entertainment Bureau and the far more numerous scripts from the Office of Bell and Drum are fully written out and provide the complete dialogues for every character. Late Ming evidence indicates that play scripts were submitted to court censors before performance, and this most likely also applied in earlier years of the dynasty. This practice probably also goes a long way to explain the standardization of the texts, which is already observable in the Yu Xiaogu texts but which is even more observable in the palace texts emanating from the Office of Bell and Drum. The manuscripts deriving from the Office of Bell and Drum usually conclude with an encomium to the emperor who was watching the play. For instance in the Three Kingdom's play *Prior Emperor Liu: A Meeting at Xiangyang* (*Liu Xianzhu Xiangyang hui* 劉先主襄陽會), Liu Bei's judgment that wraps up the action of the play concludes with

> For a thousand antiquities [my men's] names will be spread and carried on,
> As they support the altars of state for hundreds upon hundreds of generations.
> We pray that
>
> OUR EMPEROR
> Will live ten thousand upon ten thousands of years!

It would have been impossible for Liu Bei, at this point, to utter these words to Xiandi of the Han within the context of the play, and they are clearly meant as a eulogy for the Ming emperor.[62] In contrast, seven of the Yu Xiaogu texts are followed by the phrase "This is the end of the *zaju* text" (*Zaju juan zhong ye* 雜劇卷終也) or by a variant of that phrase, followed by a rhymed passage that may have been either sung or chanted. Unlike the conclusion to palace plays performed before the imperial presence, the Yu Xiaogu texts concluded by "the end of the *zaju* text" have much more generalized summations, often self-referential to the actors or acting troupes and praising the contributions to imperial rule of the civil and military officials in front of whom the Court Entertainment Bureau often performed. While the phrase "the end of the *zaju* text" occurs in only seven of the dramas, we have one example of a full structure in the play *The Story of Sima Xiangru and His Inscription on the Bridge* (*Sima Xiangru tiqiao ji* 司馬相如題橋記), where the following occurs immediately after the coda of the last act:

(眾云)雜劇卷終也。(外云)道甚。(眾答云)瀛洲開宴列嘉賓,祝讚吾皇萬萬春。武將提刀扶社稷,文官把筆佐絲綸。

THE ENSEMBLE *speaks*: This is the end of the *zaju* text.
EXTRA *speaks*: What are you going to say?
THE ENSEMBLE *responds*:

Set out a feast on Fairy Isle and array the fine guests,
We pray to celebrate Our August One's myriads of springs;
The military officials raise the swords to support the altars of state,
The civil officials hold their brushes to help the silken words[63] spun by the king.[64]

The invocatory line ("end of the *zaju* text") has been lined out in a few texts with an ink stroke (by Zhao Qimei?) (see fig. 8),[65] since it must have been puzzling to later editors.

And, while we cannot argue ex nihilo that it was expunged entirely in some texts of the Yu Xiaogu collection, there is good circumstantial evidence to suggest that this closing scene was a standard part of the performance as represented in the Yu Xiaogu materials—a set of actions, songs, or recited passages that were done after the fourth act, after the play itself was finished. In some dramas we find text that resembles the last couplet of the response just cited (military officials . . . civil officials) and that exists as an independent couplet unrelated to the main action. While not noted in the text itself, it is probable that these lines were uttered by the dramatic company as a whole in response to a prompt, as in the preceding example, by the "extra," a person who was offstage and not part of the troupe onstage.[66] The linguistic and stagecraft artifacts found in the Yu Xiaogu collection are represented in this volume by the rewrite of *Tippler Zhao Yuan Encounters the Prior Emperor*. The Yu Xiaogu texts can be dated with some reliability to the 1480s, and, according to evidence adduced by Komatsu Ken, there is a probability that some were performed as early as 1464, more than fifty years before the palace editions of the Jiajing reign. This allows us not only to sharpen our understanding of the various strata of Ming court editions but also to begin to sort out the transmission of texts and their possible influence on later collections. For instance, differences between printed texts of the same play that show a great discrepancy in late sixteenth and early seventeenth century editions may be due not only to editorial intervention (by Zang Maoxun, for instance) but also to the different Ming manuscripts on which they were based.

The one thing that all the Ming manuscripts have in common is that they do away with the "imperial role" (*jia* 駕), due to proscriptions in the Ming from portraying emperors onstage:

"Detailed Explanations" from *The Great Ming Legal Code*

Now, for entertainers who act out northern comedies or southern plays: they are not allowed to costume as emperors or kings, empresses or consorts, loyal ministers, or brave warriors of historical dynasties nor former sages, former worthies, or images of gods; those who violate this will be caned a hundred times. Those who allow or order such costuming in the houses of officials in charge of the people shall share the same punishment. Those who costume as immortal Daoists, as well as righteous husbands, chaste wives, filial sons, and compliant grandsons, or any who compel people to goodness do not

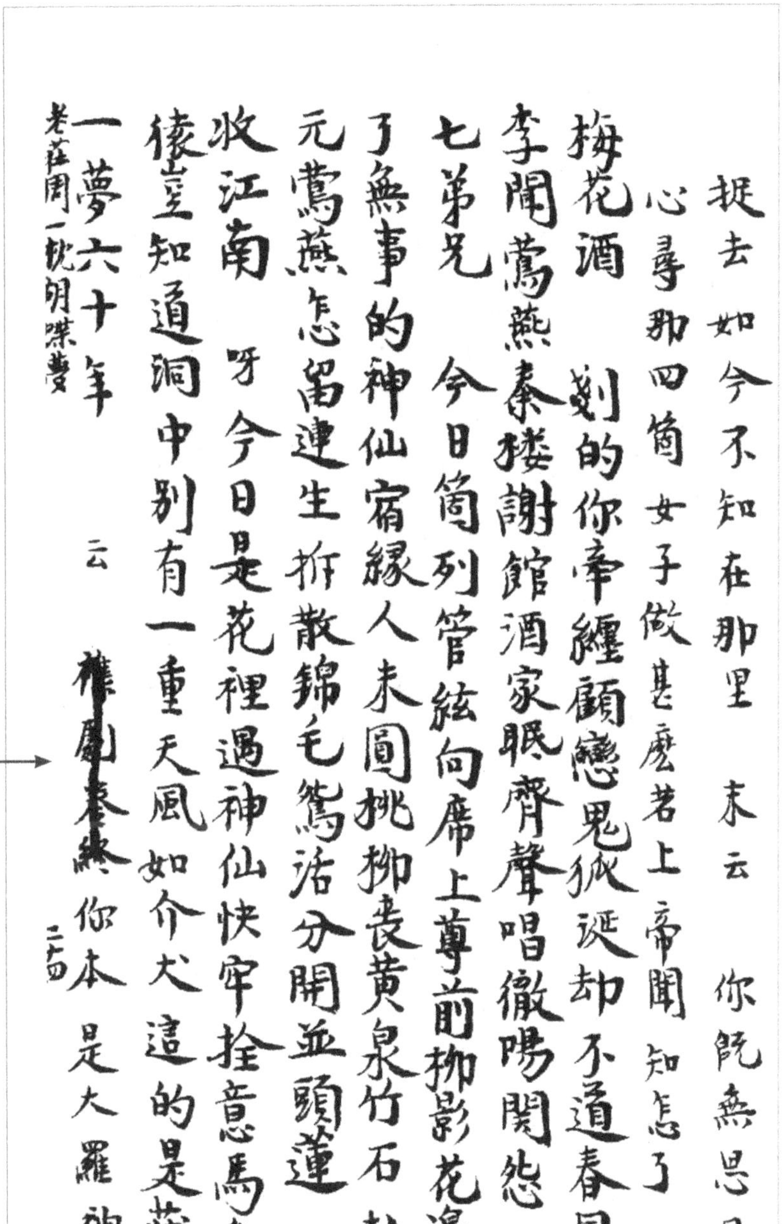

挺去如今不知在那里　末云　你既無思凡的
心尋那四箇女子做甚麼若上帝聞知怎了　唱
梅花酒　剗的你牽纏顧戀鬼狐涎却不道春風桃
李鬧鶯燕秦樓謝館酒家眠齊聲唱徹陽關怨
七弟兄　今日箇列管絃向席上尊前柳影花邊做
了無事的神仙宿緣人未圓桃柳喪黃泉竹石却還
元鶯燕怎留連生拆散錦毛鴛活分開並頭蓮
收江南　呀今日是花裡遇神仙快牢拴意馬與心
猿豈知道洞中別有一重天風如介大這的是莊周
一夢六十年　云　~~雜劇卷終~~　你本是大羅神仙
老莊周一枕胡蝶夢　二十四

FIGURE 8 Page 24 of *Zhuang Zhou's Dream of the Butterfly*, showing the lined-out phrase "this *zaju* play is finished" 雜劇卷終

lie within this proscription. 凡樂人搬做雜劇戲文,不許妝扮歷代帝王、后妃、忠臣、烈士、先聖、先賢、神像,違者杖一百;官民之家,容令妝扮者與同罪。其神仙道扮及義夫、節婦、孝子、順孫、勸人為善者,不在禁限。(大明律講解卷二十六刑律雜犯).[67]

The importance of this proscription is brought into relief when we consider that fourteen of the thirty Yuan print editions list an emperor role (*jia* 駕) in the stage directions, referring either to an emperor or to a king of the preimperial Zhou (there are fifteen if we count He Huang's manuscript transcription of *Wang Can Ascends the Tower*). It is also possible that the role of Liu Bei in *Dream of Western Shu* was played by an emperor role, but since no stage directions are extant, we cannot tell. Conversely, while the emperor in person disappeared from the stage in the Ming, palace editions strongly emphasize imperial power as the ultimate arbiter. A fine example of that is provided by the rewrite of *The Orphan of Zhao*. Whereas the Yuan printing strongly suggests that the grown-up Orphan will kill his father's murderer in a private act of bloody revenge, a fifth act that is found in the *Yuanqu xuan* version and most likely derives from a palace script has him ask permission to kill the murderer, turning private revenge into state punishment. Palace editions also tend to tone down explicit social criticism and gory violence. Reflecting their new performance venue, where ensembles of the finest actors in all role types were clamoring for expanded roles, many palace scripts cut down the number of arias assigned to the male or female lead and expand the part of other actors by assigning them poems and other recitation pieces.

THE *THIRTY PLAYS* IN MODERN SCHOLARSHIP AND CRITICISM

Despite their rediscovery and subsequent reprinting nearly a hundred years ago, the thirty independent editions of Yuan northern drama have had little effect on the study of *zaju* as a genre of literature.[68] Their primary influence has been in providing earlier recensions of stories used in drama as well as data for examining the structure, tonal patterns, and lexicon of early northern theater. This has been due, in our estimation, to the fact that the study of drama itself is a modern phenomenon that has assembled the corpus of early *zaju* retrospectively under the influence of reading practices that were a legacy of literati culture that continued into the modern age. This has created a situation, nearly unknown in other cultures, in which the early texts of drama (or portions of dramas) are unnaturally divided into two major categories: performance scripts and literary editions. This is certainly due to the fact that in China—as distinct from cultures in which narrative and drama stand as foundational genres—lyric poetry and historical or philosophical prose stand at the fount of cultural production and have ineluctably shaped the reading practices of literati.

Moreover, the distinctly modern discipline of drama studies does not start in China until the cusp of the twentieth century. Prior to this time the majority of formal writing by traditional critics on *zaju* and other forms of drama was limited primarily to structure (tonal patterns, rhymes), music, performability, audience, biography, and bibliography. Wang Guowei is usually singled out as the progenitor of modern drama studies in China, and his book *Song Yuan xiqu kao* 宋元戲曲考 has been canonized in the secondary literature, becoming the default starting point for students of drama.[69] As is well-known, Wang Guowei and those who follow him treat *zaju* as literature rather than performance text. As Ren Zhongmin pointed out in a lecture transcribed in 1983,

> Wang Guowei was a literatus through and through; he was not a performer. His appreciation of *The Story of the Western Wing*, *The Story of the Lute*, and all Yuan drama is limited to the texts of the northern and southern songs; he did not emphasize the prose dialogue, the stagecraft, or the structure. His eyes were always on the literary compositions, therefore [in writing his book] he had to choose the term *xiqu* [the narrower term, literally, "the songs of plays"] and reject the idea of *xiju* [the broader term, literally, "plays"]. Because his knowledge of drama is so one-sided, we do not need even bother with his notions of "real drama" or "strong and complete" drama. What is unfortunate is that those who followed him blindly, like the historians of drama Zhou Yibai and Zhang Geng, had no choice but to call their works histories of *xiqu*, not daring to call them histories of *xiju*.[70] 王國維是個徹底的文人,不是藝人。他欣賞《西廂》、《琵琶》和一切元劇，乃以其南北曲的文章為限，至于賓白、排場、結構等等，亦非他所重了。他的著眼僅在詞章，故他取文體名時，就不得不用『戲曲』，而放棄『戲劇』，他對戲劇的認識如此偏差，就不必于所謂真戲劇、健全的戲劇上找他的麻煩吧。可嘆的是盲從他的一些人，如周怡白和張庚等戲劇史家，都不敢稱『戲劇史』而稱『戲曲史』.

This is not the place to debate the value of Wang's contribution, which has created a minor cottage industry of text,[71] but to pursue the line of questioning that Ren opened up about Wang's reading preferences. In this lecture, Ren goes on to say that as a literatus trained in classical literature, Wang subscribed to the hegemonic status of textual learning, which for Ren is encapsuled in the phrase "Everything else is worthless, only reading is the highest achievement" 萬般皆下品，唯有讀書高. Furthermore, according to Ren, Wang's book was highly popular because it resonated with an overarching scholarly preference for textual learning; and by relocating the authority to judge drama from the performers themselves (and their patrons) to the scholar and the norms of their literary tradition, it simply trumped the question of performers' status as interpreters of culture. That is, the values of an elite meritocracy were interposed between the object of study—drama as a whole—and cultural discourse, effectively effacing both performer and nonelite writer. This was not something new. In the early fifteenth century, Zhu Quan 朱權 (1378–1448) included this short passage in his *A Formulary of Correct Sounds for an Era of Great Peace*:

Zaju: those performed by actors are called "prostitute-entertainer plays" and therefore called "of the stage." Zi'ang, Master Zhao[72] said,

> The *zaju* performed by playboys from good families is called "the work of the professional entertainer"; that performed by prostitute-entertainers is called "layman acting." Now good families value a sense of shame, so there are very few who actually perform. Now they have become very few and, paradoxically, those performed by the professional prostitute-entertainer are now called "professionals." This has missed it by a mile. Someone asked me, "What is the reason for this?" And I responded by saying, "*Zaju* comes from great Confucian scholars and men of deep learning, composed by men of poetry and scholarship. They are all from good families. If they were not created by our kind, would the prostitute-entertainer have anything to perform? I have traced this to its root in order to bring its principles to light and therefore take them to be lay amateurs."
>
> Guan Hanqing said, "It is not they who are skilled in their own profession, it is the work of our group. They do no more than perform the labor of slaves, providing laughter and working diligently to please and thereby serve our likes. What these disciples act out is the 'wind and moon'[73] of our whole group." I have seized on this because, although it was said in jest, it conforms to principle.

Among the sons of good families are those who are thoroughly versed in the rules of rhymes and metrics; moreover they are born into an era of burgeoning peace, and delight under a rule of harmony. They want to revert to antiquity in order to affect the present in order to adorn this great peace. That which they now act out was called "play of happy streets" in the Sui, "music of the Pear Garden" in the Tang, "play of the garden of pleasure" in the Song, and "music of ascendant peace in the Yuan."[74]

雜劇，俳優所扮者，為之『娼戲』，故曰『勾欄』。子昂趙先生曰：『良家子弟所扮雜劇，謂之行家生活，娼優家所扮者，謂之戾家把戲。良人貴其恥，故扮者寡，今少矣，反以娼優扮者謂之行家，失之遠也。』或問：『其何故哉？』則應之曰：『雜劇出於鴻儒碩士，騷人墨客所作，皆良人也。若非我輩所作，娼優豈能扮乎？推其本而明其理，故以為戾家也。』關漢卿曰：『非是他當行本事，我家生活。他不過為奴隸之役，供笑獻勸，以奉我輩耳。子弟所扮，是我一家風月。』雖是戲言，亦合于理，故取之。良家之子有通于音律者，又生當太平之盛，樂雍熙之治，欲返古感今，以飾太平。所扮者，隋謂之『康衢戲』，唐謂之『梨園樂』，宋謂之『華林戲』，元謂之『昇平樂』.

This short passage is perhaps the earliest extended discussion of the break between performers and literary specialists. There seems to be little doubt that, while writers trained for the examinations did not create the performance genre of *zaju*, they were instrumental in changing it from simple skits to a more sophisticated dramatic genre. The metrical requirements of composition, the cultural knowledge needed to sustain a complex and multilayered subjectivity presented through the lead singer, and the linguistic and stylistic ability to write poetic lyrics probably lay outside the reach of all but the most educated entertainers. This calculus is further complicated in this passage by the implied relationship between learning and status. When Zhao Mengfu comments that the writing is produced by great Confucian scholars, we do not think he meant that eminent Confucians actually wrote the plays but that the "sons of good families" were raised in a family tradition (*jiafeng* 家風) in which classical learning was part of everyone's life when growing up. This knowledge was put to use in drama; but that very act was further complicated by having to adapt this classical knowledge into a universal colloquial language and the specific cultural world that stamped fiction and drama. Of course not every entertainer was incapable of this—as witnessed by the coauthors of Ma Zhiyuan, Hua Li Lang, and Hongzi Li Er[75]—but for the most part entertainers simply did not have the training and therefore did not possess the stylistic gifts or ethical weight that this training necessitated.[76]

In a sense, then, Wang Guowei was simply the last in a long line of elite writers that stretched back to the fourteenth century who all chose to emphasize writing and text over performance. Wang held a quite equivocal view about the quality of *zaju*, recognizing its beauty but also (in terms of literati culture) its flaws. He was less sanguine about what Zhu Quan had called "Confucian scholars and men of deep learning" and actually reified the divide between the social and cultural status of early text producers and those he thought of as "real dramatists" from the elite world of the literati. In his *Luqu yutan*, published in 1909, he wrote,

> Bai Pu was the only scholar-official to write *zaju*. None of the other writers, like Guan Hanqing, Wang Shifu, Ma Zhiyuan, or Zheng Guangzu, held an important position, but they resided somewhere between the scholar and the actor. Therefore, there is something about their writing that stands out by itself, but so does the shallowness of their learning and the vulgarity of their minds. The reason that *xiqu* never was part of even the most insignificant literature was probably due to this. When it came to the Ming, then many literati began to dabble in *xiqu*. In the early period there was Gao Ming ([given name] Dongjia) and in the later, Tang Xianzu ([given name] Linchuan)—both were widely learned and elegant gentlemen. It was only when it reached Kong Shangren ([given name] Jizhong) and Hong Sheng ([given name] Fangsi) of our dynasty [that is, the Manchu Qing dynasty] that they began completely to sweep away several hundred years of rankness, but the vitality [of drama] was about to be exhausted.[77] 士大夫之作雜劇者，唯白蘭谷樸耳。此外雜劇大家，如關、王、馬、鄭等，皆名位不著，在士人與倡優之間。故其文字誠有獨絕千古者，然學問之弇陋，與胸襟之卑鄙，亦獨絕千古，戲曲之所以不得與於文學之末者，未始不由於此。至明，而士大夫亦多染指戲曲。前之東嘉、後之臨川，皆博雅君子也；至國朝孔季重、洪昉思出，始一掃數百年之蕪穢，然生氣亦略盡矣.

At the time that Wang wrote this, neither the trove of 242 texts from the Maiwangguan nor the *Yuankan zaju sanshi zhong* had come to light,[78] and it was inevitable that he would turn to Zang Maoxun's 1615–1616 anthology as his basic source material. He explained his choice thusly:

> The world often criticizes Zang Jinshu ([proper name] Maoxun) for making so many unnoted changes in his printing of the *Selection of Yuan Plays*. From my perspective the early Ming manuscript of Zheng Tingyu's *zaju*, *King Zhao of Chu*: *The Most Distant Relative Goes Overboard*, which was in the Jiahui Tang library of the Ding family in Qiantang,[79] is full of errors and execrably inferior, and is a long way from [the quality] of the edition found in a *Selection of Yuan Plays*. Now many Yuan plays underwent unseen changes at the hands of entertainers and had long lost their authenticity. The printing by Jinshu derived from editions of the Office of Imperial Theater obtained from Liu Yuanbo, and as he mentioned in his preface, "were not the same as current commercial editions."[80] Later people discussed [Zang's texts] by holding up examples from commercial editions and selections from the *Songs from the Music Bureau in an Era of Peace and Joy* (*Yongxi yuefu*), so it is logical that there would be so many conflicts. 世多病臧晋叔（懋循）刻元曲選，多所改竄;以余所見錢塘丁氏嘉惠堂所藏明初鈔本鄭廷玉《楚昭王疏者下船》雜劇，謬誤拙劣，不及元曲選本遠甚。蓋元劇多遭伶人改竄，久失其真。晉叔所刊，出于黃州劉延伯所得御戲監本，其序已云，『與今坊本不同』。後人執坊本及《雍熙樂府》所選者而議之，宜其多所牴牾矣.

As Wang points out in this remark, Zang Maoxun took his selection of one hundred from texts he had stored in his own library and from two hundred plays from the Imperial Theater Office. As Zang's prefaces to the *Selection of Yuan Plays* show, he also picked his own texts based primarily on the criterion of how well they would educate southern writers to the wonders of *zaju*. In essence, then, Wang selected a text of the play to canonize what had previously been selected by a late Ming literatus as a representative work from a group of plays that had in turn been selected (or created) by the eunuch agency in charge of providing scripts for imperial performance.

Moreover, Zang Maoxun's prefaces are written in the context of dramatic debates of the sixteenth and seventeenth centuries. In his second preface to the *Selection of Yuan Plays*, in particular, he sets forth his own criteria for drama (summarized here):

1. That *qu*, including both *zaju* and *xiwen*, are in a direct line of descent within the orthodox genre of poetry and therefore are subject to the same standards of critical ethical judgment
2. That *qu*, nevertheless, is a broader form, drawing from a wide range of sources and therefore more difficult to write

3. That it must not only present a seamless combination of these sources but also meld the refined (*ya* 雅) and vulgar (*su* 俗) into a realm of "sentimental diction" (*qingci* 情辭) that is "stable and balanced"
4. That it must create an organic space onstage, created from the appropriate register and dialect of the characters' language and from a representation of events that is of "true color"—a recognizably mimetic and accurate reproduction of any event's "basic appearance."[81] This space is separated from the outside not by physical barriers but by a virtual landscape that language generates from the center and which remains as a centripetal force.
5. That it must recognize the difference in regional forms of language but that it must be clear about tonal distribution, appropriate dialect and register in terms of rhyme and tone, and that it must abide by accepted rules of composition

Finally, the perfect presentation of drama relies, according to Zang, on the skilled writer and the skilled performer, each working in their respective spheres. As in Zhu Quan's essay, Zang's preface is careful to keep the two spheres of writer and performer separate. Zang also clears space for his own emendations to the text, particularly his rewritings of the fourth act, by claiming that *zaju* authors were "worn out" by the fourth act.[82] One of the ways of looking at Zang's prefaces is that they are in conversation with the writings of Wang Jide 王驥德 (d. 1623), He Liangjun, and Wang Shizhen 王世貞 (1526–1590) at a critical moment in the sixteenth century when *zaju* is in decline and southern drama is on the ascendancy. Zang finds his greatest affinity with He Liangjun and clearly accepts the idea that *qu* as song was derived from a poetic legacy that could be traced back to the *Book of Odes*.[83] Thus, it had to undergo editing to bring the songs into the ethical realm that such a tradition denoted.[84] Consequently, there are clear agenda in Zang's prefaces that center on the relationship between genre, culture, and prosody, as well as a personal anxiety about establishing his own point of view as authoritative in a moment of contending and powerful voices.

Our point here is that the canon of *zaju* and the modern study of the history of drama are both retrospective creations based on later, even modern, conceptions of what they should be. As opposed, say, to the tradition of *shi* poetry, which has a long history of development in terms of canon formation (a canon that has changed over the years) and a parallel development in poetic theory and criticism, drama is discovered as a literary genre only as it emerges into elite literati consciousness in the early Ming. And when it emerges into their consciousness, it is fraught with issues of class status, ethical status, as well as where it should be placed within an already well-defined constellation of culturally orthodox literary genres. Moreover, reading practices that had been shaped by years of education had inculcated aesthetic values that included complicated homologies between genre, linguistic usage, class, interiority, and ethics. So, in addition to the actual social class differences between performers and authors, a respectable canon had to be formed that would also adequately represent these more abstract and culturally determined values of elite culture. As opposed to what we might call the natural and symbiotic development of a canon and its accompanying critical apparatus, the corpus of *zaju* (and to some extent early southern drama as well) that was selected to appear in print retrospectively created an artificial and imaginary canon into which earlier textual antecedents, discovered after the fact well into the twentieth century, did not fit.

The relatively little attention paid to the *Yuankan* texts may also stem from the fact that they have been introduced into the field primarily in three ways: (1) as "original" *zaju* texts (原本) that preserve the "original features of *zaju*" (元雜劇本來面目),[85] (2) through textual scholars who are interested purely in a history of editions or in setting a text, and (3) as a data set for linguists working both in syntax and phonology. In the case of setting texts, the emphasis has been on providing "corrections" to variant forms of graphic representation, or replacing homophonic "borrowings" with the "real" characters. In nearly all cases emphasis has been laid on the poor quality of the received text of the Yuan printings: "There are many incorrect characters, the simplifying of written characters does not conform to normative conventions, there are critical instances of omissions, the characters are unclearly written, and the printing blocks are worn-out—none of which makes it easy for the reader" 錯別字多，簡寫不規範，脫漏情況嚴重，白字漫漶不清，版子又斷爛，頗不便于閱讀.[86] As Zheng Qian wrote in the preface of his pioneering critical edition of the thirty Yuan plays,

> These texts are aria scripts published by commercial presses in the Yuan. The cutters were extremely careless and inferior; incorrectly written characters, missing characters, homophonic borrowings, simplified and vulgar characters are found all over the pages. Sometimes it is cut in such a way that it makes no recognizable character. If we discuss the format and style of the lines, we find the prose sections and arias are indiscriminately mixed, and the song titles are often incorrectly carved or missing altogether. And in addition [the texts] have another deficiency, which is that the prose dialogue is incomplete, either retaining only simple prose lines of the male or female lead or lacking any dialogue altogether. In this case, if there is no other edition available, the plot details often cannot be clearly understood. Since it has these two major deficiencies, even seasoned readers of Yuan drama experience the effort needed to read these texts, let alone beginners. And this is precisely the reason that these texts are not widely circulated, although they are fine and important.[87] 這部書是元代書坊所印的『小唱本』，刻工非常草率拙劣，錯字、掉字、同音假借字、簡體俗字、滿紙都是，有時簡直刻得不成字形。講到行款格式，則賓白與曲文常是混在一起，分不出來，曲調牌名嘩常有誤刻或漏刻。此外還有一種毛病，就是賓白不全，只有正末或正旦的簡單說白，或竟全無賓白。於是，別無他本諸劇的情節常是弄不清楚。有了這兩個缺點，對于元劇修養有素的人，對此書也有時頗感吃力，更不必說初學。此書雖好雖重要而不太通行，就是這個緣故.

Zheng goes on to remark that it took him nearly thirty years to create his own edition, due in part to the need to learn the conventions of Yuan printings,[88] to master the formal features of prosody, and to have access first to the collotype edition from Kyoto and then to the Ming woodblock and manuscript editions.[89] His ultimate aim was to provide a general reader for early drama (一般通用的讀本).

Despite Zheng's desire to make a reading edition, his work is still consulted today mostly as a philological text. The same holds true for the other collated editions of *Yuankan* texts. The dominant classroom and scholarly text remains the *Yuanqu xuan*. The reasons why are well expressed by the late Xu Shuofang in his article "Zang Maoxun and His *Yuanqu xuan*," in which he addresses the problems inherent in giving up the eminently readable *Selection of Yuan Plays* for the earlier editions. He points out that while the Yuan editions may be thought by some to "be closer to the original text" (接近于原本),[90] their lack of dialogue makes them difficult to use. Xu considers the fact that Wang Guowei (and, by extension, others) legitimize the *Yuankan* as "authentic" by accepting Zang Maoxun's proposal that "the dialogue was created by actors while they were performing. So, it is often coarse and repetitive." Xu counters by pointing out the necessity of the dialogue to move the plot along, which cannot be accomplished by the arias alone. He cites several examples of compelling prose passages that he attributes to the literate authors of the writing societies (*shuhui* 書會) and notes that elite readers are always biased toward the poetry of the arias, seldom taking serious note of the dialogue as an integral part of the dramas. "To attribute such fine dialogue," he says, "to momentary inspiration of the actor, in which anyone can add or subtract at will, if not a momentary slip of the tongue [on Zang's part] then is to let the point of view of orthodox literature become a bane" 把。。。中的科白歸之于演員的即興之作，人人得以自由增減，不是一時失言就是正統文學觀點在做祟.[91] On the contrary, Xu argues, because they contain the dialogue, Zang Maoxun's texts are closer to the original dramas. The *Yuankan* texts, "with incomplete dialogue, difficult to understand arias, even having undergone meticulous putting in order . . . still are hard for a general readership to accept as literary texts" 賓白不全，曲文難懂，即使經過細心整理，元刊本也難以作為文學作品為一般讀者所接受.[92]

In sum, the reading practices of a Jiangnan literatus (Zang Maoxun) and his community of readers in the seventeenth century are imposed retrospectively on a set of texts that have their own, hidden, evolutionary nature. Not only do the standards of this group become the basis for selecting and anthologizing earlier texts, they are enacted as a practice that is free from the traditional prescriptions for editing, collecting, and printing that hold for other forms of literary text. And, when drama studies become a discipline under the pressure of modernization in the twentieth century, these texts are canonized as the representative body. Moreover, later scholars who mature intellectually reading the same texts of orthodox literature maintain a standard mode of reading that subsumes dramatic texts to the more standardized and culturally comfortable realm of traditional poetics. Literati, as Xu points out, will always prefer the arias because they are poetry.

The constant stress on the difficulty of reading the Yuan editions is due to the fact that their conventions are *not* those of the seventeenth century or those of that particular group of Suzhou literati who were creating the corpus of drama and *xiaoshuo* as reading material in the early seventeenth century. Only Zheng Qian, of all modern scholars, has a notion that they can be readable as literature—and he openly acknowledges the difficulty of preparing oneself for that task. But his positive example only highlights the larger failure to see these texts historically, and to accept the fact that they represent a reading practice of an audience for whom these texts were perfectly understandable. For example, "wrong" characters often turn out to be homophones (*baizi* 白字), simple phonetic prompts to the correct pronunciation of a word or term. In that context they are perfectly understandable. Difficult orthography turns out to be conventional;[93] missing dialogue would be about well-known stories or plots; and different arrangements or length point to a differing sensibility or strictures onstage.[94] That the texts have remained underutilized as literature—due to this complex combination of social class, ethical status, easy acceptance of literati recensions as "authentic" texts, and completeness of other editions—should not deter us from seeing them at the fount of a written legacy. They are difficult to read, but we should attempt to read them in their own context, appreciate the literary quality they have, try to understand the literary quality they had in the eyes of their readers (and listeners), and see how they contribute to a legacy of textual materials. Too often the thirty Yuan plays are completely separated from later Ming editions as an anomaly, but as we hope to have shown, they form a natural unit not only with Li Kaixian's *Revised Plays of the Yuan Masters* (*Gaiding Yuanxian chuanqi* 改定元賢傳奇) but also with the Yu Xiaogu manuscripts in the collection of the Studio of the Transformed Bookworm and other early manuscripts from the Ming Court Entertainment Bureau (Jiaofang Si 教坊司). In context, they allow us not only to understand textual development but also to comprehend how literary taste changes over the ages before it is codified by the tradition of high learning.

NOTES

1. By "comedy," we mean a play in the colloquial tongue that generally portrays ordinary people or popular representations of historical figures, has loosely connected scenes, and ends in a moment of happy reunion.
2. That is, scripts that were produced for either the single female or male lead to use.
3. See Idema 1996 and West 2004.
4. Shi Junbao 石君寶, *Wind and Moon in the Courtyard of Purple Clouds* (*Fengyue Ziyun ting* 風月紫雲庭), in Idema and West 1982, 236–77; Guan Hanqing 關漢卿, *A Beauty Pining in Her Boudoir: The Pavilion of Praying to the Moon* (*Guiyuan jiaren baiyueting*閨怨佳人拜月亭), in West and Idema 2010b, 77–103; *Zhuge Liang Burns the Stores at Bowang* (*Zhuge Liang Bowang shao tun* 諸葛亮博望燒屯), in Idema and West 2012, 197–235; Guan Hanqing, *The Great King Guan and the Single Sword Meeting* (*Guan dawang dandao hui* 關大王單刀會) and *In a Dream Guan and Zhang, a Pair, Rush to Western Shu* (*Guan Zhang shuangfu Xi Shu meng* 關張雙赴西蜀夢), in Idema and West 2012, 236–95, 296–315.

5. West and Idema 2010b, ix–xxxv.
6. For a general overview of prosimetric narrative, see Idema 2010b, 343–67; for a basic introduction to the features of northern drama, see West and Idema 2010b, ix–xxxv.
7. On the use of role types in drama rather than characters, see West and Idema 2010b, x, xvii–xix.
8. While some texts claim to have been compiled in Dadu, only one text claims to have been printed in Dadu.
9. Huang Pilie 1958, 23b; preface dated Dec. 18, 1804.
10. Ibid., 1a–4a.
11. Ibid. (sec. 2), 1a.
12. See n. 19.
13. Iwaki 1961, 80–87; see also Miao 2004, 15–17. On Li Kaixian, see Idema 2005–2006; Tan 2009; and Zhen 2008.
14. For a succinct description of the extant editions of *zaju*, see West and Idema 2010b, xix–xxxi; on Ming palace editions, see Du 2008; Zheng Li 2007; and Komatsu 2001.
15. Guan 1958, 25b; see also Cai 1989, 2:637.
16. Meng 1958, 32b; see also Cai 1989, 2:790.
17. Zheng Tingyu 1958b, 31b; see also Cai 1989, 2:774.
18. Gong 1958, 32b; the arias to which he alludes are found in act 1, 9a–11b, and act 2, 15b–17b; see also Cai 1989, 2:796.
19. Zhen 2008, 65.
20. Ibid. Li Kaixian, with the aid of a number of assistants, produced his own anthology of Yuan drama titled *Gaiding Yuanxian chuanqi* 改定元賢傳奇 (*Revised Plays by Yuan Authors*). To judge from the few surviving plays of this project, it appears that they worked on the basis of Yuan printings or manuscripts in his collection. While Li and his collaborators retained the full suites of songs and made only minimal changes to the arias, they provided full dialogues for all characters in the play on the basis of a careful reading of the arias, the preserved stage directions, and the cue lines. While we know that sixteen plays were printed, only six have been preserved. Later Ming editions of plays with these titles appear to be based on these editions. See Idema 2005–2006 and Tan 2009.
21. Zheng Guangzu 1958, 21b, and Cai 1989, 2:793.
22. Ibid.
23. Zhou Deqing 2006. On the rhyme categories in *Zhongyuan yinyun*, see Stimson 1966.
24. Zhou Deqing 2006, 299.
25. Zheng Guangzu 1958, 20a.
26. That is, female entertainers.
27. A poet.
28. From the story of a person who dreamt of an entire lifetime during the time it took to cook a pot of millet. See chap. 4, n. 19.
29. Zhou Deqing 2006, 298.
30. Ma 1958, 4a.
31. Zhong 1982, 117. See also 204n606, which includes Jia Zhongming's 賈仲明 (1343–1422) note that the authors, Ma Zhiyuan 馬致遠, Hongzi Li Er 紅字李二, Hua Li Lang 花李郎, and Li Shizhong 李時中, all belonged to the Yuanzhen Writing Society 元貞書會. Hongzi Li Er (literally, "Red-Writing Li the Second") and Hua Li Lang (literally, "Esquire Li the Flowered") both probably sported tattoos.
32. Compare He Huang's use of the autograph text that Li Kaixian seems to have copied from a Yuan printed version; see n. 16.
33. In modern theaters the text of arias is projected over the stage for the benefit of the audience.

34. Stage directions can be extremely detailed in the way they instruct the lead actor or lead actress about how to perform his or her role, at times demanding them to exhibit contradictory emotions. For specific examples, see Idema 1993.
35. Bao and Hu 2010, 45.
36. See Xia 1996, passim; Idema and West 1982, 145–69. We are referring here to the famous exchanges between Guan Hanqing, Hu Zhiyu 胡祇遹 (1227–1293), Feng Zizhen 馮子振 (1257–1327), and Pearl Screen Beauty, Zhu Lianxiu 珠簾秀. See Idema and West 1982, 166–67, and Xia 1996, 82–90.
37. This tune does not occur in the repertoire of southern drama, and the song appears to have come directly from the play's northern antecedent. See West 2008, 89–94.
38. *Zhangji* 掌記 were hand-copied scripts small enough to be put into one's clothing and carried around. Extant evidence suggests that they contained the text of an act of a play and were annotated with musical notations for quick reference. See Idema and West 1982, 93; Tseng 2009, 353–57.
39. Translation revised from Idema and West 1982, 207.
40. Following the notes in Hu 2008, 312–16.
41. Following Hu Ji's suggestion that 恰 may be a mistake for 招.
42. As Hu indicates, this line has room for reinterpretation given that it may refer to the "venal official" role type.
43. Li Kaixian remarked in his preface to the *Revised Plays of the Yuan Masters* that he had more than a thousand scripts in his possession. See Li Kaixian 2004, 1808, translated in Idema 2005–2006, 49.
44. We should note, however, that in his 1332 work, *Rhymes of the Central Plain*, Zhou Deqing uses the term *zhe* 摺 at least once to mark act divisions.
45. Bao and Hu 2010, 44.
46. Zheng Qian's remarks are pertinent here. He has rectified this suite by inserting a more normal first song, *Fen die'er*, based on the *Guming jia* edition. But he also notes that there are other instances in which the song *Zui chunfeng* begins a suite, and therefore keeps the original arrangement open as an option. He takes the term *zimu diao* as denoting a particular singing method (*changfa* 唱法) and expresses uncertainty about whether or not it is linked to the first song. If it were a "singing method," then it could be understood perhaps as "sung in contrasting light and heavy manner." See Zheng Qian 1962, 240–41.
47. Fan Kang 1958, 7a–b.
48. See West and Idema 2010b, 346–47.
49. Wang Bocheng 1958, 9b.
50. Jin 1958, 8b.
51. Guan 1958, 26a.
52. Huang Tianji thinks Zhou Cang may sing these last songs. See Huang Tianji 2001, 107.
53. See Idema 2005–2006, 61–64; Shi 1958, 7a; Idema and West 1982, 276.
54. The actress Wei Daodao 魏道道; see Xia 1996, 136.
55. See particularly Komatsu 2001, 38–43.
56. Di 1958, 8b.
57. Yang Zi 1958, 7a.
58. Zheng Guangzu 1958, 8b.
59. Information drawn from Komatsu 2001, 124–42; Zheng Li 2007, 98–99; Du 2007, 48–52.
60. Du 2007, 49.
61. Zhao's family had long been acquainted with the Yu family. Zhao's father, Zhao Yongxian 趙用賢 (*jinshi* 1571), had, along with Yu's father, Yu Shenxing 于慎行 (1545–1607), criticized the high Ming official Zhang Juzheng 張居正 (1525–1582) for his failure to carry out proper mourning rites. As a high official himself, Yu Shenxing had many opportunities to be in and out of the court and to have access to court

plays, particularly those from the Court Entertainment Bureau, which were often performed for officials rather than the emperor.

62. See Idema and West 2012, 181, 195–96.
63. Imperial edicts.
64. Anon 1958a, 41b.
65. Komatsu 2001, 136–37.
66. This function of the extra has to be distinguished from the extra as an actor performing secondary male roles. This particular extra sometimes made intrusive comments from offstage in direct questioning of a particular actor or set of actors.
67. Cited in Wang Liqi 1981, 11. This proscription was first issued on the twenty-fifth day of the third month of the twenty-fifth year of Hongwu, April 21, 1389, and was restated in several other edicts during the rest of the dynasty. See ibid., 11–16.
68. A very recent article by Bao Jianqiang and Hu Chengxuan has finally begun to challenge the use of Ming editions as a basis for examining early text. In their work, they write, "Since the Yuan texts are performing texts that are stamped by the performance of artists and stagecraft, those who edit the texts should value and respect the basic quality of the texts, and move along the path of popular performance and should not measure them or shape them according to the standard or frame of literati editions" 既然元本是藝人性和劇場性的民間通俗演唱腳本，那麼，校勘元本應尊重其版本性質，走民間文藝一路，不以文人版本的標准、框架來衡量、斧鑿它. See Bao and Hu 2010, 44–49.
69. On Wang Guowei's early opinions on drama and his subsequent shift in attitude under the influence of Japanese scholars, see Huang Shizhong 2009; He Yuming 2007; and Llamas 2010.
70. Ren and Ji 1983, 34–35.
71. In this respect, see He Jinli 2006.
72. The great Yuan literatus and painter Zhao Mengfu 趙孟頫 (1254–1322).
73. This highly ambiguous term here means "literary elegance," although it might be tinged with its other connotation, "romantic affair."
74. Zhu 2010, 39–42. Another version of this passage is found in Fei 2002, 44–45.
75. See n. 31.
76. See Zhu 2010, 42–44.
77. Wang Guowei 1964, 274; see also *Luqu yutan* in Wang Guowei 1983, 4b.
78. Ibid., 279 and 8b.
79. Gao Sixi 1976, 32–35.
80. Zang 1998, 1b.
81. This does not necessarily mean an empirical mimesis; a philosophically or conceptually hypothetical reality can also have its "basic color."
82. Zang and many of his contemporaries believed that the Yuan dynasty used *zaju* in its official examinations and the examination candidates were exhausted by the time they reached the fourth act.
83. Zang 1998, 1b. The *Shijing* (*Book of Odes*) is a collection of over three hundred songs. The collection was one of the Five Classics, and tradition credited Confucius with the selection and editing of the texts that were included.
84. This would, of course, also place Zang in the tradition of Confucius, who supposedly edited the folk songs of the *Shijing* for court use.
85. Sun 1953, 153; Wang Guowei's preface to the Shanghai reprint of the Kyoto edition of the thirty plays, cited in Zheng Qian 1962, i.
86. Xu Qinjun 1980, iii. Xu's statement is a bit harsher than either Zheng Qian 1962 or Ning 1988.
87. Zheng Qian 1962, ii.

88. Ibid., 3: "My own knowledge of novels and short stories in the colloquial and drama had grown; moreover, I had seen several kinds of commercial Yuan woodblocks in photoprint, like the *Yuefu xinsheng* and *Sanguo zhi pinghua*, and I could recognize all the simplified and alternative-form characters in these works, and all that was left were a few malformed characters that could not be recognized" 我對於戲曲小說，所知已較前為多，並已見過若干種元代坊刻書的影印本，如《樂府新聲》、《三國志平話》之類，此書的簡體別體字已經都能認出，只剩下一些不成形體根本無從辨識的字.
89. In reference to the printing of the Maiwangguan collection.
90. Xu Shuofang 1993, 14.
91. Ibid, 15.
92. Ibid, 17.
93. See, for example, Ning 1988, 13–17.
94. The oft-cited example of *The Orphan of Zhao* is the primary example of this. The *Yuankan* text has only four acts, while the *Selection of Yuan Plays* version has five, leading most scholars to claim that the Yuan play is somehow incomplete, as Xu Shuofang remarks, "like an arrow nocked, its power lies in the necessity of firing it; it's hard to leave off halfway" 如箭在弦，勢在必發，難以半途廢. See Xu Shuofang 1993, 16.

Conventions

There are considerable differences in the physical format of the editions that we have used, and we have striven to maintain these distinctions in the translation. A typical *zaju* drama, stripped to its skeletal form, will have a title, a wedge (optional demi-act), four acts, and be concluded by a "title" and a "name." Each act will consist of a suite of songs in a single mode arranged in order, written to the same rhyme, sometimes concluded by a coda (*wei*, or *sha*). As we noted in the introduction, the early plays may also be concluded by a "dispersal scene" (*sanchang* 散場). The play proper will then be concluded with the title and name of the drama. For instance, in the fourteenth-century edition of *Tippler Zhao Yuan Encounters the Prior Emperor*, the structure looks thus:

[ACT 1] [XIANLÜ MODE]	[ACT 2] [NANLÜ MODE]	[ACT 3] [ZHONGLÜ MODE]	[ACT 4] [SHUANGDIAO MODE]
(*Dian jiangchun*)	(*Yizhi hua*)	(*Fen die'er*)	(*Xinshui ling*)
(*Hunjiang long*)	(*Liangzhou*)	(*Zui chunfeng*)	(*Qiaopai'er*)
(*You hulu*)	(*Muyang guan*)	(*Ying xianke*)	(*Tianshui ling*)
(*Tianxia le*)	(*Gewei*)	(*Shang xiaolou*)	(*Zhegui ling*)
(*Nezha ling*)	(*Gan huang'en*)	(*Reprise*)	(*Qi dixiong*)
(*Que ta zhi*)	(*Hong shaoyao*)	(*Shi'er yue*)	(*Yan'er luo*)
(*Jisheng cao*)	(*Pusa Liangzhou*)	(*Yaomin ge*)	(*Desheng ling*)
(*Zui zhong tian*)	(*Coda*)	(*Shua hai'er*)	
(*You simen*)		(*Second from Coda*)	
(*Shanghua shi*)		(*Coda*)	
(*Reprise*)			
(*Coda*)			

Title:	Father-in-law and mother-in-law have venomous hearts, The official concerned abuses his power to get a rouged beauty.
Name:	In the snow a government runner takes great revenge, Tippler Zhao Yuan Encounters the Prior Emperor.

✤ ✤ ✤

We use brackets for several purposes: (1) to add information that the Chinese implies but does not state (e.g., I see three golden-saddled [horses] tied to an aged mulberry tree), (2) to indicate a missing subject (e.g., [ZHANG QIAN *speaks*:] Face the judge) or (3) a missing object (e.g., If I write out [the divorce writ] . . .), and (4) to indicate acts and wedges in the early print editions (e.g., [Act 1]). These are meant only as a convenience to the reader. It is clear that these early editions did not conceive of hard-and-fast divisions between acts except as units of the play marked by the suites. It is clear that in many cases action was continuous between what later editors would stipulate as a separate acts. The change between "[Act 2]" and "[Act 3]" of *Xue Rengui Returns Home* provides an excellent example of the fluidity between suites of a drama.

✤ ✤ ✤

Normally a play is composed of three basic kinds of text: stage directions, plain speech, and lyric songs (translated as free verse). Role types appear as small-capital text, stage directions as italic text, arias are inset three spaces, lines spoken within the arias are inset six spaces in reduced type. Poems are centered in the text. Recited text from other forms of performance (for instance, sections of ballad verse and the judgments pronounced at the end of the plays) that are not delivered in plain speech are inset two spaces and flush left. Tune titles are in italics, and the mode to which the suite is written is in small capitals.

✤ ✤ ✤

The fourteenth-century print and Ming manuscript editions separate stage directions with only a large space to signal separation of the stage directions from each other, from the arias, and from spoken passages. To note these we utilize em dashes to separate the stage directions from other parts of the text:

EMPEROR *speaks*:—Zhao Yuan, do you want to see your enemies?—MALE LEAD *speaks*:—Your Majesty, I certainly do.—EMPEROR *speaks*:—Personal attendants, bring in the Prefect of the Eastern Capital along with Zhao Yuan's in-laws and his wife Moon Fairy Liu.—CHU *speaks*:—Understood! The whole group go in and face Him.—*Acts out taking* OLD MAN, OLD WOMAN, PAINTED FEMALE, *and* COMIC *and they all kneel.*—EMPEROR *speaks*:—You miscreants, do you know your offenses?—COMIC *speaks*:—I don't, Your Majesty.—EMPEROR *speaks*:—Why did you forcibly take a commoner's wife?—COMIC *speaks*:—I certainly wouldn't dare do such a thing. She made me be a live-in son-in-law.—EMPEROR *speaks*:—This miscreant knows nothing about how to act.—MALE LEAD *sings*:

Zang Maoxun's *A Selection of Yuan Plays* editions use parentheses to enclose the stage directions:

(CHEN JIQING *speaks*:) Wife, I have to go off to the examinations. (FEMALE *speaks*:) Scholar, you just got home, how can you leave and abandon me? (*She acts out grieving.*) (CHEN JIQING *speaks*:) How could I ever set aside the feelings between us? It's just that the time of the examination is pressing in, and in the blink of an eye another three years will be gone. What then? (MALE LEAD *sings*:)

We have annotated the text with primarily advanced students in mind. But, by the time these texts were created, many of the gems of Chinese poetry had entered the colloquial lexicon and had become standard, even cliché parts of ordinary speech. Unless a poem has special significance in the text or is rarely used, we have identified these passages by simply putting them into quotation marks. They function as a form of speech similar to what the Chinese call "set phrases" (*chengyu* 成語) or "colloquial sayings" (*suyu* 俗語), which are handy aphorisms that are spoken to capture the moment linguistically as a precise category of behavior or feeling. These clichés and set phrases are also enclosed in quotation marks.

✤ ✤ ✤

The reader should also bear the following in mind:

1. Chinese texts seldom use personal pronouns, except for the first person. Instead, the common form of address is to use terms denoting kinship, social status, or official position. To make the text more readable, we have often emended these to simple pronouns, except in cases where they specify a key relationship of the speaker to the person being addressed.
2. We use serial periods to denote missing or blurred text. We do not include the actual character count of words missing. The reader who desires to investigate the number of characters missing or putative reconstructions of text should consult the annotations of Zheng Qian 1962, Xu Qinjun 1980, and Ning Xiyuan 1988.
3. We have attempted to follow the original printed edition or manuscript copy as closely as possible. This means that spoken text that is in smaller characters (often set flush right in the column) in the original is rendered in smaller type and placed apart from the lyrics of the aria (as shown in the preceding example). The text in smaller

characters is either speech inserted between lines as part of the song or padding words (*chenzi*; see the introduction). Zang Maoxun's text does not mark padding words, and we have, as he has, made them part of the lines of the arias, maintaining their original size.

4. The *jing* role includes both comics and villains. We have identified the *jing* role in the dramatis personae contextually as either a comic or a villain. Ming editors introduced a role type unknown in the earlier editions, the *chou* 丑, which we have translated as "clown."
5. Finally, it should be noted that the fourteenth-century Yuan texts do not use the stage direction "sing" in their texts. This is because these are role texts written for only one actor to use and therefore omit the redundant stage direction.

1

The Orphan of Zhao

INTRODUCTION

The Orphan of Zhao (*Zhaoshi gu'er* 趙氏孤兒) is one of three plays for which the Yuan printing provides only tune titles, lyrics of the songs, and a very few padding words. No stage directions or prose dialogue, however fragmentary, are to be found. The Yuan printing represents *The Orphan of Zhao* as a regular *zaju* of four suites of songs preceded by a wedge. All songs are assigned to a male lead who plays four different characters: Zhao Shuo 趙朔 (in the wedge), Han Jue 韓厥 (in the first act), Gongsun Chujiu 公孫杵臼 (in the second and third acts), and the grown-up Orphan (in the fourth act). An extremely heavily edited version of the play is also preserved in Zang Maoxun's *Yuanqu xuan*. The extent and nature of the differences between these two versions are suggested by the fact that the *Yuanqu xuan* edition includes a fifth act, a rarity among *zaju*. We provide a translation of the *Yuanqu xuan* version of *The Orphan of Zhao* following the translation of the Yuan printing.

The *Yuanqu xuan* version of *The Orphan of Zhao* has the distinction of being the first Chinese play to be translated into a European language. Joseph Henri Marie de Prémare's (1666–1736) French translation of the early eighteenth century, subtitled a *tragédie chinoise*, however, limited itself to the stage directions and prose dialogues—since the dialogues in this play are extremely extensive and detailed, the play lent itself very well to such a treatment. Prémare's translation exerted a considerable influence on eighteenth-century European drama, culminating in Voltaire's *L'Orphelin de la Chine* (1755), which was one of the most successful plays of its age. The characterization of *The Orphan of Zhao* as a tragedy by its French editors helped to ensure a special reputation for the Chinese play in twentieth-century modern Chinese scholarship on traditional drama, starting with the writings of Wang Guowei, who highlighted *The Orphan of Zhao* alongside

Guan Hanqing's *Injustice to Dou E* (*Dou E yuan* 竇娥冤) as rare examples of a Chinese tradition of tragedy. The characterization of these plays as "tragedies," a term that carries with it all the theoretical baggage of Greek tragedy and the ensuing Western tradition, was roundly rejected by the great comparative literary scholar Qian Zhongshu 錢鍾書 (1910–1988) in 1935.[1] Despite his sensible evaluation of the differences between the Chinese and Western traditions of plays of a tragic nature, his article carried little weight in the historical process that canonized these plays—most likely because the article appeared in China in English.

Although Yuan printings of drama provide no authorial attribution, *The Register of Ghosts* credits a certain Ji Junxiang 紀郡祥 with a play by the same title. Ji's name occurs in the section of *The Register of Ghosts* titled "Already Deceased Lords and Poets of the Former Generation Whose Plays Now Circulate in the World," which would date his activities roughly to the second half of the thirteenth century. The biographical data provided by *The Register of Ghosts* are limited to the following laconic statement, "A man of Dadu, who was a contemporary of Li Shouqing and Zheng Tingyu" 大都人,李壽卿、鄭廷玉同時.[2] Apart from *The Orphan of Zhao*, Ji Junxiang is credited with the authorship of five other plays. *A Formulary of Correct Sounds for an Era of Great Peace* lists the same six titles under his name and remarks of Ji's style, "The lyrics of Ji Junxiang are like plum blossoms in the snow" 如雪裡梅花.[3] Now, Ji Junxiang's song texts may indeed be said to display an unadorned simplicity, but the mood suggested by the phrase "plum blossoms in the snow" better describes the one remaining song suite of an otherwise lost play on the topic of Buddhist enlightenment, *Chen Wentu Realizes the Way: A Dream in the Shade of a Pine* (*Chen Wentu wudao songyin meng* 陳文圖悟道松陰夢).[4] The description clearly is not a good fit for Ji's lyrics on loyalty, self-sacrifice, and bloody violence in *The Orphan of Zhao*.

None of the other titles listed under the name of Ji Junxiang in *The Register of Ghosts* have been preserved. Their subject matter ranged from contemporary scandal and romance to classical fairy tales and Daoist deliverance plays. We find the same variety of subject matter when we have a look at the ten titles credited to Li Shouqing 李壽卿, who hailed from Taiyuan and had a very minor official career.[5] Zheng Tingyu 鄭廷玉, who hailed from Zhangde (in Henan province), was the most prolific playwright of the trio: our sources credit him with twenty-three *zaju*, six of which have been preserved. In view of the wide variety of their subject matter and the simple style they employ it

1. Ch'ien 1935, 37–45.
2. Zhong 1982, 112.
3. Zhu 2010, 26, 53.
4. Also known by an alternative title, *Li Yuanzhen: The Story of the Shade of a Pine* (*Li Yuanzhen songyin ji* 李元真松陰記); see Zhong 1982, 112.
5. Ibid., 110–11.

would appear that these three authors wrote primarily for the contemporary commercial theater of Dadu.[6]

The action of *The Orphan of Zhao* is set in the early sixth century BC in the powerful state of Jin. Centered in the area of the modern province of Shanxi, Jin originally held sway over all adjoining regions, but the ruling house gradually lost power as that of the other six great noble clans of the state increased. After lengthy internecine warfare, three clans—Han, Wei, and Zhao—survived to carve up the state of Jin into three independent kingdoms that would continue to play major roles in the political history of China during the period of the fifth to third centuries BC.

The first work to provide a coherent account of the feud between Tu'an Gu 屠岸賈 and the Zhao clan is the "Hereditary House of Zhao" (Zhao shijia 趙世家) in the *Records of the Historian* (*Shiji* 史記), by Sima Qian 司馬遷 (ca. 100 BC), who created his text from scattered references in the *Zuozhuan* 左傳, a set of narrative stories attached to the laconic *Spring and Autumn Annals*, an annual history of the states of China between 722 and 468 BC. According to Sima Qian, Zhao Dun 趙盾 had dominated the court of Jin during the reign of Duke Ling (r. 620–607 BC), whose ascension to the throne Zhao Dun had engineered. Duke Ling was a cruel man who eventually tried to kill Zhao Dun. Zhao fled the capital, and in his absence the duke was murdered by one of Zhao Dun's clansmen. Even though many held Zhao Dun responsible for Duke Ling's death, he returned to dominate the court during the reign of Duke Cheng (r. 606–600 BC). Zhao Dun's son, Zhao Shuo, who inherited his father's post, was married to one of the duke's sisters. During the reign of Duke Jing (r. 599–581 BC), Tu'an Gu, a former favorite of Duke Ling's and then the commander in chief, set out to exterminate the Zhao clan. Han Jue tried to dissuade Tu'an Gu of this idea but to no avail. Neither did Han meet with success when he tried to persuade Zhao Shuo to flee. Han Jue then retired from public life under the pretext of illness, and Tu'an Gu exterminated all male members of the Zhao clan.

According to the *Records of the Historian*, the pregnant wife of Zhao Shuo hid herself in the palace. Two retainers of Zhao Shuo's thereupon conspired to ensure the survival of the clan. When Zhao Shuo's wife had given birth to a boy, Cheng Ying 程嬰 smuggled the child out of the palace and purchased another baby to replace him. When Tu'an Gu started to search for the Zhao baby, Cheng Ying stepped forward and accused Gongsun Chujiu 公孫杵臼 of hiding the Orphan of Zhao. Gongsun Chujiu's house was searched, and when the false Orphan was discovered, the baby and Gongsun Chujiu were both slain. Cheng Ying raised the true Orphan in the countryside. Many years later, in the fifteenth year of the reign of Duke Jing, the duke fell ill, and oracles informed him that his illness was due to "a great house left without an heir." Han Jue thereupon stepped forward and told the duke that the house concerned was the exterminated Zhao clan, of which a single male descendant miraculously had survived. He then brought the Orphan to court

6. A more detailed discussion of the similarities between these playwrights is provided in Idema 1988, 162–69.

and in turn exterminated Tu'an Gu and his clan. When the Orphan, named Zhao Wu, had been reinstated in his hereditary position and had regained his lands, Cheng Ying committed suicide in order to join Gongsun Chujiu.[7]

Ji Junxiang may well have been the first dramatist to adapt these materials for the stage. It has been suggested by certain similarities between the play and the historical circumstances accompanying the downfall of the Song dynasty (960–1279) that the drama is an expression of Ji's loyalty to the defunct Song. The imperial family of the Song was also surnamed Zhao, and the Song had at various times lavished great posthumous honors on Cheng Ying and Gongsun Chujiu. Moreover, the last emperor of the Song dynasty, an infant, died in 1279 when, during a sea battle near present-day Hong Kong, the last prime minister of the Song leapt into the sea with the infant tied to his back.[8] But it should also be borne in mind that the Beijing area, which had served as the capital of the Jurchen Jin (1115–1234) for almost a century, had never been part of Song territory. The Latter Jin dynasty (936–946) had long ceded it to the Khitan Liao dynasty.[9]

In Ji Junxiang's version of the events, the action is concentrated in the reign of Duke Ling and recounts events after a direct confrontation between Zhao Dun and Tu'an Gu. The wedge takes up the story after Zhao Dun has literally been hounded to death. The songs in the wedge are assigned to Zhao Shuo, who has been ordered to commit suicide as a part of the purge of his clan. Before his death he instructs his pregnant wife to ensure the survival of their child should she give birth to a boy in order that he may exact revenge for the clan. The songs of the first suite are assigned to Han Jue, who has been ordered by Tu'an Gu to guard the palace where Zhao Shuo's wife is staying. Zhao Shuo's wife entrusts the baby to a physician, Cheng Ying, and then commits suicide. When Cheng Ying attempts to smuggle the baby out of the palace in his medicine box, the plot is discovered by Han Jue, who subsequently allows him to escape with the Orphan and commits suicide in order to cover up any trace of the child.

The next two suites of songs (acts 2 and 3) are assigned to Gongsun Chujiu. In the first of these, Gongsun Chujiu promises to die together with the only-born son of Cheng Ying, whom they agree to substitute for the Orphan. In his second suite of songs in act 3, when Tu'an Gu interrogates Gongsun Chujiu, he denies hiding the Orphan. After a search of his house results in the discovery and murder of the false Orphan, Gongsun commits suicide. The final suite of songs is assigned to the grown-up Orphan, who has been adopted by the childless Tu'an Gu (who believed him to be the son of Cheng Ying)

7. For an English translation of the "Zhao shijia," see "Chin, Hereditary House 9," in Ssu-ma Ch'ien 1995a, 347–57.

8. See, for instance, Chen Zhongfan 2003, 20–35; Zhou Yibai 1979, 184–86; Zhang and Guo 1980, 218–19; and Luo 1977, 377–80.

9. Other scholars have preferred to read the play as an expression of anti-Mongol patriotism more generally. See, for instance, Xu Shuofang 1956, 39–44.

and given the name of Tu Cheng 屠成 ("he who brings Tu to completion"). Just as Tu'an Gu (with the full support of Tu Cheng) is on the verge of toppling Duke Ling to take the throne for himself, Cheng Ying shows Tu Cheng a painting of successive scenes of the feud between Tu'an Gu and Zhao Dun. At first Cheng Ying does not disclose the names of the protagonists of the depicted story, but, after recognizing the characters, Tu Cheng is filled with indignation at the behavior of the villain of the piece. Cheng Ying then reveals to him that he, Tu Cheng, is the sole survivor of the Zhao clan and that his adoptive father is his clan's archenemy. In the final scene of the play, the Orphan concludes that he must exact revenge and envisions the grisly violence of his future actions.

While the full title of this *zaju* (*Injustice Repays Injustice: The Orphan of Zhao*) draws attention to the theme of revenge, the actual revenge never takes place onstage. For Ji Junxiang it was enough that the Orphan had become aware of his true identity and the duties involved. Also, the revenge as envisioned in the final songs of the play was probably simply too grisly to stage. Loyal self-sacrifice is the major theme of the enacted version of the story: the wedge and the first three suites of songs show a series of suicides that increasingly become acts of free choice. But the play also contains a number of references to other cases of sacrificial suicide inspired by the virtuous behavior of Zhao Dun. In the end, the promise of revenge exacted substantiates the meaning of all these acts of truly selfless loyalty.

The Yuan printing of our play, in its references to incidents preceding the stage action, mentions the characters of Chu Ni 鉏麑 and Ling Zhe 靈輒. Chu Ni had at one time been hired by Tu'an Gu to murder Zhao Dun. However, when he had sneaked into the Zhao mansion at night and had observed the reverential seriousness with which Zhao Dun prepared himself for the court audience at dawn, he was overcome with remorse and committed suicide by butting his head against a tree.

The story of Ling Zhe is more complicated. Once, when Zhao Dun made a trip to the countryside, he observed a large man lying on his back beneath a mulberry tree with his mouth open. The man explained that he was a farmhand but that he had such a voracious appetite that no one was willing to hire him. As a result he was starving, but because he did not want to be accused of stealing, he had laid himself down under the tree, waiting for the mulberries to drop into his mouth. Zhao Dun thereupon provided him with a decent meal. Later, Tu'an Gu had trained a dog, the Demon Mastiff (Da'ao 大獒), to attack Zhao Dun in court. When the attack came, Zhao Dun tried to flee, but the duke had earlier arranged to have one of Zhao's chariot wheels loosened. When it came free, Ling Zhe jumped forward to carry the axle on his shoulder, allowing Zhao Dun to escape for the moment. The stories of Chu Ni and Ling Zhe, and of Tu'an Gu's attempts on the life of Zhao Dun by using the Demon Mastiff, are recounted in great detail at the opening of the wedge in the *Yuanqu xuan* version of the play.

The story of *The Orphan of Zhao* remained popular onstage well into the twentieth century. We know that it was adapted as a *xiwen* 戲文 (a southern-style drama) at an early moment, and one of the earliest preserved *chuanqi* 傳奇 plays is also an adaptation of these materials. In later years, adaptations of the story of *The Orphan of Zhao* came to be known under the title *Bayi ji* 八義記 (*The Story of the Eight Righteous Heroes*), which drastically rewrote the story of the Zhao clan. *Bayi ji* was also the title under which these materials entered the Peking opera repertoire.

Critical discussion of *The Orphan of Zhao* by modern scholars is usually based on the *Yuanqu xuan* version of the play. As with many of the scripts in the *Yuanqu xuan*, the text of this edition directly or indirectly derives from a late script from the Office of Bell and Drum in the Ming imperial palace. While some of the differences between the two editions of *The Orphan of Zhao* are probably due to Zang Maoxun, the heavy-handed compiler and editor of the *Yuanqu xuan*, many of them may also have derived from the extensive revisions of the play at court in order to make it suitable for performance in front of the emperor. While the multiple cases of self-sacrifice displayed in this *zaju* will have encountered no objection, the code of clan loyalty and revenge was unacceptable, and an exceptional fifth act was added to turn the Orphan's murder of Tu'an Gu from a private (and ferocious) act of revenge into the state-mandated execution of a traitor and rebel, reasserting the state's monopoly on violence. And whereas Tu Cheng had only been too eager to support his adoptive father in toppling their rightful ruler in the earlier Yuan version, the *Yuanqu xuan* version turns him into a loyal vassal of the ruling house. Few *zaju* have been rewritten as drastically as *The Orphan of Zhao* as it moved from the commercial theater of the Yuan to the imperial stage of the Ming, and from the imperial stage in Beijing to the scholar's study in Jiangnan: practically every preserved aria has been completely rewritten, many arias have been dropped, and new ones have been added, resulting in an utterly different play.

The difference between the two versions of *The Orphan of Zhao* is also conspicuous in their portrayal of Cheng Ying. Even though Cheng Ying is present onstage in each of the four acts of *The Orphan of Zhao* and is clearly the play's "moral Machiavelli," Ji Junxiang did not assign any arias to him but had the male lead impersonate such diverse roles as Zhao Shuo (a young prince), Han Jue (a middle-aged general), Gongsun Chujiu (an elderly retired civil official), and the Orphan (a twenty-year-old youth). While this must have made the play a perfect vehicle for a great actor to showcase his versatility, another reason for the author to choose these four persona was that he anticipated that the audience might not be able to fully sympathize with a man who is willing to sacrifice his only male heir in order to save the life of another infant, the single survivor of a noble line to whom he is indebted. Since Ji Junxiang did not assign any arias to Cheng Ying, and since the Yuan printing does not provide any dialogue, Cheng Ying, for all his importance to the plot, is absent from the text of the play in its earliest printing. The *Yuanqu xuan* version of the play (and most likely the palace script on which we assume it was based), however, pays due attention to the central role of Cheng Ying by assigning him a large number of opportunities to speak—including one passage in ballad verse and many poems—as he first entices Han Jue and then Gongsun Chujiu to sacrifice themselves for the sake of the Orphan. And eventually, twenty years later, he informs the Orphan of his true identity in such a way that the Orphan burns to take revenge. Sima Qian's historical version stressed Cheng Ying's selfless devotion by having him commit suicide to join Gongsun Chujiu as soon as the Orphan had taken revenge and been given his ancestral titles and lands. Such a suicide, however, was unacceptable as the conclusion of a play, and the *Yuanqu xuan* version of the play has Cheng Ying rewarded with a farm and continuous sacrifices by the Zhao clan, which in the eyes of some may compromise Cheng Ying's morality.

Many modern critics have compared *The Orphan of Zhao* as preserved in the *Yuanqu xuan* with Shakespeare's *Hamlet*, as both plays require a son to take revenge for his father. These critics often compare the decisive Orphan unfavorably with the doubtful and hesitating Hamlet, who is praised as a quintessential modern hero. In contrast to Hamlet, the characterization of the Orphan is often faulted as superficial.[10] The act in which Cheng Ying discloses his true identity to his ward, however, shows more psychological realism than these critics are willing to credit. Cheng Ying piques the Orphan's interest, slowly discloses the full enormity of the injustice his family had suffered, and simultaneously affirms the necessity of revenge. It is only at the height of suspense that he discloses to the Orphan that his adoptive father is also the murderer of the young prince's own father and entire family. Confronted with that revelation, the Orphan is so overwhelmed that he faints, but as soon as he comes to, he realizes that his own moral compass allows him only one course of action. While the earlier version of the play does not suggest the Orphan will tarry to take revenge, it does not specify how and when that revenge will actually take place—we are left with a vision of the Orphan contemplating revenge and relishing the anticipated violence. After all, if the main theme of the play is self-sacrifice rather than revenge as such, the promise of revenge may well be enough. It is only in the *Yuanqu xuan* version (in the rather lame fifth act) that the revenge is swiftly enacted, and then only after being legitimized by the authorities.

Joseph Henri Marie de Prémare was the finest linguist among the French Jesuits at the Manchu court in Beijing in the early decades of the eighteenth century.[11] He prepared his (partial) translation of *The Orphan of Zhao* as an example of vernacular Chinese for the benefit of Étienne Fourmont, an influential orientalist in Paris who had developed an interest in the Chinese language.[12] It is not clear what made Prémare choose this play in particular, because it cannot have been its status in Chinese critical opinion at the time. It is more likely that the very detailed dialogues made the play very suitable for his purpose. As the only play in the *Yuanqu xuan* of five acts, with a serious action set in high circles, it must have appealed to Prémare's notions of a proper tragedy. It will also have helped

10. See, for instance, Shih 1976, 42, and Lau, 1985, 367–71.

11. Lundbaek 1991.

12. Leung 2002.

that the play had no love interest and no comic interludes. The (threatened) murder of innocent toddlers also may have reminded him of the massacre of innocent infants by Herod the Great.

Prémare's translation started to become more widely known only when it was included as *Le petit orphelin de la maison Tchao, tragédie chinoise* by Jean Baptiste du Halde in his *Description géographique, historique, chronologique, politique, et physique de l'empire de la Chine et de la Tartarie chinoise* of 1735, a four-volume compendium of European knowledge of the Chinese world, based largely on materials provided by Jesuit missionaries in China. This was the high tide of chinoiserie and the European (especially French and German) fascination with all things Chinese, and Prémare's translation was quickly rendered into other European languages. His translation also provided inspiration to playwrights as diverse as Hatchett, Metastasio,[13] Murphy,[14] and Voltaire. The most important work to be inspired by Prémare's translation was of course Voltaire's *L'Orphelin de la Chine.* Voltaire's other Chinese source of inspiration was the Manchu conquest of the Ming, which in the seventeenth century had inspired a number of European playwrights. The place of action was relocated from a minor dukedom to the capital of China itself, close to the Great Wall; and the time of the action was moved to the eve of the Mongol conquest of the Southern Song (some Chinese critics have praised Voltaire for grasping the true patriotic intent of Ji Junxiang's play!). Voltaire's play, which was performed all over Europe in both the original French and in translation, holds a special place in European theater history because it was one of the earliest popular plays in which actors performed in "authentic costume."[15]

Prémare had declined to translate the arias in his *Yuanqu xuan* version of the play because of the different conventions of Chinese and French poetry. The first complete translation of the *Yuanqu xuan* version of the play, including the arias, was produced a century later by the eminent French Sinologist Stanislas Julien and published in 1835, on the eve of the Opium War. By that time the West's attitude toward China had changed, and Julien's work exerted hardly any influence outside academic circles.

SUGGESTED READINGS

Ch'en Shou-yi 1936; Ch'ien Chung-shu 1935; Hsia 1988; Idema 1988; Lau 1985; Leung 2002; Liu 1953: Lundbaek 1991; Shih 1976; Ssu-ma 2006; Trauzettel 1975; Wang 1978; Ward 2010; Yang 2011; Yu 2005–2006.

13. Ward 2010, 98–115.
14. Chi-ming Yang 2011, 148–83.
15. Voltaire's play has also recently been translated into Chinese. See Fan and Arouet 2010.

THE ORPHAN OF ZHAO, A FOURTEENTH-CENTURY EDITION

DRAMATIS PERSONAE IN ORDER OF APPEARANCE

Role type	*Names and family, institutional, or social role*
MALE LEAD	ZHAO SHUO, father of ORPHAN
MALE LEAD	HAN JUE, guard
MALE LEAD	GONGSUN CHUJIU, elder statesman
MALE LEAD	ZHAO WU (aka TU CHENG), the ORPHAN

✣ ✣ ✣

THE ORPHAN OF ZHAO

[WEDGE]

[ZHAO SHUO *sings*:]
([XIANLÜ MODE:] *Shanghua shi*)
The rivers and mountains of Duke Ling of Jin should come to an end,
That traitorous Tu'an Gu holds all power in his hands.
He manipulates the Son of Heaven[16] to command the liege lords,
And me he decapitates at the execution ground—
This is the finale to it all—everything for which I've worked so hard!
(*Reprise*)
I'll wind up without a single tumulus in which to lay my body,
After I gave her my instructions, showers of tears flowed down her cheeks.
I will leave behind no other words
But these: after this child grows to manhood,
Let him take revenge for both the son and the father.

16. In Yuan printings of *zaju*, the various feudal princes of the Zhou dynasty (1122–256 BC) may all be designated as "sons of heaven" (*tianzi* 天子) and are played by a role type called the emperor (*jia* 駕). Feudal princes are also referred to by terms that in more strict usage are reserved for the king or emperor, employing words such as "imperial." Later editors, finding this practice unacceptable, made changes accordingly.

[ACT 1]

[HAN JUE *sings*:]
([XIANLÜ MODE:] *Dian jiangchun*)[17]
Only after he repulsed and matched Qin of the west,[18]
Established and completed Jin in the east,
Were we safe and secure.
But that traitorous official Tu'an Gu
Destroyed that noble minister[19] below the golden steps.
(*Hunjiang long*)
Duke Ling of Jin is partial to him[20] and compliant,
So all the court puts its trust in this kind of person!
The loyal and upright are decapitated in the marketplace,
Sycophants and toadies take their ease in palace bureaus.
Those who earned merit for their ruler gained the harshest sentences,
Those who profit not the citizens enjoy the lord's grace.
He is so out of control that he abuses the Son of Heaven,
And scares the liege lords witless—
Those who go against him are exterminated to the last man,
Exterminated to the last man: prime ministers at court
And generals in the field.
(*You hulu*)
Right at this moment, the whole world is in turmoil, the dust of battle rises,
Each now marks out a border on their own—
Trusting slanderous words, Tu'an Gu has sold out the universe of Jin.
The world is in chaos, heroes are rendered powerless—
When will law be just and compliant to Heaven's will?
That scoundrel mocks the blue above,
And destroys the people below.
Let me interrogate that infinitely azure, high heaven blessed with sun,
Will it, with embarrassed blue face, spare no man?
(*Tianxia le*)
I am sure that

17. In this song, Han Jue lays out the successes of Zhao Dun and his demise at the hands of Tu'an Gu.
18. The feudal state of Qin occupied the Wei valley in present-day Shaanxi and so lay to the west of the state of Jin, which had its center in the present-day province of Shanxi.
19. Zhao Dun.
20. Tu'an Gu.

"It is visited as distantly as upon your sons and grandsons, or as close at hand as yourself."
He wanted to gobble up the rivers and mountains
And because Zhao Dun would not fall in line, he marked well his hatred.
He came up with a plan, worked his evil design,
Claimed a good minister rebellious,
Obscured the truth, sent up lying memorials to his lord and king, all of which were approved.
(*Nezha ling*)
Remember how Zhao Dun came to the aid of the people,
And shared his own rice with his guests?
How he shamed Chu Ni into being a man—
Who gave up his life by butting the acacia tree?
And saved Ling Zhe from starvation—
Who repaid the favor by lifting up the axle?
Governing the Hundred Surnames,[21] Zhao Dun earned great merit,
Supporting the One Man,[22] he showed no selfish whim,
Yet wound up unable to keep body and head together.
(*Que ta zhi*)
All in vain
He swept away miasma and dust,
Established his merit and deeds.
Unable to rest in peace behind the unicorns[23]—
His old grave is now a rank tumulus.
The father—neck severed and corpse split in half,
The son and grandsons—suddenly the targets of a vicious and evil heart.
(*Jisheng cao*)
That child
Will have no escape,
But Tu'an Gu will suffer history's verdict—
Slanderous ministers are always manipulative in the way of slanderous ministers,
Enemies will always bear an enemy's hatred,
Sons and grandsons will always assume the lot of sons and grandsons.
From reign to reign they carry their hatred—when will it stop?
Injustice repays injustice—when will it end?

21. Hundred Surnames: here an archaic reference to liege lords' households, not to "common people."
22. The One Man: a conventional designation for the ruler.
23. The road to the graves of high officials was lined on both sides with stone statues of men and beasts, including such miraculous creatures as the unicorn (*qilin* 麒麟).

(*Houting hua*)[24]
You say you are a household client of Prince Consort Zhao,
I am a retainer-in-waiting of Tu'an Gu.
You say you are hiding a one-year-old unicorn foal,
But it can't fly out of these ninefold dragon and phoenix gates.[25]
If I profess no concern
And do not interrogate you....
Well, those who are favored must repay in kind.
(*Jinzhan'er*)
I see
On his cheeks the streaks of dried tears,
And at the corners of his mouth, the froth of his mother's milk.
He turns his little eyes—so he recognizes people!
He's swaddled so tightly inside the medicine case,
So narrowly cramped he cannot turn and toss,
So miserably short he cannot stretch his limbs.
True it is, "To grow to manhood, one must suffer a lack of freedom;
With too much freedom, one cannot grow into a man."
(*Zui zhong tian*)
If I were to offer up this little windfall and scheme for a titled lot,
This would be no more than "pleasing myself to destroy others."
Three hundred family members beheaded to extinguish the line—
Every leaf of every branch exterminated.
If he sees this little child,
He's certain to pound his bones to dust, dismember his body,
And leave not even a milk tooth behind.
Why do other's work by digging out the grass, root and all?
(*Coda*)
I will "slow slice" my own body,[26]
Rather than endure torture and interrogation by that lot.
Better I slice my own throat with my three-foot-long Dragon Spring.[27]
In a moment's time they will paint his likeness, sketch his shape, search for him long and hard—
So hide yourself in deep mountains and deserted fields.
As soon as this child approaches his first decade,

24. In the intervening scene between these two songs, we assume that Han Jue uncovers Cheng Ying's attempt to smuggle the Orphan out.
25. A metaphor for the royal palace.
26. Han Jue decides to release Cheng Ying and the Orphan and kill himself.
27. Dragon Spring: a conventional term for a keen sword.

Then make him practice the military arts, cultivate the civil.
And, when he has finally mastered both military and civil learning,
Let him then mark his hatred for his enemy well,
And search out, too, his benefactors—
When he has killed his enemies, let him not forget those who helped him.

[ACT 2]

[GONGSUN CHUJIU *sings*:]
([NANLÜ MODE:] *Yizhi hua*)
A fine man unjustly killed,[28]
A true pillar destroyed.
How powerful the minister has grown, this Tu'an Gu,
How weak the lord has become, this Duke Ling of Jin
Who now heeds and follows that sycophant and toady—
That traitor, who holds all power over the army—
So that meritorious ministers cannot exert their loyalty.
It makes my breast fill with rage,
Truly my lord and king has fallen into the snare of a child.
(*Liangzhou*)
From the time he dominated court and country, was ennobled, made prime minister,
It scared me so that I came to this remote village, gave up my post, and returned to the land,
Unwilling to get involved, even if there were others desiring to bring peace and order to the people of the state.
His offices have risen to the highest rank, number one,
His position has reached the level of the Three Dukes.[29]
He has been enfeoffed with the households of eight districts,
And for salary enjoys a tax harvest of a thousand catties.
He has eyes to see injustice, but is blind to it,
Ears to hear people's curses, but is deaf to them.
Now he who manipulates the Son of Heaven is promoted in rank and heaped with titles,
The one who harms the Hundred Surnames seeks his salary by paying court,

28. Referring to Han Jue.
29. The Three Dukes are the paramount counselors of the ruler and the highest officials of the land.

And he who commands the liege lords receives rewards when asking for merit.
For the while, in dire straits
I'll suffer deprivation,
And heed not whether I'll be buried in a unicorn grave after I die.
It's not that I take pleasure in plowing and sowing,
But I've jumped out of a lair of hungry and predatory tigers,
And for the while will nurture my indifference.
(*Gewei*)[30]
You say
Sycophantic ministers have been used at court from antiquity,
And for sure,
"This good thing has always been the same under heaven."
The more
Myriads of people curse him,
Thousands of people despise him,
The more the One Man values him—
He becomes evermore impure and unfair,
Unfilial and disloyal.
And now
Every citizen under heaven, each and every one, grumbles.
(*He xinlang*)
Who dares send a sealed letter to challenge the imperial palace?
If Tu'an Gu should look to the east, to the east [the duke] flows,
He has manipulated Duke Ling to the point that his every whim is followed.
He has frightened the two divisions of civil and military officials until they live in constant terror,
And in the ranks of their assemblies they all feign befuddlement.
They hide themselves by holding the tablet of office in front of their chests—
It's just as if fish paste glued their mouths shut
Or fish bones were stuck in their gullet!
They lower their heads like a mute lost in a dream.
Yes, indeed
"Every single thing that happens in the world
All lies in what is unsaid."
(*Muyang guan*)
Before he was born, he had lost all his relatives,[31]
While still in the womb, his whole lineage had been extinguished.

30. Gongsun Chujiu discusses Tu'an Gu's treachery with Cheng Ying.
31. He discusses the infant.

If he lives until manhood, it'll be a life of little luck and much disaster.
His father was decapitated at the execution ground,
His mother died prisoner in her cold palace.[32]
This is no bloodthirsty white-clad minister,
But rather an abandoned black-headed grub.
You say he's a real man who'll avenge his father and mother,
But I
Say he's the very seed of disaster that brought his parents down.
(*Hong shaoyao*)[33]
In twenty years you can avenge your noble father,
That will be the time for you to rise to glory.
I must die sooner or later, and then everything will be gone—
My spirit and energy are not what they used to be.
But abandoned, how could this child establish his merit?
In all your insistence you refuse to budge an inch—
Wouldn't I like to have one more day of life to display my awesome might?
But I find it hard to stand these evening drums and morning bells.[34]
(*Liangzhou*)
In this marionette's booth
Drum and fife manipulate us.
And the flower of youth is dispatched by a finale,
A finale that brings every hero to his end in old age.
"To meet an enemy and take no vengeance is a useless act,"
"No courage counted to see an injustice and not to act,"
"What use are words spoken without trust?"
You don't have to make more of me than I am,
No real man sorrows over his own death,
Less so me, with white hair flowing free.
(*Ma yulang*)
Which of the two of us will act the leader, which the accomplice?[35]
For we'll both wind up beheaded in the marketplace.
You are in pain because of the grace shown you by the family Zhao—
For you, my brother,

32. When empresses or other palace ladies had lost the favor of their lord, they were banished from the main palace and housed instead in the "cold palace."

33. This aria is sung to the Orphan.

34. That summon one to court.

35. Assents to Cheng Ying's plan to switch the babies and induce Tu'an Gu to slay the false orphan.

I am filled with the same respect,
As if we were born from the same mother.
(*Gan huang'en*)
I fear no tip of a three-foot frost-cold sword,
Not even the nine tripods of a state cauldron,[36]
Execution by a sharp blade,
Being fed poisonous herbs,
Or boiled in roiling oil.
May my heroic soul dissolve into darkness,
And in the somber mists, hazy and vague,
Disperse into sorrowing clouds,
And follow the setting sun,
Aloft on a mournful wind.
(*Chujiang yun*)
This old rustic
And this little baby[37]
Are both forlorn in the bright moon's light.
Ethers of enmity rush out, hatred knows no end,
Ten years of the past are rendered useless in a moment.
(*Second from Coda*)
That one
Is seed of a minister of merit whose portrait should grace the Unicorn Hall.[38]
I don't believe one finds dog tracks in front of a tiger's gate—
After grown to manhood, he will set things right.
To slice Tu'an Gu ten thousand times would be too slight
To avenge all the suffering of a patriarchal line of three hundred.
There will be no need for any mass for the dead—
Wrench out the blood from his breast and let it gush into the sky
As an offering for your father and grandfather.
(*Coda*)
Relying on the thousand-year lineage, those branches and leaves of the house of Zhao,[39]

36. This is a conflation (found only in Yuan editions of dramas) of two terms, "nine tripods" (*jiuding* 九鼎) and the common phrase "tripod and cauldron" (*dinghuo* 鼎鑊), the implements used to boil people as punishment for severe crimes. The "nine tripods" are the ritual tripods of state (each holding earth of one of the ancient divisions of China). The *huo* is a torture implement, a pot used for boiling people alive. In both cases, the phrase occurs in a context in which the instruments of the state are used to satisfy personal interests.

37. Referring to Cheng Ying's son.

38. The original Unicorn Hall was erected by Emperor Wu of the Han dynasty (r. 140–87 BC). Emperor Xuandi (r. 73–49 BC) displayed there the portraits of eleven meritorious ministers.

39. That is, the lineage of the family tree.

We will prop up the hundred-two[40] might of the mountains and rivers of the dynasty of Jin.

In this way,

By displaying his might to the eight directions, he can lead masses of troops,
And, arranging two ranks of scarlet-clad outrunners, he can line up his retinue of chariots.

I think back

To Ling Zhe who held the axle, whose resolve was fierce,
To Chu Ni who smashed his head against the acacia, whose life was so ended,
To the palace officer who guarded the gate, who committed suicide.
Gongsun, who will now sacrifice his life, is old and useless,
The child, who is just newly born, will suffer sword's point,
Cheng Ying, who gives up his own child, is unshaken in his heart.
In the register of names in the history of the state, we will unjustly be omitted,
But the future will know and value us.
No need to erect a memorial stele amid the densely scattered graves,
But at Beimang Hill[41] simply inter my empty casket within its burial mound.

[ACT 3]

[GONGSUN CHUJIU *sings*:]
([SHUANGDIAO MODE:] *Xinshui ling*)

All I see is dust rising as they fly over the small bridge,[42]
Surely it is the rebellious minister who has commandeered the liege lords.
Massed in orderly fashion—his officers and troops array themselves;
Glistening, shimmering bright—their lances and swords stand in rows.
What's clear to me now is that I die this very morning,
I can escape this painful, brutal abuse no more.

(*Zhuma ting*)

For me it's thus:

"The general is old, his soldiers slack."
With Zhao Dun, I swore brotherhood to the death.

---

40. While the original meaning of the expression "hundred-two" is a matter of dispute, it is clear that in later literature it is used in the meaning of "overpowering, very powerful." Another reading may be in reference to the designation of the area around modern Xi'an as "hundred-two," meaning a strategic site that can be held by an army only 2 percent of the size of the attacking force.

41. The Beimang Hill, north of Luoyang, are the proverbial grave site.

42. Tu'an Gu's army arrives.

I did say, "The minister is all-powerful, the lord weak."
And I know my tongue is the very sword that will cut off my own head.
A real man, heroic and brave, makes his pact with heroes and the hardy,
The sage once said, "Those who possess the Way chastise those without."
[Tu'an Gu] has cut off the descent of the whole house,
O, heaven,
"A hard frost first kills a grass without roots."
(*Chenzui dongfeng*)
Don't think that the soul of a real man will fly in fright to the ninth heaven.
Let Tu'an Gu use a thousand cudgels—
If I confess quickly, he'll easily get to the bottom of it,
But if I confess slowly, he'll find my story hard to doubt.[43]
Every stroke I can bear is a stroke of merit.
If we don't want him uprooting the tree to trace the roots to their lowest point,
Then I'd better
Suffer as much as I can of being trussed tightly, strung up, and beaten.
(*Yan'er luo*)
Manipulating me, you got me into this,[44]
Falling in line with the traitor, you've informed on me.
You scare me so,
I can't still my quivering, shaking, quaking kneecaps,
Or subdue my thumping, racing, jumping heart.
(*Shui xianzi*)
The two of us decided—I confess first,
As it rises to the tip of my tongue, I choke it back down.
Should I die, don't think I'll say even one "Cheng Ying"—
How can I start something I won't end?
And not just beating,
Even if they prop up nine tripod vats of boiling oil,
I've had enough experience not to get ruffled.
If I am to die, I will die well—
Even if you send down a whole storm of hail!
(*Chuan bo zhao*)
You—
In those days you kept the Demon Mastiff,
That tore at loyal ministers and good generals.

43. Assuring Cheng Ying that he will not give up the real Orphan.

44. These songs are in the form of a false accusation of Cheng Ying in front of Tu'an Gu to remove any suspicion of complicity.

You—
You wanted to usurp the power of the imperial court
And scheme against ministers and officials.
Him—
His whole household, three hundred strong, old and young,
Everyone within his gates was decapitated in the marketplace,
And his whole lineage was completely wiped out.
Now you have searched out this small child
And fly into a pounding rage.
(*Qi dixiong*)
He has utterly changed
His outward look.
He'll never show mercy,
His countenance[45] is red from the tip-top down.
Over his lion-buckle belt he lifts the brocade battle gown,
And draws his Dragon Spring sword from its sharkskin sheath.
(*Meihua jiu*)
Ah!
There he lies in a puddle of blood.[46]
Testimony to the toil of growing up.
He couldn't escape Heaven's predestination,
You cannot enjoy the offspring of sons.
Cheng Ying, will you ever raise a son to prepare for your old age?[47]
I cannot believe you aren't disturbed.
This child, from his birthing mat just lifted—
Counting today, only ten days hence—
Has been cruelly cut in two by Tu'an's blade.
(*Shou Jiangnan*)
Say not the phrase "If the family is rich, the child is pampered."
I see him[48] over there, with an itch in his heart he can't scratch,
He dares not let a single teardrop fall from his pupils,
Furtively wiping them all away,
As if all his living organs were scalded by boiling oil.

45. The Chinese term we translate as "countenance" is *wuyunshan* 五雲山 (literally, "the mountain of the five skandhas"). The five skandhas are the five components of an intelligent being: form, sensation, conception, evaluation, and cognition.

46. The false orphan is slain.

47. This song is an aside, praising Cheng Ying for giving up his own son.

48. That is, Cheng Ying.

(*Coda*)
If my dying at sixty cannot be counted as reaching old age,
How young this child who dies in his first year?
We two, who die here in this one place,
Should at least end up with a name that will last ten thousand generations.
And so
I urge you, Cheng Ying, remember well the cruelly slain Zhao Shuo,
And raise this child to manhood,
So he may avenge the injustice of his parents' murder,
And with a thousand hacks of his own blade, turn that bastard into mincemeat—
I will not lightly let you off!

[ACT 4]

[ORPHAN, *as man of twenty, sings*:]
([ZHONGLÜ MODE:] *Fen die'er*)
No need
For the armed troops under my command—
The Son of Heaven, aided by the hundred gods,
Wants my father to call himself "We, This Orphan."[49]
To desire these rivers and mountains,
Or steal away the Altars of Earth and Grain,
Is as easy as taking something from the folds of a gown.
On his golden throne or in his simurgh palanquin,
He is as frightened of us as if we were scorpions.
(*Zui chunfeng*)
I want to
Rebel against our old master Duke Ling of Jin
And aid our new lord, Tu'an Gu.
Let the Crown Equal to Heaven,
The belt of lapis lazuli,
And the gown of coiling dragons
Change to a new master.
Master!

49. Kings and emperors in China designated themselves as "This Orphan," "This Unfortunate One," etc.

Who cares about a sage lord? A wise minister?
If the father is loving and the child filial,
Who cares that "the worries of the master are the shame of the ministers"?
(*Ying xianke*)
Why
So many stains of tears wiped away?[50]
Or such heavy sighs as these?
I had come forward with folded arms only to pay my respects—
You are cranky and cross, your anger has been stirred up,
Mean and nasty, you've worked up a rage.
I lower my head and wonder,
Which of my words was off the mark?
(*Hong xiu xie*)
Painted
In darkest, deepest green—some mulberry trees,[51]
A clamoring, shouting crowd—a bunch of rustic villagers.
This one here, dripping with blood, supports a cart on his arm,
And this one here dies below the acacia tree.
The point of a sword executes this one,
And this old man,
Turns over an infant with some advice.
(*Shiliu hua*)
Now this one, mean and nasty, grasps a saber in his hand,
And this one here kneels below the steps.
This infant here loses his life under the point of a sword,
And a woman is slain,
Splayed out in a puddle of blood.
And why is this old man put to death?
This one here, wearing his red gown, is really rotten to the core!
I've thought this story over, but don't have the slightest clue.
It's painted in such a way that it puzzles me, leaves me confused and depressed.
(*Dou anchun*)
Whose child is it in this bloody affair?
Whose ancestors are these on the execution ground?
This one has no sons and grandsons to call his own,
And that one can't save his own father and mother.

---

50. Spoken to Cheng Ying.
51. Cheng Ying displays a hand scroll on which the story of the extermination of the Zhaos is painted. In narrative paintings the characters were often identified by their names, and a short written account of each episode also might be provided. Such aids are missing in this case.

Whose family history does this hand scroll depict?
Tell your son everything, from beginning to end:
Did this man here transgress the law and all of its codicils?
Did that man there suffer injustice? Harbor vengeance?
(*Putian le*)
I want to hear everything from the beginning,
Pull out my blade to come to their aid.
　　It makes
Sorrow knot in my heart,
Rage pound in my breast.
　　So
It was *my* father who was done in,
And the ancestors of *my* family!
And if we speak of the most desolating and heartbreaking points,
Even a man of iron
Would weep and cry without restraint.
　　Tu'an Gu,
You were to be emperor and lord,
And I prime minister—
What was heaven thinking?
(*Shang xiaolou*)
Father, if you hadn't looked out for me,
And hadn't raised me, your child,
From twenty years ago,
My head would have been separated from my body
And I would have perished in the wilds outside town.
Tu'an Gu,
That common miscreant,
Uprooted the tree to search for its roots,
Decapitated my whole family, extinguished our house, exterminated our clan.
(*Reprise*)
Since that bastard is betraying the One Man,
How fitting to exterminate *his* entire lineage.
Really! All the armies in the empire,
The people who fill the realm,
Were put in the hands of that bastard.
All the time it was you who masterminded it,
You who protected him
And let him abuse the liege lords.
All the time it was you who set him to murder his lord and kill my father.

[(*Shi'er yue*)]
    Thinking about
My father and mother, harboring their injustice—
I'll grab that toadying traitor,
Make him ride the wooden donkey,[52]
Cut the bastard's body to pieces,
And chop his pampered sons and young daughters into a pulpy mess—
I'll not let a single relative get away!
[(*Yaomin ge*)]
    Today
Someone will do away with you, how does that feel?
And it was you who became the magic amulet that protected the life of the Orphan of Zhao!
So, let the whole family of that bastard—master and servants—be executed.
Just see how smeared with blood my three-foot-long Dragon Spring will be!
In a moment,
In a moment,
What you owed and shorted me on in my previous life,
Will be collected in full today.
(*Shua hai'er*)
If I meet my blood enemy in the morn,
I'll block the path of that traitor in the Long Street,[53]
With Dragon Spring clenched in my hand, I'll clutch his gown,
And halting his bearlike horse, I'll just stretch out my gibbon arms,
Jerk his jade-bridled, golden-saddled horse to the ground,
And mangle his golden-flowered, black-canopied chariot.
There'll be no easy pardon,
"A fierce tiger may hesitate
And be no match for the sting of wasps and scorpions!"
(*Third from Coda*)
If I do not cleanse this vengeful hatred,
I cannot rid myself of this hated injustice.
I can see my cruelly slain father, the mother who bore me dying in captivity.
If I don't avenge the hatred of my parents in their graves,
I'll be ashamed to meet that starving man among the mulberries.[54]

---

52. Criminals condemned to be killed by slow slicing were paraded through town before their execution nailed to a "wooden donkey," a trestle on wheels.
53. Long Street: common term for the main streets of towns.
54. The "starving man" refers Ling Zhe.

Have no doubts nor plan too much—
There's no need to distinguish between strong and weak,
Or delve into right or wrong!
(*Second*)
That bastard—
I'll scoop out his eyes,
Rip open his belly,
Pull out his heart and liver,
I'll cut off his arms and legs,
And break that bastard's back, cracking and snapping, in a single throw.
So it's said, "A man without hatred is no man of honor,
A man with no venom is no man at all."
He cannot be shielded—
I fear no
Guards to the front and runners behind,
No troops to the right or left.
(*Coda*)
I want to repay the favor of my father and mother, cruelly slain,
Relying on the good fortune of our sagely and enlightened, august emperor.
If the Imperial Guard is willing to protect the Orphan of Zhao,
Then I will act the advocate for our lord and king on his golden throne.

Title: Han Jue saves a hero who risks his life,
Cheng Ying convinces one jealous of valor and gives up his own child.
Righteousness meets righteousness: Gongsun Chujiu,
Injustice repays injustice: the Orphan of Zhao.

The Orphan of Zhao, the end.

THE ORPHAN OF ZHAO GREATLY WREAKS VENGEANCE, A SELECTION OF YUAN PLAYS EDITION

DRAMATIS PERSONAE IN ORDER OF APPEARANCE

Role type	*Name and family, institutional, or social role*
VILLAIN	TU'AN GU
ADDED MALE	ZHAO SHUO, father of the ORPHAN
FEMALE LEAD	ZHAO SHUO's wife, PRINCESS OF JIN
EXTRA	MESSENGER
EXTRA	CHENG YING
MALE LEAD	HAN JUE
SOLDIER	A sergeant in HAN JUE's squad
MALE LEAD	GONGSUN CHUJIU
SOLDIER	GUARD at TU'AN GU's office
MALE LEAD	CHENG BO (aka TU CHENG, the ORPHAN)
EXTRA	WEI JIANG, court dignitary of Jin
ZHANG QIAN	Aide to WEI JIANG

✤ ✤ ✤

THE *ZAJU THE ORPHAN OF ZHAO GREATLY WREAKS VENGEANCE*

WRITTEN BY JI JUNXIANG OF THE YUAN

COLLATED BY ZANG JINSHU OF WUXING IN THE MING DYNASTY

WEDGE

(VILLAIN, *dressed as* TU'AN GU, *enters leading foot soldiers and recites*:)

Humans have no mind to harm the tiger,
But a tiger has the will to injure humans;

If you don't exhaust your emotions at the moment,
After the fact your feelings will be stirred up.

I am Tu'an Gu, mighty general of the Jin. Our ruler now seated, Duke Ling, has a thousand each of ministers civil and martial. But those he trusts number only one of each, Zhao Dun, head of the civil ranks, and me, head of the martial. The two of us, civil and martial, don't get along, and I've always had a mind to harm Zhao Dun. But try as I could, there was nowhere to set my hand to it. Zhao Dun's son is called Zhao Shuo and he is now the duke's son-in-law. I once dispatched the brave knight Chu Ni to leap across the wall holding his short knife to assassinate Zhao Dun, but who'd figure that Chu Ni would bash his head against a tree and die? Now Zhao Dun had once gone out to the suburbs as the Exhorter of Agriculture and he saw a man dying from hunger under a mulberry tree. He fed him his fill of rice and wine, and that fellow fled without even a single good-bye. Later the state of the Western Rong sent a hound as tribute, a dog they called the Demon Mastiff, and Duke Ling gave him to me. I've had a plot to kill Zhao Dun ever since I took possession of this Demon Mastiff. I locked him in an empty room and skipped feeding him for four or five days. Then I strung a straw man up in the rear garden, dressed him in purple robes and a jade belt, an ivory tablet of office, and raven-black boots—just like the way Zhao Dun dresses. I hung a pair of sheep's entrails inside this straw dummy and brought the Demon Mastiff out. I tore open the purple robes of Zhao Dun, gave the hound his fill of food, and then put him back, as before, into an empty room. Then I starved him again for a few days, and then he attacked the dummy, bit into it, broke open the purple robe, and ate his fill of sheep's entrails again. After I had trained him this way for a hundred days and I figured that he was ready to use, I went to see Duke Ling. I simply told him that there was a man neither filial nor loyal in our midst who was set on duping the duke. As soon as Duke Ling heard this, he got angry and asked me who it was. I told him, "This Demon Mastiff that was offered up by the Western Rong is a creature of preternatural wonder; he can sniff him out." Duke Ling was overjoyed and said, "Back in the times of Yao and Shun, the Single-Horned Beast[55] gored all the evil people. Who'd have thought that our own state of Jin would possess this Demon Mastiff? Where is it?" I led out that wonder hound, and as soon as it saw Zhao Dun, who was standing in his purple robes and jade belt by the duke's seat, it attacked and bit him. Duke Ling said, "Tu'an Gu, you let that Demon Mastiff loose. Isn't this the slanderous minister?" I set the mastiff loose, and it chased Zhao Dun around the hall. But, alas, someone stepped in angrily from the sidelines—that Grand Pacifier of the Force Before the Hall, Timi Ming—and knocked the Demon Mastiff down with his

55. This was a legendary creature, the Xiezhi (獬豸), that could distinguish the good from the bad, the righteous from the corrupt. It looked like a goat and had a single horn with which to gore the evil and corrupt.

melon-gourd club. Then with one hand he picked the dog up by the loose skin of his head and with the other grabbed hold of his jawbone. And with a single rip, he split the Demon Mastiff in half. As soon as Zhao Dun got out of the door, he looked for the four-horse chariot he came in. But I had already sent someone to unbuckle two of the horses and take off one of the wheels. He got onto the chariot, but he couldn't go anywhere. Running in from the sidelines another brave warrior held up the wheel with one shoulder and drove the horses on with one hand, opening up the road in front of him and giving Zhao Dun an escape route. And who do you think this person was? Ling Zhe, the guy who was starving under the mulberry. I persuaded Duke Ling in a face-to-face encounter to exterminate all three hundred relatives, noble and base, who filled Zhao Dun's gates. Only Zhao Shuo, who was in the palace with the princess and was the royal son-in-law, couldn't be assassinated. I wanted to cut out all the grass and extirpate all the roots so that no sprouts should tendril out. So I faked an order from Duke Ling and sent a minister to deliver the three court measures for dealing with crimes—bowstring, poisoned wine, and dagger—and ordered Zhao Shuo to pick whichever measure he liked to end his life. I told that man to get back here soon and report to me. (*Recites*:)

Three hundred household dependents: a house already extinguished,
All that's left is one royal relative: Zhao Shuo.
No matter by which measure he should die,
All the grass will be cut and the roots all dug up.

(*Exits.*)

(ADDED MALE, *costumed as* ZHAO SHUO, *and* FEMALE LEAD [*costumed as*] *princess, enter.* ZHAO SHUO *speaks*:) I am Zhao Shuo, and my office is that of commandant-escort. Who would have thought that Tu'an Gu would be so incompatible with my father and would manipulate Duke Ling to the point that he would assassinate all three hundred household dependents of our clan, whether noble or base? Ah, Princess, listen to the words I leave behind. Your belly now holds our child. If it is a girl, there is nothing to be said, but if it is a little boy, I am going to name it in the womb and give it the baby name of the Orphan of the Family of Zhao. When he is fully grown, let him cleanse this injustice and take revenge for my father and mother.

(FEMALE LEAD, *acting out crying, speaks*:) Oh, I'm dying with the pain of it all.

(EXTRA, *costumed as* MESSENGER, *leads a retinue on and speaks*:) I am bearing the mandate of our ruler, the duke. I am to deliver the three court measures for dealing with crimes—bowstring, poisoned wine, and dagger—and give them to Consort Zhao Shuo and let him pick the one of his choice to quickly end his life. Afterwards I am to lock the princess in her quarters as prisoner. I dare not hesitate or stop; I must deliver this mandate in a hurry. Here I am already at the gate of their residence. (*Acts out greeting them, speaks*:) Zhao Shuo, kneel. Listen to the mandate of our lord, the duke.

Because your family is disloyal and not filial, because they have deceived the duke and despoiled the law, your entire family, whether noble or base, has been exterminated; yet there remains a miscreant. Pausing to think that you, Zhao Shuo, have a relationship to my own blood, I cannot bear executing you and so have bestowed on you the three court measures for dealing with crimes. You may select one by which to die. The princess shall be locked up in her residence, cut off from her relatives, and forbidden all intercourse with any of them.

Zhao Shuo, the royal mandate may not be countered or delayed. Quickly do yourself in.

(ZHAO SHUO *speaks*:) It has come to this and there is nothing left to be done. (*Sings*:)

([XIANLÜ MODE:] *Shanghua shi*)

All in vain—the loyal goodness with which I repay my lord is ended in a morning,
While that traitorous official, poisonous worm of state, wields power in his hands.
He has without reason employed his snares and plots,
And sent me to have my head lopped off in Yunyang Market.[56]
Isn't this the final result of all my energy and effort?

(FEMALE LEAD *speaks*:) Heaven! Pity our family so abused that they die without a place to bury them! (ZHAO SHUO *sings*:)

(*Reprise*)

It will never come to pass that my body will be buried in our ancient tumuli!

(*Speaks*:) Remember well, My Princess, the words that I spoke to you. (FEMALE LEAD *speaks*:) I know, I know. (ZHAO SHUO *sings*:)

I enjoin her as tears stream like rain along her cheeks,
Every sentence I speak becomes a single moment of sorrow.
Wait until that child of mine has grown to manhood
And say, "For the three hundred of us—
Revenge! Take revenge for our injustice."

(*He acts out dying and exits.*)

(FEMALE LEAD *speaks*:) My husband! You're killing me.

(*Exits.*)

(MESSENGER *speaks*:) Zhao Shuo used the short knife to end his life. The princess is locked away in her residence. I must now go and report to our lord the duke. (*Recites*:)

The very day the Western Rong presented the Demon Mastiff as tribute,
Sealed the inescapable fate of the hundred members of the Zhao family.
Pity the princess still locked away in her room,
Could Zhao Shuo have not decided on the short knife?

(*Exits.*)

56. Yunyang Market is the conventional designation of the execution grounds.

ACT 1

(TU'AN GU *enters and speaks*:) I am Tu'an Gu. As for the princess—I'm afraid she's added a boy child who will eventually become a grown-up man. Won't he become my enemy? I've already locked the princess up in her residence, and she should have reached parturition by now. Why hasn't the person I sent to check on her returned yet? (FOOT SOLDIER *enters, acts out reporting, speaks*:) I am reporting to you, Grand Marshal, that the princess, locked inside her chambers, has given birth to a boy that she has named the Orphan of Zhao. (TU'AN GU *speaks*:) So it's true. She's called him the Orphan of Zhao. I'll wait until the first month is up;[57] that'll be time enough to kill the runt. Messenger! Send forth my command, "Send Lieutenant General Han Jue to hold the doors of her residence secure. Don't check anyone going in but search everyone coming out. If anyone tries to spirit away Zhao the Orphan, their whole family will be decapitated and none of their nine mourning grades[58] will be left alive." Also hang up a notice for me to tell all generals that they had better not contravene or mistake this order lest they bring down the same punishment on themselves. (*Recites*:)

It was because the princess of Jin grew pregnant,
And the Orphan she bore is my enemy;
Wait I must for the full month and then hack him to death with an iron sword,
Before I can claim that I have pruned the grass and ripped out its roots.

(*Exits.*)

(FEMALE LEAD, *cradling the boy, enters and recites*:)

Every vexation under heaven,
Lies upon this heart of mine;
Just like the rain of an autumn night,
Every drop, every sound is sorrow.

I am a princess of the house of Jin. That traitor of an official Tu'an Gu slew everyone, exterminated the house of Zhao without regard to their status. And now for my only begotten son I remember that my husband left a testament as he neared death: if it was a boy, he was to be called Zhao the Orphan. When he grows up

57. The Chinese term for puerperium; the first month after childbirth is lived in confinement in the women's quarters.

58. There are several theories as to what these nine relations or nine grades of mourning were. One proposes that it was the patrilineal clan of ego's lateral generation, four generations before ego and four generations afterward; another suggests that it was four generations of the patrilineal clan, three generations of the matrilineal, and two generations of the wife's clan. The Ming codified the punishment as four generations and before after ego, as well as ego and his brothers, cousins, and second cousins.

to be a man, he's to cleanse away the injustice done to his parents and repay their enemies. O, Heaven. How can I get this child out of here? Any way I can will have to do. Let me think; there are no relatives left. There's only our retainer Cheng Ying, whose name was never affiliated with the family. I'll wait until he arrives—I have an idea.

(EXTRA, *dressed as* CHENG YING, *enters bearing a medicine chest on his back and speaks*:) I am Cheng Ying. I was originally an itinerant physician, but when I was a retainer in the house of the consort, I was treated very, very well—better than the average person. But that murderous official Tu'an Gu slew everyone, noble and base, exterminating the house of Zhao. Fortunately my name did not appear on the family register. Now the princess is locked away in her residence and I send her tea and food every day. Even though she has given birth to a boy—he is called the Orphan of Zhao and when he grows up to be a man he's to cleanse away the injustice done to his parents and repay their enemies—I'm afraid he'll never escape the clutches of that traitorous butcher Tu. This is all wrong. I hear that the princess summoned me, and I guess that she needs some liquid and herbal medicine.[59] So, I'd better go. (CHENG YING *acts out greeting her and speaks*:) Why did you call me, Princess?

(FEMALE LEAD *speaks*:) We Zhaos have suffered to death. Cheng Ying, I've asked you here for only one reason; I've had a son who was given the name of the Orphan of Zhao by a father on the verge of his own death. Cheng Ying, in all the time you've been with our Zhao family, we've never treated you badly. You must think of a way to hide this baby away so that later, when he's a man, he can pay back the enemy of the Zhaos. (CHENG YING *speaks*:) Don't you know, Princess, that Tu'an Gu knows you've given birth to this boy and that on each of the four city gates has hung up this announcement: "If anyone tries to spirit away the Orphan of Zhao, their whole family will be decapitated and none of their nine relations will be left alive." How can I hide him away? (FEMALE LEAD *speaks*:) Cheng Ying, (*recites*:)

Is it not said, "Think of kin when encountering an emergency,
Rely on old friends when approaching danger"?
If you rescue this child that I gave birth to,
Then the family of Zhao will have left a single root behind.

(*Kneels and speaks*:) Cheng Ying, have pity on the Zhaos, whose three hundred souls are vested in this one child! (CHENG YING *speaks*:) Princess, arise. If I hide this little master away and Tu'an Gu finds out about it and asks you about the Orphan of Zhao, you just tell him you have given the child to me. If my own family should

59. This does not mean that she was sick. In terms of Chinese medicinal practice, in which the body is an amalgam of properties that need to be kept in harmonic balance, she needed to replenish certain elements in her body that the process of childbirth had depleted.

die, so be it. But don't hope this child will get away alive. (FEMALE LEAD *speaks*:) Enough, enough, enough. Cheng Ying, I'm telling you to go with an easy mind. (*Recites*:)

Cheng Ying, let your heart find no turmoil,
A thousand tears will fall when I finish speaking.
His father died willingly by the point of a knife

(*Takes off the belt of her skirt to hang herself, speaks*:) Enough! Enough! Enough!

His mother now follows with her own death.

(*Exits.*)

(CHENG YING *speaks*:) I never guessed that the princess would hang herself. I'd better not linger or tarry. Let me open this medicine chest and put the little master inside and then cover his body with some fresh herbal medicines. O, Heaven, how pitiful! Three hundred souls of the Zhao family were wiped out and all that's left is this one little child. I'll try and get him out safe now. If you have any luck at all, I'll be successful. If you're found, you'll lose your life and the lives of my whole family will be beyond protection. (*Recites*:)

Cheng Ying, let your heart make a plan:
This family of Zhao is truly worth grieving over.
I just want to get you outside these nine-deep concentric circles of the marshal's headquarters,
So you can escape those calamities of heaven's net and earth's snare.

(*Exits.*)

(MALE LEAD, *costumed as* HAN JUE, *enters leading foot soldiers, speaks*:) I am Lieutenant General Han Jue, an aide under the aegis of Tu'an Gu. He has sent me to guard the doors of the princess's residence. And why? Just because the princess has borne a child that is called the Orphan of Zhao. He's afraid someone will steal it away. He told me if I find it in searching people leaving the residence, then the whole family of that person is to be decapitated and all nine relations wiped out. Captain, hold the gate to the princess's compound securely. Damn, Tu'an Gu, when will we see the end of people like you, who so destroy the loyal and good? (*Sings*:)

(XIANLÜ MODE: *Dian jiangchun*)

The enfeoffed states now in tangled confusion,
None is stronger than Jin.
When just so securely settled,
Why such a tyrannical minister as Tu'an Gu?
He simply destroys the loyal and filial grandees of state.

(*Hunjiang long*)

And just when the winds are fair and the rain seasonal—
In such years of high peace such a man as this is favored!
The loyal and filial have their heads lopped off in the marketplace,

While that traitor and toady takes his ease in the marshal's compound.
And now he exercises all the power and makes all the fortune—
We cannot say that it is "Half from the lord, half from the minister."
He, he, he—claws and fangs he has packed into the gates of the court:
Those who resist even a little are cut down, finished one by one.
True it is, he's a source of evil among men,
He's no "general to be trusted beyond the gates."

(*Speaks*:) I don't believe that such a deep enmity that knotted Tu'an Gu and Zhao Dun together can ever be undone. (*Sings*:)

(*You hulu*)
He wants to cut down the grass, prevent sprouts, cut out the root of disaster,
And makes me hold tight the compound gate.
I, too, am a longtime minister of house and state.
He who hides the child—it is not right to conceal him.
He who slays the child—can his heart bear to do it?
(*Continues in speech:*) Tu'an Gu, you're tyrannical. (*Sings:*)
One day you'll enrage Heaven above
And vex the people below.
Why don't you fear the myriad mouths will boil over in competing condemnations?
Or that heaven, showing its blue face, will grant no pardon to man?
(*Tianxia le*)
Is it not said, "It reaches as far away as sons and grandsons, and comes as close as one's self"?[60]
Ai! Such an oh-so-treacherous official,
How could you and Zhao Dun
Have been colleagues for twenty years and yet you still lack any friendly feelings?
But you came up with the plan to work your evil design
And fingered a good minister as an evil man.
And if these two were to be carefully evaluated,
Which one will wind up to be the crueler?

(*Speaks*:) Officer, watch the gate. If you see anyone coming out of the compound gate, let me know. (SOLDIER *speaks*:) Yes sir! (CHENG YING *runs on in a panic, speaks*:) Inside this medicine box in my arms I have the Orphan of Zhao. Heaven, take pity! Fortunately, it is General Han Jue who is guarding the compound gate. He is someone who was promoted by the old minister. The young master and I both may live.

60. That is, sooner or later there will be a response for any action a man takes, whether good or bad.

(*Acts out going out through the gate.*) (MALE LEAD *speaks*:) Sergeant, bring me that man who is holding a medicine box in his arms! Who are you! (CHENG YING *speaks*:) I am an itinerant physician and my name is Cheng Ying. (MALE LEAD *speaks*:) Where are you coming from? (CHENG YING *speaks*:) From brewing up infusions and administering simples in the princess's compound. (MALE LEAD *speaks*:) What kind of medicine did you supply? (CHENG YING *speaks*:) I gave her a postpartum infusion. (MALE LEAD *speaks*:) And what do you have in this box? (CHENG YING *speaks*:) Only simples. (MALE LEAD *speaks*:) What kind of simples? (CHENG YING *speaks*:) Bellflower, licorice, and peppermint. (MALE LEAD *speaks*:) What is between the layers? (CHENG YING *speaks*:) Nothing. (MALE LEAD *speaks*:) Then you may go. (CHENG YING *acts out fleeing*. MALE LEAD *acts out calling, speaks*:) Cheng Ying, come back! What do you have in that box? (CHENG YING *speaks*:) Only simples! (MALE LEAD *speaks*:) Is there anything you are carrying hidden in between? (CHENG YING *speaks*:) There's nothing hidden in between! (MALE LEAD *speaks*:) Go! (CHENG YING *acts out fleeing*. MALE LEAD *acts out calling, speaks*:) Cheng Ying, come back! You have to be hiding something. When I tell you to go, you're like an arrow leaving the string. But when I call you to come back, it's like pulling hair over felt. Cheng Ying, did you think I don't recognize you? (*Sings*:)

(*Hexi Houting hua*)

You were once upon a time an honored guest in the house of Zhao Dun,
But I am definitely a retainer in the service of Tu'an Gu.
You're hiding that unicorn seed that has yet to reach a month in age!
(*Continues in speech:*) Cheng Ying, don't you see? (*Sings:*)
How can you get out of this tiger and leopard lair that even the wind can't enter?
And if I were not the lieutenant general,
I would not subject you to questioning!

(*Speaks*:) Cheng Ying, I know that you have received many favors of the Zhao family. (CHENG YING *speaks*:) Yes indeed. One who acknowledges a favor, repays that favor. That goes without saying! (MALE LEAD *sings*:)

You say "one who acknowledges favor" should "repay that favor,"
But I don't think you'll escape with your life even if you wanted:
Front and rear, the gates are guarded,
On earth or in heaven you've nowhere to run.
If I bring you back and find out the truth
And go and report, taking the Orphan with me,
To live will be impossible,
To die a certainty!

(*Speaks*:) Sergeant, move back! Come if I call you, but if I don't, don't! (SOLDIER *speaks*:) Yes sir! (MALE LEAD *acts out opening the box and noticing the baby, speaks*:) Cheng Ying, you said you had bellflower, licorice, and peppermint, but now I've

found ginseng![61] (CHENG YING *acts out kneeling down in panic and prostrating himself.*) (MALE LEAD *sings*:)
(*Jinzhan'er*)
I see the Orphan, his forehead covered in sweat
And at the corners of his mouth the froth of his mother's milk.
He opens wide his eyes, sparkling and bright, and recognizes me.
Quiet and silent inside the box, he seems to swallow his voice,
Closely swaddled, he cannot stretch a limb,
So tightly cramped, he cannot turn over.
True this is: "If one is to grow into a man, one must suffer lack of freedom,
But too much freedom, then one cannot grow into a man."

(CHENG YING *recites in ballad verse*:)
Your Excellency, please still your rage and rest your anger,
And listen to me explain the matter from the very beginning:
Because Zhao Dun was the worthiest official of the house of Jin,
Tu'an Gu in his heart was consumed by jealousy and spite.
He had the Demon Mastiff attack a man so loyal and good,
And through the gate of the palace Zhao Dun fled for his life.
Steering that one-wheeled chariot Ling Zhe repaid a favor,
Then disappeared into the deepest mountains, no one knows where.
But Duke Ling heeded and trusted words of a slanderer
And let that traitor Tu do as he liked!
He bestowed death upon the ducal son-in-law, who fell on his sword,
And exterminated nine mourning grades of the family—none was left alive.
He confined the princess to the cold palace
And would not allow any relatives to help.
In conformity with her husband's last words she called her child "the Orphan."
But mother and child were unable to remain together.
For barely had she given birth, when her life returned to the shades,
But she ordered me, Cheng Ying, to conceal him and protect him
So later he can eventually grow up and become a man
Who will look after the ancestral graves of the Zhao family.
By lucky chance I have encountered you, General,
And I fully hope that you will draw your sword and come to his rescue.
If you once again cut off and uproot this last little sprout,
Won't you be finishing them off, the whole family extirpated and gone?

---

61. "Ginseng" (*renshen* 人參) is a pun here on *rensheng* 人生 (literally, "man's life" or "a living person"), referring also to the fact that the root is in the shape of the character for a human (人).

(MALE LEAD *speaks*:) Cheng Ying, if I were to take this child and deliver it up, I would live in riches and honor for the rest of my life! But I am a real man who stands on earth with heaven above him—how could I willingly do such a foul deed! (*Sings*:)

(*Zui zhong tian*)

If I were to offer him up for the sake of glorious advancement,
Would they not say, "He profited himself by destroying others"?
How sad that none of his three hundred blood kin survive,
So who is left to wipe out this everlasting wrong?
(*Continues in speech:*) If that Tu'an Gu sees this child, (*sings:*)
I'm sure he'll take skin, tendons, and all
To knead him into a meaty paste!
But I have no reason at all
To establish such blind merit!

(*Speaks*:) Cheng Ying, carry this child on out. If Tu'an Gu asks, I'll answer myself for it! (CHENG YING *speaks*:) Thank you, General! (*Acts out walking out carrying the box, but returns again and kneels down*) (MALE LEAD *speaks*:) Cheng Ying, I said you're free to go. Do you think I am playing with you? Get out of here now! (CHENG YING *speaks*:) Thank you, General! (*Acts out going and again returning to kneel.*) (MALE LEAD *speaks*:) Cheng Ying, why have you come back once more? (*Sings*:)

(*Jinzhan'er*)

You must be guessing that I am putting you on and am being insincere.
Don't you know that "the orchid sighs, lamenting that the basil is burned?"[62]
Go, now, go, a number of times I've set you free,
Why do you keep coming back to the gate?
(*Continues in speech:*) Cheng Ying! (*Sings:*)
If you don't have enough courage to protect yourself,
Who forced you to make yourself the Orphan's protector?
Isn't it said, "A loyal minister does not fear death,
Whoever fears death is no loyal minister!"

(CHENG YING *speaks*:) General, if I get out of this compound and you tell Tu'an Gu, he'll send another general to run me down and arrest me. There's no way that the Orphan can survive. So be it! General, arrest me, request your merit and take your reward! I am willing to lay down my life together with the Orphan's! (MALE LEAD *speaks*:) Cheng Ying, go on and don't worry! (*Sings*:)

(*Zui fu gui*)

You want to preserve the last scion for the sake of the Zhao,
But I feel no closeness to that traitor Tu!

62. Both are fragrant plants; this is to lament something bad that happens to someone or something of like kind.

Why would I want to pretend to have human feelings,
Then dispatch a mass of troops to form a whirlwind battle formation?
But if you are loyal, I too can keep my word,
If you are willing to sacrifice your life,
I willingly will slit my throat!
(*Qing ge'er*)
Really, this is something that cannot be expressed in a single word, in a single word!
(*Continues in speech:*) Cheng Ying! (*Sings:*)
And for you nothing is treasured in your eyes, in your eyes!
Take the Orphan and hide him in the deepest recesses of the deepest mountains,
And there teach and guide him to manhood,
Let him practice martial and civil arts,
So he may take command of the army,
Arrest that traitorous minister—
Crush his head and dismember his body
To repay the souls of the dead!
Then that will not betray our determined steps through the gate of right and wrong,
Or the way we shouldered danger and distress!
(*Continues in speech:*) Cheng Ying, go without fear! (*Sings:*)
(*Zhuansha Coda*)
It's better that he gets clarification from my very body,
But how can I put up with being interrogated in front of that traitor?
I will rashly bash my head against the steps to end my own life.
I might not leave a fragrant name to be renowned for all eternity,
But I can still keep Chu Ni company, twin souls of loyal men.
You, you, you be diligent, look after him morning and dusk,
For he is the only life root of the house of Zhao!
And just wait until he has reached manhood,
Before you tell him the tale from the very beginning:
And tell him, he who takes revenge,
To not forget me, his great benefactor!
(*Slits his throat, exits.*)

(CHENG YING *speaks*:) Ah, General Han has slit his throat! I'm afraid that when the soldiers find this out, they will report it to Tu'an Gu. So what to do now? I'll have to flee for my life, carrying the Orphan in my arms! (*Recites*:)

General Han was truly a soldier loyal and good,
Who slit his throat and perished, all for this Orphan.
Now I can go on ahead without having to worry,
And in Great Peace Village make further plans.

(*Exits.*)

ACT 2

(TU'AN GU *enters leading soldiers, speaks:*) "Let nothing bother me, those who are bothered go crazy."[63] Because the princess bore a little one whom she called the Orphan of Zhao, I, Tu'an Gu, dispatched Lieutenant General Han Jue to guard the gates of her compound and to search out any traitors or spies. On the other hand I had announcements posted that if anyone smuggled the Orphan of Zhao out, he and his whole family would be punished by decapitation—none in the nine grades of mourning would be left! I don't have to worry that the Orphan will fly off to Heaven, do I? But I haven't seen anyone bring the Orphan to me yet, so I can't stop worrying. Runner, go keep watch outside the gate! (SOLDIER *acts out reporting, speaks:*) Marshal, a disaster! (TU'AN GU *speaks:*) What kind of disaster? (SOLDIER *speaks:*) The princess hanged herself with the belt of her skirt in her compound, and General Han Jue, who was guarding the gate, has died by slitting his throat! (TU'AN GU *speaks:*) Why did Han Jue slit his own throat? He must have allowed the Orphan of Zhao to escape! What to do now? "One wrinkle at the tip of the brow, and a new scheme arises in the heart": I now have no other way but to counterfeit an edict by Duke Ling, according to which all newborn babies in the state of Jin younger than six months but older than one month will be rounded up and brought to me. Every single one I see I will chop to pieces with three strokes of my sword! The Orphan of Zhao will surely be among them. This will do away with any future harm to me. Runner, post announcements ordering that all newborn babies in the state of Jin who are younger than half a year and older than one month must be rounded up and taken to my marshal's office to await further orders. Anyone who disobeys will be decapitated along with his whole family, and no one in the nine mourning grades will be left. (*Recites:*)

If I round up all the infants in the state of Jin,
The Orphan, I reckon, will have no place to hide.
Let him be a golden branch, a leaf of jade,[64]
He will never escape the disaster of death by my sword!

(*Exits.*)

(MALE LEAD, *costumed as* GONGSUN CHUJIU, *enters leading a servant boy, speaks:*) I, this old codger, am Gongsun Chujiu. At the court of Duke Ling of Jin I was a grandee

63. This is simply a common phrase meaning that if one allows things to bother oneself, it is impossible to keep a clear and tranquil mind; here, however, it may carry a second meaning, "Nothing is on my mind; what is on my mind is rebellion." Since the word *luan* 亂, which we have translated here as "crazy," also has the meaning of "against rule and reason, disorderly, rebellious," a third level of meaning would be "those who are bothered will become rebellious."

64. A scion of royalty.

of the second order. Because of my advanced age and because I saw that while Tu'an Gu monopolized power I could no longer carry out the affairs of the lord, I retired from my post and resumed farming. A thatched cottage, dozens of acres of fields, and a hoe upon which I can rest my hand! I am living in Lülü Great Peace Village. I usually sleep at night within my bed-curtains and listen to the bugle blowing in the cold. Now I am leaning against the brushwood gate and counting the lines of geese. How it makes one ponder things! (*Sings*:)

(NANLÜ MODE: *Yizhi hua*)

You really have unjustly humiliated a great man,
Completely destroyed a true "roof beam of the state."
Like a foul and filthy butcher of dogs[65]
You abused this old codger who "fishes out giant turtles."[66]
It was my misfortune to live in the time of Duke Ling, one without the Way,
Who loved that traitor and heaped favor and grace on him,
While the worthy suffered privation and distress.
If I had not pulled my feet out of that rushing torrent,
I probably would have delivered my head to that bustling market![67]

(*Liangzhou diqi*)

He, he, he, in his marshal's office, flaunts his power, shows off his valor,
I, I, I, in Great Peace Village, have retired from my post to resume farming.
Don't think there are any more heron ranks and leopard tails to come for me![68]
At this very moment his office has topped out at the highest rank,
And he has reached a level equal to the Three Dukes;
He has been enfeoffed with the tax harvest of eight districts
And enjoys a salary of a thousand bushels.
He sees injustice, but his eyes seem blind,
Hears them curse and revile him, but his ears seem deaf.
He, he, he simply lets those who know to toady and flatter lay out tripods of food in rows and double up their cushions;
Those who harm the loyal and good he raises in office, presents with emoluments,
Those who scourge both state and family are all given noble rank according to their "merit"!
They, they, they only think of their present pleasure,
And forget that the higher you climb, the worse the sprain when you stumble.

---

65. Since the word "butcher" (*tu*) is also the first part of Tu'an Gu's surname, this could be understood as "foul and filthy men like that dog Tu."
66. "To fish out giant turtles" is to perform heroic acts, or to have designs to do so.
67. Executions were normally carried out in the marketplace.
68. Heron ranks are the orderly formation of officials at morning court; leopard tails are hung on the chariots of high officials.

How can they compare to me, keeping to field and garden, learning to plow and sow?
I have jumped out of that lair of man-eating starving tigers,
And now I am so at ease!

(CHENG YING *enters, speaks*:) Cheng Ying, you are such a wreck! Young Master, you are in such danger! Tu'an Gu, you are so cruel! I, Cheng Ying, may have dashed out of the city at the risk of my life, but I have heard that Tu'an Gu, informed that the Orphan had escaped, wants to collect at his offices all the babies in the state of Jin younger than six months but older than one. Whether they are orphaned or not, he will personally hack each of them into three pieces. Where should I take the young master now? I've got it! I'm thinking of Gongsun Chujiu in Lülü Great Peace Village. He was a colleague of Zhao Dun's and they were the best of friends. Now he has resigned from his post and resumed farming. That old minister is a loyal and upright person. He'll be willing to hide him there! Now I have arrived in the village. I'll put my medicine box under this mat shed. Young Master, sleep for a while, I will come back to look after you after I have seen Gongsun Chujiu. Servant, say that Cheng Ying is here and wants to see your master. (SERVANT *acts out reporting, speaks*:) There's a Cheng Ying at the gate. (MALE LEAD *speaks*:) Invite him in. (SERVANT *speaks*:) Please come in. (MALE LEAD *acts out greeting him, speaks*:) Cheng Ying, what brings you here? (CHENG YING *speaks*:) My reason for visiting you here in Great Peace Village is that I have a special request. (MALE LEAD *speaks*:) How have the other ministers been doing since I retired from office? (CHENG YING *speaks*:) Ah, these are not like the times when you were a minister. Now Tu'an Gu monopolizes power and nothing is the same as it was. (MALE LEAD *speaks*:) Well, then the other ministers should remonstrate with him again and again. (CHENG YING *speaks*:) Minister, there has always been this kind of traitorous officials. Even in the time of Emperor Yao there were the Four Disasters.[69] (MALE LEAD *sings*:)

(*Gewei*)
You say from antiquity many have been manipulated by evil ministers,
And that even the age of the Sages was replete with its own Four Disasters.
But who, like this one, is cursed by myriads, hated by thousands, but valued by
The One!
He is unjust and unfair,
Neither filial nor loyal—
And all alone he killed the entire clan of Zhao Dun until not one seed is left!

(CHENG YING *speaks*:) Minister, fortunately august Heaven has eyes: the seed of the house of Zhao has not yet been destroyed! (MALE LEAD *speaks*:) His whole household, high and low, more than three hundred souls, have all been exterminated. Even the royal son-in-law suffered the "three court measures" and slit his throat with a

69. Yao exiled four mythical beasts—Hundun, Qiongqi, Taowu, and Cantie—to the perimeter of his kingdom.

dagger. The princess too hanged herself by the belt of her skirt. What seed is left and where? (CHENG YING *speaks*:) The above-mentioned facts you already know, so I don't have to explain them. But recently the princess, while confined to her compound, gave birth to a son, whom she called the Orphan. If he isn't a seed of the house of Zhao, who is? But I fear that if Tu'an Gu finds out, he'll want to kill him too. If he kills this baby, then truly the seed of the house of Zhao will be destroyed! (MALE LEAD *speaks*:) Where is this child now? Could someone have rescued him? (CHENG YING *speaks*:) Since you, Minister, show this inkling of compassion, I dare not hide the truth from you. Before her death the princess handed the child to me, Cheng Ying, and ordered me to take good care of him, so that when he grows up and becomes a man, he can take revenge for his father and mother and wipe out this injustice. When I carried the child out through the gate, General Han Jue wanted to arrest us and report to Tu'an Gu, but after I reproved him, he set me free to go out through the gate. He then slit his throat and died. Now I have no place to hide this child and I came to seek shelter with you. Since you were a colleague of Zhao Dun's I thought you must have been extremely close. Find a way to pity us and to save this Orphan! (MALE LEAD *speaks*:) Where is the Orphan now? (CHENG YING *speaks*:) He's under the mat shed right now. (MALE LEAD *speaks*:) Don't frighten the Orphan but quickly bring him inside! (CHENG YING *acts out getting the chest, opening and looking, speaks*:) Thank heaven and earth! The young master is still asleep! (MALE LEAD *acts out taking him in his arms, sings*:)

(*Muyang guan*)
This child—before he was born he had lost all his relatives,
While still in the womb, his whole lineage had been extinguished.
If he lives until manhood, it'll be a life of little luck and much disaster.
His father was decapitated on the execution ground,
His mother was confined inside the palace.
How can a white-clad minister carry the stench of fresh blood?
He is just a black-headed grub without a thought of gratitude.[70]

(CHENG YING *speaks*:) The whole Zhao family relies only on this young master to take vengeance. (MALE LEAD *sings*:)

You say he'll be a real man who'll avenge his father and mother,
But I say he's a seed of disaster that brought down his mommy and daddy!

70. A white-clad minister usually refers to a student who has yet to pass the examinations and become an official. A black-headed grub refers to the folk belief that "black-headed grubs" and "yellow-mouth *chen* birds" were two creatures that ate their parents, therefore completely unfilial. These two lines should be read in concert with the last two of the song, and seem to mean, "He'll just wind up a meek civil official who won't be able to take revenge, or he'll be an unfilial son that not only will not take revenge but will cause the death of his parents as well."

(CHENG YING *speaks*:) What you don't know, sir, is that because the Orphan of Zhao was set free, Tu'an Gu is rounding up all the babies in the Jin state, and he is going to finish them all off. Now the reasons I smuggled the Orphan out and want to hide him with you are first, I want to repay Consort Zhao's fine treatment of me and second, I want to save the lives of all infants of the state of Jin. Now I'm nearly forty-five and have only one son, less than a month old. I want to pretend he is the Orphan of Zhao and have you denounce me to Tu'an Gu by telling him that I am hiding the child. The two of us, father and son, will be put to death on the same spot. You, Minister, may then raise the child at leisure, and when he has grown up and become a man, he may take revenge for his father and mother. Wouldn't that be the best? (MALE LEAD *speaks*:) Cheng Ying, how old are you? (CHENG YING *speaks*:) I've turned forty-five. (MALE LEAD *speaks*:) This child, I reckon, will have to be twenty before he can take vengeance for his father and mother. With another twenty years, you'll be only sixty-five. But with another twenty years, I'll be ninety. At that time most likely I'll be dead. What revenge then would be possible for the house of Zhao? Cheng Ying, if you are willing to give up your child, hand him over to me. You denounce me to Tu'an Gu by telling him that Gongsun Chujiu is hiding the Orphan of Zhao at Great Peace Village. Tu'an Gu will come with his soldiers to arrest me, and I will die together with your son. Then you will raise the Orphan of Zhao to manhood so he can take revenge for his father and mother. This seems a better strategy. (CHENG YING *speaks*:) Minister, you are right, but how could I impose on you like this? You just dress my child up as the Orphan of Zhao and denounce me to Tu'an Gu, so that we, father and son, may die at the same spot. (MALE LEAD *speaks*:) Cheng Ying, I have given you my word, why do you still doubt me? (*Sings*:)

(*Hong shaoyao*)

A little master who needs twenty years to take vengeance,
Will take that long before he is satisfied,
And I worry that it would come to nothing should I eventually die.

(CHENG YING *speaks*:) Minister, you are still full of a hearty spirit. (MALE LEAD *sings*:)

My vigor and energy are not what they used to be.
And if left behind, how could this child achieve success?
You won't age right away—
You are the one to put yourself out front on behalf of the Zhao family!

(*Continues in speech*:) Cheng Ying, you just do as I say! (*Sings*:)

I will not last through those evening drums and morning bells.

(CHENG YING *speaks*:) Minister, you were doing fine at home when I, without any sense of timing, just barged in and turned over this bag of sorrow to you. That's why I cannot set my mind at rest. (MALE LEAD *speaks*:) Cheng Ying, you're talking nonsense. I am a man of seventy and death is nothing out of the ordinary. It makes no difference when it happens! (*Sings*:)

(*Pusa Liangzhou*)
In this marionette's booth
We perform to drum and flute,
But it's no more than acting out a short little dream.
Turn your head quickly to the past and all the heroes have died.
"How can one meet one's benefactor if grace is still unrequited?"
"No courage counted to see injustice and not act."

(CHENG YING *speaks*:) Minister, you have consented. Don't break faith! (MALE LEAD *sings*:)

"To speak but be without trust—then what's the use of speaking?"

(CHENG YING *speaks*:) Minister, if you make it possible for the Orphan of Zhao to survive, your name will be recorded in the history books and you will leave a reputation for all eternity. (MALE LEAD *sings*:)

There is no need to try to get in my good graces now—
"A real man does not sorrow over his own death,"
How much more so me, my white locks loose and tangled?

(CHENG YING *speaks*:) Minister, there is yet one other thing. Can you withstand the three investigations and the six questionings once Tu'an Gu has arrested you? You're bound to finger me. My and my son's deaths lie within our allotted fate. But it would be a pity if the Orphan of Zhao winds up dead anyway and I have dragged you into this for nothing. (MALE LEAD *speaks*:) Cheng Ying, you are right. When I think of Tu'an Gu and the Consort Zhao . . . (*Sings*:)

(*Third from Coda*)
These two families had become deadliest enemies,
His only aim was to find some trace of the Orphan.
He's bound to surround Great Peace Village with his troops
As tight as an iron bucket—not a breath of air will get through.

(*Speaks*:) After Tu'an Gu arrests me, he'll shout in his loudest voice: "You old geezer, didn't you see the announcement that was posted three days ago? And yet you stubbornly had to hide the Orphan of Zhao to oppose me! Please, please!" (*Sings*:)

He'll only say to this old geezer, "Please, 'You step into the vat first.'"[71]
You knew quite well that all of heaven quaked when the announcement was hung!
But you, retired-from-office, back-to-the-fields, single old peasant
Had to poke this scorpion and nettle this wasp in public!"

71. Someone reported to Wu Zetian that a certain Zhou Xing was plotting rebellion. Empress Wu ordered someone to question him. The person asked Zhou Xing one day how he would make a prisoner confess to a crime. Zhou responded, "That is easy. Just take a huge vat, put charcoal around its four sides, and get it red-hot. If you make the accused get into it, what won't they confess to?" The official ordered up a vat and said, "Please, Old Brother, get into the vat." Of course Zhou Xing quickly confessed. This phrase later came to mean "to step into danger of one's own accord." Here, something like, "Go ahead, hang yourself."

(*Second from Coda*)
He'll use every method, strip me naked, bind me with a rope, hang me upside down, and beat me,
Just to wring out every little detail at the root of this case.
And when my parched skin and decayed old bones can't stand the pain,
I'm bound by my truthful confession to implicate you—
Of course you, Cheng Ying, are afraid!
(*Continues in speech:*) Cheng Ying, set your mind at rest! (*Sings:*)
A single "Yes" from me has always weighed as much as a thousand pieces of gold.
Even if he sends me up the mountain of knives and the peak of swords,[72]
Never will I be one who "has a beginning but no end."

(*Speaks*:) Cheng Ying, set your mind at rest and go on with raising this Orphan, so he may grow to manhood and take revenge for his father and mother, wiping away all injustice. The single death of an old man is not worth mentioning! (*Sings*:)

(*Sha Coda*)
He'll rely on his noble descent from the house of Zhao, a thousand years old,[73]
And the hundred-two[74] might of the mountains and rivers of the state of Jin.
He will display his radiant heroism and lead army troops,
Overawe and suppress all the other states, which will all submit.
He will visit all the dukes and nobles and narrate his bitter experience,
And all the disaster that originally arose below the palace;[75]
Then tell how pitiably three hundred relatives all tasted the sword
And only a lonely and forlorn little child was left.
Waiting patiently for this morn
To inherit his father's position,
He will bring up his hated enemy
And his tears will burst out.
He will request a tablet- and standard-bearer to go down into the deepest layers of the palace
And arrest that fiendish official in his marshal's office.
He'll cut off his head, dismember his body, and offer it up in sacrifice to his ancestors,
The nine mourning grades will all be executed, none will be spared.

---

72. Typical underworld tortures.

73. That is, the lineage of the family tree.

74. See n. 40.

75. The enmity between Tu'an Gu and Zhao Dun began over the cruelty of Duke Ling. The duke had constructed a tower in his palace, from which he shot pellets from his crossbow at people who walked by below. Zhao Dun strongly remonstrated with him for finding his pleasure in such an inhumane way and became involved in a dispute over this with Tu'an Gu, who then began to plot against Zhao.

At that time he will show he did not betray you, who risked death to protect the Orphan as repayment to your lord,
And even I will be at peace, buried close to Yao Li's grave by the side of the road.[76]
(*Exits.*)

(CHENG YING *speaks*:) The time is critical now. As I was going to do before, I will carry this Orphan home and send my own child to Great Peace Village. (*Recites*:)

Willingly I take the child that I fathered
To secretly exchange for the Orphan of Zhao.
This is what I should do by what is right—
But I lament I have dragged Old Minister Gongsun into this affair.

(*Exits.*)

ACT 3

(TU'AN GU *enters leading soldiers, speaks*:) The Orphan of Zhao has escaped me! But I have already distributed announcements to the effect that if no one comes forward with the Orphan within three days, I will round up all the infants in the state of Jin of less than half a year and more than one month in my marshal's office and execute all of them. Soldier, keep watch in front of the gate, and if there is someone who comes forward with information, report back to me. (CHENG YING *enters and speaks*:) I am Cheng Ying. I took my child to Gongsun Chujiu yesterday and today I will go to Tu'an Gu to denounce Gongsun. Soldier, report to your master that the Orphan of Zhao has been found. (SOLDIER *speaks*:) Just wait here. Let me go inside and report. (*Acts out reporting, speaks*:) I report to the marshal that there is someone who is claiming that the Orphan has been found. (TU'AN GU *speaks*:) Where is he now? (SOLDIER *speaks*:) He is outside the gate. (TU'AN GU *speaks*:) Order him to come in. (SOLDIER *speaks*:) Come inside! ([CHENG YING] *performs greeting rituals.* TU'AN GU *speaks*:) You there, who are you? (CHENG YING *speaks*:) This humble person is the itinerant physician Cheng Ying. (TU'AN GU *speaks*:) Where is the Orphan of Zhao now? (CHENG YING *speaks*:) He is hidden in the house of Gongsun Chujiu

76. Yao Li was a famous assassin from the state of Wu during the Spring and Autumn era. The King of Wu wanted to get rid of a rival, Prince Qingji, who had fled to Wei. Yao Li proposed that he pretend to have committed an offense against the king and endure punishments so that when he fled to Wei, Qingji would believe him. He cut off his right hand and fled; the king then burned Yao Li's wife in the marketplace. Yao Li lived in Wei for a while, then made an alliance with Qingji to invade Wu. As they crossed the river, Yao Li stabbed Qingji. Before dying, Qingji persuaded his retainers not to kill Yao Li, claiming that it would be a deep wrong to "kill two heroic men in the same day." Yao Li later regretted his actions, cut off his own hand and feet, and then fell on his sword. Here, of course, Gongsun means that he will also endure suffering but in the end die a righteous man.

in Lülü Great Peace Village. (TU'AN GU *speaks*:) How did you come to know this? (CHENG YING *speaks*:) I happen to know Gongsun Chujiu. I went to visit him and to my surprise I saw an infant in the bedroom, lying in a brocaded baby harness on an embroidered cushion. I thought, "Gongsun Chujiu is a man of seventy who had never had son or daughter, so where did this one come from?" And I said to him: "This little one must be the Orphan of Zhao!" Immediately he turned pale and he didn't know what to say. That's how I came to know that the Orphan is at the house of Gongsun Chujiu. (TU'AN GU *speaks*:) Bah! You rascal! Do you think you can put one over me? No enmity existed between you and Gongsun Chujiu in the past and there is no grudge in recent times. So why do you accuse him of hiding the Orphan of Zhao? You must be an accomplice! If you tell me the truth, everything is fine, but if not . . . Soldiers, sharpen your swords! Kill this guy first! (CHENG YING *speaks*:) Marshal, still your thundering rage and restrain your tiger- and wolflike might! Allow me to tell you the complete story. Between Gongsun Chujiu and me there exists indeed no enmity or strife. I do this only because you announced that you want all the infants in the state of Jin rounded up in your office to kill them all. First of all I want to save the lives of the infants in the state of Jin. Secondly, at the age of forty-five I have just become the father of a boy who is not yet one month old. I wouldn't dare not to offer him up, but then I too would be left without posterity! As I see it, if the Orphan of Zhao is found, the living souls in the whole state will be saved from harm, and my child too will be safe. That's why I came forward. (*Recites*:)

I beg you, Your Excellency, to still your rage for a while!
This is the one and only reason why I came forward.
Even though I save all the living souls in the state of Jin,
What I really feared was the extinction of the house of Cheng.

(TU'AN GU *acts out laughing, speaks*:) Aha! Yes, indeed! Gongsun Chujiu once was a colleague of Zhao Dun's. Of course he's the one to do a thing like this. Soldier, today I summon the men and horse under my command and with Cheng Ying I will go to Great Peace Village to arrest Gongsun Chujiu!

(*All exit.*)

(MALE LEAD, [*costumed as*] GONGSUN CHUJIU, *enters and speaks*:) I am Gongsun Chujiu. Yesterday Cheng Ying and I discussed how to save the Orphan of Zhao. Today he went to the offices of Tu'an Gu to denounce me. By this time that scoundrel Tu'an Gu must be on his way. (*Sings*:)

(SHUANGDIAO MODE: *Xinshui ling*)

All I see is stirred-up dust flying over the small bridge,
It must be that traitor who harms the loyal and good who has arrived.
Precise in their ranks are the officers and troops he has massed,
Shimmering and glistening their lances and swords are arranged in rows.
What's clear to me now is that I die this very morning,
And cannot avoid a painful beating and torture.

(TU'AN GU *enters together with* CHENG YING, *leading his soldiers, and speaks*:) Here we are in Lülü Great Peace Village. Soldiers, surround Great Peace Village. Cheng Ying, where's the house of Gongsun Chujiu? (CHENG YING *speaks*:) It's that one. (TU'AN GU *speaks*:) Bring that old fella over here! Gongsun Chujiu, do you know your crime? (MALE LEAD *speaks*:) I am not aware of any crime. (TU'AN GU *speaks*:) I know that you, old fella, were a colleague of Zhao Dun's. How dare you hide the Orphan of Zhao? (MALE LEAD *speaks*:) Marshal, do I have the heart of a bear or the gall of a leopard? I wouldn't dare hide the Orphan! (TU'AN GU *speaks*:) No beating, no confession! Soldiers, pick out a big club and thoroughly thrash him! (SOLDIERS *act out beating him.* MALE LEAD *sings*:)

(*Zhuma ting*)

I realize that even though I quit my office to take leave of the court,
I was once renowned for my sworn-to-the-death brotherhood with Zhao Dun.

(*Speaks*:) Who revealed this? (TU'AN GU *speaks*:) Cheng Ying, who informed on you, is right here. (MALE LEAD *sings*:)

Which one sold me out and informed on me?
None other than Cheng Ying, whose tongue is the sword that will cut off my head!

(*Speaks*:) You've already killed the three hundred souls, noble and base, who filled the gates of the Zhao family and left only this child. Now you want to take his life! (*Sings*:)

You are just a wild wind to aid the sky-striking eagle,
A severe frost that strikes first the grass with withered roots.[77]
If now the Orphan is also slain,
Who will take revenge for the injustice done to those three hundred souls?

(TU'AN GU *speaks*:) Where have you hidden the child, old fella? Confess quickly, so you can spare yourself this torture! (MALE LEAD *speaks*:) What child do I have to hide anywhere? Who saw him? (TU'AN GU *speaks*:) So you won't confess! Soldiers, lay hold of him and beat him soundly! ([SOLDIERS] *act out beating him.* TU'AN GU *speaks*:) This old fella is an obstinate bag of bones unwilling to confess. Cheng Ying, you were the one to denounce him. You apply the club on my behalf! (CHENG YING *speaks*:) Marshal, I am an itinerant physician, my wrists are too weak to even collect simples! How can I apply the club? (TU'AN GU *speaks*:) Cheng Ying, if you don't apply the club, it must be because you fear he will implicate you! (CHENG YING *speaks*:) Marshal, I'll apply the club! (*Acts out taking a club.* TU'AN GU *speaks*:) Cheng Ying, I see you cull through the clubs and then take a skinny one. Are you afraid he will implicate you when the pain starts? (CHENG YING *speaks*:) Then I will beat him with a thick stick. (TU'AN GU *speaks*:) Stop! First you picked a thin stick. Now

77. That is, "the strong always get help to make them stronger, the already weakened receive further harm." He is cursing Cheng Ying for aiding Tu'an Gu, who is already in a position of supreme power. A "sky-striking eagle" refers to a large and strong eagle.

you take the biggest one. But if you beat him to death with two or three strokes, you will have no one to testify against you because he is dead. (CHENG YING *speaks*:) If I take a thin stick, it isn't right, and if I take a thick one, it isn't right either. What am I supposed to do? (TU'AN GU *speaks*:) Cheng Ying, just take a middle-sized stick. Gongsun Chujiu, you old fella, are you aware that it's Cheng Ying who will apply the club? (CHENG YING *acts out applying the club, speaks*:) Confess quickly! (*After acting out beating him three times,* MALE LEAD *speaks*:) *Aiya*! I've been beaten all day, but no stick has hurt me like this one! Who's beating me? (TU'AN GU *speaks*:) Cheng Ying is beating you! (MALE LEAD *speaks*:) Cheng Ying, why are you beating me? (CHENG YING *speaks*:) Marshal, I've beaten this old fart until he has started spouting nonsense. (MALE LEAD *sings*:)

(*Yan'er luo*)
Who on earth so thoroughly canes me with the thickest club?
He beats me so painfully that my fine soft skin falls away.
What enmity ever existed between you—cruel Cheng Ying—and me
To make this old man Gongsun suffer such torture?

(CHENG YING *speaks*:) Quickly confess! (MALE LEAD *speaks*:) I'll confess, I'll confess! (*Sings*:)

(*Desheng ling*)
You've beaten me until there's not the slightest crack through which to flee,
And since I have a mouth, I will be wrongly forced into a confession.
It must be that he knew about the Orphan
And pointed me out with certainty!

(CHENG YING *acts out panicking*.) (MALE LEAD *sings*:)

This is really hard to endure,
But I still force myself to clench my teeth and suffer.
I secretly steal a peek at him,
And see that he is already so scared his calves are shaking!

(CHENG YING *speaks*:) Quickly confess and be done with it, lest I need to beat you to death. (MALE LEAD *speaks*:) Alright! Alright! (*Sings*:)

(*Shuixianzi*)
The two of us discussed how to save this little child.

(TU'AN GU *speaks*:) Of course he would implicate someone! He says, "The two of us." One of these is you. Who is the other one? If you tell me the truth, I'll spare your life! (MALE LEAD *speaks*:) If you want me to tell you who, I'll tell you! (*Sings*:)

Aiya! Now I have to swallow those words that sprang to my lips.

(TU'AN GU *speaks*:) Cheng Ying, are you part of this? (CHENG YING *speaks*:) You old fart, don't wrongly finger a good man! (MALE LEAD *speaks*:) Cheng Ying, what are you so worried about? (*Sings*:)

Why would I ever say "Cheng Ying"
And fail to carry out the affair to its end?

(TU'AN GU *speaks*:) At first you said there were two, so how can you now say there were none? (MALE LEAD *sings*:)

You've beaten me so much I don't know up from down.

(TU'AN GU *speaks*:) If you won't tell me, I'll beat you to death, old fella! (MALE LEAD *sings*:)

Even if you beat me until my skin all splits
And my flesh is gone,
Don't think that I will utter half a word to implicate others!

(SOLDIER *enters, carrying child in his arms, speaks*:) Congratulations, Marshal! We discovered the Orphan of Zhao in a hole in the ground. (TU'AN GU *acts out laughing, speaks*:) Bring that little one over here. I will hack him into three pieces with my own hand. You old fella, do you still say there is no Orphan of Zhao? So who is this? (MALE LEAD *sings*:)

(*Chuan bo zhao*)
In those days you trained the Demon Mastiff
To attack a loyal official and sink its teeth into him,
Driving him out into the wilds to die.
One slit his throat and died by a steel blade,
Another hanged herself with the belt of her skirt.
You executed a whole household, young and old, of three hundred,
Leaving not half a person alive.
But that still didn't quell those thoughts growing in your mind!

(TU'AN GU *speaks*:) When I see this Orphan, I can't help but get angry. (MALE LEAD *sings*:)

(*Qi dixiong*)
All I see is him glance left,
Glance right,
And bellow in rage—
A fiery redness alters his hideous and vicious features.
Over his lion-buckle belt he lifts the brocade battle gown
And draws his Dragon Spring sword from its sharkskin sheath.

(TU'AN GU *speaks in a rage*:) I've drawn my sword. One stroke! Two strokes! Three strokes! (CHENG YING *acts out being startled and pained.* TU'AN GU *speaks*:) I have hacked this little seed of disaster into three pieces. Haven't I achieved my lifelong desire? (MALE LEAD *sings*:)

(*Meihua jiu*)
Ah!
I see the child lying in a puddle of blood!
That one weeping and wailing,
This one fuming with rage.
And even I tremble and shake.

Such an evil deed
Could happen only because there is no Heavenly Way.
Ah!
Considering that from the birthing mat this child was lifted
Just these ten days—
How can we forgive his judgment under the sword?
In vain was he born,
For naught his mother's worry,
What need to "prepare for old age"!
(*Shou Jiangnan*)
Ah,
Isn't this a case of "If the family is rich, the child is pampered"?[78]

(CHENG YING *acts out covering his tears.*) (MALE LEAD *sings:*)
I see Cheng Ying, his heart as if scalded by boiling oil,
Not daring to shed a single teardrop in front of others,
But behind their backs wiping them all away.
Without reason he parted with his own flesh and blood merely to see it cut in three!

(*Speaks:*) Tu'an Gu you traitor, just look! Above there's a heaven that will not pardon you! My death isn't of any importance. (*Sings:*)
(*Yuanyang Coda*)
I die at seventy, will get no older,
This child dies at one—I know this is young!
We two, who die here in this one place,
Will leave behind a name to be remembered for ten thousand generations.
I urge you, this Cheng Ying who will live on,
Don't turn your back on that cruelly slain Zhao Shuo!
The proverb says: "Time passes quickly,
Revenge for an injustice follows fast."
Hack this bastard ten thousand times with a thousand blades
And never, ever let him get easily away.

(MALE LEAD *acts out dashing his head, speaks:*) I find a proper place to die by bashing my head against the steps.
(*Exits.*)

(SOLDIER *acts out reporting, speaks:*) Gongsun Chujiu has died by dashing his head against the steps. (TU'AN GU *acts out laughing:*) Now that old bastard has died, we can let it lie. (*Acts out laughing, speaks:*) Cheng Ying, I owe you for this whole incident. If it hadn't been for you, how would I have ever slain the Orphan of Zhao? (CHENG YING *speaks:*) Marshal, I harbored no grudge against the Zhao family. But

78. Spoken sarcastically.

first of all I wanted to save all living creatures in the state of Jin, and secondly I myself have a child who is not yet one month old. If the Orphan of Zhao hadn't been found, this child of mine also would have had no chance to survive. (TU'AN GU *speaks*:) Cheng Ying, you're a man I can trust. Why don't you become a retainer in my household? I will raise your son to manhood. When he has grown up, he will study the civil arts with you and you can send him to me to practice the military arts. I am already approaching fifty and still have no son. I will treat your child as my adopted son. I'm already advanced in years, but I will hang on so your son can later ask to succeed me in office. What do you think of that? (CHENG YING *speaks*:) How can I thank you, Marshal, for this extraordinary favor? (TU'AN GU *recites*:)

Just because the mainstays of the court only glorified Zhao Dun,
My heart unconsciously grew enraged.
Now that I have rubbed out this tiny little sprout,
I will forever be free of future trouble!

(*All exit together.*)

ACT 4

(TU'AN GU *enters leading* SOLDIERS, *speaks*:) I am Tu'an Gu. Twenty years have passed already since I slew the Orphan of Zhao. Now there's that child of Cheng Ying's, who is called Tu Cheng[79] because I adopted him. I have instructed him in the eighteen kinds of martial arts and there are none he hasn't grasped or any he doesn't comprehend. His horsemanship and skills with the bow even surpass mine, and relying on the power and might of my son, I will finalize a plan. After killing Duke Ling I'll wrest away the state of Jin. I will give all my official posts to my child to fulfill. Only then will my lifetime ambitions have been fulfilled. A moment ago my child left for the training field to practice his riding and shooting. When he comes back, I'll discuss this with him then. (*Exits.*)

(CHENG YING *enters holding a scroll in his hand, recites*:)

Revolutions of suns and moons harry one to grow old,
Alternations of light and shade chase away one's youth.
The limitless affairs in my heart
I have not yet dared clearly reveal.

How quickly time passes! It's already been twenty years since I moved into Tu'an Gu's mansion. He has raised my child, who has now reached the age of twenty. Officially he is called Cheng Bo. He has studied the civil arts with me and with Tu'an Gu,

79. The literal meaning of the name is "brought to completion by Tu," but it can also be understood as "completed through butchery."

the military. He is full of clever stratagems and excels at riding and shooting. Tu'an Gu is completely pleased with my child. But there's no way he can know the inside story! There's only one thing: the child too has been left in the dark. This year I am sixty-five. In case something should happen, who can explain it to my child so he will know that he must take revenge on behalf of his Zhao family? That's the reason why I am in a dither, toss and turn, and cannot sleep by day or by night. On this painted scroll I have now depicted the loyal officials and fine generals who earlier died unjustly. In case my child asks me about them, I will explain all of these events of the past to the last detail. Then he cannot but take revenge for his father and mother. I'll sit here sullenly in this study, and when my child shows up, I will know what to do. (MALE LEAD *enters costumed as* CHENG BO, *speaks*:) I am Cheng Bo. My father on this side is Cheng Ying, and my father on that side is Tu'an Gu. During daytime I practice the martial arts, and in the evening I study the civil arts. Now I'm returning from the practice field, so I will go and see my this-side father. (*Sings*:)

(ZHONGLÜ MODE: *Fen die'er*)

Leading these army troops under my command,
I show not the slightest inkling of fear for anyone's murderous intent.
Each day I study and practice strategic writings.
Because of the fact that I
Find joy in battle,
And am capable of facing off enemy camps,
All other states are made to submit and surrender.
My father has no equal in heroic valor,
And I support him, unhesitatingly, with all my heart!

(*Zui chunfeng*)

I want to support the enlightened ruler, Duke Ling of Jin,
And assist his wise minister Tu'an Gu.
Capable in the civilian, skilled at the martial, I can stand alone against ten thousand,
My father approves,
Approves of me.
Can it not be said, "If horses are sturdy and men are strong,
If the father is loving and the child filial"
There is no fear that "the worries of the master are the shame of the minister"?

(CHENG YING *speaks*:) I unroll this scroll. How sad! So many wise ministers and heroic men were sacrificed for this one Orphan of Zhao! Even my own child died as one among them. (MALE LEAD *speaks*:) Soldier. Take my horse. Where is my father on this side? (SOLDIER *speaks*:) He is reading in his study. (MALE LEAD *speaks*:) Soldier, report that I am here. (SOLDIER, *acting out reporting, speaks*:) Cheng Bo is here. (CHENG YING *speaks*:) Tell him to come in. (SOLDIER *speaks*:) Come in. (MALE LEAD *acts out greeting, speaks*:) My father on this side, I'm back from the training ground. (CHENG YING *speaks*:) Go get something to eat. (MALE LEAD *speaks*:) As I come out of this gate I am starting to wonder: every day my father on this side is usually happy to see me. But today when he saw me, he was really upset and wept ceaselessly. I don't know what's on his mind. I'll go over and ask him. Who is bullying you? Tell me, you know I won't let him off! (CHENG YING *speaks*:) Even if I were to explain it to you, you couldn't set things straight for your mother and father. Just go and have something to eat. (CHENG YING *acts out crying and covering his tears.*) (MALE LEAD *speaks*:) This really is strange! (*Sings*:)

(*Ying xianke*)

Why so many tears wiped away?

(CHENG YING *acts out heaving a sigh.* MALE LEAD *sings*:)

Or such heavy sighs as these?
I had come forward with folded arms only to pay my respects—
(*Continues in speech:*) My father on this side, (*sings:*)
Cranky and cross, your anger has been stirred up,
In a roaring fire, you've worked up a rage.
(*Continues in speech:)* Who has dared bully you? (*Sings:*)
Here I lower my head to wonder—
(*Continues in speech:*) Since no one has bullied you, (*sings:*)
Which of my words was off the mark?

(CHENG YING *speaks*:) Cheng Bo, you do some reading here in this study, while I go to the back rooms for a moment. (*Acts out dropping the scroll and makes a false exit.*) (MALE LEAD *speaks*:) Ah, he actually left a scroll behind here. What kind of document is this? Let me unroll it and have a look. (*Acts out looking, speaks*:) How strange! That one clad in red is leading a vicious dog that's attacking someone in purple. Then there's one holding a melon-headed cudgel, beating that vicious dog to death. This one is holding up a one-wheeled chariot with his hands right where the other wheel should be. This one is committing suicide by bashing his head against an acacia tree. What kind of story is this? And no names have been provided either! How am I supposed to understand? (*Sings*:)

(*Hongxiuxie*)

What's painted here are—in darkest, deepest green—a few mulberry trees,
A clamoring, shouting crowd—a bunch of rustic villagers.
This one is holding aloft a single-wheeled chariot grinding away,
This one is raising the melon-headed cudgel by himself,
This one delivers up his body by butting an acacia tree.
And then there's that vicious dog that keeps on attacking the one in purple.

(*Speaks*:) Let me have another look. In front of this general are laid out a bowstring, poisoned wine, and a dagger; and he takes the dagger to slit his own throat. And just why does this other general draw *his* sword to slit his throat and die? And there is a physician who is kneeling, holding a medicine box in his arms. This woman bears an infant in her arms, but it seems as if she intends to hand him over to the physician. Ah! Actually that woman also commits suicide by hanging herself with the belt of her skirt. How sad! (*Sings*:)

(*Shiliu hua*)

All I see is one clad in brocaded everyday clothes,

Taking the string of a bow, poisoned wine, and a dagger for his execution.

But why is there another general too, all smeared with blood from his own slit throat?

This one holds up a medicine box while kneeling down,

This one carries an infant to hand over.

How sad this woman of a good family, wearing her pearls and jade—

She hangs herself by the belt of her skirt; but what was her crime?

I have pondered it deeply for quite a while but don't know what to say,

It's painted in such a way that it puzzles me, leaves me confused and depressed.

(*Speaks*:) Let me look carefully. How vicious is the one in red! Here he is again, mercilessly beating a white-bearded old man! (*Sings*:)

(*Dou anchun*)

I only see how that red-clad scoundrel

Canes and humiliates the white-bearded one.

This confuses and upsets my seat of emotions,

Fills my lungs and innards with rage.

(*Continues in speech*:) Should this family be linked to me— (*Sings*:)

I'm no man if I don't kill that traitor!

I'd dare set matters right!

The one who's lying in this puddle of blood, I know not whose relation he is,

Nor who the ancestors of those killed on the execution ground might be.

(*Speaks*:) In the end I don't understand it. I'll have to wait till my father on this side comes back to ask him to explain it all. Then I will be free of doubt and suspicion. (CHENG YING *enters, speaks*:) Cheng Bo, I have been listening quite a while. (MALE LEAD *speaks*:) Father, please explain it to me. (CHENG YING *speaks*:) Cheng Bo, you want me to explain this story, but it will concern you! (MALE LEAD *speaks*:) You just explain it to me very, very clearly! (CHENG YING *speaks*:) Cheng Bo, listen. The history of this affair is very long. At the beginning this one clad in red and this one clad in purple were colleagues in the same court. But, one an administrator and one a fighting man, they did not get along and became longtime enemies. The one clad in red thought, "The first to strike becomes the stronger, the second to strike will suffer." Secretly he sent an assassin hiding a dagger and who was called Chu Ni to scale a low wall to murder the one clad in purple. Who would have thought that this old minister nightly burned incense to pray to heaven and earth, that his whole heart was intent only on repaying his country, and that he showed not the slightest inclination to favor his own family. That man Chu Ni thought, "If I kill this old minister, I will commit a heinous crime against heaven. I definitely cannot do this. But if I go back to see the one clad in red, I'm sure to die. So be it!" (*Recites*:)

His hands carrying a keen blade, he hid away in the darkness,
But because he saw such loyalty and goodness he felt remorse.
This shows that the impartial Way shines as clearly as the sun—
That very night Chu Ni butted his head against the acacia tree.

(MALE LEAD *speaks*:) So the one who died by ramming into an acacia tree was Chu Ni? (CHENG YING *speaks*:) Yes, indeed. In springtime, this one clad in purple went out to the fields on the outskirts of town to exhort the farmers. Under a mulberry tree he saw a strong man lying on his back and with his mouth wide open. The one clad in purple asked him the reason. That strong man told him, "I am Ling Zhe. Because I eat a peck of rice at every meal, not even the biggest landlord can afford to provide me with food and they all eventually drive me out. I would like to pick some mulberries and eat them, but then they would say that I stole what is theirs. Therefore I'm lying here on my back, waiting for the mulberries to drop into my mouth. And if they don't drop into my mouth, I'll have to die of starvation, because I won't be humiliated by them." The one clad in purple said, "This man is a hero!" Thereupon he gave wine and food to the starving man. After he had eaten his fill, he left without a word of thanks. But this one clad in purple felt no rage or anger whatsoever. Cheng Bo, this shows the measure of the minister's virtue. (*Recites*:)

Because in spring he urged the farmers to begin the plowing,
He toured the outskirts and plains before the dusk.
On whom was the jug of gruel, the basket of food bestowed?
Just to help that one starving fellow beneath the mulberries.

(MALE LEAD *speaks*:) Ah, the starving fellow under the mulberry tree was called Ling Zhe. (CHENG YING *speaks*:) Cheng Bo, keep his name in mind! On another day, the western barbarians offered a Demon Mastiff in tribute. The Demon Mastiff was a dog—those with bodies four feet tall are called mastiffs. Duke Ling of Jin bestowed the Demon Mastiff on the one clad in red. He really wanted to murder the one clad in purple so he strung up a straw man in his back garden, and dressed it just like the one clad in purple. He hung a set of sheep entrails in the stomach of the straw man. After he had starved the Demon Mastiff for some five or six days, he cut open the stomach of the straw man and let the dog eat its fill. He trained him like this for a hundred days before he went to Duke Ling and said, "At present there must be disloyal and unfilial people in court who harbor the intention to deceive their lord." Duke Ling asked him who those people were. The one clad in red said, "The Demon Mastiff that you gave me can sniff them out." The man clad in red led out the Demon Mastiff, while the one clad in purple stood upright in the palace hall. The demon Mastiff took him for the straw man, attacked him, and chased him around the palace hall. That angered someone nearby—the colonel of the guard, Timi Ming. He raised his golden melon-headed cudgel and beat down the Demon Mastiff. With one hand he grabbed the skin on the back of its head and, ripping once, he ripped him in two. (*Recites*:)

The devilish schemes of the traitorous minister included a thousand evil tricks,
He persecuted the loyal and good until they had no place to flee.
Before the hall there was a heroic man
Who used his terrible hands to rip the Mastiff apart.

(MALE LEAD *speaks*:) This vicious dog was called the Demon Mastiff. And the one who beat that vicious dog to death was Timi Ming. (CHENG YING *speaks*:) Yes. When that old minister had gone out through the palace gate, he wanted to mount his chariot. Who could have known that the one clad in red had taken away two horses from the team of this four-horse chariot and had also removed one of the two wheels. When he could go no further, a strong man appeared by his side, lifting the axle with one arm and whipping the horses on with his other hand. The axle ground his clothes until his skin appeared, ground his skin until flesh appeared, ground his flesh until the tendons appeared, ground his tendons until bones appeared, and ground his bones until marrow appeared. Supporting the axle and pushing the wheel, they fled to the wilds. Who do you think this man was? It was none other than that starving fellow under the mulberry tree—Ling Zhe. (*Recites*:)

When the one in purple fled disaster through the palace gate,
One wheel had been removed from his four-horse chariot.
But Ling Zhe was there to support him with strength off into the wilds
And so repaid the favor of a single meal among the mulberry trees.

(MALE LEAD *speaks*:) I remember: That was the Ling Zhe who was lying on his back under a mulberry tree! (CHENG YING *speaks*:) Yes. (MALE LEAD *speaks*:) Father on this side, that bastard clad in red is quite vicious! What's his name? (CHENG YING *speaks*:) Cheng Bo, I have forgotten his name. (MALE LEAD *speaks*:) And what is the name of the one clad in purple? (CHENG YING *speaks*:) This one clad in purple was surnamed Zhao. He was the chancellor Zhao Dun. He is related to you. (MALE LEAD *speaks*:) I've heard it said that there was such a Chancellor Zhao Dun, but I've never given him much thought. (CHENG YING *speaks*:) Cheng Bo, you have to remember very carefully what I am telling you now. (MALE LEAD *speaks*:) There's still more on that scroll. Please go on and explain. (CHENG YING *speaks*:) The one clad in red exterminated Zhao Dun's whole household, high and low— more than three hundred souls. The only one left was Zhao Shuo, who was a ducal son-in-law. The one clad in red forged a command by Duke Ling to bestow on Zhao "the three court statutes," that is, a bowstring, poisoned wine, and a dagger, so he might commit suicide by choosing one. At that time the princess was pregnant. Zhao Shuo's final words were, "If you give birth to a little boy after I die, you must call him the Orphan of Zhao, so he may take revenge for us, these three hundred souls." No one expected Zhao Shuo to slit his throat with the dagger and die. The one clad in red confined the princess to her compound, where she gave birth to the Orphan of Zhao. As soon as the one clad in red knew about this, he dispatched the Lieutenant General Han Jue to guard the gates to the compound, for the very purpose of preventing anyone from smuggling the Orphan out. This princess had a trusted retainer, who was called the itinerant physician Cheng Ying. (MALE LEAD *speaks*:) Father, that must be you! (CHENG YING *speaks*:) There are so many people in the world that have the same name and the same surname! He is a different Cheng Ying. The princess handed the child over to that Cheng Ying, and then died after hanging herself with the belt of her skirt. That Cheng Ying came with the child in his arms to the gate of the compound, where he ran into General Han Jue. Han discovered the child, but he was persuaded to act by just a few words from Cheng Ying. No one expected that General Han Jue too would draw his sword and slit his own throat. (*Recites*:)

That physician showed no fear at all,
And smuggled that Orphan out.
He ran smack into that loyal and righteous general
Who would rather die than arrest the pair.

(MALE LEAD *speaks*:) What a fine man this general was, to slit his throat and die on behalf of the Orphan of Zhao. I will remember that he was called Han Jue. (CHENG YING *speaks*:) Yes, yes indeed, he was Han Jue. But who would have thought that, after the one clad in red found out about it, he would round up all the infants in the state of Jin who were younger than half a year and older than a month, and bring them to his headquarters, where he could cut them all into thirds with three strokes of his sword and be certain to kill the Orphan of Zhao. (MALE LEAD *acts out being enraged, speaks*:) The one clad in red was too vicious! (CHENG YING *speaks*:) He was truly vicious! But it happened that this Cheng Ying also fathered a boy who had not yet reached one month of age. He dressed him as the Orphan of Zhao and brought him to Gongsun Chujiu in Lülü Great Peace Village. (MALE LEAD *speaks*:) Who was this Gongsun Chujiu? (CHENG YING *speaks*:) This old minister had been a colleague of Zhao Dun's. Cheng Ying said to him, "Minister, you take this Orphan of Zhao. Then you go to the one clad in red and report to him that I am hiding the Orphan. We, father and son, will die in the same spot, but you will raise the Orphan to manhood, so he may take revenge for his father and mother. Wouldn't that be the best thing to do?" But Gongsun Chujiu replied, "I'm already old. If you are able to part with your child and dress him up as the Orphan of Zhao, you should hide him with me, and go and denounce me to the one clad in red. I will die together with your son. And you will hide the Orphan, so he later may take revenge for his father and mother." (MALE LEAD *speaks*:) Was that Cheng Ying capable of parting with his child? (CHENG YING *speaks*:) He was willing to give up his own life, so you can imagine that child was not so important! So he dressed up his own child as the Orphan and brought him to Gongsun Chujiu, and he denounced the latter to the one clad in red. That one subjected Gongsun Chujiu to the three questionings and the six interrogations, had him beaten, trussed, and tossed over the wall upside down. He tracked down the false Orphan of Zhao, and hacked him apart with three blows of his sword. Gongsun Chujiu committed suicide by ramming his head into the steps of the hall. This all happened twenty years ago and now the Orphan of Zhao is twenty years old. If he does not take revenge for his father and mother, then what else can he do? (*Recites:*)

His appearance is impressive, a seven-foot frame,
He has mastered the civil and martial arts, but now what?
Riding a chariot—where did his grandfather wind up?
A whole household, noble and base—all executed.
In the palace of disfavor his mother hanged herself from the rafters,
On the execution ground his father drew out the knife to die.
Injustice and hatred unavenged until now—
As a man among men he is useless!

(MALE LEAD *speaks:*) You've spoken the whole day about this, but I still don't get it—it seems like I'm asleep or in a dream. (CHENG YING *speaks:*) So you still don't understand? Now the one clad in red is no one else but that traitorous minister Tu'an Gu. Zhao Dun was your grandfather, Zhao Shuo was your father, and the princess was your mother! (*Recites:*)

Now that each and every thing has been explained in detail:
Do you really not see the beginning and end?
I am old Cheng Ying who saved the Orphan by sacrificing his child,
And that Orphan of Zhao is none other than you!

(MALE LEAD *speaks:*) So I was the Orphan of Zhao all this time! This makes me so angry! (MALE LEAD *acts out collapsing.* CHENG YING *acts out helping him up, speaks:*) Young Master, come to your senses! (MALE LEAD *speaks:*) This is too much to bear! (*Sings:*)

(*Putian le*)
I had to hear you explain it from the beginning,
Before I could understand what happened.
I have wasted these twenty years of my life
And was given this strapping body for nothing.
So my father was the one who slit his throat,
And it was my very mother who hanged herself.
If we speak of the most desolate heartbreaking points,
Even a man of iron
Would cry and holler.
I'll capture that old scoundrel at the risk of my own life—
I want him to pay for those ministers and officials of our entire court,
And for all the relatives of our extended household!

(*Speaks:*) If you hadn't explained it, how would I ever have known? Father, please sit down and accept this obeisance from your child. (MALE LEAD *acts out bowing.* CHENG YING *speaks:*) Today I have kept the branches and leaves of the Zhao family

tree alive, but I have turned my own family, all of it into naught but mown-down grass and plucked-out roots. (*Acts out weeping.* MALE LEAD *sings*:)
(*Shang xiaolou*)
If it weren't for the fact that you cared for me, Father,
And for the fact you raised me as your child,
Twenty years ago
I would have already met the blade
And been long buried in some ditch.
What I hate now is that common miscreant Tu'an Gu,
Who sought out every root to uproot a tree
And nearly exterminated my whole family!
(*Reprise*)
He, he, he had our whole clan executed,
I, I, I will return the favor by butchering nine generations of his.

(CHENG YING *speaks*:) Young Master, don't carry on so loudly. I'm afraid Tu'an Gu will find out. (MALE LEAD *speaks*:) As for him and me: "Once I get started, I'll finish it up!" (*Sings*:)
Let him lead on the Demon Mastiff,
Be surrounded by his private guard,
Or employ all his power and tricks—
Just look at this one,
And at that one,
On whose account did they die?
Can I, the son, simply act as calmly as before?[80]

(*Speaks*:) Father, don't you worry. Tomorrow, after I will first go see our lord the duke, then I will personally murder that traitor, together with all the officials and ministers at court. (*Sings*:)
(*Shua hai'er*)
If I meet my blood enemy tomorrow morning,
I will block his path, meeting him head-on.
I will have no further need for troops and soldiers,
But will lightly stretch out my gibbon arms,
Jerk his jade-bridled, golden-saddled reins,
Drag him down from his golden-flowered, black-canopied chariot,
And drag him off like a dead dog,
And simply ask, "Where was your human heart?
What is heavenly principle for?

---

80. This line may also be understood as a reference to his new status as the Orphan: "Can I now, this person who is *their* son, simply act as calmly as before?"

(*Second from Coda*)
"What made you so excessive in the use of your heroic valor?
Or so vicious in carrying out the righting of wrongs?
It's unavoidable—every act will be repaid without hesitation or mistake.
In the beginning you questioned old Gongsun under torture,
But today the Orphan of Zhao is still alive.
Don't think that I will show you any clemency!"
Lightly, ever so lightly I'll toss him down
And slowly, ever so slowly open him up.
(*First from Coda*)
I'll pluck that one big seal of his, as big as a peck measure,
I'll strip off his layers of gowns, covered with flowers.
With ropes of hemp I will tie him to the general's post,[81]
With pincers of iron I will rip out his rotten tongue,
With an awl I will prick out the eyes of the traitor while he's alive,
With a knife I will chop his whole body to mincemeat,
With a hammer of steel I will pound his bones to smithereens,
And with a sickle of bronze I will chop off his skull!
(*Coda*)
Even then my roaring rage will not be quenched,
My deep and dark grudge will be left unresolved,
Because for twenty years I, this unfilial son, took him as my father—
It is only today that the ghosts of three hundred wrongly slain
Will find their champion!
(*Exits.*)

(CHENG YING *speaks*:) Tomorrow the young master definitively will arrest that old traitor. I will have to follow him to be of assistance.
(*Exits.*)

ACT 5

(EXTRA, *costumed as* WEI JIANG, *enters leading* ZHANG QIAN, *speaks*:) I, this humble official, am a high court dignitary of the state of Jin, Wei Jiang. Now Duke Dao sits on the throne. A certain Tu'an Gu monopolized all power and killed off the whole household, noble and base, of Zhao Dun. Who could expect that a certain Cheng Ying of the household of Zhao Shuo would hide away the Orphan of Zhao?

81. The post to which criminals destined for execution were tied in the marketplace.

Now some twenty years have passed. [The Orphan's] name was changed to Cheng Bo. This morning he has sent a memorial to let our lord and duke know that he wants to arrest Tu'an Gu and take revenge for his father. I now have received a command from our duke, stating that, since the military power of Tu'an Gu is too great and we fear that he may rebel anytime, Cheng Bo is to go ahead in secret to catch him. No one, noble or base in his household—not even a baby tooth—should be left. Upon the successful completion of this mission, he will be further rewarded and enfeoffed. I do not dare to divulge this lightly and will have to deliver this command to Cheng Bo in person. (*Recites*:)

Loyal officials were butchered,
This deep injustice lasted twenty years.
This morning we will take the treacherous traitor,
And finally know that injustice repays injustice.

(*Exits*.)

(MALE LEAD *enters astride a horse and with drawn sword, speaks*:) I am Cheng Bo. This morning I have sent a memorial to our lord and duke letting him know that I want to arrest Tu'an Gu and take revenge for my father and grandfather. This old traitor was really too reckless! (*Sings*:)

(ZHENGGONG MODE: *Duanzheng hao*)

There's no need to put the soldiers in formation,
Or arrange the officers,
Or rouse all the broad swords and long lances.
Today I will wreak vengeance,
And risk my life to execute that gang of traitors.
In short, it's his life that is over, he's bound to die!

(*Gun xiuqiu*)

Here in this busy neighborhood marketplace
We'll fight it out.
There's no way I'll let him off easily—
It'll be just like a tiger attacking a wooly sheep.
There's no need for panic,
No need for haste.
I have my martial skills well prepared,
We'll see if that rascal can defend himself!
I'll requite this injustice stored up for twenty years,
And seek recompense for those three hundred people who have died!
What does it matter if I lose my own life?

(*Speaks*:) I will wait for him here in this crowded market. That old traitor will have to pass by sooner or later. (TU'AN GU *enters leading soldiers, speaks*:) Today I am on my way back from the headquarters to my private residence. Soldiers! Bring out the road-clearing unit and go slowly! (MALE LEAD *speaks*:) It must be that old traitor who is coming! (*Sings*:)

(*Tang xiucai*)
Look at those ranks of brave and mighty point riders,
Those clamoring and shouting followers trailing on either side.
Look how he puffs up his chest
To affect the guise of power.
Here, I spur my horse that runs like flowing water,
Unsheathe my sword that shines like autumn frost,
And go forward to fight it out!

(TU'AN GU *speaks*:) Tu Cheng, what are you doing here? (MALE LEAD *speaks*:) You old traitor, I am not Tu Cheng, I am the Orphan of Zhao! Twenty years ago you killed off completely three hundred souls, a whole household noble and base. Today I arrest you, scoundrel, to take revenge for my family's injustice! (TU'AN GU *speaks*:) Who told you all this? (MALE LEAD *speaks*:) Cheng Ying told me so. (TU'AN GU *speaks*:) This boy's martial skills are really good! I'm no match for them. I'd better make a clean getaway. (MALE LEAD *speaks*:) Where are you running to? (*Sings*:)

(*Xiao heshang*)
I, I, I display on all eight sides the fullness of my might,
You, you, you are unable to rouse yourself, unable to block me.
Already, already, already he's so scared his souls are gone with the wind,
Don't! Don't! Don't try to talk yourself out of this.
Right, right, right! I will not negotiate.
Come! Come! Come! In one fell swoop I will lift you from your saddle!

(MALE LEAD *acts out grabbing him firmly.* CHENG YING *enters in panic, speaks*:) I'm so afraid something will happen to the young master. I have to follow him and help him out. Thank Heaven and Earth! The young master has arrested Tu'an Gu! (MALE LEAD *speaks*:) Bind this scoundrel up and let's see our lord and duke.

(*Exit together.*)

(WEI JIANG *enters with* ZHANG QIAN, *speaks*:) I am Wei Jiang. Cheng Bo has gone to arrest Tu'an Gu. Soldier. Look out at the gate, and report to me when he arrives. (MALE LEAD *enters together with* CHENG YING, *holding* TU'AN GU. MALE LEAD *speaks*:) Father, you and I will go and see our lord and duke. (*Acts out greeting rituals, speaks*:) Minister! Take pity on the grave injustice suffered by the three hundred souls of my family. Today I have arrested Tu'an Gu. (WEI JIANG *speaks*:) Bring him here! You, Tu'an Gu, you vicious traitor who murdered the loyal and good, now that Cheng Bo has arrested you, what is there to say in your defense? (TU'AN GU *speaks*:) Successful, I would have been a king; defeated, I am a prisoner. Now that things have reached this point, I only wish to die quickly. (MALE LEAD *speaks*:) Minister, set matters right for me! (WEI JIANG *speaks*:) Tu'an Gu, you may want to die quickly, but we want you to die slowly. Soldiers! Nail this traitor to the wooden donkey and slice him carefully with three thousand slices. Only after all the flesh and skin are gone shall you cut off his head and open up his chest! Don't let him die quickly! (MALE LEAD *sings*:)

(*Tuo bushan*)
Nail that scoundrel to the wooden donkey
And push him to the execution grounds,
Don't cut off his head or open up his chest,
But slice away until he has become one big pile of meat sauce—
Even that cannot dissolve the anger and frustration that fill my bosom!

(CHENG YING *speaks*:) Young Master, now that you have avenged this injustice and have reclaimed your own surname, take pity on this lonely old man who is bereft of support. (MALE LEAD *sings*:)

(*Xiao Liangzhou*)
Who was willing to abandon his own child to hide one of another surname?
A virtue and grace like yours can never be forgotten!
I will ask a fine artistic hand of extraordinary skill
To depict your true likeness,
To be honored in my family's shrine!

(CHENG YING *speaks*:) What virtue and grace do I have that my young master should show me such consideration! (MALE LEAD *sings*:)

(*Reprise*)
You never were remiss in the three years of nursing and feeding;
Doesn't that surpass the ten months of pregnancy?[82]
Fortunately today you've escaped from ten thousand deaths
And your body is in good health.
Even if I would day and night burn incense to honor you,
I could never repay you who raised me as father and mother.

(WEI JIANG *speaks*:) Cheng Ying and Cheng Bo, kneel down in the direction of the palace and listen to the command of our lord and duke. (*Recites in ballad verse*:)
Just because Tu'an Gu injured the loyal and good,
In a hundred ways the stability of the court was disturbed.
He caused Zhao Dun and his whole household, high and low,
To all one day suffer disaster, though guiltless.
In those times many held to righteousness,
How could it truly be said that Heaven's Way grew indistinct.
Fortunately the Orphan could repay his grudge of many years

82. In traditional China a pregnancy was said to last ten months, counting lunar months from the time of conception to the month of birth.

And separate head and body of that vile minister.
Let him resume his surname, and we bestow on him the name Zhao Wu,
And let him inherit his ancestors' title and office.
The descendants of Han Jue will become commander in chief,
And Cheng Ying shall be provided a homestead of many acres.
For old Gongsun a grave will be built and a stele erected,
Timi Ming and the others will all be glorified.
The state of Jin today marks a new beginning—
Let us gaze together upon the boundless virtue of our lord!

(CHENG YING and MALE LEAD *act out expressing their gratitude.* MALE LEAD *sings:*)

(*Huangzhong Coda*)
We thank our lord for his grace that rains down on the state of Jin,
And exterminated the entire family of that vile minister.
On the Orphan he bestows a new name,
And makes him heir to his ancestors and thus a minister.
Heroes loyal and righteous are all praised and rewarded,
Those who were military officers are restored to their commands,
Those who are destitute commoners are given sustenance,
Those who had died already are awarded a noble burial,
Those who are still alive receive titles and gifts.
This grace is as broad as heaven!
And who would dare to make polite refusals?
We swear we will sacrifice our lives on the battlefield,
To make neighboring states all give us their allegiance.
In the history books we will leave our names,
For later generations to praise!

Title: Gongsun Chujiu is shamefully subjected to interrogation
Name: The Orphan of Zhao Greatly Wreaks Vengeance

2

Huo Guang Remonstrates as a Ghost

INTRODUCTION

As is customary in Yuan printings of drama, *Huo Guang Remonstrates as a Ghost* (*Huo Guang gui jian* 霍光鬼諫) mentions no author. The bibliographical section of *The Register of Ghosts* does not contain this title, and *A Formulary of Correct Sounds for an Era of Great Peace* lists it as an anonymous *zaju*. It is only Yao Tongshou 姚桐壽 (fl. 1350), in a collection of notes on the area of Haiyan (on the seacoast north of Hangzhou) called *Private Notes from a Land of Bliss* (*Lejiao siyu* 樂郊私語), who ascribes this and two more titles to Yang Zi 楊梓 (ca. 1255–1327).[1] Yang was a remarkable figure in the world of *zaju*. A southerner by birth and a high official by virtue of education and family ties, he was also a magnate of the overseas shipping trade.

The Yang family hailed from Pucheng in Fujian province. Little is revealed in historical sources about Yang Zi's grandfather Yang Chun 楊春, but Yang Zi's father, Yang Fa 楊發, held high military office under the Southern Song dynasty, attaining the rank of vice campaign commander of the Bureau of Military Affairs. During the final onslaught of the Mongols against the Southern Song, however, he switched his allegiance to the Yuan and by 1277 served under the new regime as pacification commissioner for Fujian province. When the Yuan reinstituted the Maritime Trade Supervisorates in that year, he was put in charge of the three supervisorates of Shanghai, Ganpu 澉浦, and Qingyuan 慶原 (Ganpu was the international harbor of Hangzhou, Qingyuan is the modern city of Ningbo). The Ganpu Maritime Trade Supervisorate was officially abolished in 1298, but Yao Tongshou's *Lejiao siyu* indicates that it continued to

1. Yao 1936, 26b.

function as late as 1360. It would appear that members of the Yang family remained in control of Ganpu international trade and ocean shipping for some generations and amassed an enormous fortune.[2]

Yang Zi probably was born sometime around 1250–55 since his two elder sons were born to separate concubines in 1283. He served with distinction in the unsuccessful Mongol campaign against eastern Java of 1292–1293. Later, in 1314, he attained the rank of vice pacification commander for Zhedong and soon afterward was appointed Hangzhou route commander. Hangzhou is also the most likely place for Yang to have met and befriended the famous songwriter Guan Yunshi 貫雲石 (1286–1324), who lived in Hangzhou for the last six years of his life.[3] Yang Zi's eldest son, Yang Ying (1283–1303), was groomed for an official career but died at a relatively young age. Yang Ying's younger brother, Yang Shu 楊樞 (1283–1331), took to sea. Starting in 1301 he made a number of trips to the countries bordering the Indian Ocean. In 1327, the year of his father's death, he took up the post of sea transport vice battalion commander, and in 1331 his rank was raised to that of battalion commander, but he died before assuming the post. Yet a third brother was in charge of the business operations in Ganpu.

According to Yao Tongshou, the Yang family was a great patron of drama. Yao states that Yang Zi wrote his three plays "in order to give expression to the feelings of his grandfather and father" (*yi yu zu fu zhi yi* 以寓祖父之意).[4] Each of the three plays deals with an instance of conspicuous loyalty following a switch of allegiance from an undeserving patron to a more deserving lord. In southern China, Marco Polo assures us, anti-Mongol sentiment ran very high, and Yang Zi apparently felt a need to defend the behavior of his forebears, proving by historical example that turncoats can be heroes too.

The materials for Huo Guang Remonstrates as a Ghost are derived from the biography of Huo Guang (d. 68 BC), whose career is chronicled in great detail in the *Hanshu*, the dynastic history of the Western Han dynasty (206 BC–AD 8). Huo Guang rose to preeminence at court during the later years of the reign of Emperor Wu, upon whose death he became the real power behind Emperor Zhao (r. 86–74 BC). When Emperor Zhao passed away, Huo Guang and other court officials called the Prince of Changyi (Changyi Wang 昌邑王) to the capital in order to place him on the throne. When the prince failed to behave as expected, he was quickly deposed. In a solemn court meeting, the Prince of Changyi had to listen to a list of his 1,117 crimes, and Huo Guang personally removed the imperial seal from his belt. After sending the Prince of Changyi back to his fief, Huo Guang and his fellow officials installed a grandson of Emperor Wu's, a minor who had the status of only a commoner. Known to history as Emperor Xuan (r. 73–49 BC),

2. Ibid., 7a–8a.

3. On Guan Yunshi, see Lynn 1980.

4. Ibid., 26b.

this monarch entrusted the administration of the realm to Huo Guang, whose sons and nephews reached the highest bureaucratic positions and whose daughter, Chengjun 成君, became Xuan's main wife upon the death of Empress Xu. When Huo Guang fell ill, the emperor even visited him in person to inquire about his health. But following Huo Guang's death, the emperor moved quickly: the Huo clan was gradually stripped of their power, accused of rebellion, then arrested and executed.

The *Hanshu* also recounts that Huo Guang's wife prepared the way to glory for her daughter by having Emperor Xuan's empress, née Xu, killed after childbirth. When Huo Guang first heard of this, it is said, he was greatly perturbed and wanted to inform on her, but in the end he could never bring himself to do so. Just before the final downfall of his clan, his ghost appeared to his wife in a dream, warning her of impending doom. Her unbridled lust for wealth and power earned Huo Guang's wife a substantial section in the supplementary biographies of the *Lienü zhuan* 烈女傳 (Biographies of Exemplary Women) as a negative example. This potted biography stresses the virtue of Huo Guang in contrast to the shameless behavior of his wife, daughter, and sons, and it is this characterization that seems to underlie that of Huo Guang in *Huo Guang Remonstrates as a Ghost*. Huo's loyalty to Emperor Xuan, whom he had personally installed on the throne, outstripped even the interests of his own family.

The likelihood of the *Lienü zhuan* as the direct source of Yang Zi's play is further strengthened by the remarkably prominent role that Yang Chang 楊敞 (d. 74 BC), a person who is relatively unimportant in history, plays in the drama. In the *Lienü zhuan*, the biography of the wife of Yang Chang immediately precedes that of Huo Guang's wife. This biography shows a Yang Chang who is completely paralyzed by fear when Huo Guang and others ask him to participate in deposing the Prince of Changyi but who decides to join them following the resolute intervention of his wife.

Huo Guang Remonstrates as a Ghost is a regular *zaju*. It consists of four suites of songs assigned to a male lead who plays Huo Guang in each act. The contents of the play may be summarized as follows: In act 1, the Prince of Changyi, who has been summoned to the throne by Yang Chang and Huo Guang, is berated for his 1,117 infractions by Yang Chang, whose remonstrations are completely unsuccessful. Huo Guang decides to speak to the new emperor. He enters the palace, observes the Prince of Changyi at his carousals, and also remonstrates with him, but he also meets with no success. After consultation with Yang Chang, Huo Guang now calls Emperor Xuan to the throne, and the Prince of Changyi is banished. Emperor Xuan summons the two good-for-nothing sons of Huo Guang, Huo Shan 霍山 and Huo Yu 霍禹 (both committed suicide in 66 BC), and appoints them to high positions—despite the loud and repeated protests of their father, who is sent off on an inspection tour of the south.

In act 2, during Huo Guang's absence from the capital, his two sons conspire with their mother and succeed in installing their sister, Chengjun, in the palace. Upon his return from the south, Huo Guang is met at home by his wife. Surprised at the absence of his children, he is informed by his wife about their positions. Infuriated, he departs for the palace. Huo Guang gives vent to his fury to Yang Chang and berates his two sons. Huo Guang visits the emperor and asks him to dismiss his sons and confine his daughter. A greatly angered Emperor Xuan flatly refuses to do so and orders Huo Guang to leave. Huo Guang thereupon voices his disappointment to Yang Chang.

A chagrined Huo Guang falls ill in act 3 and approaches his death. He admonishes his sons and urges his daughter to assist the emperor in the cultivation of virtue. When Emperor Xuan comes to visit him on his sickbed, Huo Guang first urges him to practice benign government and, afraid that his sons will soon rebel, requests a pardon beyond the grave. He then dies.

In act 4, Huo Shan and Huo Yu do indeed plot rebellion. To warn Emperor Xuan, the ghost of Huo Guang appears to him in a dream and informs him of his sons' conspiracy. The next morning, Huo Shan and Huo Yu are arrested and executed, and an offering is presented at Huo Guang's grave.

As is clear from this summary, Yang Zi made very free use of his sources. The historical roles of Huo Guang and Emperor Xuan are reversed: in the play it is the emperor who takes the initiative to raise the relatives of Huo Guang to high positions despite Huo's own urgent and sincere protests. The text of our play contains no explicit references to Huo's wife's murder of the earlier empress—perhaps our author deemed that crime too heinous for inclusion. In the play Huo Guang also castigates his sons for prostituting their sister for their own advancement. No historical source provides a basis for Huo Guang's long mission to the south and his subsequent absence from court, which seems to have been introduced in the play to explain Huo's ignorance about his family's schemes.

The historical Huo Guang, a bureaucrat bent on increasing the power of his own house, is changed in the play to a loyal official who informs against his own wife and sons. This characterization, first hinted at in his wife's biography in the *Lienü zhuan*, is completed in act 4 when his ghost appears not to his wife but to the emperor. When caught between loyalty to his lord and protection of his relatives, who shamelessly exploit the emperor's gratitude, Huo Guang unwaveringly opts for loyalty. But the very severity of Huo's denunciation of his sons betrays the intensity of such a tragic conflict of interest, from which the protagonist can escape only in an undisturbed grave.

SUGGESTED READINGS

Idema 1989; Kinney 2014; Loewe 1974; O'Hara 1945; Pan 1944; Wagner 1998; Watson 1974a, 1974b.

NEWLY PRINTED IN HANGZHOU WITH PLOT PROMPTS: *HUO GUANG REMONSTRATES AS A GHOST*, A FOURTEENTH-CENTURY EDITION

DRAMATIS PERSONAE IN ORDER OF APPEARANCE

Role type	*Name and family, institutional, or social role*
MALE LEAD	HUO GUANG
MINOR FEMALE	CHENGJUN, HUO GUANG's daughter
OLD WOMAN	MADAME HUO, HUO GUANG's wife
COMIC	HUO SHAN, HUO GUANG's son
COMIC	HUO YU, HUO GUANG's son
EMPEROR	EMPEROR XUAN
EXTRA	YANG CHANG

✤ ✤ ✤

NEWLY PRINTED IN HANGZHOU WITH PLOT PROMPTS: *HUO GUANG REMONSTRATES AS A GHOST*

[ACT 1]

After PRINCE OF CHANGYI *enters and opens and after* EXTRA *speaks—after* EXTRA *enters, remonstrates, and is not heeded—wait until* EXTRA *has departed.* [*You,*] MALE LEAD, *enter, dressed in armor as* HUO GUANG *with a sword at your belt, and open.* I am Huo Guang, newly appointed as Grand Marshal. After Emperor Zhao passed away, the Prince of Changyi ascended the throne. Chancellor Yang Chang, from the ranks of civil officials, and I, from the ranks of the military, both set him up. I've been sick and haven't been to morning court for several days. I heard a report that the Prince of Changyi, having been lord for less than a month, has committed one thousand, one hundred and seventeen major crimes. Officials in court and out all say, "It was that old fellow, Huo Guang, and no one else who set him up in the first place." *Hai*! What should I do now? I recall that it was no easy thing for the Exalted Ancestor, the first emperor, to establish this great realm, this dynasty of Han.

(XIANLÜ MODE: *Dian jiangchun*)
King Huai, newly set up,
Sent out Liu Bang and Xiang Yu,
And they drove forth their troops and commanders.[5]
Western Chu and the state of Qin—
Both had a heroic aura that rose ten thousand feet high.
(*Hunjiang long*)
Manifesting the expectations of the people,
The Duke of Pei, with halberd and spear, entered Xianyang.
Ziying
Was resigned to surrender at the crossroads,
And the Hegemon King cut his own throat at the Rook River.
Extinguishing Chu and destroying Qin,
The state altars of Liu:
All thanks to
The High Ancestor of Han, who began the enterprise and laid the foundations of state.
Later . . .[6]
. . .
Who, all day among the music ensemble,
In the sounds of strings and pipes,
Where voices in song warble and wind,
And postures of dance flutter and float.
. . .
. . . dressed in dragon robes,
And yet still
Sodden, drunk as mud all day.

---

5. This song and the following provide a potted history of the wars following the death of the First Emperor of the Qin dynasty in 210 BC. When Xiang Yu 項羽 (232–202 BC) had risen in rebellion, he searched for a scion of the royal house of the former state of Chu and set him up as Emperor Huai, while he himself assumed the title of Hegemon King of Western Chu. Liu Bang 劉邦 (256 or 247–195 BC) rose under his command to the position of Duke of Pei 沛公. When the rebellious troops marched toward northwestern China, the area of the Qin dynasty capital Xianyang was promised as domain to the commander who would be the first to occupy the city. Liu Bang's troops captured the city and accepted the surrender of Ziying 子嬰, the last emperor of the Qin dynasty. However, Xiang Yu robbed him of his spoils by enfeoffing him not with the capital area but with the mountainous area of Hanzhong, where Liu Bang became known as the Prince of Han. In the ensuing war, Liu Bang eventually emerged victorious, and Xiang Yu, deserted by his troops and trapped, fled. When Xiang Yu reached Rook River (Wujiang 烏江) on his final retreat, the post guard told him he had boats that Xiang could use to ferry across. Xiang Yu refused, saying that he had "no face left" to see the fathers and elder brothers of the young men he had led out from there and who had been killed in his defeat. See Ssu-ma Ch'ien 2002, 17–49. Episodes from the Chu-Han story cycle were highly popular on the Yuan stage; see Idema 1990a.
6. A portion of the text is missing here due to a torn page.

He listens to naught but
The tuning of strings, the blowing of bamboo flutes,
Where is any
"Discussing the Way or ordering the state"?[7]

Speak: Here I am, outside the court gate. I am afraid of bumping into Yang Chang, and I'd better just enter through the ministers' back gate.—*After* YANG CHANG *has bumped into you and spoken*: [*You speak*:] Your remonstrance was not heeded, Chancellor. Rest easy! I will go in and remonstrate with him.

(*You hulu*)
Tipsy the whole day, he enters the Land of Drunkenness,
And right now,
He will have surely returned to his grotto chamber,[8]
Ai!
Already the silver candles are burning on high to shine on rouged beauties.
All one hears
Is the clamorous din of the entrance and exit of singers and dancers,
Or the wavering harmony of the clear tones of Tibetan flutes.
On this very day, I am concerned about peace in the empire.
I must remonstrate with the Prince of Changyi:
When I've set aflight songs sung before goblets of Bamboo Leaf,[9]
He'll have a change of heart,
Repair the administration of the state,
And put in order the mainstays of the court.

(*Tianxia le*)
Still
Rotten drunk by the side of a beauty and her patterned zither!
I have passed the Screen of Reverence[10]—
I must have audience with the Imperial King.
I do not hear
The three cracks of the whistling whip of silence,
I do not see the civil officials arrayed along the left,
Or the military officers
Arrayed on the right.[11]
Only the twelve ranks of golden hairpins arrayed as always.

---

7. The last lines of this song, starting from "Later . . . ," evidently describe the behavior of the Prince of Changyi since his ascension to the throne.
8. Grotto chamber: a secluded inner chamber; often used to indicate "bedchamber."
9. Bamboo Leaf: a high-quality rice wine
10. The Screen of Reverence was a screen or wall behind the main gate into the palace hall; upon passing it, the minister who entered the hall was expected to act with utmost circumspection.
11. The retinue normally in attendance upon the emperor. The golden hairpins following are metonymy for women.

After having audience with PRINCE OF CHANGYI—*after* [*he*] *speaks*:—[*You speak*:] Do you know your crimes, My Lord?—*After* PRINCE OF [CHANG]YI *speaks—speak*: Having been lord for less than a month, you have committed one thousand, one hundred and seventeen crimes—and you still are aware of no wrongdoing?

(*Nezha ling*)

My lord, it is said
That you are as depraved as the King of Yue, who was infatuated with Xishi,[12]
As besotted with lust
As the King of Chu, who raped Wu Xiang.[13]
And you have committed incest in the palace
Like King Zhou, who was infatuated with Da Ji.[14]
In front of the host of ministers,
The many grandees and councilors,
We should
Go over all of this, and carefully.

(*Que ta zhi*)

One who so harms the family and state
Or injures the loyal and good
Should, as fast as possible, hand over these rivers and mountains,
And abdicate the Dragon Throne.
Now the troops and citizens of all four corners all praise *him*[15] to the skies,

---

12. During the sixth and fifth centuries BC the state of Wu 吳 (with its capital in present-day Suzhou) and the state of Yue 越 (with its capital at present-day Shaoxing) were engaged in extensive wars. Following a victory over his adversary, the King of Wu imprisoned the King of Yue, Goujian 勾踐, who was released only after many years of servitude. Upon his return to his country, Goujian vowed revenge. In order to make the King of Wu neglect his duties as head of state, Goujian selected the most beautiful maiden in the state of Yue, Xishi 西施, and had her groomed in the arts of seduction, whereupon she was presented to the King of Wu. She succeeded in her mission: the King of Wu became besotted with her and the state of Wu was easily overrun by the troops of Yue. According to one version of the legend of Xishi, she was thereupon killed by the King of Yue as a dangerous temptress, but according to another version she left the state of Yue together with the man who had first discovered her and went on to live a happy life with him, roaming the rivers and lakes. According to yet another version, to which our author refers, she was taken back to Yue by King Goujian, who now became the victim of her beauty and neglected the affairs of state, with disastrous consequences.
13. Wu Xiang 無祥 (literally, "misfortunate one") is the name of the daughter of the Duke of Qin who was brought to Chu by King Ping 平王 to be a daughter-in-law. He later took her as his own wife (technically speaking, thereby committing incest).
14. Da Ji 妲己 was the favorite concubine of King Zhou 紂王, the last king of the Shang dynasty (traditional dates, 1766–1122 BC). Under her influence, later tradition claimed, King Zhou had naked men and women copulate among mountains of meat and ponds of wine, and he completely neglected the affairs of state. As a consequence, his lords rebelled and his dynasty was supplanted by the Zhou dynasty (traditional dates, 1122–256 BC).
15. The last two lines of this aria praise the future Emperor Xuan, who is here compared with sage emperors of mythic antiquity. Yao 堯 (traditional dates, 2356–2255 BC) ceded the throne to Shun 舜 (traditional dates, 2255–2205 BC), who in turn ceded the throne to Yu 禹 (traditional dates, 2205–2197 BC), the founder of the Xia dynasty (traditional dates, 2205–1766 BC). Tang is Cheng Tang 成湯, the founder of the Shang dynasty.

And his virtue surpasses
Yu and Shun, Yao and Tang.
(*Jisheng cao*)
About him, I've heard this—
His air of benevolence is replete,
His imperial enterprise is brilliant.[16]
Emperor Zhao has long been buried in his tumulus,
And the Prince of Changyi knows nothing of the manner of the court.
But now
A new Son of Heaven will take the coiling-dragon couch.
This is a case of
"The fields of those before are reaped by those who come after,"
True it is
"On the Yangtze River, waves from behind press on those that went before."

Wait until PRINCE OF CHANGYI *finishes speaking*:

(*Liuyao xu*):
He blocks me head-on,
Lunges directly toward me, and
To my face
Turns black into white, white into black.
He flaunts his
Indomitable hot-blooded gall,
A martial skill not to be vanquished.
But in my eyes he's merely insignificant and ordinary.
Involuntarily my
Heroic aura rises ten thousand feet!
In a flash, disaster will overtake you at the Screen of Reverence,
And,
Another five steps and blood will spatter the gold steps.
And in that place
Don't draw out the years and months,
Don't hang on to an hour of time.
(*Yao*)
He replies,
Haughty and arrogant,
He flees the dragon couch.
I grab his clothes,
And in this

16. Imperial enterprise: the founding of a new state.

Very Hall of the Golden Simurgh,[17]
We two
Square off for a bout.
What I see
Are his words flustered and confused,
His gestures wild and crazy.
When this crisis peaks, he can only panic—
Cross a hero like me, and there'll be no end to it.
Haven't you heard that
Zhuan Zhu was able to stab the King of Wu?[18]
And today, for us
The righteous bond of master and vassal is severed beyond hope.
Since you imitate Li Ji's destruction of Jin,[19]
I find it hard to imitate Yi Yin's support of Tang.[20]
Speak:

Chancellor, the Prince of Changyi is without the Way. Let the two of us, without the Hundred Officials, civil and military, arrange the proper insignia and the simurgh chariot and proceed to invite our new master. *After acting out welcoming* EMPEROR, *who enters—speak*: The Prince of Changyi was without the Way and was unfit to preside over the ancestral temples. Today we establish a new ruler. In unison let our two bodies, civil officials and military officers, shout hurrah. *After* THE RETINUE *speaks—speak*: Prince Changyi, the new lord, in his ○○ [Sagely Decree][21] has spared you from the death penalty and granted you a fiefdom. Quickly leave the court! *After* PRINCE OF CHANGYI *speaks—after* EMPEROR *appoints you to office—speak*: I request with all my heart to be allowed to retire and live in seclusion.—*After* EMPEROR *summons two* COMICS *onstage—After he appoints them to office—speak*:

17. Hall of the Golden Simurgh (Jinluan Dian 金鸞殿) was, in Tang times, the name of one of the buildings of the Hanlin Academy; as such it is mentioned in the first poem in the collected works of Bai Juyi 白居易 (772–846). By Yuan times the term was used as a designation of the main hall of the imperial palace.

18. Zhuan Zhu 專諸, who had hidden his dagger inside a fish, stabbed the King of Wu Liao (r. 526–515 BC) to death on behalf of a disgruntled prince. As soon as he had committed the murder, Zhuan Zhu was killed by the king's guards.

19. Li Ji 驪姬 ("Barbarian Beauty") was a princess of the Li-Rong 驪戎 tribe who had been captured by the ducal army of Jin (r. 676–51 BC) in a raid against that tribe and became a consort of Duke Xian of Jin 晉獻公. When she had borne the duke two sons, she started to plot against the sons of the duke by an earlier marriage. As a result, the duke had the crown prince, Shensheng 申生, executed, while his two younger brothers fled the state. Li Ji and her children were eventually all killed during the troubles upon the death of Duke Xian.

20. Yi Yin 伊尹 was the loyal and wise minister of Tang the Completer (Cheng Tang 成湯), founder of the Shang (ca. 1600 BC).

21. Because it was taboo to write them out, the two words "sagely direction" (*shengzhi* 聖旨) are omitted in the text and replaced by two circles. This convention is not followed in all cases (see the beginning of act 2).

Your Majesty, how can you appoint two such unfilial sons to so high an office? Truly, one still bears his fetal hair! [(*Sing*:)]

(*Houting hua*)

Why should they enjoy the emolument and position of a thousand-stone weight?[22]
They cheat the myriad people out of their possessions,
But now receive official appointment of the second rank
And control the silver seals of the Three Terraces.[23]

Them—how can they

Put in order the mainstays of the court?
Truly, these two brats are vulgar louts, uncouth bumpkins.
Two lines of text are too much for them to read,
A single bow is one too many for them to draw.
Just this morning they were bumpkins from the paddy fields,
But tonight they ascend the hall of the Son of Heaven.

(*Qing ge'er*)

How can they be prime ministers at court, at court?
All in vain, the hopes of the people are now lost, lost.
These two brats grew up in a house that never leaked, that was filled with fine rice and dry firewood.

But you now award them

Purple-corded golden seals,
Feathered banners, and oxtail pennants,
Allow them to sit in state in the central office,
To support and assist my emperor,
To judge and decide the mainstays of court,
To order and regulate both family and state.

What I fear

Is that they will destroy the order of yin and yang,
And so incite the rage of the vaulted blue,
That heaven will send down disaster and calamity,
And set frost flying in the sixth month.[24]

Drought will kill

---

22. A stone is a weight of 120 catties (pounds). In Han times, officials were paid in grain, and their rank was often indicated by referring to their yearly allowance of grain.

23. The Three Terraces (Santai 三臺) refer to the positions of the three highest-ranking government officials, the Three Dukes (Sangong 三公).

24. Zou Yan 鄒衍 (ca. 305–240 BC) was a loyal minister to his king. He was slandered and thrown into prison. He raised his head to weep to heaven, and in the middle of the summer it began to snow. This later became a common allusion to injustices severe enough to evoke Heaven's displeasure.

The harvest, the mulberry trees,
    Waters will flood
The fields, the villages.
The four borders will fill with famine and starvation,
And ten thousand people will flee and fly.
    Just look!
They are fiercer than jackals and wolves,
More crude than pigs and goats.
Their countenance: sunken eyes and hollow cheeks,
Their appearance: yellow faced and weak limbed.
Pampered by their daddy's rice and their mommy's soup,
They've no hope for "noble husband and glorious wife,"
And as a result, bad bones broken, they're even more unstable.
They are boats without rudders, baskets without bottoms.
    My King you must
Reach back and model yourself after Tang of the Shang,[25]
Subjugate and make vassals of the Rong and Qiang.[26]
Go to the outskirts to greet those who can govern,
Choose and advance those wise and good,
Select and employ the loyal and good,
Be upright and square in all your actions,
Outstrip the ordinary in talent and wisdom,
Discuss the Way, order the state,
Extend the realm, expand its borders,
And make the myriad countries submit in surrender.
Then the myriad people will have peace and prosperity—
You will live a myriad of lives without end,
And a myriad generations will sing your praise.
But deep-fried monkeys like them
Are frivolous and crazed by nature,
    In truth,
Can one believe their portraits will ever be painted in the Unicorn Hall?[27]

---

25. Tang of the Shang is, as noted, Cheng Tang.
26. Rong 戎 and Qiang 羌 are the names of non-Chinese tribes. Victories over these tribes by the early kings were celebrated in the classics.
27. The Unicorn Hall (Qilin Dian 麒麟殿) had been erected by Emperor Wu upon the capture of a unicorn. Emperor Xuan had painted here the portraits of eleven meritorious officials, including Huo Guang.

After EMPEROR *speaks—speak*: Now, I, this single official, this very day bid My Lord adieu and go off to inspect the Five Southern Provinces.[28] [(*Sing*:)]
(*Zhuansha Coda*)
The emperor has ascended the throne,
Heaven has hung down its signs:
On this very day,
The sky is clear, the sun is bright.
The days of Shun and the years of Yao resonate with the high azure.
Over his head hovers a purple mist, a red aura,
That spreads evenly over the Land of the Five Clouds.[29]
He, all alone and forlorn, at the bank of the autumn river,
Will hear, year after year,
The echo of springtime thunder that shakes the cosmos in response to heaven.[30]
One ascends the throne in Jianzhang Palace,[31]
The other hides himself at ocean's shore—
This is truly "A true dragon appears in the world, the false dragon goes into hiding."
Exit.

[ACT 2]

After EMPEROR *exits after speaking—two* COMICS *enter, open and stop—After* OLD WOMAN *finishes speaking—After two* COMICS *greet* [*her*], *they exit*—EMPEROR *and retinue enter, open, and stop—After two* COMICS *enter and offer up* MINOR FEMALE—OLD WOMAN *enters, speaks again, exits.*[32] *You,* MALE LEAD, *enter riding a bamboo horse, open*: Under commission of the Sagely Directions of our emperor I have made a tour of inspection of the Five Southern Provinces. How quickly has half a year passed! Oh, what a pleasure to reach home today.

28. The Five Southern Provinces are identified as Jiangnan 江南 ("South of the River," modern-day southern Jiangsu and surroundings), Hunan 湖南 ("South of the Lake"), Lingnan 嶺南 ("South of the Range," modern-day Guangdong and Guangxi), Hainan 海南 ("South of the Sea"), and Yunnan 雲南 ("South of the Clouds"). However, the expression as such refers to the southern border areas in general.
29. The Five Clouds are auspicious five-colored clouds; the Land of the Five Clouds is a designation of the realm of immortals; as such the term can refer to the seat of the emperor.
30. These two lines refer to the banished Prince of Changyi.
31. The Jianzhang Palace 建章宮 was a palace and garden complex built in 104 BC by Emperor Wu (r. 140–87 BC) and was so large that it had a thousand gates and ten thousand doors. Later the term was used as a general designation for the imperial palace.
32. The characters for "male lead" (*zhengmo* 正末) are raised one character space here. The term "male lead" occurs infrequently in the earliest Yuan plays, and we usually translate it as an imperative or command, "you, as the male

([ZHONGLÜ MODE] *Fen die'er*)

A lean horse, a long whip—
The road stretched on and on, yet could I shirk from this tiring duty?
Worn out by the journey; oh, how bleak a traveler's lot!
But on behalf of the August One,
I have expended all my energy—
Let him use me to my limits and I will die without resentment.
On this occasion I have undone injustices against the people
And happily return home,
My happy heart's desire fulfilled.

(*Zui chunfeng*)

I went a full distance of twenty rest stops,
Passing from one to the other for three or four thousand miles;
In the Five Southern Provinces I was gone for half a year—
Never was a road so distant, so far.
When I thought—of my wife, leaning with anticipation on the door,
Or of my children—in dreams,
They appeared live before my eyes.

Act out returning home: Servants, take my horse.—*After* OLD WOMAN *receives you and stops—After she speaks*:

(*Hong xiuxie*)

I brush the dust from my face,
Overjoyed that we, husband and wife, are together again.
Here at home you must have had a hard time because of the children—
Even though
I have a good salary,
And some public lands—
I think
It's hard to get by on such a poor income.

Speak:—On the whole trip I thought only of those two. Why didn't they come to greet me?—*After* OLD WOMAN *speaks—Speak*:—And isn't my daughter, Chengjun, coming from her embroidery chamber to greet me? *After* OLD WOMAN *speaks act out collapsing from anger*. [(*Sing*:)]

lead," do such and such an action, in keeping with the function of the text as a role text written for that lead. Its raised placement here marks the beginning of a new scene in the play that represents a major break from what precedes it. In this case, it is also possible to see the stage directions preceding "male lead" as a short scene that takes place between acts 1 and 2. We have chosen to add them to the second act. As we noted in the introduction, these plays do not designate act divisions, only scene divisions, so adding the scene to either act 1 or act 2 is merely a convention imposed by editors of modern editions or by us on the translation.

(*Ti yindeng*)
In carrying out their duties, they had no other gift to present
Except to turn over their sister on a platter to the emperor?
No doubt,
A commoner has rushed into a hall of pure gold.
Is this the summoning of worthies, the selection of talent by my emperor of Han?
Think of those days—
One at the foot of the cliff,[33]
One on the bank of the Wei,[34]
Even that youngster from Huaiyin who begged for food[35]—
(*Manqing cai*)
They never did any
Reaching glory in a single leap,
Never
Offered up their little sister for a bit of cash,

---

33. Fu Yue 傅說 was working as a convict laborer in the area of Fuyan (modern Shanxi), where he worked on constructing walls of rammed earth (he is often wrongly credited as the inventor of the form system for these walls). According to the *Records of the Historian*, the Shang thearch Wuding (d. 1192 BC) dreamt of obtaining a wise sage:

> At night Wuding dreamt of attaining a sage, who was named Yue. Based on what he had seen in his dream, he looked at the assembled ministers and hundred clerks of his government, but none of them matched. At that point he sent his hundred officers to seek him in the wilds, and he obtained Yue from the precipices of Fu. At this time Yue was a slave, forming walls in the precipices of Fu, and when he was seen by Wuding, Wuding said, "This is he." He got him and conversed with him, and indeed Yue was a sagely man, so he was raised to be minister and the state of Yin was grandly governed. Therefore, he consequently bestowed on him the surname Fu because of the precipices of Fu and called him Fu Yue.

Thanks to the wise advice of Fu Yue, King Wuding succeeded in the restoration of the Shang dynasty. See "Basic Annals of Yin" 殷本紀 in Sima Qian 1959, 102.

34. Lü Wang 呂望, who is also known as Lü Shang 呂尚, Jiang Shang 姜尚, Jiang Taigong 姜太公, or Jiang Ziya 姜子牙, was a hermit who spent his days angling on Pan Creek near the Wei River until he was brought to court at the age of seventy by King Wen of the Zhou. At the age of eighty Lü Wang would assist King Wu in his conquest of the Shang and the establishment of the Zhou dynasty. In imperial times Lü Wang was credited with the authorship of a military handbook titled *Six Tactics*. For his biography see "T'ai-kung of Ch'i, Hereditary House 2" in Sima Qian 2006, 31–46.

35. In his youth Han Xin 韓信 (d. 196 BC), also known as Marshal Han, who eventually would become one of Liu Bang's most effective generals, survived by begging in his hometown of Huaiyin 淮陰. After Liu Bang had defeated all his opponents and established the Han dynasty, he began to be paranoid about those around him who posed a threat to his rule. Liu Bang's wife, the cruel Empress Lü 呂后, sent the powerful minister Xiao He 蕭何 to summon Han Xin to the capital, where he was relieved of his command and beheaded. Since Xiao He was instrumental in both Han Xin's success and failure, it has given rise to a common saying in Chinese, "Success by Xiao He, defeat by Xiao He" (Cheng ye Xiao He, bai ye Xiao He 成也蕭何, 敗也蕭何), which is used to indicate the fickle and inconstant nature of the world and the foolishness of counting on current circumstances. Han's biography is found in English in "The Marquis of Huai-yin, Memoir 32," in Sima Qian 2008, 61–98, and in Sima Qian 1993, 91–98.

Bartered her for a steady salary.
This breath of rage won't subside, it chokes my throat,
I am so enraged my hands and feet tremble and shake.

Speak: This very day I will see the Son of Heaven at court and offer my remonstration. *Wait for* EMPEROR *to enter, open, and stop—After* EXTRA MALE *enters and remonstrates—You,* MALE LEAD, *enter conveniently—Act out greeting* YANG CHANG—*After he speaks*: Chancellor, call out those two scoundrels for me. *After two* COMICS *enter, speak, and exit.*

(*Shiliu hua*)
I have
Exerted myself for twenty years on behalf of the emperor,
And I once
Occupied the office of commander in chief, controlled all military power.
Now today,
In the central office, they channel the emperor's edicts,
Barely able to get a promotion,
They act the official.
I once
Braved death fighting on sandy fields,
I once
Slept in frost and camped in snow,
Behind the battle lines and at army's vanguard.
I recall my
Water-mill whip,
Leather-ridged stave,
And eagle-feathered arrow.
I doffed my metal armor,
To barter for a purple robe to wear.[36]

(*Dou anchun*)
Beat these scoundrels who are appointed officials because of an oiled topknot,
Who receive their commissions on account of her powdered face.
Your food and clothing were earned at the belt of a woman's skirt,
Sword and armor earned my salary and emoluments.
If I don't beat you to death, I can't rid myself of this wrong.
Is this what I looked forward to for half a year?
Ask for no consideration of those feelings proper to father and sons,
For we've nearly lost the correct demeanor of lord and minister.

36. That is, change from a military to civil position in government.

After being received in audience by EMPEROR—*After* EMPEROR *speaks*:
(*Shang xiaolou*)
Beat these scoundrels
Who are low in talent, shallow in wisdom.
How could they
Attend you at court, be promoted, transferred?
How can they
Extend the realm, expand the borders,
Order the country, bring peace to the state,
Offer up policies or set out criticism?
To my mind, these scoundrels
Have no exalted insights or long-range vision,
How could they
Occupy the central office and be enfeoffed with an estate of eight districts?
After EMPEROR speaks:
(*Reprise*)
Should they be allowed
To embezzle money from the Hundred Surnames,
Then betray
The emperor's edict,
In order, with all gall,
To abuse and oppress the good citizens?
Or annoy and offend the heavenly countenance,
Commit crimes to call down punishment,
And in the end suffer execution in the marketplace?
I fear
It will implicate my whole household, noble and base.

Speak: I beg Your Majesty to degrade these two scoundrels to commoners and to set Chengjun aside in the Cold Palace. May your sagely wisdom be not deluded! *After* EMPEROR *speaks, he and his retinue exit—After* YANG CHANG *speaks—Speak*: The emperor does not heed my remonstration. Enough, enough, enough.

(*Shuahai and Four from Coda*)
Once it becomes hard to defend myself before the sagely anger of my lord and king,
I can see my aged life trickle away before my eyes.
How can I bear today's humiliation?
It makes me
Hang my head in silence.
The fulsome rage of the heavenly countenance I could not dispel,
And I irritated him so much
That an immediate beheading was before my eyes.

Everyone is fed up—
In the lightest case, I should be caned a hundred strokes,
In the worst, banished three thousand miles away.
(*Three from Coda*)
Yes, indeed,
Bi Gan was ripped open at Star-Plucking Tower,[37]
Qu Yuan drowned in the Miluo River,[38]
And Fan Li bade Gou Jian adieu at Gusu Terrace.[39]
Forever have disordered states lacked the Way.
And from antiquity,
Deluded lords have neither valued the worthy,
Nor distinguished between the pure and the muddied.
I'm afraid
They are Robber Zhis who eat the hearts of men[40]—
How can they be
Yan Yuans, reverential and full of virtuous acts?[41]
(*Two from Coda*)
Why did I
Wear myself out as an official,

37. Bi Gan 比干 was an uncle of King Zhou's, the evil last ruler of the Shang dynasty. When King Zhou had had enough of the remonstrations of Bi Gan, he had him killed in order, he declared, to see whether the heart of a sage really had seven chambers. The Star-Plucking Tower (Zhaixing Lou 摘星樓) was a pleasure loft erected by king Zhou.

38. This refers to the narrative of Qu Yuan 屈原 (ca. 340–278 BC), who wrote a poem called "Embracing Sand" (Huaisha 懷沙) just before he clasped a stone to his chest and threw himself into the river. He had held high position at the Chu court but was exiled because of slander. "Embracing sand" is thought by some to have the meaning of "clasping sand and gravel to the chest in order to sink into the river." For treatments of this famous poem and others by Qu Yuan, see Hawkes 1985, 169–82, and Owen 1996, 155–215.

39. Gusu Terrace (Gusu Tai 姑蘇台) is located near Suzhou. Fan Li 范蠡 worked on behalf of Goujian 勾踐, King of Yue, to destroy the kingdom of Wu. To do so, he presented the most beautiful woman in the land, Xishi 西施, to the King of Wu, who (as described in n. 12) became infatuated with her to the point he paid no attention to government. There are two alternative endings to the story of Fan Li. Fan Li became convinced that Goujian was someone he could help when in difficulty but not someone he could abide in good times. So, in one ending, Fan Li took Xishi off by boat and was never seen again; in the other, he moved to the county of Tao 陶, took the name Master Zhu (Zhugong 朱公) and became a rich merchant. Tao Zhugong later became a catchphrase for a wealthy person. In one version of the story, Goujian has a statue of Fan Li cast in gold to keep by his throne as a reminder of his goodness.

40. Robber Zhi 盜知 is a character in chapter 29 of the *Zhuangzi*, where he is introduced as the younger brother of the virtuous Liuxia Hui. The first paragraph of the chapter paints a lurid picture of the gruesome cruelties and rampant acts of violence he commits as a bandit-king. The chapter continues with a dialogue between Robber Zhi and Confucius, in which Robber Zhi holds forth on the violence and cruelty of the sage-kings.

41. Yan Yuan 顏淵 (Yan Hui 顏回) was the brightest and most morally advanced of Confucius's disciples, as illustrated in *Analects* 6.11: "What a worthy man was Yan Hui! Living in a narrow alley, subsisting on a basket of grain and a gourdful of water—other people could not have borne such hardship, yet it never spoiled Hui's joy. What a worthy man was Hui!" see Slingerland 2003, 56.

Why didn't I
Covet money?
All I considered was that my pure reputation would shine in later years.
I never sought gold or jade, nor noble title upon noble title.
What
Offspring have I who are "each worthier than the other"?
Unfulfilled is my life's ambition.
Get out of my sight,
Stay away from me!
(*Shou shawei Coda*)
Even though raised to the very first rank,
And on top of that given extra commissions.
After YANG CHANG *speaks*:
Who wants to rely on a grand air to manifest his might?
After EXTRA *speaks*:
I fear
Breeding virgins to gain official title will wind up with only the shallowest good fortune.
Exits.

[ACT 3]

After two COMICS *speak*—EMPEROR *does one scene*—EXTRA *opens one scene* —[*You*] MALE LEAD, *act out being violently ill and enter being supported, open*: Since I beat those two miscreants, I have been bedridden for twenty days. How it vexes me. All my merit and labors of earlier days have been wiped out in a single stroke. *Act out heaving a long sigh*:

([ZHONGGONG MODE] *Duanzheng hao*)
For my family I've labored hard in vain,
On behalf of the state I've suffered for naught.
From the very founding of the Han, I've supported the fiery Lius,[42]
I sorrow over my failure, uselessly hang my head.
Without cease
Tears moisten the sleeves of my battle garb.
(*Gun xiuqiu*)
On that day I came back,
I contracted these symptoms,

42. The house of Liu, the imperial family of the Han dynasty, was believed to rule by the virtue of fire, one of the Five Phases.

All because of
These beasts who shame our family name.
And so this
Damned life was spent, but spent in vain.
Stifling my anger caused incessant coughing,
And now I leave this detailed testament to my wife:
It's just because
Of the humiliation to our family that I can't dispel the anger in my heart,
The offering up of their little sister can never conceal the shame on our faces.
Life is like the foam that floats on water's surface.

Wait until two COMICS *enter and act out asking about your illness—Speak*:—I'm old.—Both my legs hurt. *After two* COMICS *stretch your legs*:

(*Tang xiucai*)
You have matched the phoenix companion and the simurgh mate,
And have won some rich food and imperial wine.
For you it's precisely
"That autumn when real men achieve their ambition."
I will soon
Return to the underworld,
Be buried in a desolate mound—
That will be my final fall harvest.

After MINOR FEMALE *speaks—Speak*: My child, I'm far from ascending to heaven but close to entering earth. Yet, I have a few words to leave to you. Heed what I say. *Wait until* MINOR FEMALE *finishes speaking*:

(*Dai guduo*)
It looks like your
Revered father may die any moment,
So I ask you to listen to my testament:
Have the emperor
Recruit gentlemen and summon worthies,
Don't let him
Be led astray by flowers or lust for wine.
I'm afraid these miscreant sons will slander loyal ministers.
You should
Circumspectly, carefully, present your memorial to the lord king himself.
You should imitate
Lady Wuyan, who established the state of Qi,[43]

---

43. Lady Wuyan 無鹽 was extremely ugly. When at forty she still had found no husband, she offered herself to King Xuan of Qi 齊宣王 (r. 319–301 BC), who was so struck by the wisdom of her words and forthright criticism of his behavior that he raised her to the position of queen.

Don't imitate that
Empress Lü who deranged the dynasty of Liu.[44]

Wait until EMPEROR *enters—speaks and stops—You, as* MALE LEAD, *speak*: Ah, I merit ten thousand deaths.

(*Tang xiucai*)
I, this minister,
Cannot put on the golden seal and its purple cords,
And can barely say, "I bow my head with true trepidation."
I, this minister,
Cannot carry out the dancing steps that raise the dust in a triple kowtow.
I am moved by Your Majesty's special concern
For your old court noble,
Whom you've come to ask after in person.

After EMPEROR *asks after you, speak*: There are several affairs in which Your Majesty must heed my petition.

[(*Reprise*)]
Your Majesty,
Write out writs of amnesty and set the prisoners free,
Lessen taxes and imposts and so show mercy to the populace.
In every route, prefecture, and city, restore the temple buildings.
In executions, do not spare your relatives,
In rewards, do not shun your enemies.
"Grace flows from above."

(*Gun xiuqiu*)
Your Majesty, have
Padded uniforms frequently distributed to the army,
And rations of grain daily made available to the troops.
So, even if you use them to their limits, they will not shirk from hardship,
But will risk their lives against sword and halberd, spear and lance.
It's only when you press for grain or press for taxes,
That, then,
Most likely the grain is not harvested or the wheat will not ripen,
And you will vainly pressure them to the point that each and every family flees—
How can they not fear
Flogging, caning, banishment, or exile?

44. Upon the death of Liu Bang in 195 BC, his wife, Empress Lü, became the real power at court. From behind a lowered screen, she ruled with an iron hand and did not hesitate to execute some of the most meritorious officials from the founding years of the dynasty. She was completely partial to members of her own clan, and the power of the Lü clan was destroyed only upon her death in 180 BC.

Your Majesty,
Open the granaries to save the impoverished people,
Then won't they likely
Enjoy their work, be settled in their homes, and not wander in search of food?
These and only these
Are the prime sources of the ordered state.

The whole entourage enters, report to EMPEROR, *stop—Speak*:—Your Majesty, these two miscreant sons are bound to rebel in the future—I request a single writ of reprieve to pardon my crimes.—*After* EMPEROR *speaks*:

(*Tang xiucai*)
I, this minister, fear
That they will implicate all of Huo Guang's family, young and old,
These scoundrels
Are bound to rebel against the universe of our Liu dynasty.
This is
Something that lies ahead that I have already perceived.
These few words—
Mark them in your heart,
Don't let them slip away!

(*Gun xiuqiu*)
These two,
Worthy of the sword,
In the end will die worse than pigs or dogs.
I, this minister, fear
That they will implicate my three-foot-high lonely tumulus.
Just because of you two,
They will split open my coffin,
And cut off the head to desecrate my corpse.
A single writ of reprieve will protect this old minister,
And, as if it were a life-protecting amulet, I will guard it tightly within my bosom.
Let them
Cleave open the new grave mound of your deceased father,
But let no person spit and curse over the damned bones of this humble minister—
Great achievement now gone forever!

After EXTRA *speaks*:

(*Three from Coda*)
"He who has known to the full the affairs of the world is slow to open his mouth"—
Why
Did you serve our lord and king, but not to the full?
I just want you
To order the country and bring peace to the state,

Leave the wicked and return to the upright,
Attract gentlemen and summon worthies,
Establish the Han and raise the Lius.
    Take your example from our noble founder:
Be open-minded and magnanimous,
Have a tolerance as deep as the sea,
Accept remonstrance without interruption.
Rely on the tender protection of high heaven.
    I just desire
Your Majesty can comprehend your officials—civil and military—and esteem dukes and nobles.
(*Two from Coda*)
    O, Heaven,
You lengthen the years of those whose evil hearts blind their consciences,
But when it comes to me, who's served state and family, I've drawn the shorter lot.
    It is also
Earlier karma from a former life,
That caught up now so that I suffer,
Suffused with illness, sunk in disease—
For a thousand deeds, a thousand ends.
    I've wound up with nothing but
My three souls fading, fading,
My four limbs burning, burning,
My seven spirits moving away, away.
    It makes me
Lower my head in silence,
Tears—that are not just teardrops—flow.
(*Coda*)
The pulse in my two wrists diminishes to nothing, I am now beyond saving,
The one breath from my mouth does not return—so it is now the end.
I conclude that my spent life will not last long.
After I, this humble minister, have died—now any moment—
I don't hope for a burial mound on a high plain.
What need for the vain effort of a memorial mass,
Or reading and reciting the scriptures until hoarse?
Don't think that by these actions the souls of the dead will be spared anxiety.
My reward must be, My Lord and King, that you bestow rich benefice,
And keep in mind my deeds when I administered the state,
Then, when my funeral cortege goes out, meet it at the crossroads,
Ascend the Meridian Gate, and then, My Lord and King, gaze at my catafalque,

If Your Majesty has pity on me, this humble official,

Gaze from afar on my hearse and pour out a libation of a single cup of wine!

Exit.

[ACT 4]

EMPEROR *enters, opens. After he signals falling asleep,* [*you*], MALE LEAD, *enter, costumed as the sentient soul, and open*: Huo Shan and Huo Yu are going to revolt, I had better go and inform the Son of Heaven. *Ai*! The realm of the Overseer of Darkness is vastly different from the human world.—EXTRA, *after performing one scene, exits.—Wait until* EMPEROR *enters to open a second time.—Two* COMICS *explain their plans for one scene and exit.*

([SHUANGDIAO MODE] *Xin shuiling*)

Cold, chill, and gloomy, the wind flutters the pennant that summons back sentient souls,[45]

Yet I, because of this state [of Han]—my whole soul has yet to scatter.[46]

They raise on high the gauze-globed road shiner,

While lightly shaking the horse's cinch rings.[47]

I had better study

How to pile eggs carefully, how to cling to the railing,[48]

And then

Remonstrate with that humane and virtuous emperor and king of mine.

(*Zhuma ting*)

The night is still, the watch near midnight,

As I swirl up the ridge and climb the mountains, seek out the old passes leading home.

---

45. A banner used to summon the soul of the departed; it was hung on a long pole and carried by mourners garbed in funeral clothes at the front of the funeral procession.

46. The "whole soul" (*yi ling* 一靈) was made up of two souls: a corporeal element (*po* 魄) that returned to earth and a purely sentient part (*hun* 魂) that became spirit alone.

47. These two lines seem to refer to actions of the funeral cortege: the kenning "road shiner" (*zhaodao* 照道), which usually refers to the lamps leading a procession or a signal to give people a direction for travel, is perhaps here symbolically used to light the way in the afterworld. Clinking the horse's cinch rings may likewise represent some ritual during the procession.

48. "To pile eggs"—to approach a precarious situation. "To cling to the railing"—from the story of a certain Zhu Yun 朱雲, who wrote a memorial to Emperor Cheng of the Han requesting that the emperor execute one of his favorite ministers for malfeasance. The emperor ordered Zhu Yun executed, but when he was being hauled away from court, he clung to a railing and refused to go any further. He clung so tightly that the railing broke. Emperor Cheng, having the affair explained to him, not only pardoned Zhu Yun but also commanded that the railing in the palace be left broken as a reminder of Zhu's righteous remonstration.

Clouds gather away, fog disperses
As I enter Chang'an under this cloak of stars, this belt of the moon.
Before, when alive, I summoned my energy to protect these rivers and mountains,
And now, my allotted years finished, I will fulfill my honor in support of the fiery Han.
You watch me now,
Supporting the king or protecting the emperor, I'll neither shirk nor fear.

Act out entering the palace.—Do the action of standing behind the lamp and waiting until EMPEROR *acts out being deeply shaken—after he finishes speaking—speak*: I have frightened my master. I, your humble servant, am no malignant spirit.—*Wait until* EMPEROR *speaks.*

(*Yan'er luo*)
I, this humble servant,
Cannot form ranks with the court ministers,
Because my two souls are scattered by the wind.
An incident on the border will be brought up tomorrow,
And in the morning levee, you will hear righteous remonstrance.

Wait until EMPEROR *finishes speaking.*

(*Desheng ling*)
Tomorrow it will be a grand minister, in the cold of the fifth watch,[49]
Right now, it is me, at the third drum, before the watches are finished.

After EMPEROR *speaks.*

So you want
To banish me from these palace halls,
There's no
"Please stay behind my aged Mount Tai"?[50]
In the normalcy of days past
You treated me as if I were Yi Yin or Dan, the Duke of Zhou,
Yet today
You take me to be a malignant apparition, a ghostly demon.

MALE LEAD *speaks*: Your Majesty, someone is plotting rebellion!—EMPEROR *speaks.*

(*Yan'er luo*)
His Majesty says,
"From the east at Hangu Pass,
Westward to the Cloud-Climbing Trestle Way,[51]
Who is there to spy on me?
Who is there to lightly cross me?"

---

49. The period 3–5 A.M.
50. "Aged Mount Tai," a polite term for father-in-law.
51. The road to Sichuan, located west of the capital in Chang'an.

(*Gua yugou*)

Your Majesty.

Should be preparing against armor-clad generals crossing the passes in the night,
Instead you treat me, your minister, with no respect.

What I fear—

"It's too late to patch the boat when it's in the middle of the river!"
And you will see the Hundred Surnames mired in mud and muck.[52]
I
Am neither a military genius like Wu Zixu,[53]
Nor a civil minister to equal Dan, the Duke of Zhou,

O, how pitiful,

Our heaven and earth, conjoined from six directions,
And our rivers and hills that stretch on for ten thousand li.

[*Speak*]: Your Majesty, Huo Shan and Huo Yu are plotting revolt. Tomorrow they will request that my master go to their private residence. On the signal of striking a metal gong, they will disorder all under heaven. I have come especially to inform you, my master. *Exit.*

After EMPEROR *has indicated that it is dawn—after two* COMICS *are apprehended and enter—After* EMPEROR *makes his judgment and after sending him off with sacrifice.*

(*Luomei feng*)[54]

Nine branches of the clan exterminated, all the young slain,
The whole family decapitated, all the family wealth seized.
How pitiful: Twenty years of public service,
The moist, rich earth on his grave has yet to dry—

This was

"In the Palace of Receiving Sages' Wisdom, Huo Guang Remonstrates as a Ghost."

Dispersal Section

Title: In the walled city of Chang'an, Huo Shan plots rebellion,
In the district of Haihun, the deposed Prince of Changyi runs into trouble.

Name: In the Hall of Lasting Trust, Emperor Xuan assumes the throne,
In the Palace of Receiving Sages' Wisdom, Huo Guang Remonstrates as a Ghost.

In the Palace of Receiving Sages' Wisdom, Huo Guang Remonstrates as a Ghost, the end.

---

52. Literally, "mud and charcoal ash," a dangerous situation facing the citizens.
53. Wu Zixu (d. 484 BC) helped the King of Wu defeat Chu. For more detail on Wu, see chap. 4, n. 105.
54. We take it that Huo Guang, now offstage, would not sing this song. Since the song appears to be a summary of the play, we think that it may have been sung by the company as a whole.

3

Xue Rengui Returns Home Clad in Brocade

INTRODUCTION

Once the Sui dynasty (589–617) had reunified the Chinese world at the end of the sixth century, it also tried to extend its power into the Korean Peninsula. But whereas centuries earlier the Han dynasty (206 BC–AD 220) had been able to establish prefectures in what is now northern Korea, the Sui encountered stiff resistance from the Koguryo kingdom, which extended from modern-day northern Korea to the east banks of the Liao River in modern-day Manchuria. The three Korean campaigns of Emperor Yang of the Sui (r. 605–618), an archetypical "bad last ruler," are characterized by historiographers as dismal failures. Following the collapse of the Sui and the establishment of the Tang (618–906), the second and third rulers of that dynasty, Taizong (r. 627–649) and Gaozong (r. 650–683), once again waged war on Koguryo. During the reign of Taizong, the Koguryo court was dominated by Yŏn Kaesomun (Yuan Gesuwen 淵葛蘇文, d. 666), who sported the title of *mangniji* (*molizhi* 摩離支), roughly translatable as "commander of the army." As long as Yŏn was alive, the Chinese campaigns were inconclusive at best, and it was only following his death that the generals of Gaozong eventually succeeded in destroying Koguryo, after which its territory was taken over by Silla, one of the other states on the Korean Peninsula.

In the minds of later generations the memory of these campaigns came to focus on the seaborne invasion of Korea of 645 led by Taizong. In the Chinese tradition this invasion had been deliberately provoked by Koguryo's dictator of that time, and the campaign had ended in a proper Chinese victory, resulting in the execution of the evil dictator and the reestablishment of proper (and properly submissive) royal authority by a benevolent Taizong. The victory, however, had been hard-won, and Taizong had repeatedly been in danger of losing his life. On one occasion, as he had dreamt before setting out on the campaign, he was saved from danger in the nick of time by a soldier dressed all in white. This white-clad warrior was Xue Li 薛禮 (613–683), better known by his given name, Rengui 仁貴. In the continuous Chinese retellings of the Korean campaign, the war was increasingly reduced to a simple account of Xue's heroic exploits alone. In these later legendary tales the emperor learns Xue's name and his value only at the very end because Xue Rengui's jealous commander, Zhang Shigui 張士貴 (d. 656), claims all the merit for himself (and even attempts to murder Xue in order to maintain secrecy). The historical Xue Rengui did indeed serve with distinction in the Korean campaign and also later in the campaigns of the Tang in central Asia, at one moment awing the Sogdians into submission with his perfect archery:

> At that time the nine surnames [that is, the Sogdians] had a host of more than 100,000, and they sent out ten light-horse cavalry to initiate the attack. Rengui shot three arrows that immediately killed three men. At this point the bravery of the caitiffs quailed and they all surrendered. Rengui anticipated that this would result in problems later and buried them all, immediately turning his attention to subduing the remaining host in the Northern Barrens [the Mongolian steppe], where he captured three brothers of the False Yabghu Turks and returned. In the army they sang,
>
> With three arrows the General settled the Heavenly Mountains,
> With long songs the brave soldiers come back through the passes to Han.
>
> Consequently, the Sogdians went into decline.[1]

The saga of Xue Rengui must have been extremely popular in the vernacular literature of the thirteenth to fifteenth centuries. One long prose account of Taizong's Korean campaign and Xue Rengui's stellar contribution to it was preserved in manuscript in the *Yongle dadian* 永樂大典—a huge compendium presented to the throne in 1407—as *A Brief Account of Xue Rengui's Subjugation of Korea* (*Xue Rengui zheng Liao shilüe* 薛仁貴征遼事略).[2] A prosimetric rendition of the legend, focusing more exclusively on the exploits of Xue Rengui and titled *Newly Cut, Completely Illustrated: The Story of How Xue Rengui of the Tang Crossed the Sea and Subjugated Korea* (*Xinkan quanxiang Xue Rengui kuahai zheng Liao gushi* 新刊全相唐薛仁貴跨海征遼故事), has been preserved in a printing from the Chenghua period (1465–1487).[3] Both these texts, however, may well have been composed at a much earlier date. The story was also adapted for the stage by Zhang Guobin 張國賓 of the late thirteenth century. Zhang Guobin held a position in

1. See Ouyang and Song 1975, vol. 10, chap. 111, 4141.
2. See Zhao Wanli 1957.
3. See Anon. 1979.

the Court Entertainment Bureau. He was most likely an actor who wrote plays for performance at the imperial palace in Dadu (the capital of the Mongol Yuan dynasty at the site of Beijing). The earliest catalogues of *zaju* credit him with four titles, of which two have survived.

Since Zhang Guobin refers to Xue Rengui as the "General Clad in White" in the first line of the full title of his play ("The General Clad in White: At Court His Blessings Are Hidden" 白袍將朝中隱福), he certainly knew the tale of Xue Rengui's military service in Korea as told in the prose account or the prosimetric version. But he does not deal with these battle scenes. All he presents of Xue's military career is, in act 1, the culminating moment: the final confrontation of Xue Rengui and Zhang Shigui in front of Emperor Taizong that was adjudicated by High Minister Du Ruhui 杜如晦 (585–630).[4] This is then followed in act 2 by a dream visit of Xue Rengui to his hometown, which alerts him to the poverty of his parents. When, in act 3, he arrives in his hometown, a boyhood friend, before he recognizes Xue, roundly curses him for his lack of filial piety. Act 4 is devoted to Xue Rengui's glorious homecoming. His parents, too, do not recognize him at first and are scared out of their wits when they learn their son has married the emperor's daughter. When the newlywed couple bows to the old man and his wife, the old man collapses on the floor, but he is picked up by Xue Rengui's servants and carried in a procession to a new mansion.

Zhang Guobin's play is a regular *zaju*, consisting of a wedge and four acts. The text as it has been preserved in a fourteenth-century printing is a typical male role text, and as such is very complete. All arias are sung by the leading male, who plays the part of Du Ruhui in act 1; that of Xue Rengui's father, Old Uncle Xue, in the wedge and act 2; that of Xue Rengui's boyhood friend in act 3; and that of his father once again in act 4. The wedge and each of the first three acts are indicated in the text by printing the final stage direction, "Exit," in a smaller size immediately following the last words of the last arias. In the arias, the "padding words"—extrametrical phrases (*chenzi* 襯字)—are indicated by printing them in somewhat smaller size than the other words of the aria.

Actors in Kaifeng of the first quarter of the twelfth century, we know, amused their urban audiences by making fun of country folks in skits called *zaban* (雜扮 or 雜班). Zhang Guobin's play was probably written very much in that tradition and may well be one of our best sources to suggest what those earlier skits may have looked like. The confrontation of a local peasant who has stayed in the village with his boyhood friend who has moved away and made a career (here reenacted in act 3) is best known from a song set by Ju Jingchen 睢景臣 (ca 1275–1320), "The Exalted Ancestor Returns to His Home Village" (Gaozu huanxiang 高祖還鄉), which describes Liu Bang's famous visit

4. Du Ruhui was one of the high ministers in the early years of the Tang dynasty.

to his hometown after he had become the emperor of the Han. The song tells the story as observed through the eyes of a fellow villager who realizes that this high and mighty lord is none else than the good-for-nothing Liu Bang, who still owes him money! Xue Rengui's first visit back to his home village as a common soldier in act 2 is also reminiscent of chapter 11 of the *Liu Zhiyuan in All Keys and Modes* (*Liu Zhiyuan zhugongdiao* 劉知遠諸宮調), in which Liu Zhiyuan, a former farmhand and now a provincial governor, tests the loyalty of his wife—whose rich brothers had chased him away—by visiting the village as a common soldier. Finally, Xue Rengui's final homecoming shows some similarity with the scene in the ballad story on the youth and early career of Judge Bao, in which yamen runners come and ask Bao's father for Magistrate Bao. But his father believes that his son is simply a dimwit who has disappeared.

The relations between father and son are put into the foreground in the play. The story focuses on the underside of the pursuit of fame and glory. Xue Rengui is very much portrayed as the typical unfilial son who refuses to provide for his parents and runs away from home at first opportunity to join the army. He simply leaves his elderly parents to fend for themselves—with terrible consequences. In many parallel situations, this conflict between filial piety and personal ambition (or more positively phrased, loyalty to the ruler) would have been mitigated by providing the hero with a devoted wife, who stays at home and promises to take care of her husband's parents, which she will do whatever the price to herself. Sources from as early as the eleventh century provided Xue Rengui with such a supportive wife, who actually urges her husband to grasp the unique opportunity of the Korean campaign to make a career. The ultimate virtue of such a wife in many stories and plays would then be further underlined by showing that she lacks any jealousy when her husband eventually returns in the company of a highborn trophy wife (the latter eagerly cedes the first position in the marriage to the original wife, and the two women promise to treat each other like sisters, although this was technically illegal). Two later court plays on the career of Xue Rengui from the early Ming indeed highlight the role of Xue Rengui's wife, stressing that filial piety to one's parents and loyalty to one's ruler do not have to be in conflict but can exist side by side. One is therefore tempted to conclude that Zhang Guobin ignored the existence of Xue Rengui's wife on purpose in order to achieve his own vision. It also gave him an opportunity to provide the play with an original and hilarious ending.

Under a slightly different title a heavily edited version of Zhang Guobin's play has also been preserved in Zang Maoxun's *Selection of Yuan Plays*. Zang Maoxun most likely based his edition on a palace version. It is now impossible to say which of the changes are due to the palace actors and their censors and which are due to Zang himself. In this version from the early seventeenth century, Xue's parents and wife warmly support his departure for the army, and his wife promises she will take good care of his parents during his absence. In the first act the role of the emperor, in line with the Ming-dynasty prohibition of the portrayal of any emperor onstage, has been removed. Taizong has been replaced by one of his high ministers, who later also becomes Rengui's father-in-law. Whereas the arias by Zhang Guobin are extremely colloquial and almost free of literary allusions, in the *Selection of Yuan Plays* edition, the language of the songs is more literary, and some songs are laden with allusions. As is common in palace editions, the number of arias in each act has been reduced, and each of the roles in the play has extensive dialogue. While the action in the second and third acts remains largely the same, the version in *Yuanqu xuan* has a completely new final act. Since Xue Rengui's first wife was already introduced in the wedge, we now have a highly conventional conclusion in which the two wives become best of friends.[5] While the *Yuanqu xuan* version of the play is still in many ways a quite enjoyable work, it lacks the freshness of Zhang Guobin's composition and exhibits a much more mainstream Confucian morality.

The legend of Xue Rengui would remain popular throughout the Ming and Qing dynasties. The story would be written up as a novel, best known as *Xue Rengui Subdues the East* (*Xue Rengui zhengdong* 薛仁貴征東), which would be followed by novels on the martial exploits of his sons and grandsons, which appeared under titles such as *Xue Dingshan Subdues the West* (*Xue Dingshan zhengxi* 薛定山征西) and *Xue Gang Revolts Against the Tang* (*Xue Gang fan Tang* 薛剛反唐). Some of the stories from these novels would also enjoy a great popularity on the Peking opera stage.

SUGGESTED READINGS

Crump 1972; Crump and Dolezelová-Velingerová 1971; Hsia 1974; Idema 1990b, 2007b, 2010b; McLaren 1998, Shu 2008; Twitchett 1979, Wang 2008, Yen 1970.

5. No mention of her presence is made in the intervening acts.

A NEWLY CUT FULL TEXT: *XUE RENGUI RETURNS HOME CLAD IN BROCADE*, WITH THE COMPLETE PROMPTS, A FOURTEENTH-CENTURY EDITION

DRAMATIS PERSONAE IN ORDER OF APPEARANCE

Role type	*Name and family, institutional, or social role*
EMPEROR	EMPEROR TAIZONG of the Tang
VILLAIN	ZHANG SHIGUI
EXTRA MALE	XUE RENGUI
MALE LEAD	XUE DABO, XUE RENGUI's father, elderly peasant (wedge, acts 2, 4)
OLD FEMALE	MOTHER XUE
MALE LEAD	DU RUHUI (act 1)
COMIC	CONSTABLE
MALE LEAD	BAHE, rustic villager, XUE RENGUI's childhood friend (act 3)
EXTRA MALES	XUE RENGUI's entourage

✤ ✤ ✤

[WEDGE]

The EMPEROR *enters and opens—when that one scene is done—the* VILLAIN *enters for one scene—the* EXTRA MALE *for one scene—You, the* MALE LEAD, *and the* OLD FEMALE *enter—open*: I am registered as an inhabitant of Longmen Township in Jiangzhou. For generations we have devoted ourselves to agriculture. My surname is Xue, and because I am advanced in years, the common people all simply call me Old Uncle Xue. My family consists of three persons. I have a son called Xue Rengui. From his youngest years he refused to work on the farm. He loved only to twirl the lance and use the cudgel, and he has completely mastered all eighteen of the martial arts. He just heard that the state will conduct a campaign across the sea against the Liao and is recruiting volunteers to fill the ranks, so he is going to join the army! Alas, what can I do about this? My son, how cruel you are, abandoning the two of us to join the army so far away! *After the* EXTRA MALE *speaks—the* MALE LEAD *speaks*: My son, if your heart is gone already, I'm afraid I cannot hold you back. So go if you must, but come back home as soon as possible, whether you obtain an office or not!

([XIANLÜ MODE:] *Duanzheng hao*)
Today you
Leave your farming village,
Depart from your hometown,
And bid adieu to
Your aged parents
Because you want
To risk your life on the battlefield.
Awe imposing,
Full of vigor and pluck:
An imposing body,
A terrifying physique!
On the front line,
On the battlefield,
You'll wear battle dress,
And hold sword and lance.
When you have achieved merit,
And displayed your lofty power,
At that very moment
Come home quickly!
My son,
Don't let the two of us each and every day
Lean on the gate and wait with eager eyes for nothing!
Exit.[6]

[ACT 1]

The EMPEROR *enters and opens for one scene—the* EXTRA MALE *enters for one scene—the* VILLAIN *enters and speaks—after the* VILLAIN *and the* EXTRA MALE *have disputed each other's merits—the* EMPEROR *enters, opens, and stops—after he has ordered an imperial proclamation to be read—the* MALE LEAD *enters dressed as* DU RUHUI*—and opens*: I am Du Ruhui, and I serve as counselor for the military command. I am in charge of the registers of merit. His Majesty has summoned me by OO [Sagely Direction][7] to establish the merits of the various generals. The mutual

6. In this text the stage directions are printed in regular-size characters, and they are (usually) separated from each other and from dialogue and song by open spaces. The "exit" at the end of this wedge and at the end of each act is written immediately following the last word of the preceding song and in smaller size and flush right in the line.

7. See chap. 2, n. 21.

accusations this time around are quite extraordinary! I will go according to the guile of each!

([XIANLÜ MODE:] *Dian jiangchun*)

Just like

A hungry tiger blocking the road:
Who dares "walk the streets of Chang'an"?

He just desires

"To hate the purple and seize the vermilion,"[8]
And stubbornly refuses to recommend capable men.[9]

(*Hunjiang long*)

A murder may be forgiven,
But who dares mess up another man's merits?
You just want to contrive plans to have tigers lie in wait,
Use beheading or slowly slicing[10] as a resourceful strategy.

You just say,

"A general noble and bold, awe-inspiring on all eight sides,"
But the Son of Heaven, enlightened as a sage, is supported by the hundred gods!
Let me straighten my gauze gown,
Put on my formal headdress,
Buckle my golden belt,
Grasp my ivory tablet,
And quickly hurry to the jasper steps.
I will establish merit and blame,
And distinguish between true and false.

After performing the rites of greeting the EMPEROR*—after the* EMPEROR *speaks—after the* EXTRA MALE *and the* VILLAIN *have spoken:*

(*You hulu*)

Facing this humane and sagely lord who created the empire and laid the foundations,
With his civil officials and military officers on both sides,

They both claim

The three shots that pacified the Heavenly Mountains—neither submits!
There is no need, General, to fight over the registers of merit—

8. Originally a phrase meaning to hate that the upright have been replaced by the deviant, it later came to mean exactly the opposite, "hated purple has replaced vermilion." Here, to take what is not rightfully his. The original quote is from *Analects* 17.18, "The Master said, 'I hate that purple has usurped the place of vermilion, that the tunes of Zheng have been confused with classical music, and that the clever of tongue are undermining both state and clan.'" See Slingerland 2003, 207.

9. This is speaking about Zhang Shigui.

10. Use capital punishments.

Just be like
A phoenix bird alighting on a *wutong* tree.[11]
Other people may have accomplished ten great merits,
He doesn't even have an inch![12]
He just wants to release the eagle to grab roe deer or hares on the level plain,
And is unwilling to fish out the giant turtle from the deep blue sea!
(*Tianxia le*)
Don't be
A real man, a stalwart hero for nothing—
I have no selfish desire
To give you a handsome appointment.
You do not know the books of Lü Wang about the six *ren* days avoiding *jia*,[13]
And yet you want
To lead the Bureau of Military Affairs,
Head the Office of Commander in Chief—
But have
Men without merit ever received a salary?

After the EXTRA MALE *and the* VILLAIN *have spoken—after the* EMPEROR *speaks—*

speak: I know what's on your minds!
(*Jinzhan'er*)
One of them
Holds on to his crafty schemes;
The other
Relies on the *Hidden Correspondences*;[14]

---

11. The phoenix will eat only the purest of sustenance and not compete with other birds for unclean food like "rotten mice." In other words, Zhang Shigui as a general should not fight with a common soldier such as Xue Rengui over merit.

12. Despite the change from the second-person pronoun to the third-person pronoun these two lines would appear to refer to Zhang Shigui, just like the preceding two lines. The change in the use of personal pronoun may indicate that in the preceding lines Du Ruhui was trying to argue with Zhang Shigui but now has turned away from him in desperation and voices his personal opinion of the man.

13. Lü Wang 呂望, also known as Lü Shang 呂尚, Jiang Shang 姜尚, Jiang Taigong 姜太公, or Jiang Ziya 姜子牙, was a hermit who spent his days angling until he was brought to court at the age of seventy by King Wen of Zhou. At age eighty, Lü Wang assisted King Wu in his conquest of the Shang and establishment of the Zhou dynasty. The six *ren* are the six *ren* days in a sexagenary cycle. This was a prognostication procedure for auguring fortune on the battlefield. In the ten heavenly branches, *jia*, *yi*, *bing*, *ding*, *xu*, *ji*, *geng*, *xin*, *ren*, and *gui*, the last two are attached to "water" among the Five Phases (water, fire, wood, metal, and earth). *Ren* is active (yang) water and *gui* is passive (yin) water, so *ren* is the preferred sign. Since there are six *ren* cycles in a sixty-day cycle, they represent auspicious days. Two bowls are used, one inscribed with the ten heavenly stems, the other with the twelve earthly branches; heaven is placed on top and rotated, and the resulting cyclical signs determine auspicious times to move. "Escaping the *jia*" (*dunjia* 遁甲) ("following the *jia*," *xunjia* 循甲, in some readings) is another method of prognostication, in which one avoids yin combinations of the cycle of sixty as days on which to act.

14. A work of military strategy attributed to Lü Wang.

One of them
Wants to display love and righteousness;
The other
Defies all authority,
And we want them to sign together to be in charge of military supplies!
Have you not heard, Your Majesty,
"Those who are close will always be so;
Those who are distant will remain so"?
The two of them,
Wise and stupid, cannot live together,
Like fire and water cannot share one stove!

After the EXTRA MALE *and the* COMIC *have spoken—the* EMPEROR *speaks—[sing:]*
(*Zui fu gui*)
The Son of Heaven
Has me head the Executive Office, I receive his salary,
So I should
Effect the Kingly Way, transform customs and morals.
You must have heard:
"If you raise up the crooked and apply them to the straight, the people will never submit,"[15]
So let the two of them
Here in front of the palace determine winner and loser.
After the EMPEROR *speaks*:
He who wins will serve his lord at court in a glorious position;
He who loses will have to hoe and dig in the deepest mountains.

After the EMPEROR *has spoken—after the* EXTRA MALE *and the* VILLAIN *have spoken*:
(*Yi wangsun*)
Xue Rengui as a gentleman is certain about where to begin;
Zhang Shigui as a scoundrel finds out his gallbladder is completely empty.[16]
The first immediately assents to the proposal;
The second is only mumbling and grumbling.
Xue Rengui is secretly pleased,
But Zhang Shigui, like a centipede on a hot spot—no escape.

---

15. *Analects* 2.19; see Slingerland 2003, 14; here slightly changed in its intent, "If you raise up the crooked and wrong the upright, the people will never submit."

16. That is, Xue understands the proper rituals concerning archery. The gallbladder was believed to be the seat of courage.

The EMPEROR *speaks—after shooting at the target*:

(*Zui fu gui*)

Xue Rengui's arrow, loosed, swerves not the slightest,
His technique is out of the ordinary.
Zhang Shigui
Pulls a stiff bow, comes near the target but is nothing special.
Xue Rengui's
Arrow—*clink*—sticks fast in the eye of a coin.
Zhang Shigui
Pulls the string full and looses the whistling arrow:
That arrow lands thirty paces from the target!

After ZHANG SHIGUI *speaks*:*—after the* EMPEROR *speaks*:

(*Nezha ling*)

Under protection of the Sagely Son of Heaven
Who possesses great blessings equal to Heaven
I have been ordered to provide a full account of all merits.
You, General Xue Rengui—
Listen as I appoint you caitiff slayer.
But this other general: no matter where his horse goes,
He finds no gateway to his goal—
Is it not said, "Heaven's justice always wins"![17]

(*Que tazhi*)

The [Koguryo]
Wanted to settle their plans and schemes,
To show who would be victorious.
Under the protection
Of the sagely and enlightened Son of Heaven,
And the concerted assistance of the hundred gods,
You slew them until their last men were driven before and pursued from behind,
Chasing them on until not a single one was left!

After the EMPEROR *speaks*:*—speak*: Your Majesty, no need to say so.

(*Jinzhan'er*)

We have revealed winner and loser,
Determined glory and shame.
What is rewarded is done on the basis of each general's merit:
One

17. Understanding the phrase *tianli he ru* 天理何如 in this context as the second half of the phrase *qi yu renxin tianli he ru* 其於人心, 天理何如, "What is heaven's will compared with the desires of men?" This is spoken in reference to Zhang Shigui.

Will be stripped of his office, deprived of his rank;
The other
Will attach the golden fish to his jade belt.
Zhang Shigui,
Fill your belly from a twenty-acre farm,[18]
A farmhand with a single hoe.
Xue Rengui, will you not thank him, He who grants this favor?
You take these twelve lances to array in front of your gate,
And these paintings of "Eight Pepper" for your door.[19]

After the EXTRA MALE *expresses his gratitude for the imperial grace:*

(Zhuansha Coda)

His Majesty wants
To repay you for the red of the blood that stains your battle dress,
For the green of your army boots dyed by weeds.
Your single
Heavenlike lance surpasses past and present.
Just look at Zhang Shigui—
His face looks as gray as ashes;
His theft of merit was an infraction of Heaven's justice.
[Our Emperor] dominates this august metropole,
And the four seas are without a worry,
Thanks to this
Strong imperial abode of a hundred and two mountains and rivers.
Because you ordered the wind and called forth the rain,
He grasped the clouds and arrested the mists,
But without me, how could you get
This one letter of appointment from the Son of Heaven?
Exit.

18. Ning 1988, 2:3, has altered the original text here—*Bao zhuang sanqing di, /fushou yizhang chu* 飽莊三頃地, / 伕手一張鋤—to *Baozhong sanqing di, /fushou yizhang chu* 刨種三頃地, / 扶手一張鋤, which would change the meaning to "take this twenty acres on which to plant your seeds / Support your hands on a single hoe." Unfortunately, Ning's reading would remove the parallelism of the lines. We have followed the original text.

19. In legend, "Eight Pepper" (Bajiao 八椒) is the eighth son of the dragon and is something like a freshwater snail, because it seals up its mouth like a snail does. Because of this peculiar quality, the term "pattern of eight *jiao*" (*bajiao tu* 八椒圖) or simply "pepper pattern" (*jiaotu* 椒圖) became attached to the creatures that hold the ring on a door pull, probably from the idea that they will not open their mouths to release the ring. The pattern itself is a whirl of small spirals that crown the heads of the animals and look like small snails.

[ACT 2]

After the EMPEROR speaks—the EXTRA MALE acts out knocking on the gate in a dream—the MALE LEAD, dressed as an ELDERLY PEASANT, and the OLD FEMALE enter:

([SHANGDIAO MODE:] *Ji xianbin*)

I hear someone
Repeatedly calling my name, "Old Uncle Xue"!
Heaven,
Who is that little good-for-nothing who is pestering me?
I cannot stand on my feet,
As I bend forward and backward;
I cannot walk on my own,
Swaying to the east and the west.
I am so bent by age that my body has wasted away to nothing,
I am so racked by sorrow that my hair has turned right to gray.
Where is my son who has gone off to become a soldier?
Even a man with an iron head would be moved to sad sighs![20]
Failing to become
Commander in chief of the six armies,
Probably all you achieved
Was a nailed-up sign, "From foreign parts."[21]

(*Xiaoyao le*)

Because you, my son, had to travel to foreign lands,
I've been bereft of all energy, robbed of all strength;
And my two souls have scattered.
My son,
Out there you are scorched by sun, scourged by the wind;
Most likely you're blinded by dust and buried by sand on the battlefield.
How I hoped you'd establish merit with one shot and change our status,
That you'd glorify the ancestors of the Xue family!
But you have left me without kith, without kin,
Without support, without assistance,
Without rice and without firewood.

20. An obvious pun on the expected phrase, "Even a man with an iron heart will be moved."

21. The sign on the grave of someone who died and was buried far away from home.

After the OLD FEMALE[22] *speaks*:

(*Wuye'er*)

When Bodhisattva, the daughter of Old Master Liu,
Took in Wang Two from our village as her husband,
All relatives and kin were told to put a pin in her hair,
But when she came to me, she was not allowed to bow.
And then when I asked what the reason might be,
One single sentence made tears run down my cheeks.[23]

My son, Xue Rengui,

Because of you your father and mother are at a loss!

After the OLD FEMALE *speaks*:

(*Gua jinsuo*)

It must be

Because of my earlier karma in an earlier life,
That I owed you an archenemy's[24] debt!
This longing day after day, morning after morning,
Has ruined your father and mother!

My son! Xue Rengui! Where are you?

If you would sneak back to this village,
The smile on my face would squeeze a line right through my cheeks.

But failing to see you, my son,

Makes me cry all the way out the door.

After the EXTRA MALE *speaks:—after the* OLD FEMALE *speaks*:

(*Houting hua*)

A clean break:[25]

Once you got going, you didn't think twice;
You followed your whim in a hundred, a thousand ways.
You joined the army at the age of twenty-two,

How come

You show up precisely at thirty-three?
On that day when you left home to set out on "those purple paths,"
You displayed your heroic might in Carmine City.[26]

---

22. The original has here "official" role type (*gu* 孤) rather than "old female." We have emended it following Ning 1988,2:11.
23. Elders with children were believed to bring luck to the bride; to be childless was considered unlucky.
24. The word "archenemy" is often used for "lover," but here the old man uses it in reference to his son. The term designates a person to whom one is tied by karma from a former life.
25. Following Ning 1988, 2:12, emending *he jiu le* 合旧子 to *geshe le* 割舍了.
26. Jiangzhou 絳州, here translated literally to capture the play on color words. "Purple paths" are the roads in the outskirts of a city.

By joining the militia and manifesting your skills,
You hoped to change the status of our family—
Who could have ever expected it would be more than ten years!
(*Liuye'er*)
I was just wondering where my son might be,
Who could have imagined
You would "advance a thousand ranks every day"![27]
He
Bows in the dust, extending his legs and stretching his waist.
Let me forgive you for the moment,
I only thought you "had left to deliver a lampstand,"[28]
But once you had left, you came right back!

After the EXTRA MALE *speaks*:

(*Cu hulu*)
You don't have
To "knead like a cake,"[29]
To guess like a riddle:
I have assembled my fortune by moving booze and carrying water.
Flattened-out old woks served as sturdy "bottoms" for the ends of my carrying pole,
And so I have acquired this great fortune of two pieces,
Which, if you got them, would bring you only disaster.

After the EXTRA MALE *speaks*:

(*Reprise*)
My wife,
Run and buy some wine,
Hurry and kill the pig!
Go to the shop and pawn your old hemp shoes!
You're afraid Xue Rengui has a capacity for drink like the ocean,
But below the bed we still have five pints of buckwheat.
I have to laugh so much that spittle soaks my chin!

After the COMIC *has entered to arrest the* EXTRA MALE:

(*Reprise*)
Seeing him so dreadfully and anxiously open the imperial edict,
Scares me so my face turns a parched yellow.

---

27. This sentence is clearly intended ironically.

28. That is, that he had left for good; from the common saying "Old Zhao went to deliver a lamp stand; once gone, he never returned" 趙老送燈台，一去更不來.

29. "To knead" also has the meaning "to guess."

I see some
Oh-so-vicious constables line up on both sides.
I beg you, this Guanshiyin from south of the southern sea who saves us from suffering,[30]
I kowtow to you and make my bow:
Set my son free and that good deed surpasses a meal for a myriad of monks!

After [soldiers] have entered and arrested the EXTRA MALE:

(*Langlilai Coda*)
Rough and rude they push my son out through the village gate,
Brutal and bloodthirsty, they want to kill him.
What I see ahead: agony and pain—his corpse stretched out in a pool of blood—
How can he wriggle his way out of the hempen rope tied behind his back?
The only way in which your miserable life can survive,
My son,
Would be if a writ of pardon came swirling down from highest heaven!
Exit.

After they have exited, pushing the EXTRA MALE *off*—[31]

30. The bodhisattva Guanyin (or Guanshiyin) is one of the most widely venerated deities of East Asia. In China, one of her main pilgrimage sites was Putuoshan, a small island off the Ningbo coast. Guanyin as she manifested herself on Putuoshan was venerated as Guanyin of the Southern Sea.

31. This passage provides an excellent example of how little the concept of "act" comes into play in Yuan editions that are designed as role texts. After the last aria, we have a stage direction placed at the end of the aria in smaller font that is a simple imperative, "exit" (*xia* 下). This is then followed by a sequence of stage directions concerning the other actors with aspect markers ("After . . .") before the next imperative ("You enter . . . and speak" [*Shang yun* 上云]). The first of these stage directions, "pushing the extra off," concludes the scene of the arrest; the second ("after the emperor enters and opens") begins a new scene in which Xue Rengui narrates his dream to the emperor and is allowed to return home ("announces the decree") and then thanks the emperor for his grace ("after extra male speaks"). The next imperative is directed again to the male lead. Thus, there is no clear act division, only a series of actions that the male lead must pay attention to as he rests (and, as in this case, changes costume) offstage after being carried off by soldiers. This is, thus, a clear example of the fact that these stage directions are meant for the male lead only (the imperatives) and that act divisions are arbitrary and further that scenes intervening between musical suites are merely consecutive entrances and exits conceived of as independent scenes that do not necessarily stop or start where a later editor makes an act.

[ACT 3]

After the EMPEROR *enters and opens—after he has ordered the* EXTRA MALE *by decree to return to his hometown—after the* EXTRA MALE *speaks—You, the* MALE LEAD, *enter dressed as an* ELDERLY PEASANT *and speak—shout*: Bangu'er,[32] you're drunk! Wait for me!

([ZHONGLÜ MODE:] *Fendie'er*)

The annual seasons have turned to the Cold Food Festival:
Each family goes to the graves to prepare![33]
They have stewed and fried some food to offer in sacrifice:
Some vegetable-stuffed steamed buns;
Noodles dribbled through a sieve,
Chicken, shoats, dog, and swine.
Who knows what the fuck she has been up to—
She's drunk so much she really kills the mood!

(*Zui chunfeng*)

You have lost your paktong[34] hairpin,
So your oiled bun droops to one side.
Now, there are drunk wives aplenty at the grave sites,
But none as drunk as you,
As you,
As you!
You've drunk so much you reel from east to west,
Bend backward and forward.
  You've quaffed so much
You're puking up heaven and earth!

After FEMALE *has become drunk*:

(*Chao tianzi*)

  Every day
Now here,
Now there,

32. Bangu (伴姑) is a conventional stage name for a young peasant woman, here perhaps used ironically for his old wife. The term is often used for a daughter, the mate to the term for a young son, Bange (伴哥), which is used in the *Selection of Yuan Plays* edition of this play.

33. The Cold Food Festival was celebrated on the 105th day following the winter solstice. During this period in the third month of spring one was not allowed to light a fire for three days. In the late imperial period Cold Food became increasingly identified with Qingming (Clear and Bright), which was celebrated on the third day of the third month. On this day families would visit the graves of the ancestors to clean and repair the graves, offer sacrifice to the ancestors, and have a picnic in the open air.

34. An alloy of tin and lead used in soldering. Traditionally also used as a cheap substitute for silver.

You drink until you're drunk as a skunk.
The old sayings and modern proverbs have it right:
In truth,
"Wine is cheap, but yellow mud[35] expensive."
I'll go over here,
And grab her tightly.
She is a woman without reason!
I'm man enough to curse you,
And man enough to give you a beating,
Give you a beating for being drunk and drunk again!
(*Shi'er yue*)[36]
 You
Pinch and twist my face,
 I
Hold you by your sleeve.
You don't try to spin flax or weave cloth,
But throw down the shuttle, tip over the loom;
 You don't try
To be pure and honest,
 You only want
To share your cups and pass the pot.
[(*Yaomin ge*)]
In the whole city there is no one worse than you!
When I die, you can stop bringing winter clothes.[37]
And climb that green hill to turn into a husband-watching rock[38]—
Don't do anything more for this old fellow.
Damn,
These women and wives
Only want to be drunk as skunks every day!

---

35. Used to seal a jug of wine.

36. In the original the tune title given here is *Yaomin ge*, and what we have marked here *Shi'er yue* and *Yaomin ge* are one song under the latter title. We are following the emendations proposed in Ning 1988, 13, which is based on Zang Maoxun's emendations in *A Selection of Yuan Plays*.

37. The tale of Meng Jiangnü 孟姜女 is one of the most popular themes in Chinese popular literature. During the reign of the cruel First Emperor of the Qin dynasty, Meng Jiang's husband was drafted to work on the construction of the Great Wall. When winter approached, Meng Jiang made the long and arduous trek from her hometown to the northern border to take her husband winter clothes. When she arrived at the work site, she learned that her husband had died from exhaustion and that his remains had been buried in the Great Wall. She wept by the side of the wall until it collapsed on the spot where her husband had been buried. In this way, she became a model of wifely devotion. See Lee 2005 and Idema 2008.

38. Many places in China claim that a local rock is the transformation of a faithful wife who, long ago, when her husband failed to return from a trip, climbed a hill each day to watch for his return—until she turned to stone.

After the EXTRA MALE *has entered with his party and spoken—act out being frightened*:

(*Shang xiaolou*)
I see people talking,
I hear horses whinnying,
As they come towards me.
I'm so frightened I'm shaking all over,
I'm swaying and unsteady,
My spirit scatters, my souls fly away.
Here; there; nowhere to hide,
So I can only
Kneel, *kerplonk*, right in front of the horse.

After the EXTRA MALE *speaks*:

(*Reprise*)
It's just
That frown on your brow,
And your pursed lips—
It's all quite different from your behavior earlier,
All boorish and ill behaved—
But if we little ones misspeak only as little as a hair's breadth,
Our bodies
Will not be given a burial upon death.[39]

After the EXTRA MALE *speaks*:

(*Manting fang*)
It's not that
I make all kinds of excuses,
I only fear
My words will not come out right,
Or what I say will be at odds with you.
Here in Longmen Township
We have supplied corvée labor for generations,
But our strength is limited, our manpower small.
My uncle has a deformed shin and he limps,
My father is old and weak and handicapped.
I fear my duties and tasks—
In my township everybody knows:
Whatever it is you want me to do, I'll go along.

---

39. That is, as soon as we little people displease those in power, we will be punished in a most cruel way.

After the EXTRA MALE *speaks*: I know that Xue Rengui!

(*Kuaihuo san*)

The two of us—

Out on the threshing ground we stripped ears of grain,
And from the tops of trees plucked green plums.
Facing backward we rode on the black oxen, playing the Tibetan flute,
And stole fresh melons to eat, rind and all!

(*Hong shaoyao*)

The two of us

Have been friends since our earliest days,
And ran around together, everywhere.

From his youngest days

He fervently trained with lance and with staff,

Unwilling

To pull the harrow or steer the plow.
He indeed rejected the farmer's life
To practice the military arts.
He became the champion of each band or group.
Give him a bow and arrows, and he could shoot;
Give him a broken-down nag, and he could ride it

Without having to use

Either horsewhip or spurs.

(*Baolao'er*)

A golden-coin-spotted leopard's tail hanging down from the top
Of the painted shaft of the squared-heaven lance he employed;

Later

He became the best of the volunteers,
To the great pleasure of Commander Zhang Shigui!

He wanted to

Campaign in the south, pacify the north,
Root them out in the west, stamp them out in the east,
And kill every opponent who stood against him.
He could do it all: twirl a lance, use a sword,
Grab the men and arrest the officers,
Snatch their drums and steal their banners.

(*Shaobian*)

For sure, as a man he made a career for himself,
But he didn't treat his parents like Heaven and Earth.
The two of them are really wasted and exhausted,
They are so worn they are bent and crooked and their heads hang low.
When in this village

Shan Sa, Niu Biao, Bange, and Wang Liu[40]
Mention him, they heave a heavy sigh.
Raising children is for providing for one's old age—
He at present rides in the saddle and burdens his horse,
To obtain preferred appointments for his sons and ennoble his wife.
The only way sons and daughters can repay their own parents' great favors
Is by
Carrying their father and mother on their shoulders,[41] reciting "Amituofo."
May that scoundrel die quickly and have a tardy rebirth,[42]
May he be dumped in a ditch or thrown into a pit!
On his final exit,
I am sure, he will be seated on a donkey of wood.[43]

After the EXTRA MALE *speaks*:

(*Shuahai'er*)
His parents suffer bitterly but he enjoys riches and glory,
Of course he'll be struck by a thunderbolt in high summer![44]

After the EXTRA MALE *has asked a question—speak*: I would recognize Xue Rengui, but . . . *After the* EXTRA MALE *speaks again*:

Well you are plumper and fatter than in those days,
And have grown a moustache that covers your lips.
Don't take offense at the words I maligned you with just now—
It's because so much time has passed that I couldn't recognize you.
You on your horse, so high and mighty,
You must remember
How we raced up the trees to grope doves,[45]
And competed to move the roller![46]

---

40. These four names are all conventional names onstage of country folks.
41. See *Fumu en zhong jing* 父母恩中經 (*Sutra on the Great Favors of Our Parents*): "Even if someone would carry his father on his left shoulder and his mother on his right shoulder and the skin was ground away to the bone and the bone was pierced to the marrow and he walked around Mount Sumeru for a hundred thousand kalpas while blood flowed down and immersed his ankles, he still would not be able to repay the great favors of his father and mother."
42. That is, may he suffer for a long time in hell before being reborn.
43. Criminals who had been condemned to death were taken from prison to the execution grounds riding a wooden donkey.
44. It was widely believed that the thunder gods executed unfilial sons by striking them with their thunderbolts. Emending *bude* 不的 to *shaobude* 少不得, following Ning 1988, 2:14.
45. "Groping doves" probably means groping under a dove on her nest in order to steal the eggs.
46. Emending *liuzhou* 六軸 to *liuzhou* 碌軸, following Ning 1988, 2:14. The roller is a heavy tree trunk used to crush grain or flatten earth.

After the EXTRA MALE *has asked a question*:

(*Five from Coda*)

Your mother is approaching seventy,
Your father is exactly eighty,
And you have absolutely no siblings of any age!
That
Single, orphaned, lonely, isolated father of yours endures the cold;
That
Old, weak, worn-out, and sick mother of yours suffers hunger.
To no avail you've reached the age of thirty;
All in vain
You stand between heaven and earth,
Have eyes and eyebrows, seem to be human.

(*Four from Coda*)[47]

The two of them really do not have enough clothes to cover their bodies
Or enough food to fill their mouths.
This is something all neighbors and villagers know.
You think I'm lying or prevaricating to your face?
The proverb says:
"The mouths of passers-by surpass a stele!"[48]
What I've told you can be known:
They have suffered through stormy cold and steamy summers,
Starvation and bitter toil!

After the EXTRA MALE *speaks*:

(*Third from Coda*)

I collected some firewood for them,
And I helped them out with some food,
But even though I
Could find them something to eat, they had nothing to wear.
Your father suffered the cold of deepest winter in the last month of the year
While your mother stirred a whole night's ashes in the cold stove.
They suffered such hunger their innards shattered.
For them no succulent lamb and white noodles;
They only had
Bland rice and yellowed pickles.

---

47. The original writes here *ersha*, "second from coda."

48. Inscriptions on stelae often exaggerate or provide a completely false picture of a man's qualities, but the opinion of the common people will be honest and correct.

After the EXTRA MALE *speaks*:

(*Second from Coda*)[49]

He carried good water for other people,
And exchanged it for filthy;
He also didn't know how to "buy cheap in the south and sell dear in the north."
You enjoyed a salary of a thousand bell weights in the jade hall of ministers,
But in your joy completely forgot to return to your parents in their thatched cottage.
They shed tears of desperation,
Only managing vexation and sorrow,
And heartrending sadness.

(*Coda*)

They wept from deepening dusk until early evening,
Then from early evening until late at night,
Their only thoughts of Xue Rengui who quit home and hearth!

Continues in speech: Now you today have obtained an office, a beautiful girl supports your arm, and a strong warrior offers the whip. Go home as soon as possible!

Your aged parents do nothing but wait for you!

Exit.

[ACT 4]

After EXTRA MALE *speaks*[50]—MALE LEAD, *once again dressed as* ELDERLY PEASANT, *enters with the* OLD FEMALE:

([SHUANGDIAO MODE:] *Xinshui ling*)

All because of

This son who was to be our provider, I've wept until my eyes have grown blurry.

My son,

I've been worried for the whole ten years you have been gone.
You have probably returned to the courts of the underworld,
There covered by yellow sand.

What

Has happened to you? Success?
Expel these vexations! When will they end?

(*Zhenzhen ying*)

You have

Abandoned both your aged parents—

49. The original writes here "fourth from coda."

50. Most likely the actor performing Xue Rengui enters the stage to announce his intention to visit his parents now the construction of a new mansion is complete and then leaves the stage.

Why didn't you come home after you had left?
You must be wandering at the ocean's rim;
You must be stranded at the edge of heaven!
I keep watch for you like a butterfly playing with a flower in a mirror!
My thoughts for you will be my death!
O, son.[51]
(*Douye huang*)
You, my little archenemy,
Have worn me out with thinking about you.
In the Yellow Springs there are no inns,
So at whose house will we lodge later this evening? This very night?
Your parents soon will be seventy and eighty:[52]
When the time of our death will come,
Who will wear cloth and hemp[53] on our behalf?
Who will pour out wine and tea as libations?
(*Qing dongyuan*)
The way you treat me is impossible to bear:
You tease me,
Treat me like a joke!
In dreams you've caused me so much suffering, I'm afraid to sleep.
My son, if you are alive, you're a flame emerging from cold ashes!
My son, if you are alive, you're an earthen pot growing tusks!
My son, if you are alive, it can only be a rotten tree putting forth flowers!
My son
Failed to receive the summons of the Son of Heaven
And will become merely a tale for fishermen and woodcutters.[54]

After the EXTRA MALE *speaks—after others have spoken—after the whole party comes to a stop—after the* EXTRA MALE *speaks —*

(*Qing Xuanhe*)
At my house we have no fodder at all,
Where am I going to get a feeder or scythe?
These last few years
We've had so many setbacks our family funds are all wiped out!

51. Here we have, along with Zheng Qian, abided by the original printing. Zheng Qian 1962, 225, points out that this is a version of the tune *Desheng ling* but has a completely different metrical system. He can find no other equivalent but wisely leaves it untouched. Xu Qinjun 1980, 2:405, and Ning 1988, 2:7, suggest that there are characters missing in this line. They are making these suggestions, however, on the basis of parallel texts and rhyme formularies, which are either anachronistic or based on ideal models (in the latter case, ideals broken with regularity in the early Yuan texts).

52. Emending *shangba* 上八 to *qiba* 七八.

53. Clothes of the simplest materials and without any adornment (therefore white) are worn when in mourning.

54. "A tale of fishermen and woodcutters" refers to a tale of past glories.

Continues in speech: I don't even have a donkey to ride,
So how would I have a service horse or a second horse?[55]

After the EXTRA MALE *speaks—speak*: Dear officials, have pity! I am so poor that I don't have a thing!

(*Chuan bo zhao*)
When I hear
Them say "roots and sprouts"
I'm totally confused for a while:
Why need to brag about yourself,
"Martial arts so accomplished and smooth,"
"Battle strategies so successful,"
"Wearing battle robes and armor when joining the fray,"
"Defeating the Liao army in a single battle,"
And that you have been "tagged to become a Reserve Horse"?
(*Qi dixiong*)
This just provokes laughing!
Laughing!
What kind of glory is this!
For nothing I'll suffer the whole village's cursing!
What I can do is crawl about and creep along to feel for some fish and shrimp,
Or carefully creak along handling a plow handle.
(*Luosiniang*)
Mine is a plastered mansion, half a hall with a leaky roof,
And I don't have any wicker stores of grain.
The rats and mice run and rush all around,
Bitterly complaining they're starving to death!
(*Yan'er luo*)
I'm wearing a worn-out vest
With nits as thick as hemp.
Pick them out and crush them with your fingernails on the bricks,
You'll get no fewer than three or four handfuls!
(*Dao lianzi*)
It is my fate to find no success:
I survive by pushing the plow or turning the mill for others.
A holey bamboo hat is strapped to my head
And my feet tread on old hempen sandals.

55. We follow the emendation and interpretation of Ning 1988, 2:15, which points out that in Yuan-dynasty times farmers were required to provide the government with one horse in time of need and to keep a second horse in reserve. The word for "second horse" (*fuma*) has the same pronunciation, however, as the common designation for a son-in-law of the emperor, which was also "reserve horses" (*fuma* 駙馬), an abbreviated form of the title commander of the reserve horses (*fuma duwei* 駙馬都尉), which was an honorific title commonly awarded to the husbands of imperial princesses.

After the EXTRA MALE *speaks—speak*: Is that my son Xue Rengui?

(*Meihua jiu*)

What do you mean "fine form"?
My posture is way too rustic,
My clothes are a mess.
My eyes are red and blind;
I cling tightly to my staff.
We don't have half a handful of straw for burning,
And on the earthen *kang* our items are a scattered mess:[56]
We're just like beggars!
Despised by the whole village,
So, Xue Rengui, check it out carefully yourself!

(*Shou Jiangnan*)

How could I dare be a "matching family" to the Great Tang's ④④ [Son of Heaven]?
If the boy and the girl get into a fight,
There are these melons of purple-gold as big as bowls[57]
That I really fear.
Grandma, don't scare the little baby!

After the EXTRA MALE *speaks:—speak*: If you bow to me, that's not the right way.[58]

(*Taiping ling*)

Just wait till I'll have brought home the harvest in autumn,
And I'll scare up some money and give you some hemp.[59]
And if that's not enough, I'll add two loads of melons next year.
That face of hers is perfect,
Her body quite seductive,
And with those artificial flowers in her hair
She resembles the bodhisattva Samantabhadra.

Come on!

Let the two of them[60] bow to these two toads turned monsters.

---

56. A kind of stove that has a large square earthen platform with a heating chamber underneath, used both to heat a room and to serve as a bed.
57. Globed staffs used as (ceremonial) weapons.
58. This is the possible moment for Xue Rengui's bride to enter onstage. Also note that a proper marriage demands the exchange of gifts between the family of the groom and the family of the bride. So as long as the father of the groom has not presented gifts to the bride's family (and which then often become part of her dowry), the marriage cannot be concluded, and it would not be right for the bride to bow to the groom's father as her father-in-law.
59. Tentative translation. The choice of "hemp" (*ma* 麻) may simply be a matter of satisfying the requirements of rhyming.
60. For *lai er da* 來二大 we read *lai er ren* 來二人. The modern editors of this text read *er* (二) as a reduplication sign (=) following *lai*, but the size of the character argues against such a reading. The size suggests that the character *er* is part of the text of the aria. *Da* is probably a mistake for *ren*. At this moment Xue Rengui and the princess, as groom and bride, bow in front of Xue's father and mother as prescribed by marriage protocol.

After acting out collapsing:

(*Desheng ling*)

I suddenly saw

A hand as big as a winnowing basket draw near,

Tightly grab the short hair on my head,

And slam me down in front of the steps,

Hitting me right on my old nose!

Why, her father is the current emperor!

Just give it some thought:

How can I, this poor guy, deal with this?

After the EXTRA MALES *have acted out carrying the* MALE LEAD:

(*Dianqian huan*)

If the local authorities see this, they're bound to have me punished.

Continues in speech: Temple festivals have been prohibited![61]

Secretly they carry a local god of the soil right into a house![62]

You walk with such a grand air that I cower for fear.

The two rows of the escort are all lined up.

There's something I want to say:

Let me tell you: Don't step on the tiles,

Because you'll slip and slam me down in front of the steps,

And if you don't shatter my skull,

At the very least you'll break my nose!

Dispersal Scene

Title: The general dressed in white: at court his blessings are hidden;
The black-hearted scoundrel: frost is added on top of snow.

Name: Taizong of the Tang summons the wise and appoints gentlemen;
Xue Rengui Returns Home Clad in Brocade.
A Newly Cut Complete Text

Xue Rengui Returns Home Clad in Brocade
with the complete prompts.

61. "Temple festivals for supplicating the gods, questioning the divinities by use of the planchette, gathering at night and only dispersing at dawn, and also those people who wound their own body, hang themselves from hooks and flagellate their back and beg for money obstrusively—these too should be prohibited." Fang Linggui 方齡貴, *Tongzhi tiaoge jiaozhu* 通制條格校注 (Beijing: Zhonghua shuju, 2001), 673, as quoted in Wang Shipei 2008, 146n21.

62. The old man is carried in a sedan chair, we may assume, to a new house that Xue Rengui has had prepared in advance.

A SELECTION OF YUAN PLAYS EDITION OF THE *ZAJU XUE RENGUI RETURNS HOME IN GLORY*

DRAMATIS PERSONAE IN ORDER OF APPEARANCE

Role type	*Name and family, institutional, or social role*
MALE LEAD	OLD UNCLE XUE, XUE RENGUI's father (wedge, acts 2, 4)
MINOR FEMALE	LADY LIU, XUE RENGUI's wife
OLD FEMALE	MADAME XUE, XUE RENGUI's mother
OPENING MALE	XUE RENGUI
VILLAIN	KING OF KOGURYO
COMIC	THE *molizhi*, commander of Koguryo army
EXTRA	XU MAOGONG, chief of staff, duke of Yingguo
SOLDIERS	SOLDIERS in XU MAOGONG's entourage
VILLAIN	ZHANG SHIGUI, commander in chief
MALE LEAD	DU RUHUI, president of Ministry of War, duke of Cai (act 1)
SOLDIERS	SOLDIERS in ZHANG SHIGUI's dream entourage
CLOWN	Peasant woman, BANGU
MALE LEAD	Peasant male, BANGE (act 3)

✤ ✤ ✤

THE *ZAJU XUE RENGUI RETURNS HOME IN GLORY*

WRITTEN BY ZHANG GUOBIN OF THE YUAN DYNASTY

COLLATED BY ZANG JINSHU OF WUXING OF THE MING DYNASTY

WEDGE

(MALE LEAD *dressed as an elderly farmer enters with* OLD WOMAN *and* FEMALE.) (MALE LEAD *speaks*:) I am registered as an inhabitant of Big Huang Village of Longmen Township in Jiangzhou. Surnamed Xue, everyone calls me Old Uncle Xue. There are four of us in the family, and my old lady is surnamed Li. I have a son called Donkey

Xue, whose school name is Rengui, and who has a wife from the Liu family. We come from farming folk, but my child Donkey Xue refuses to make a living as a farmer. Every day he practices thrusting with a spear and twirling his cudgel, practicing some military art or the other. My wife, where did our son go? (OLD FEMALE *speaks*:) My husband, he went off to the market. (MALE LEAD *speaks*:) Tell him to come and see me when he gets back. (OPENING MALE, *dressed as* XUE RENGUI, *enters, and recites*:)

A horse is saddled for battle, a general wears his battle robes;
At the tips of the willow branch outside the gate, the moon is high.
If a real man wants to wear a seal of noble rank[63]
A bloodied sword must always hang at his waist.

I am Xue Rengui, twenty-two years old, and I live in Big Huang Village of Longmen Township in Jiangzhou. Both my parents are still alive, but I don't want to make a living as a farmer, so I spend every day thrusting with my spear and twirling my cudgel, or practicing shooting with bow and arrow. I have fully mastered and completely understand each of the eighteen military arts. I spend every day shooting geese at the river ford for fun. I have heard that a yellow imperial poster has been put up in Jiangzhou, summoning volunteer heroes for the militia. I have a mind to join the army as a volunteer. So let me now return home to report to my parents and then set off on that long journey. Here I am at the gate. (*Acts out greeting. Speaks*:) Mother, Father, I'm home. (MALE LEAD *speaks*:) Son, where did you go? (XUE RENGUI *speaks*:) My dear parents, you don't understand. A poster has just been put up in Jiangzhou: they're summoning hardy volunteers for the militia. Your son has mastered the eighteen military arts and boned up on books about strategy. I've made up my mind: I want to join the militia. What do you, my parents, think about it? (MALE LEAD *speaks*:) My son, I'm afraid the two of us completely rely on you to be our one set of eyes and pair of arms. If you join the militia—we're so old now—who will take care of us if something happens? (OLD FEMALE *speaks*:) Son, do what your father says. Don't go off to join the militia! (XUE RENGUI *speaks*:) Dear father, with all due respect, I've learned that what was called the greatest act of filial piety in ancient times was to establish a career and make a name in order to bring glory to one's parents. To wait on you dawn and dusk, to ask after your well-being or look after your food—these are the most trifling gestures a son can make and cannot be considered true filial piety. Right now is the moment the state needs men to wipe out the eastern barbarians and to pacify the border regions. With the military arts I have mastered and with my unsurpassed wisdom and valor, I am bound to achieve success as soon as my horse reaches the battlefield. And after I attain the measliest office of some kind, I will come back and change the status of our family and bring glory and luster to my parents. Otherwise, I would just stay here at this thatched cottage and be a farmer—wouldn't that be a

63. The seal of office, usually a small brass square cuboid, was worn at the waist on a belt.

total waste of my capacities! (OLD FEMALE *speaks*:) My son, as long as you give it your all! Just go! (MALE LEAD *speaks*:) So be it then! You have made up your mind to go! My wife, get together some silver and give it to our son as travel money. My son, be careful while traveling. Whether you obtain an office or not, send us letters as often as you can, so the two of us won't have to worry. (XUE RENGUI *acts out bowing down, speaks*:) Today is a lucky day and propitious time. My father and mother, please let me say good-bye to you, as I have to set out on my journey. (MALE LEAD *sings*:)

(XIANLÜ MODE: *Duanzheng hao*)

Today you leave your village and farm,
Say good-bye to your hometown,
Bid adieu to your elderly parents.

(XUE RENGUI *speaks*:) On this journey I definitely want to repay the state for its favors with a loyal heart, expand its territory and extend its borders, and be ennobled as a lord or appointed as a general—then I'll return. Father, don't worry! (MALE LEAD *sings*:)

You want to risk your life on the sandy battlefield.
You are majestically martial,
Filled with an arching spirit,
An awe-inspiring body,
A stern and robust presence!
I've no idea when you'll be able to come home!
My son,
Don't make the two of us lean against the gate each and every day gazing with hope for your return!

(*Exit with* OLD FEMALE.)

(MINOR FEMALE *speaks*:) My husband, I'm here at home and happy to take care of your parents, so please go on without any worries! Let me accompany you to outside that brushwood gate and there say good-bye. (XUE RENGUI *speaks*:) My wife, Mother and Father have no one else, so please go back and wait on your parents-in-law. There is no need to see me off. (*Acts out taking his leave with a bow.*) (XUE RENGUI *recites*:)

As I today leave for distant parts to join the army,
My only hope is that you will serve my parents with filial deference.

(*Exits first.*)

(MINOR FEMALE *acts out being overcome by sadness, recites*:)

Even though a couple like intertwined branches in our fragrant years,
For the sake of glory and fame there is no option but separation.

(*Exit.*)

ACT 1

(VILLAIN, *dressed as* KING OF KOGURYO, *enters, leading* SOLDIERS. *He recites*:)

I alone occupy a small state east of the Liao;
Oh Great Tang, do not blame me for my refusal to submit:
Let it have its million heroic generals—
Who among them dares sneak a peek across the Yalu River!

I am the king of Koguryo. From the time the viscount of Ji was enfeoffed with this territory,[64] our state has enjoyed an uninterrupted transmission down to Us. For generations We have maintained Koguryo and proclaimed Ourselves the rulers of all lands east of the Liao. East of Koguryo there are still another sixteen kingdoms, and these kingdoms yearly offer tribute to the Great Tang. It is only my country that does not obey the Great Tang. And why? Because We have the Heavenly Mountains and the Yalu River for Our impenetrable natural defenses, which need to be guarded by only a single man! Let the Great Tang have a million men and horses, they cannot fly across these barriers. Recently I also found a great general by the name of Ge Suwen, whom I appointed as *molizhi*. He has such great valor that even a myriad of men are not his match! I have heard that the Great Tang has lost Qin Qiong to death and worn out Jingde,[65] and now lacks any heroic or fierce generals. I now have assigned a hundred thousand troops to the *molizhi* and ordered him to encamp in front of Whitebrow Slope near the Yalu River, there to send out a declaration of war, inciting the famous generals of the Great Tang to engage him in battle. If they can defeat Us, We are willing to offer yearly tribute to the Great Tang just like the other sixteen countries. But if they cannot, We will be the superior state and the Great Tang will be the inferior, so they will have to offer tribute to Us! Wouldn't that be splendid? *Molizhi*, where are you? (COMIC, *dressed as* MOLIZHI, *enters, and speaks*:) I am Ge Suwen. My chieftain calls for me, so I will have to go over and see him. (*Acts out greeting, speaks*:) Your Majesty, why have you summoned me? (KING OF KOGURYO *speaks*:) *Molizhi*, I have called you only for the following reason. We have heard that the Great Tang lost Qin Qiong to death, wore out Jingde, and now lacks any heroic or fierce generals. So We now assign a hundred thousand troops to you and order you to set up camp in front of Whitebrow Slope near the Yalu River, there to send out a declaration of war, inciting the famous generals of the Great Tang to engage you in battle. If you, as I reckon, will be victorious and successful, you will receive

64. According to Sima Qian's *Records of the Historian* (*Shiji*), the Viscount of Ji was a virtuous uncle of Zhou's, the evil last ruler of the Shang dynasty (1460–1045 BC). When the Shang dynasty was overthrown by King Wu of the Zhou dynasty, he enfeoffed the Viscount of Ji as the independent ruler of the Korean Peninsula. See Sima Qian1959, vol. 5, 1620, and Ssu-ma Ch'ien 1995a, 269–76, for the story of the Viscount of Ji.

65. Qin Qiong 秦瓊 (d. 638) and Yuchi Gong 尉遲恭 (Jingde 敬德; 585–658), later widely revered as door gods, were both major generals in the founding of the Tang (617–906).

promotions and rewards! (MOLIZHI *speaks*:) Understood! This very day I will lead a hundred thousand men and horses to Whitebrow Slope near the Yalu River, and challenge the famous generals of the Great Tang to come out and fight me. Officers and soldiers, listen to my orders! (*Recites*:)

Obeying the orders of my lord, I lead my hardy troops;
At Whitebrow Slope I will erect fortifications and set up camp.
I reckon the Tang does not have a single man who can fight me,
So it's a done deal: a thousand battles, a thousand victories.

(*Exits.*)

(KING OF KOGURYO *speaks*:) The *molizhi* definitely will be successful in his mission, but I still have to mobilize all the men and horses of my country to follow him in support from the rear.

(*Exit.*)

(EXTRA, dressed as XU MAOGONG, *enters, leading soldiers, and recites*:)

Since earliest years clad in brocade wearing a cloak of purple sable;
An armored horse, the western wind, an autumn of grasses sere.
Due to this single three-feet-long sword in my hand
I effortlessly won a noble position.

I, this old man, am Xu Shiji, and my style is Maogong.[66] My family hails from Lihu District in Caozhou.[67] Because of my support of the Great Tang I have been appointed to the office of chief of staff and ennobled as Duke of Yingguo. Lured by the *molizhi* of the land to the east of the Liao who challenged us to battle, Commander Zhang Shigui led an army out to meet him head-on in front of Whitebrow Slope near the Yalu River, but he was greatly defeated. Suddenly an officer in a white robe rode out to take the challenge and with three arrow shots pacified the Heavenly Mountains. He inflicted a defeat on the Liao troops, and led our army back to court. I have been appointed by His Majesty to determine promotions and rewards on the basis of merit here in the office of commander in chief. Zhang Shigui still claims it was all his merit. Then there is this petty officer Xue Rengui, who explains it was his merit. I'm still not certain which claim is true, I have given orders to summon those two men. Soldiers, keep watch in front of the gate, and report back to me when these two men arrive. (SOLDIERS *speak*:) Yes sir! (VILLAIN, *dressed as* ZHANG SHIGUI, *enters and recites*:)

I am supreme commander and my surname is Zhang;
From birth I've loved to chew on candy.
As soon as I hear the call of the battle drum,
The skin of my face is first to turn as yellow as wax.

66. Xu Shiji 徐世勣 (594–669) was one of the major generals in the founding of the Tang dynasty. In recognition for his contributions to the founding of the dynasty, he was granted the imperial surname Li and is therefore also known as Li Ji 李勣.

67. On the Shandong Peninsula, directly across the bay from the Korean Peninsula.

I am Commander Zhang Shigui. When I led my troops and engaged in battle with the *molizhi*, I never had any idea I would lose to him. Who could have known that in the thick of battle suddenly a flying knife would come my way? I was so scared my soul fled from my head, so I pulled my horse around and gave it free rein to run away. If that minor officer in a white gown Xue Rengui had not come out on his horse and taken on the challenge, how could I have escaped with my life? At present Xue Rengui has settled the Heavenly Mountains with three arrow shots and sent the *molizhi* in retreat. These were of course all his merits. But who has witnessed these feats? I will snatch them away for my own! I have reported these feats of arms to His Majesty, and he has now ordered Xu Maogong and Du Ruhui to determine promotions and rewards on the basis of merit here in the Office of the Commander in Chief. I'd better go. Well, here I am. Soldiers, please report that Commander Zhang Shigui has arrived. (SOLDIERS *act out reporting, speak*:) Sir! We report to Your Excellency the Chief of Staff that Zhang Shigui has arrived! (XU MAOGONG *speaks*:) Tell him to come inside! (ZHANG SHIGUI *acts out greeting him.*) (XU MAOGONG *speaks*:) Commander, that pacification of the Heavenly Mountains by three shots—whose merit was that? (ZHANG SHIGUI *speaks*:) Chief of Staff, if it hadn't been for me, Zhang Shigui, how would Koguryo have so quickly submitted? In this battle, the pacification of the Heavenly Mountains by three shots and the defeat inflicted on the *molizhi* are all due to my merit. Who else was there apart from me, Zhang Shigui? (XU MAOGONG *speaks*:) Was this really your merit? There are people who say it is the merit of a minor general in a white gown, Xue Rengui. (ZHANG SHIGUI *speaks*:) That's right. This is all my merit. I was wearing white that day! (XU MAOGONG *speaks*:) I don't believe it. Soldier, call in Xue Rengui! (SOLDIER *speaks*:) Xue Rengui, where are you? (XUE RENGUI *enters, recites*:)

As a general I pacified the Heavenly Mountains with three shots;
As a hero I reentered through the passes of the Han,[68] singing a long song.
Only then did I know that the many strange features of distant parts
Cannot be captured in the minute space filled by brush and ink.

I am Xue Rengui. I have served under Commander Zhang Shigui from the time I bid adieu to my parents to join the army. Going off to campaign against Koguryo, the harbor[69] was secured by me, and after I had pacified the Heavenly Mountains with three shots, I forced the *molizhi* to retreat, and I led the army back to the capital in victory. Today merit will be determined in the Office of the Commander in Chief;

68. In poetry, the Tang is often referred to as the Han dynasty (206 BC–AD 220) because of their comparability in terms of longevity and extent of territory.

69. According to both the *Xue Rengui zheng Liao shilüe* and the *Xue Rengui kuahai zheng Liao gushi*, Xue Rengui took the lead in establishing a beachhead for the invasion fleet despite stiff opposition from the Koguryo defense troops. In the first work he leads five hundred soldiers in landing on the beach; in the second work he downs the commanding Koguryo officer with a single shot.

promotions will be granted and rewards handed out. The chief of staff has called for me, so I must go. Here I am! Soldiers, report that Xue Rengui has arrived. (SOLDIER *acts out reporting, speaks*:) Sir! I report to Your Excellency the Chief of Staff that Xue Rengui has arrived! (XU MAOGONG *speaks*:) Tell him to come in. (XUE RENGUI *acts out greeting, speaks*:) For what commission did Your Excellency the Chief of Staff summon me, Xue Rengui? (XU MAOGONG *speaks*:) The pacification of the Heavenly Mountains by three shots and the defeat inflicted on the *molizhi*—whose merits were these? (XUE RENGUI *speaks*:) The pacification of the Heavenly Mountains by three shots and the defeat inflicted on the *molizhi* are both due to my merit. But it is not just these—every one of my fifty-four feats of arms in crossing the sea to pacify Liao have been falsely claimed by Zhang Shigui. If you hadn't asked me today, Chief of Staff, I would not have dared raise the issue. Chief of Staff, please set the matter straight on my behalf! (XU MAOGONG *speaks*:) Zhang Shigui, if you want to falsely claim his merit, that is not a minor matter indeed! How could you claim this merit as your own? But who was in charge of the battle formations that day? (XUE RENGUI *speaks*:) The official who supervised the battle that day was Du Ruhui. Chief of Staff, if you do not believe me, just ask the army supervisor to come over, and you will learn the truth. (MALE LEAD *enters dressed as* DU RUHUI, *and speaks*:) I am Du Ruhui, and my style is Keming. I hail from Duling in the Metropolitan Prefecture, where my ancestors have lived for generations. Together with Fang Xuanling[70] I am in charge of imperial administration. The emperor in his grace has appointed me to the office of the president of the Ministry of War and ennobled me as Duke of Cai. Because Koguryo has lately refused to obey the commands of the court and has invaded our borders, His Majesty dispatched generals to lead an army on a punitive campaign against the eastern regions. There was one minor general in a white gown, a certain Xue Rengui, who pacified the Heavenly Mountains with three shots of his bow and forced the *molizhi* to retreat. These feats of arms are truly no minor merits. Now Xu Maogong at the Office of the Commander in Chief has sent people to invite me over, I trust, for the matter of determining merit. I've personally seen the heroic courage of the *molizhi*—who could have forced him to retreat except for Xue Rengui?

(XIANLÜ MODE: *Dian jiangchen*)

He was just like a ferocious tiger blocking the road:
Who'd dare resist?
There was one soldier in a white gown
Who courageously charged forward,
And fought so hard that *molizhi* had no way to flee!

70. Fang Xuanling 房玄齡 (579–648) was one of Li Shimin's most trusted advisers and rose to the highest administrative positions in the central bureaucracy following the establishment of the Tang.

(*Speak*:) But that Commander Zhang Shigui falsely claimed Xue Rengui's merits. I've witnessed these feats of arms on the battlefield with my own eyes, so how can he falsely claim them? (*Sings*:)

(*Hunjiang long*)

Such men may be pardoned for murder,
But he deliberately muddles up another man's merits!
Coveting a single moment's title or reward,
He plies a hundred tricks of bribery and lies.
I simply ask you: Whose strength was it in front of Nine-Mile Mountain?[71]
Yet you want to be portrayed in the Gallery Soaring Beyond the Mists![72]
Kowtowing below the golden steps I will provide a detailed exposition—
How can you turn white into black and black into white?
This is no more than "hating the purple and seizing the vermilion"![73]

(*Speaks*:) I reached the Office of the Commander in Chief while I've been talking. Soldiers, report that Du Ruhui has arrived. (SOLDIER *acts out reporting, and speaks*:) Chief of Staff, sir, I report that Army Supervisor Du has arrived. (XU MAOGONG *speaks*:) Invite him in. (MALE LEAD *acts out greeting, and speaks*:) Duke Ying, why did you summon me? (XU MAOGONG *speaks*:) I wouldn't dare invite you with no reason. On that day, the pacification of the Heavenly Mountains by three shots, and the defeat inflicted on the *molizhi*—Duke Cai, only you were in charge of the battle formations, and you must have seen things clearly. Now Zhang Shigui claims that it was his merit, but Xue Rengui also explains it is his. It is hard for me to make a decision at the moment on something so far away, so I would like Duke Cai to provide me with a true account. (MALE LEAD *speaks*:) These are all feats of arms by Xue Rengui. (ZHANG SHIGUI *speaks*:) Your lordships, today all civil officials and military officers are assembled here. Who else in this battle could have come close to the *molizhi* except for me, Zhang Shigui? The pacification of the Heavenly Mountains with just three shots and the defeat inflicted on the *molizhi* are clearly both my merits. So why do you now want to snatch them away from me and reward that Xue Rengui? (MALE LEAD *speaks*:) Zhang Shigui, these are both feats of arms by Xue Rengui. How can you falsely claim them as yours? (XUE RENGUI *speaks*:) Lord Army Supervisor, you

71. Nine-Mile Mountain is the sight of fierce battles between Liu Bang, the founder of the Han dynasty, and his main rival, Xiang Yu; a common metonymy for "battlefield."

72. The Lingyan Ge (凌煙閣), a gallery in which Li Shimin 李世民, the founding emperor of the Tang, had portraits painted of twenty-four meritorious officers and officials who helped him found the dynasty. Here used metaphorically to indicate honors heaped on high ministers in historical remembrance. For a study of the imaginative re-creation of the portraits in the gallery and the discursive space that the name implies, see Burkus-Chasson 2010, 163–255.

73. See n. 8.

are an enlightened minister. When some time ago we crossed the sea to pacify the Liao, I, Xue Rengui, established fifty-four great merits, but Zhang Shigui has falsely claimed them all. Lord Army Supervisor, please be so kind as to serve as my witness! (MALE LEAD *sings*:)

(*You hulu*)

On that day the battle lines were drawn on the banks of the Yalu.

(ZHANG SHIGUI *speaks*:) If you say that the merit of the pacification of the Heavenly Mountains by three shots wasn't mine, whose was it? (MALE LEAD *sings*:)

Now you're facing the civil officials and military officers.

(XU MAOGONG *speaks*:) Pacification of the Heavenly Mountains by three shots: this was the greatest merit. But you are wrangling over it, so how can I know whose merit it was? (MALE LEAD *speaks*:) I have witnessed this with my own eyes. This is truly Xue Rengui's merit. (*Sings*:)

The three shots pacifying the Heavenly Mountains precisely resembled pearls on a string!

(ZHANG SHIGUI *speaks*:) I am an officer with the rank of commander, so I can be listed on the register of merits. That Xue Rengui is only a foot soldier running before the cavalry, so how could he be listed in the register of merits? (MALE LEAD *sings*:)

There is no need for you, General, to fight over the register of merits.
No matter what, isn't it always the phoenix that winds up on the *wutong* tree?[74]

(ZHANG SHIGUI *speaks*:) When Xue Rengui got to Koguryo, he broke out in hives all over his body, and all he did every day was scratch himself. How many times did he fight? He didn't even have an inch of arrow, so what merit could he have? (MALE LEAD *sings*:)

That Xue Rengui had ten great merits,
You are the one without an inch of arrow.
You just want to play that Zhao Gao who called a stag a horse in the court of Qin—
Why can't you imitate the Longbo and pull leviathans up from the depths?[75]

(ZHANG SHIGUI *speaks*:) It's not that I, Zhang Shigui, like to brag, but who can ride a nag like me? Pull a stiff bow like me? Eat cold food like me? Chew fat onions like me? If you have good wine, pour me three pints. I am a truly stout fellow made of ringing iron! (MALE LEAD *sings*:)

74. The phoenix does not compete for foul food with lesser birds.

75. Following the death of the First Emperor of the Qin dynasty, the eunuch Zhao Gao controlled the court. When a stag was presented to the Second Emperor and Zhao Gao called it a horse, none of the courtiers dared contradict him. Longbo, here used as the name of a person, is actually the name of a mythic country inhabited by giants who pull up six leviathans at once when fishing.

(*Tianxia le*)
You dare brag about being a real man, a stalwart hero?
Unlike all others?
Just mull it over!
Are you some Yang Youji who can hit a poplar leaf from a hundred paces away?[76]

(ZHANG SHIGUI *speaks*:) When Xue Rengui got to Koguryo he spent all his time catching locusts, feeling around for crabs, and digging out crickets. When was he capable of fighting? (MALE LEAD *sings*:)
And who was leading the grand army?
And who was running the marshal's office?

(ZHANG SHIGUI *speaks*:) Don't you boast! Where is your merit? (MALE LEAD *speaks*:) You tell me! (*Sings*:)
Who requests a salary without first showing merit?

(ZHANG SHIGUI *speaks*:) Let's evaluate me: on the civil side, I am conversant with the *Three Strategies*,[77] on the military, I understand the *Six Tactics*.[78] I'm there with the best! (MALE LEAD *speaks*:) Shut up! (*Sings*:)
(*Nezha ling*)
If we were to speak of the civil:
Can you compare to Guan Zhong and Bao Shuya?[79]

(ZHANG SHIGUI *speaks*:) And as for the military? (MALE LEAD *sings*:)
If we were to evaluate your martial qualities,
Are you a match for Zhou Yu or Lu Su?[80]

(ZHANG SHIGUI *speaks*:) And what about my intelligence and capacity for planning? (MALE LEAD *sings*:)
As for that:
Can you match Recumbent Dragon or Fledgling Phoenix?[81]

---

76. Yang Youji is an archer of legendary fame who was able to hit a poplar leaf dead center one hundred out of one hundred times. A Chinese "pace" (*bu* 步) is the equivalent of two steps, roughly five feet.

77. The *Three Strategies* (*Sanlüe* 三略) is a handbook of military tactics ascribed to the Yellow Lord (Huanggong 黃公 or Huangshi Gong 黃石公), a mythical Daoist sage who taught Zhang Liang (d. 186 BC), one of Liu Bang's main advisers in the early Han. On Zhang Liang, see n. 82.

78. A military manual attributed to Lü Wang.

79. Guan Zhong 官仲 (d. 645 BC) and Bao Shuya 鮑叔牙 are exemplary friends of ancient times. When Guan Zhong took more than his fair share of profits from a common trading enterprise, Bao did not complain because he knew that his friend had to take care of his ailing mother. This pair later came to signify a friendship that accepts the idea that one person is due more than the other and that equality is not the issue.

80. Zhou Yu 周瑜 (175–210) and Lu Su 魯肅 (172–217) are the two best-known strategists serving Sun Quan 孫權 (182–252), the ruler of Wu in the Three Kingdoms. See Idema and West 2012, passim.

81. Recumbent Dragon is Zhuge Liang 諸葛亮 (181–234), the famous strategist serving Liu Bei 劉備 (161–223). Fledgling Phoenix is his fellow strategist Pang Tong 龐統 (179–214). The story of Pang Tong and his wise counsel to Liu Bei is well described in the anonymous Ming play *Liu Xuande Goes Alone to the Xiangyang Meeting* (*Liu Xuande du fu Xiangyang hui* 劉玄德獨赴襄陽會); see Idema and West 2012, 152–96, esp. 175–78.

(ZHANG SHIGUI *speaks*:) When it comes to military books and battle tactics, I'm stuffed to the gills! Sometime later on I will be appointed as minister, ennobled as lord, and get a really important office! (MALE LEAD *sings*:)

If you are going to resemble Zhang Liang,[82]
You'd better leave the court and go back to the hills
To study a few more battle plans and military books!

(ZHANG SHIGUI *speaks*:) I hold the office of a commander, yet I don't measure up to some village peasant who started out as a common soldier? As foul as my temper is, would I submit to this? (MALE LEAD *sings*:)

(*Que tazhi*)
You say that he was a lowly peasant,
Who began a common soldier.

(*Continues in speech*:) Just think of Zhuge Liang!

If he wasn't hiding his traces in Nanyang,
Could he happily have plowed and hoed?

(ZHANG SHIGUI *speaks*:) So what happened to him later? (MALE LEAD *sings*:)

His fate changed, he met up with an imperial ruler,
Who in a single year thrice visited his thatched cottage.[83]

(ZHANG SHIGUI *speaks*:) That Zhuge Liang hoed the field and tilled the land, and that First Lord Liu[84] wove mats and plaited sandals—why would you want to mention such people? (MALE LEAD *speaks*:) Since ancient times loyal ministers and great generals come from poor families. I will tell you one more example. (*Sings*:)

---

82. Zhang Liang (Zifang) was descended from one of the ministerial families of the kingdom of Han, one of the three states that had resulted from the tripartition of the dukedom of Jin in the fifth century BC. After the First Emperor had annihilated his home state, Zhang Liang tried to have him murdered but failed in this attempt. Later Zhang Liang served Liu Bang in establishing the Han dynasty. But once the dynasty had been established and Liu Bang grew suspicious of his erstwhile supporters, Zhang Liang retired from the court, according to legend, to become a hermit. By the end of the Western Han his identity as a Daoist was firmly established, and in his eulogy to the "Marquis of Liu, Hereditary House 25" (Liuhou shijia ershiwu) in the *Records of the Historian*, Sima Qian expresses some skepticism about the prevailing idea that Zhang received the texts of the *Laozi* from Laozi himself, which was firmly part of the tradition by that time. See Ssu-ma Ch'ien 2002, 99–114. One of the commentarial notes to this passage cites a work that declares, "The Lord of the Wind was the commander of the Yellow Emperor's army, and he later transformed into Laozi, who bestowed his text on Zhang Liang." In later religious traditions Zhang Liang became a Daoist immortal. He once displayed his humility by retrieving a slipper that Master Yellow Stone had thrown down a bridge, and the latter instructed him in military strategy (that is, the *Three Strategies*).

83. For the early career of Zhuge Liang and the third of the three famous visits, see *Zhuge Liang Burns the Stores at Bowang* (*Zhuge Liang Bowang shao tun* 諸葛亮博望燒屯) in Idema and West 2012, 204–27.

84. First Lord Liu refers to Liu Bei, who came from a humble background. See Idema and West 2012, xv–xvii, and the description of Liu Bei's early life in the Ming play *Liu, Guan, and Zhang: The Tripartite Oath of Brotherhood in the Peach Orchard* (*Liu Guan Zhang Taoyuan san jieyi* 劉關張桃園三結義) and in the *Records of the Three Kingdoms in Plain Language* (*Sanguo zhi pinghua* 三國志平話), in Idema and West 2012, 1–39 and 321–23, respectively.

(*Jisheng cao*)
Once long ago, I remember, Marshal Han
Begged food from a washerwoman.[85]
If Xiao He[86] had not recommended him as the generalissimo,
Could the Prince of Han have done in Double Pupils?[87]
This shows that the loyal and great mostly come from impoverished households.

(ZHANG SHIGUI *speaks*:) Army Supervisor, if it were up to me we would separate Xue Rengui from the army and send him back home to plant his crops as he did before. Now that would bring pleasure to my heart. (MALE LEAD *sings*:)
Your road laid with gravel would overturn a bridge of purple-gold,[88]
That's no match for that washing pool for soaking hemp that sets up a heaven-bearing pillar![89]

(XUE RENGUI *speaks*:) Chief of staff, there's no mistaking what the army supervisor saw, how can you register my merits under Zhang Shigui's name? This would make a mockery of the Tang emperor's divine sageliness! It also would mean that the enlightened ruler would be unaware of the corruption of his underlings. (XU MAOGONG *speaks*:) Stop! Stop! You two generals stop arguing! Duke of Cai, if you want to settle these merits, it's easy enough. We will set up a target with a red bull's-eye, on that we'll place a golden coin, then set up the target at a distance of one hundred paces, and have them each fire three arrows. We will list the merit of pacifying the Heavenly Mountains with three shots under the name of whoever hits the golden coin in the center, and he will be promoted and rewarded. But whoever cannot hit the golden coin will be dismissed from office, have his salary discontinued, and have his status reduced to that of a mere commoner. (MALE LEAD *speaks*:) Chief of staff, you are right! (ZHANG SHIGUI *speaks*:) So now you order Xue Rengui and me to shoot at this target of a golden coin. Well, Chief of staff, please allow me to ask: How about the one who can hit the target? How about the one who cannot hit the target? Even those who made it into the Gallery Soaring Beyond the Mists couldn't hit such a target. Xue Rengui, just settle down! You wanted to claim my feats of arms as your own merit and now force me to hit the target. You shoot first! (MALE LEAD *speaks*:) Chief of Staff, let's watch as they shoot their arrows, and then we'll know the truth. (*Sings*:)
(*Jinzhan'er*)

85. Han Xin 韓信 (d. 196 BC) rose from being a beggar to one of the three prominent generals under Liu Bang 劉邦 (256 or 247–195 BC), founder of the Han dynasty.

86. Xiao He 蕭何 (d. 193 BC) is best known in later times for the severity of the law code that he had promulgated.

87. The Prince of Han refers to Liu Bang, and "Double Pupils" refers to Xiang Yu 項羽 (232–202 BC), his main rival to replace the Qin.

88. In the Tang capital of Chang'an, the home of the prime minister was linked to the palace by an elevated gravel road. Here, "Your fine background leads to destruction" (a bridge of purple-gold [that arches across the sea] means a stalwart minister or famous general.)

89. That is, the washerwoman who aided Han Xin.

The two of you compete to win or lose,
In this way finding out the truth.

(XU MAOGONG *speaks*:) We need to get this cleared up today, before we can distribute rewards in accordance with merit. (MALE LEAD *sings*:)

In this way the register of merit will be free of the slightest error.

(XU MAOGONG *speaks*:) The one who cannot hit the golden coin will be dismissed from office and deprived of rank; the one who hits the golden coin—let him wear a purple gown and golden belt. (MALE LEAD *sings*:)

Miss the target and be stripped of office and rank;
The one who can hit the target: a golden fish[90] will hang from his jade belt.

(XU MAOGONG *speaks*:) The one who cannot hit the target will be reduced in rank to the status of mere commoner, while the one who hits the target will be appointed to a position above those of the Three Dukes.[91] (MALE LEAD *sings*:)

For the one who cannot hit the target a thatched homestead, three *qing* of land,
And for tools to hold in his hand, a single hoe.
The one who'll hit the target definitely will achieve "twelve lances arrayed in front of your gate,"[92]
"Eight Pepper patterns" arrayed on your door.[93]

(XU MAOGONG *speaks*:) Now move the target with its red bull's-eye out. Can you see that golden coin on the target? Each of you will shoot three arrows in this match. (XUE RENGUI *speaks*:) Chief of Staff, this is fair. Get me my bow and arrows, and I will shoot three arrows. (*Acts out shooting and hitting the target three times.*) (SOLDIER *acts out reporting, speaks*:) Chief of Staff, Xue Rengui has hit the bull's-eye with each of his three arrows. (XU MAOGONG *speaks*:) A fine general! He has hit the center of the golden coin! Zhang Shigui, it's your turn to shoot. (ZHANG SHIGUI *speaks*:) He shot his arrows? His bowmanship is just the same as mine. (XU MAOGONG *speaks*:) Just keep quiet and shoot your three arrows! (ZHANG SHIGUI *speaks*:) In my opinion none of those who first made it into the Gallery Soaring Beyond the Mists could hit such a target. Xue Rengui, just settle down! You wanted to claim my feats of arms as your own merit and now force me to hit the target. Well fine, I'll shoot. Push the target out! (SOLDIER *speaks*:) Check out the target! (ZHANG SHIGUI *speaks*:) What is the distance of this target? (SOLDIER *speaks*:) It is one hundred paces. (ZHANG SHIGUI *speaks*:) Bring it back seventy or eighty paces. (SOLDIER *speaks*:) That's too close! (ZHANG SHIGUI *speaks*:) You come somewhat closer. If I manage to hit the target, I will be your son! Soldier, get me my bow and arrows. I've been a commander

90. A small golden tally in the shape of a fish worn at the belt of high officials.
91. The Three Dukes is a collective reference to the highest dignitaries of the empire.
92. A ceremonial guard.
93. See n. 19.

for thirty years, but I've never realized that a bow is actually so stiff. I'll shoot! A hit! (SOLDIER *speaks*:) A miss! (ZHANG SHIGUI *speaks*:) It's not that I didn't hit the target, it's just that the target is too far away. Let me shoot one more time. (*Acts out shooting again, speaks*:) Hit! (SOLDIER *speaks*:) Miss! (ZHANG SHIGUI *speaks*:) This bow is not my bow! The strength of my bow is that of three and half quarts of rice.[94] Let me shoot again. (*Acts out shooting again, speaks*:) Hit! (SOLDIER *speaks*:) Another miss! (ZHANG SHIGUI *speaks*:) Now what? Didn't I say I couldn't hit it? (XU MAOGONG *speaks*:) Bah, you missed every shot. Soldiers, arrest Zhang Shigui! (SOLDIER *speaks*:) Yes sir! (*Acts out arresting* ZHANG SHIGUI.) (XU MAOGONG *speaks*:) At the command of His Majesty I determined the proper course of action here in the Office of Commander-in-Chief because the two generals were fighting over merit. It turned out that Zhang Shigui falsely claimed the merits of Xue Rengui. According to military law he should be beheaded, but for the time being he will spared from the sword and reduced to the status of commoner. "A thatched homestead, three *qing* of land / And for tools to hold in his hand a single hoe." Soldier, take him outside. (SOLDIER *speaks*:) Yes sir! (ZHANG SHIGUI *speaks*:) Xue Rengui's original status was that of a farmer, yet he is now made an official. My original status was that of an official, yet I am made into a farmer. Chief of Staff, you are truly muddleheaded! Fine! Fine! Fine! He has had his say now, but I've yet to have mine! (*Recites*:)

In my capacity as commander I was way too vicious:
This morning I'm stripped of my office and become a farmer.
No need for me to study anymore the Yellow Lord's *Three Strategies*—
When I get home I'll guzzle down tofu and three flagons of wine!

(*Exits*.)

(XU MAOGONG *speaks*:) Today merit and crime have been made clear, so I'll have to return to His Majesty and report.

(*Exits*.)

(XUE RENGUI *speaks*:) Army Supervisor, today would have never happened if it hadn't been for you! Some other day I will have to repay your favor doublefold. (MALE LEAD *speaks*:) General, it is well deserved! (*Sings*:)

(*Zhuan Coda*)

You will accomplish what was begun with the bloodstained red of your battle dress
The green of your campaign boots tucked into the stirrups,
That one "square-heaven" lance of yours[95] surpasses past and present.
Look at that merit-stealing thief with a face like dung
Exiting the yamen gate like a scurrying pig or fleeing wolf!
Quite unlike you, filled with joy,

94. The stiffness of a bow was measured in terms of the weight that had to be suspended from the string in order to make the bow curve. Three and a half quarts of rice would be a ridiculously low weight for a good stiff bow.

95. A long lance with a sharpened metal tip with two crescent-shaped blades attached toward the top.

With well-wishers pressing around you, front and back.
That phrase "For a single general to achieve success myriads of men must die" means nothing here![96]

(XUE RENGUI *speaks*:) I can't think of any kind of merit that I may possess to earn Your Excellency's recommendation? (MALE LEAD *sings*:)
It's all because you opened the borders and expanded our territory,
Grasped the clouds and controlled the mists,
Supported by the sagely enlightened Son of Heaven and the hundred gods.
(*Exits.*)

(XU MAOGONG *enters and speaks*:) Xue Rengui, because you have achieved such great merit by pacifying the Heavenly Mountains with three shots and vanquishing Koguryo, by order of His Majesty you are hereby appointed as the empire's commander in chief of the infantry and cavalry. Face the court and give expression to your gratitude. (XUE RENGUI *acts out expressing his gratitude, and speaks*:) Your Excellency Chief of Staff, many thanks for your recommendation! (XU MAOGONG *speaks*:) Commander in Chief, His Majesty offers you three cups of wine. Soldier, bring the wine. (XUE RENGUI *speaks*:) Chief of Staff, I can't drink. (XU MAOGONG *speaks*:) This is His Majesty's command. Who would dare to refuse? (XUE RENGUI *speaks*:) As it is His Majesty's command, I will drink this wine. (*Acts out drinking the wine, and speaks*:) *Aiya*! I'm drunk! (*Acts out falling asleep.*) (XU MAOGONG *speaks*:) The commander in chief is drunk and has fallen asleep. Soldiers, don't make any noise, and report to me when the commander in chief wakes up. I will go to the rear hall.
(*Exits.*)

(XUE RENGUI *acts out having a dream, and speaks*:) I'm Xue Rengui. I've been away from home for ten years. My father and mother are old now and have no one to take care of them. Today I will secretly leave the border regions and, with some twenty or thirty cavalry men with light bows and short arrows and with fine steeds and trusted men, go back home to see my parents. (*Recites*:)

Because the merit of my three shots established peace,
I've been appointed commander in chief to guard the borders.
For ten long years I never dreamt of going home,
And in sadness I heed the cry of the "compassionate" crow out beyond the sky.[97]

---

96. This line quotes the last line of the first of two quatrains by Cao Song 曹松 (ca. 830–after 901) titled "Two Poems of the Year 819" (Jihai sui liangshou 已亥歲兩首). This poem can be translated as follows:
Marsh and city, rivers and hills are caught up in the schemes of warfare;
Common people cannot live happily even as woodcutters and fishermen.
I beg you, sir, do not talk about the business of achieving noble rank:
For a single general to achieve success, myriads of men must die.

97. So called because it was believed that fledgling crows would return to feed their parents in the nest as they had been fed when they were chicks.

ACT 2

(OLD FEMALE *enters and speaks*:) I am Donkey Xue's mother. Ten years have passed since our son joined the army and we have never even received a letter. The two of us are now advanced in years and we thankfully rely on the care of our daughter-in-law. After we eat breakfast there's nothing left for evening. We scorch the earth to sleep, and cook the dirt to lie down.[98] I keep an urgent lookout but never see my son return. Nor do I have a clue whether he obtained an office or not. *Aiya*! My son Donkey Xue, pining for you has done me in! (*Acts out weeping*.) (XUE RENGUI *enters and speaks*:) I, Xue Rengui, am coming back to see how my parents are doing, and here I am already! Ah, my old home. Open the gate! Open the gate! (OLD FEMALE *speaks*:) Who is calling at the gate? Let me open the gate. (*Acts out greeting, and speaks*:) Officer, who are you? (XUE RENGUI *speaks*:) It's me, Donkey Xue! (OLD FEMALE *acts out weeping, and speaks*:) My son, how I longed for you! Let me call your father. (*Acts out calling, speaks*:) Old Uncle Xue! (MALE LEAD *enters dressed as an elderly peasant, holding a cane, and sings*:)

(SHANGDIAO MODE: *Ji xianbin*)

Who keeps calling "Old Uncle Xue"!

(OLD FEMALE *speaks*:) That was me calling you! (MALE LEAD *sings*:)

I would have said that it was that little good-for-nothing pestering me again!
I can't move: I bend forward then backward;
I can't stay still; I sway to the east and the west.
I am so bent by age that my skinny and shrunken old body has wasted away to nothing,
I am so racked by sorrow that my dry and desiccated beard and hair have turned all gray.

(*Acts out weeping, and sings*:)

Oh, my son who has joined the army!
Alas,
Where can he be?
Even if I were a man of iron or stone I'd be moved to sad sighs.
You failed to become commander in chief of the six ministers![99]

(*Acts out weeping, and sings*:)

Alas, my son,
All you achieved was a nailed-up sign, "From foreign parts."[100]

---

98. That is to say, they are so poor they have no proper bed and have to sleep on the ground, which they warm first with a small fire.

99. The six ministers are the commanders of the king's six armies.

100. See n. 21.

(XUE RENGUI *speaks*:) Father, how did you get so old you seem barely alive?[101] (MALE LEAD *sings*:)

(*Xiaoyao le*)
Aiya! My son,
Ever since you joined the army and left for foreign parts,
I've every day been bereft of all energy, robbed of all strength;
I've lost my souls and my spirit has scattered.
Aiya! My son,
Who knows where you might be scorched by the sun, scourged by the wind,
Or gambling for glory and fame, so that joy will follow upon suffering.
I only hope that the success of a single shot by you will change our status,
That you'll glorify our ancestors and all preceding generations!
But at present I'm without kith, without kin,
Without support, without assistance.
(*Acts out weeping, and sings*:)
Aiya! My son,
Every day we have no rice and have no firewood.

(MALE LEAD *acts out greeting* OLD FEMALE, *and speaks*:) My wife, what are you calling me for? (OLD FEMALE *speaks*:) My husband, you are always in a stew no matter what you do. Why are you crying and weeping like this? Where were you when I was calling for you a moment ago? (MALE LEAD *speaks*:) I was over at the eastern side of the village, having some wine at a wedding party. (OLD FEMALE *speaks*:) My husband, if you were over at the eastern side of the village having some wine at a wedding party, whose daughter was bringing home whose son? Tell me the whole story! (MALE LEAD *speaks*:) My wife, listen to me. (*Sings*:)

(*Wuye'er*)
Bodhisattva, the daughter of Old Master Liu,
Took in Wang Two from our village as her husband.
And all her kith and kin put a pin in her hair.

(OLD FEMALE *speaks*:) Did that girl bow to you? (MALE LEAD *speaks*:) My wife, you've hit the nail on the head! She first bowed to her father-in-law, to her mother-in-law, to the elder uncles, to the younger uncles, and to all the aunts, but when she came to me and started to bow, I heard them say: "Don't!" (*Sings*:)
But when she came to me, they stopped her from bowing,
And I asked, "Why did you stop?"

(*Speaks*:) The people more advanced in years didn't say a word, but those younger folks all together started to make a ruckus and said: "Don't bow to that old geezer. He has

101. Spoken by Xue Rengui to himself.

only one son, who went off to the army ten years ago and may be dead. If you bow to him, who will be left to carry on our family's rites? This single sentence— (*Sings*:)
Once it was said, it made tears fill my cheeks.
Aiya! Donkey,
Because of you your father and mother are overcome by depression!

(OLD FEMALE *speaks*:) My husband, be happy! Donkey Xue has come back! (MALE LEAD *speaks*:) Where is he? (OLD FEMALE *speaks*:) My son, come and bow to your father! (XUE RENGUI *acts out greeting* MALE LEAD *and bowing to him, and speaks*:) My father, I have come back to see how you and mother are doing. (MALE LEAD *speaks*:) You ungrateful little thief, you've really come back! Wife, let me give this scoundrel a beating! (OLD FEMALE *acts out dissuading him, speaks*:) He just got home! How can you beat him? Husband, still your anger! (MALE LEAD *sings*:)
(*Houting hua*)
A clean break: once you got going, you didn't think twice!

(*Acts out raising his cane.* OLD FEMALE *acts out grabbing it.*) (MALE LEAD *speaks*:) Wife, let go! (OLD FEMALE *speaks*:) Husband, still your rage! (*They act this out three times.*) (MALE LEAD *sings*:)
I'll beat you in a hundred, a thousand ways for following your whims!

(MALE LEAD *speaks*:) Donkey, how long have you been gone? (XUE RENGUI *speaks*:) Your son has been away for a full ten years. (MALE LEAD *sings*:)
You joined the army at the age of twenty-two,
How come you show up precisely at thirty-three?

(XUE RENGUI *speaks*:) Father, because I fulfilled the duties of loyalty, I could not fulfill those of filial piety. (MALE LEAD *sings*:)
On that day when you left home to set out on "those purple paths,"
You displayed your heroic might in Carmine City,[102]
And showed off your martial skills in Longmen Township.
You said you would promptly change our family status—
Who could have ever expected that another ten years would pass!
(*Shuang yan'er*)
You are exactly like Zhao Gao, who delivered a candlestick but never returned.[103]
Aiya! My son,
I thought that father and child were cut off forever
And didn't believe that you would be here in the flesh.
Your mother has lost all her strength,
And your father's hair has turned gray.

(XUE RENGUI *speaks*:) Father and Mother, you should know that I did not come back home openly, but slipped away from the border regions to see how you were doing, so

102. See n. 26.

103. See n. 28.

I am going to have to leave. (MALE LEAD *speaks*:) Wife, treat our son to a meal! (OLD FEMALE *speaks*:) With what, husband? (MALE LEAD *sings*:)

(*Cu hulu*)

Buy some wine

And kill a chicken.

(OLD FEMALE *speaks*:) What should I buy some wine and a chicken with? (MALE LEAD *sings*:)

At the eastern side of the village,[104] pawn that old pair of hempen sandals for me!

(OLD FEMALE *speaks*:) Even if I can buy a little wine and some snacks, it won't be enough for him to get drunk. Donkey can hold his liquor! (MALE LEAD *sings*:)

You say that Donkey Xue can hold an ocean of liquor. . . .

(*Continues in speech*:) No problem! (*Sings*:)

We still have those two pints of buckwheat under the bed.

Oh, my son,

I have no idea which wind blew you, swirling and twirling, home!

(ZHANG SHIGUI, *leading* SOLDIERS, *suddenly enters, and speaks*:) Isn't that Xue Rengui? Listen to His Majesty's command: because you neglected your military duties and slipped away to go home, His Majesty has ordered me to arrest you and take you back to the palace for punishment. Soldiers, grab Xue Rengui and bind him up tightly. (XUE RENGUI *acts out panicking and weeping, and speaks*:) What to do now? Father, who can save me? (MALE LEAD *sings*:)

(*Reprise*)

Seeing him so dreadfully and anxiously open the imperial edict,

Already scares me so much that my face turns a parched yellow.

(ZHANG SHIGUI *speaks*:) Soldiers, arrange yourself on both sides and don't let that old geezer approach. (OLD FEMALE *acts out weeping*.) (MALE LEAD *speaks*:) My son! (*Sings*:)

I see those oh-so-vicious constables line up on both sides:

None can help but Guanyin of the southern sea who saves everyone from suffering.[105]

(ZHANG SHIGUI *speaks*:) Keep that old geezer away and don't let him snatch the criminal away! (MALE LEAD *sings*:)

I'm so scared I kowtow to you and make my bow—

(*Continues in speech*:) Your Excellency! (*Sings*:)

You forgiving my son,

Would far surpass [in merit] feeding a myriad of monks.

(ZHANG SHIGUI *speaks*:) Soldiers, take him away! (XUE RENGUI *speaks*:) My father and mother, I cannot take care of you! (MALE LEAD *acts out weeping, and sings*:)

---

104. The term we have translated "village" here is *dian* (店), which means the area of a small village occupied by people who are not farmers: they are shopkeepers, tradesmen, etc.

105. See n. 30.

(*Langlilai Coda*)

Rough and rude they push my son out through the gate,

(ZHANG SHIGUI *speaks*:) Drag him outside, kill him, and be done with it. (MALE LEAD *sings*:)

He, wide-eyed in terror, is about to be killed—

Uselessly I strain my mind and muster my thoughts—what can be done?

(ZHANG SHIGUI *speaks*:) Bind him up tightly, don't let the scoundrel escape! (MALE LEAD *sings*:)

All I know is that it'll be hard for him to wriggle out of the hempen rope tied behind his back.

Who will come to forgive my child?

Aiya! My son,

The only chance for us to meet again is that highest heaven sends a writ of pardon!

(MALE LEAD *and* OLD FEMALE *exit.*)

(ZHANG SHIGUI *acts out pushing* XUE RENGUI *and speaks*:) Don't pretend this is happening only in your sleep and in a dream!

(*Exits.*)

(XUE RENGUI *acts out waking up, and speaks*:) I slept really well. Well, so it turned out to be a dream of Southern Branch,[106] but it terrified me! A moment ago I had three cups of wine and got drunk, accidentally fell asleep, and went straight home in a dream. When I saw my father and mother they were so poor and miserable! When will I be able to see them? (*Acts out being sad.*) (XU MAOGONG [*enters and*] *speaks*:) I am Xu Maogong. I wonder why Xue Rengui in the front hall is so upset? I'll have to ask him why. (*Acts out greeting, and speaks*:) Commander in Chief, why are you so upset? Perhaps because you find your office too small? (XUE RENGUI *speaks*:) Your Excellency Chief of Staff, if you don't mind a long story, please listen as I give you a full account at leisure. (*Recites*:)

From my earliest youth I grew up in a farming village,
And all my life I knew only the taste of village wine.
When did I ever smell the carefully sealed imperial brew?
When I had taken three cups, I was as drunk as a skunk!
My single soul, my true nature, traveled back home,
Where I was happily reunited with my father and mother.
But suddenly we heard a loud shouting outside the gate,
Announcing the arrival of Commander Zhang Shigui.

106. This was, first, a famous story by the Tang writer Li Gongzuo 李公佐 (778–848) and then a series of plays about a person who fell asleep and dreamt that he went to a land called Acacia Peace (Huai'an 槐安). He married the princess of the state and was made magistrate of Nanke (literally, "Southern Branch" 南柯), where he enjoyed wealth and nobility. Later, he was defeated in a battle, his wife died, and he came under the king's suspicion. Dispirited, he returned to his own home, and then awoke from his dream to find that Nanke district and the state of Acacia Peace were nothing more than ant colonies in the roots of an acacia tree—here, of course, meant to signal that human life is nothing more than a dream, or that a lifetime can be lived in the space of a dream.

He said that I had left the border regions on my own,
And that he had been dispatched to punish me.
He bound my arms behind my back and brought me before the steps—
With one blow of the sword my skull was shattered!
All of a sudden I woke up with a start from my dream,
I had been sleeping in the army headquarters' front hall!
From afar I gaze at my hometown—where may it be?
Thinking of my father and mother, my tears fall freely.
I implore you this, Chief of Staff, who opened the borders and expanded the territory:
Take pity on me, Xue Rengui, who abandoned his village and left his home.

(XU MAOGONG *speaks*:) So that's the situation! I will propose to His Majesty that you, Commander in Chief, be allowed to return to your hometown, clad in brocade. I will also give you my own daughter as your wife, so she can accompany you and meet with your parents. The husband glorious, the wife noble, and both enjoying Heaven's favor—wouldn't that be wonderful? (XUE RENGUI *speaks*:) Many thanks, Your Excellency Chief of Staff. I dare not stay longer or tarry. With a hundred ounces of yellow gold and a thousand jugs of imperial wine I will return home to see my parents. (XU MAOGONG *recites*:)

Because you pacified the Heavenly Mountains with three shots,
You were given the golden seal and appointed as general with all honors.

(XUE RENGUI *recites*:)

Once long ago, weeping and crying, I abandoned my father and mother;
On this day, laughing and smiling, I return in glory, clad in brocade.

(*Exit.*)

ACT 3

(COMIC, *dressed as* PEASANT WOMAN, *enters, and sings*:)
(SHUANGDIAO MODE: *Douye huang*)[107]

Where, oh where?
To the west of the jujube orchard!
My mother told you to come on home early,
Afraid that wolves and tigers would bite you.
Pick the jujubes, pick the jujubes, pick your mother's brains!
You say you never picked any jujubes?
Where did those pits in your mouth come from?

---

107. As Shao 1955, 86, remarks, this rendition of *Douye huang* appears to be an inserted popular song from the Ming. Not only does it not rhyme with the rest of the suite but also the metrical structure of the song is different from the metrical structures for the tune by this title found in the music formularies of northern and southern drama.

I round things up, set them right.
If I see a wolf,
I'll spring across the wall,
And scare your mother!

(*Speaks*:) Bange, I am leaving for the graves. You also should hurry up! (MALE LEAD *enters dressed as* BANGE *and speaks*:) You should wait a minute for me. Today is the Cold Food Festival. The weather is really nice. (*Sings*:)

(ZHONGLÜ MODE: *Fendie'er*)

Today the sun is warm, the wind light;
Each family goes to the graves, well prepared![108]
They have prepared some festival foods:
Some vegetable-stuffed steamed buns;
Noodles dribbled through a sieve,
Chicken, shoats, dog, and swine.
What stupid thing is she up to now
That she has drunk so much she's killed the mood!

(*Zui chunfeng*)

You just had to lose your paktong[109] hairpin,
So your oiled bun sags to one side.
Plenty of people visit the graves,
But none the likes of you,
You!
Drinking until you cannot even walk,
Cannot even stand:
Drunk and drunk again!

(PEASANT WOMAN *speaks*:) Bange, hurry up! Let's go look at the sprouts. (MALE LEAD *speaks*:) Do you see that? Who's coming there in the distance? (PEASANT WOMAN *acts out panicking, and speaks*:) Bange, that's a whole bunch of people. That's really scary! (MALE LEAD *sings*:)

(*Shi'er yue*)

It must be bunch after bunch out "trodding the green";[110]
Band upon band seeking out the paddies along the paths:
All I see is a cloud of red dust rising up.

The song occurs in one other Ming drama, in act 2 of *Liu Xuande Drunkenly Flees the Yellow Crane Tower* (*Liu Xuande zui zou Huanghe lou* 劉玄德醉走黄鶴樓), where it is followed by a second song, titled "Sprout Lyric" (He 禾詞); see Anon. 1958a, 15a–16b. The lyrics of the two songs show a few variations that involve transcriptions of common words but are otherwise nearly identical.

108. See n. 33.

109. See n. 34.

110. "Trodding the green" (*taqing* 踏青) refers specifically to taking in the sights of spring at the time of the Qingming Festival; it resulted in far more social occasions than the family-centered rituals at the grave site.

(XUE RENGUI *enters, astride a horse and leading troops, and speaks:*) I am Xue Rengui. Preceded by my ceremonial guards, I leisurely travel on. (MALE LEAD *sings:*)

So it turns out to be a mounted warrior, speeding on like a flash of lightning.
His entourage wears brocade from top to bottom,
So why is the general alone wearing a plain white top and bottom?
(*Yaomin ge*)
Wow,
Could it be that the god of snow has descended from heaven?

(XUE RENGUI *speaks:*) Hey, you, farmer, stop! (MALE LEAD *sings:*)

When he shouts his booming voice resembles spring thunder!

(XUE RENGUI *speaks:*) Don't get flustered, I just want to ask you a question. (MALE LEAD *sings:*)

It scares me so much my mind and my courage both quiver and quake in delirium;
My hands and feet tremble and shake like an idiot.
Let me steel myself—
How can I move my body?
Best I fake drunkenness without the need of wine!

(XUE RENGUI *speaks:*) Hey fellow, I want to ask you something! (MALE LEAD *sings:*)

(*Shang xiaolou*)
Suddenly I hear him talk, his horse whinny:
A power and prestige of terrifying power!
It scares me so much I quiver and quake,
Am flurried and flustered,
And only want to wail and weep, cry and sob.
Here; there; nowhere to hide,
And this makes me kneel, *kerplonk*, right in front of the horse.

(XUE RENGUI *speaks:*) You fellow, I have some questions for you. And don't come up with all kinds of excuses. (MALE LEAD *speaks:*) How would I dare? (*Sings:*)

(*Manting fang*)
How would I dare make all kinds of excuses?
I only fear my words will not come out right,
Or what I say will be at odds with you.

(XUE RENGUI *speaks:*) Are you a local? Or are you a sojourner? What labor service are you on? (MALE LEAD *sings:*)

We, your children, are inhabitants of Longmen Township and fulfill our corvée.

(XUE RENGUI *speaks:*) What are you doing here in such large groups all together? (MALE LEAD *sings:*)

Today is day one-oh-five, Cold Food Festival:
Those who are visiting the graves are our fellow villagers—
When drinking wine we use earthen jugs and pottery bowls.

Your Excellency must be here to collect taxes due,
So I will go to the village and report your arrival.
Your Excellency,
Just say what you want, and I will do it!

(XUE RENGUI *speaks*:) Let me ask you: Old Uncle Xue in this village had a son called Donkey Xue. Do you know him? (MALE LEAD *speaks*:) Your Lordship, I know that Xue Rengui! (*Sings*:)

(*Kuaihuo san*)
Out on the threshing ground the two of us stripped ears of grain,
And from the tops of trees plucked green plums.
Facing backward we rode on the black oxen, playing the Tibetan flute,
And stole fresh melons to eat, rind and all!

(XUE RENGUI *speaks*:) As you were such a good friend of Donkey Xue's, what craft did he learn in his youth? (MALE LEAD *sings*:)

(*Ya gu'er*)
He, he, he—from his earliest youth—
He, he, he did not behave in a proper way!
He fervently trained with spear and with staff,
Unwilling to pull the harrow or steer the plow.
He indeed rejected the farmer's life,
Practiced the military arts,
And became champion of each band or group.
You gave him a bow and arrows, and he could shoot;
You gave him a fiery steed, and he could ride it,
And he employed a squared-heaven lance with a painted shaft.

(XUE RENGUI *speaks*:) Who now takes care of his father and mother? Tell me everything, and I will listen carefully. (MALE LEAD *speaks*:) That elderly couple are now quite advanced in years. They only had this one child but he joined the army; for ten years they've had no news. His parents at home lack rice and firewood, and they anxiously keep watch for a return still unseen. What suffering! (*Sings*:)

(*Baolao'er*)
As soon as that child had become a grown man,
He didn't treat his parents like Heaven and Earth.
I have no idea who his lover may be in some whorehouse or other,
But he never remembers their profound favor of feeding and raising him.
How pitiable, his father and mother,
Advanced in years, bereft of strength,
Nothing to rely on, nothing for support.
That scoundrel should die before his time,
And be tossed in a hole or dumped in a ditch—
He is truly a good-for-nothing!

(XUE RENGUI *speaks*:) You fellow, would you still recognize that Donkey Xue? (MALE LEAD *speaks*:) How would I not be able to recognize him? If I would see him, I would go and punch him in the face about fifty times! (XUE RENGUI *speaks*:) You fellow, now lift your head and open your eyes. I am that Donkey Xue, am I not? (MALE LEAD *speaks*:) If I had known that from the start, I wouldn't have said a word! (XUE RENGUI *speaks*:) And you have cursed me enough. How could you know that at present I am the commander in chief of the infantry and cavalry of the whole empire, and that at the command of His Majesty I am returning home clad in brocade to visit my parents at home. (MALE LEAD *sings*:)

(*Shuahai'er*)
While your old parents suffer bitterly, you enjoy riches and glory,
And your appearance has changed into a heroic and stalwart figure.
Well you are plumper and fatter than in those days,
And have grown a moustache that covers your lips.
Don't take offense at the words I maligned you with just now—
It's because so much time has passed that I couldn't recognize you.

(XUE RENGUI *speaks*:) I will not blame you. Forgive me for not coming down from my horse. (MALE LEAD *sings*:)

Ai!
Just look at his high and mighty air on horseback!
How we raced up the trees to grope for doves' eggs,
And went into the muck and mire to snag frogs.

(XUE RENGUI *speaks*:) How have my father and mother been doing since I joined the army? Tell me everything and I will listen carefully. (MALE LEAD *sings*:)

(*One from Coda*)
Your mother is more than seventy,
Your father is exactly eighty.
And you have no siblings of any age:
In his dilapidated house your father bitterly suffers the cold of deepest winter;
While your mother stirs a whole night's ashes in the cold stove.
They suffer such hunger their innards are shattered.
For them no succulent lamb and white noodles;
They get through with bland rice and yellowed pickles.

(XUE RENGUI *speaks*:) Do my father and mother ever think of me? (MALE LEAD *sings*:)

(*Coda*)
They weep from deepening dusk till early evening,
Then from early evening till late at night,
They weep for that Xue Rengui who quit home and hearth!

(*Speaks*:) Your father and mother are leaning on the gate from early till late, waiting for Donkey Xue, without any idea when he may return. How terrible! (*Sings*:)

Your aged parents do nothing but wait for you!

(*Exit together with* PEASANT WOMAN.)

(XUE RENGUI *speaks*:) So my father and mother are suffering in such a terrible way. How could I dare tarry here any longer? I have to hurry back home to see my father and mother. (*Recites*:)

Returning from Koguryo I enjoy my lord's favors:
A hundred ounces of yellow gold, a thousand jugs of wine.
When I come home I will present these to my two parents:
This will best being a peasant by a long shot!

(*Exits*.)

ACT 4

(DU RUHUI *enters and speaks*:) I am Du Ruhui. After Xue Rengui had defeated the troops of Koguryo, pacified the Heavenly Mountains with three shots, and returned to court, he was appointed commander in chief of the infantry and cavalry. Xu Maogong's daughter was bestowed upon him as his wife, and he was ordered to return to his hometown clad in brocade. Now I have been ordered by His Majesty to relay to Xu Maogong by edict that he should proceed straightaway to Longmen Township in Jiangzhou to ennoble Xue Rengui's family and distribute rewards. I have transmitted this edict to Xu Maogong, and I can tarry here no longer since I have to return and report to His Majesty. (*Recites*:)

All because Xue Rengui crossed the sea and fought against Koguryo,
And repeatedly established great merits on the banks of the Yalu River,
He was bestowed yellow gold to return home and celebrate his parents' old age,
He will be given further noble rank, heavy reward, and then summoned back to court.

(*Exits*.)

(MALE LEAD, *dressed as elderly peasant*, *enters with* OLD FEMALE *and* MINOR FEMALE, *and speaks*:) I am Old Uncle Xue. My wife, it's been ten years since our son joined the army and we have received no news nor has he come back home. Will this ever end? (OLD FEMALE *speaks*:) My husband, it is all your fault! You let him go off and join the army! If you are having a hard time now, what can you say? Husband, last night I had a dream that our son had obtained an office. Could it be that he has enjoyed such luck? (MALE LEAD *speaks*:) Dreams are the longings of the heart. My son, come home quickly whether you got an office or not. This yearning for you is killing me! (*Sings*:)

(SHUANGDIAO MODE: *Xinshui ling*)

Because of you, a son who was supposed to be our provider, I've wept till my eyes have grown blurry.
Alas, I've been worried for the whole time you've been gone.
My son, if you haven't gone off to the courts of the underworld,

Why have you tarried for ten years at the edge of the earth?
How can that be so-called "high rank at court or in the provinces"?
It makes me so vexed—when will it end?

(OLD FEMALE *speaks*:) He'll come back in none of our lifetimes, so there's no point to your vexations. (MALE LEAD *speaks*:) Let me get some sleep. (OLD FEMALE *speaks*:) My husband, you get some sleep. I'll keep watch at the gate. (XUE RENGUI *enters with* YOUNG FEMALE *and* SOLDIERS, *and speaks*:) I'm home. Soldiers, take my horse! Isn't that person outside the gate my mother? (OLD FEMALE *speaks*:) You, official coming from over there, who are you? Don't scare me, this old woman! (XUE RENGUI *speaks*:) Mother, do you recognize your son Xue Rengui? Today I've come home after obtaining an office. (OLD FEMALE *speaks*:) Of course you are my child Xue Rengui! I will go and tell your father. My husband, congratulations! Our son has come home after obtaining an office. (MALE LEAD *speaks*:) Is that true? My wife, let's go outside see if it is true. (*Acts out greeting, and speaks*:) Which one is Xue Rengui? (XUE RENGUI *speaks*:) I am Xue Rengui! Receive your child's obeisances. (MALE LEAD *sings*:)

(*Dianqian huan*)

Our son has finally been able to come home:
But what honor guard of men and horses is that in his entourage?

(XUE RENGUI *speaks*:) Father, I can't believe ten years have passed. (MALE LEAD *sings*:)

These ten years have become an empty tale:
What is true? What is false?
I harbored doubts that the magical magpie would leak any secrets at the evening yamen session,
Or that the daddy longlegs would spin its web at the front of the eaves,[111]
But my dreaming soul could not abandon them.
A few days ago my eyes fluttered and jumped;
Last night the candlewick's snuff suddenly popped.[112]

(XUE RENGUI *speaks*:) Father, after I had pacified the Heavenly Mountains with three shots and inflicted a defeat on the *molizhi*, I was appointed as commander in chief of the infantry and cavalry of the whole empire, and by imperial decree the daughter of the Duke of Ying was awarded to me as a wife. Today I have come back to my hometown clad in brocade to see my father and mother. Miss, please bow to my parents. (MINOR FEMALE *acts out bowing, and speaks*:) Father-in-Law and Mother-in-Law, please allow your daughter-in-law to perform eight bows. (OLD FEMALE *speaks*:) So you are the daughter of the Duke of Ying. That is really too much of an honor for us! (MINOR FEMALE *speaks*:) Today father and son and husband and wife are all reunited.

111. The magpie was thought to have extrasensory powers that enabled it to tell when a loved one would arrive; it revealed the arrival by its call at evening court. The daddy longlegs (*xizhu'er* 喜蛛兒) is also known as the "happy one" (*xizi* 蟢子) and would spin a web when a wish was granted.

112. Two more happy omens.

My dear parents-in-law, please be seated, and allow your daughter-in-law to congratulate you with a bow. (OLD FEMALE *speaks*:) My son, we owe much to our daughter-in-law for taking care of us old folks in the last ten years. (MALE LEAD *sings*:)

(*Tianshui ling*)

We have experienced interminable years,
Desolate winter months,
Long hot summers,
Hopefully gazing in expectation with aching hearts and eager eyes.
For all the work and all the provisions during that time,
The gathering of leeks, the harvesting of vegetables,
The sewing of clothes, the mending and patching,
We relied on your first wife, the woman Liu!

(XUE RENGUI *speaks*:) First wife, I am deeply grateful to you for taking care of my parents for these ten years. Miss, you and I should show our gratitude by making a bow to Madame Liu. (YOUNG FEMALE *speaks*:) Elder Sister, I am deeply indebted to you for taking care of our parents-in-law. Allow your younger sister to make a few bows. (FEMALE *speaks*:) Miss, I am only the daughter of common folks, while you are the precious darling of a family of officials. Please take your ease. (TWO FEMALES *act out bowing together*.) (MALE LEAD *speaks*:) My daughters-in-law, from now on the two of you should not make any distinction between first and second, nor any between elder and younger. It would be best if you would treat each other as sisters. (MALE LEAD *sings*:)

(*Zhegui ling*)

It has to be stressed our family already had a wise and worthy daughter-in-law,
But who could know that by imperial grace
You would be gifted with such a pretty beauty?
One is a staunch and courageous man,
One, the wife who withstood poverty,
And one is the daughter of a prime minister.
That one knows the rites, displaying modesty;
This one is very caring, free from any mistake.
The two of you are both admirable and praiseworthy,
And without blemish or flaw.
This one, a village wife,
Lifted the tray as high as her eyebrows;[113]
That one, an official's daughter,
Resembles a flower added on to brocade.

---

113. Meng Guang, the wife of the first-century poor recluse Liang Hong, displayed her respect for her husband by lifting the tray as high as her eyebrows when serving him his food.

(XU MAOGONG *enters leading soldiers, and recites:*)

Yesterday I left the Phoenix Towers,[114]
Today I arrive here in Dragon Gate.
One entire family enjoys happiness,
For a thousand years we will praise the emperor's grace.

I am Xu Maogong. Xue Rengui achieved merit in the campaign against Koguryo, and he has gone back to his village clad in the brocade that he was granted. Now I have been ordered by His Majesty to take this edict to Longmen Township, to ennoble and reward his parents and his wife Madame Liu, and to summon him back to court. Now I have arrived at his gate. Soldiers, report that Xu Maogong has arrived bearing the order of His Majesty. (SOLDIER *speaks:*) Sir! Commander in Chief, Xu Maogong has arrived in front of the gate at the order of His Majesty. (XUE RENGUI *speaks:*) Prepare some incense, and let me welcome him in person. (*Acts out greeting.*) (XU MAOGONG *speaks:*) Xue Rengui, I have been ordered by His Majesty to deliver this edict, ennobling and rewarding your whole family. (XUE RENGUI *speaks:*) Your Excellency, if I had known you were coming, I would have met you further out on the road. Please forgive me for this crime. (MALE LEAD, OLD FEMALE, *and* FEMALE *act out changing into cap and gown.*) (MALE LEAD *sings:*)

(*Xi Jiangnan*)

Oh, could anyone guess that such glory would come our way?
Even a simple village peasant of weathered face and hoary head like me
Can be robed in scarlet, carry an ivory tablet, and be belted in raven-black silk.
My son, you should be happy now:
Not in vain did you once study the martial arts!

(XU MAOGONG *speaks:*) Xue Rengui, let your whole family kneel facing the palace. Listen to His Majesty's edict:

Because of your merit that arches over the world, We raise your noble rank to that of Koguryo-pacifying duke, and you are given tax rights over ten thousand households. Upon your father and mother are bestowed a hundred ounces of yellow gold. Both Madame Liu and Madame Xu are bestowed the noble rank of lady of Liao. You will have to return to court within the next three months. Express your gratitude for the imperial grace!

(*They all act out expressing gratitude.*) (XU MAOGONG *speaks:*) At that time, I remember, the *molizhi* had bivouacked his troops in front of Whitebrow Slope on the banks of the Yalu River and challenged the famous generals of our Great Tang to battle. At that time some of the famous generals of our Great Tang had passed away, and some were just too old. It was all due to your three shots, Commander in Chief, that we

114. Phoenix Towers is one of the many terms to designate the imperial palace.

were able to inflict a defeat on the *molizhi* and that you achieved this great merit. It is not without reason that today His Majesty has raised your office and distributed rewards. (MALE LEAD *sings*:)

(*Gu meijiu*)

So the Great Tang lacked famous generals,
And our son was ready to show his mettle.
It was just because he requited the state with his whole loyal heart
And fought a pitched battle with the troops of the Liao,
That we can finally put an end to this warfare.

(XUE RENGUI *speaks*:) Father, when I crossed the sea I established fifty-four merits in the campaign against Koguryo, but they were all falsely claimed by Commander Zhang Shigui. If His Excellency the Chief of Staff had not clarified merit and crime, how could I have lived to see this day? (*All act out expressing their gratitude to* XU MAOGONG.) (XU MAOGONG *speaks*:) This was all because His Majesty ordered me to promote and reward in accordance with merit. Why should I be thanked? (MALE LEAD *sings*:)

(*Taiping ling*)

Even though the Son of Heaven of the Tang determines life and death,
How could he be a match for the dirty tricks of Commander Zhang?
If it had not been for the divine perspicacity of you, Chief of Staff,
The merits of our general clad in white would have surely been wiped out.
Today our ranks are raised, our rewards are increased:
We enjoy such spectacular success!
Oh, how can we ever rightly pay our great benefactor back?

(XU MAOGONG *speaks*:) Commander in Chief, to have one's whole family enjoy glory and status and to be summoned to court are the most joyous events of a man's life. Today let's slaughter a sheep and brew wine in order to have a large celebratory banquet! (*Speaks in ballad verse*:)

The white-clad general is peerless in this world;
He pacified Koguryo and his prestige shook the border regions.
He supported us until the cosmos was peaceful and stable,
And polished our luster until the sun and moon shone with brilliant light.
Old Uncle Xue, like the tree of long life, will never age;[115]
Madame Xue will share this joy in the daylily hall.[116]
A prime minister's daughter happily takes second place;
A wife from the porridge days shows herself very wise.

115. The Chinese mahogany tree (*Cedrela sinensis*) grows very slowly and is reputed to live for thousands of years; the "noumenal *cedrela*" is a tree that exists in ancient legend that never dies. It is used as a metaphor for the father.

116. Daylilies are planted in front of a mother's apartment because one of the alternative names of this plant is "forget all worries."

By imperial decree the whole family is ennobled and given riches;
Now their status has been changed, their glory is exceptional.
If Xu Maogong had not ordered a shooting match at the army headquarters,
Could Xue Rengui have returned home clad in brocade?

Title: Xu Maogong orders a shooting match at the army headquarters.
Name: Xue Rengui Returns Home in Glory.

The End of The *Zaju Xue Rengui Returns Home in Glory*

4

The Bamboo-Leaf Boat

INTRODUCTION

The story of the bamboo-leaf boat stems from an anonymous classical tale of the late Tang dynasty that is found in several recensions.[1] Known alternatively as "Chen Jiqing" (陳季卿), the name of the protagonist, or "The Bamboo-Leaf Boat" (Zhuye Zhou 竹葉舟), it formed the basis of a play by the mid to late Yuan playwright Fan Kang 范康, who was also known as Fan Zi'an 范子安 or Fan Ziying 范子英. Fan's name occurs in the section of the *Register of Ghosts* titled "Those Famous and Talented Men Who Are Already Dead Whom I Knew Personally." Since this section includes people who were listed as "still alive" in the first edition of 1330 but moved to the "already dead" section in Zhong Sicheng's last revisions of 1345, we can date Fan's passing sometime between 1330 and 1345. The *Register of Ghosts* provides us, in fact, with what little we know about Fan's life and part of his literary production:

> Fan Kang, also known as Zi'an, was a man of Hangzhou. He understood human nature and natural principle and was skilled at exposition and explanation; he was capable in writing, and also thoroughly versed in the rules of music. He composed the play *Du Zimei Roams the Serpentine* because Wang Bocheng had written *Li Taibai Banished to Yelang*,[2] and as soon as his pen touched paper, it was new and original. This was most

1. See Wang Meng'ou 1971, 33–37, esp. 37.
2. Wang Bocheng 王伯成was one of the most outstanding dramatists of the second part of the thirteenth century, but little of his work has come down to us. His *Li Taibai bian Yelang* 李太白貶夜郎has been preserved in a Yuan edition. The play deals with the famous poet Li Bai's 李白 (701–762) principled and prescient criticism of the adulterous couple Yang Guifei 楊貴妃and An Lushan 安祿山. For a study of this play, including extensive

likely because that with which heaven had endowed him was superb and distinct, unreachable by others.

[His plays:]
On Serpentine Reservoir Du Fu Roams in the Spring[3]
Chen Jiqing Is Enlightened to the Way on a Bamboo-Leaf Boat[4]
[An Elegy:]
Poems inscribed on Goose Pagoda, limning autumn's clarity,
Wine filling the horn flagon, rowing in the evening breeze;
Poetic tallies from "wine commands"[5] and leisurely chanted songs,
On the battlefield of letters he achieved the greatest merit;
Sweeping away a thousand troops, he was commander in chief in the arena of
brushes.
Dreams of dragons and snakes,
Traces of fox and hare[6]—
Half of his life spent
In the sound of a finger snap.[7]

In addition to these plays, only the latter of which is extant, Fan also has a few surviving colloquial poetic works (*sanqu* 散曲): four "little songs" (*xiaoling* 小令) titled

quotations in translation, see Idema 2004; for an extensively annotated translation with copious notes, see Akamatsu et al. 2011. Wang Bocheng treated Emperor Xuanzong's passion for Yang Guifei, her adulterous relation with a Sogdian general in Chinese service, An Lushan, and the latter's eventual rebellion (resulting in the elderly emperor's flight from his capital Chang'an and the death of Yang Guifei) in much greater detail in his *Tianbao yishi zhugongdiao* 天寶遺事諸宮調, which has been preserved only in fragments (see Fan Ben Li Chen 1992 and 2005–2006). Fan Kang's *Du Zimei you Qujiang* 杜子美遊曲家江 (or, its alternative title, *Qujiang chi Du Fu youchun* 曲江池杜甫遊春) has not been preserved. Its main character must have been China's most famous poet, Du Fu 杜甫 (712–770), lamenting the decline of the Tang dynasty on the eve of the An Lushan rebellion. Plays on this topic are discussed by Tan 2010, 55–68.

3. The alternative title found in n. 2.
4. Li Kaixian mistakenly attributes the fourth act of the play *Fan Li Returns to the Lakes* (*Fan Li gui hu* 范蠡歸湖) to Fan Kang rather than to Zhao Mingdao 趙明道, who is normally considered the author. See Li Kaixian 1982, 318.
5. Wine commands, or "wine songs" (*jiuling* 酒令), were commands issued by a game master at drinking bouts. The commands were normally based in the composition, use, or violation of various textual forms, including both prose and poetic works. If one failed in carrying out the command, one had to immediately drink or was issued a wine tally that had to be cleared by a drink at a later time in the evening. See Harper 1986.
6. Zhong 1982, 120; Lü and Wu 2000, 463–67. The precise referents in the last four lines of this song are highly ambiguous. "Dreams of dragons and snakes" probably refers to his lack of success as a writer. The phrase "not yet created the dream of dragons and snakes" (*weizuo longshe meng* 未作龍蛇夢) is often used in elegies (*wan'ge* 挽歌) written after Southern Song to describe an incompletely fulfilled artistic life. "Traces of fox and hare" usually refers to a deserted place or a place of splendor now filled with the tracks of foxes and rabbits, extended perhaps to mean a land of former glory (Song) now crisscrossed with the tracks of wild animals (Mongols).
7. The sound of snapping fingers means a flash or an instant, as in the common phrase "One hundred years pass in the sound of snapping fingers" (*Tanzhi sheng zhong guo bainian* 彈指聲中過百年).

"Wine," "Sex," "Wealth," and "Anger" (*jiu se cai qi* 酒色財氣), and an extended suite of songs called *Finding Joy in the Way* (*Ledao* 樂道). Both sets of songs have a tangential relationship with Daoism, particularly the Quanzhen (Perfectly Realized) sect. The early figures of this sect considered the emotions inspired by alcohol, sex, riches, and anger as the "four harms" (*sihai* 四害), giving in to which would dissipate the vital essence and virtue of the body and spirit.[8] The second suite, *Finding Joy in the Way*, is a rather conventional set of songs about the joys of Daoist life; it bears a close resemblance to an inserted suite of songs found in the *Yuan Edition* of the play. We should, however, remember that these are rather cliché songs, and that the warnings against sex, alcohol, material possessions, and anger have a very old tradition reflecting an emphasis on restraint that is shared by many schools of Chinese thought and religion. Still, they do point to Fan Kang's general interest in Daoism and exploring the idea of "the world as a dream."

THE ORIGINAL STORY

The story of Chen Jiqing as it exists in the Tang makes no direct connection to Daoism, but it does speak of a hermit from Zhongnan Mountain, south of Chang'an. This mountain is particularly famous for its anchorites, as well as its relationship to the formative tradition of Daoism.[9] The story in its entirety reads as follows:

> Chen Jiqing's home was in the area south of the Yangtze, and he had been gone from home for ten years to take the advanced scholar examinations. His ambition was such that it was impossible for him to return unless he had succeeded. He stayed in the capital, where he sold calligraphy and writing in order to clothe and feed himself. He often visited a monk at Green Dragon Monastery. It so happened that he went there on a day when that monk had gone somewhere else, so he rested in a heated room to wait for his return.
>
> An old codger from Mount Zhongnan was also waiting for the monk, and he had just sat up near to the stove and he welcomed Jiqing to come close to it. They sat for a while, and he said to Jiqing, "It's already late afternoon, you must be famished." Jiqing replied, "Indeed, I am hungry, but since the monk is not here, what's to be done?" The old man loosened a little bag that had been tied behind his wrist and took out an herbal simple about an inch square, which he steeped in a cup and gave to Jiqing, saying, "This can pretty much cure your hunger." Jiqing swallowed it and then he felt pleasant and full, the suffering of cold and hunger washed from his body.

8. See Komjathy 2007, 104–6, for a general discussion and bibliography on this topic. He translates *sihai* as "four hindrances."

9. Ibid., 41, and sources cited there.

There was a map of the world on the eastern wall where Jiqing traced the road to south of the river and then sighed deeply to himself, "If I could get to float out on the Yellow River from the Wei, roam along the Luo, swim in the Huai, and ford across the Yangtze to get to my home, then I would not regret that I went back without any success." The old man laughed and said, "This is easy to bring about." So he ordered the monk's acolyte to snap off a leaf from a bamboo in front of the steps, and he made a little leaf boat, placing it on the Wei River on the map and said, "You concentrate your gaze on this boat, sir, and it will be just as you had just desired. But when you reach your home, you must be careful not to stay too long."

Jiqing stared at it for a long time and had just slightly perceived the waves of the Wei River when the leaf suddenly expanded, and the mat sails had already been set—it was just like he had boarded a boat. He first went from the Wei to the Yellow River, and he anchored his boat at a Chan meditation cave at a secluded monastery, where he inscribed a poem on the southern fore pillar, which read,

When the frosty gong rings, the evening winds quicken,
A chaos of crows once again roost in the cold forest;
At this time I quit the oars, grieve, and murmur:
Standing alone facing Lotus Blossom Peak.[10]

The next day he overnighted at Tong Pass and went ashore, where he inscribed some lines on the gate at Putong Monastery east of the gates of the pass, which read,

Crossing the pass grieving over ambitions lost,
Ten thousand thoughts disorder heart's plans;
Even going down the slope, the horse lacks energy,
The dust from "cleaning the doorway" fills my clothing.[11]
My plots and plans, most not reached—
Heart and mouth naturally turn against each other.[12]
But, having already set a plan to return home in shame
Is still better than not returning home because of shame.

From the eastern part of Shaanxi onward, every place he passed was a replication of his former desire. In ten days or so he reached home and his wife and children, and his brothers older and younger all welcomed him at the gate. That evening he wrote a poem titled "Evening Gazes from a Pavilion on the Yangtze" that he inscribed in his study:

I stand facing the Yangtze pavilion with a sorrow that fills the eyes,
Events past in the last ten years truly seem long gone and far away;

---

10. The westernmost peak of Mount Hua.

11. Originally from the story of a young man who wanted an audience with a noble official and had no other way but to arrive and clean the doorways of that official's gate. From its earlier meaning of seeking audience with a noble or the powerful, by the Song it had come to mean simply "to expend energy in order to accomplish something you are seeking." Here, a reference to the energy he put into seeking office.

12. That is, his former oral promise to succeed in the examinations and his current state of mind.

Fields and gardens[13] have already dispersed like floating clouds,
Kinsmen and fellow villagers have half disappeared with the passing water.
On the banks of that stream I nowhere encounter those fishermen and woodcutters—
At the edge of the eddy it is hard to find the sand-spit gulls of older days.
Do not reason that because I still have my hair and teeth that I am not yet past my prime,
For facing those distant mountains and chanting is capable of turning the hair white.

On this evening, he told his wife, "My examination time nears, and I cannot tarry long. I should set off immediately." Thereupon he intoned a stanza to separate from his wife:

The moon falls aslant, cold dew whitens,
This night I depart, but leave my heart behind;
Wine comes, filling us with sorrow as we drink,
The poem completed, it is intoned to a harmony of tears.
A song of separation from the "perching phoenix" pipes,
"Parting Cranes"[14]: we resent the jasper zither.
And tomorrow night, at my lovelorn spot,
The autumn wind will ruffle a half-empty coverlet.

As he was about to get on the boat, he left one more poem behind for his brothers:

In planning my life it is not that I was not early enough,
But, alas, that my fate comes too slow.
All of my old friends populate the Celestial River,[15]
But this body of mine is still out on the road.
The northern wind comes after a slight snow,
The evening scene still has a few clouds.
Disconsolate and dreary out on the clear river,
This petty little person must make this examination deadline.

After the first watch, he once again boarded his leaf boat, floated out on the river, and disappeared. His siblings and his wife and children wept and wailed on the bank, taking him now to be a "ghostly thing."[16]

The single leaf floated as if to take flight on the wind and he traced his old route back to the banks of the Wei. Thereupon he rented a mount, and once again visited Green Dragon Monastery. He clearly saw the old codger sitting there wrapped in his coarse clothes, and Jiqing thanked him, saying, "Well, I did return. But wasn't it just a dream?"

---

13. The family fortune.
14. A traditional song of separation between husband and wife, contrasted with the paired phoenixes above.
15. That is, the brilliant stars in the Milky Way are those of his friends who have succeeded. Passing the examinations and making a career in the imperial bureaucracy are often compared to ascending to heaven.
16. That is, as good as dead.

The codger laughed, "You'll know for sure only after sixty days have passed." The day was drawing toward evening and the monk had still not returned. The codger left, and Jiqing went back to the host [of the house where he was staying].

Two months later, Jiqing's wife and children brought gold and cloth from south of the river [in order to pay for his burial]. They were of the opinion that Jiqing had passed away and therefore came to find out. His wife said, "You came home on such and such a day in such and such a month, and on that night you wrote a poem for the western studio, and also left behind two parting poems." He then became aware that it had not been a dream.

In the spring of the next year Jiqing failed the examinations and returned eastward, and he saw the poems he had left at the Chan meditation cave and the secluded monastery at the pass—the ink was still fresh. In his later years, Jiqing did pass the examinations, but then "gave up the grains"[17] and went off into Zhongnan Mountain.[18]

This is one of the many Tang tales that teaches the illusionary quality of human existence through a dream. The two most famous examples of such tales are Li Gongzuo's *Tale of the Prefect of Southern Branch* and Shen Jiji's *Inside a Pillow*. In the first story the protagonist experiences a splendid official career as prefect of the county of Southern Branch in a dream only to realize once he awakes that it was a career in the kingdom of ants below the acacia tree in his courtyard. In the second story a young student on the way to the examinations experiences an even more splendid and eventful career while taking a nap in an inn on a headrest given to him by an elderly man at Handan while waiting for the yellow millet porridge to be cooked—when he wakes up, the yellow millet is still not done.[19]

THE DRAMA

Fan Kang made several changes to this story when he converted it into a play, adapting the Tang version to a subgeneric classification of *zaju* known as "deliverance plays" (*dutuo xi* 度脫戲).[20] This designation was first used by Aoki Masaru (1887–1964) in his *Introduction to the Zaju Drama of Yuan Writers* (*Genjin zatsugeki kaisetsu* 元人雜劇序說) published in 1938 and then supplemented and corrected by Sui Shusen and Xu Tiaofu in their 1941 translation of this book. In that work, Aoki remarked, "These are plays in which an immortal explains the Dharma to a mortal, causes him to be liberated from

17. He went off to perfect the rituals of becoming a Daoist.

18. See Li Fang 1986, 462–63; Wang Rutao 1987, 569–72.

19. For extensively annotated translations of both tales, see Nienhauser 2010, 189–232 and 73–129, respectively.

20. For a thorough introduction to the deliverance plays, see Zhao Youmin 1975a, b. For a general introduction to the subgenre in English, see Idema 1985, 63–69.

worldly cares, and leads him into the way of the immortals."[21] The term *dutuo* is considerably older than Aoki's adoption, however, and in its frequent use in both the Daoist and Buddhist canons has the clear meaning of "to lead someone beyond [their current existence] and shed [worldly cares]." Of course, that other possible existence varies in Buddhism or Daoism. Aoki's clear intent was to bring thematic specificity to the vague classification of "Immortals Transforming Others Through the Way" (Shenxian Daohua 神仙道化)[22] in Zhu Quan's *Twelve Categories of Zaju* (*Zaju shier ke* 雜劇十二科), the earliest attempt to categorize *zaju* by theme. In addition to *Bamboo-Leaf Boat*, fourteen other Yuan and Ming plays are usually classified as deliverance *zaju*:

Daoist

Anon., *Lü Dongbin in Peach and Willow: A Dream of Ascending to Immortality* (*Lü Dongbin taoliu shengxian meng* 呂洞賓桃柳升仙夢)

Anon., *Old Zhuang Zhou's One Dream of the Butterfly* (*Lao Zhuang Zhou yizhen hudie meng* 老莊周一枕蝴蝶夢)

Anon., *Zhongli of the Han Leads Lan Caihe to Enlightenment* (*Han Zhongli dutuo Lan Caihe* 漢鍾離度脫藍採和)

Dai Shanfu 戴善甫, *Cripple Li Yue: Poetry and Wine at the River-Gazing Pavilion* (*Que Li Yue shijiu Wangjiang Ting* 瘸李岳詩酒望江亭)

Gu Zijing 谷子敬, *Lü Dongbin Thrice Leads the Willow South of the City to Enlightenment* (*Lü Dongbin sandu chengnan liu* 呂洞賓三度城南柳)

Jia Zhongming 賈仲明, *Iron Crutch Li Leads Golden Lad and Jade Lass to Enlightenment* (*Tieguai Li du Jintong Yunü* 鐵拐李度金童玉女)

Li Haogu 李好古, *At Shamen Island Student Zhang Brews Up the Sea* (*Shamen dao Zhang Sheng zhuhai* 沙門島張生煮海)

Ma Zhiyuan, *Lü Dongbin Gets Drunk Three Times in Yueyang Tower* (*Lü Dongbin sanzui Yueyang Lou* 呂洞賓三醉岳陽樓)

Ma Zhiyuan, *Ma Danyang Thrice Leads Crazy Ren to Enlightenment* (*Ma Danyang sandu Ren fengzi* 馬丹陽三度任風子)[23]

Ma Zhiyuan, Li Shizhong 李時中, Hua Lilang Xueshi 花李郎學士, Hongzi Li Er 紅字李二, *Gaining Enlightenment at Handan: The Dream of Yellow Millet* (*Handan dao xingwu huangliang meng* 邯鄲道省悟黃粱夢)

21. Aoki 1941, 32.

22. This may also be understood as "Immortals Transforming Through Revealing the Change That Lies Behind the Way," from its earlier use in Sima Qian's *Records of the Historian*, where the term *daohua* is related to how the *Book of Changes* reveals the inner workings of the Way.

23. This is the only deliverance play besides *Bamboo-Leaf Boat* to have been preserved in a Yuan edition. Unfortunately, the text of the second act of that edition is heavily damaged. For a discussion of this play and its subsequent editions, see Idema 2007b, 70–76; for a list of translations of these plays, see West and Idema 2010b, 283–313 and 469–72.

Yang Jingxian 楊景賢, *Ma Danyang Leads Head of the Guild Liu to Enlightenment* (*Ma Danyang dutuo Liu hangshou* 馬丹陽度脫柳行首)

Yue Bochuan 岳伯川, *Lü Dongbin Leads Iron Crutch Li to Enlightenment* (*Lü Dongbin dutuo Tieguai Li* 呂洞賓度脫鐵拐李)

Buddhist

Li Shouqing (?) 李壽卿, *The Monk of Moon's Light Leads Liu Cui to Enlightenment* (*Yueming heshang du Liu Cui* 月明和尚度劉翠)

Zheng Tingyu 鄭廷玉, *The Monk with a Burden and the Story of "Patience"* (*Budai heshang renzi ji* 布袋和尚忍字記)

For a more complete survey of the deliverance plays of the period 1250–1450 we should, moreover, add the deliverance plays composed by the early Ming princes Zhu Quan and Zhu Youdun written in the late fourteenth and early fifteenth centuries. Zhu Youdun informs us that deliverance plays were performed at major birthdays, and at one time in his life he would write a new deliverance play every year for the celebration of his own birthday, bringing his total of deliverance plays to seven. Zhu Quan's only surviving deliverance play was clearly intended to be performed at his own birthday too. To what extent the performance of deliverance plays throughout the Yuan were limited to birthday celebrations is, however, not clear, but the large casts and special effects required by at least some deliverance plays may suggest that they too have been written for performance at court. This is also suggested by the collaboration of court actors in the composition of at least one deliverance play.

Fan seems to have been very interested in Daoism and the possibility of literary expression of its basic concepts. It is dangerous, of course, to create conclusions about a person's inclinations based solely on a miniscule amount of material, and the extant poems and dramas of Fan Kang may reflect nothing more than appreciation by anthologists and bibliographers for these poems. But from what is left, we can assume that Fan knew and appreciated Quanzhen Daoism, and this appreciation is reflected in the way he changed the Tang story. For instance, he converts the "old codger from Zhongnan" into Lü Dongbin, one of the Eight Immortals as well as one of the lineage patriarchs of the Quanzhen sect of Daoism. Like all authors of deliverance plays, Fan Kang had to choose between the person to be delivered and the deliverer as the lead of his *zaju*. A choice for the person to be delivered would have resulted in many songs praising the pleasures of the flesh and reviling the mendicant as a crook; a choice for the deliverer will result in arias extolling the superior joys of the immortals. Fan Kang takes the second option and so shifts the focus of the story from Chen Jiqing to the Daoist patriarchs Lü Dongbin and the ancient magician Liezi 列子 (Master Lie, also known as Lie Yukou). The first act of the play on Chen Jiqing's meeting with a stranger at Green Dragon Monastery is clearly modeled on the classical tale, as is the third act, which is devoted to Chen Jiqing's nighttime visit to his parents and his wife back home. The second act, which dramatizes a meeting of Chen Jiqing with the immortal Liezi and his companions has no direct counterpart in the classical tale, but it may have been suggested by the reference to visiting a Chan meditation cave. But whereas in the classical tale Chen Jiqing returns to Chang'an following his visit home, the play does not allow for this and ends his journey in a dream with an abrupt near drowning at the end of the third act. Whereas in the Tang tale the dream is recounted in the vein of the traditional Chinese "tales of the strange" (*zhiguai* 志怪), in which Chen Jiqing begins his ascetic pursuit of enlightenment only after succeeding in the examinations, the dream sequence in the play brings Chen to the edge of death to reveal to him the uselessness of pursuing an official career, or any other worldly endeavor. In the final act, an awakened Chen Jiqing sets out in pursuit of his deliverer, Lü Dongbin, who once again explains the meaning of the Way and then takes Chen to meet the other members of the Eight Immortals.[24]

The play follows the pattern of most deliverance plays. As in them, the person to be brought to enlightenment is usually someone of low status but with a level of material comfort. There are three basic patterns to the deliverance plays.[25] The first appear as stories of immortals who have been banished to earth to suffer for some misdeed stemming from rekindled desire or some faux pas in the transcendent realm. They are turned into mortal human form, from which they are delivered back to their original immortal being. The second pattern involves people who are not explicitly identified as banished immortals but who have some innate capacity to become an immortal—they "have what it takes to become an immortal" (*you shenxian zhi fen* 有神仙之分) or "half of what it takes" (*you ban shenxian zhi fen* 有半神仙之分). This is signaled to heaven by "a blue or purple ether" (*qing, ziqi* 青、紫氣) that radiates into the heavens. These humans are either students or "mean people" such as courtesan-entertainers, butchers, actors, or minor officials. The third pattern involves protagonists who are either inanimate objects or ghosts. These include spirit beings and the essentialized spirits (*jing* 精) of trees: most notably the peach, the apricot, and willow. In their inanimate form, they are all hindered from becoming immortal, even though they possess the "wind of an immortal and the bones of the Way" (*xianfeng daogu* 仙風道骨). Thus they must first be reborn as humans.

The human protagonists all cling to the world. They are characterized either by their burning ambition for success (as in the case of students) or by their brazen enjoyment of material comfort (as in the case of low-class characters like actors, courtesans, and butchers). They are confronted by their deliverer, who is often dressed as a mendicant. They are presented with their worst nightmare: a descent into poverty and the onset of all the material deprivation and discomfort of such that their mind could imagine.[26]

24. Song and Yu 2003, 43–44.

25. See Zhao Youmin 1975a, 155.

26. Such imagined fear would have been given more weight by the ascetic practices of early Quanzhen, which included sleep deprivation, exposure to severe weather, beatings, and being forced to beg. See Komjathy 2007, 47, and Eskildsen 2004, 38–66.

Comfortable, and often surrounded by friends and colleagues, they are reluctant to leave their families and friends and, therefore, extremely resistant to the delights of the Daoist life relayed to them orally by their deliverer. To counter this resistance, the deliverer has no other recourse but to create, through either dreams or a carefully arranged minidrama that enlists the help of his immortal fellows, a situation that brings the targeted person to the understanding that unlimited desire is associated only with the "material self" that has a limited life span.[27] It is only at the end of the play when the person, suffering the trauma of the dream or event, is finally persuaded to join after realizing the power of the deliverer to create other worlds and manipulate time.

The majority of those who convert these souls are members of the Daoist lineage of patriarchs, and with the exception of the Spirit of Venus (Taibai Jinxing 太白金星) and Iron Crutch Li, they are all Quanzhen masters. The lineage of patriarchs in this school are, in order,[28] the Imperial Lord of Eastern Florescence (Donghua Dijun 東華帝君), Zhongli Quan 鍾離全, Lü Dongbin, Wang Zhe 王嚞, and Ma Danyang. Many scholars therefore assume a close link between Quanzhen Daoism and deliverance plays. There is a congruence between those converted—financially comfortable—and those who do the converting in the drama and in the doctrinal texts of Quanzhen. One of the early precepts of the school was the issue of charity: of giving up one's wealth to a religious institution that would redistribute it to the poor in the form of medicine and food.[29] The point is that there is a definite audience in the minds of the writers and perhaps a theatrical audience that is reflected in the class status of those portrayed as waiting to be delivered.

The Buddhist agents of deliverance—the Monk of the Bright Moon and the Monk with the Burden—show no significant difference, despite their being Buddhist, from those who are Daoists. The essential generic rules of the deliverance play still hold. This should at least give us pause in considering any of these plays as "belonging" to a certain sect. Even the catchphrases that are often associated with Quanzhen asceticism—the monkey of the mind and the horse of the will, or the four deadly vices of wine, sex, anger, and material goods—are in fact shared not only by these two religions but by Confucianism as well. The main difference is that where Buddhism and Daoism argue for complete abnegation of desire and pleasures of the senses, Confucianism argues for moderation; and that plea to moderation exists at a very early, perhaps even pre-Confucian, stage in such works as the *Book of Documents*. Such concepts may more logically be considered as general cultural and social modes or norms that become more specifically and more stringently applied as they are incorporated into and shaped by the doctrines and praxes of various religions or schools of thought.

---

27. Zhao Lingxia 2009, 50–51. *Bamboo-Leaf Boat* is an excellent example of how a dream sequence is used to terrify the one to be delivered. For a staged scenario, see the last two acts of *Zhongli of the Han Leads Lan Caihe to Enlightenment*, translated in its entirety in West and Idema 2010b, 283–313.

28. For an excellent brief introduction, see Goossaert 2008a.

29. See Eskildsen 2004, 161–66.

The Daoist deliverance plays often feature members of the Eight Immortals. This is a grouping of immortals that is first encountered in the thirteenth century and reached its final makeup in the fifteenth. While two of the members of the group (Zhongli Quan and Lü Dongbin) are also counted as Quanzhen patriarchs, other members such as the cripple Li Yue (Iron Crutch Li) and the actor Lan Caihe have no link to the sect. Many deliverance plays are concluded by a scene in which the company of the Eight Immortals introduces the new immortal to the Queen Mother of the West, a mythical creature whose history predates that of Quanzhen Daoism by more than a thousand years. Only two of the fifteen plays, in fact, deal specifically with one, and only one, of the human members of the Quanzhen sect: Ma Danyang.

One of the small ironies of the deliverance plays is that when the object of deliverance emerges from whatever parlous state in which he or she had been put, their transformation is not complete until the deliverer points out the significance of that state. It is only then, when these tremulous souls are still in a hazy state of uncertainty about their experience, that the magical nature of these immortals is displayed by their power of interpreting the state—the staged scene, dream, or death—that they had crafted. It is this magical power to create and interpret that finally erases all doubt and allows the delivered to be whisked off to the paradise of the Queen Mother of the West in like company.[30]

The *Bamboo-Leaf Boat* itself is extant in two versions: the early fourteenth century Yuan edition and one heavily edited by Zang Maoxun, who has exercised his Confucian, anti-Daoist stance in several ways.[31] Most noticeable among his changes is in the name itself. In the early Yuan edition, the play is known as

[Title:] Lü Pure Yang appears in transformed form in a dream of blue waves
Lü Chunyang xianhua canglang meng 呂純陽顯化滄浪夢
[Name:] Chen Jiqing Is Enlightened to the Way on a Bamboo-Leaf Boat
Chen Jiqing wudao zhuye zhou 陳季卿悟道竹葉舟

Zang Maoxun changes these to

Title: Lü Dongbin Appears in Transformed Form in a Dream of Blue Waves
Lü Dongbin xianhua canglang meng 呂洞賓顯化滄浪夢
Name: Chen Jiqing Mistakenly Boards the Bamboo-Leaf Boat
Chen Jiqing wushang zhuye zhou 陳季卿誤上竹葉舟

30. The ancient Daoist philosopher Liezi is not included among the Quanzhen patriarchs, nor is he ever counted as one of the Eight Immortals.

31. Perhaps not all changes can be attributed to Zang Maoxun, who, as a rule, worked on the basis of texts that directly or indirectly came from the court and may have been heavily revised there. The addition of a wedge at the beginning of the play, and the introduction of the abbot, Hui'an, may have already happened in the source text used by Zang. The court stage is also a much more likely source of the foul language of the acolyte than Zang's study.

While this may seem, in fact, only a minor change, it captures the whole tenor of changes that Zang makes to the play. In the *Yuan Edition*, the emphasis is on Chen's transformation, the expected result of Lü Dongbin's creation of the boat and dream. In Zang's version, it makes it seem as though Chen, as Song Ke and Yu Ying say, "has boarded a pirate ship and fallen into the clutches of Lü Dongbin."[32] The meaning of the change becomes clear in the play in the fourth act, where Zang Maoxun added an extra song that did not exist in the earlier edition:

> (*Gun xiuqiu*)
> You say I drove that little boat across the blue waves,
> Held the bamboo fishing rod and threw on that green rain cape—
> This I did!
> You came within an inch of your life foolhardily crossing that river,
> (CHEN JIQING *speaks*:) Master! Once you decided you would lead me to enlightenment, why did you dump me in the river, putting me at death's door? You really know how to manipulate people! (MALE LEAD *acts out pointing to* LIE YUKOU, *sings*:)
> *If I hadn't laid out that little snare* [italics ours],
> How could I have persuaded these immortal ones to bring this scene to an end?
> I have seven other brothers among my old friends as well.

The intent of this addition seems clear enough: to suggest that Lü Dongbin is a charlatan whose interest lies not in enlightening Chen but in demonstrating to the rest of the Eight Immortals his own cleverness. This agenda of revealing the chicanery of the Daoists is carried out in minor and major ways throughout Zang's *Selection of Yuan Plays* edition. For instance, minor changes in the padding words can produce significant changes in tenor. If we compare the following aria in the two editions, we can see how cleverly Zang makes these small changes:

Yuan version:

【天下樂】 (*Tianxia le*)	
早經了一將功成萬骨枯。	I've already been through "One general's success is ten thousand bleached bones,"
嘆你區區,文共武,	*Ai*, you insignificant little civil and military officials:
好辛苦麼紫羅袍、白象笏。	So much trouble, those purple silk court robes, and white ivory tablets—

32. Song and Yu 2003, 45.

爭如我誦《黃庭》《道德經》，	How can they compare to my chanting the *Yellow Court* and *Canon of the Way and Its Virtue*,
持金符《太素書》，	Holding a golden tally and *The Text of Great Plainness*—
傳清風一萬古。	That transmits a freshening wind across myriad antiquities.

Zang Maoxun's *A Selection of Yuan Plays* version:

【天下樂】(*Tianxia le*)	
早經了一將功成萬骨枯。	I've already been through "One general's success is ten thousand bleached bones,"
哎,你區區,文共武,	*Ai*, you insignificant little civil and military officials:
說甚麼榮耀人也紫羅襴、	Say what you want about those purple silk court robes that glorify a person,
烏紗帽、	Those raven's black gauze hats
白象笏。	And white ivory tablets—
爭如我誦《黃庭》《道德經》，	How can they compare to my chanting the *Yellow Court* and *Canon of the Way and Its Virtue*,
諷《金精》《太素書》，	Or intoning *Golden Essence* and *The Text of Great Plainness*
倒落的播清風一萬古。	That *unexpectedly* wound up sowing a freshening wind across myriad antiquities.

The introduction of the phrase "unexpectedly" (*dao luode* 倒落的), italicized in the last line of the table, breaks what is a continuous flow in the final three lines of the *Yuan Plays* song—which culminates in a natural transmission of the freshening wind—and therefore creates a slight disjuncture in which activity and outcome seem not to have any natural connection.[33]

More major changes involve shortening the suite of eight inserted songs that come between acts three and four to a suite of four, and changing the singer from Lü Dongbin to Liezi. Not only does this destroy Lü Dongbin's long meditation on the nature of human activity and how enlightenment releases one from the vexations it produces, but Zang's changes subtly undermine Liezi's expression of similar pleasures by an introduced emphasis on the hedonistic, even lazy, nature of the life that Liezi describes: sleeping

33. Ibid.

late, cadging food, a completely disinterested existence. Whereas the *Yuan Plays* edition allows Lü to ruminate about the difficulties he faced in coming to his decisions and about the contrast between historical awareness and rational judgments on one side and an enlightened intuitive knowledge on the other, Zang's changes make Liezi seem simply like a social dropout who rationalizes his choice to be completely lazy.

Likewise, Zang changes the singer of the second act, Liezi in the *Yuan Plays* edition, to Lü Dongbin, and his choice seems dictated by a desire to bring about confrontation.[34] In this act, Zang introduces a theme that is not present in the earlier play: he has Chen Jiqing accuse Lü of completely one-sided knowledge. That is, that Lü Dongbin "had never been an official" so could not possibly "know about the happiness of being an official." This effectively destabilizes Lü's constant reference to the role of experience over learning and of nonhistorical time over the power of history, asking how one can make a judgment without knowing both sides.

These changes seem part and parcel of Zang Maoxun's distrust of Daoism and a strong impulse to introduce—if not Confucian values—a sense of the function and value of history and human community built on interconnected social roles and responsibilities. Song and Yu suggest that these changes may not have been Zang's alone but reflect a growing dissatisfaction with Daoism and its relationship to court and culture at large. They suggest that Ming rulers adopted a "pragmatic approach" to Daoism and exploited it for what it could offer in terms of lengthening one's life span, which included not only drugs but also techniques of the bedchamber, which resulted in a heightened interest in sexual techniques and literary representation in the great pornographic novels of the Ming. As they point out, "There is not a single good Daoist" portrayed in the *Journey to the West*, one of the four major classics of fiction in the Ming.[35]

Whatever the reason, there are significant differences between the two editions, and we have translated both in order that readers can investigate these differences and their significance for themselves.

SUGGESTED READINGS

Crump 1994, Katz 1996 and 1999, Song and Yu 2003.

34. Zang Maoxun also suggests that the fisherman in act 3 is actually Lü Dongbin in disguise. In this way, the leading male plays a single character throughout the four acts of the play.

35. Ibid.

NEWLY CUT WITH PLOT PROMPTS: *CHEN JIQING IS ENLIGHTENED TO THE WAY ON A BAMBOO-LEAF BOAT,* A FOURTEENTH-CENTURY EDITION

DRAMATIS PERSONAE IN ORDER OF APPEARANCE

Role type	*Name and family, institutional, or social role*
EXTRA MALE	CHEN JIQING
ACOLYTE	Young ACOLYTE at Green Dragon Monastery
MALE LEAD	LÜ DONGBIN (acts 1, 4)
MALE LEAD	LIEZI (act 2)
COMICS	DAOIST IMMORTALS
OFFICIAL	DAOIST OFFICIAL
MALE LEAD	FISHERMAN (Lü Dongbin) (act 3)
OLD MAN	CHEN JIQING's father
OLD WOMAN	CHEN JIQING's mother
FEMALE LEAD	CHEN JIQING's wife
EIGHT IMMORTALS	EIGHT IMMORTALS

✤ ✤ ✤

NEWLY CUT WITH PLOT PROMPTS: *CHEN JIQING IS ENLIGHTENED TO THE WAY ON A BAMBOO-LEAF BOAT*

EXTRA MALE *costumed as* CHEN JIQING *enters and speaks*—I am named Chen Jiqing and am from Yuhang in Wulin.[36] I studied the Confucian curriculum when young and came to the capital to take the examinations. I did not pass the examinations and am drifting around here. I'm now facing winter, and the thick and tossing snow is falling fast. Oh! Such bad luck. I just suddenly thought: the abbot of Green Dragon Monastery is an old hometown friend. I'll go off and see him now.

36. Modern Hangzhou.

Wait until EXTRA MALE *has come on, opened, then stopped—Wait until after* ACOLYTE *speaks—After* EXTRA MALE *finishes inscribing the lyric "Fragrance Fills the Courtyard"—You, as* MALE LEAD *costumed in a stork-feather overcoat and carrying a thorn basket, enter and open*—I, this humble Daoist, am named Lü Yan, with a second name of Dongbin; my name in the Way is Master of Pure Yang. [I'm here by] command of my master. Because in the mortal world there is a certain Chen Jiqing who is destined to be an immortal, I have been ordered to enlighten him. Far off, I see a shaft of purple light coming from Green Dragon Monastery, and that means he is probably there.

In the morning I rove the northern seas, at eventide Cangwu,[37]
With Green Snake[38] in my sleeve I am rashly courageous;
Three days at Yueyang Tower,[39] not a soul recognized me,
Reciting a poem in a clear voice I flew over Lake Dongting.

([XIANLÜ MODE:] *Dian jiangchun*)

I have just visited northern Yue and Cangwu[40]
And already the progressions of the seasons have passed many times
To evolve into past and present.
I sigh over the prosperity and decline of worldly events,
Who actually recognizes the path to long life?

---

37. These lines are based on a poem attributed to Lü Dongbin in early Song works. Lü Dongbin does not appear in any Tang-dynasty materials and appears to have been a figure created during the early Song. The earliest textual reference is found in the *Categorized Garden of Song-Dynasty Affairs* (*Songchao shishi leiyuan* 宋朝事實類苑), a work by Jiang Shaoyu 江少虞 that collects and categorizes citations from other texts covering a span of 120 years from 960 to 1085. In his citation from a collection of Yang Yi's 楊億 (974–1020) conversations, recorded by his student, we find the following:

朝辭百越暮三吳,	In the morning I depart the land of the Hundred Yue, at evenfall reach the Three Wus*,
袖裹青蛇膽氣粗。	Green Dragon in my sleeve, I was rough and ready;
三入岳陽人不識,	Three times I entered Yueyang but no one recognized me,
朗吟飛過洞庭湖。	Chanting loudly, I flew across Lake Dongting.

*Wuxing, Suzhou, and Kuaiji in Jiangsu and Zhejiang

See Jiang 1981, 560–61. The poem varies considerably from source to source, particularly in the first line. For a general discussion, see Fu Xuanzong 1990, 1:393–404.

38. A sword.
39. Located on the Yangtze in modern Wuhan.
40. The term "northern Yue" is written here as 北粵. This *yue* is interchangeable in old texts with another *yue* 越 (see the early geographical record *Shuijing zhu* 水經注, "the two *yue* characters are interchangeable, just like the Hundred Yue become the Hundred Yue 粵與越通,猶百粵之為百越). See Chen and Li 1999, 1287. This may stem from the fact that both characters have the same initial and share a final stop (*k*). At the time they began to be interchangeable, we have no way of determining the medial vowels across a wide range of dialects. The term "Hundred Yue" is a common designation of the ancient peoples that lived in an area of southern China stretching from modern Zhejiang in the east to Guangxi and Yunnan in the west and southward to Cangwu in Hunan. Cangwu, also known as Mount Jiuyi, was often considered the southern end of the civilized world.

(*Hunjiang long*)
I've measured that dollop of the cosmic realm,
And passed through the remains of pitched battles where dragons contested and tigers fought.[41]
From the time that swirling confusion was split open,[42]
I have trod through to the empty void—
Hills and valleys, high and deep, have all changed apace,
Mountains and rivers, atmosphere and appearance, reflect in the blue void.
I have cultivated myself until my spirit is like water,
And the color of my face like vermilion.
Moreover, I take no mica of mysterious spirit,
No pound of lead to form a myriad-year gem,
I ingest no goji berries or rhizomes of *cangshu*,[43]
Pluck no China root or osmanthus seeds,
And wear no miraculous tallies or precious spells at my belt.
I just harness that monkey heart and horse will tight:
So let the stars turn and things change one for the other,
Rocks rot and mulberries wither.

MALE LEAD *acts out greeting* EXTRA MALE, [*speaks*:] What are you doing here? Don't plot for riches and wealth, or covet fame and fortune. Are you willing to leave with me?

(*You hulu*)
I laugh at this road to fame and fortune of yours, with its windblown waves ten thousand feet high;
Heading to the land of right and wrong, you'll suffer all in vain—
Even if you had Su Qin's very ministerial seals at your belt, what good would it do?[44]
Just look: in that Gallery Soaring Beyond the Mists,[45] who are the true heroes?
In the precinct of the Golden Valley[46] they are all beclouded boys and girls.

---

41. The king or emperor is the dragon, his generals, tigers.
42. Here, the expression means both "from the time I left my deluded secular state" and "from the beginning of the universe."
43. *Cangshu* is *Atractylodes chinensis*; these two items (goji berries and *Atractylodes*) are still used to prepare a prophylactic rice gruel, good for "strengthening the liver" and "improving eyesight."
44. Su Qin 蘇秦 was a politician of the Warring States period famed for his rhetorical skills who led an alliance of six states against Qin. At one time, he was prime minister of each of them and carried the seals of each of these states on his belt. See "Su Ch'in, Memoir 9," in Ssu-ma Ch'ien 1995b, 97–121.
45. See chap. 3, n. 72.
46. Golden Valley was an estate owned by the fabulously rich Shi Chong 石崇 (249–300). It later became a stock metaphor for an elegant estate of the rich. "Boys and girls" is a term used by inferiors when addressing superiors as a self-reflexive humility; its use here is clearly sarcastic. While it might refer to both genders, it is most likely one of those terms in which only the first word carries meaning. Thus: those little boys who are vulgar and immoral. See Knechtges 2006.

Wait until EXTRA MALE *speaks*, [*speak*:] There are the worthy.

What kind of worthiness can you discern,
What kind of dullness?
Even if you cast a likeness of Zhugong of Tao in yellow gold,[47]
In the end he would still float on the misty waters of Dongting Lake.
(*Tianxia le*)
I've already been through "One general's success is ten thousand bleached bones,"
Ai, you insignificant little civil and military officials:
So much trouble, those purple silk court robes,
And white ivory tablets—
How can they compare to my chanting the *Yellow Court*[48] and *Canon of the Way and Its Virtue*,[49]
Holding a golden tally and *The Text of Great Plainness*[50]—
That transmits a freshening wind across myriad antiquities.

After EXTRA MALE *speaks*.—[*Speak*:] The *Yellow Court* and *Canon of the Way and Its Virtue*. . . . Aren't you cold and hungry, scholar?—*Wait until* EXTRA MALE *speaks*.—[*Speak*:] I have some small techniques to free you from hunger and cold.—*Act out taking out herbal simples and giving them to* EXTRA MALE.—*After* EXTRA MALE *takes the simples*.—EXTRA *asks* MALE LEAD [. . .] the secret practices of above.—MALE LEAD *speaks*: In old days the Four Hoary Heads hid themselves on Mount Shang. Nestman and Xu You attained it at Ying River.[51] These were all immortals who had attained the way.—*Wait until* EXTRA MALE *has spoken*.

(*Nezha ling*)
You must have heard of Lie Yukou
Who rode upon the freshening wind to enter the eight domains of the world?[52]

---

47. This is a name later adopted by Fan Li 范蠡. See chap. 2, n. 39.

48. The *Huangting jing* 黄庭經, a text concerning visualization of the inner gods that animate the body. One of the earlier and more influential of the Daoist texts, it was related to the tradition of "nourishing life" (*yangshen* 養生). See Robinet 2008b.

49. That is, the *Daode jing* 道德經, the "Daoist bible." See Robinet 2008a.

50. This may refer to a section of the *Inner Scripture of the Yellow Emperor* (*Huangdi neijing* 黃庭內經) called the "Great Plainness" (Taisu 泰素), which exists only in an eleventh-century copy of an eighth-century manuscript. See Hsu 2008, 507.

51. Chaofu 巢夫 ("Nestman") and Xu You 許由 were famous hermits who lived during the time of Yao. When Xu You told Chaofu that Yao had offered him the empire, Chaofu answered, "Why didn't you hide your body and cover your brilliance? You are not my friend!" He thereupon went to a brook and rinsed out his ears. According to another legend, Xu You rinsed his ears after Yao had offered him the empire.

52. From the *Zhuangzi*: "Lie Tzu could ride the wind and go soaring around with cool and breezy skill, but after fifteen days came back to earth. As far as the search for good fortune went, he didn't fret and worry." See Watson 1968, 32.

And there was Master Zifang
Who accompanied Red Pine in his return to the Grotto Gates.[53]
Zhang Qian floated his raft to the Thearch's Capital,[54]
And there was that Ye Jingchan too[55]
Who welcomed the Lustrous Emperor to go off
And roam the byways of Heaven.
(*Que ta zhi*)
The sights in that place of ours are not common at all,
And there, none of you from the lower realms dwell.
What you will see are rainy mists and cloudy sunsets,
Their colors penetrating the heavenly avenues.
There the immortals of Grand Canopy Heaven[56] freely pass by.
I've come down to this dusty realm
To transform the obtuse and doltish—like you.

[*Speak*:] Do you know these things, scholar?—EXTRA MALE *speaks again*: What things?

(*Jisheng cao*)
Just think of that day when Liu, the Exalted Ancestor,
Drove Xiang Yu of Chu to his ruin.
Xiang Yu had displayed his "strength to uproot mountains,"
And single-handedly lifted a bronze tripod—
All these heroic acts.
But he was cast into the red dirt and lost his way on the road to Yinling,
And quickly reached Rook River—it was not a ferry crossing with no boat![57]
You should study Zhang Liang of the Han, who quit office, gave up his post:
"Better to hear 'quickly return to the mountains.'"[58]

---

53. Red Pine was a mythic figure of antiquity who, over time, had been considered the Master of Rain (Yushi 雨師), a magician, and a Daoist sage who specialized in the "circulation of breath" techniques (*xingqi* 行氣), which he taught to Zhang Liang (Zifang). See Raz 2008. On Zhang Liang, see chap. 3, n. 82.
54. As an ambassador of Emperor Wu of the Han, Zhang Qian 張騫 (d. 114 BC) repeatedly made extensive journeys to central Asia. Later legend claimed that he had boarded a raft floating on the Yellow River that had taken him up to the Silver River (the Milky Way) before bringing him back to earth.
55. The Daoist master who accompanied the Tang emperor Xuanzong on his visit to the moon is usually identified as Ye Fashan 葉法善. The story is also included, however, in a long prose account of the miracles wrought by the Daoist master Ye Jingneng 葉竟能. This latter text, known as *Ye Jingneng shi* 葉竟能詩, was found at Dunhuang.
56. The highest heaven that covers all other heavens; see Miller 2008.
57. See chap. 2, n. 5.
58. From a couplet attributed in the Song period to Red Pine, who sent the lines to Zhang Liang:

    不如聞早歸山去 Better to hear early on, "go back to the mountains,"
    免事君王不到頭 To avoid, in service to one's lord, not making it to the end.

    The poem is found as here in Jiang 1981, 881, and with a slight emendation to the first line (聞→閒) in Zeng 1982, 962 (56.31a), cited from *Liu Gongfu shihua* 劉貢父詩話, now lost.

Wait until EXTRA MALE *has spoken.*—MALE LEAD *speaks*: Can you find where I live?

(*Reprise*)

In vain you'll wear out Wang Qiao's sandals, he who ascended to immortal state,[59]
You'll never see the simples-refining stove of Ge Hong.[60]
That house of mine: I come and go as I please, stop wherever I want,
No wind, no rain, hard to throw it over,
No repairing, no fortifying, yet it is always rock solid.
Nor have the grotto gates been deeply locked amid the mountains far,
Truly it is a place you can't find in a land filled with snowy clouds!

Wait until EXTRA MALE *has spoken.*—*After* MALE LEAD *speaks.*—EXTRA MALE *acts out ignoring him.*—MALE LEAD *acts out looking at the map of China and foreign lands and inscribing a poem.* [MALE LEAD *recites*:]

Let your eyes roam in leisure over the *Record of the Nine Areas*:
Just like it is all here before your eyes;
Raise your head to gaze at the military districts,
The border courts are just an inch away.
One hundred thousand markets listed for each county,
Five thousand mountains sequestered in each province.
There may be no road home,
But you should check the map thoroughly.

EXTRA MALE *acts out ignoring* MALE LEAD.—*After* MALE LEAD *finishes getting up and reciting* EXTRA MALE*'s "Fragrance Filling the Courtyard."*—*After* EXTRA MALE *finishes speaking and reciting "The Phoenix Rests on the* Wutong *Tree."*—*After* MALE LEAD *finishes getting up and reciting* EXTRA MALE*'s "Fragrance Filling the Courtyard."*[61]—MALE LEAD *acts out laughing sarcastically*, [*speaks*:] You doltish fellow, you are still thinking about your home. Scholar, before I came here you had recited

59. Wang Qiao 王喬 (or Wangzi Qiao 王子喬) is one of the best-known immortals of ancient times. According to one tradition he was a son of King Ling of Zhou (r. 571–545 BC) who disappeared into the skies riding a white crane after studying the techniques of immortality for thirty years on Mount Song. See Raz 2008.

60. Ge Hong 葛洪 (283–343) was an alchemist and also the author of the famous *Master Who Embraces Simplicity* (*Baopu zi* 抱朴子), which is an important source for the history of Daoism and its practices. See Miura 2008; Pregadio 2008a, 2008b. Here the playwright rejects the discipline of exterior alchemy in favor of the meditation techniques of inner alchemy.

61. "The Phoenix Rests on the *Wutong* Tree" and "Fragrance Filling the Courtyard" are names of song lyric tunes. Each of these tunes would have its own demands in terms of number of lines, number of syllables in each line, distribution of level and deflected tones, and the placement of rhymes. Chen Jiqing apparently wrote one poem to the tune "Fragrance Filling the Courtyard" and one poem to the tune "The Phoenix Rests on the *Wutong* Tree." The names of these tunes are conventional and give no indication of the contents of the lyrics. The repetition of the line "After MALE LEAD finishes getting up and reciting EXTRA MALE's 'Fragrance Filling the Courtyard'" is removed from some modern editions of the play. We have left it since it may indicate some scene in which it was necessary to repeat the action. However, there does seem to be some confusion in the lines.

a lyric poem that I still remember.—*Wait until* EXTRA MALE *has spoken*, [*speak*:] If you are willing to go with me, I'll give you a full sail of freshening wind and you'll reach there without using any travel money. *Pointing to the leaf on the wall.* This one path is truly the road to home.

(*Zui zhong tian*)

This poem is better than Wang Can's "Rhapsody on Ascending a Tower,"[62]
Just like Zhang Han's "recollections of water mallow soup and sliced sculpin."[63]

MALE LEAD *pastes the leaf on the wall.*

Look—barely visible, a leaf of a vessel across the blue waves,

Wait until EXTRA MALE *speaks.* MALE LEAD *speaks*: Dolt! You'd better take the correct path!

Don't guess that no one crosses waters in the wild;
You gave it your all to take the examinations in Chang'an,
And when you failed, like Tao Yuanming you wanted to return to your home[64]—
But these two actions are no more than the single dream of Hua Xu.[65]

MALE LEAD *speaks*: Dolt! Do you see the road you should take?

(*Jinzhan'er*)

Look at Jing and Wu, hidden by misty waves,
The distant waters bearing the homeward skiff.
Go ahead and
Let the windblown waves rise and surge, krakens and dragons grow angry!

---

62. This rhapsody written by Wang Can 王粲 (177–217) couples the general motif of "climbing to a height" and writing about the vastness of nature and insignificance of man with Wang Can's own sense of nostalgia for his home and frustration at the constant and dangerous warfare of the period. See "Climbing the Tower," translated by Burton Watson, in Lau and Minford, 2000, 311–13. For a discussion of Zheng Guangzu's 鄭光祖 *zaju Drunk and Longing for Home Wang Can Climbs the Tower* (*Zui sisiang Wang Can denglou* 醉思鄉王粲登樓), see Idema 2005.

63. Zhang Han 張翰 (ca. 300) had taken a position in North China. When autumn came, he "longed for the wild rice, water mallow soup, and sliced prickly sculpin of Wu." This later became a simple allusion to a strong desire for one's home, or simple homesickness. For the story itself, see Liu and Liu 2002, 213–14.

64. When the famous poet Tao Yuanming陶淵明 (aka Tao Qian 潛; 365–427) had become a magistrate and learned he had to bow to his superiors, he promptly abandoned his position and wrote a rhapsody titled "Let's Return Home" (Guiqulai ci 歸去來辭). For a complete translation, see, for instance, Robert Hightower's translation, "The Return," in Hightower 1970, 268–70.

65. A reference found in the *Liezi* to the dream journey of the mythical Yellow Emperor through the Land of Hua Xu, where there was no ruler, where people lived without desire, completely at ease with their lives. Because they did not fear death or contend for things out of desire, they lived in a world where there was no hatred or struggle for self-benefit. When the Yellow Emperor awoke from his dream, he became aware that the Way could not be sought through passion. Hua Xu thus becomes a standard trope for a utopian paradise. See Graham 1990, 34–35, and Zhou Shaoxian 1983, 158–59.

After MALE LEAD *speaks,* [*sing*:]
You just close your two eyes tight,
Lay your body down.
Oars pierce the river's moon, cold,
The sail is raised in the sea clouds, floating.
Cold mists arise over ancient fords,
Ahh . . .
There are the thatched huts of your former home.
Speak: Dolt! Don't open your eyes! Don't forget the correct path!
(*Coda*)
You and I will kick down the portals to the land of ghosts,
And our dreams will circle the road to Acacia Peace,
And wake up to "a pillow of the southern branch."[66]
Ensnared by the bridle of fame and the fetters of profit—
In the nodding of the head it is "mulberry and elm in the sunset scene."[67]
If you become my disciple,
We will cut off the vulgar and common together—
This is: "The Green Snake in my sleeve, rough and ready"—
Rely on this companion of misty sunsets,
Go back dancing in the west wind—
And I'll have you "Chanting aloud as you fly across Dongting Lake."
(*Exits.*)

[ACT 2]

After EXTRA MALE *speaks.*—MALE LEAD[68] *enters with* COMICS *and* OFFICIAL, *four people in total, costumed as Daoists in free-wandering costume, and speaks*: How delightful this all is, my fellow spirits!
([SHUANGDIAO:] *Xinshui ling*)
I've rambled over the five lakes and three isles
With just these two wind-sweeping sleeves of my robe.
I've summoned noumenal lads to pluck grass of good augury[69]

66. See chap. 3, n. 106.
67. Both "sunset" and "old age."
68. Here costumed as Liezi.
69. Noumenal lads (*lingtong* 靈童), also known as "jade lads" (*yutong* 玉童) or "transcendent lads" (*xiantong* 仙童), are young attendants at the court of the Queen Mother of the West.

And gone down to Immortals' Islet[70] with fellow immortals.[71]
Free and untrammeled,
I sigh for all those days and nights in the dusty world.
(*Zhuma ting*)
I roamed as a god through my old domain,
Saw so many things change and so many stars make their transit.
I completely figured out that floating life,
Saw my share of "evening suns setting west" and "the Yangtze flowing east."
I sigh over dynasties' rise and fall, frown over the sorrow of the imperial court;
For merit and fame alone a person will "grow as emaciated as the yellow blossoms."[72]
Return and be done!
See how imposing, layer after layer, are the silver mountains and iron walls.[73]

EXTRA MALE *acts out entering unobtrusively.*—MALE LEAD *speaks*:—Chen Jiqing, you stupid dolt! What did you come here for?—*Wait until* EXTRA MALE *is startled and speaks.*

(*Yan'er luo*)
You swallowed that hook of fame and fortune all by yourself,
Who will save you from this sea of misery?
Fortunately, your ethers did not soar through the clouds to pierce the Dipper and Buffalo constellations[74]—
In vain would have been your kowtow, all atremble, at the Cinnabar Steps![75]

EXTRA MALE *speaks*: What are the names of the four of you?

(*Gua yugou*)
Silence!
I disparage those Marquises of Ten Thousand Households in that human realm,
I see their tears soaking the gauzy silk sleeves of their robes.

[(*Speaks*:)] The four of us play the pipes and strum the strings, sing to ourselves and dance for ourselves. What joy!
True it is: "Wherever there is music and song there is sorrow."
You'll wind up as emaciated as Bo Yi and Shu Qi![76]

---

70. Literally, Yingzhou 瀛洲, a mountain in the Eastern Sea where immortals dwell.
71. *Xianzi* 仙子, a common designation for Daoists.
72. A famous quote from female poet Li Qingzhao (1084–ca. 1151).
73. Obstacles that cannot be torn down; insurmountable obstacles.
74. That is, beyond the highest point of the heavens.
75. That is, "Fortunately you did not pass the examinations and spend the rest of your life in fear serving at court."
76. Two paragons of virtue, the eldest and youngest sons, respectively, of the lord of Guzhu, who mutually deferred the throne to each other and then fled together rather than either of them take the throne. They later decided to cast their lot with King Wen of the Zhou, but when they had reached his state, they found that he had died. They berated his son, later to become King Wu of Zhou, for attacking his enemies before burying his deceased father. They fled to Mount Shouyang, where they, refusing to eat "the grain of Zhou," eventually perished from their diet of mountain bracken. See "Po Yi, Memoir 1," in Ssu-ma Ch'ien 1995b, 1–6.

So don't go in front of the Phoenix Galleries
Or behind that Simurgh Terrace.[77]
Once your name is listed on the Golden Plaque[78]
You suddenly do your spiritual roaming in a strange land.[79]
Wait until EXTRA MALE *has spoken.*
(*Gu meijiu*)
You shut up!
Do you really want to be a magistrate in the red dust?
To leave your name in the green books of history?
You tighten up your sleeves to "clamber up to the toad and snap the cassia branch."[80]
Stop this desire for merit and fame,
Plumb the Mysterious Pass[81] as quickly as you can!
[(*Taiping ling*)]
Look at the bright mountains and luxuriant rivers in the Garden of Immortals,
So much better than Confucius, out of grain in Chenzhou![82]
For nothing have you studied and mastered "Kuang Heng boring through the wall,"[83]
For nothing have you suffered the hardship of Sun Kang and his reflected snowlight.[84]
Even if you were one of the Five Liege Lords
In a Phoenix Tower
Drinking imperial wine—
So much pain—
Those "golden seals and purple tassels."

77. "Phoenix Galleries and Simurgh Terrace" can refer to both the imperial court and the high offices of the central government. Here the latter is probably meant since this is the way the expression is used in other dramatic contexts.
78. That is, as a successful examination candidate and hence in line for an official position.
79. It is unclear here whether this refers to the peripatetic life of a lower official who must travel every third year to a different post in the empire or if it is a reference to death away from home at an official posting.
80. The toad lives in the moon, where a rabbit also pounds out the elixir of life under a cassia tree; this is a metaphor for passing the examinations.
81. The primordial chaos that contains a unity of yin and yang that is beyond cognition and discursive speech. See Esposito 2008.
82. Besieged in the state of Chen, Confucius ran out of grain. His disciples were extremely weak with hunger, and one asked him, "Does the gentleman encounter hardship?" Confucius of course responded with a "yes" and took advantage of the situation to instruct his disciple, "The difference is that the petty man, encountering hardship, is overwhelmed by it." From *Analects* 15.2; see Slingerland 2003, 174.
83. Kuang Heng was so poor that he had to work all day just to make ends meet. At night, too poor to purchase candles, he bored a whole in the wall that separated him from his neighbor so that he could steal enough light to read. He later rose to become a noted minister in the Han.
84. Sun Kang was another poor student, whose solution was to read by the moonlight reflected from the snow.

MALE LEAD *speaks*: You stupid dolt, do you remember arguing with that old man on Mount Zhongnan about the four immortals?—EXTRA MALE *speaks*: I remember.—MALE LEAD *speaks*: Do you recognize these four?—EXTRA MALE *speaks*: I don't recognize any of them.—*Wait until all four immortals have spoken.*

(*Didi jin*)
I drive the winds of heaven,
Caress the stars and constellations.
This one once fervently set critical policy;[85]
This one floated his nimble raft alone
And saw right through the Pass to Heaven.[86]
This one roamed at will through the Moon Palace.[87]
(*Zhegui ling*)
Fortunately I did not broadcast an empty name over the distant past,

After MALE LEAD *has spoken. After* EXTRA MALE *has spoken.*

Nor did I leap over the dragon's gate in a single try
To stand alone on the tortoise's head,
Then suddenly pack my lute and books to go to some distant place,
Bitter and depressed like Song Yu grieving over autumn.[88]
You faced that aloof old codger at Mount Zhongnan,
Put your pillow on high and slept without a care at Green Dragon Monastery.
You rode that leaf of a boat
Over ten thousand miles of the River's current.
If you now go in your dream into Acacia Peace,
Then both sides will concentrate their sorrow.

---

85. This probably refers to Han Yu, who had been enlightened by Han Xiangzi, one of the Eight Immortals (and also, in legend, considered Han Yu's nephew). When Han Yu (the Literary Duke) was banished for his "Memorial on the Bone of the Buddha," he was on his way to Chaoyang but was halted by a snowstorm at Indigo Pass (Languan 藍關) in Shaanxi. When impeded, he wrote a poem titled "To Show to My Nephew Xiang When I Reached Indigo Pass After I Had Been Banished" (Zuo qian Languan shi zhizun Xiang 左遷至藍關示姪孫湘), which included the lines

雲橫秦嶺家何在	Clouds lie across the Qinling Mountains, where is my home?
雪擁藍關馬不前	Snow stuffs Indigo Pass, the horse will not go forward.

Prior to this time, Han Yu's legendary nephew, Han Xiangzi, had forced a peony to blossom during early winter, and on its petals was this couplet, which he showed to Han Yu, who did not understand the meaning of these lines. Later, when Han Yu was banished, Han Xiangzi traveled to meet him when he was stuck in the snow at Indigo Pass, and they then understood the meaning of the poem. They overnighted at the pass, and Han Yu followed Han Xiangzi to become an immortal.

86. That is, Zhang Qian; see n. 54.
87. That is, Ye Fashan/Ye Jineng/Ye Jingchan; see n. 55.
88. The poet Song Yu (third century BC) is famous for the lines "Alas for the breath of autumn! / Wan and drear! Flower and leaf fluttering fall and turn to decay. / Sad and lorn! As when on a journey far one climbs a hill and looks down on the water to speed a returning friend." See Hawkes 1985, 209.

After MALE LEAD *has spoken.—Wait for* EXTRA MALE*'s [lyric] "The Immortal Draws Near the River."—You, as* MALE LEAD, *speak*: This boy can be taught!—*Wait until* EXTRA MALE *speaks.*

(*Chuan bo zhao*)
No use for you to suffer and blame yourself,
Just shut tight that busy mouth that "discusses heaven and discourses about earth."
Even if you destroyed Qin and helped Han arise,
Were made a prime minister or enfeoffed as a lord,
Aided the Exalted Ancestor of Han, spreading your merit to the entire cosmos,
Even if you truly are a helping hand to patch up heaven and earth,
(*Qi dixiong*)
Quickly nod your head
And shake your sleeves to leave
On your travels through the five-colored auspicious clouds.[89]
Cast away that golden seal of the minister of education, as heavy as a peck measure.
Beside jade creeks misty waters unceasingly flow,
In front of the green cliffs, wind and moon remain as always.
(*Meihua jiu*)
Do not wait until the hair at your temples turns autumn white,
So you "can share anxiety with the emperor."
Or sigh that years and months, so hard to slow,
Turn one's head white all too soon.
You offer up your own "Rhapsody on Tall Poplars Palace"[90] and approach the imperial pylons,
I will clamber onto that bright-colored phoenix and ascend to Immortals' Islet,
We three are old friends.
This one faces the cliffs, blowing his jade flute,
This one paces Cangzhou, relying on his silver-toned zither,
And this one boards a flat boat, strumming a brocade dulcimer.
(*Shou Jiangnan*)
I lie and blow the pipe, going to Yangzhou,
Availing myself of the fresh wind, blown into the blue above to roam with the clouds;

89. While this phrase can also signal high achievement or refer to the imperial palace, it is used here as an invitation to join Liezi on his trips through the heavens. Certainly an ironic jab is intended.

90. Yang Xiong was given rank at court ("purple steps") on the basis of his rhapsodies in celebrating imperial power. As Knechtges notes, these rhapsodies also included subtle reprimands for extravagance. See Knechtges 2008, 63–80, 85–88; for a translation of the "Rhapsody on Tall Poplars Palace," see Knechtges 1987, 137–50.

You sit astride the golden tortoise ascending steadily to the Phoenix Tower!
Instead of grasping for clouds, put your hands in your sleeves for the time being,
And pay attention to one scene of Zhuangzi's dream of the butterfly.[91]

MALE LEAD *speaks*: You cannot stay here long! Your hometown is near. You'll reach it in just a minute. Just don't forget the true Way!

(*Litingyan Coda*)
Riding this freshening wind in the bright moon, after yellow dusk,
The tired traveler at heaven's edge has suffered for nothing.
Trusting to a short sword and long zither,
You roamed all over the Seven States of the Springs and Autumns.
True it is,
You "Wrestled a tiger and forded the River,"[92]
You "studied butchering a dragon"[93] but were left with your hands in your sleeves!
If you want to be free and unfettered,
Then wash clean all of the filth from your heart.
I will roam freely through the Garden of Immortals
And never trod again down that path to Handan.[94]

After EXTRA MALE *has spoken, act out calling for a fishing boat, then speak and exit.*

[ACT 3]

Wait for one scene of OLD MAN, OLD WOMAN, *and* FEMALE LEAD *to be finished*—MALE LEAD *enters costumed as* FISHERMAN, *dressed in rain cape and swinging a boat* [*as though sculling it*], *enters and opens.*

Beneath the moon I punt my little leaf of a boat,
Before the wind I gather in my fishing hook;
With bamboo hat covering my head, I endure the days and months,
With rain cape thrown on my body, I pass the springs and autumns.

Ah, how happy we fisherfolk are!

---

91. Once upon a time the philosopher Zhuang Zhou dreamt he was a butterfly, as happy as could be. When he woke up, he wondered whether he perhaps was a butterfly dreaming it was Zhuang Zhou.

92. From *Analects* 7.9, later a common saying about someone who is brave but heedless of danger; one who gives no forethought to what one is doing.

93. A story of a certain Zhu Pingman 朱泙漫, who spent years studying how to butcher a dragon but had no place to employ his skills. The hands he had used to perfect his skills rest idly in his sleeves.

94. From a Tang-dynasty tale by Shen Jiji 沈既濟 (ca. 750–800) titled "Inside a Pillow" (Zhenzhong ji 枕中記) about a certain student named Lu 盧生 who meets a Daoist named Codger Lü (Lü Daoweng 呂道翁) at an inn in Handan. Lü gave him a pillow so he could take a nap, and he dreamt of passing the examinations, attaining a

([NANLÜ MODE:] *Yizhi hua*)

A squat brushwood window is newly woven,
The fine ropes of my net have been neatly rearranged.
Facing the westerly wind, I rolled up my line and hook,
And now row my skiff following the bright moon—
Mist and water stretch on and on,
I have brewed my own Master Huang's wineshop wine,[95]
And lift up this speckled bamboo sieve myself.
I'll drink until I'm dizzy drunk, the moon is clear, the wind fresh,
And, at ease and happy, defy that vastness of time and space.[96]

(*Liangzhou diqi*)

I pay no heed to seeing off greening spring, or the late sun's setting in the west;
Let those unfeeling waters of the Yangtze flow on to the east.
"Light mists and drizzly rains obscure front and rear."
Hanging poplars along the twisting banks,
Sand spits and islands in the stream.
A rain cape is thrown over my body
And a bamboo hat covers my head.
This is the fisherman's grand lifestyle—
We befriend the wild egrets and sand gulls.
I have just left that level stretch of lake that was Master Zhu of Tao's,[97]
Brushed by the Three Rivers' Ford of Master Zhuge of Shu,[98]

high position, having a family, and finally dying. When he died, he awoke from the dream to find that the yellow millet that the innkeeper was cooking was not yet ready. In later traditions the story is grafted into the hagiographies of Lü Dongbin, who becomes Student Lu, and Zhongli Quan, who becomes Codger Lü, and the story is turned into a tale of Lü Dongbin's enlightenment. For the original story, see "The World Inside a Pillow" in Nienhauser 1987. For the hagiographical materials about Lü and their representations, see Katz 1996 and "Taoist Immortals" in Little and Eichman 2001, 324–27.

95. Note the following passage from *A New Account of the Tales of the World*:

> Once while Wang Rong was serving as president of the Imperial Secretariat in 301–302, he passed by Master Huang's wineshop wearing his ceremonial robes and riding in a light one-horse carriage. Looking back, he remarked to the guests in the carriage behind him, "Long ago I used to drink and make merry in this wine shop with Ji Kang and Ruan Ji and, in the outings in the Bamboo Grove, I also took a humble part. But ever since Ji Kang's premature death and Ruan Ji's passing I've been hemmed in by the times. Today as I look on this place, even though it's so near, it seems as far away as the hills and rivers."

Translation adapted with minor changes in romanization from Liu and Liu 2002, 346.

96. Literally, "Heaven goes on and on, oh, earth lasts forever."
97. See chap. 2, n. 39.
98. A generalized reference to the fords across the three rivers of Shu that empty into the Yangtze: the Min, Pei, and Tuo. Zhuge Liang was the great tactician and strategist who was employed by the Shu-Han in their contestation for the empire in the Three Kingdoms era. See Idema and West 2012, 302.

And have now reached the head of Yan Ling of Han's Seven-Mile Rapids.[99]
The blue waves and old trees are my bosom friends,
The duckweed of the Yangtze in Chu is better than the finest food,[100]
What I enjoy are sculpin newly from the hook and wine sieved on the spot—
I am happy enough to forget my troubles!

Wait until EXTRA MALE *has spoken.*—MALE LEAD *acts out listening to him.*

(*Gewei*)
Isn't that Wen Qiao, burning a rhinoceros horn and walking midriver?[101]
Or the Spirits of the Xiang River [102] thrumming the zither and floating over
the water?
I will concentrate my gazing eyes and wait patiently beside the bulrushes.
This is a gap in the bank of that sandy dike—
Not the front of the house or the backyard—
So how come this traveler, calling a boat to ferry him across, is standing there?

Wait until EXTRA MALE *has seen the* OLD FISHERMAN *and called out to cross.*—MALE LEAD *speaks*: Where are you going, scholar?—EXTRA MALE *speaks*:—What are you doing asking me?[103] [MALE LEAD *sings*:]

(*He xinlang*)
You want to ferry across the river,
So I have to ask why.
Are you some trader or traveling merchant?
Looking for your old friends or family?
You are just waiting dull-wittedly at the bank beside the blue waves.

---

99. Yan Guang 嚴光, *zi* Ziling 子陵 (ca. 20 BC–AD 20) was a hermit of the Eastern Han period who lived at Seven-Mile Rapids (Qilitan 七里灘) on the Fuchun River 富春江 near Hangzhou, where he fished to provide for himself. His old schoolmate Liu Xiu, who had restored the Han after ascending the throne and defeating the usurper Wang Mang, tried many times to enlist him in service to his court, but Yan Guang always rebuffed him.

100. From a story about King Zhao of Chu, who gathered duckweed seeds as he crossed the Yangtze to visit Confucius. Confucius told him that the seeds could be split and eaten and were an augury of good fortune. Later, duckweed seeds became a common metaphor for things that augur propitious events. Here, perhaps this is just a general reference to aquatic plants that are good to eat.

101. From the story of a certain Wen Qiao 溫嶠 of the Jin who crossed the Yangtze to reach Buffalo Jetty (Niuzhu Ji 牛渚磯) and heard strange sounds underwater. He was told that there were monsters under the water, so he asked someone to light a rhinoceros horn (which was believed to go on burning below the water) so he could look in the water, where he saw many strange apparitions and monsters.

102. The term *xiangling* 湘靈 refers to the Spirits of the Xiang River (Xiang Shen 湘神). In some traditions, there are two spirits, the daughters of the sage-king Yao, who became the two consorts of his successor, the sage-king Shun, Nühuang 女皇 and Nüying 女英. The tears they shed on Shun's death fell on bamboo stalks and permanently stained them, whence a new kind of bamboo, "tear-spotted bamboo," began to grow along the riverbank. This allusion is implicit as well in the reference to Jiaofu of Zheng. See n. 225.

103. More equivalent to the English expression "What business is it of yours?"

You're not one of the Three Grandees of Chu,[104] embracing sand to throw himself in the River, are you?
Or Wu Zixu, intent on taking vengeance for wrongs done to your father?[105]
Or imitating the Banished Immortal Li, off to embrace the moon?[106]
Or perhaps imitating Fan Li wanting to take a boat home?

Wait until EXTRA MALE *has spoken.* [MALE LEAD *sings*:]

So it turns out to be some local yokel student who had set off to take the examinations but failed.
He wanted to hold the white ivory plaque in springtime breezes at the Imperial Garden,[107]
But having failed he wants to take a little fishing boat out on the misty waves and bright moonlight.

Wait until EXTRA MALE *has spoken.* [MALE LEAD *sings*:]

(*Ma yulang*)
The dew is cold and has soaked through my raincoat;
I wave my short oars and dip them into the main current,
Passing by a span of bridge, a lonely footbridge as thin as a dragon's waist.
I see the several dots of gulls
Chasing each other ahead,
Little beauty spots on the autumn river's elegance.
(*Gan huang'en*)
Reflections of the clouds glide on and on,
The force of the wind blows strong and chilly.
Winding my way by the green poplar dike,
Shores of fragrant grass,
Islets of water pepper flowers.[108]

---

104. See chap. 2, n. 38.

105. King Ping of Chu, after heeding slander, slew Wu Zixu's father, who had protested when the king took his own son's fiancée as his wife. Wu Zixu escaped to the state of Wu, where he helped the King of Wu defeat Chu. The exacting of revenge involves Wu Zixu's draining a lake to unearth King Ping's grave and whip the corpse three hundred times. Here, the allusion is more clearly directed toward the death of Wu, who was slain because he remonstrated with the King of Wu. The constant remonstration caused the king to lose trust in him, and Wu Zixu was ordered to commit suicide. Wu's body was then sewn up in a leather sack and dumped into the river. According to legend, Wu Zixu then became the "spirit of the waves." For a detailed account, see Johnson 1980.

106. This is the famous poet Li Bai (701–762), whose many poems on wine and the moon earned him the sobriquet of "the Banished Immortal." According to one legend, he died after drinking too much and trying to embrace the reflection of the moon in the river.

107. This refers to the banquets the Song emperors held at the Garden of Chalcedony Forest (Qionglin Yuan 瓊林苑) outside the eastern gates of Kaifeng, which was then known as the Eastern Capital or Bianliang.

108. This could be either *Polygonum hydropiper*, the mild water pepper, or *Polygonum senticosum*. No accepted English common name seems to exist for *senticosum*, according to the Global Biodiversity Information Facility.

EXTRA MALE *speaks*: Where are we? [MALE LEAD *sings*:]
We have passed to the headwaters of the Huai,
And to where the Bian River splits its flow.[109]
We already draw near your native village,
Approach your old home,
So don't stop or slow down!

EXTRA MALE *speaks*: How strange! I am already at the gate to my home. Why, it's only the second watch![110] [MALE LEAD *sings*:]
(*Caicha ge*)
You don't need to ask, "What watch or wooden slip?"[111]
Just look at how the clouds on the water disappear:
Drippingly bright, that half wheel of remnant moon is at the tip of willow's branch.

Act out making the boat stop.—MALE LEAD *speaks*: Scholar, we have arrived in your village. Come back after you see your family.—*Wait until* EXTRA MALE *speaks.*—[*Speak:*] This is the house. Just allow me a moment and then disembark.
I'll tie the boat to this little stump of a peg here so you can disembark,
You can hear the woofing hounds bark in the depths of the bamboo forest.
They both exit.

Wait until OLD MAN, OLD WOMAN, *and* FEMALE LEAD *all enter.—Speaking stops.—You, as* MALE LEAD, *and* EXTRA MALE *enter together.*—EXTRA MALE *speaks*:—You wait here and I will come back after I have seen my parents.—*After* FEMALE *opens the door and speaks.—Wait until* EXTRA MALE *speaks.—Wait until* OLD MAN *speaks.—Wait until* EXTRA MALE *speaks.—Wait until* OLD MAN *finishes.—Act out offering wine.—You, as* MALE LEAD, *laugh coldly and speak*: Jiqing, hurry up, come on! [*Sing*:]
(*Muyang guan*)
Quickly sing that "Golden Threads" at the feast mat,[112]
And raise that jade wine server before the goblet—
As soon as that single meal of yellow millet is done.
Quickly take leave of your white-haired parents
And set aside forever your perfect match of verdant spring.
You oh-so-simpleminded, dull-witted stupid dolt!
Quickly achieve enlightenment, you prisoner to officialdom.
If you are so attached to the idea of Shi Chong's thousand weight of wealth,
How can we dispatch this little boat of Master Zhu of Tao's?

109. Where the Bian Canal is diverted from the Yellow River.
110. The second watch corresponds to the period 9–11 P.M.
111. The wooden slip is a counter in the water clock, a notched stick that rises with the water level in the pot to mark time. Here, "You don't need to calculate by human mechanical time."
112. A conventional lyric sung to accompany drinking at banquets.

Wait until MALE LEAD *speaks.—Wait until* FEMALE *acts out grieving.*

(*Ku huangtian*)
All she can do is go on and on to try and beguile him,
Her overflowing tears ever streaming.
Hurry and take off that golden cangue and those jade-link fetters,[113]
Be done quickly with those swallow companions and oriole mates.
Prepare raincoat and bamboo hat, line and pole, hooks, and boat,
And go off to the side of Pan Stream,[114]
The head of the Wei River,
And become a fisherman on the misty waves,
So free and untrammeled,
With loose gown and full sleeves.
Oh, to the paradises of Lang Garden or Immortals' Isle
Let us both go and there rest, defying the western winds.
We'll pay no heed to dragons fighting and tigers brawling,
To the raven flying or hare running.[115]

Wait until EXTRA MALE *acts out finding brush and paper and writes a lyric poem.*

(*Wu ye ti*)
You vie with Sui He[116] but waste those lips in vain,
And don't think I'll "let any old wind carry me off east on an eastern rill."[117]
Recite:

The moon slides down and cold dew grows white,
This night I go, but leave my heart behind;
Songs of separation are perched in a phoenix pipe,
Tears of parting sprinkle on the jasper zither.
The wine arrives, drinking it increases our sorrow,
The poem finished, we recite it with matched tears;
On moonlit nights I will have dreams of love,
And in the empty bed, lie beneath half the quilt.

[*Sing*:]
And now, you raise your eyebrows, as emaciated as a bare autumn cliff,[118]
Turn your heads to hold each other's eyes

113. Conventional reference to attachment to one's children.

114. This is where Qiu Chuji 丘處機 (1148–1227), the most famous of human Quanzhen Daoists, studied the Way.

115. The sun is inhabited by a three-legged metal raven, while the moon is the home of a jade hare pounding out the medicine of immortality: reference to the passing of time.

116. One of Liu Bang's ministers whose glib tongue persuaded Ying Bu to defect from Xiang Yu and join Liu Bang.

117. That is, "Don't think I am going to give up control and turn it over lightly to someone else" or "just go blithely along with someone else."

118. Bare autumn hills, denuded of their foliage, are on occasion characterized in poetry as "emaciated."

As the vexation of separation goes on and on.
One looks at the carved saddle, brows furrowed, in sorrows for the court;
One is filled with enmity at Yang Pass,[119] tears soaking her spring robe's sleeves.
Let's go,
Stop suffering—
For my grass sandals and hempen robe
Far outdo fat steeds and fine sables!

Wait until OLD MAN, OLD WOMAN, *and* FEMALE *exit.*

(*Three from Coda*)
On these softly plied oars with their creaking groan we leave the river's mouth,
To see a single dot of a flickeringly bright fishing lamp at the head of the ancient ford.
All I can see are snowy waves on the springtime river crashing against the heavens,
The moon growing blacker, the clouds ever more sorrowful.
Whipping wind grows wild, lashing rain violent—
To what part of what season should this weather belong?
An endless expanse of white, the silver waves flow unbroken—
Where is the end of Chu and beginning of Wu?

(*Two from Coda*)
All I see are
Krakens and dragons howling in the swirling abyss,
Ghosts and sprites sorrow in the blank emptiness of the hoary moon:
The roiling river and stirred-up sea shake the God of the Waves.[120]
It scares me so much I grow cowardly and meek—
This has to happen to me: a dark sky, a sinking boat!
I grasp the short oar—who will save us?[121]
This leaf of a boat nearly flips,
And our lives are like a floating bubble on the water's surface.

[EXTRA MALE *speaks*:]The waves are rising! What shall we do? Who will save us?

Act out invoking the Buddha. [MALE LEAD *sings*:]

(*Shouwei Coda*)
In vain now you beseech the Dark Abyss, pay homage to the Spirit of the River, and bow with folded hands again and again.

119. A reference to the last line of a famous parting poem by Wang Wei 王維 (701–761): "Beyond Yang Pass you will have no friends."

120. Also known as Yanghou 陽侯.

121. These lines are spoken directly to Chen Jiqing.

Just settle your state of mind, make firm your soul, and close your eyes tight.
The waves billow and rise,
The river flows upstream,
Crashes against the Three Mountains,
Overflows into the Nine Kingdoms,
Shakes the Gates of Heaven,
Shifts the Axis of the Earth.
Rolling turtles of gold
Float on the sea:
You tremble and shake,
Cold sweat flows,
Your soul has left your body,
Your life is near its end—
And you will be unable
To be buried in your village
Below a three-foot overgrown mound—
Who will sacrifice a cup of wine over your grave at Beimang?[122]

Wait until EXTRA MALE *cries out*: *Save me*! *And he acts out falling into the water and waking up.—After* ACOLYTE *enters and speaks.—Wait until* EXTRA MALE *signals understanding and speaks.—After* ACOLYTE *speaks.—* EXTRA MALE *acts out chasing after the master and seeing the basket* [*and speaks*:] The master is gone, but there's this basket. There is nothing in it except this scrap of paper with writing on it. I'll take a look. . . . [*Recites*:]

A single leaf was so kind as to send a traveler home,
Long bamboos with kingfisher leaves stand against each other;
Jade pipes at the banquet seat, on that day a message was left,
A marvelous song in one rendition was when he knew his mistake.
Upon meeting, incapable of expressing enough words,
He then left a poem on his wife's makeup stand.
That beauty wept bitterly after the yellowing dusk—
You thought that this mountain codger knew nothing at all.

EXTRA MALE *acts out deeply sighing* [*and speaks*:] He is indeed a good man, for he knew everything I did in that dream. I am going to chase that master down!
[*Exit.*]

122. The Beimang Hills north of Luoyang were the favorite location for graves during the Eastern Han dynasty.

[ACT 4]

MALE LEAD *enters beating on the drum that enlightens*[123] [*and recites:*]

Yesterday Eastern Zhou, today the dynasty of Qin;
The lamp fires of Xianyang, and the Luoyang dust.[124]
A hundred years is but a single dream of blue waves
That brings laughter to us here on the very peak of Kunlun.[125]

There's nothing to do this morning, so I'll go to the street and collect alms.

(*Jiejie gao*)

All because
A hundred years of fame and fortune
Result in a single exemplary case.[126]
Just try to look
At those officials and ministers of the Golden Horse Gate and the Jade Hall;
They all want to reside forever in the corridors and ancestral halls of the imperial capital
And accumulate merits for all eternity.
They reach the highest ranks,
Enjoy salaries of thousands of measures,
Ai!
They're already at the top of the hundred-foot pole![127]
How could they know I've already handed in those black boots and ivory tallies?

(*Yuanhe ling*)

In my hut I sit in quiet meditation;
For merit and fame you busy yourself everywhere.
If that road of thorns[128] is linked to the gates of heaven,[129]

---

123. This musical instrument is identified either as *yugu* 漁鼓 (fisherman's drum) or, as here, as *yugu* 愚鼓 (a drum to enlighten the doltish), which appears to be a Yuan designation that rarely occurs in texts after the early Ming. Wang Qi 王圻, a late Ming compiler of an encyclopedia, described how they were made in the Ming: "Current method of construction: cut a bamboo tube three or four feet long and cover the head of it with skin (the thinnest portion [of skin] over the intestinal fat of a pig is superior). Strike with two fingers." Wang Qi 1988, 154.9414–15.

124. That is, these two cities, one the capital of the Qin and the other the capital of the Eastern Han, were both burned to nothing.

125. The abode of immortals and the portal for them between heaven and earth.

126. There is the possibility "case" here may refer to a Chan (Zen) *gong'an* (koan).

127. This is probably a reference to the common saying "On a hundred-foot pole take one more step" (*Baichi gan geng jin yibu* 百尺竿更進一步), which means "to try for even more success even though one has reached a high level of accomplishment," "to never be satisfied."

128. That is, the path to office.

129. That is, the court.

People would still clamber up, even if it grows more difficult with each step.
They pay no heed to the fresh blood in Yunyang[130] that has yet to dry,
Or the vile windblown waves that have passed by their eyes.
(*Shangma jiao*)
Even if you are clever in all things,
And crafty in all that you do,
Who has ever reached a state where "both horse and man are at peace"?
Better to be Yan Ziling fishing alone on the autumn river,
Facing the red pepper-weed rapids,
Leisurely clutching the fishing rod.
(*You simen*)
When confronted with the difficulty of the world's way, with its windblown waves ten thousand feet high—
We must admit that fame and fortune do not equal leisure.
I see the yellow cranes dancing as a pair by the green pine brook,
Unbothered by any vulgar business of the world.
Rein in your horse of will
And topple that mountain of right and wrong!
(*Sheng hulu*)
So much better than "A general in iron armor crosses the pass at night."
He drives wild beasts before him,
Sits astride a carved saddle,
But one day when the battle is done, white bones will grow cold in the overgrown wilds.
Can this compare to my thatched hut, my grass shack,
My rush cushion[131] and paper enclosure,
Resting at ease in pure leisure?
(*Reprise*)
When no affair deceives the heart, one sleeps self-secure—
I urge you in the dusty world, do not sorrow or worry.
Pack up your zither and books[132] and return to your old mountains,
Search out the simples-refining stove and scriptures,
Face the stone table and the incense stand,
For in the end this surpasses the human world.

130. The official execution grounds.

131. A round cushion used for meditation.

132. The two essentials a scholar or student carries along with him when going somewhere to study or to take the examinations.

(*Houting hua*)
Look: the dirt on the tumulus has yet to dry,
But the bones of heroes are already cold.
Where are they, those at Hegemon King of Chu's feast at Goose Gate,[133]
Or at Marshal Han's altar when he was commissioned as a general?[134]
They are now completely deserted:
Human life is an empty illusion.
I sigh that human life is like [fleeting clouds] passing our sight.
On that old road to Handan, I
Grew weary of constant travel through the red dust.
I tied up my lame donkey outside the door,
Discarded success and fame as though it were nothing,
And in an instant became an immortal.
(*Liuye'er*)
I ate that meal of the immortal's yellow millet
And it was better than the nine-times-refined noumenal cinnabar pill of Ge Hong.[135]
I was used to coming to the streets of Chang'an,
Where I dissembled as a crazy man.
And temporarily took on the face of a drunkard;
Then in the nod of a head I fully understood the human realm.
([ZHENGGONG MODE:] *Duanzheng hao*)
I'll not go and roam the Jade Hall,
Nor go to sleep at the Eastern Hills[136]—
When you can wander freely, then freely wander as you will!
I beat out a few cadences from the drum that enlightens as I go to the dusty realm—
That is *my* leisurely daily ritual out beyond the world.

---

133. This refers to a feast given for Liu Bang by Xiang Yu, who planned to kill Liu Bang but hesitated and lost the opportunity and subsequently the empire as well. A "Goose Gate meeting" has come to mean any treacherous or otherwise unpleasant meeting where someone will metaphorically be killed.

134. See chap. 2, n. 35.

135. Here the playwright rejects the discipline of exterior alchemy in favor of the meditation techniques of inner alchemy.

136. The Eastern Hills (Dongshan 東山) refer to the place where Xie An 謝安 (320–385) lived in opulent retirement before he joined the administration and rose to a high position.

(*Gun xiuqiu*)
I passed by the tip of Penglai
To visit my old friend Lan Caihe.
Leading my old companions, we eight brothers who roam in leisure,
I watch the steeply rising Silver Pylons on the mountain in the sea.[137]
With Ge Hongya,[138] I'll stroke the starry constellations,
With Fei Changfang call for the dragon staff to stop.[139]
I'll tell the immortal lad not to lock the Grotto Gate;
Facing Cinnabar Mound, I will pour rippling golden waves,[140]
I keep time to Shuangcheng's[141] trim-waist dance at Spreading Cold Palace,[142]
And listen to Magu's song from white teeth at Penglai Mountain.[143]
Drunk, I enter into nothingness.

Wait until EXTRA MALE *acts out running in a hurried way with hat askew.*—[EXTRA MALE *speaks*:] Master, save me, your disciple!—*Speak and* [*make false*] *exit.* [*Sing*:]

(*Tang xiucai*)
Look at him, trembling and shaking, frightened and fearful, running all afluster.
This completely dumbstruck imbecile stares intently at me.

Wait for EXTRA MALE *to speak*:—[EXTRA MALE *speaks*:] Master, deliver me, and send me toward the Way of long life!—[EXTRA MALE] *acts out bowing.* [*Sing*:]

As if boldly unrestrained—why is he bowing to me?
I'm just a poor Daoist
Who lives far off at mountain's bend,
How could *I* lead *you*, a Confucian scholar, to enlightenment?

137. The Silver Pylons were the two gates in front of the Jade Capital on Jade Capital Mountain in Great Canopy Heaven, where all the immortals gather.

138. This seems to be a name for Ge Hong, who refined cinnabar at Cinnabar Cliff.

139. Fei Changfang, whose biography is found in the biographies of magicians in the *History of the Latter Han*, was given a bamboo staff by an old herbal simples salesman, who told him, "Ride this and let it go where it will, and it will reach the place by itself. Once you have arrived, throw it on an overgrown bank." Changfang rode it around and went home; he thought it had taken him fewer than ten days to make the trip, but it turned out he had been gone for ten years. When he got home, he threw it on the bank of a pond, and it turned into a dragon.

140. That is, wine.

141. Shuangcheng 雙成 ("Double Complete") was a serving girl of the Queen Mother of the West. Shuangcheng later became a common designation of beautiful dancers.

142. The palace of the moon goddess, Chang'e 嫦娥.

143. Magu is an immortal who descends as a girl of eighteen or nineteen and performs magic tricks at the house to which she was summoned. Her looks are deceptive, however, since she says she has seen the "mulberry groves change to blues seas" three times, which indicates she has seen the world transformed over a very long period. She comes from Penglai. See Penny 2008b, 731–32.

Wait until EXTRA MALE *speaks.*—[*Sing*:]
(*Gun xiuqiu*)
This poem is seeking a first place pass at the immortals' altar,
Do you know what this poem means?
[EXTRA MALE *speaks*:] Your disciple doesn't get it. *Sing*:
If you cannot see through the Gate of Mystery in this little poem,
Then don't raise your "hairs of purple frost"[144] to adjudicate the empire!
Do you know that the glory of the world is like froth on the water,
And merit and fame like sparks from a flint?
EXTRA MALE *speaks*:—I don't get it.—*Act out bowing.*
Oh, how I wish I had punctured your façade in the lecture hall!
I will sweep the vulgar dust from you as I raise my sagely hand to rub.
You have been the victim of time, that has frittered away your youthful face,
Have been so buried by the affairs of the world that your white hair flourished—
You were gradually worn down.
EXTRA MALE *speaks*:—Where are you going, Master? I want to go with you!
(*Daodao ling*)
There we have dark-green pines crooked and twisting: krakens and dragons at rest,
Virescent hills and high peaks: a wash of clearing mists.
Unmoved by fragrant winds, pine flowers fall,
Grotto gates are closed away in the deep, no one locks them.
Follow me, oh,
Follow me—
To pay court to the Realized we will ascend together the Galleries of Penglai.[145]
Arrange the formation of the Eight Immortals and enter.—EXTRA MALE *speaks*: Master, tell me, who are these people?
(*Yaomin ge*)
This one sticks flowers in his cap and once roamed in the Great Canopy Heavens.[146]
This one blows an iron flute with beautiful harmonies and pleasant sounds.[147]
This one has an ample mouth and her hand holds a wicker strainer.[148]

---

144. That is, your brush.
145. Penglai Galleries is an actual place on Cinnabar Cliff Mountain in Shandong that offers a vista over the sea. Here used to gesture toward the galleries of Penglai Island, an immortals' isle in the Eastern Sea.
146. Zhang Guolao.
147. A historical Daoist noted for both his uncanny prognostications and his outspokenness, Xu Shenweng 徐神翁 (1033–1108) was honored at the court of Huizong of the Song. In texts of the Ming dynasty he disappears to make room for He Xiangu 何仙姑 (Immortal Maiden He) in the list of Eight Immortals, but here he has dislodged Cao Guojiu 曹國舅 (Imperial In-Law Cao).

This one with ragged beard drags an iron crutch behind him.[149]
This one converted that Huayang woman.[150]
This one in the long green robe dances wildly and sings out loud.[151]
[(*Yaomin ge*)]
This one has a beard on his chops and is always drunk, red in the face.[152]

EXTRA MALE *speaks*: Master, you? (*Sing*:)

At an inn in Handan I passed through the yellow millet dream,
And when I awoke they had completely altered, those mountains and rivers.
It was all a dream of rise and fall at the southern branch.
True it is:
In the beginning, we all might suffer,
But today, a fresh wind for all eternity is set free.

Dispersal Scene

[Title:] Lü Pure Yang appears in transformed form in a dream of blue waves
[Name:] Chen Jiqing is Enlightened to the Way on a Bamboo-Leaf boat

Newly Cut with Plot Prompts:
Chen Jiqing Is Enlightened to the Way on a Bamboo-Leaf Boat

The End

148. He Xiangu, the only female member of the Eight Immortals.

149. Li Tieguai.

150. The Huayang woman refers to Xie Ziran 謝自然, who was supposedly led to immortality by the Shangqing Daoist Sima Chengzhen 司馬承貞 (647–735). There are varying accounts of her life, and the one found in Shen Fen's 沈汾 *Continuation of the Biographies of Transcendents* (*Xu Xianzhuan* 續仙傳) was purportedly written by Han Yu 韓愈 (768–824), the late Tang poet and essayist. See Penny 2008c, 1123–24; Kirkland 2008, 911–13. In this context the one who converted the Huayang woman must be Han Xiangzi.

151. Lan Caihe.

152. Zhongli Quan.

A SELECTION OF YUAN PLAYS EDITION OF THE *ZAJU CHEN JIQING MISTAKENLY BOARDS A BAMBOO-LEAF BOAT*

DRAMATIS PERSONAE IN ORDER OF APPEARANCE

Role type	*Name and family, institutional, or social role*
OPENING MALE	CHEN JIQING (act 1)
EXTRA	HUI'AN, abbot of Green Dragon Monastery
ACOLYTE	ACOLYTE
MALE LEAD	LÜ DONGBIN (acts 1, 2, 4)
LIEZI	LIEZI, Lie Yukou
ZHANG LIANG	ZHANG LIANG, Zhang Zifang
GE HONG	GE HONG, Ge the Immortal Codger
MALE LEAD	FISHERMAN (Lü Dongbin)
EXTRA MALE	OLD MAN CHEN, CHEN JIQING's father
OLD FEMALE LEAD (old woman)	MADAME FANG, CHEN JIQING's mother
FEMALE LEAD	MISS BAO, CHEN JIQING's wife
CHILD	ASHENG, CHEN JIQING's son
OPENING MALE	IMPERIAL LORD OF EASTERN FLORESCENCE (act 4)
ZHANG GUO	ZHANG GUO, one of the Eight Immortals
ZHONGLI QUAN	ZHONGLI QUAN, one of the Eight Immortals
IRON CRUTCH LI	LIE TIEGUAI, one of the Eight Immortals
XU SHENWENG	XU SHENWENG, one of the Eight Immortals
LAN CAIHE	LAN CAIHE, one of the Eight Immortals
HAN XIANGZI	HAN XIANGZI, one of the Eight Immortals
HE XIANGU	HE XIANGU, one of the Eight Immortals
DIVINE CODGER XU	DIVINE CODGER XU, Daoist Immortal

✣ ✣ ✣

CHEN JIQING MISTAKENLY BOARDS A BAMBOO-LEAF BOAT

WRITTEN BY FAN ZI'AN OF THE YUAN DYNASTY

COLLATED BY ZANG JINSHU OF WUXING IN THE MING DYNASTY

[WEDGE]

OPENING MALE *costumed as* CHEN JIQING *enters and recites*:

Ashamed now of my insignificant name, failed at the Ministry of Rites,[153]
I am tossed and buffeted, no different from a swallow flying alone;
In the great buildings that stretch to heaven there are no places to roost,
Next year just like this one—returning, but not.

I am named Chen Jiqing and am from Yuhang in Wulin.[154] I studied the Confucian curriculum when young and was known for my literary talent. But because time and fate never matched, I did not pass the examinations and I am drifting about, unable to return home. And to top it off, I've run smack into late winter, and although the rain and snow have cleared, the cold becomes more and more unbearable. How can someone like me—"No relatives wherever I look"—avoid "sighing over hunger and cold"? (*Acts out sighing, speaks*:) Oh! Such bad luck. I just started to think, though, about Green Dragon Monastery on Zhongnan Mountain and the abbot Hui'an, an old hometown friend. He has often written and asked me to visit him at the monastery. Perhaps he can rescue me from this. But it's no sure thing. I might as well go off to Zhongnan Mountain and see Abbot Hui'an.

(*Exits.*)

EXTRA *costumed as pure esquire*[155] HUI'AN *enters leading an ugly* ACOLYTE, *recites*:

A bright heart will twirl no flowers from hidden valleys,[156]
To visualize the Buddha nature, what need for transmission of palm-leaf texts?
The sun comes out, ice melts: it was water all the time,
Refracted rays, when the moon sets, never leave the heavens.[157]

---

153. The branch of government that in the Tang held the qualification examinations.

154. Modern Hangzhou.

155. *Jielang* (潔郎 or 傑郎) is a Song and Yuan slang term for a monk, referring to monks' baldness and celibacy.

156. The "bright heart" is a heart cleared of random thoughts and in which the Buddha-nature will appear. The flower represents a method of transmission of the Dharma outside language, from the story about the origin of Chan by the Buddha's showing a flower to the progenitor of Chan, who smiled in understanding.

157. One's Buddha-nature is always there.

I am monk Hui'an from Green Dragon Monastery here on Zhongnan Mountain. I was originally a man from Yuhang and from a young age worked hard at the Confucian enterprise, but in my middle years I shaved my hair to become a monk. Serendipitously, I came here to Green Dragon Monastery in my wanderings as an acolyte, and I so delighted in its scenery that I remained here to become the head monk. I have an old friend I studied with, called Chen Jiqing. This fellow has filled himself with the classics and histories, has gone through the whole of the Hundred Schools, has a talent that can weave all of heaven and earth together in perfect harmony, and the ability to drink the pure dew and course across the clouds. But because he has yet to realize success or fame, he is adrift for a while and cannot go home. I have sent him many letters asking him to come visit me in the monastery, but he's sent not a single word in reply. Acolyte, go to the main gate and keep an eye out, and when Master Chen arrives, immediately inform me! (ACOLYTE *speaks*:) Understood! (CHEN JIQING *enters and recites*:)

I have just left those paths of purple[158]
To enter into clouds of white.

Here I am at the gate of Green Dragon Monastery. Little monk, is Abbot Hui'an at home? (ACOLYTE *speaks*:) Faugh! You ought to open up your donkey eyes and take a closer look! How can you call a monk as tall as me a "little monk"?[159] You know nothing about proper ceremony! I'm beginning to see—you are wearing such a tattered old gown that's holding up this yellow and dried skinny old face—you must be here to throw yourself on our master of the house. Well, how come you're so arrogant? (CHEN JIQING *speaks*:) Ohh, what an unlucky little fellow. (*Acts out bowing to him and speaks*:) Please forgive me, Young Master. May I beg you to trouble yourself to report to Abbot Hui'an that his old friend, Chen Jiqing, has come to visit him? (ACOLYTE *speaks*:) You finally come out with it. No wonder that you Confucianists and my house have been at such odds since antiquity. Enough! Enough. Stand here and I will go and report for you. (*Acts out going to report, speaks*:) Hey, wait a minute. Let me have a little fun with Baldy first. (*Acts out entering and greeting, speaks*:) Master, an old friend is outside, who calls himself Che-en-ji-yi-qi-ying, has come just to visit you. (HUI'AN *speaks*:) This is gibberish. Who in the world would have a name like that? (ACOLYTE *speaks*:) You old bald good-for-nothing, you still want to be enlightened to the Dharma Law? Then you have to steal a glance at other fellows' wives when you're looking at the sutras. (HUI'AN *speaks*:) This guy's gone mad! Go on back out and get it clear this time. (ACOLYTE *speaks*:) What's not clear? Che-en-ji-yi-qi-ying has come just to visit you. (HUI'AN *speaks*:) I don't get it. (ACOLYTE *speaks*:) Ask your old lady to come out, she'll know. (HUI'AN *speaks*:) Pshaw! (ACOLYTE

158. The "paths" are the roadways to the capital.

159. Playing on the fact of the bald head of monks, the term "little monk" is also a slang word for penis.

speaks:) Alright, I'll tell you. I was having fun playing the word-splitting game. Che-en is Chen, Ji-yi is Ji, and qi-ying is qing. Hasn't your old friend Chen Jiqing come to see you? (HUI'AN *speaks*:) Hurry out and invite him in. (ACOLYTE *acts out going to greet him, speaks*:) Mister Chen, my master just consistently refused to see you, but thanks to my cursing that bald old good-for-nothing, he's relented and asks you to go on in. (CHEN JIQING *acts out going in and greeting him, speaks*:) This humble student has been remiss in visiting you for the past several years. (HUI'AN *speaks*:) This poor monk has known for a while that my beloved brother has been unsuccessful on the field of letters, and I sent you several letters asking you to come. That you have now stooped to make a visit is all to my good fortune! (CHEN JIQING *speaks*:) Abbot, I have continuously received your written summons, and it is not that I was unmoved by them, but I have labored for many years by the firefly-lit window[160] and by reflected snow light.[161] I would have said that success and fame could be had as easy as spitting into my hand, and I never expected to fail time after time, or be too frightened to go home. For this reason, I had little face left to come and visit you. I just pray that you will forgive me. (HUI'AN *speaks*:) You are wrong, my beloved brother. Have you not heard the ancient's saying, "To be without learning: this is poverty; to learn and be incapable of putting it into action: this is illness."[162] Based on your expansive talent and accumulated learning, there should be no worry about attaining success and fame. In the old days Yi Yin plowed in the state of Shen,[163] and Fu Yue was wearied with forms for building walls.[164] Later, they encountered enlightened rulers and ended up in the positions of mentors and ministers. Although you are in a bad state and dispirited now, when the day comes when luck and timing converge, you too will be a mentor and a minister. How hard will it be then to carry out the work of someone like a Yi Yin or a Fu Yue? (CHEN JIQING *speaks*:) Well said, but excessive! I am returning now. (*Sings*:)

160. Che Yin 車胤, also known as Wuzi 武子 (333–401), was a man of Nanping 南平. His great-grandfather, Jun 浚, was the grand protector of Kuaiji 會稽 in Wu, where he lived with his entire family. Che Yin's family was poor and could not always get lamp oil, so in the summer he would stuff dozens of fireflies into a gauze sack in order to have them reflect their light on his texts, and he went on into the night from there.

161. See n. 84.

162. An altered version of famous lines quoted in various forms in classical texts, in which Zigong, one of Confucius's disciples, went to visit another disciple, Yuan Xian, who lived in utter poverty. Zigong arrived on a fine chariot that was too large to enter Yuan Xian's alleyway. Yuan greeted him, and Zigong asked, "What is wrong with you?" Yuan Xian answered that he had heard that "to be without wealth is called poverty; to study but be unable to effect the Way, this is an infirmity. Now I am poor, not infirm!" Zigong was shamed by his comments. See the one version of the story in "Confucius' Disciples, Memoir 7," in Ssu-ma Ch'ien 1995b, 77.

163. See *Mencius* 1A.7. Yi Yin 伊尹 was a farmer in the outskirts of Shen, where he "delighted in the Way of Yao and Shun." King Tang the Completer 成湯王 asked him several times to enter his service, but he refused, being unmoved by any kind of reward. Finally, he joined Tang and helped establish the Shang dynasty.

164. See chap. 2, n. 33.

([XIANLÜ MODE] *Shanghua shi*)

All because I spent ten years by the firefly-lit window, diligently studying texts,
I am totally ashamed that I have not yet set my body on the ten thousand mile Peng-bird path[165]—
And because of this I willingly wander around in the wind and dust.
How many times in secret have I scorned myself,
Because I have so little face left to see my fellow villagers?

(*Exits.*)

(HUI'AN *speaks*:) Brother! Why are you leaving? Turn back. *Aiya*! He's really gone. Acolyte, hurry out and tell him to turn back. Say that I have more to say to him.

(ACOLYTE *speaks*:) I'll scurry on out of the main gate and ask him to leave, lest my master's wife won't let him stay.

(*Exits.*)

(HUI'AN *speaks*:) Just look at how anxious my brother is about success and fame. I'm sure he wants to go back to his lodging to review all those classics and histories. My monastery may be desolate and dreary, but it doesn't lack congee or gruel. It would have been better to keep him here, provide him some food and clothing, and let him wait for the next examination. That would have both let him succeed with his "ambitions of wind and cloud" and also let me display some of the affection I have for someone from my old home. (*Recites*:)

This old friend, alas, his time unmet,
Can avail himself of this mountain retreat;
I'm only afraid that once he ascends to high office,
He will never inquire again about a grass-woven hut.

(*Exits.*)

ACT 1

(CHEN JIQING *speaks*:) I am grateful for Abbot Hui'an's feelings of friendship and loyalty for someone from his old home and that he has detained me to review the classics and histories and wait for the next examination. This is my fortune amid misfortune. There's nothing happening today, so I'll wait until Hui'an comes out of meditation,

165. This is the path toward an official career. The metaphor stems from the *Zhuangzi*, "In the northern darkness there is a fish and his name is Kun. The Kun is so huge I don't know how many thousand li he measures. He changes and becomes a bird whose name is Peng. The back of the Peng measures I don't know how many thousand li across and, when he rises up and flies off, his wings are like clouds all over the sky. When the sea begins to move, this bird sets off for the southern darkness, which is the Lake of Heaven." See Watson 1968, 28 (with changes in romanization)

and ask him to point out to me where I might take a walk and see some old sites. (HUI'AN *enters leading* ACOLYTE, *acts out greeting him, speaks*:) Brother, you have humbled yourself to stay here; this mountain monastery is decrepit and dreary and I have been negligent in many things. Is there anything you would like to bring to my attention? (CHEN JIQING *speaks*:) How can you say that, Brother? I have disturbed you now for many months, and I am entirely grateful. But I have often heard that Mount Zhongnan is the most famous mountain in the empire, so there must be many sights to see here. I beseech you to point them out to me so that I might go and gaze upon them; it would certainly not be in vain. (HUI'AN *speaks*:) Well then, let me lead the way; you simply follow along and enjoy the sights of our temple. (CHEN JIQING *acts out inspecting the monastery, speaks*:) What a fine monastery this is! Look how the halls penetrate into the blue welkin, how the trees brush wispy stratus clouds, how the water winds about Ripple Lake, and how the peaks look down on the Purple Galleries of the Imperial City. Truly, "Never enough of gazing, ever an excess of joy!" (*Acts out gazing far away, speaks*:) Abbot, what is that indistinct ribbon of water there in the southeast corner? (HUI'AN *speaks*:) This is the waterway that runs into and out of Ripple Lake, and from here it runs into the Han River. It is the road home to our old village. (CHEN JIQING *acts out sighing, speaks*:) When I am confronted with this, Abbot, suddenly thoughts of return come unbidden. If you have a brush and inkstone, may I borrow them? I want to compose a lyric to the tune "Fragrance Fills the Courtyard" and write it on a blank wall—would that be alright? (HUI'AN *speaks*:) I'd love to see it. Acolyte, go and fetch the "four treasures of the studio."[166] (ACOLYTE *speaks*:) Here they are. You think you've composed a good one. If you think you've composed a good one and can write it out well,[167] then write it out. Otherwise don't write it out lest other people laugh at you as the "Hangzhou idiot." (CHEN JIQING *acts out writing it out, speaks*:) Abbot, let me recite it for you. . . . (*Recites*:)

I sat until I wore out my blanket against the cold,
Ground through an inkstone of iron,
Boasting all the time that the classics and history would flow like water,
That gathering with others in purple and blue strings of ministerial caps
Would be as easy as spitting in the hand, and not worth a worry.
Time after time in Chang'an I sat for the tests—
I submitted my myriad word policy paper to the dragon's throne.
But my talent of jade, worth a string of cities, was left unused,
And I was bereft of plans to seize official rank.

166. A brush, paper, ink, and an inkstone.

167. In good calligraphy.

Pitiful, and dispirited too,
I set out to return to my old home,
Yet idly lingered in those August Precincts.
Moved by the weight of your feelings,
I tarried here in the cells of monks.
On your day of leisure you led me to climb high to gaze,
And from this high perch,
We looked out over the expanse with the eyes of poets—
The mountains of home are far away,
How can we go back?
We commit it all to a dream's roaming.

(HUI'AN *speaks:*) What a talent! (ACOLYTE *speaks:*) It'll do. (HUI'AN *speaks:*) What would you know? Go get the tea ready.

(ACOLYTE *exits.*)

(MALE LEAD *costumed as* LÜ DONGBIN *enters carrying a thorn basket, speaks:*) You people of worldly ways! Follow me and leave your family![168] I will make each and every one understand the Way, each and every one become an immortal. Oh, there's no one here. I am Lü Yan, known as Lü Dongbin, and my name in the Way is Master of Pure Yang. Because I did not pass the examinations and my road home passed through Handan, I got to meet my master, Master of Correct Yang, who transformed me in my "dream of the yellow millet."[169] And I completed the Way of the Immortal. I now bear the command of my master to go lead a certain Chen Jiqing—a man from Yuhang who is destined to be an immortal—to enlightenment. I was just descending on my cloud tip when I saw a shaft of blue light—he's at Mount Zhongnan. I'm going to have to go to Green Dragon Monastery. (*Sings:*)

(XIANLÜ MODE: *Dian jiangchun*)

"I have just left the northern seas and also Cangwu,"[170]
And already the progressions of the seasons have passed many times,
To evolve into past and present.
I sigh over the prosperity and decline of generational events,
Who actually recognizes that path to long life?

168. That is, become a Daoist; for the sake of readability, we translate this phrase, in the following, simply as "follow me" or "go off with me."

169. See n. 94.

170. "Northern seas" (*beihai* 北海) is the area along the southern coast of China, just west of the peninsula that leads to Hainan Island. These lines are based on a poem attributed to Lü Dongbin in early Song works. Lü Dongbin does not appear in any Tang-dynasty materials and appears to have been a created figure during the early Song. For more information, see n. 37.

(*Hunjiang long*)

I've measured that dollop of the world's realm,
And passed through the remains of pitched battles of former courts and later dynasties.
From the time that swirling confusion was split open,[171]
I have trod through to the empty void —
I use no Nine-Sublimating Pill to complete my thousand-year life span,
No pound of lead to form a myriad-year pearl,
Pick no rare sprouts or strange grasses,
And carry no noumenal tally in precious seal script.
I just needed to nurture my spirit until it was like water,
And refine my bones until their marrow was like butter.
Every day I harnessed my monkey heart and horse will tight:
Let the mountains and valleys switch places
And rocks rot into these desiccated pines.

(ACOLYTE *enters and speaks*:) I'll go off to the main gate and keep watch. (MALE LEAD *speaks*:) I've reached the gate of Green Dragon Monastery. Little monk, go on in and tell Chen Jiqing that a Daoist elder has come to visit him. (ACOLYTE *speaks*:) I'm just out of luck today. First that penurious scholar called me a little monk, and now this cow nose[172] is calling me a little monk. Well, *this* little monk will carry *your* mother away! Look, cow nose, Chen Jiqing isn't here. (MALE LEAD *speaks*:) I can augur the ethers, so I know he's here in the monastery. (ACOLYTE *speaks*:) Well, augur away at your fucking impotence and scrotal pain! Even if you were the Most Venerated Laozi, Zhongli of the Han, or Lü Dongbin and you can augur ethers, I'm not going to report for you. I'm going off to my cell to enjoy some spirits and dog meat. (*Exits*.)

(MALE LEAD *speaks*:) Since he wasn't willing to announce me, I'll just go on in. (*Acts out entering and greeting, speaks*:) Scholar! Abbot! I bow to you. I am a cloud-roving Daoist, and I have come here for nothing else but to lead a disciple to enlightenment, to "leave his home" and go with this poor Daoist. (CHEN JIQING *speaks*:) You've made a mistake, sir. This is Abbot Hui'an, and Buddhism and Daoism are two different religions. It is impossible for him to be your disciple. Could you be here to lead me to enlightenment? (MALE LEAD *speaks*:) You know it! Scholar, you're a failed candidate right now; if you go with me, you'll be an immortal tomorrow. This won't put you to shame, scholar. Just bid the abbot good-bye, and go off with me. (CHEN JIQING *speaks*:) Listen, you Daoist, I don't know you at all. How can you expect me to go off with you? I've studied until "my belly is stuffed with learning" and I am just

---

171. See n. 42.

172. A term that makes a satirical jab at Daoist priests, whose swept-up hairdo looked like a cow's nose.

getting ready to be an official. Honestly, I tell you, I can't go off with you. (MALE LEAD *sings*:)

(*You hulu*)

I sigh over this road to fame and fortune of yours, fraught with waves of danger,[173]

Truly, you'll suffer all in vain—

I ask: even if you had Su Qin's very ministerial seals at your belt, what good would it do?[174]

Just look: in that Gallery Soaring Beyond the Mists, who are the true heroes?[175]

In the precinct of the Golden Valley they are all affected boys and girls.[176]

(CHEN JIQING *speaks*:) Well, you have to discern between the worthy and the dull. How can you call them all fake in one fell swoop? (MALE LEAD *sings*:)

What kind of worthiness can you discern?

What kind of dullness?

Even if you cast a likeness of Zhugong of Tao in yellow gold,[177]

In the end you can't carry off Xishi to float on river and lake![178]

(CHEN JIQING *speaks*:) If I become an official, this body will be dressed in a purple silk court robe, my head capped with a hat of raven's black gauze, and my hands will be grasping a white ivory tablet—what glory and honor! You who've "left the family" just "dress in grass and eat bark."[179] Where will you wind up? (MALE LEAD *sings*:)

(*Tianxia le*)

I've already been through "A single general's success is ten thousand bleached bones of others,"

Ai, you insignificant little civil and military officials:

Say what you want about those purple silk court robes that glorify a person,

Those raven's black gauze hats

And white ivory tablets—

How can they compare to my chanting the *Yellow Court*[180] and *Canon of the Way and Its Virtue*,[181]

Or intoning *Golden Essence* and *The Text of Great Plainness*[182]—

That unexpectedly wound up sowing a freshening wind across myriad antiquities.

---

173. Literally "windblown waves ten thousand feet high."

174. See n. 44.

175. See chap. 3, n. 72.

176. See n. 46.

177. See chap. 2, n. 39.

178. See chap. 2, n. 12.

179. That is, to live a rustic life.

180. See n. 48.

181. See n. 49.

182. These two texts are probably made-up titles. For instance, the *Yuankan* version of this song uses the term *jinfu* 金符 (golden talley) instead of *jinjing* 金精 for the first. The second title may refer to a section of the *Inner Scripture of the Yellow Emperor* (*Huangdi neijing* 黃庭內經) called the "Great Plainness" (Taisu 泰素), which exists in one copy only, an eleventh-century copy of an eighth-century manuscript.

(ACOLYTE *enters to serve tea, speaks:*) Look: old baldy in the middle, a cow's nose on the left, and a penurious scholar on the right, covering everything from past to present, pretending to be as smart as the very sages of the three religions.[183] (*Acts out delivering the tea.*) (CHEN JIQING *speaks:*) I've been so tied up with this Daoist I haven't even eaten. (MALE LEAD *speaks:*) Scholar, if you are willing to chant the *Scripture of the Yellow Court,* then you won't be cold or hungry. (ACOLYTE *speaks:*) Mister, don't listen to this cow nose's lies. I chant sutras all day long and my stomach is always so hungry that it is constantly rumbling. (MALE LEAD *speaks:*) You don't think that you really won't be cold and hungry after chanting this classic? It is precisely after you have completed the way of the immortal that you won't be hungry or cold; and that comes after chanting this text. (CHEN JIQING *speaks:*) Daoist—how many can you name who have actually attained the way of changing into an immortal over the centuries? (MALE LEAD *speaks:*) Well, let me briefly mention a few for you. (*Sings:*)

(*Nezha ling*)
You must have heard of Lie Yukou
Who rode the cold wind to roam through the eight domains of the world?

(CHEN JIQING *speaks:*) That's one. Others? (MALE LEAD *sings:*)

There was that Zhang Zifang,
Who left the imperial capital following Master Red Pine.[184]

(CHEN JIQING *speaks:*) Others? (MALE LEAD *sings:*)

There was Immortal Master Ge,
Who plucked cinnabar sands to go into the cave abode.
Even though they started out with frames as insensate as clay and wood,
These turned out to be the bones of spiritual immortals,
Nothing like you mortal fellows with your common eyes.

(CHEN JIQING *speaks:*) May I ask, my Daoist, are there beautiful sights in that place where immortals reside? (MALE LEAD *speaks:*) Of course there are! (*Sings:*)

(*Que ta zhi*)
That place of ours there is called the Pot of Penglai[185]
And is near the Capital of Heaven—
All cowry shell pylons and pearl palaces,
Paths through the sunsets, tracks through the clouds—
A place only an immortal from Grand Canopy[186] Heaven can dream of reaching.

(CHEN JIQING *speaks:*) Well, if it's so great, what are you doing down here in our lower world? (MALE LEAD *sings:*)

I've come down to this dusty realm
To transform the obtuse and doltish like you.

183. Confucius, Laozi, and the Buddha.

184. See n. 53.

185. The fairy island of Penglai in the Eastern Sea was graced with a mountain in the shape of a wine pot.

186. See n. 56.

(CHEN JIQING *speaks*:) Look, Daoist, don't exaggerate. Where, in honest truth, is that immortal's realm? (MALE LEAD *speaks*:) Since you've asked me, I'll tell you, but you can't find me there. (*Sings*:)

(*Jisheng cao*)

For nothing will you wear through those roaming-immortal boots of yours,
Because you'll never find that simples-refining oven of mine.
I come and go as I please, stop wherever I want:
No wind, no rain, hard to throw it over,
No repairing, no fortifying, yet it is always rock solid.
At that place are grotto gates deeply locked amid the mountains far,
Truly it is a place you can't find in a land filled with snowy clouds!

(*Speaks*:) Scholar, leave with me now! (CHEN JIQING *speaks*:) I want to be an official, how can you persuade me to join you? Running off at the mouth like this results in a lot of fine words that mean nothing to me! (*Acts out ignoring him.*) (MALE LEAD *speaks*:) Don't think about glory and riches, scholar! Just leave with me! (CHEN JIQING *acts out looking at a map with his hands on his back, speaks*:) Here on this wall is a map of China and the foreign lands. Let me take a look at it. (MALE LEAD *speaks*:) Well that scholar is ignoring me and has gone off to look at a map of China and the foreign lands. Let me go and inscribe a poem on this map for him to look at. (*Acts out inscribing a poem.*) (CHEN JIQING *speaks*:) So, this Daoist can write poems. Well, let me read it out. . . . (*Recites*:)

Let your eyes roam in leisure over the *Record of the Nine Realms*:
The whole seems to lie within a foot rule,
One hundred thousand markets listed for each county,
Five thousand mountains sequestered in each province.
For You and Yan, you have to gaze toward the north,
For Wu and Yue, look toward the south;
There may be no road home,
But to go off as a spirit is not hard at all.

What tremendous talent! Daoist, how did you know I wanted to go home? (MALE LEAD *speaks*:) How could I not? When you inscribed that "Fragrance Fills the Courtyard" you wrote, "The mountains of home are far away, / How can we go back? / We commit it all to a dream's roaming." Didn't this mean that you wanted to go home? (CHEN JIQING *acts out sighing and speaks*:) Och, it's just that I've drifted to here and don't know when I'll get to go home. (MALE LEAD *acts out laughing and speaks*:) Scholar, if you leave with me, I'll find a boat to take you home. That's not a problem. (HUI'AN *speaks*:) Brother Daoist, where is your boat? You should avail yourself of it to send my old friend home. (CHEN JIQING *speaks*:) When did you see my "Fragrance Fills the Courtyard"? (MALE LEAD *speaks*:) I saw it as soon as you wrote it. (*Sings*:)

(*Zui zhong tian*)
This poem is better than Wang Can's "Rhapsody on Ascending a Tower,"[187]
Just like Zong Bing's painting of "Roaming While Abed."[188]
(*Acts out taking a bamboo leaf and sticking it on the wall, sings:*)
Look at this barely visible leaf of a vessel across the blue waves.

(*Speaks:*) Presto! Scholar, isn't this a boat now? (CHEN JIQING *speaks:*) It was just a sliver of a leaf pasted on the wall. . . . How could it change into a boat? Strange, strange indeed! (HUI'AN *speaks:*) This is a really small boat and not reliable enough to take my friend home. (MALE LEAD *speaks:*) Dull-witted one! It's perfect to use. (*Sings:*)
Don't guess that no one crosses waters in the wild;
Originally you wanted to "clasp three proposals," become a noble by passing the examination,
But when it was clear you would not pass, like Tao Yuanming you wanted to return to your home—
How could you know that both of these are the same dream of Hua Xu?[189]

(*Speaks:*) Can you see your road home? (CHEN JIQING *speaks:*) I already found it on the map of the world. (MALE LEAD *speaks:*) Look at this. (*Sings:*)
(*Jinzhan'er*)
Don't you see the distant trees covering Jing and Wu?
Or dark waters bearing the homeward skiff?
Go ahead and let the windblown waves rise and surge, krakens and dragons grow angry,
You just close your two eyes tight,
And fix your body firm.
Let the oars pierce the cold of river's moon
And the sail be raised in the loneliness of sea's clouds.
Cold mists arise over ancient fords,
Ahh . . . there are the thatched huts of your former home.

(ACOLYTE *speaks:*) Don't say this boat is made from a bamboo leaf, even if it were real, all it lacks is a single foot of mine, and it would be tipped over already. (CHEN JIQING *yawns, speaks:*) Why am I suddenly so tired? All I want to do is sleep. (MALE LEAD *speaks:*) This dull-witted one is asleep, I'll wake him up from his "big sleep." (*Sings:*)

187. See n. 62.

188. Zong Bing 宗炳 (375–443) was a painter and musician. He loved to travel through mountains. When he grew old, he painted remembered landscapes on the walls of his room and lived contentedly with his lute and brush, roaming in spirit through the many mountains he had traveled. See Bush and Murck, 1983, 105–31.

189. See n. 65.

(*Zhuan Coda*)
You and I will kick down the portals to the land of ghosts,
And open up the road to Acacia Peace
And wake up from "a pillow of the southern branch."
Don't be ensnared in the bridle of fame or the fetters of profit—
A quick turn of the head and already it is "mulberry and elm in the sunset scene."
If you become my disciple,
We will cut off the vulgar and common together—
Will you fear "hard to leap out of a sea of bitterness that extends forever"?
Rely on this companion of misty sunsets,
Climb aboard this floating raft and depart—
Won't you "Chant loud as you fly across Dongting Lake"?

(*Leaving the thorn basket behind, he exits.*)

(HUI'AN *speaks*:) How strange, indeed! This crazy Daoist just pasted a bamboo leaf on the wall, and it turned into a tiny little boat. What a fine magic trick. Chen Jiqing is asleep now. Acolyte, prepare a meal for us to eat when he awakens. I'm going back to my cell to meditate. (*Recites*:)

I will restrain my mind beneath the front window,
And pay no heed to right and wrong in the world of men.

(*With* ACOLYTE *trailing, he exits.*)

(CHEN JIQING *dreams and acts out awakening, speaks*:) What a great sleep, I'll get on this boat now and return home with this favorable wind.
(*Exits.*)

[ACT 2]

(MALE LEAD *enters leading* EXTRA MALES LIEZI, ZHANG LIANG, *and* GE HONG, *speaks*:) I am Lü Dongbin. This is Lie Yukou, this is Zhang Zifang, and this is Ge the Immortal Codger. I went down to Green Dragon Monastery on Mount Zhongnan to lead Chen Jiqing to enlightenment. But this fellow is infatuated with success and fame, and he did not come to a realization. I pasted a bamboo leaf on the wall and magically turned it into a small boat, which he immediately wanted to get on and ride on favorable winds to go home and see his parents, his wife, and his children. My dear Superior Immortals, let's wait here, and when he comes we will slowly transform him, and return him to the Correct Way. We will strike out both life and death from the Hall of the Yama King, and put his name among the ranks of Immortal Clerks.[190]

190. An unhappy translation for *xianli* 仙吏, immortals who hold various bureaucratic positions at the Daoist celestial court.

Point to and open the road to heaven's edge at the corner of the sea,
Lead the lost ones to walk upon the Great Way.

(LIEZI *speaks*:) That obtuse Chen Jiqing—we'll bring him along sometime. (MALE LEAD *sings*:)

(SHUANGDIAO MODE: *Xinshui ling*)

I've rambled over the five lakes and four seas,
With just these two wind-sweeping sleeves of my robe.
I've summoned the noumenal lad to pluck grass of good augury,
And gone down to Immortals' Islet[191] with fellow immortals.
With such untrammeled freedom as this,
I sigh for all those days and nights in the dusty world.

(LIEZI *speaks*:) I think those people mired in common custom are greedy, angry, covetous, and full of desire, in the same way bottle flies have a fetish for blood, or a mass of ants love rotten meat. They just rush forward for profit, forgetting in the end that they will drown in it. They are so stupid and lost! (MALE LEAD *speaks*:) I can see that Chen Jiqing was originally endowed with a portion of an immortal, but that his dust-loving heart is too heavy. I tried two or three times, but just couldn't get him to realize the truth. Ah, when will he get to complete the Correct Way? (*Sings*:)

(*Zhuma ting*)

Roaming carefree through the immortals' gardens,
So many autumns where things have changed and the stars have made their transit.
I have completely penetrated through the Mysterious Pass,[192]
And seen my share of "evening suns setting west" and "the Yangtze flowing east."
One life emptily holds in its arms a whole life's sorrow,
Can a thousand years have a thousand-year life span?
One should just turn one's head as soon as possible,
And forever abide with idle clouds and cranes in the wild.

(CHEN JICHING *enters and speaks*:) I am Chen Jiqing. I met a crazy Daoist at Abbot Hui'an's place, Green Dragon Monastery, who just kept on urging me to go away with him. He pasted a sliver of a bamboo leaf on the wall, and it magically transformed into a boat. I should not have been so quick to be moved by thoughts of home and board this boat to go back, because now I've reached here and have completely lost my way. There's no one in front or behind to ask. . . . What shall I do? (MALE LEAD *speaks*:) Chen Jiqing, what did you come here for? (CHEN JIQING *acts out looking over his shoulder with alarm and speaks*:) Oh my, is someone calling me from somewhere? (MALE LEAD *sings*:)

---

191. Yingzhou 瀛洲, a mountain in the Eastern Sea where immortals dwell.

192. See n. 71.

(*Yan'er luo*)
All too quickly you mistakenly swallowed that hook of fame and fortune,
And, emptily aflutter in the end, forgot me, this old guy of misty sunsets;
In a hazy murky blankness you've come to the end of your road, where can you return?
Eyes wide open in this sea of misery with no one to save you.

(CHEN JIQING *speaks*:) Who's calling me? Can you point out the main road for me?

(MALE LEAD *sings*:)
(*Desheng ling*)
Oh-ho. Didn't you say "that the classics and history would flow like water,"
That you didn't need to worry about "purple and blue strings of ministerial caps"?
Why didn't you take that "jade worth a string of cities" and memorialize at the cinnabar steps?[193]
Or wrestle away an Earldom of Ten Thousand Families in Lingyang?[194]
Today you've become withdrawn and meek,
And this is truly the unexpected scourge of wanting to be an official—
Better, indeed, to just give it up,
And quickly follow me off to freedom.

(CHEN JIQING *speaks*:) Oh, so it turns out to be the Daoist I met at the monastery. Please save me! (MALE LEAD *speaks*:) Quiet! (*Sings*:)
(*Gua yugou*)
You said I was no ardent friend, that we didn't speak the same language,
And then went off to exhaustively research the *Record of the Nine Realms*.
But all that did was stir up a bit of desire to go home, and your tears secretly flowed
Until the drops saturated the sleeves of your traveling robe.
And now you've lost your way, and the road is hard to find.
On that map you took them for the mountains of home—
You couldn't know it was a spiritual journey in a dream.

(CHEN JIQING *speaks*:) As there are actually three more of you, I would like to exchange names with them. (MALE LEAD *speaks*:) These are all my friends in the Way. This is Lie Yukou, this is Zhang Zifang, and this is Ge the Immortal Codger. (CHEN JIQING *speaks*:) I am completely unenlightened at the moment and do not know, which dynasty are you from? What were the reasons that allowed you to complete the Way of the immortal? Please, each of you explain in turn, and I will listen with

193. To present to the emperor at the vermilion-lacquered steps of the palace.

194. There are two Earls of Lingyang 陵陽侯. The first was Boshen 波神 (Spirit of the Waves), a mythical figure. According to legend, the Earl of Lingyang was drowned in a flood and was then turned into a spirit who sometimes created violent waves. The second, clearly referred to here, was Ding Chen 丁綝 of the Eastern Han, who was enfeoffed by the Guangwu Emperor (r. 25–57) in the Eastern Han for his support of Guangwu's campaign against Liu Mang. This granted him the right to collect taxes from ten thousand households under his aegis.

a reverent bow. (LIE YUKOU *speaks*:) I am Lie Yukou, a man of Zheng. During the time of Duke Mu of Zheng, I witnessed Ziyang as prime minister. He was completely inclined toward corporal punishments and fines, and because of this I gave up my salary and went home to plow. Later I met the Master of Wide Attainment who passed on his great Way,[195] so I was able to become an immortal. (ZHANG ZIFANG *speaks*:) I am Zhang Liang, a man of the state of Han, and a ninth generation minister to Han.[196] The First Emperor of the Qin was a person without the Way and he exterminated my state. I made a secret alliance with a stout fellow to ambush the First Emperor at Bolangsha, but he mistakenly struck at the secondary chariot. The emperor searched for me for three days, but I hid out in Xiapi. Later, when I saw that the armies of the Ancestor of Han[197] had risen, I raised up my sword and gave my allegiance to Han, raising the Liu clan to power and squelching Xiang Yu—so I was able to take revenge for Han. The Ancestor of Han enfeoffed me as the marquis of Liu. But because he was also killing the meritorious officials who had helped him to power, I gave up my seal of office and followed Red Pine into the mountains, and consequently perfected the way of the immortal. (GE THE IMMORTAL CODGER *speaks*:) I am Ge Hong,[198] a man from Wuxing, and I was magistrate of Julou in the time of Mingdi of the Jin.[199] Because I was plucking cinnabar from the ground, I met the Realized One of the Luofu Mountains,[200] and he taught me the techniques of the Nine Cycles of Reverted Elixir.[201] From that time on, I shed my post and perfected the Way, and consequently was able to complete the Way. (CHEN JIQING *speaks*:) I have lost any courage to speak to you! According to what you say, you have all given up your offices to perfect the Way, and by this were able to enter into the ranks of the arrayed immortals. But I "have spent ten years beneath the cold window," and put in so much hard work that right now I can only think of being an official. I can't make these high-sounding claims. (MALE LEAD *speaks*:) Idiot! (*Sings*:)

(*Gu meijiu*)

You say you were stuck for ten long years by the firefly-lit window,
And want to leave your name on the inscribed Goose Pagoda[202]—

195. This is Guangchengzi 廣成子, who, according to legend, was the Yellow Emperor's teacher. In another tradition, he was presumed to have been one of the early avatars of Laozi. See Penny 2008a.

196. See chap. 3, n. 82.

197. The founding emperor, Liu Bang.

198. See n. 60.

199. In 332 or 333, he was appointed to a post in Julou (句漏) in what is now Vietnam, but he never reached there, retiring instead to the Luofu Mountains of Guangzhou. See Pregadio 2008b.

200. This was Bao Jing (d. ca. 330) of the Jin, not only Ge Hong's master but also his father-in-law. See Espesset 2008.

201. See Pregadio 2008c.

202. After the Shenlong 神龍 reign period (705–707) it became a custom for the advanced scholars who had passed the examination to inscribe their names on the Great Goose Pagoda (大雁塔) in the Monastery of Compassionate Beneficence (慈恩寺) in Chang'an.

Your strong ambition leaps and vaults to pierce the Dipper and Buffalo constellations.[203]
You hope for that chance meeting of wind and cloud, of lord and minister—
Would you settle to follow along behind others?
(*Taiping ling*)
You just talk about "the golden seals and purple tassels of being an official,"
I just speak of "three fairy isles and ten magic kingdoms of leaving the family."
You just talk about "the merit completed and fame won by being an official,"
I just speak of "the prolonged years and augmented life span of leaving the family."
You—leave off, shut your mouth and just look at my friends of the Way:
All of them abandoned their offices like so much filth.

(CHEN JIQING *speaks*:) You yourself say all three of these were officials, and I have seen their names in the historical records. But have you ever held office? (MALE LEAD *sings*:)

(*Tianshui ling*)
I once clambered up those phoenix pylons of the capital,
Leapt over the Dragon's Gate,[204]
My horse's hooves rushed forward,
In that autumn when I reached high to snap the cassia branch.[205]
But I, by chance, passed through Handan
And was transmuted when I met my master;
Awaking from the dream of yellow millet—
I wiped away my heart of dust with a single stroke!

(CHEN JIQING *speaks*:) I knew you'd never been an official! (MALE LEAD *sings*:)

(*Zhegui ling*)
Fortunately I never was disappointed about this "standing on the tortoise's head" of yours.

(CHEN JIQING *speaks*:) You've never been an official—how would you know about the happiness of being an official? (MALE LEAD *speaks*:) Stupid dolt! Where is your position? (*Sings*:)

Weren't you already too ashamed to return home?
And just hung around the capital?

---

203. That is, beyond the highest point of the heavens.

204. A common idiom for passing the advanced scholar examinations, found first in the *San Qin ji*: "Every year at the end of spring yellow carp from the ocean and all the streams fight their way to a place just below the Dragon's Gate [located on the Yellow River]. Seventy-two of them ascend the gate every year, and when they first get into the passage, clouds and rain soon follow closely behind them. From behind a heavenly fire sets their tails alight as they transform into dragons."

205. That is, to succeed in the examinations.

(CHEN JIQING *speaks*:) But I want to go home now. (MALE LEAD *sings*:)
Hadn't Ruan Ji already turned his cart around?[206]
And Liu Fen failed?[207]
And Wang Can climbed the tower?
You had already put your head together with your old friend on Zhongnan Mountain,
And were all smiles in your leisure days at Green Dragon Monastery.
You rowed a little leaf of a skiff,
And floated many twists in the flow of this river.
It's clearly all a single pillow of Acacia Peace,
So why make it a case of "both parties feel the sadness of parting" instead?

(LIE YUKOU *speaks*:) Scholar, while it may be true that those who become immortals have immortal flesh and Daoist bones bestowed by heaven, these must be transferred to and received by extraordinary individuals before one can complete the Way of the immortal. Today, we companions in the Way have tried to lead you across three or four times so you will follow us, but you are still unable to realize enlightenment. Isn't this making everything we do worth nothing? (CHEN JIQING *speaks*:) You fellows don't understand; it's not that I'm unwilling to follow him and leave my family, it's that I simply cannot do it. There is no need to talk about failing the examinations—I have aged parents at home, a wife and children. How can I leave? Let me recite a lyric poem to the tune of "The Immortal Draws Near the River" to justify what I am saying:

From the time I came to Chang'an to sit for the examinations,
I was plotting for that wealth, nobility, and glory—
Who knew I would fail and have to return home?
My wife and children are still young in years,
The temple locks of my parents are dappled with frost.

Now in midpath I've lost my way, where could I ask?
Then you group of immortals came down to board my raft.
I hesitate, have nothing to say, just uselessly sigh.
Brokenhearted, we have all lost our way,
Sticking out our trembling necks, each at heaven's edge.

---

206. Ruan Ji 阮籍 (210–263) is one of "the Seven Sages of the Bamboo Grove" (Zhulin Qixian 竹林七賢). He was an eccentric with much pent-up anger who would take his cart out and travel random paths until he came to an end and could go no farther. Thereupon, he would weep copiously and return. See Holzman 1976.

207. Liu Fen 劉蕡 (d. ca. 838) sat for a special examination to select talented men in 828, but he was banished because of his wholesale criticism of the eunuchs who held power at that time. His classmate remarked, "That Liu Fen failed and we have passed is because we are shameless!"

(LIE YUKOU *speaks*:) Scholar, do you think your parents, wife, and children will stay with you to the end? You are stupidly deluded! (CHEN JIQING *speaks*:) Daoist, just point out the road to me so I can go home, and see how surely I will wrest away the title of Top of the List this time! (MALE LEAD *speaks*:) Stupid dolt! (*Sings*:)

(*Chuan bo zhao*)
I laugh at you, you stupid dolt,
If you match deed to word and wrest away this Top of the List,
And employ it so that you have outriders ahead and runners behind,
Painted galleries and vermilion lofts,
Dancing sleeves and singing throats,
That will be of no use to the cosmos.

(*Acts out pointing to* LIE *and sings*:)
How can that compare to our Lie Yukou, who rides on the fresh wind?

(*Acts out pointing to* ZHANG *and sings*:)
(*Qi dixiong*)
Or compare to our Han Marquis of Liu, planning strategies and deciding plans?

(*Acts out pointing to* GE *and sings*:)
How can that compare to our Magistrate Ge, refining cinnabar sands and resigning from Julou?
Just look beside Jade Creek where misty waters unceasingly flow,
Or in front of the green cliffs, where wind and moon remain as always.

(CHEN JIQING *speaks*:) Daoist! Just point out the road for me so I can go home. Don't wait until I've turned into an old man. (MALE LEAD *sings*:)

(*Meihua jiu*)
Don't wait until your temple hairs have turned autumn's white,
So you "can share anxiety with the emperor."
Or sigh that years and months, so hard to hold back,
Turn one's head white too soon.
You offer up your own "Rhapsody on Tall Poplars Palace" and approach the purple steps,[208]
I will search for great herbal simples and return to Cinnabar Hill,
Where I will go back with these three to rest.
This one paces Immortals' Islet, relying on his silver-toned dulcimer,
This one retires to the seclusion of cliffs, blowing his iron flute,
And this one boards a lonely boat, strumming a brocade zither.

---

208. See n. 90.

(*Shou Jiangnan*)

Och! And me? I once was "three times drunk in Yueyang Tower,"[209]

Striding on the strong wind, blown into the blue above to roam with the clouds!

So in vain, the attempt of this immortal from Great Canopy Heaven to lead a prisoner awaiting execution to enlightenment!

For nothing did I make fun of that willow south of the city

Just to make you dream Zhuangzi's dream of the butterfly.

(LIE YUKOU *speaks*:) Scholar, since you won't follow us away, you cannot tarry here. Go on back. (CHEN JIQING *speaks*:) But I'm lost. (MALE LEAD *speaks*:) Stupid dolt! It's straight ahead, not far, you're close to your home. Just don't forget the proper Way! (*Sings*:)

(*Yuanyang sha Coda*)

Just because you were seduced by the two words "merit" and "fame,"

You took on this dangerous thousand-mile journey.

Trusting to your short sword and long zither,

You roam all over the heartland of this divine kingdom.

True it is, "all those places of songs and music

Are just households of suffering and anxiety."

It won't take long before it will starve you until you're as emaciated as Bo Yi and Shu Qi.[210]

There's no comparison to me, desiring nothing in this world,

Never to trod again down those paths of red dust.

(*The four exit together.*)

(CHEN JIQING *speaks*:) All four have gone. That crazy Daoist said I was close to home and wasn't supposed to "forget the proper Way." Well, I guess that "the proper Way" means "the main road." I'll just trundle along the main road a little further and then I'll reach home. (*Recites*:)

> I gradually become aware that my local dialect is getting closer,
> And this turns the conditions of travel more grievous;
> The road is long, I am wrapped in dreams of return—
> "When the heart hurries, the real pace slows."

(*Exits.*)

---

209. Two early *zaju* dramas are about Lü Dongbin getting drunk three times at the Yueyang Tower, located on the shores of Lake Dongting, and converting two tree spirits—one plum and one willow—and leading them to enlightenment. The first is by the noted playwright Ma Zhiyuan (1254?–1320?), *Lü Dongbin Gets Drunk Three Times in Yueyang Tower* (*Lü Dongbin sanzui Yueyang lou*), translated as "The Yüeh-yang Tower" by Richard Yang 1972. The second is Gu Zijing's 谷子敬 (ca. 1368–1392) *Lü Dongbin Thrice Converts the Willow South of the Wall* (*Lü Dongbin sandu chengnan liu* 呂洞賓三度城南柳).

210. See n. 66.

[ACT 3]

(EXTRA MALE *costumed as* OLD MAN *enters, leading* OLD FEMALE LEAD [*costumed as*] OLD WOMAN, FEMALE LEAD, and CHILD, *and speaks*:) I am a man of Yuhang, named Chen. Because I am well-off, everyone calls me Magnate Chen. I have five people in my family: my wife Madame Fang, my daughter-in-law Miss Bao, my grandson Asheng, and one who has gone off to take the examinations, Chen Jiqing. Now he's been gone a long time, and there's been neither message nor letter, all of which has made our family anxious. Wife, close the gates and sit inside for a while so I can go to the market and check to see if there is any news. (OLD WOMAN *speaks*:) I know. (*Exits together with* OLD MAN.)

(MALE LEAD, *costumed as* FISHERMAN, *enters and recites*:)

Out on the river I punt my leaf of a boat,
On my rod tip I gather in the hook that gets the fish;
My rain hat and rain cape are always at hand—
No need to fret about wind-driven drizzle.

Ah, how happy we fisherfolk are! (*Sings*:)

[NANLÜ MODE] (*Yizhi hua*)

This squat brushwood window is newly woven,
The fine ropes of my net have been neatly rearranged.
With my back to the westerly wind, I just gathered in line and hook,
And now row my skiff into the bright moon—
Mist and water stretch on and on.
I have brewed my own chrysanthemum wine,
And lift up this speckled bamboo sieve myself.
I'll give myself up to splendid drunkenness until the Dipper revolves and Orion sets,[211]
And enjoy to the full this unhurried pleasure amid the vastness of time and space.[212]

(*Liangzhou diqi*)

I pay no heed to arranged times of arrival, or sun's setting in the west,
And I let those unfeeling waters of the Yangtze flow to the east.
How often the case "light mists and scattered rains obscure front and rear."
I have already passed some hamlet bridges and wilderness inns,
Sand spits and islands in the stream.
I already have a rain cape to drape askew,

211. That is, until dawn's light.

212. See n. 96.

And a rain hat to lightly cover my head.
We fishermen are never in the dumps and know no sorrow,
For we befriend the bathing egrets and roosting gulls.
I have just left that level stretch of lake that was Master Zhu of Tao's,
Brushed by the Three Rivers' Ford of Master Zhuge of Shu,[213]
And have now reached the head of Yan Ling of Han's Seven-Mile Rapids.[214]
And which, would you say, were my finest friends?
No more than this: the blue waves and old trees are longtime bosom friends,
The duckweed of the Yangtze in Chu is better than fat meat,[215]
And then there is that short-neck bream newly on the hook—
I'll not stop until I'm drunk with it all!

(CHEN JIQING *enters and speaks*:) I've reached this ford where the road ends. How can I get a boat to ferry me across? (*Acts out looking in the distance and speaks*:) Isn't that a fishing boat I see off in the distance? (*Acts out summoning him with his hand and speaks*:) Fisherman, punt your boat over here. (MALE LEAD *acts out ignoring him.*) (*Sings*:)

(*Gewei*)
Aren't you Wen Qiao, burning a rhinoceros horn and walking midriver?[216]
Or the Spirit of the Xiang River[217] thrumming the zither and floating on
the water?
This makes me dumbstruck, yet I patiently abide beside the bulrushes.
This is no regular ferry at some narrows,
Nor in front of someone's house or behind their backyard,
So how come this traveler, calling me to ferry him across, is standing there?

(CHEN JIQING *acts out calling him and speaks*:) Fisherman, punt your boat over here and ferry me across! (MALE LEAD *speaks*:) Where do you want to go? (CHEN JIQING *speaks*:) What's the point of asking me? (MALE LEAD *sings*:)

(*He xinlang*)
So you say we fishermen should ask for no rationale or reason?
I'm just asking if you're some trader or traveling salesman.

(CHEN JIQING *speaks*:) I'm not. (MALE LEAD *sings*:)

Looking for your home or old relations?

(CHEN JIQING *speaks*:) I'm not. (MALE LEAD *sings*:)

Well, if not then, why are you waiting for me at the bank of the Yangtze?

---

213. See n. 98.
214. See n. 99.
215. See n. 100.
216. See n. 101.
217. See n. 102.

(CHEN JIQING *speaks*:) I want to go across the river. (MALE LEAD *sings*:)

You're not one of the Three Grandees of Chu,[218] embracing sand to throw himself in the River are you?
Could you be Wu Zixu, intent on taking vengeance for wrongs done to your father?[219]
Or are you the Banished Immortal Li, off to embrace the moon?[220]
Or perhaps Zheng Jiaofu toying with the pearls of his journey?[221]

(CHEN JIQING *speaks*:) I need to get across the river quickly; I can't take this fisherman's wrangling discourse over past and present. All of this interrogation of me is just so much blabber. Fisherman, you've guessed them all wrong, just take me across the river and be done with it. (MALE LEAD *sings*:)

So it turns out to be some local yokel student who had set off to take the examinations.
If he had passed them, he would have spurred through the spring winds holding the bridle of a five-colored dapple,
But having failed, all he wants is one little fishing boat to float on the blue waves.

(CHEN JIQING *speaks*:) That's right. I'm going back to Yuhang in Wulin to see my family, and I want to use your boat. I still want to go back and take the examinations again, so what if I give you a bit more money to hire the boat then? (MALE LEAD *speaks*:) Yeah, that'll do. Hurry, get aboard, and I'll get under way. (CHEN JIQING *acts out boarding the boat.*) (MALE LEAD *sings*:)

(*Ma yulang*)

My rain cape has been soaked through by a heaven's worth of dew,
I wave my short oars and dip them into the main current,
Passing by this span of bridge, a lonely footbridge thin as a dragon's waist.

---

218. See n. 104.

219. See n. 105.

220. See n. 106.

221. The last two characters in the line, *zhuyou* 珠遊, are drawn directly from a poem by Bao Zhao 鮑照 (ca. 414–468):

淚竹感湘別	Tears sprinkle bamboo, moved by parting on the Xiang,
弄珠懷漢遊	Playing with pearls, remembering roaming on the Han.

The lines, in turn, refer to the story of Jiaofu of Zheng 鄭交甫, who encountered two female spirits of the Han River, "who wore at their belts two pearls as large as chicken eggs." They presented them to him, but after he took a few steps, both the women and the pearls had disappeared. This story is found in Li Shan's commentary to the *Wenxuan*. See Knechtges 1982, 314, 316, n. L.29, whence the preceding text comes. Together, these last few allusions, all about experiences along riverbanks, are a sarcastic reply to Chen's refusal to say why he wants to go across the river: is he there to commit suicide out of grief (Qu Yuan) or happiness (Li Bai), to look for apparitions (Wen Qiao), is he a spirit returned from the dead (Wu Zixu), or is he lost in memory of other experiences along rivers (the consorts of Shun weeping over his death, or the strange encounter of Jiaofu)? The fisherman knows, of course, why he is there.

I see the light gulls chasing each other ahead,
Dotting beauty spots on the autumn river's elegance.
(*Gan huang'en*)
Reflections of the clouds glide on and on,
The force of the wind blows strong and chilly.
Winding my way out beyond the green poplar dike,
Shores of fragrant grass,
Islets of water pepper flowers. . . .

(CHEN JIQING *speaks*:) Where are we? (MALE LEAD *sings*:)

We have traveled to the headwaters of the Qinhuai,[222]
Unawares come to the flow that splits Wu and Yue,[223]
And already draw near your native village,
Approach your old home,
So don't stop or slow down!

(CHEN JIQING *speaks*:) How strange! I am already at the gate to my home. (*Acts out listening to the drums marking the night watch and speaks*:) Why, it's only the third watch![224] (MALE LEAD *sings*:)

(*Caicha ge*)
You don't need to ask, "What watch or wooden slip,"[225]
Just look at how the clouds on the water disappear,
And that half wheel of a moon rises to the tip of willow's branch.

(*Acts out stopping the boat and speaks*:) Scholar, I will wait here for you with my boat. Come back after you see your family. (*Sings*:)

I'll just secure the boat line to this little stump of a peg here,
And listen to the woofing hounds bark in the depths of the bamboo forest.

(*Exits for a moment with* CHEN JIQING.)

(OLD MAN, OLD WOMAN, FEMALE LEAD, *and* CHILD *enter*, OLD MAN *speaks*:) This drives me nuts! My son has gone off to take the examinations, and I can find no information about him in town. Wife, let's just close the gate for a while. (OLD WOMAN *acts out closing the gate*.) (MALE LEAD *enters with* CHEN JIQING *and speaks*:) Isn't this your home? (CHEN JIQING *speaks*:) Wait until I knock on the door. Fisherman, I want to go back to take the examination again as soon as I have seen my family, so don't take your boat anywhere. (MALE LEAD *speaks*:) Just hurry and get off the boat, I don't have the spare time to sit around and wait for you. (CHEN JIQING *acts*

222. That is, they left the Yangtze at Nanjing and went south along the Qinhuai River, following one of the feeder canals that goes south toward Hangzhou.

223. The Qiantang River, which separates the ancient states of Wu and Yue.

224. The third watch (11 P.M. to 1 A.M.) is equivalent to saying in English "Why, it's only midnight!"

225. See n. 112.

out knocking on the gate and speaks:) Wife! Open the gate! Open the gate! (FEMALE LEAD *speaks*:) Who's calling at the door? Let me open the door and take a look. (*Acts out greeting and speaks*:) I wondered who it was, and it turns out Jiqing is here! (CHEN JIQING *speaks*:) Where are my parents? (FEMALE LEAD *speaks*:) They are in the hall. (CHEN JIQING *acts out entering and making obeisance, speaks*:) Father, Mother; your son has come home. (OLD MAN *speaks*:) Child, have you gotten a post? (CHEN JIQING *speaks*:) My time is yet to come. I didn't get a post, and so was too embarrassed to come back, and just drifted around away from home. I have been remiss in "serving you the sweet and flavorful."[226] Now that "the field of selection" is about to open again, I have come especially to see you, my parents, and then, like before, go off to take the examinations. (MALE LEAD *speaks*:) Son, you've been gone for many years and you just got back. Stay here for a few days. (CHEN JIQING *speaks*:) Father, Mother, the day draws near and I'm afraid I won't get to the examination field on time. (MALE LEAD *speaks*:) Since the day is drawing near. . . Servant! Bring some wine so we can send our son off properly. (MALE LEAD *acts out laughing and speaks*:) Chen Jiqing! Get a move on! (*Sings*:)

(*Muyang guan*)

You sing that "Golden Threads" at the feast mat,[227]
And raise that jade wine server before the goblet—
Isn't this the time that yellow millet cooking in the pot is finally done?
You'd better take leave of your white-haired parents soon,
And set aside forever your perfect match of youth.

(*Continues in speech:*) If you don't go now what else are you waiting for? (*Sings:*)

You oh-so-simpleminded, dull-witted stupid dolt!
It seems in vain I was sent to quickly enlighten this fine Confucian type.
If you are so attached to the idea of imitating Laolaizi's dance in colored clothes[228]
How can we dispatch the tethered boat of the Posthouse Captain of Rook River?[229]

(CHEN JIQING *speaks*:) Wife, I have to go off to the examinations. (FEMALE *speaks*:) Scholar, you just got home, how can you leave and abandon me? (*She acts out grieving.*) (CHEN JIQING *speaks*:) How could I ever set aside the feelings between us? It's just that the time of the examination is pressing in, and in the blink of an eye another three years will be gone. What then? (MALE LEAD *sings*:)

---

226. Figuratively, "I have been remiss in my filial service to you."

227. A conventional lyric sung to accompany drinking at banquets.

228. Laolaizi is a paragon of filial piety. At age seventy he would dress up in the colored clothes of a child and dance, falling down and crying like a baby to amuse his senile parents.

229. These two lines, which refer to the historical Xiang Yu's refusal to cross the river to save his life, may be understood as, "If you are so attached to your parents, you'll miss the boat that will ferry you out of the mortal world of life and death." On the original episode, see chap. 3, n. 8.

(*Ku huangtian*)
All she can do is go on and on to try and beguile him,
Her glistening tears ever flowing.
Hurry up and follow these nice and orderly companions
And for the time being, cast away that charmingly pretty phoenix mate.
Better now to prepare line and pole, line and pole, hook, and boat,
And go off to the side of a Fuchun islet,[230]
The bank of the Wei River,
To be companion to the fisherman on the misty waves,
The idler of wind and moon,
Yet, the one who winds up with untrammeled freedom, freedom from a hundred cares.
Let those mountains crumble and the sea leak away,
That crow fly and rabbit run.

(CHEN JIQING *speaks*:) Wife, bring a pen and inkstone and let me compose a poem on the spot to leave as I part. (*He acts out writing.*) (MALE LEAD *sings*:)
(*Wu ye ti*)
From this point on, keep your babbling trap shut,
And don't think I'll "let any old wind carry me off east on an eastern rill."[231]

(CHEN JIQING *speaks*:) There, the poem is finished. Let me read it out loud so you can listen to it. (*He acts out reciting.*) (*Recites the poem*:)

The moon slides down and cold dew grows white,
This night is the hardest to bear;
Songs of separation choke the jade pipe with sobs,
And thoughts of parting sunder the jasper zither.
Wine arrives, we drink with linked sorrow,
The poem finished, we recite it with matched tears;
On moonlit nights, we'll treasure dreams of the other,
And in the empty bed, lie beneath half the quilt.

(FEMALE *speaks*:) Jiqing, this poem is so heartrending and full of passion, it makes my glistening tears fall as I read it. Oh, it pains me to death! (CHEN JIQING *acts out making obeisance and parting, speaks*:) Father, Mother, your son is off to the examinations. (MALE LEAD *sings*:)
At your leisure you dillydallied until your poem was finally sung,
But why a piece on separation's sorrows,
That holds both in concentrated gaze?
This one raises a golden whip, far away brushing wineshop doors,

230. See n. 99.
231. See n. 121.

And that one weeps at Yang Pass, secretly splattering on sleeves of fragrant gauze.
Let's go,
Stop suffering—
For my grass sandals and hemp rope belt,
Far outdo those fat steeds and fine sables of yours!

(CHEN JIQING *speaks*:) Father, Mother, I am leaving for the examinations. (FEMALE *acts out escorting him to the door.*) (CHEN JIQING *speaks*:) Wife, go on back now. (*Acts out going out the door and speaks*:) Fisherman, where is your boat? (MALE LEAD *speaks*:) Hurry and get on the boat, how many hours do I have to wait?

(*They exit together.*)

(OLD MAN *speaks*:) Our son has gone off to take the exams. Wife, close the gate for a while. . . .

Our eyes will watch for the pennants and flags of victory,
Our ears will listen for good news.

(OLD WOMAN, FEMALE LEAD, *and* CHILD *exit together* [*with* OLD MAN].)

(MALE LEAD *enters with* CHEN JIQING *and speaks*:) Scholar, we've reached the Yangtze already! (*Sings*:)

(*Three from Coda*)

On these softly plied oars with their creaking groan, we have come to the mouth of the creek,
And already see those little dots of fishing lamps with their round brightness at the head of the ancient ford.

(CHEN JIQING *speaks*:) Fisherman! Turn the boat closer to the bank. . . . It's getting really windy! (MALE LEAD *sings*:)

All I can see are snowy waves on the autumn river billowing up to crash against the heavens,
Then the moon grows black, the clouds more sorrowful.
Whipping wind grows wild, lashing rain violent—
To what part of what season should this weather belong?

(CHEN JIQING *speaks*:) Fisherman! This violent storm, these waves rising steep scare me to death! (MALE LEAD *sings*:)

Dissolving indistinct white, the silver waves flow unbroken,
Then the moon grows black, the clouds more sorrowful.
There is no "riding a crane to Yangzhou."[232]

---

232. This is a pointed comment about the search for fame and wealth still beclouding Chen Jiqing's heart and mind. The reference is to a story from Yin 1999, 1038:

> Some men were traveling together, and each expressed his ambition. One wanted to be the prefect of Yangzhou, one wanted to be wealthy, and one wanted to ascend to the heavens on a crane. One of them said, "With 100,000 strings of cash at my waist I'll ride a crane to Yangzhou." He combined the three. 有客相從各言所志,或願為揚州刺史,或願多資財,或願 騎鶴上升。其一人曰:"腰纏十萬貫,騎鶴上揚州。"欲兼三者.

(*Two from Coda*)
Suddenly I hear thunder swirl in the steep cliffs—krakens and dragons howl,
And then see lightning circle the empty forest—ghosts and sprites sorrow.
This angry God of the Waves,[233] roiling the river and stirring the sea,
Scares him so much he grows cowardly and meek—
How can we keep from tipping over,
Who will save your life?[234]
My fishing boat has nearly been trampled apart,
To become but floating scum on water's surface.

(CHEN JIQING *speaks*:) Alas! The boat has broken apart! Fisherman, save me! (*He acts out reciting a scripture, speaks*:) O, Great One, Celestial Worthy[235] who rescues us from peril! (MALE LEAD *sings*:)

(*Huangzhong Coda*)
In vain now, bowing with folded hands, you beseech the God of the Abyss and pay homage to the Spirit of the River,
All you have to do is settle your flighty soul, secure your vital spirit, and close your eyes tight.
The wind abruptly blows,
The waters flow backwards,
And slap against the three mountain ranges,
Overflow the Nine Kingdoms,
Shake the Gates of Heaven,
And shift the Axis of the Earth.
It has scared you so much you quake all atremble,
Just like the prisoner of Chu,
Who gave himself up to death—
Your whole life is over
And you cannot
Be buried in those old tumuli of home.
From this time on, for autumns eternal,
Who will sacrifice a cup of wine over your grave at Beimang?

(CHEN JIQING *acts out falling in the water, speaks*:) Help! Save me! (*He acts out startling himself awake.*) (ACOLYTE *speaks*:) Sir, my master requests your presence at

233. See n. 107.

234. These lines are spoken directly to Chen Jiqing.

235. The Great One (太乙) was a supreme deity of Daoism and often equated with the Jade Emperor. There was also a Daoist sect, The Teachings of the Great One, that was popular during the Yuan period. See Andersen 2008 and Goossaert 2008b, 959–60. This invocation is, however, of an actual Lingbao deity. See *The Golden Text for Rescuing and Salvation of the Lingbao Sect* (*Lingbao jidu jinshu* 靈寶濟度金書), "The Green Mysterious Supreme Emperor of the Eastern Extremity Transformed into the Great One, the Heavenly Worthy Who Rescues Us from Peril" 東極青玄大帝化為太乙救苦天尊.

a vegetarian feast. (CHEN JIQING *speaks*:) Where did the Daoist go? (ACOLYTE *speaks*:) You were asleep here, I am asking you to a meal here, who knows where the mad Daoist went? (CHEN JIQING *speaks*:) I just went home, and he was waiting for me midway, and he had some Daoist friends, who tried three or four times to get me to go away with them. These Daoists were a bit weird. . . . Let me catch up to them. (*Acts out running over to look in the bramble basket, speaks*:) That Daoist left this basket here. Let me take a look. There's nothing inside this bramble basket but one piece of paper. Let's see what he wrote. (*Acts out a verse recitation*:) (*Recites a poem*:)

A single leaf in a moment's time sent a traveler home,
Mountains' glow and waters' radiance collapsed against each other;
We had barely passed the place where Qu Yuan sang his song,
Before we then passed the jetty where Yan Ziling fished.
His parents neglected, he was ashamed, so inattentive to their support—
So on his wife's makeup stand why did he leave a second poem?
And when parting, wept in the yellowing dusk?
They thought that I knew nothing at all.

(*Acts out being startled, speaks*:) How can he know everything that happened in my dream? He is indeed an immortal. I think of the saying, "Human form is hard to achieve, the Middle Kingdom is hard to be born into, and an extraordinary person is hard to meet!" How could I have missed the signs? I'd guess that this Daoist hasn't gone far. Little Master, please send my regrets and thanks to the abbot, but I'm not going to have this meal, I'm going to carry this bramble basket and go off after that Daoist! (*Exits*.)

(ACOLYTE *speaks*:) Well, this scholar is really a pudding head. In broad daylight he falls asleep on an empty stomach, wakes up all flustered from I don't know what kind of dream, and now wants to take off after that Daoist. Who knows how crazy monks and wild Daoists wind up, or where he's gone? I'll go back and report to my master. Whatever shit hunger squeezed out of this pudding head is none of my business in the least!

[ACT 4]

(LIE YUKOU *enters leading* ZHANG ZIFANG *and* GE THE IMMORTAL CODGER *carrying drumming sticks and long clappers*[236] *and recites a poem*:)

Yesterday Eastern Zhou, today the state of Qin;
From the lantern globes of Xianyang to Luoyang's dust.[237]

---

236. See n. 110.

237. That is, from the height of Qin and Western Han to the end of the Eastern Han.

A hundred years is but a single dream of blue waves
That brings laughter to us here on the very peak of Kunlun.

I am Lie Yukou. That Master of Pure Yang, desiring to lead Chen Jiqing to enlightenment, relied on me, Zhang Zifang, and Ge Xianweng to help encourage him to enter the Way. But the dust lay too heavy upon his heart and, for the moment, we have yet to turn his head. But the Master of Pure Yang showed us the power of his magic and he created a completely different realm to give him a look, and this certainly must have enlightened him. Chen Jiqing hasn't come yet and we have nothing to do, so we'll go down into the marketplace and sing some "Songs of Daoist Sentiments" as a way to provoke people of the world into waking up! (ZHANG ZIFANG *speaks*:) This is the best! You first, Elder Immortal. (LIE YUKOU *sings*:)

(*Cunli yagu*)[238]
Here, deep in our grotto heavens,
Is a place, indeed, where no mortals come;
I just want to bury away all my names—
No glory, no shame, no troubles or vexations.
Look at that "snail's horn" fame,
And that "fly's head" profit,
All, more or less, the same.
I want to sleep at night until it turns bright,
Sleep in the bright until it turns night,
Sleep straight through until I awake!
Ai! Now light, now dark, time passes like wind ruffling a horse's ears.
(*Yuanhe ling*)
What I eat is a half gourd of food, begged from a thousand households,
What I wear is a single set of clothes patched together from a hundred scraps;
This kind of coarse clothing and bland food is enough to linger over—
Let the Lord of Heaven grant it or not!
I just want to snuggle up at mountain's waist inside a bamboo fence and thatched hut—
I close the brushwood gate, soundlessly silent and still,
And sigh over human life that is so muddled and befuddled in vain.
(*Shangma jiao*)
You want your fame to swell,
Your position to be high—
These are just knives to kill another!
When will you get to relax, enjoy, ease the feelings in your chest?

238. These "Songs of Daoist Sentiments" are not part of the regular suite, but they also are written as a suite to a single rhyme, although that rhyme is different from that used in the suite itself.

True it is,
"Burning anxieties finally destroy both brow tips!"[239]
(*Sheng hulu*)
You have to worry day and night, ponder a myriad plans,
Can that compare to my careless feelings of pleasure?
Here no grass withers, neither spring, summer, winter, nor fall.
I "lean against the bright window where I entrust my proud spirit,"[240]
Use a short bamboo as a staff and concentrate my gaze
To look for those Peaches of Immortality ripening on the sea.[241]

(LIE YUKOU *speaks*:) Master of Pure Yang has arrived before we had a chance to finish these "Songs of Daoist Sentiments." (ZHANG ZIFANG *speaks*:) Let us withdraw to one side.

(*Exit*.)

(MALE LEAD *sings*:)

[ZHENGGONG MODE] (*Duanzheng hao*)
I'll not go and roam the northern abyss,
I'll not go to sleep at the eastern peak—
When you can wander freely, then freely wander as you will!
In that dusty realm I'll beat out a few cadences from the drum that enlightens—
That is *my* leisure daily ritual act.
(*Gun xiuqiu*)
I sigh over "now day, now night, it passes like a shuttle thrown,"
And over "who knows how long a life will last?"
In a quick turn of the head, a hundred years pass,
Then, facing the burnished bronze mirror your temples are speckled white.
Watch Wang Liu play his silly skit,
And listen to Sandy Three sing his satiric song.[242]

---

239. From the tips of the brow moving up and down when one frowns out of anxiety.

240. Adapted from two lines from Tao Qian's "Let's Go Home":

依南窗以寄傲	I lean against the southern wind in order to entrust my proud spirit,
審容膝之易安	Consider how easy to feel secure in "room for just the knees."

For a complete translation, see Robert Hightower's translation, "The Return," in Hightower 1970, 268–70.

241. Literally, "twisting tree peaches," from a legend that they grew on a huge tree that spread out in a twisting pattern for three thousand miles. According to the *Inner Biography of Emperor Wu of the Han* (*Han Wudi neizhuan* 漢武帝內傳), the Queen Mother of West descended to the emperor on the seventh day of the seventh month and gave him four immortals' peaches. He ate them and immediately kept the seeds to plant. She told him, "These peaches ripen once every three thousand years, the earth is too thin in the Central Xia, and they will not grow if you plant them" 七月七日西王母降，以仙桃四顆與帝，帝食輒收其核，欲種之，母曰「此桃三千年一生實,中夏地薄,種之不生。」. For a complete translation, see Schipper 1965; Robinet 2008b; and Yoshikawa 2008b.

242. Wang Liu and Sandy Three are typical names for country yokels.

We send to the burial place those vainglorious do-nothings who schemed out of greed—
What can they keep when the end comes?
Can't you see: old friends at your window grow fewer with each harvest,
The new graves beyond the suburbs multiply with each year,
This is all only a dream of the southern branch!

(CHEN JIQING *enters in a fluster carrying the bramble basket and speaks*:) Master! I have eyes but I'm blind. I can only hope, Master, that you will save me through conversion. (MALE LEAD *sings*:) Let us withdraw to one side.

(*Tang xiucai*)
Look at him running there all afluster.

(*Acts out waving him away with his hand, sings*:)
Ai! You stupid imbecile, stop following me!

(CHEN JIQING *acts out catching up to him and grabbing him, making him stop, speaks*:) Great Immortal! I only hope for your compassion that will free me from suffering[243] and point out the road to long life. (*Acts out making obeisance.*) (MALE LEAD *sings*:)
Let me ask you, "Why are you bowing up and down in the road like you were pounding garlic in a pestle"?
I'm just a poor Daoist
Who lives far off at mountain's bend,
How could *I* lead *you*, a Confucian scholar, to enlightenment?

(CHEN JIQING *speaks*:) Inside this bramble basket you left behind a poem that betrayed complete knowledge of my trip home to see my family. Doesn't that mean you are an immortal? I want to follow you now with all my heart, leave the family, and become your disciple. (MALE LEAD *speaks*:) Dolt! Go on to the examination fields and wrest away your Top of the List. Why are you bowing to me? (*Sings*:)

(*Gun xiuqiu*)
With all your heart you want to meet your lord and king, get a first on the examination,
So why are you kowtowing to an immortal to seek a final outcome?

(CHEN JIQING *speaks*:) Master! Your disciple here has read the poem and now I don't want to be an official anymore. (MALE LEAD *sings*:)
You say you read the poem and then saw through the Gate of Mystery,
I just fear that my "hairs of purple frost[244] have wrongly adjudicated this state"!

---

243. The term used here, *pudu* 普度, more correctly written 普渡, is a Buddhist term that literally means "to ferry everyone across."

244. The finest hairs for writing brushes, taken from the backs and tails of hares.

(MALE LEAD *speaks*:) Dolt! Are you enlightened now? (CHEN JIQING *speaks*:) I am! (MALE LEAD *sings*:)
Since you already know that the glory of the world is but froth on the water,
And merit and fame like sparks from a flint,
Why did you take so many digs at me in the lecture hall?

(CHEN JIQING *speaks*:) I had only common and vulgar sight! How could I know a true immortal had descended from heaven! I only hope that you will raise your noble hand high and sweep dusty customs from me. (MALE LEAD *sings*:)
And now, I will sweep the vulgar dust from you as I raise my sagely hand to rub,
And then explain in detail why that Hall of Bright Radiance of the Son of Heaven within the ninth wall
Can never be the equal of the little tunnel of peace and security of us immortal folk on our three isles,
And you will never want to bustle around in the busy world again.

(*The three, including* LIE YUKOU, *enter and he speaks*:) Elder Brother of the Way, is that Chen Jiqing finally willing to follow you off? (CHEN JIQING *enters and speaks*:) So, all three of the great immortals have been here all the time. (*Acts out bowing to them.*) (MALE LEAD *speaks*:) We had to go down into the mortal world three times for this one dolt. (*Sings*:)
(*Tang xiucai*)
Yesterday, oh,
You couldn't take off that golden cangue and those jade-link fetters.
But today, well,
You want to have "audience with the Prime Origin to verify completion of your discipline tasks"[245]—
So we know you know "Who is freely wandering!" and "Who is full of frustration!"
Raise your head: the mountain colors are fine,
Let it into year ears: the sound of water is mellifluous—
This is exactly the way we Daoist immortals live our lives!

(CHEN JIQING *speaks*:) I know it wasn't one of these three, but was that old fisherman who ferried me home a transformation of you? (MALE LEAD *speaks*:) Dolt. (*Sings*:)
(*Gun xiuqiu*)
You say I drove that little boat across the blue waves,
Held the bamboo fishing rod, and threw on that green rain cape—
This I did!

245. That is, to become an immortal (*chaoyuan zhengke* 朝元證課). These practices seem to refer to inner cultivation techniques of "complex practices of visualization and inner concentration leading to transfiguration" that are associated with the Zhongli Quan and Lü Dongbin schools. The carefully graded path to transfiguration is found in manuals such as *The Complete Methods of the Numinous Treasure* (*Lingbao bifa* 靈寶畢法). See Baldrian-Hussein 2008a and the works cited therein, including Baldrian-Hussein's translation. See also Baldrian-Hussein 2008b.

You came within an inch of your life foolhardily crossing that river!

(CHEN JIQING *speaks*:) Master! Once you decided you would lead me to enlightenment, why did you dump me in the river, putting me at death's door? You really know how to manipulate people! (MALE LEAD *acts out pointing to* LIE YUKOU, *sings*:)

If I hadn't laid out that little snare,
How could I have persuaded these immortal ones to bring this scene to an end?
I have seven other brothers among my old friends as well.

(CHEN JIQING *speaks*:) Master! Just exactly where are the Eight Grotto Precincts of the Upper Realm?[246] (MALE LEAD *acts out gesturing with his hand in a direction, sings*:)

The Grotto Precincts of which you ask are still cut off by the high peaks of Penglai's range,
How would I have persuaded these immortal realized ones to bring this scene to an end?

(*Continues in speech:*) If you want to dance,

We have the slim waist twirl of "Rainbow Skirts and Feathered Sleeves,"[247]

(*Continues in speech:*) If you want to sing,

We have the white teeth songs of the Crimson Tree and Green Zither,[248]
So let us waste no more time.

(CHEN JIQING *speaks*:) Master! Can you tell me just about the sights you have there? (MALE LEAD *sings*:)

(*Daodao ling*)

There we have dark-green pines crooked and twisting: krakens and dragons at rest,
Virescent mountains and high peaks: waves of glaucous mist.
Unmoved by fragrant winds, pine flowers fall,
Grotto gates are closed away in the deep, no one locks them.
Let's go, you and I,
Let us go—
To perfect realization we will ascend together the Galleries of Penglai.[249]

246. The abode of the immortals; there are eight upper-realm and eight lower-realm grotto precincts.

247. Also known as Rainbow Skirts and Feathered Jackets, a dance of nearly mythic status, introduced into China from either central Asia or India during the Tang. Legend, however, claims that the Xuanzong Emperor of the Tang discovered it when he roamed on a magical trip through the palace of the moon, where the dance was performed by sylphlike immortals. Although Xuanzong tried to memorize the tune, he lost a part of it with each step across the bridge that led back to the mortal world. He immediately ordered his court entertainers to try and approximate the music and choreography.

248. Crimson Tree was a beautiful singer immortalized in a poem by Cao Pi; Green Zither was a beautiful female spirit; these two are commonly used together as a general reference for a beautiful singing girl.

249. See n. 149.

(OPENING MALE *costumed as* IMPERIAL LORD OF EASTERN FLORESCENCE[250] *enters, holding a tally and leading* ZHANG GUO,[251] ZHONGLI QUAN, IRON CRUTCH LI,[252] DIVINE CODGER XU,[253] LAN CAIHE,[254] HAN XIANGZI,[255] *and* HE XIANGU.[256])

(CHEN JIQING *speaks*:) Oh! So many great immortals and I recognize none of them. Could you tell me who they are, Master? (MALE LEAD *points to* ZHANG *and sings*:)

(*Shier yue*)

This one rides on a donkey backward, as fast as going downhill.

(CHEN JIQING *speaks*:) So it turns out to be the great immortal Zhang Guo (*Acts out bowing.*) (MALE LEAD *points to* XU *and sings*:)

This one blows an iron flute with beautiful harmonies and pleasant sounds.

(CHEN JIQING *speaks*:) It's the great immortal Divine Codger Xu (*Acts out bowing.*) (MALE LEAD *points to* HE *and sings*:)

This graceful beauty holds a wicker strainer.

(CHEN JIQING *speaks*:) It's the great immortal He Xiangu (*Acts out bowing.*) (MALE LEAD *points to* LI *and sings*:)

This one with ragged beard drags an iron crutch behind him.

(CHEN JIQING *speaks*:) It's the great immortal Iron Crutch Li (*Acts out bowing.*) (MALE LEAD *points to* HAN *and sings*:)

This one converted the Literary Duke at Indigo Pass.[257]

(CHEN JIQING *speaks*:) It's the great immortal Han Xiangzi (*Acts out bowing.*) (MALE LEAD *points to* LAN *and sings*:)

This one in the long green robe clacks his clappers and sings out loud.

(CHEN JIQING *speaks*:) It's the great immortal Lan Caihe (*Acts out bowing.*) (MALE LEAD *points to* ZHONGLI *and sings*:)

(*Yaomin ge*)

This is the one with twin coifs who always drinks until he's red in the face.

(CHEN JIQING *speaks*:) It's the great immortal Zhongli of the Han (*Acts out bowing and speaks*:) May I ask, Master, what your name is? (MALE LEAD *speaks*:) You dolt! Didn't I already tell you? (*Sings*:)

---

250. Donghua Dijun was the mythical first patriarch of the Quanzhen Daoist sect. See Smith 2008. A thousand years earlier, in Han-dynasty times, he was often paired with the Queen Mother of the West in visual arts.

251. This begins a list that offers one rendition of the so-called Eight Immortals. See Yoshikawa 2008a, 2008c, and West and Idema 2010b, 284.

252. See Yoshikawa 2008a, 220.

253. See n. 132.

254. On Lan Caihe, see West and Idema 2010b, 283–313, which includes a translation of *Zhongli of the Han Leads Lan Caihe to Enlightenment.*

255. Sometimes thought to be Han Xiang, a nephew of Han Yu's (764–824), the great Tang writer; see Yoshikawa 2008a.

256. Ibid., 222.

257. See n. 85.

I once—in the moment when the yellow millet was boiling in the pot—
Had whiled away fifty years of life unknown.

(CHEN JIQING *speaks*:) Oh, you already said that! I was just too deluded to understand. (*Acts out bowing and speaks*:) Let me pay my deep respect now. (MALE LEAD *sings*:)

Now he knows I am Master of Pure Yang Lü and no one else.

(*Speaks*:) Dolt! Could you still be dreaming? (CHEN JIQING *speaks*:) I am truly enlightened now, I am not dreaming anymore. (MALE LEAD *sings*:)

Go now and think carefully about what has happened,
Don't make us sneer at you,
We just want you to see how damn meaningless is that field of fortune and fame!

(IMPERIAL LORD OF EASTERN FLORESCENCE *speaks*:) I have received the emperor's command: since Chen Jiqing already possessed the fate to become an immortal, and to become Master of Pure Yang Lü's disciple, all of the assembled immortals can lead him off to the west to the feast of the Immortal Peaches. (*Recites in ballad verse*:)

To the west we gaze at the Porphyry Pool where all the Realized gather,
From the east comes a purple aura that pervades the Gates of Heaven;
From this point on, at the chalcedony feast mats of the Queen Mother,
One more will be added when the Peaches of Immortality are handed out.

(CHEN JIQING *and the group all act out bowing*.) (MALE LEAD *sings*:)

(*Coda*)
We gather at the Porphyry Pool and celebrate with Peaches of Immortality;
They fill to the brim the golden platter and are bestowed in Great Canopy Heaven.
They extend our fortune-allotted years beyond measure,
And secure our eternal bliss.
Take this feathered cloak and raven-black head cloth and tie it on yourself,
And arrange the straps on your kudzu-vine sandals.
Let that black mule be stabled and fed,
For now you ride with me on an auspicious cloud.
Even though it be some million-mile journey of the Peng,
We will fear the breadth of neither heaven nor sea.

Title: Lü Dongbin reveals a transformation in a dream of blue waves
Name: Chen Jiqing Mistakenly Boards the Bamboo-Leaf boat.

5
Tippler Zhao Yuan Encounters the Prior Emperor

INTRODUCTION

Biographical information is extremely limited on Gao Wenxiu 高文秀 (second half of the thirteenth century), a prolific playwright from Dongping 東平 (in modern Shandong), a major performing center in the early history of *zaju*. The *Register of Ghosts* reveals that he "hailed from Dongping, was a prefectural student, and died young."[1] A manuscript edition of the *Register* adds that the people of the capital called him a "minor Hanqing" (*xiao* Hanqing 小漢卿), which would seem to suggest that he was also active, or at least his works were well known, in Dadu, home of Guan Hanqing. In his extended edition of the *Register of Ghosts*, Jia Zhongming 賈仲明 (1343–1422) inserted the following elegy poem for Gao:

> In the flower encampments and brocaded formations he led buckler and spear,
> In the halls of the Xie and the lofts of Qin he arrayed song and dance,[2]
> At the altars of poetry and the gatherings of wine he relaxed chatting and talking,
> And he composed the play *Liu Shuahe*.[3]
>
> From younger years to sixty he never succeeded in the examinations
> And—except for that one Hanqing
> And sorting out the other early worthies—
> None had as many dramas as he did![4]

1. Zhong 1982, 106.
2. The "halls of the Xie and lofts of Qin" usually refer to courtesan houses but here probably are also intended to include theaters.
3. Liu Shuahe 劉耍和 was a noted actor of the Jin-Yuan period and Group Leader of the Court Entertainment Bureau, about whom both Jin farces and Yuan comedies were written.
4. Zhong 1982, 157n191.

Of the more than thirty *zaju* credited to Gao Wenxiu, eight include in their titles the name of the "Black Whirlwind" (Hei Xuanfeng 黑旋風).[5] Evidently, Gao Wenxiu felt a special affinity for the Black Whirlwind, who was Li Kui 李逵, a conspicuous member of a band of Robin Hood–like bandits who roamed the Liangshan Marshes in Gao's home province in the early twelfth century.[6] Gao and Kang Jinzhi, another Shandong playwright who also wrote on the Lianghsan bandits, are called the "two pillars of Li Kui plays" (*Hei Xuanfeng shuangbi* 黑旋風雙壁).[7] Of Gao Wenxiu's many recorded works, only five plays have been preserved:[8]

Tippler Zhao Yuan Encounters the Prior Emperor (*Haojiu Zhao Yuan yu Shanghuang* 好酒趙元遇上皇)

The Black Whirlwind Twice Brings Heads as Tribute (*Hei Xuanfeng shuan xiantou* 黑旋風雙獻頭)[9]

Xu Jia Belittles Fan Sui (*Xu Jia sui Fan Sui* 須賈誶范雎)[10]

Guaranteeing Duke Cheng's Safety, Going Straightaway to the Meeting at Mianchi (*Bao Chenggong jingfu Mianchi hui* 保成公徑赴澠池會)[11]

Liu Xuande Goes Alone to the Xiangyang Meeting (*Liu Xuande dufu Xiangyang hui* 劉玄德獨赴襄陽會)[12]

The attribution of the last two plays to Gao Wenxiu is suspect, and certainly in the case of the final one, it bears little likeness to the quality of the language in those plays that are well attested as Gao's and is more than likely a product of court entertainers in the Ming.[13]

5. Either thirty-three or thirty-four plays are normally attributed to him. See Wang Xiaojia 2004, 87–88.
6. There are several plays about (or that include) Li Kui available in English: Kang Jinzhi's 康進之 *Li K'uei Carries Thorns* (*Liangshan bo Li Kui fujing* 梁山泊李逵負荊) (Kang 1980), and two by Zhu Youdun, *A Leopard Monk Returns to the Laity of His Own Accord* (*Baozi heshang zi huansu* 豹子和尚自還俗) and *Black Whirlwind Li Spurns Riches out of Righteousness* (*Heixuan feng zhangyi shucai* 黑旋風仗義疏財). For these latter two plays, see West and Idema 2010b, 314–88.
7. See Wang Xiaojia 2004, 88.
8. Gao Wenxiu's plays have recently been collected and annotated in Chen, Xu, and Zhang 2011, 1:119–220.
9. In this play, Li Kui tracks down and kills a philandering wife and her paramour, the local prefect, and brings their heads back to Liangshan. For a summary of the play, see Li, Li, and Hou 2003, 13.
10. A retelling of the story in the *Records of the Historian* of Xu Jia and Fan Sui, a tale of political jealousy and betrayal in the Warring States period. The drama is little changed from the biographies of Fan Sui and Cai Ze. See Li, Li, and Hou 2003, 14–15, and "Fan Sui and Ts'ai Tse, Memoir 19," in Ssu-ma Ch'ien 2002, 233–46.
11. A story of Lin Xiangru's 藺相如 skill as a civil minister for Zhao and of his conflict, eventually resolved, with Lian Po 廉頗, the great general of Zhao during the Warring States period. See Li, Li, and Hou 2003,15, and the original source, "Lian P'o and Lin Xiangru, Memoir 21," in Ssu-ma Ch'ien 2002, 263–71.
12. This play, preserved in the Maiwang Studio collection, dramatizes Liu Bei's first meeting with Liu Biao in Jingzhou, Liu Bei's flight across Sandalwood Creek, and an account of the activities of Xu Shu, Liu Bei's field marshal. For a translation of the complete play, see Idema and West 2012, 152–96.
13. Ibid., xxix.

Of these five plays, only *Tippler Zhao Yuan Encounters the Prior Emperor* survives in a Yuan printing. The play is also known in a late Ming manuscript from the Maiwangguan collection. We provide translations of both plays in this chapter.

The setting of this play is Bianliang (modern Kaifeng), also known as the Eastern Capital, which served as the capital of the Northern Song (960–1127). As the capital of the most populous empire of the contemporary world, one that had known undisturbed domestic peace for over a century and a half, Kaifeng had grown by 1100 into a bustling metropolis with a population of over a million. The bickering of factions at the highest echelons of the imperial court bureaucracy hardly affected the crowds that thronged its streets. The lively bustle of the city is described well in coeval accounts of its pleasures, most notably the recollections of its last years as capital, written in 1147 as *A Record of My Dream of Paradise in the Eastern Capital* (*Dongjing meng Hua lu* 東京夢華錄). But the unprecedented material and popular splendors of Kaifeng were wiped out in a single stroke when the city fell to the invading Jurchen in 1126.[14]

This collapse of Song peace and prosperity was presided over by Emperor Huizong 徽宗 (r. 1101–1125), a flamboyant personality, a great patron of Daoism and the arts, and quite a distinguished painter himself. His romantic adventures outside the walls of the palace, especially his incognito visits to Kaifeng's most renowned courtesan, Li Shishi 李師師, became the stuff of popular legend. Following a first siege of Kaifeng by the Jurchen in the summer of 1126, Huizong abdicated to be succeeded by one of his sons, known to history as Qinzong (r. 1126–1127). Following his abdication, Huizong was known as the Prior Emperor (Shanghuang 上皇), and this was the title by which he was remembered in the following decades. During the Jin dynasty (1115–1232), founded by the Jurchen, there even existed a special category of farce, "Farces on the Prior Emperor" (Shanghuang Yuanben 上皇院本), which was devoted to Huizong's merry adventures. The fourteen farces under this heading listed in Tao Zongyi's 陶宗儀 (b. 1316) *A Record of Resting from Plowing* (*Nancun chuogeng lu* 南村輟耕錄) are for the most part about Huizong's luxury palaces—taking place in Yanfu Palace 延福宮 and Genyue Park 艮岳—or about his dalliance with Li Shishi and perhaps other women he visited incognito.[15] In due time, however, his personality was invested with more and more traits of the "bad last ruler," a picture that was fixed in such vernacular works as *Remnant Tales of the Xuanhe Reign* (*Xuanhe yishi* 宣和遺事).[16] Yet the direct cause of the downfall of the Northern Song was not so much due to the personality of Huizong as to Song foreign policy. Ever since the founding of the Song, the dynasty had lived in an uneasy truce with its northeastern neighbor, the Liao (916–1119), a regime founded by the Khitan, a non-Chinese ethnic group hailing from southern Manchuria.[17] The Liao occupied sixteen

14. See West 2000, 2002, 2005, 2006.

15. See Tao Zongyi 1959, 307.

16. See Ebrey and Bickford 2006, Anon. 1981, Hennessey 1984, and West 2006.

17. See Levine 2009.

northern Chinese prefectures, including the area of modern Beijing, that had been ceded to it by Shi Jingtang in exchange for support in the founding of his short-lived Jin dynasty (936–945). Furious attempts by the Song in the early decades of its existence—remembered in literature of later centuries as the exploits of the generals of the Yang family[18]—to dislodge the Liao from the sixteen prefectures had all failed. Thus, in the early twelfth century, the Song eagerly entered into a joint alliance with the Jurchen, a Tungusic tribe from northern Manchuria, to wage a two-front war against the Liao.

The Jin quickly succeeded in destroying the Liao, then, claiming the Song had failed to honor its commitments, turned against its southern ally. To its surprise, the Jin met with almost no opposition, and in the summer of 1126 the Jurchen troops stood before the gates of Kaifeng. Withdrawing after receiving a huge ransom, the Jurchen quickly returned in the winter of 1126–1127, this time to stay. Again, the Song mounted no effective military resistance and Kaifeng quickly fell. Huizong, Qinzong, and many others were taken to the far north as prisoners, never to be released. Within a few years, the Jurchen controlled China as far south as the Huai River, and the Song was reduced further in size, squeezed into China south of that river. Huizong's sixth son, known posthumously as Gaozong 高宗 (Zhao Gou 趙構, r. 1127–1163), declared himself emperor, and after many years of warfare eventually located the capital of this Southern Song court in Hangzhou. After the border had become stabilized, Gaozong, in turn, abdicated and also assumed the title Shanghuang.

The use of the title Prior Emperor[19] for Huizong would seem to imply that the action of *Tippler Zhao* is set in the afterglow of the glory of the Northern Song, sometime between his abdication and the fall of Kaifeng. Since the final act of the play portrays Huizong very much as a reigning emperor holding court, however, it is much more likely that the title Prior Emperor had become so identified with Huizong that it was used anachronistically to refer to him before his abdication. This would also solve the problem presented in this play by the mention of Yang Jian (d.1121), a eunuch who enjoyed the favor of Huizong and rose to the highest military position. In later assessments of the fall of the Song, Yang Jian was considered one of the so-called seven scourges responsible for the debacle of 1126 and 1127.

One may, of course, read the play as just one more colorful incident in the life of a fun-loving emperor whose life would end tragically. Comparable anecdotes are told about Gaozong as Prior Emperor: he would make the reputation of poor students and impoverished soup vendors after meeting them incognito. However, the setting of *Tippler Zhao* also seems to demand a political interpretation. It is difficult not to read the play as an indictment of soldiers, portrayed as total and hopeless drunks, and of officials who care

18. See Idema and West 2013.

19. The term "prior emperor" (*shanghuang* 上皇) is bestowed on monarchs who abdicate their throne.

nothing for their underlings. Even the Prior Emperor himself comes under suspicion for neglecting his duties in order to frequent places of ill repute with his cronies and for promoting a sot to the position of metropolitan prefect. In such a reading, soldiers, officials, and emperor may well be seen as equally responsible for the disgrace of the Chinese loss of the north to barbarian rulers.

The editor of the Maiwang Studio manuscript of the play may have tried to make such an interpretation impossible by moving the action of the play to the reign of Emperor Taizu 太祖 (r. 960–975), the founder of the Song dynasty. Taizu also had a reputation for leaving the palace in disguise; but he did so to visit his wise councilors to discuss issues of statecraft in the informal privacy of their homes. The Maiwang Studio manuscript has created a fictional brother for the emperor, Zhao Guangpu, from the famous Northern Song official Zhao Pu, by using the word *guang*, which is a generational marker in the proper names of the brothers of Song Taizu and Taizong. It also makes every effort to turn Zhao Yuan into an exemplar of probity.[20] With such a moral protagonist, the play could then be interpreted as a paean to an emperor's concern for the common soldier and make it much more suitable for performance at the imperial court.[21] From the collation note at the end of the manuscript we learn that the text had once belonged to Yu Xiaogu, whose play manuscripts would appear to have originated mostly from the late fifteenth century Court Entertainment Bureau. As is well-known, the Ming imperial court did not allow the portrayal onstage of any emperor, and most Yuan-dynasty *zaju* featuring emperors that were adopted into the Ming court repertoire were revised in such a way that the role of the emperor was removed.[22] While perhaps it might have been permissible to portray an emperor in disguise, an emperor in function—as in the last act of this play—would be unthinkable. Perhaps the Court Entertainment Bureau from which Yu Xiaogu had obtained his manuscripts was not the Court Entertainment Bureau at Beijing but the Court Entertainment Bureau in Nanjing, where, in the physical absence of an emperor since the early fifteenth century, the rules may have been applied less strictly than in Beijing.

Despite the considerable number of parallel stories in the unofficial historical accounts of the Song, no direct source is known for Gao Wenxiu's play. The plot might either be his own invention or derive from some popular legend.

---

20. While making these changes, the anonymous editor also made changes to the geographical setting of the play. During the Song dynasty the capital, Kaifeng, was also known as the Eastern Capital, but the anonymous editor apparently understood the Eastern Capital and Kaifeng as referring to two different places. This means that Zhao Yuan now meets with the emperor in disguise after he has left his hometown and is on his way to the capital, whereas in the earlier version he meets with the emperor after leaving the capital.

21. Even the most up-to-date academic writing still argues that "prior emperor" refers to Song Taizu and feels the need to legitimize that choice by dredging through historical records to find the slimmest of evidence. This line continues because these scholars work solely from the later Ming manuscript edition, which, as we note in the introduction and elsewhere, is a product of severe court censorship. A simple look at the *Yuan Edition* of the play and its place in the entertainment literature of the Jin and early Yuan would put this argument to rest. See Yu Xuejian 2012.

22. Tan 2008. Other Yuan plays that kept an emperor in their cast in late Ming editions would appear to have come down to us from Li Kaixian's *Gaiding Yuanxian chuanqi*, which would appear to have been edited on the basis of preserved Yuan editions.

Tippler Zhao is a regular *zaju* consisting of four suites of songs. These four suites of songs are all assigned to the male lead, who plays the part of Zhao Yuan. The action of the play can be reconstructed as follows. Zhao Yuan, a lowly yamen runner with a lovely wife, is a habitual drunk. His wife and her family demand a writ of divorce because his superior, the prefect of Kaifeng, wants the woman for his own. The prefect sends Zhao Yuan off on an impossible mission. He must deliver some documents to another prefect (as it later turns out, an imperial relative) at some unspecified place (presumably at Luoyang) in the coldest month of winter. The documents must be delivered within a specified number of days. If late, he will be beheaded. Thus beleaguered, Zhao eventually consents to the divorce (act 1).

Outside town at Strawbridge Inn, in the midst of a snowstorm, Zhao Yuan arrives at a wineshop at the same time as the emperor, disguised as a student and accompanied by two followers. Zhao offers the "student" a cup of wine, and the emperor returns the gesture. The emperor is unable to pay for the wine—emperors do not carry any cash— and is beaten up by the innkeeper. Zhao Yuan comes to the rescue of the "student." The emperor asks him about his name, and, since they both share the surname Zhao, he swears brotherhood with Zhao Yuan. After being told about Zhao Yuan's impossible situation, the emperor writes a letter to his "brother," the prefect, on Zhao Yuan's bare arm (act 2).

Zhao Yuan eventually arrives at his destination, but late. When he presents himself, the prefect flies into a rage and orders him executed. Zhao Yuan then cries out that he is also bringing him a letter from his "elder brother." After he bares his arm and the prefect reads the letter, Zhao Yuan is immediately seated in a place of honor and treated with great respect. He is informed that the emperor has appointed him prefect of Kaifeng (act 3). The final act is devoted to Zhao Yuan's presentation at court, where he is extremely ill at ease in his official dress and vows to spend his time drinking, leaving the populace alone.[23] In the end his wife and her lover are brought in and duly punished.

The songs of this play are extremely lively and very much in character—the language is simple and nearly free of allusions. The few that are to be found all relate stories that were clichés on the Yuan stage. In view of its subject matter, drinking, it is of course only to be expected that the text is sprinkled liberally with the names of famous brews: Spring in the Vat, Bamboo Leaf, Nine Times Brewed, Spring's Color, and of course the finest wine, Gaoyang.

READING SUGGESTIONS:

Bickford and Ebrey 2006; Hennessey 1981, 1984; Weng 2006; West 2000, 2006.

23. For an interesting take on the relationship between this play and the cultural meaning of drinking, see Weng Minhua 2006.

NEWLY CUT WITH PLOT PROMPTS: *TIPPLER ZHAO YUAN ENCOUNTERS THE PRIOR EMPEROR*, A FOURTEENTH-CENTURY EDITION

DRAMATIS PERSONAE IN ORDER OF APPEARANCE

Role type	*Name and family, institutional, or social role*
OLD MAN	ZHAO YUAN's father-in-law
FEMALE LEAD	MRS. ZHAO, ZHAO YUAN's wife
MALE LEAD	ZHAO YUAN, the tippler
EXTRA MALE	PREFECTURAL OFFICIAL (act 1); also called COMIC and OFFICIAL.
WAITER IN WINESHOP	WAITER IN WINESHOP
EMPEROR	FORMER EMPEROR (Huizong)
EXTRA MALES	EMPEROR'S ENTOURAGE (act 2)
OFFICIAL	HIGH OFFICIAL, brother of EMPEROR
EXTRA MALE	COURT ATTENDANT
YAMEN RUNNERS	YAMEN RUNNERS
YANG JIAN	YANG JIAN

✤ ✤ ✤

NEWLY CUT WITH PLOT PROMPTS: *TIPPLER ZHAO YUAN ENCOUNTERS THE PRIOR EMPEROR*

[ACT 1]

Wait until the one scene of OLD MAN *and* FEMALE LEAD *is finished—wait until one scene of* EXTRA MALE *is finished—[you]* MALE LEAD *enter acting drunk—immediately belt out*:

([XIANLÜ MODE:] *Dian jiangchun*)

Tilting east, listing west,
Falling backwards, bumping forwards—
I leave my seat.

This wine has made me crazy,
And my drunken souls head off toward home.[24]
(*Hunjiang long*)
Suddenly I observe the wine flag,
And see the windblown green banner[25] hailing, "Gaoyang wine!"
To drink some dreggy wine or strained ale
Beats sap of jade or chalcedony liquor.
What makes me happy
Are two sleeves filled with fresh wind and a curving moon,
One pot of Spring's Color and its perfume seeping through the crock.
Before the flowers I drink my wine,
Under the moon I stroke my beard.
Tangled hair, smudged face,
I drum on my belly and croon a tune,
In the thatched hut beside the wine crock I sing, "Tra-la-la."
Three cups in the stomach,
And it will carry you away forever.

Act out going into a wineshop and drinking. Wait until OLD MAN *and* FEMALE LEAD *have entered and spoken.*

(*You hulu*)
You say,
I love my wine and lust after the cup, that I will cause trouble—
But you are the rustic boors,
And rightly nicknamed "a den of wolves."
Before you see the peach blossoms rise to my cheeks,
Already
You have scattered them with your shouting before my cup of Bamboo Leaf.
Cursing and cussing you grab my hair,
Kick me with your feet,
Keep boxing my ears—
You've ripped all my clothes to shreds.
(*Tianxia le*)
You've abandoned it all now, and have made a real scene this time,
What kind of dirty tricks do you have now for beating and cursing your son?
I've never stirred up any trouble by loafing around and hanging out,

24. Or perhaps "to my home where the wine flag hangs."
25. Wine houses advertised their presence by a banner or bundle of straw hung from a high pole.

You keep after me for a handprint[26]
And try every means to get a writ of confession;[27]
You bully this poor hungry and cold, destitute army runner to death.

Wait until OLD MAN *has spoken.* The reason I've been drinking these three days is due to the kindness of friends.

(*Nezha ling*)
Day before yesterday it was Blind Wang the Fifth, raising the roof beam,
Yesterday it was the rustic Li Hu sacrificing a goat,
And today it was the lush Liu Hong, celebrating his birthday.
I didn't want to go—
It was *they* who visited *me*,
They fetched *me* and dragged me away.

Speak: Wine has its good points!

(*Que ta zhi*)
Only after you have wine can you gather together your relatives,
Only after you have wine can you meet friends wise and good.
Haven't you heard the old saw and proverb:
"Wine can dispel all sorrows in the heart"?
After I have wine, my tolerance is as capacious as the seas,
But without any wine, my stomach burns and my guts writhe.

Wait until EXTRA MALE *has spoken. Speak*: Stop drinking?

(*Jisheng cao*)
I could be a clerk,
Become a peddler,
Use a buffalo to grow beans and furrow the fields,
Smear on lime, daub on clay, and learn to act and sing,
Or shave my head, cut my hair, and become a monk—
But make me give up the spring from the vat that melts away sorrow and dispels depression—
I can't give it up!
I'd far rather stretch out my neck in the bustling marketplace at the execution ground.

Wait until [*they*][28] *have spoken. Speak*: I couldn't give it up for a year, even if I tried. I'll explain why I can't give it up in each of the four seasons.

(*Zui zhong tian*)

---

26. Since he cannot write his name.

27. That is, a writ of divorce, a "confession" that he is a bad husband.

28. Subjects and agents are omitted in the stage directions. There are two possibilities here for someone to urge Zhao Yuan to stop drinking: the old man and his wife. Of course, we may restore these agents from the Ming edition, but that would be to assume that the Ming edition is a true replication of the action of the Yuan play. We have therefore opted to leave the stage directions as unclear as they are in the original.

Give it up in spring?

In spring's warmth, flowers' fragrances are all set free.

Give it up in summer?

In summer's heat, caltrop and lotus are redolent.

Give it up in autumn?

At the golden well, the *wutong* tree drops leaves of yellow.

Give it up in winter?

Auspicious snows flurry about our heads.

Heaven has its days and nights, clear and cloudy, men have mornings and eves, good luck and bad.

Alive, dead—a man's life lies in the single moment:
To give up the golden rippled green brew
Would have been to pass uselessly from one season to another.

Wait until [someone] *has spoken. Speak*: You want me to live in a village, where there's surely no wine. Two things now that will make it even more impossible to stop!

[(*Jinzhan'er*)]

You want me to keep company with Esquire Sprout in a village
And nourish this skin sack in some hamlet quarter,
Where each day, blown by winds, scorched by the sun, I will furrow the fields,
And suffer wind and frost along with Sha the Third and Zhao the Fourth?
How could I spend the hundred years allotted to me besotted with wine
Or enjoy those thirty-six thousand drunken days?

These two things—

"Don't let the wildflowers[29] pop out of the ground."
What I fear is "the perfume of village brew seeps through the crock."

Wait until OLD MAN *drags you to see* EXTRA MALE—*wait until* OFFICIAL[30] *has entered and spoken—greet* COMIC. *After* COMIC *speaks—act out being frightened. Speak*: It's someone else's turn to go, it's not my job. *After* COMIC *speaks—wait until* FEMALE LEAD *requests a writ of divorce—act out hesitating. After it has been written out—act out weeping.*

(*You simen*)

They want me to hand over this fine flower to some rich gent—
Husband and wife will be torn apart.
There is no turning back from the documents I have before me.
I see that I will perish,
And she will mate up with a simurgh or phoenix.

29. Other women.

30. The text uses three terms for this prefectural official: comic, extra, and official. It switches in midact. See Xu Qinjun 1980,127, 129.

(*Liuye'er*)
Really, the official is completely on her side.
And if I have to take this trip, snow will pile on top of frost.[31]
Silently, secretly I'm scared, so scared my soul floats away.
Where can I submit my own complaint?
If I write that out, I can avoid disaster and misfortune,
Ah,
If I don't write it out, then what harm will come?
Act out coming outside after having turned over the writ of divorce, weeping and wailing.
(*Shanghua shi*)
All because of her one face that is not plain, I am forced to leave my home—
That two-faced official knows how to work a plot,
Those three are evil at heart.
For less than four years we've been husband and wife,
But they've been to court five times ten.
(*Reprise*)
Inside the six dimensions,[32] I've suffered your rottenness,
Seven generations of my ancestors you have reviled at will,
And, from all eight directions, have accused me wildly, discussed me at length,
We've been man and wife—consider it well, nine times nine:
Don't hope that I'll die by the time you count ten.
(*Coda*)
You, with a tenfold adulterous heart,
Fear no neighbor's comments after nine,[33]
In all eight directions, you will walk the streets and cruise the alleys.
Don't curse seven generations of mothers
Because your six relatives are flustered when they see you.
Think on it yourself:
Think, with head propped on hands, in the fifth watch of the night,
How easily we woke our four neighbors, who called the local elder.
I want to lay out three cups by the side of the road[34]—
In less than two weeks my life will be lost.
Summon my soul from nowhere else
For my one spirit will never leave the brewery!
[*Exit.*]

31. That is, a bad situation will become worse.
32. North, east, south, and west, and up and down.
33. Here using the homophone "long time" (*jiu* 久), which would literally render "you fear no neighbor's gossip will occur after a time."
34. As a sacrifice to assure his safe completion of the task.

[ACT 2]

Wait until WAITER IN WINESHOP *enters and speaks—and until* EMPEROR, *leading his party, enters, seats himself, and speaks—enter acting braving a snowstorm—belt out*:

([NANLÜ MODE:] *Yizhi hua*)

Battling the wind, I face into the willow floss,
Braving the snow, I brush the pear blossoms away.[35]
Snow mantles a thousand trees until they grow old with age,
Wind trims them until ten thousand branches wither.
Such a journey as this of wind and snow—
Snow veils the road to heaven's edge.
The wind is strong,
The snow heavy—
Just like it was sprinkled by a spade or tossed by a winnowing basket,
Just like combed cotton or plucked floss.

(*Liangzhou*)

It's just like Han Yu, who couldn't get his steed to go forward through Indigo Pass,[36]
Or Meng Haoran, who refused to ride his donkey across the Baling Bridge.[37]
I'm so frozen that my hands and feet have goose bumps like grain.
The heavens are cold, the days short,
The boundless fields, desolate and empty,
Passes and mountains, hard and bitter,
Wind and snow mix and mingle.
My whole body wrapped only in an unpadded gown
That flaps in the eastern wind, randomly flecked with true pearls.
I raise my head just like a baby badger coming out of its hole,
Hunch my shoulders just like an old rat soaked with water,
Bend my waist just like a human dried shrimp.
When will I get to the imperial capital?
Scraping the sky, scraping the earth, a wild wind beats,
Who has suffered such misery as this?
I see three golden-saddled horses tied to an aged mulberry tree—
Must be some relatives of the emperor's or scions of the state.

---

35. Willow floss and pear blossoms are conventional images for snowflakes.

36. See chap. 4, n. 106.

37. During a yearlong visit to the capital Chang'an (present-day Xi'an) in 728–729, the poet Meng Haoran 孟浩然 (689–740), in order to enjoy the first flowering of the plum, rode on his donkey to the suburbs on a day of heavy snowfall. The incident was adapted for the stage; it was also a popular subject in painting.

Act out going inside, going to the fire, sniffing the odor of the wine. Speak: Bring me two hundred coppers' of wine! *Wait until* [*waiter in wineshop*] *acts out bringing wine.*

(*Muyang guan*)
After I see the wine, I hurry to bow in obeisance,
After I drink the wine, I pay my respects again,
Reunited today with my old buddy wine.
O, wine,
I would have said we'd never meet again,
Never imagined we'd be together at one place and time.
Because of wine, I suffered with storm and snow,
Because of wine, I trod this long road.
But now this wine-soaked head meets you again—
Ah,
Papa Wine, have you been well?

Act out offering a cup of wine to EXTRA MALE—*wait until* EXTRA MALE *has drunk a cup with you.*

(*Gewei*)
I'm just a good-for-nothing who follows donkeys and handles horses,
You must be grandees who discuss the past and discourse on texts.
It's all heaven's fate, a man doesn't make that himself.
Even though I'm a stupid and vulgar lout
Who cannot hold forth on the rites of former kings,
I can chug it, gurgling and gulping, right down my throat.

Wait until EXTRA MALE *fights—listen, then stop.*

(*Gan huang'en*)
I am just about to drink my fragrant ale,
But who is this, shouting and yelling, quarreling and screaming?
All I hear is endless censure, ceaseless curses, "You penniless pedant!"
He keeps on shoving him, pushing him around,
Grabbing, dragging, seizing, shaking.
But you must know that once Li Bo pledged his sword for a drink,
And pawned his zither to pay up his tab.[38]

38. The poet Li Bai (701–762) established a great reputation as a drinker, not only by his actual behavior but also because of his poetry—in his many poems on the pleasures of wine, he repeatedly states that he will pawn his possessions such as his fine sword or his precious coat in order to buy the best wine. Later legend had it that he not only wrote his best work but also offended the highest powers in the land while drunk, and that he died by drowning when, in a drunken stupor, he tried to embrace the reflection of the moon in the water of a lake. These colorful adventures of Li Bai were of course adapted for the stage in Yuan times.

(*Caicha ge*)
One pulls at his clothes,
The other is smeared with blood.
Scholar,
You can't say here, "Flowers' shadows cover the body, ask for help getting up"![39]
Why should you three learned men have any reason to fear?
I'll put out my own coppers to pay for what you owe.

Wait until EMPEROR *swears brotherhood with you—act out going over and drinking wine. Act out weeping and wailing. After* EMPEROR *asks why—after acting out explaining the plot.*

(*Hong shaoyao*)
My mother- and father-in-law have venomous hearts,
The official who was part of it screwed up his duties.
Indeed, this beauty has betrayed her husband,
And that guy wanted to be with her, like fish in water.
The finest of appearances
Hide evil schemes.
Blind to the facts,
They wanted a divorce.
Relying on the official's coercion, they broke apart husband and wife.
Really they are horses and oxen in human dress!
(*Pusa Liangzhou*)
I may be all alone in the world,
So who will hear my complaint?
I harbor my wrongs and carry my injustice,
And so rage fills my breast and tears rain down like pearls.
This writ—one raised the frost-tipped brush,
One pulled me by the arm,
And, as one held me up,
They said that these two lines of characters were my passport to heaven,
And would see me safely back to home and friends.
This good deed[40]

---

39. A line from "Matching a Poem by Ximei When Awaking from a Stupor on a Spring Night" (He Ximei chunxi jiu xing 和襲美春夕酒醒), written by Lu Guimeng 陸龜蒙 (d. 881?) in response to one sent him by Pi Rixiu 皮日休 (834?–881?). The line is the second of a couplet:

覺後不知明月上	After awaking, unaware that the bright moon has risen,
滿身花影倩人扶	Flowers' shadows cover the body, I ask for help getting up.

40. "This good deed" refers to paying for the wine the (incognito) emperor is unable to pay.

Must be done.
Who would have thought that two full strings of a hundred cash could buy a man's life?
Brother,
You don't need paper to write this letter.

After taking leave—wait until EMPEROR *speaks*:
(*Coda*)

I never imagined that now, as I was about to die an unjust death, [you'd save] my head.
Pointing afar to among the clouds: a goose delivering a letter.
My two feet
Will never stop.
This anxious sorrow,
This fitful fear,
This vexatious worry—
To whom shall I complain?
How can I raise my voice,
I bear too much injustice.
Prior Emperor Zhao, you sit securely in your august capital,
How can you know of the unjust misery of an army runner who so endures wind and snow?
[*Exit.*]

[ACT 3]

Wait until OFFICIAL *enters, speaks, and stops—immediately enter and belt out*:
([ZHONGLÜ MODE:] *Fendie'er*)

Six-pointed flowers fly,[41]
At blue heaven's rim, frozen clouds linger.
Hugging my shoulders, I tuck my head low.
My wine soul has disappeared,
I've just sobered up from the wine
And my limbs have no strength.
Soon my life will be buried in the mud of the Yellow Springs.
How can I avoid such a disaster?
(*Zui chunfeng*)

41. Six-pointed flowers are snowflakes.

You've done me in, this Spring in the Vat, this Bamboo Leaf,
This wife I loved with all my heart, this sprig of pretty flowers.
Just because of my passion for fragrant brew,
I finally found the stirrup cup of eternal separation.
How can I have regrets?
How can I have regrets?
And it is also predestined fate from former lives,
Something we alone create, something we alone suffer—
Blame heaven, blame earth!
(*Ying xianke*)
His retinue is lined up,
His runners are lined up—
Thus death comes in the dark, unbeknownst to man,
And we can't grow wings to fly away.
Unstoppable, my tears seem pushed out by a hoe,
Hei!
This is a punishment without a crime that I've brought on myself.

After greeting OFFICIAL—*after* EXTRA MALE *has pushed you and you have turned around—act out being flustered and speak*: Excellency, I am bringing you a letter from your brother. *Wait until* OFFICIAL *speaks.*

(*Shang xiaolou*)
I have a letter from your elder brother.
At the foot of these steps, allow this humble person to explain—
Quickly, so quickly, speedily, so speedily,
Correct, so correct, exact, so exact,
I will enumerate all the true facts—
And if I, Zhao Yuan, should make only the slightest error in my explanation,
I'd be happy to let my life return to the world of the springs.[42]

Wait until you have been interrogated.

(*Reprise*)
It was a party of three,
Who insisted on offering me a cup.
They came up short on their tab, the owner shouted and screamed and got all worked up,
And without a second thought, I paid two hundred coppers on their behalf.
For this reason
He swore brotherhood with me.

42. The world of the springs is the underworld, often called the Yellow Springs.

Wait until you have been interrogated. Speak: I was on my way to deliver documents when I came to the inn at Strawbridge. There I saw three scholars drinking wine, and when they had no money, I paid their bill. He asked me what I was surnamed, and I responded, "My name is Zhao." He said, "My name is Zhao, too." So I gave him my respects as elder brother. And because of this, he wrote this letter. He said that he was Your Excellency's elder brother. *Wait until* OFFICIAL *speaks—and acts out having seen what is on your arm—wait until* OFFICIAL *grasps his tablet of office*[43]*—and* YAMEN RUNNERS *have put you in a chair—act out being scared out of your wits.*

(*Shi'er yue*)
They've put me into this folding chair to sit,
And are dancing[44] around me hand and foot.
They spread an embroidered carpet on the ground,
While perfume wafts from the golden lion.
Call a doctor! What's my pulse?
These stricken eyes will be hard to cure!

(*Yaomin ge*)
Who ever saw the god of the soil in his poor house bow to Zhong Kui?[45]
Or the judge of hell in his court consult a quack?
Call for divine needles or dharma moxa—it's that kind of illness.
Like a Lan Caihe who can't dance, yet sees flowers whirling.[46]
I smirk ever so slightly over
The emperor's edict appointing me
To judge the affairs of Kaifeng prefecture.

Wait until [*he*] *speaks—Speak*: I'm appointed the prefect of the Southern Capital?[47]
Is there any wine there in the yamen?

(*Shua hai'er*)
I can't be an official, but there are plenty of precedents by which to accomplish it,
And the codes of the five punishments are all there in regular order.

---

43. In order to make a formal bow.
44. "Dancing" here means "performing rituals."
45. Every town and hamlet has its own god of the soil, who is part of an empirewide ghostly bureaucracy, headed by the Great Emperor of the Eastern Marchmount and King Yama and the other judges of hell. The gods of the soil all have their own (often very modest) temple or shrine. Zhong Kui was and is widely venerated as a demon queller and door god, but no temples are dedicated to him.
46. Lan Caihe is one of the Eight Immortals. Nowadays he is often depicted as a youth carrying a basket of flowers, but in Yuan times he was believed to have been an entertainer.
47. Southern Capital is an anachronistic designation of Bianliang (modern Kaifeng). Under the Northern Song dynasty, Kaifeng was called the Eastern Capital. Only during the Jin dynasty, which had its own capital at present-day Beijing, did Kaifeng come to be called the Southern Capital.

But I never studied the laws and regulations of Xiao and Cao,[48]
So whenever there's a case, I'll hand it over to the head clerk to solve.
Let none without wine enter the yamen,
I know nothing of the world but a good sleep.
Without entanglements,
There's no need to care about any runners or clerks,
I'll just drink, and then go back home to a feast.[49]
(*Second from Coda*)
I'll drink wine in the manner of Li Taibo,[50]
Be as muddleheaded as Rescriptor-in-Waiting Bao.[51]
Call me "the bottomless jug," and all the world will know who it is.
"There is a path to the blue empyrean, and finally I've arrived."[52]
"If fine wine has no name, I swear I will not return."[53]
Every day I'll be stewed with wine.
Who cares about the three deductions and six interrogations?
Better to hit the wine and crash every banquet.
(*Coda*)
Who cares about Autumn Springs and Bamboo-Leaf Green,
Nine Times Brewed in its lotus-leaf cups?
It makes no difference if it's your Canglang waters or mine,[54]
It's far better than enduring storm and snow, hunger and cold, halfway down the road.
[*Exit.*]

---

48. Xiao and Cao are Xiao He (d. 193 BC) and Cao Can 曹參 (d. 190 BC), ministers of Liu Bang's, the founder of the Han dynasty (206 BC– AD 220). Xiao He was responsible for the draconian law code of the early Han dynasty, and he recommended Cao Can as his successor when he lay dying. Cao Can followed Xiao He's laws to the letter.
49. That is, he'll drink all day on the job and then go home to a banquet.
50. See n. 7.
51. Rescriptor-in-Waiting Bao is Bao Zheng (999–1062), also known as Bao Longtu (Bao Dragon Design) or Judge Bao. Already during his lifetime, Bao Zheng had established a reputation as a stern and incorruptible official. By Yuan times, he had become proverbial as an incorruptible and perspicacious judge who judged the living in his yamen in daytime and judged the dead in the underworld at night. He is the main character in a great number of *zaju*. On numerous occasions he is described as "muddleheaded" by impatient plaintiffs and unjustly imprisoned victims; the term comes to mean something like a feigned obtuseness that conceals great wisdom. The reputation of Judge Bao would continue to grow well into this century. See, especially, acts 2 and 3 of Guan Hanqing's *Rescriptor-in-Waiting Bao Thrice Investigates the Butterfly Dream* (*Bao Daizhi sankan hudie meng* 包待制三勘蝴蝶夢), translated in West and Idema 2010b, 37–76. See also Idema 2010a.
52. This line is usually spoken of examination candidates who get high positions on passing the examinations.
53. This, too, is an ironic turn on a favorite quote of students bound for the examinations, "If I have not made a name for myself, I'll not return."
54. That is, the waters in which one washes the cords of one's official hat, pondering the value of the life of an official.

[ACT 4]

Wait for one scene of OLD MAN, COMIC, *and* FEMALE LEAD. *After* EMPEROR *enters and speaks, and the official summons are completed. You, as* MALE LEAD, *enter holding tablet of office with* YANG JIAN—*Wait until* EXTRA MALE *speaks.*

([SHUANGDIAO MODE:] *Xinshui ling*)

Who wants two rows of underlings in noisy confusion?
They're no match for the ten poles of wine jugs carried before my horse.
This gauzy cap of office and genuine official purple gown
Are no match for my stiff white belt and old threadbare shirt.
I can't speak any highfalutin language,
Let alone be some corrupt official.

Wait until EXTRA MALE *speaks, Speak*: There's dragons and tigers there,[55] I can't go there!

(*Qiaopai'er*)

These words have not been weighed with care,
You know, deep water has to be probed with a pole.
Don't trap a simple man in front of our lord and master,
Zhao Yuan's addiction to wine is a foul mess.

(*Tianshui ling*)

I don't lust for high position—
Don't try and deceive me,
I really can't bear all this hassle.
When you say I've met him, it scares me to death.
. . .[56]
Better I live in a straw hut or a rush shed.

(*Zhegui ling*)

No office for me, I'm afraid of the snarling commotion of the tiger's lair and dragon abyss;
As you know, this dragon has its wind and clouds,
The tiger its mountains and cliffs.
When tigers fight and dragons war, I fear,
They'll stir up some traitorous slander.
Who in court and province is the likes of me:
Beclouded, dumb, dim-witted, and dull.
First mumbling and grumbling, then silent and still.

---

55. The emperor is a dragon, his generals are tigers.
56. According to the prosodic formula of this song, there is a line missing here.

Who'd guess that prime ministers and royal nobles
Have it worse than Li the Fourth and Zhang the Third.[57]

Act out appearing before EMPEROR.

(*Qi dixiong*)
How would I—
Your insignificant subject—
Dare carry out a high official's obeisance?
I only know bitter, stringent, sour, full, and light.[58]
Let everyone else covet luster and smoothness,
Your subject is easily duped, but never corrupt.
(*Meihua jiu*)
Your insignificant minister is the greatest coward of them all,
All I want is to be stewed each day in sweet drunkenness.
Please, my sagely master, consider it well
And do not ask me time and time again.
I can be no clear judge, no investigator of hidden matters,
Nor viscount or earl, duke or baron.
I'm ashamed:
If my office is high, the vexations would be a mess;
If my salary is large, I would grow too covetous.
(*Shou Jiangnan*)
In the city of Bianliang, I will be Director in Chief of the Bureau of Wine,[59]
I'll pour my own, dance alone, carry on pure conversations with myself.
Without worry, without vexation, I'll just dither on.
You'll find no me in places of right and wrong,
These morsels from the Jade Hall are no match for the sweetness of the vat.

Wait until the party of COMIC *and* FEMALE LEAD, *who are in custody, enter, and speak.*

(*Yan'er luo*)
You, venerable elder Jiang, were daring in the wrong cause,[60]
You, righteous woman of Lu, had thought it carefully through[61]
And in league with the magistrate's office, demanded my handprint.
But today you are the ones who have been ensnared in a trap.
(*Desheng ling*)

57. Li the Fourth and Zhang the Third are proverbial representatives of the common people.
58. That is, flavors of wine.
59. During the Song dynasty, the production of wine was a government monopoly.
60. See chap. 2, n. 34.
61. The righteous woman of Lu is a proverbial term for a virtuous woman. According to the *Lienü zhuan* 列女傳 (*Exemplary Women*) by Liu Xiang 劉向, once, when the state of Qi had attacked the state of Lu, a woman from the state of Lu was fleeing with her son and a nephew. When she could no longer manage both children, she left her son behind rather than her nephew. This earned her the reputation of "the righteous woman of Lu."

Isn't it said, "Hoist the carrying pole of breeze and moon"?[62]
It was never more than "a dragonfly trying to shake Mount Tai."[63]
In days past, you were stupid and corrupt,
But now you will lose your head under the knife.
I was unable to bear your clutching fists,
And you tricked me out into the wind and snow.
You're so scared your face is blue,
You, who were so courageous when demanding the writ of divorce.

EMPEROR *pronounces the judgments and sends them off.*

Title: Father-in-law and mother-in-law have venomous hearts,
The official concerned abuses his power to get a rouged beauty.
Name: In the snow the government runner takes great revenge,
Tippler Zhao Yuan Encounters the Prior Emperor.

Newly Cut with Plot Prompts: *Tippler Zhao Yuan Encounters the Prior Emperor*

The End

62. We take this to mean something like "get involved with silly business (here, an affair) and suffer the consequences."
63. That is, "you didn't calculate your own strength," continuing the metaphor of the carrying pole: "You wanted to be together but didn't know what it would cost you."

TIPPLER ZHAO YUAN ENCOUNTERS THE PRIOR EMPEROR, A MING MANUSCRIPT EDITION

DRAMATIS PERSONAE IN ORDER OF APPEARANCE

Role type	*Name and family, institutional, or social role*
EXTRA	OLD MAN, Squire Liu the Second, ZHAO YUAN's father-in-law
OLD WOMAN	MRS. CHEN, ZHAO YUAN's mother
PAINTED FEMALE LEAD	LIU YUEXIAN (Moon Fairy), ZHAO YUAN's wife
EXTRA	INNKEEPER in Eastern Capital
MALE LEAD	ZHAO YUAN, the tippler
COMIC	PREFECT ZANG
ZHANG QIAN	ZHANG QIAN, a clerk
WINE TENDER	WINE SELLER at Strawbridge Inn
EMPEROR	FORMER EMPEROR (Taizu)
CHU ZHAOPU	MEMBER OF EMPEROR'S ENTOURAGE
SHI SHOUXIN	MEMBER OF EMPEROR'S ENTOURAGE
ZHAO GUANGPU	EMPEROR'S BROTHER, prefect of Luoyang
ATTENDANT	ATTENDANT to ZHAO GUANGPU
BUREAU CLERK	BUREAU CLERK in Luoyang prefectural offices

✤ ✤ ✤

A MING COURT MANUSCRIPT EDITION: *TIPPLER ZHAO YUAN ENCOUNTERS THE PRIOR EMPEROR*

GAO WENXIU OF THE YUAN

ACT 1

EXTRA, *costumed as* OLD MAN, *enters with* OLD WOMAN *and* PAINTED FEMALE LEAD.—OLD MAN *speaks*:

My hair like silver threads, my two sideburns of autumn,
Old now, crooked at the waist, I must go with lowered head.
When the moon passes the fifteenth, its radiant light diminishes,
When a person reaches the last years of life, all affairs cease.

I am surnamed Liu, and because I am ranked second among my generation, everyone calls me Squire Liu the Second. I am a man of the Eastern Capital. My wife is named Chen, and we have no other children except for this one young daughter, whose child name is Moon Fairy. She's a perfect ten in everyone's eyes, and she is really a beauty, but I never betrothed her to anyone until I found a live-in son-in-law in Zhao Yuan. But that guy turned out to be worthless—he loves to drink and is always in his cups. He never pays attention to our family livelihood nor does anything to make a living. All he does is drink all day. This daughter of mine really despises him. I've heard that there is a new prefect of Kaifeng named Zang who has taken a liking to my daughter, and she wants with all her heart to marry him. But there's this Zhao Yuan to deal with. Wife! Daughter! How are we going to deal with this?—OLD WOMAN *speaks*:—Old fella, this guy Zhao Yuan does nothing but drink all day. He never pays any attention to making a living. How will this end if it goes on like this?—PAINTED FEMALE *speaks*:—Father, it will not do in the long run for me to stay with that dreg head. If it were up to me, I'd go straight down to those wineshops on the main street, find Zhao Yuan, give him a sound thrashing, and ask him clearly for a writ of divorce. If he gives it, then fine. If not, then we should drag him off to the prefectural yamen and then, no matter what, we'll get the divorce writ. After he divorces me, I can marry that Prefect Zang. What do you think, Father?—OLD MAN *speaks*:—You've hit it on the head, Daughter. Let the three of us go down to the wineshops on the main street and find him!

Exit together.

EXTRA, *costumed as* INNKEEPER, *enters and speaks*: —

Coming back from doing business, I'm still wet with sweat,
When I go to bed I am always thinking of the morning to come.
Why is the head of the house always first to turn gray?
Day and night he's always thinking about a million plans.

I am an innkeeper and live here in the Eastern Capital. I don't have any other way to make a living, so I opened this little wineshop. Still, all those travelers and merchants who come and go from every direction all stop here to have a drink. It's a clear morning, so I'll open the shop, hang out the wine flag, and start a fire to get this wine warmer hot. Let's see who comes along.—MALE LEAD *costumed as* ZHAO YUAN *enters drunk and speaks*:—I am Zhao Yuan, a man of Bianliang, the Eastern Capital. I am a live-in son-in-law of old Squire Liu the Second here, and my wife's child name is Moon Fairy. Normally, I like to have a few, and my wife and her father really detest me and have beaten and cursed me many times to try and get me to divorce her. When I think what it's like to be me in these times—if it weren't for these cups of wine, it would be impossible to get this sorrowful depression out of my heart. Well, there's not much happening today, so I'll go down to the wineshops on the main street and have a few cups of wine to dispel my depression!—*Sings*:

(XIANLÜ MODE: *Dianjiang chun*)

Tilting east, listing west,
Falling backwards, reeling forwards—
I leave my seat.
This wine has made me crazy,
And my drunken soul heads off toward home.[64]

(*Hunjiang long*)

Here I suddenly observe the wine flag:
The wind blowing the green pennant, calling out, "Gaoyang wine!"
Drinking this awful unstrained wine, pure lees,
Is so much better than jade liquor or chalcedony nectar.
What is pleasing are two sleeves filled with wind and the curving moon,
One pot of Spring's Color with its perfume seeping through the crock.
Drinking wine before the flowers,
Flipping my beard under the moon;
Tangled hair, smudged face,
I drum on my belly and croon a tune.
In the thatched hut beside the wine crock I sing, "Tra-la-la."
Three cups in the belly
And it will carry on forever.

Speaks:—Well, here I am already. Innkeeper! Bring out two hundred coins' worth of wine. Warm it up slowly and I'll drink it.—INNKEEPER *speaks*:—Of course. I have wine, lots of it. Please, sir, sit down.—*Acts out pouring wine and speaks*:—Sir, here is two hundred coins' worth of wine.—MALE LEAD *speaks*: Bring it over and I'll drink a few cups and see who comes along.—OLD MAN *enters with* OLD WOMAN *and* PAINTED FEMALE *and speaks*:

When the heart is beset, the road here is long,
When affairs are urgent, go out of the home.

Daughter, I'll ask if Zhao Yuan is drinking wine here in this shop. Let me take a look.—*Acts out greeting.*—OLD MAN *speaks*:—You're something, Zhao Yuan! There's not a single day you do anything productive. You love to drink and are always in your cups. You are worthless, and here you are again in a wineshop drinking.—PAINTED FEMALE *speaks*:—Zhao Yuan! Here you are, not doing what you should be doing. You drink every day, you don't do what you should be doing, you just lust after wine,

64. Or perhaps "to my home where the wine flag hangs."

so greedy for the cup. When will this end? Boy, do you exasperate me!—MALE LEAD *sings*:

(*You hulu*)

You say I "lust after wine and am greedy for the cup" and cause you grief.

OLD MAN *speaks*:—You are a worthless good-for-nothing. I'll smack this wino bastard!—MALE LEAD *sings*:

You really are a rustic boor.

OLD WOMAN *speaks*:—Old man! Smack this bastard!—OLD MAN *speaks*:—I know, Wife. What do I have to fear if I hit him?—MALE LEAD *sings*:

It's really clear why your nickname is "a den of wolves."

PAINTED FEMALE *speaks*: You hick bastard! You sleep drunk every day, you lie down drunk every day, and you freeze me out every day at home. What good comes of drinking? MALE LEAD *sings*:

Don't you see: before the peach blossom rises to the cheeks,

You have already scattered their leaves with your "shouting before the cup."[65]

PAINTED FEMALE *speaks*:—Father! What's there to say to a thing like this? What reason can we speak? Ivory won't grow out of the mouth of a dog![66] Go on up and hit this wine-loving son-of-a-bitch who won't do anything to make a living!—OLD MAN *speaks*:—You're right, Daughter! I'll beat this bastard.—*Acts out hitting him.*—MALE LEAD *sings*:

Snicker-snack, they've grabbed me by the hair.

PAINTED FEMALE *speaks*:—Father, hit him with your fists, kick him with your feet! Turn him into a rotten sheep's head.—OLD MAN *speaks*:—I'll kick this worthless animal.—MALE LEAD *sings*:

He keeps on kicking me with his feet.

OLD MAN *speaks*:—I'll box the ears of this son-of-a-bitch!—MALE LEAD *sings*:

He keeps boxing my ears.

PAINTED FEMALE *speaks*: Didn't I make that "corpse skin" you're wearing? I'll rip yours to shreds.—MALE LEAD *sings*:

Fiercely and ferociously she rips my clothes to shreds.

OLD WOMAN *speaks*:—Every day, you do nothing about making a living. All you do is drink—when is it going to end?—MALE LEAD *speaks*:—What's it to you if I drink?—PAINTED FEMALE *speaks*:—Oh, that's good. You still want to argue! Every day, you get drunk, sober up, get drunk again, fall down and sleep in the alleyway. Well this time I'm going to make sure that you're taken care of. Father, I can't stand him!—MALE LEAD *sings:*

---

65. *Zunqian chang* 尊前唱: the word *chang* can mean both "to perform at a banquet" and "to create a ruckus"; here he is making a sarcastic statement.

66. A comment on his sarcastic statement.

(*Tianxia le*)
You've abandoned it all now, and have made a real scene this time,
What kind of dirty tricks do you have now for beating and cursing your son?
I've never stirred up any trouble by loafing around and hanging out.

PAINTED FEMALE *speaks*:—You're a stray arrow shot, an unexpected spear stabbed, a needle that pricks to destroy it all! You stir up trouble and I'll report you to the officials who, I dare say, will strip off your skin, and break every bone in your feet. All you do is lust after wine and covet the cup—you don't look after me enough to keep me alive. Hand over the writ of divorce!—MALE LEAD *sings*:

You keep after me for a handprint,[67]
Try every means to get a writ of confession;[68]

PAINTED FEMALE *speaks*:—You drunken short-lived fool, skipping all the way to your death. If you have any money, you drink. I can't even squeeze any rouge or powder out of you when I want to put on makeup. You are a real man, but you don't attempt to make a living, you just drink. What do I want you for? Why would I want to be with you?—MALE LEAD *sings*:

You bully this poor hungry and cold farm boy to death!

OLD MAN *speaks*:—Zhao Yuan, I told you not to drink. Why have you been drinking the last couple of days and staying away from home?—MALE LEAD *speaks*:—Well, I got a few "gifts"[69] the last couple of days, so I've been drinking. No problem.—PAINTED FEMALE *speaks*:—Liar! What gifts? A dog invited you to drink! Father, don't listen to him.—MALE LEAD *speaks*:—Father! Listen to me explain.—*Sings*:

(*Nezha ling*)
Day before yesterday it was blind Wang the Third, raising the roof beam on his new house.

OLD MAN *speaks*: Where did you drink yesterday?—MALE LEAD *sings*:

Yesterday it was the rustic Li Hu sacrificing a goat.

OLD MAN *speaks*: You're drunk again today. Where did this bout of drinking come from?—MALE LEAD *sings*:

Today it was the lush Liu Hong, celebrating his birthday.

PAINTED FEMALE *speaks*:—That whole group of friends of yours are a pack of good-for-nothing lazy dog slicks![70]—OLD MAN *speaks*:—You jerk! All you do every day is drink. You don't pay attention to making a living at all—what's to be done?—MALE LEAD *sings*: —

Well I didn't want to go out—
It was *they* who visited *me*,
They fetched *me* and dragged me away.

67. See n. 26.

68. See n. 27.

69. That is, bribes.

70. Literally, "dog-oil things," an idiom for people who "can eat a lot but are lazy."

PAINTED FEMALE *speaks*:—You reputation-ruining, family-destroying, hick son-of-a-bitch. All you do all day is covet the cup and lust after wine, let your wife freeze and your mother go hungry. Is there anything good about drinking?—MALE LEAD *speaks*:—Oh, wine has its good points.—PAINTED FEMALE *speaks*:—This rice-wine-soup-for-brains is defending himself? What good points? Tell me! Spit them out!—MALE LEAD *sings*: —

(*Que ta zhi*)

Only after you have wine can you gather together your relatives,
Only after you have wine can you meet friends wise and good.

PAINTED FEMALE *speaks*:—Pshaw! You have absolutely no shame. Every day you pal around with these fox buddies, this pack of dogs—are any of them any good? And how do they make drinking any better?—MALE LEAD *sings*:

Haven't you heard the old saw and proverb:
"Wine can dispel all sorrows in the heart"?

OLD WOMAN *speaks*:—After you're drunk, you'll stir up trouble and end up dragging our whole family into it.—MALE LEAD *sings*:

After I have wine, my tolerance is as capacious as the seas,
But when I have none, my stomach burns and my guts writhe.

PAINTED FEMALE *speaks*:—You dreg-drunk donkey, dreg-drunk beast, dreg-drunk set of dog bones—after a while you'll simply die dreg drunk. Other people drink, but at the right time. Anytime is good for you. Father! Don't let him off! Make him stop the wine!—OLD MAN *speaks*:—You are right, child. Zhao Yuan, come here. You better stop drinking today for my sake. If you don't give up the wine, I'll beat you to death with a hundred yellow-mulberry clubs.—MALE LEAD *speaks*:—You want me to cut out wine? I'll do any kind of occupation you want, but I just can't give up this wine.—PAINTED FEMALE *speaks*:—Pshaw! So your addiction is this bad.—OLD MAN *speaks*:—How can you work if you aren't willing to give up wine?—MALE LEAD *speaks*:—I'll do any kind of work there is, but I cannot give up wine.—*Sings*:

(*Jisheng cao*)

I could be a clerk,
Become a peddler,
Use a buffalo to grow beans and furrow the fields,
Smear on lime, daub on clay, and learn to act and sing,
Or shave my head, cut my hair, and become a monk.

PAINTED FEMALE *speaks*:—I am not going to play the drunken liar with you. Give up the wine!—MALE LEAD *sings*:

But make me give up the fragrance from the vat that melts away sorrow and dispels depression—

PAINTED FEMALE *speaks*:—Give it up! Give up the wine!—MALE LEAD *speaks*:—I can't! I can't!—*Sings*:

I'd far rather stretch out my neck in the bustling marketplace, that execution ground.

PAINTED FEMALE *speaks*:—Give it up for one year for me!—MALE LEAD *speaks*:—I can't give it up even for a year. There's something good about drinking wine in every season of a year.—OLD MAN *speaks*:—Why can't you give it up in these four seasons? Tell me.—MALE LEAD *speaks*:—I say I can't give it up in any season.—OLD MAN *speaks*:—What about giving it up during the spring sights?—MALE LEAD *speaks*: To give it up in spring . . .

(*Zui zhong tian*)

In spring's warmth, flowers' fragrances are all set free.

OLD MAN *speaks*:—What about summer?—MALE LEAD *speaks*: To give it up in summer . . .

In summer's heat, caltrop and lotus are redolent.

OLD MAN *speaks*:—Giving it up in autumn?—MALE LEAD *speaks*: To give it up in autumn . . .

At the golden well, the *wutong* tree drops leaves of yellow.

OLD MAN *speaks*:—Giving it up in winter?—MALE LEAD *speaks*: To give it up in winter . . .

How could we ward off those auspicious snows that flurry about our heads?

Speaks:—Heaven has unfathomable winds and rains[71] and men have fortune or calamity at each of those times.—*Sings*:

Alive, dead—a man's life lies in the single moment:
To make me give up the golden-rippled green brew—
Wouldn't that mean passing uselessly from one season to another?

PAINTED FEMALE *speaks*:—So many flowery words and clever phrases. Looks to me like you just love wine. You really are a dreg-drunk bastard who's not long for this world. Father, since he isn't willing to give it up, don't let him stay in the city. Tell him to go back to our place in the village to live. There's surely no wine to drink there.—OLD MAN *speaks*:—You're right, child. Zhao Yuan, sooner or later your drinking wine will implicate me somehow. Don't stay in the city, but go with me today back to our place in the village to live. You'll have to give up drinking.—PAINTED FEMALE *speaks*:—If you don't give up wine, I won't give you anything to eat. You'll starve until you're as flat as a pancake. Go back to the house!—MALE LEAD *speaks*:—You want to make me live in the village because there's no wine there. That would make it even harder to give it up.—OLD MAN *speaks*:—Why can't you give it up?—MALE LEAD *sings*:

(*Jinzhan'er*)

You want me to keep company with Esquire Sprout in a village
And nourish this skin sack in some hamlet quarter,

71. Vicissitudes, unplanned disturbances.

Where each day, blown by winds, scorched by the sun, I will furrow the fields,
And suffer wind and frost along with Sha the Third and Zhao the Fourth?
How could I spend the hundred years allotted to me besotted with wine,
Or enjoy those thirty-six thousand drunken days?

Speaks: Father! There are two things I can't give up in wine.—OLD MAN *speaks*:—What two?—MALE LEAD *sings*:

The saying goes, "Wildflowers[72] pop up out of the ground,"
And what I fear, "The perfume of village brew seeps through the crock."

PAINTED FEMALE *speaks*:—Father. This short-lived, cup-coveting wine-loving, never-working beggar of a bastard—I can't be his wife. But even so, he isn't willing to divorce me. Let's drag him off to see the prefect and let the officials put an end to it. I'll give all my effort there to make my case, and then I can be married off to someone else.—OLD MAN *speaks*:—You're right, child. I'll go off to the yamen with you.

Act out dragging MALE LEAD *and exit together.*

COMIC *costumed as* PREFECT ZANG *enters leading* ZHANG QIAN *and speaks*: —

The magistrate is as clear as water,
The yamen clerks as white as flour;
Mix up a batch of flour and water
And all you get is one messy lump.

I am the prefect here, named Zang. Prefect Zang,[73] that's me. There's a woman here named Moon Fairy. I've wanted to take her as a wife, and she has a mind to marry me. But, alas, she has a husband. I'll find some minor infraction sometime and do his life in, so I can take that woman to wife. Then all of my life's desires will be fulfilled. I'll ascend the bench today and see who brings along an indictment.

OLD MAN, OLD WOMAN, *and* PAINTED FEMALE *enter leading* MALE LEAD.—OLD MAN *speaks*:—Injustice! Injustice!—COMIC *asks*:—Who is yelling "Injustice" outside? Bring them in.—ZHANG QIAN *speaks*:—Understood.—*Acts out summoning them in.*—[ZHANG QIAN *speaks*:] Face the judge.—*All act out kneeling.*—COMIC *speaks*:—You, old fellow. How have you been wronged? Speak.—OLD MAN *speaks*:—Have pity, Great One. This live-in son-in-law of mine, Zhao Yuan, pays no attention to making a livelihood, freezes out his wife and starves her to death; all he does is drink all day. My daughter really requests a writ of divorce from him.—COMIC *speaks*:—Please rise, old man. I have figured it out today. The reason you want a writ of divorce is that she has to divorce to be given to someone else.[74]—OLD MAN *speaks*:—Great One, please have pity and act as my advocate!—COMIC *speaks*:—Hey, wait a

72. See n. 25.

73. The surname Zang is a homophone for the term *zang* 臟 (dirty), here meaning "corrupt"; hence, "I am named Zang, the corrupt prefect—that's me!" It is also a homophone for *zang* 贓 (booty, swag, stolen goods).

74. That is, someone besides Prefect Zang.

minute! It has to be this way. . . . Let's make him go off to deliver some documents to the Western Capital, the prefecture of Henan.[75] Higher authorities have a clearly written rule: miss the deadline for being there by one day, and it's forty strokes of the club; two days, eighty strokes; three days, beheading. This guy is a sot, if I send him he won't come out alive. Once I get rid of this guy, wouldn't it be great if I married her? Zhang Qian, ask all of the clerks in the Six Bureaus: who should carry the documents off to the Western Capital?—ZHANG QIAN *speaks*:—I've asked, sire, and it should be Zhao Yuan from here.—COMIC *speaks*:—Well, if it is like this . . . Zhao Yuan, come forward. I'm having trouble deciding about the divorce with your wife. Right now, you should deliver these documents to the Western Capital at Henan prefecture. Higher authorities have a clearly written rule: miss the deadline for being there by one day, and it's forty strokes of the club; two days, eighty strokes; three days, beheading. You leave today.—MALE LEAD *speaks*:—Someone else should go, not me.—COMIC *speaks*:—No, it has to be you.—PAINTED FEMALE *speaks*:—Since you are going to deliver these documents, Zhao Yuan, you have to give me a writ of divorce! Whether you live or die on this trip is no concern to me, once you're out of my eyesight, then it's all over.—MALE LEAD *while acting out kneeling—sings*:

(*You simen*)
They want me to hand over this fine flower to some rich gent—
Husband and wife will be torn apart.
There is no turning back from the documents I have before me.
I see that I will perish,
And she will mate up with a simurgh or phoenix.

COMIC *speaks*:—Don't miss the deadline. Get on with taking the documents. If you want to write out a writ of divorce, then give it to her now, don't beg for another beating. MALE LEAD *sings*:

(*Liuye'er*)
I really have to take these to higher authorities.
And if I have to take this trip, snow will pile on top of frost.[76]
It scares me so much that far off and floating, my sentient soul is swept away.
Where can I submit my own complaint?
If I write out [the divorce writ] I can avoid disaster and misfortune,
If I don't write it out then what harm will come?

Speaks: Alright! Enough! I'll write it out for you.—*Sings*:

(*Shanghua shi*)
All because of one extraordinary face, I am forced to leave my home—
That two-faced official knows how to work a plot.

---

75. Modern Luoyang.

76. See n. 27.

All because those three are evil at heart.
For the four years or so we've been husband and wife,
They've sued in court five times ten.

PAINTED FEMALE *speaks*: Give me a writ of divorce. If you are run over by a cart, trampled by a horse, or opened up and skinned by some badman—it will have nothing to do with me. I'll just be free of worry to marry another.—MALE LEAD *sings*:

(*Reprise*)
Inside the six dimensions,[77] I've suffered your rottenness,
Seven generations of my ancestors you have reviled at will,
And from all eight directions accused me wildly, discussed me at length,
We've been man and wife—consider it well, nine long times:
Don't hope that I'll die by the time you count ten.

(*Coda*)
A mind to keep lovers, ten times strong,
Fears no neighbor's gossip after nine,[78]
In all eight directions, you will walk the streets and cruise the alleys.
Don't go overboard cursing seven generations of mothers,
Because your six relations are trembling with fright when you are in sight.
Think, with head propped on hands, in the fifth watch of the night,
How easily we woke our four neighbors, who called the local elder.
I want to lay out three cups by the side of the road—
In less than two weeks my life will be lost.
But my one spirit will never leave the brewery!

Exits.

COMIC *speaks*:—I've sent Zhao Yuan on his way, and I see him now as a dead man. Big Sister, let's select an auspicious day and a good hour, and make the engagement visits. Don't marry anyone else. Zhang Qian, bring my horse, I'm going back to my private residence for a while.

Exits.

OLD MAN *speaks*:—Child. You've gotten your writ of divorce from Zhao Yuan. And when he leaves this time, it sure looks like he's a goner. You should marry that prefect. Child, do you have any money with you?—PAINTED FEMALE *speaks*:—Why do you want it?—OLD MAN *speaks*:—I'm going to buy two wicker baskets, and go off to the main gates and scoop up some horseshit with the baskets.[79]

Exits with OLD WOMAN *and* PAINTED FEMALE.

77. See n. 32.
78. See n. 31.
79. For fuel, but used here as a comic reference.

ACT 2

WINE TENDER *enters and speaks*: —

At the head of the crooked staff hangs a grass bundle,
In the shade of the poplar a pipa is played;
Lords of the wine cup—don't pass by for nothing—
This is no ordinary wine-seller's place.

I am a wine seller and have opened up a wineshop here at Strawbridge inn outside of the Bian Capital walls. It's dead winter and swirling and whirling a huge snowstorm falls. It's so cold. I'm opening up the wineshop in the early morning. I have raised up the wine-flag pole, and heated up the wine warmer until it's nice and hot. Let's see who comes to have a drink.—EMPEROR *leads on* CHU ZHAOPU *and* SHI SHOUXIN, *all dressed as young scholars, and speaks*:

The founding enterprise rose with mighty swells, I came up with extraordinary plans,
With books on warfare and military strategies I brought an end to spear and lance;
In times of leisure if I had had no good officials to help,
How could I have so quickly added four hundred districts?

I am the August Thearch, Grand Progenitor of the Song. Since I have ascended the throne, the four seas have been peaceful and the eight directions have lain quiet. Today I have brought my private attendants Chu Zhaopu and Shi Shouxin with me—all dressed as students—to travel incognito out beyond the city walls. I dispatched Zhao Guangpu to be Defender of the Capital. In the dead winter falls a snowstorm, swirling and whirling. You two walk slowly along with me.—CHU *speaks*:—My Lord, the snow is getting worse, so for the moment let's go into that wineshop. On one hand, we can temporarily escape this wind and snow, on the other, we can drink a few cups of this village brew. How about it?—EMPEROR *speaks*: Since it is getting worse, let's go on in for a bit to escape this storm.—*Act out going into the shop and sitting down.*—CHU *speaks*:—Wine tender! Prepare two hundred coins' worth of wine.—WINE TENDER *speaks*:—Understood. Please, scholars, sit down and I will prepare the wine.—*Acts out preparing wine, presenting it, then speaks*: Gentlemen, here is your two hundred coins' worth of wine. Please enjoy it.—SHI *speaks*:—Bring the wine here. Student Zhao, please drink this cup to the full.—EMPEROR *speaks*:—Please, you two drink!—CHU *speaks*:—Student Zhao, please drink to the full.—EMPEROR *acts out drinking and speaks*:—Please, you two, sit down and drink.—SHI *speaks*:—The two of us will drink too.—EMPEROR *speaks*:—Let us three drink at leisure and see who comes along.—MALE LEAD *enters leaning into the wind and speaks*:—I am Zhao Yuan. Who could have ever expected the head of the local office, Prefect Zang, would steal away my wife for his own, and then make me deliver documents to the capital? Miss the deadline for being there by one day, and it's forty strokes of the club; two days, eighty strokes; three days, beheading. Unawares, I have already gone half a month over the deadline on my journey—I'm as good as dead. It's dead winter and swirling and whirling the "auspicious omens for the state"[80] are falling. What a storm!—*Sings*:

(NANLÜ MODE *Yizhi hua*)

Battling the wind, I face into the willow floss,
Braving the snow, I brush the pear blossoms away.
Snow mantles a thousand trees until they grow old with age,
Wind trims them until ten thousand branches wither.
Such a journey as this of wind and snow—
Snow veils the road to heaven's edge.
The wind is strong,
The snow heavy—
Just like it was sprinkled by a spade or tossed by a winnowing basket,
Just like combed cotton or plucked floss.

(*Liangzhou*)

It's just like Han Yu, who couldn't get his steed to go forward through Indigo Pass,[81]
Or Meng Haoran, who refused to ride his donkey across the Baling Bridge.[82]
I'm so frozen that I shiver and shake and can't control hands or feet.
Even more, how can I bear that the heavens are cold, the days short,
The boundless fields are desolate and empty,
Passes and mountains, cold and lonely,
Wind and snow mix and mingle?
My whole body wrapped only in an unpadded gown
That flaps in the eastern wind, randomly flecked with true pearls.
I raise my head just like a poisonous snake coming out of its hole,
Hunch my shoulders just like an old rat soaked with water,
Crook my back just like a human shrimp or maggot.
When will I get to the imperial capital?
Scraping the sky, scraping the earth, a wild wind beats,
Who has suffered such misery as this?
I see three golden-saddled [horses] tied to an aged mulberry tree—
Must be some relatives of the emperor's or scions of the state.

Speaks: I've come to a wineshop, and there are three horses at the door. Must be someone inside. I'll go on in and get out of the storm for a spell. *Acts out entering the wineshop*.—EMPEROR *speaks*:—You two have another cup!—CHU *speaks*:—We will

80. Snowflakes signaling good harvests for the next year.
81. See n. 34.
82. See n. 35.

drink another.—MALE LEAD *speaks*:—Let me get closer to the stove and face the fire.—WINE TENDER *speaks*:—Sir traveler, do you want some wine?—MALE LEAD *speaks*:—Prepare two hundred coins' worth.—WINE TENDER *speaks*:—Sir, here is your wine.—MALE LEAD *speaks*:—Ah, wine! I haven't seen you for days on end. Who knew that we would meet here again? Oh, how wonderful!—*Sings*:

(*Muyang guan*)
After I see the wine, I hurry to bow in obeisance,
After I drink the wine, I pay my respects again,
Reunited today with my old buddy wine.
O, wine, I would have said we'd never meet again,
Never imagined we'd be together at one place and time.
Because of wine, I suffered with storm and snow,
Because of wine, I trod this long road.
But now this wine-soaked head meets you again—
Papa Wine, have you been well?

MALE LEAD *acts out pouring wine and speaks*:—Let me first sprinkle some wine here in sacrifice: My first wish is that Our August Highness enjoy ten thousand years! My second, that our ministers and high officials are safe and healthy! My third, that the winds are fair and the rains timely, so that all the black-haired people in the empire work happily at their jobs.—EMPEROR *speaks*:—Are there such worthy people out there? He looks rustic and unkempt, but his thoughts are broadly encompassing. This person has the way of the sages and worthies.—MALE LEAD *acts out greeting the three*:—Please receive this bow, honorable students. Let me offer a toast to you three.—MALE LEAD *acts out making a toast*:—EMPEROR *speaks*:—Oh, no we dare not. You, Brother, please drink first.—MALE LEAD *speaks*:—Please, honorable students, drink to the full!—MALE LEAD *acts out drinking*.—MALE LEAD *speaks*:—Please, you two students, please drink a cup.—CHU *speaks*:—Please, sir, you drink.—MALE LEAD *speaks*:—Please, drink your cups to the full, my two students.—THE TWO *act out drinking*.—EMPEROR *speaks*:—Brother, please drink a full cup. What virtue do we have to move you to treat us so well, Brother? Please drink this cup of wine.—MALE LEAD *sings*:

(*Gewei*)
I'm just a good-for-nothing who trails donkeys and leads horses,
You must be grandees who discuss the past and discourse on texts.
Man has never been in charge of heaven's fate—
Even though I'm a stupid and vulgar lout
Who cannot hold forth on the rites of former kings,

EMPEROR *speaks*:—A gentleman like you should drink this cup!

I can chug it, gurgling and gulping, right down my throat.

EMPEROR *speaks*:—Brother! Enjoy your wine, we three have had enough and have to go back first.—*They act out standing up*.—WINE TENDER *speaks*:—You three students have no sense of how to act. You drank my wine but gave me no money! Where are you going?—EMPEROR *speaks*:—I don't have any money with me right now. I'll pay you back another day.—WINE TENDER *speaks*:—You haven't paid after you drank. I'm not going to let you go. Beat these three imbeciles!—*Act out beating them.*—MALE LEAD *acts out listening*:—This is strange!—*Sings*: —

(*Gan huang'en*)

I was just about to drink my fragrant ale,
But who is this, shouting and yelling, quarreling and screaming?

EMPEROR *speaks*:—None of us brought any money. We'll pay you some other day.—WINE TENDER *acts out grabbing and stopping* EMPEROR *and speaks*:—Give me my money! You think I'm going to let you off lightly?—MALE LEAD *sings*:

He keeps on shoving him, pushing him around,
Grabbing, dragging, seizing, shaking.
But you must know that once Li Taibo pledged his sword for a drink,
And pawned his zither to pay up his tab.[83]

WINE TENDER *acts out grabbing and stopping him again and speaks*: What kind of act are you three putting on so you don't have to pay me?—MALE LEAD *sings*:

(*Caicha ge*)

One pulls at his clothes,
The other is drunk as mud.
You can't say here, "Flowers' shadows cover the body, ask for help getting up"![84]
Have no fear, you three learned men—
I'll put out my own coppers to pay for what you owe.

Speaks: Wine tender, why are you holding these three back?—WINE TENDER *speaks*:—They drank two hundred coins' worth of wine, but they aren't willing to pay.—MALE LEAD *speaks*:—Let the three of them go. They are the "white clothed" ministers of our state.[85] I'll pay their wine tab to you. Will that be fine?—WINE TENDER *speaks*:—Since you are going to pay their tab . . . well, fine. I'll let them go.—MALE LEAD *acts out taking out money and paying, speaks*:—Here's two hundred cash.—WINE TENDER *acts out taking it.*—MALE LEAD *speaks*:—Students, let's drink a cup together!—EMPEROR *speaks*:—May we ask your honorable name? And where you're from? What important affair brought you here?—MALE LEAD *acts out being sad and speaks*:—I am named Zhao; Zhao Yuan.—*Acts out crying.*—EMPEROR *speaks*:—Why are you so sad right now? There has to be some hidden meaning to it. Spell it out slowly and I will listen.—MALE LEAD *speaks*:—You can't possibly know. Listen to me slowly explain it. I am from the Eastern Capital, and I'm named Zhao Yuan, a live-in son-in-law to Squire Liu the Second there. I have a wife, Moon Fairy Liu, who is really attractive, but she's completely unworthy. She has reviled and cursed

---

83. See n. 36.
84. See n. 37.
85. Students destined for greatness.

me a thousand ways, and she despises me in ten thousand ways. And I have really evil and poisonous parents-in-law who are always beating and cursing me. One day the parents-in-law and my wife, Moon Fairy, dragged me to Prefect Zang's yamen, where they pressured me for a writ of divorce. I never expected that that corrupt official wanted to marry my wife, and would intentionally play around with my life, deputing me to the Western Capital to deliver some documents. Miss the deadline for being there by one day, and it's forty strokes of the club; two days, eighty strokes; three days, beheading. Unawares, I have already gone half a month over the deadline on my journey—I'm as good as dead. This is why I was crying. I never thought I'd meet up with the three of you in this wineshop.—EMPEROR *speaks*:—Too bad. I knew there was hidden meaning in all of this. Zhao Yuan—I am surnamed Zhao and you are surnamed Zhao. I want to become sworn brothers. What do you think?—MALE LEAD *speaks*:—I come somewhere between an ass and a horse, how dare I become a sworn brother of a student?—EMPEROR *speaks*:—How did your parents-in-law harm you? How did the prefect of the Eastern Capital take your wife? Explain it to me slowly.—MALE LEAD *sings*:

(*Hong shaoyao*)

My mother- and father-in-law have venomous hearts—

Bad enough—but the prefect in high place screwed up his duties.

EMPEROR *speaks*:—How is your wife so unworthy?

Indeed, this beauty dragged her husband in,

And he wanted to be like fish in water.

The finest put-on appearances

Hide evil schemes.

Blind to these facts,

They demanded a writ of divorce.

EMPEROR *speaks*:—How did that prefect of the Eastern Capital dare appropriate your wife? MALE LEAD *sings*:

He relied on the power of his office to break apart husband and wife.

Really they are horses and oxen in human dress!

EMPEROR *speaks*:—Wouldn't it have been better to go to the great yamen and report him? What's the use of weeping and crying behind their backs?—MALE LEAD *sings*:

(*Pusa Liangzhou*)

Who can I complain to

About these wrongs I harbor or this injustice I carry?

I am indeed all alone in the world—

EMPEROR *speaks*:—It's no use crying like this!

And so rage fills my breast and tears rain down like pearls.

EMPEROR *speaks*:—Zhao Yuan, what do you think about my saving your life?—MALE LEAD *speaks*:—How are you going to do that, Brother?—EMPEROR *speaks*:—Relax. I'm something of a friend to Capital Minister Zhao Guangpu. I want to write a letter for you to take, but I don't have any paper. Chu Zhaopu, pull out that frost-tipped brush from your sleeves, and bare Zhao Yuan's shoulder. Shi Shouxin, you hold him still, and I'll write two lines on the back of his shoulder and put a seal on it. When Minister Zhao sees this, you'll definitely not die!—CHU *and* SHI *act out supporting* MALE LEAD.—MALE LEAD *sings*:

One raises the frost-tipped brush,
One bares my shoulder,
And one holds me up.
They say these two lines of writing are my passport to heaven.

CHU *speaks*:—If you show these two lines of writing to Minister Zhao when you get to the capital, you will surely not die.—MALE LEAD *sings*:

Well, if they are to see me safely back home,
This good deed must be done.
I never thought that two full strings of a hundred cash could buy a man's life.
It's far better than a paper document from heaven.

Speaks:—Now that I have your letter, Brother, if I see Zhao Guangpu when I go to the capital, then he'll spare my life when he sees your seal. I had better get going.—EMPEROR *speaks*:—Be careful on the way. You most certainly will not die when he sees the seal on your shoulder.—MALE LEAD *speaks*:—Enough, enough!—*Sings*:

(*Coda*)
Who could expect that this body, destined to die a violent death, would receive such favor and concern?
Pointing afar out among the clouds: a goose delivering a letter.
My two feet
Will never stop.
This anxious sorrow,
This bitter fear,
This vexatious worry,
These constant thoughts—
How can I raise my voice?
I bear too much injustice!
Zhao Guangpu, you hold the axis of power right in the palm of your hand—
How can you know the undeserved misery of this army runner who endures wind and snow?

Exits.

EMPEROR *speaks*:—Zhao Yuan is gone. Who would have thought that such a worthy man as this was out there? When he gets to the Western Capital and sees Zhao Guangpu, after seeing Our seal of authority, Guangpu will certainly pardon this man and appoint him right away as the prefect of the Eastern Capital, a post to which he will speed by horse. If We should go the Western Capital[86] I will seize Zhao Yuan's enemies to repay his injustice. There's nothing to stop me. Let's go on our way, incognito.

86. Clearly, the Eastern Capital is meant here.

Inside this wineshop I inquired about what was wrong,
And in this chance meeting, he told me his life's story.
Zhao Yuan has now gone to seek Guangpu
And soon will rise to prefect to sit in judgment in the Eastern Capital.

Exit together.

WINE TENDER *speaks*:—The customers are all gone, it's getting dark, and I'm going to close up shop and go off to my own home.

Exits.

ACT 3

ZHAO GUANGPU *leads* ATTENDANT *and enters, then speaks*:

Two perfectly even flowers hold aloft the sun and moon,
One pair of robe's sleeves arrange the cosmos.
Don't say that the King governs all of the empire—
Half comes from the Son of Heaven, half from his officials.

I am Zhao Guangpu, known as Zeping. I aided our ruler and have been given the rank of prime minister and been enfeoffed as well as grand preceptor and duke of the princedom of Han. I am a meritorious official who helped with the founding of the state. The Sage Ruler once visited my residence at midnight and stood in the wind and snow. I was trembling in fear and went out to greet him, set up a thick comforter on the ground, lit some charcoal, and roasted some meat. My wife passed the wine around, and His Highness called her Sister, and then we set our plans for conquering the Jiangnan area.[87] Each time I decide on some important affair, I open up a piece of writing—the *Analects*. Now it is said of me that "I order the empire with half of the *Analects*." Lei Dexiang once slandered me and His Highness replied, "*Ding*s and *dang*s still have ears![88] Haven't you heard that Zhao Pu is my official of the state?" Now the ruler has gone off on a trip, incognito, with Chu Zhaopu and Shi Shouxin and has left me in charge of defending the capital. Now all of the officials in the Eastern Capital bring all of the documents for clearing here to the Superior Capital. Miss the deadline for being here by one day, and it's forty strokes of the club; two days, eighty strokes; three days, beheading. Someone unknown to me has missed the deadline by half a month, and so should be beheaded. Attendant, keep watch at the gate

87. This story is related at the beginning of Zhao Pu's biography in *The History of the Song* (*Songshi* 宋史). They gathered with the Prince of Jin, later to become the second emperor of the Song, and discussed attacking and taking Taiyuan, the capital of the Northern Han regime in Shanxi. See Tuotuo et al. 1977, 25:8932. Zhao Pu suggested, however, first to conquer the southern part of the empire and wait with an attack on Taiyuan until it would be completely isolated.

88. A *ding* 鼎 is large tripod, a *dang* 鐺, a small cooking pot. The "ears" are their handles.

and when someone comes, report to me.—ATTENDANT *speaks*:—Understood.—MALE LEAD *enters and speaks*:—I am Zhao Yuan. I've missed the deadline, so I'd better hustle along. What a snowstorm!—*Sings*:

(ZHONGLÜ MODE *Fendie'er*)

Six-pointed flowers fly,
At blue heaven's rim, frozen clouds linger.
Hugging my shoulders, I tuck my head low.
My wine soul has disappeared,
I've just sobered up from the wine
And my limbs have no strength.
Soon my life will be buried in the mud of the Yellow Springs.
How can I avoid this particular disaster?

(*Zui chunfeng*)

They've done me in: Bamboo Leaf and Spring in the Vat,
This wife I loved: a heart like a flowery twig in the wind.
Because I loved the fragrant brew we are forever separated.
And now I am filled with regret, regret, regret.
It was also predestined fate from former lives,
Something we alone created, for which we alone suffer—
Blame heaven, blame earth!

Speaks:—Here I am at the minister's gate. I have come to the formal gate.[89]—*Acts out seeing* ATTENDANT *and shaking*.—MALE LEAD *speaks*:—Oh, it scares me to death.—*Sings*:

(*Ying xianke*)

His staff are all lined up, they are like wolves and tigers,
His clerks are all in ranks, like the pinions of geese.
So death comes in the dark, unbeknownst to man,
I know no tricks to suddenly disappear
And I can't grow wings to fly away.
Unstoppable, my tears seem pushed out by a hoe,
This is a senseless punishment that I've brought on myself.[90]

MALE LEAD *speaks*:—Brother attendant, please report that the documents sent from the Eastern Capital for review are here.—ATTENDANT *speaks*:—Well, you're finally here; you must be looking to die! Wait here at the door, I'll go and report.—*Acts out reporting*.—Sire, I am informing you that the documents sent for review from the Eastern Capital have arrived.—ZHAO PU *speaks*:—This guy has a lot of gall! Tell him

89. The second gate upon entering a large residence or a government compound.

90. That is, *wutou zui* 無頭罪, which is a punishment or sentence for a crime that stems from a *wutou gong'an* 無頭公安, a case with no leads to follow—hence, senseless, with no rationale, or arbitrary. It also has a second meaning, however, of "a sentence that will result in being without a head."

to come in.—ATTENDANT *speaks*:—Understood. He's called you in.—MALE LEAD *acts out greeting*.—GUANGPU *speaks*:—You! Where are you from, courier?—MALE LEAD *speaks*:—Sire. I was sent from the Eastern Capital.—GUANGPU *speaks*:—You bureau clerk, how far behind schedule is this guy? How shall he be punished?—BUREAU CLERK *speaks*:—Late by one day, and it's forty strokes of the club; two days, eighty strokes; three days, beheading. This guy is half a month late.—GUANGPU *speaks*:—Well, in this case, gather up the documents. Attendants, take this guy out and behead him.—ATTENDANT *speaks*:—Understood!—*Acts out grabbing* MALE LEAD.—MALE LEAD *speaks*:—Father sire, I have a letter from your older brother. I've brought it with me.—GUANGPU *speaks*:—What have you brought? Servants, bring him back.—MALE LEAD *speaks*:—Listen to me explain.—*Sings*:

(*Shang xiaolou*)

I have a letter from your elder brother.
At the foot of these steps, allow this humble person to explain in detail—
Quickly, so quickly, speedily, so speedily,
Correct, so correct, exact, so exact,
I will enumerate all the true facts—

GUANGPU *speaks*:—Speak! I will listen. If you get it right, then everything is over and done; get it wrong, you'll not be let off lightly.—MALE LEAD *sings*:

If I make even the slightest error in my explanation,
I'd be happy to let my life return to the world of the springs.

GUANGPU *speaks*:—Where did you see my brother? How many people were with him? Explain and I will listen.—MALE LEAD *speaks*:—I met them in a wineshop.—*Sings*:

(*Reprise*)

It was a party of three,
Who insisted on offering me a cup.
They came up short on their tab,
The owner shouted and screamed and got all worked up.

[GUANG]PU *speaks*:—And how did you solve this?—MALE LEAD *sings*:

Without a second thought, I paid two hundred coppers on their behalf.
For this reason he swore a brotherhood with me.

GUANGPU *speaks*:—Slowly explain everything from beginning to end.—MALE LEAD *speaks*:—I was on my way to deliver documents when I came to the inn at Strawbridge. There I saw three scholars drinking wine, and they had no money for the tab, and they were being berated by the innkeeper for his money, so I paid for them. Those three students asked my name. Now, I am surnamed Zhao and he said, "I am also surnamed Zhao," and then he took me as his younger brother and I respected him as the elder. And because of this, he wrote this letter. He said that he was Your Excellency's elder brother and said, "If he sees my letter, you will surely not die."—GUANGPU *speaks*:—And where is the letter? Give it to me to read.—MALE LEAD *acts out baring his shoulder and speaks*:—Isn't this it? Because he had no paper on his trip, he wrote it on my shoulder.—GUANGPU *speaks*:—Servants, raise him up for me.—ATTENDANT *speaks*:—Help him up.—GUANGPU *looks at it and speaks*:—Servants, go and fetch some court clothing.—ATTENDANT *speaks*:—Understood! Here they are.—GUANGPU *speaks*:—Help him up, have him put on these court robes, and have him sit on a chair. If I had known my royal younger brother was coming, I would have gone out to greet you at the proper distance. Please do not fault me for not receiving you properly!—MALE LEAD *acts out being alarmed and speaks*:—You're scaring me to death!—*Sings*:

(*Shi'er yue*)
They've put me into this folding chair to sit,
Taking me by hand, foot, and body.
They spread an embroidered carpet on the ground,
While perfume wafts from the golden lion.
Call a doctor! What's my pulse?
These stricken eyes will be hard to cure!

(*Yaomin ge*)
How many times have you seen the god of the poorhouse bow to Zhong Kui?[91]
Or a judge in hell's court ask for help from a medical diviner?
It's just as fast as divine needles or dharma moxa.
Like a Lan Caihe unable to dance, watching the flowers whirl.[92]
I smirk ever so slightly over
Our emperor's edict appointing me
To judge the affairs of Kaifeng prefecture.

[GUANG]PU *speaks*:—My royal younger brother, listen: the Sage's command has accelerated you to be prefect of the Eastern Capital. You must now race to assume your position. I will prepare the documents—MALE LEAD *speaks*:—The prefect of the Eastern Capital? Is there wine there in the yamen?—GUANGPU *speaks*:—You just want to drink wine? Well you'd better start your long journey today.—MALE LEAD *sings*:

(*Shua hai'er*)
I can't be an official, but there are plenty of precedents to use,
And the codes of the five punishments are all there in regular order.
But I never studied the laws and regulations of Xiao and Cao,[93]
So whenever there's a case, I'll hand it over to the head clerk to solve.
Let none without wine enter the yamen,

91. See n. 45.
92. See n. 46.
93. See n. 48.

I know nothing of the world but a good sleep.
There will be no worries—
Who cares about runners or clerks,
I'll just drink, and then go back home to a feast.

GUANGPU *speaks*:—Take this document now but open it up inside of the yamen in the Eastern Capital.—MALE LEAD *sings*:

(*Second from Coda*)
I'll drink wine just like Li Bo,[94]
Be as muddleheaded as Rescriptor-in-Waiting Bao.[95]
Call me "the bottomless jug," and all the world will know who it is.
"There is a path to the blue empyrean, and finally I've arrived."
"If fine wine has no name, I swear I will not return."[96]
Every day I'll be stewed with wine.
Who cares about the three deductions and six interrogations?
They are no match for a hundred cups and filling in at a feast.

GUANGPU *speaks*:—You should leave today to take up your appointment in the Eastern Capital.—MALE LEAD *sings*:

(*Coda*)
Who cares about Autumn Springs or Bamboo-Leaf Green,
Nine Times Brewed in its lotus-leaf cups?
It makes no difference if it's your Canglang waters or mine,[97]
It's far better than enduring storm and snow, hunger and cold, halfway down the road.
Exits.

GUANGPU *speaks*:—This guy is gone. Who expected this fellow to meet a Prior Emperor in a wineshop who would write on his shoulder and put his seal to it? Or make him a sworn brother and accelerate him to be the prefect of the Eastern Capital, a position he should take up at all speed. When the Sage returns home there are sure to be more promotions to come. I have no more business today. Servants! Bring my horse. I'll go back to my private residence for the time being.

The Sage encounters a friend right in the wineshop,
And accelerates his rank to the prefect of the Eastern Capital.

Exits.

94. See n. 38.
95. See n. 51.
96. See n. 53.
97. See n. 53.

ACT 4

EXTRA, *costumed as* OLD MAN, COMIC *costumed as* PREFECT, *and* PAINTED FEMALE *enter.*—OLD MAN *speaks*:

When the moon passes the fifteenth, its radiant light diminishes,
When people reach the last years of their life, all affairs cease.

I am Squire Liu the Second. After my daughter successfully got a writ of divorce from Zhao Yuan, she took up with Prefect Zang from here. He sent Zhao Yuan off to deliver some documents to the Superior Capital. Miss the deadline by one day, and it's forty strokes of the club; two days, eighty strokes; three days, beheading. I never expected that when this guy got to the capital and saw the great man, that man would completely forgive him for being behind schedule. I have no idea what talents Zhao might possess, but he received the great man's orders and was appointed as the prefect of the Eastern Capital, to take up his post immediately. Well, benevolence repays benevolence and enmity repays enmity. How shall we plan for this, children?—PAINTED FEMALE *speaks*:—Now that he's an official, he'll have some gifts for me!—OLD MAN *speaks*:—Prefect Zang, what do you think?—COMIC *speaks*:—Father, what's there to say? I took his wife by force in the beginning and wanted to bring him harm. Now that he's the prefect, I'd better request to disappear like the skin off a green pea. My wife I will now return to him, and I will be dead and gone.—PAINTED FEMALE *speaks*:—Now that he's an official, I am a lady. There's no one in the world as ardently chaste as me!—COMIC *speaks*:—True it is, "Can you find a worthy wife in any house?"—OLD MAN *speaks*:—Child, let's wait until he comes, then let's the three of us take along a goat and a carrying pole of wine to congratulate him, and then 'fess up to our wrongs. Let's go back home for the time being.

Exit together.

EMPEROR, ZHAO GUANGPU, *and* SHI SHOUXIN *enter.*—EMPEROR *speaks*:—We[98] are Emperor Zhao. Before, We costumed as a student along with Chu Zhaofu and Shi Shouxin and went out for a secret excursion incognito. When we got to Strawbridge Inn, a heavy snow was falling, swirling and whirling, so we went into the inn to have some wine. Unexpectedly a man from the Eastern Capital named Zhao—that would be Zhao Yuan—also came in and had some wine. We had too much wine and We were about to leave with Our two friends when we were pulled back by the innkeeper. He asked Us for the money for the wine, but We had nothing to give to him. Zhao Yuan paid two hundred cash on Our behalf. We asked him why, and he explained that he had vile and evil parents-in-law and a perverse and stubborn wife who had a

98. The emperor uses the eidetic pronoun *guaren*, "I this person who lacks virtue" (from *guade zhi ren* 寡德之人), which is roughly equivalent to the royal "we" in English.

secret liaison with the prefect at their place. They demanded a writ of divorce, and then sent Zhao to deliver some documents to the Superior Capital. When We found out about these circumstances, We pulled out a frost-tipped brush with a mottled bamboo handle, wrote two lines of text on Zhao Yuan's shoulder, and attached Our seal. When Zhao Pu saw it, he spared his life and then accelerated this person to the rank of prefect of the Eastern Capital, which he took up at once. We have returned to the capital now, and I have summoned this person so I may see him again. I already sent Chu Zhaofu to summon him, and I sent some other people to the Eastern Capital to take his parents-in-law and his wife and the prefect into custody. We will make our decision decisive and clear. They should be here soon.—MALE LEAD *enters following* CHU ZHAOFU.—CHU *speaks*:—Mister Zhao, today the ruler has summoned you, so you should move along. Servants! Open up the fore procession, and arrange them in order. Let's go off and see the Sage.—MALE LEAD *speaks*:—You've gone to a lot of trouble!—*Sings*:

(SHUANGDIAO MODE *Xinshui ling*)

Who wants two rows of runners making a confusing noise?
Better to have ten poles of wine jugs carried before my horse.
This gauze cap of office and straight purple gown
Are no match for my old plain belt and threadbare shirt.
I can't speak any rigmarole or double talk,
So don't think I'll be some corrupt official.

CHU *speaks*:—Mister Zhao, you are seeing the ruler today and he will reward you and give you higher rank, and you can go into the Eastern Capital and become prefect. Does that sound good to you, sire?—MALE LEAD *speaks*:—I can't go, sir.—CHU *speaks*:—Why can't you go?— MALE LEAD *sings*:

(*Qiaopai'er*)

These words have not been weighed with care,
You know that deep water has to be probed with a pole.
Don't trap a simple man in front of our lord and master,
Zhao Yuan's addiction to wine is a foul mess.

CHU *speaks*:—Sire, we are here already. I'll go see the Sage first.—*Acts out greeting*.—EMPEROR *speaks*:—Chu Zhaofu, did Zhao Yuan come?—CHU *speaks*: Yes.—EMPEROR *speaks*:—Tell him to come in.—CHU *speaks*:—Understood. Sire, the ruler has expressed a command. Do him the proper honor.—MALE LEAD *speaks*:—Understood.—*Acts out greeting*.—MALE LEAD *speaks*:—Ten thousand years, Your Majesty, ten thousands of ten thousand years!—EMPEROR *speaks*:—Do you recognize Us, Zhao Yuan? We were honored by your wonderful intent at Strawbridge Inn, and We have summoned you here today to reward you and give you official rank. How does that sound to you?—MALE LEAD *speaks*:—Your Majesty, I am incapable of being an official.—EMPEROR *speaks*:—And why is that?—MALE LEAD *sings*:

(*Tianshui ling*)
With my whole heart I don't covet high position
And I don't scheme for wealth or high status.
Don't try and deceive me—
How can I bear all this hassle?

EMPEROR *speaks*:—We will rebuild your house and construct a formal hall.—MALE LEAD *sings*:
I don't want you to construct a formal hall,
Rebuild my house,
Decorate it, or build it higher and higher.
Better I live in a straw hut or a rush shed.

Speaks:—Your Majesty, I will not be an official.—EMPEROR *speaks*:—Why not?—MALE LEAD *sings*:
(*Zhegui ling*)
I'm afraid of the snarling commotion of the tiger's lair and dragon's abyss.
As you know, the dragon has its wind and clouds,
The tiger, its mountains and cliffs.
In jade halls and on golden stairways
When tigers fight and dragons war,
They stir up treacherous slander.
In court or out, who is the likes of me:
Beclouded, stupid, dim-witted, and dull?
First mumbling and grumbling, then silent and still?
Haven't you heard that prime ministers and royal nobles
Have it worse than Li the Fourth and Zhang the Third?

EMPEROR *speaks*:—If We appoint you to a high office that you can keep until you're old, what's wrong with that?—MALE LEAD *sings*:
(*Qi dixiong*)
How would I—
Your insignificant minister—
Dare involve myself in a high official's business?
I only know bitter, stringent, sour, full, and light.[99]
Let everyone else blindly covet the clear, shiny, smooth, and piquant—
When the people below are so easy to savage, why add corruption?

EMPEROR *speaks*:—We really desire to enfeoff you with high office! Why do you refuse? There must be something you're thinking of.—MALE LEAD *sings*:
(*Meihua jiu*)

99. That is, flavors of wine.

Your insignificant minister is the greatest coward of them all,
All I want is to be stewed in sweet drunkenness day after day.
Please, my Sagely Ruler, consider it well!
And do not ask me time and time again.
I can be no pure and uncorrupt investigating official,
Nor viscount or earl, duke or baron.
I'm ashamed:
Were my office high, I'd be unhappy,
Were my salary large, I would grow too covetous.

EMPEROR *speaks*:—You won't even be a pure and uncorrupt investigating official! In this case, what post do you want?—MALE LEAD *sings*:

(*Shou Jiangnan*)
In the city of Bianliang, I will be Director in Chief of the Bureau of Wine,
I'll pour my own, dance alone, carry on pure conversations with myself.
Without worry, without vexation, I'll just dither on.
You'll find no me in places of right and wrong—
Those morsels from the Jade Hall are no match for the sweetness of the vat.

EMPEROR *speaks*:—Zhao Yuan, do you want to see your enemies?—MALE LEAD *speaks*:—Your Majesty, I certainly do.—EMPEROR *speaks*:—Personal attendants, bring in the prefect of the Eastern Capital along with Zhao Yuan's in-laws and his wife, Moon Fairy Liu.—CHU *speaks*:—Understood! The whole group go in and face Him.—*Acts out taking* OLD MAN, OLD WOMAN, PAINTED FEMALE, *and* COMIC *and they all kneel.*—EMPEROR *speaks*:—You miscreants, do you know your offenses?—COMIC *speaks*:—I don't, Your Majesty.—EMPEROR *speaks*:—Why did you forcibly take a commoner's wife?—COMIC *speaks*:—I certainly wouldn't dare do such a thing. She made me be a live-in son-in-law.—EMPEROR *speaks*:—This miscreant knows nothing about how to act.—MALE LEAD *sings*:

(*Yan'er luo*)
You, venerable elder Jiang, were daring in the wrong cause,[100]
You, righteous woman of Lu, had thought it carefully through[101]—
By relying on the magistrate's office to demand my fingerprint
Today you wind up in your own trap.

(*Desheng ling*)
It might have been "Hoist the carrying pole of breeze and moon."[102]
But wasn't it like "a dragonfly trying to shake Mount Tai?"[103]
In days past, you were stupid and corrupt,

100. See chap. 2, n. 37.
101. See n. 55.
102. See n. 62.
103. See n. 63.

But now you will lose your head under the knife.
I was unable to bear your clutching fists,
And you tricked me out into the wind and snow.
You're so scared now your face is blue,
But you were mighty courageous when you demanded the writ of divorce.

EMPEROR *speaks*:—Stop! Stop! All of you, listen to My judgment:
It was all because
Squire Liu the Second did not recognize proper relations
And drove his live-in son-in-law out to live somewhere apart.
And his wife was even more vile and evil at heart—
Her poisonous heart could not distinguish the worthy from the stupid.
The wife Moon Fairy held evil intent in her heart
And boasted of her tricks to press for a writ of divorce.
Missing the deadline he bitterly encountered a decision of reprimand
And truly expected his own death.
And Zhao Yuan,
Suffering mightily, never quailed before wind and rain—
The road long and winding, he never shirked from its rise and fall.
Suddenly at Strawbridge Inn he encountered the Sagely Ruler
Who pardoned his offenses until not a speck remained.
Zhao Yuan—I make you prefect
And bestow on you colored silks and piles of real pearls.
Squire Liu the Second, husband and wife, conspired in crime but are spared punishment,
But they cannot live together with Zhao Yuan.
Moon Fairy shall be bastinadoed a hundred times
Because she stirred up trouble and destroyed good customs.
Prefect Zang destroyed the law because he lusted after sex,
And according to the legal code he is now sent away to penal exile.
Today we have settled accounts of gratitude and revenge,
And all together, loudly shout out, "Ten Thousand Years."

Title: Father-in-law and mother-in-law have venomous hearts,
The official concerned abuses his power to get a rouged beauty.
Name: In the snow a government runner takes great revenge,
Tippler Zhao Yuan Encounters the Prior Emperor.

Copied and collated from a Yu Xiaogu edition, seventeenth day of the sixth month of the *dingsi* year [July 19, 1617]. The Daoist of Pure Constancy

6

The Affair of the Eastern Window Exposed

INTRODUCTION

From the moment of its foundation the Song dynasty (960–1278) had a tense and adversarial relation with its northern neighbors. In 960 this was the Liao dynasty of the Khitan, which had its power base in southern Manchuria. The Liao dynasty was one of the most successful states to emerge from the collapse of the Tang. The Khitan leader Abaoji had assumed the imperial title in 907, and for two centuries the Liao would be the strongest military power in the region. Their support would often be the determining factor in power struggles on the Central Plain, and the warlord Shi Jingtang 石敬瑭 (892–942) would even go so far as to cede them the sixteen northeastern prefectures of the old Tang empire (including the area of modern Beijing) to secure their aid in overthrowing the Later Tang (923–935) and establishing his own Later Jin dynasty (936–945). The founding of the Song itself originated in an aborted military campaign against the Khitan: when troops of the Later Zhou (951–960) were about to set out from Kaifeng to fight the Liao, they forced their commander Zhao Kuangyin 趙匡胤 (927–976) to depose his late sworn brother's young son and assume the imperial throne himself. Over the next decade Zhao Kuangyin, now Emperor Taizu of the Song, would subdue one independent regime after the other, but not the Liao. It took the Song three large campaigns to subdue the Northern Han regime in modern Shanxi that was closely allied with the Liao, but even when Zhao Kuangyin's brother and successor, Zhao Guangyi 趙光義 (939–997; Emperor Taizong), succeeded in that objective in 979, his campaign against the Liao in 980 ended in failure, as did another large campaign in 986. While the Song stubbornly tried to regain the sixteen prefectures, the Liao held on to them just as stubbornly. Peace was established only in 1004, when Liao armies penetrated deeply into Hebei and Emperor Zhenzong (r. 1023–1063) took the field against the invaders. Both sides eventually preferred negotiations over the uncertainty of battle, however, and the Liao armies retreated behind the existing border after the Song agreed to pay a large annual tribute. Even though the amount was much less than the emperor had been willing to agree to and even though the amount was only a modest post on the Song annual budget, the fact that it had to be paid, along with the permanent loss of the sixteen prefectures, continued to rankle Chinese feelings throughout the eleventh century.

So when a new military power emerged in Manchuria at the beginning of the twelfth century in the shape of the Jurchen, who soon established the Jin dynasty (1115–1234), Song policy makers believed the moment had come to do away with the Liao once and for all and recover the territory of the sixteen prefectures. The Song and the Jin agreed to a common attack on the Liao. The Jurchen kept their part of the bargain by swiftly defeating the Liao, but the Song barely owned up to theirs. In the fall of 1125 the Jurchen armies therefore marched south and early in 1126 camped below the walls of Kaifeng. The Song court was in a panic and Emperor Huizong (r. 1101–1125) abdicated in favor of one of his sons, who succeeded him as Emperor Qinzong. The Jurchen retreated once the Song had made huge promises. It soon became clear, however, that the Song was unwilling or incapable of keeping these promises, and in the eleventh month of 1126 the Jurchen armies appeared outside Kaifeng again. The city was totally unprepared for a siege, and early in 1127 the Jurchen entered Kaifeng. If their original intention had been to loot the capital, they now decided on conquest. Both the retired emperor and the reigning emperor were deported as captives to Manchuria with thousands of others.[1]

One of Qinzong's younger brothers, the Prince of Kang, Zhao Gou 趙構 (1107–1187), escaped from the north and fled south of the Yangtze. Later legends credited his successful escape to divine intervention: the horse that one night carried him for hundreds of miles turned out in the morning to have been a clay temple statue. The Prince of Kang organized a court and ascended the throne as Gaozong (r. 1127–1161) but initially was chased all over the Jiangnan area by Jurchen troops led by the Fourth Great Prince (Si Dawang 四大王) Wuzhu 兀朮 (d. 1148). It took several years before Gaozong could establish a more or less stable regime south of the Yangtze, where Hangzhou served as the Temporary Abode (Xingzai 行在) of the court and the de facto new capital of the Song. But while the court became more successful in warding off Jurchen attacks, it also became increasingly clear that the Southern Song was incapable of mounting the massive campaign that would be required to reconquer the Central Plain, let alone push the Jurchen back into Manchuria and free the captive emperors. Voices calling for an accommodation with the Jin dynasty became louder and dominant at court once Qin Gui 秦檜 (1090–1155) became prime minister.[2] Qin Gui hailed from modern Nanjing, and had served in high court functions in Kaifeng. From 1127 to 1130 he was a captive of the Jin, where he gained the trust of a younger brother of the Jin emperor. Upon his return to the

1. See West 2006.

2. Qin Gui's name is also transcribed as Qin Kuai and Qin Hui. On Qin Gui, see Hartman 1998.

south, he soon gained the trust of Gaozong. Qin Gui, like many of his contemporaries, realized that as a precondition for a successful peace policy he would have to curtail the power of the semi-independent warlords allied with the Southern Song, all of whom had a vested interest in a continuation of the war. During the summer of 1141, when peace negotiations with the Jin were under way, the three major generals were all suddenly recalled to court, where they, now separated from their troops, were appointed to nominally high positions. One of these generals was Yue Fei 岳飛 (1103–1142). Yue Fei had served in the army since his youth and taken a leading role in the resistance against the Jin and the consolidation of the Southern Song regime. In 1140 he had pushed into Henan and recovered major cities such as Zhengzhou and Luoyang. But as effective as Yue Fei may have been as a general, he was equally inept as a politician, and upon his arrival in Hangzhou, he was thrown in jail and accused of rebellion. He refused to confess, and at the end of the year he suddenly died in prison. It was widely believed that he had been murdered at the order of Qin Gui. His adopted son, Yue Yun 岳雲 (1120–1142), and his assistant, Zhang Xian 張憲 (d. 1142), were eventually publicly executed. The other warlords heeded the lesson and agreed to be pensioned off, and in 1142 the Southern Song could sign a peace treaty with the Jin. The Huai River became the border between the two states, and the Southern Song agreed to make hefty payments to the Jin each year.

Qin Gui remained in power till his death in 1155. Soon after his death, however, both sides grew restive, and hostilities resumed in 1161. As the proponents of war now were in power at the Song court, the verdict on Yue Fei was reversed, and his full honors were restored in 1162, following the abdication of Gaozong and the succession by Xiaozong (r. 1162–1189). The hostilities came to an end in 1165 with a treaty that little changed the relation between the two states. Yue Fei had been provided in the meantime with a fine grave on the banks of Hangzhou's scenic West Lake and would soon be depicted as the embodiment of all civil and martial values. It was widely believed that at the moment that he was called back (by thirteen summons on a single day!) he had been poised to inflict a decisive defeat on Wuzhu, and to reconquer the old capital and the Central Plain. Yue Fei's grandson Yue Ke 岳珂 (1183–1240) would play a major role in shaping the posthumous reputation of his grandfather through his numerous publications. And while he recast his grandfather as a filial and loyal hero, Qin Gui has ever since been depicted as a black-hearted traitor who had insisted on a peace treaty with the Jin because he was in the pay of the Jurchen. The great philosopher Zhu Xi 朱熹 (1130–1200) pontificated in 1165, "The reasons Qin Gui's crimes permeated Heaven and could not have been redeemed even if he had died ten thousand deaths were, first, he promoted his evil policies to deceive the state, and, next, he used the power of the barbarians to coerce his sovereign, as a result obscuring proper relations between men and perverting the human heart." 秦檜之罪所以上通於天，萬死而不足以贖者，正以其始則唱邪謀以誤國，中則挾虜勢以要君，使人倫不明人心不正。[3]

3. On his "Xuwu dangyi xu" 戊午讜議序, see Zhu Xi 2010, 7:3768.

One rumor had it that the weak-spined villain Qin Gui had been able to make up his mind to have Yue Fei murdered only after his wife had told him in a private conversation at the eastern window that it was relatively easy to capture a tiger, but impossible to release the beast. Qin Gui, it was also said, had been able to achieve his position of power only because Emperor Gaozong was none too keen on the release of his elder brother Qinzong and far preferred the pleasures of an easy life in the south over the exertions of campaigning in the north. As the images of Yue Fei and Qin Gui became more polarized in the minds of the common people and the intellectual elite alike, stories soon emerged that Yue Fei had become a god and that Qin Gui was suffering eternal torture in hell. The seventeenth-century polymath Chu Renhuo 褚人獲includes in one of his compendia the following story that he credits to the *Record of the Listener* (*Yi Jian zhi* 夷堅志), a huge but incompletely preserved collection of anecdotes and gossip compiled by Zhu Xi's contemporary Hong Mai 洪邁 (1123–1202):[4]

> When Qin Gui had faked an edict and arrested Yue Fei and his sons, he had them locked up in the prison of the Court of Judicial Review. He then dispatched Moqi Xie 万俟卨 (1083–1157) to hold them over the fire. One day, when they still had not confessed, Gui was drawing in the ashes by the window of the eastern room as he was planning his next move. Gui's wife said to him, "Capturing a tiger is easy, but it is impossible to release one." Subsequently Yue Fei died in prison and Zhang Xian and Yue Yun were executed in the marketplace. The people of the Jin toasted to each other, saying, "Now none can harm us anymore!"
>
> When later Gui was visiting the West Lake with his family, he suddenly was struck by a violent disease and saw a blind man, who shouted, "You ruined the country and harmed the people. I have already lodged an accusation with Heaven and you will be beaten with iron rods in front of the palace hall of Taizu!"[5] Starting from this moment Gui fell into a deep depression that led to his death. Shortly afterward his son Xi 熺 also passed away.
>
> [During a visit to the underworld] the shaman Fu Zhang 伏章 saw Xi wearing an iron cangue, so he asked him where the grand preceptor was. A crying Xi replied, "In the Fengdu 豐都 Hell." When the shaman followed his directions to go there, he indeed saw Gui and Moqi Xie, who both were wearing an iron cangue and had been locked up inside an iron cage, where they suffered no end of torment. Gui told the shaman, "Please tell my wife that the affair of the eastern window has been exposed."[6]

4. This anecdote does not occur in the extant edition of the *Yi Jian zhi*, but it is cited in the *Compendium of Broken Treaties of Three Reigns* (*Sanchao beimeng huibian* 三朝北盟彙編) from Liu Yiqing's *Old Affairs of Qiantang* (*Qiantang yishi* 錢塘遺事). See Xu Mengxin 1987, 1495.2, and *The Affair of the Eastern Window Revealed* (*Dongchuang shifa* 東窗事發) in Liu Yiqing 1782, 2.3a–b.

5. Taizu is Zhao Kuangyin, the founding emperor of the Song dynasty.

6. See Chu 2002, 464, 47a–48b. See also Zhang Qingfa 2008.

Chu Renhuo is perplexed that this anecdote does not yet mention the yamen runner He Li 何立, who by that time had become a fixture of the legend of Qin Gui's sufferings in hell, so he goes on to quote the following story from a work titled *Miscellaneous Record from Rivers and Lakes* (*Jianghu zaji* 江湖雜記):

> When Gui had killed Yue Fei, he went to Lingyin Monastery [outside Hangzhou] to pray. There was a postulant there who criticized him in wild words. When Gui asked him where he lived, he answered with the following lines: "Prime Minister, you'll want to ask where I will go: / I live at Mountain Number One of the Southeast." Gui ordered his servant He Li to track him down. When Li arrived at a palatial hall, he saw the monk seated there and deciding a case. When Li asked one of the attendants which case, the answer was, "King Ksitigarbha is deciding the case of Qin Gui's murder of Yue Fei." Shortly thereafter he saw some soldiers leading Gui inside. Gui wore an iron cangue, had been shaved bald like a criminal, and his face was covered with grime. When he saw Li, he called to him, "Tell my wife that the affair of the eastern window has been exposed!"

The *Jianghu zaji* is not otherwise known. If the work may be identified with the *Recorded Legends of Rivers and Lakes* (*Jianghu jiwen* 江湖紀聞), it would date from the early fourteenth century and might well be based on our play for this anecdote, rather than being its source. By the fourteenth century we have records that stories of Qin Gui's villainy and his horrendous punishment were the subject of professional storytellers, had been written up into a novel, and was performed onstage. One of the best known versions is *A Sequel to the Tale of the Affair of the Eastern Window Exposed* (*Xu Dongchuang shi fan zhuan* 續東窗事犯傳) in *A Collection of Poor Imitations* (*Xiaopin ji* 效顰集) by Zhao Bi 趙弼 of the early fifteenth century. In this tale the student Hu Di 胡迪, enraged by the evil perpetrated by Qin Gui upon reading *The Tale of Qin Gui at the Eastern Window* (*Qin Gui dongchuang zhuan* 秦檜東窗傳), is invited to the underworld to witness the punishment of history's villains, beginning with Qin Gui. A vernacular version of this tale was later included by Feng Menglong 馮夢龍 (1574–1646) in his *Stories Old and New* (*Gujin xiaoshuo* 古今小說; 1620–1621).[7]

The saga of Yue Fei would only continue to grow throughout the Ming and Qing dynasties as his glorious deeds and tragic end were constantly adapted and readapted for the stage and written up as novels and ballads all over China. One of the important works in that later tradition is an eighty-chapter novel from the early eighteenth century by a certain Qian Cai 錢彩 titled *The Full Tale of Yue Fei* (*Shuo Yue quanzhuan* 說岳全傳), in which in the final episodes the sons complete the work of their father and succeed in freeing the captive emperors. While the Manchu rulers of the Qing dynasty (1644–1911) celebrated Yue Fei for his loyalty, the same Yue Fei, as a fighter against foreign aggression,

7. See Zhang Qingfa 2008, 299–300, for citations of these texts. For the tale, see Feng 2000a.

later also easily became an embodiment of the nationalistic desire to cleanse China of Manchu rule and imperialist occupation. There must be very few Chinese children indeed who do not know the story of how Yue Fei's mother on the eve of his departure for the army inked on his back the four characters meaning "Serve your country with utmost loyalty" (*jin zhong bao guo* 盡忠報國). Unfortunately the story is a pious myth that can have originated only after it had been forgotten that all soldiers were tattooed with such phrases to make desertion impossible. The temple dedicated to Yue Fei next to his grave near Hangzhou's West Lake in the 1220s has been restored time and again, and to this day displays the kneeling images of Qin Gui and his wife.[8]

The Affair of the Eastern Window Exposed (*Dongchuang shi fan*), which has been preserved only in a Yuan-dynasty printing from Dadu, may well be the earliest preserved dramatic adaptation of the legend of Yue Fei. Dating from the late thirteenth or early fourteenth century, it does not yet make reference to many episodes that would become famous and conspicuous parts of the later tradition. It is one of the most elaborate *zaju* of the period, consisting not only of four full acts but also of two wedges and a final demi-act. The songs in the play are assigned to a male lead, who has to switch roles (or at least costumes) with every wedge and act. In the opening wedge the male lead performs the role of Yue Fei, who, at the height of his career and poised to retake the north, is suddenly and urgently recalled to court. While Yue Fei has his doubts about the request, as a loyal official he has no other recourse but to obey. By the first act, Yue Fei has arrived in the capital and has been thrown into jail. The male lead now portrays Yue Fei as a prisoner wearing a cangue. Throughout this act, an indignant Yue Fei rejects every accusation of rebellion with heavy sarcasm and vaunts his merits in service to the state. Most likely his interlocutor in this act is Qin Gui (or Qin's henchman Moqi Xie, who was in charge of Yue Fei's trial), but the stage prompts in our only preserved edition are very minimal and do not specify this information (at the very end of the act Yue Fei directly addresses the emperor). By the beginning of the second act, Yue Fei has been murdered and Qin Gui visits Lingyin Monastery outside Hangzhou to appease the specters that haunt him by sponsoring sutra recitations and vegetarian feasts for the monks. At the monastery he is taunted at length by a deranged postulant, the new role of the male lead. The idiocy of the holy fool allows such a character to freely express truths that others would hardly dare utter. This holy fool does not mention his own name, but later in the play he is referred to as Ye Shouyi 葉守一. The second act is followed by yet another wedge, in which the male lead performs the role of He Zongli 何宗立, a runner who has been ordered by Qin Gui to arrest the unhinged postulant. By the time He Zongli reencounters the postulant, he realizes that the postulant is the bodhisattva Ksitigarbha, the ruler of the underworld, who has dragged Qin Gui off to the Fengdu Hell, where he suffers unspeakable torture.

8. Visitors are nowadays forbidden from spitting on the images.

In the third act of *The Affair of the Eastern Window Exposed* the male lead performs the role of the ghost of Yue Fei, who, attended by Yue Yun and Zhang Xian, appears in a dream to the emperor, requesting the verdict in his case be overturned. The identity of the emperor is not clarified in the stage prompts but would seem to refer to Gaozong following his abdication. Scenes in which deceased ministers appear to their emperor in a dream are not uncommon on the Yuan stage: Yang Zi had the ghost of Huo Guang appear to Emperor Xuan of the Han (see chap. 2), and Guan Hanqing had the ghosts of Zhang Fei and Guan Yu appear to Liu Bei. This play increases the number of ghosts to three and has them not only appeal to the emperor for help but also criticize the emperor for his failings. In act 4 the male lead returns to the role of He Zongli, who, having failed to arrest the postulant, returns some twenty years later to Hangzhou. After he has reported to Qin Gui's widow how her husband suffers in hell, he is invited to court and provides the emperor with a detailed account of his experiences. The act consists of his report to the throne. No stage directions are provided for the final demi-act, but it is obvious from the content of the arias that the male lead performs the role of a deified Yue Fei who demands from the emperor a gruesome revenge on Qin Gui. The play concludes with the appearance onstage of the bodhisattva Ksitigarbha and his retinue. We may safely assume that his final words will announce the law of karma's disposition of the heroes and villains of the piece.

As is clear from this summary, the play describes both the tragic death of Yue Fei and the final reversal of his verdict twenty years later. While the play portrays Yue Fei as an innocent and loyal martyr, Qin Gui is portrayed as a traitor who is a villain evil in every aspect of his personal and official life. But the play also highlights the divine powers of the bodhisattva Ksitigarbha. The conspicuous role of Ksitigarbha in this play is even more remarkable when we compare this play with plays about the generals of the Yang family such as Yang Ye 楊業 (d. 986) and Yang Jing 楊延昭 (958–1014), who fought the Liao in the early decades of the Song.[9] The legend of the generals of the Yang family developed at roughly the same time as the legend of Yue Fei. As in the case of Yue Fei, the heroic efforts of Yang Ye and Yang Yanzhao in fighting the Liao are continually frustrated by jealous bureaucrats, often in the pay of the enemy. In the legend of the generals of the Yang family, these treacherous bureaucrats have, however, a remarkable hold on power, and, for all the impact of popular religion on the legend, they are seldom dragged off to hell. Perhaps the reason is that in the legend of the generals of the Yang family the niche of the monk was occupied by one of Yang Jing's brothers, who had become a monk at Mount Wutai—without losing any of his qualities as a warrior. But the names of the temples involved (Lingyin Monastery vs. Mount Wutai) also may suggest the role of local cults in the differential development of these legends.

9. On the Yang family generals, see Idema and West 2013.

Our earliest catalogue of playwrights, Zhong Sicheng's *Register of Ghosts*, credits two playwrights with a *zaju* titled *The Affair of the Eastern Window Exposed*. One of these authors was Jin Renjie 金仁傑 (d. 1329) from Hangzhou. Zhong credits seven plays to Jin, almost all on historical subjects. Many earlier scholars felt that, as a Hangzhou person, Jin would be the most likely author of the preserved play, but the full title given by Zhong, who claims to have been a good friend of Jin's, is not exactly the same as that of the preserved play. Jin's play is titled *Grand Preceptor Qin's Affair of the Eastern Window Exposed*, which might suggest that Ksitigarbha did not play a role in this play. The *Register of Ghosts* was transmitted in manuscript for a long time, and the various manuscripts of the *Register of Ghosts* show major differences among one another. While one manuscript notes that Jin's play was a "second play" (a second play with the same title), one seventeenth-century printed edition states that it was a *danben* 旦本, that is, a play for a female lead. If this late evidence can be accepted, it excludes Jin Renjie as the author of the preserved play, which, as noted, assigns its songs to the male lead. Modern editors of *The Affair of the Eastern Window Exposed* therefore credit the play to the second author mentioned by Zhong Sicheng as having written a play of the title, a Pingyang 平陽playwright by the name of Kong Wenqing 孔文卿. The modern scholar Sun Kaidi suggests that the playwright may be identified with a certain Kong Xueshi 孔學詩 (1260–1341), whose style name was Wenqing and who hailed from Liyang 溧陽, but this identification has not been generally accepted.[10] It should be pointed out that the title of Kong's play, too, is given as *Grand Preceptor Qin's Affair of the Eastern Window Exposed*, but one version of the *Register of Ghosts* lists "He Zongli Arrests the Postulant of the Western Hills" as the play's title (*timu* 題目), and "King Ksitigarbha Testifies to the Crime of the Eastern Window" as its name (*zhengming* 正名), and while that does not fully correspond to the play as we have it either (in the fourteenth-century edition these two lines together serve as its *zhengming*), it is close enough for most modern scholars. The situation is further complicated by the fact that the sixteenth-century polymath Lang Ying 郎英 (1487–ca. 1566) tells us in his *Classified Essays, Seven Times Revised* (*Qixiu leigao* 七修類稿) that he had once read a play titled *The Affair of the Eastern Window Exposed* by Kong Wenzhong 孔文仲 (probably a mistake for Kong Wenqing) from Pingyang, and a novel of the same title by Jin Renjie, but then adds that he had forgotten the contents of both works.[11] Needless to say, our *Yuan Edition* of the play does not mention the name of the author.

The Affair of the Eastern Window Exposed must have made extraordinary demands on an actor as he had first to portray Yue Fei at the height of his power and next as a shackled criminal. He then had to portray an unhinged postulant, a yamen runner, the ghost of Yue Fei, the same yamen runner twenty years older, and finally the deified Yue Fei. Perhaps because the demands of this play were so high, our sources tell the name of

10. The exception is Zheng Qian 1962, iii, which states that Kong is the author of the play. Zheng simply cites Sun Kaidi's conclusion that Kong Wenqing is Kong Xueren, without offering further support for that identification.

11. Lang 1959, 352.

at least one actor who was renowned for his performance of this *zaju*. Perhaps also to distinguish Kong's play from the second play by Jin Renjie, one edition of the *Record of Ghosts* contains the information that this was the play "performed by Yang Ju'er" (*Yang Ju'er an* 楊駒兒按).[12] Our other information on Yang Ju'er is limited to the fact that he was the father of the famous actress Yang Mainu 楊買奴. The latter enjoyed the patronage of the Uighur noble and poet Guan Yunshi 貫雲石 (1286–1324), who also may have known Yang Ju'er.

The text of the play is damaged in places, especially in the fourth act. Earlier editors have been able for most of these passages to come up with convincing emendations that we have accepted and not marked in our translation.[13]

SUGGESTED READINGS

Degkwitz 1983; Feng 2000a; Hartman 1998; Hennessey 1981, 1984; Huang 2004–2005; Idema and West 2013; Liu 1972; Qian 1995; Tao 2009; Wang-Toutain 1998; West 2006; Wilhelm 1962.

NEWLY PRINTED AT THE GREAT CAPITAL, A COMPLETE TEXT WITH PLOT PROMPTS: *THE AFFAIR OF THE EASTERN WINDOW EXPOSED,* A FOURTEENTH-CENTURY EDITION

DRAMATIS PERSONAE IN ORDER OF APPEARANCE

Role type	*Name and family, institutional, or social role*
MALE LEAD	YUE FEI (wedge 1, act 1)
TWO GENERALS	YUE YUN and ZHANG XIAN
EMISSARY	EMISSARY

12. Another edition of *Record of Ghosts* writes *yi yun Yang Ju'er zuo* 一云楊駒兒做, which is usually understood as meaning "According to another source [this play] was composed by Yang Ju'er." Accordingly, Yang Ju'er has also been considered the author or coauthor of *The Affair of the Eastern Window Exposed*. But *zuo* 做 can also mean "to act," and that may well be the intended meaning here. On the various ways in which *Register of Ghosts* distinguished between multiple adaptations of the same subject materials, see Idema 1990a.

13. We have generally followed Ning 1988. This is an exceptional case, in which we note emendations to the original text when we make them on the basis of a modern edition.

MALE LEAD	KSITIGARBHA, dissembling as addled postulant (act 2)
GRAND PRECEPTOR	QIN GUI
MALE LEAD	GUARD, also known as He Zongli (wedge 2, act 4)
SOOTHSAYER	SOOTHSAYER
HERDING BOY	HERDING BOY
MALE LEAD	YUE FEI's ghost (act 3)
DOOR GODS	DOOR GODS
EMPEROR	EMPEROR GAOZU of the Southern Song
MALE LEAD	YUE FEI as a god (demi-act)
KING KSITIGARBHA	KING KSITIGARBHA
EXTRAS	KING KSITIGARBHA's retinue

✤ ✤ ✤

NEWLY PRINTED AT THE GREAT CAPITAL, A FULL TEXT WITH PLOT PROMPTS: *THE AFFAIR OF THE EASTERN WINDOW EXPOSED*

[WEDGE]

MALE LEAD, *costumed, enters leading* TWO GENERALS—*takes his seat and opens*: I[14] am Yue Fei, also known as Pengju. Since my youth I practiced the martial arts. I followed Emperor Gaozong during his Southern Crossing. We spent no more than ten days in Jinling[15] before the Fourth Great Prince of the state of Jin[16] caught up and attacked. When he arrived at the town of Qiantang[17] to the west of the Zhe, he called it the Temporary Abode and ascended the imperial throne. I lead my troops here at Zhuxian Town to stand against the enemy, and the Fourth Great Prince has locked his gates and doesn't dare come out. All my life my ambition has been the recapture of

14. It is an idiosyncrasy of this text that it uses the symbol 厶 to denote the first-person pronoun. Consistent in the beginning, later this symbol is used interchangeably with the regular first-person pronoun, *an* 俺.
15. Jinling is another name for the modern city of Nanjing.
16. This is Wanyan Zongbi 完顏宗弼 (also known as Wanyan Wochuo 完顏斡啜, Wanyan Wushu 完顏兀朮, Wanyan Wochu 完顏斡出, Wanyan Huangwochu 完顏晃斡出; d. 1148), one of the major commanders in the Jin defeat of the Song.
17. This refers to the modern city of Hangzhou.
18. That is, Kaifeng.

the Eastern Capital.[18] Recently I had a proposal submitted to His Majesty—I wish to set out on my campaign but I have not yet received an imperial edict. These last few days my thoughts have been agitated, I don't know why. [EMISSARY *enters carrying the imperial edict and the golden plaque*—MALE LEAD *receives the edict and speaks*:] I don't know what is going on at court. Zhang Xian and Yue Yun,[19] guard this border carefully. Today I better mount up and leave.

([XIANLÜ MODE:] *Duanzheng hao*)

In a single day I'm summoned by His Majesty
No less than thirteen times.
Most likely I must turn back my million brave troops.
Could it be that at court some kind of secret plot is afoot?
If not,
Why would they dispatch imperial emissaries as regularly as the nodes of bamboo?[20]
(*Reprise*)
It must be that
The Sagely Enlightened Ruler especially summons me to be feasted and rewarded;
How could he be willing
To believe words of slander and "grow branches beyond the nodes"?[21]
This can only be
A ceasefire, an end to the war, and perhaps a return to court—
I silently ponder this matter:
This must be
An appointment to office and rank by imperial grace;
A clear summons to be rewarded with gold and treasure.
When I will return with an increased number of troops,
I'll display the *Three Strategies*, use the *Six Tactics*,[22]
Recover the Nine Prefectures,[23] retake the capital city,
Slaughter their fierce generals, and bloody the slain corpses.
When I will have retaken the Four Capitals[24] and Nine Prefectures,
I will have fulfilled my lifetime's ambition!
Exits.

19. Yue Fei's adopted son (1119–1141).
20. That is, with such frequency.
21. "To grow branches beyond the nodes" means to create problems and find fault.
22. See chap. 2, n. 34, on the *Six Tactics* and chap. 3, n. 77, on the *Three Strategies*.
23. The "Nine Prefectures" refer to the area directly controlled by the capital. Here the term refers more widely to northern China.
24. The Four Capitals refer to the Eastern Capital Kaifeng (also known as Bianliang); the Western Capital, Luoyang; the Southern Capital, Shangqiu; and the Northern Capital, Daming.

[ACT 1]

MALE LEAD *enters wearing a cangue and opens*: When I was summoned and arrived at the palace gate, I was not taken to see the emperor, but Qin Gui had me sent down to the Court of Judicial Review for interrogation. His Majesty trusts treacherous ministers and rebellious sons and harms us, his meritorious ministers! "In times of Great Peace there is no need any more for the old generals." How true that is!

([XIANLÜ MODE:] *Dian jiangchun*)

I established the state and brought peace to the nation;
Was surrounded by
Tiger braves and wolf generals.
On the battlefield I slept in the snow and rested on frost.
On your behalf
I controlled strategic[25] mountains and rivers!

(*Hunjiang long*)

I recall how I "subdued men and captured generals,"
Engaged in bitter and murderous battles a thousand times,
And I have wound up
Wearing a cangue and walking in chains—
To no avail I
Extended the land and expanded the borders!
I truly believe there is
A purple seal-ribbon official who "manipulates the Son of Heaven to command the liege lords,"[26]
And wants to harm us iron-armored generals who guard the border passes and smash enemy troops!
On your behalf I
Wiped away the demonic ether,
Cleansed away that demonic miasma,
But I cannot
Enter my name into the registers.
Truly
Wrongly interrogated in front of the hall,
I consider how you all conspire in front of the emperor,
And involuntarily

---

25. Literally, where "two can withstand a hundred," that is, "strong and easily defensible."

26. Cao Cao (155–220), vilified throughout later Chinese history as an evil warlord, was said to "manipulate the Son of Heaven to command the liege lords." The colors of gowns and accoutrements were determined by rank, so purple was one of the most prestigious colors. The line refers to Qin Gui.

My hero's tears fall drop by drop on the tips of this cangue.

I imagine that

One order of our general who controls the commander's headquarters[27]

Will never supersede

The three statutes of the law[28] of those who sit in the Executive Office.[29]

Speaks: It was not Yue Fei who rebelled! August Heaven can make this clear!

(*Youhulu*)

I remember how a mere thirteen men with swirling sleeves ascended the walls overlooking Bianliang,

And imprisoned the retired emperor there at Green City.[30]

Speaks: And scared eight million men of the imperial guard so much they stripped off their armor and threw away their helmets!

At that time

There was not one precious sword in a sheath that could pull out its autumn frost!

Yang Jian[31]

Was a parasitic lazybones commander in chief;

Cai Jing,[32]

A letter-carrying, note-presenting prime minister.

One "caretaker of the household" destroyed it;

And one "supposed to bring peace to the nation" lost it.[33]

How many golden branches and jade leaves[34] were made captives and had to leave their native land!

---

27. Yue Fei.

28. When Liu Bang, the later founder of the Han dynasty, first entered the capital area of the former Qin dynasty, his minister Xiao He established a law code consisting of three statutes.

29. Qin Gui; and more generally, that field commanders are always subject to political whims of ministers at court.

30. When the troops of the Jin, led by thirteen generals, appeared outside Kaifeng in late 1126, the city was completely unprepared for war and the attackers mounted the walls without major opposition. The Jin generals then ordered Huizong and Qinzong to come out to Green City 青城, south of the capital, where the emperors stayed when performing the winter sacrifices at the altar of heaven. It was called Green City because for many years it was constructed of temporary tents and hangings of green cloth.

31. Yang Jian 楊戩 (d. 1121) was Emperor Huizong's favorite eunuch.

32. Cai Jing 蔡京 (1047–1126) served as prime minister for most of the reign of Emperor Huizong. His characterization here suggests he served as an intermediary in the emperor's dalliance with the courtesan Li Shishi 李師師, which is recounted in *Xuanhe yishi* 宣和遺事 (*Anecdotes of the Proclaiming Harmony Period*). The first two chapters of this work provide an account of Huizong's failure as a ruler, while the final two chapters describe the humiliating sufferings of the two captive emperors (Huizong and Qinzong) following the Jurchen conquest.

33. This is a not so subtle reference to the idea of governing the state by extending one's moral virtue from the self to All-Under-Heaven, as stated in the famous *Great Learning*: from perfecting the self one could order the family, by ordering the family through ethical behavior, one could govern the nation, by governing the nation with ethical behavior, one could bring peace to All-Under-Heaven.

34. "Golden branches and jade leaves" refer to members of the imperial family.

If at that time
The clay horse had not allowed the Prince of Kang to escape,
(*Tianxia le*)
Then at present
The rivers and mountains of the house of Song would all belong to the Fourth Prince!
Truly taken whole, the capital sundered, its walls in ruins!
On that battlefield[35]
Once again for you I secured the sun and moon and stabilized the four directions.
How many of us died on the battlefield?
How many wounds in defeating the enemy?
But that was just
"All the merits in the world aren't worth the paper they are written on."[36]
Since I am supposed to have planned rebellion, where are the stockpiled fodder and the assembled provisions? Who ever saw those?
(*Nezha ling*)
You think about it and consider it well:
There on the field of death, on the field of battle—
You think about it and consider it well:
I stabilized the nation, secured the nation!
You think about it and consider it well:
I established the mainstays of the court, the mainstays of its norms.
I should never have
Supported the imperial cause until it could rise again;
I should never have
Guarded the mountains and rivers until they were strongly held;
I should never have
Restored order until "earth grew old and heaven was ruined."[37]
(*Que ta zhi*)
I should never have determined survival or demise,
Arrayed swords and lances.
You truly
Made your plots and unrolled your schemes
To damage and harm the able and good.

35. Perhaps this refers to Yue Fei's victories over Wuzhu in Henan in 1140?
36. Literally part of a quote, "[A thousand generations] of merit is worth half a sheet of paper."
37. Earth growing old and heaven becoming ruined is a political metaphor for establishing a new dynasty or court. Here it refers to the fact that he kept things together until the Southern Song could establish itself in Hangzhou.

You try to drive me into the net of heaven and snares of earth;
And want to make my nine relatives[38] all suffer disaster!
(*Jisheng cao*)
I lift my head and interrogate high heaven;
My hero's rage blames the welkin above.
I questioned the Lord of Heaven, but never provoked Heaven to send down
a sign!
I governed the local population, but never made the local population unsettled;
I commanded a whole army, but never let the whole army be sacrificed.
As a result I'm now
Shackled in chains from head to toe and forced to kneel in front of the hall—
This is no
"Black parasol flying over my head"![39]
(*Cunli yagu*)
I should never have
Supported the One Man to become emperor—
I made the myriad people lose all hope.
I should never have
Served the dynasty, supported the state,
And swept away the smoke and dust both night and day.
I should never have
Depended on my skills
Or relied on my courage
To take possession until mountains and rivers grew strong,
To protect the four seas until they were peaceful,
The imperial enterprise flourished,
And the people's concerns fell away.
That was the way in which
I asked for an office and received rewards.
(*Yuanhe ling*)
I never got to enjoy any "gold getting on, silver getting off my horse,"
Even though I should have been "a general in the field, a minister at court."
For you I
Wrested away battle flags, overturned battle drums, led the braves,
Yet could not line up twelve rows of golden hairpins.[40]

38. In case of rebellion the culprit was executed together with his "nine classes of relatives." There is considerable discussion concerning which classes of relatives were included under this phrase. See chap. 1, n. 58.

39. The umbrella that shades an official when he is traveling with his retinue.

40. Crowds of beautifully dressed female servants.

But you let this herding boy, this village yokel, this coarse rustic oaf,[41]
On the other hand, be able at day's end to ascend to the Son of Heaven's hall!
(*Shangma jiao*)
There is no need to be so cruel—
Are you still afraid I'll run amok?
You say it's better
To beat me first and discuss the issue later:
I've become
The plowing ox that is whipped by its owner.
I see that the outer provinces are abandoned;
The inner provinces are protected by the Hanyang River;[42]
His Majesty has always wanted to reside in Su and Hang![43]
(*You simen*)
I only fear he doesn't know that disaster will arise behind "the screen of reverence"![44]
You intend to
Disorder the mainstays of the court:
You falsified the order that tricked me into leaving the border region.
For you "there is no world, just your official position,"[45]
And you have secretly set out swords and axes at the side of the stairs.
(*Sheng hulu*)
Quite different from
"Drunken beauties by the side of the embroidered zither"![46]
If now we accord with Heaven and abide by its proper time—
But those who go against Heaven: Heaven does not claim their lives;
And those who obey Heaven: disaster is sent down by Heaven;
Those who disobey Heaven: they are not paid back by the deities;
Those who obey Heaven: they suffer the calamities!
(*Jisheng cao*)
You say that I rebelled against the court—
I should not have aided the altars of state.
I should not have

41. Qin Gui.
42. That is, the Yangtze.
43. Su and Hang are Suzhou and Hangzhou, often described as heaven on earth.
44. The "screen of reverence" is the wall a few feet behind the entrance that blocks outsiders from viewing what is going on inside in the courtyard and in the reception hall. Upon reaching this screen, visitors act in a more respectful way than outside the compound. Disasters that arise "behind the screen of reverence" are rebellions that arise within the family or when a confidant manipulates the ruler.
45. A common saying that means you presume on your power to bully others, caring only for your own benefit.
46. A line from the Tang poet Du Fu 杜甫 (712–770).

Subdued Qi Fang, destroyed his lair, and so displayed my cunning;[47]

I should not have

Captured the bandit Li Cheng and taken him to the commander's tent.[48]

I should not have

Defeated the Jin and supported Gaozong so he might flourish.

You want to

Have me beheaded in the marketplace,

This is no

"Merits depicted in the Gallery Soaring Beyond the Mist"![49]

Speaks: August Heaven will reveal Yue Fei's loyalty and filial piety!

(*Zhuan Coda*)

You have thrown me onto death row for criminals who commit the Ten Abominations![50]

Never again will I be seated in the lotus-flower tent of Nine Tripods.[51]

But how would I ever

Willingly confess to the crime of plotting rebellion?

When I die,

I'll become a loyal and filial ghost who bears wrongs and carries injustice.

At present there are

Small states and neighboring nations that invade our borders,

And Qin Gui collaborates with them in raising sword and lance.

Your Majesty,

I have to fear you'll not be seated for long on your Dragon Throne!

When I die,

The result will be that throughout the world the common people all will say:

"Yue Fei, father and sons,

Should never have risked their lives by making the south submit and the north surrender;

Or exhausted their strength in cleaning the west and routing the east!"

After the killing of YUE FEI, YUE YUN *and* ZHANG XIAN ○ [YUE FEI *sings*:][52]

Your Majesty, you're like one who cuts down the heaven-supporting, ocean-bridging purple-gold pillar.

---

47. Yue Fei defeated Qi Fang 戚方 and his marauding troops in 1130.

48. Yue Fei defeated Li Cheng 李成 in 1134.

49. See chap. 3, n. 72.

50. The "Ten Abominations" are the most serious crimes, such as rebellion and parricide, which do not allow for pardon.

51. Of the commander in chief.

52. Great generals instrumental in founding and running the state. This last line is sung by a dying Yue Fei; the special circumstances of this shift in singer is marked in the text by a single circle (○) between the stage direction and Yue Fei's lines.

[ACT 2]

MALE LEAD *enters costumed as* ADDLED POSTULANT, *carrying a "fire pipe,"*[53] *and recites:* . . .[54]

I am the god Ksitigarbha, but I have transformed myself into a stupid postulant. Here in Lingyin Monastery I will leak the Grand Preceptor's crime of the eastern window. *A poem reads*:

Harm others, you harm yourself, your own body comes to an end:
I am mad and I'm addled, so I'm just fine.
Just think about it: in the arena of mine and thine
In the end it's hard to escape and the date of death draws near!

([ZHONGLÜ MODE:] *Fendie'er*)

Don't laugh at me for my dirty face and addled madness,
You cannot probe the main drift of my original mind—
Just because
The people of this world are too stupid to understand subtle Buddhist hints.
A head of short hair, all disheveled,
I'm toting a tattered carrying bag,
Yet inside it is hidden all of heaven and earth.
Holding my fire pipe I've left the monastery's kitchen.

(*Sings*:)[55]

I've descended to earth to leak a heavenly secret.
(*Zui chunfeng*)
I never
Worshipped, read sutras, or confessed in the Dharma Hall,
I only
Do all the heavy physical work in this monastery of ours.
All because you
Deceive the emperor above and abuse his vassals below —
Continues in speech: You may say that I am stupid, / But I say that you're a traitor. / "It may be easy to capture a tiger, / But it's impossible to set it free."[56] Grand Preceptor!
These words apply only to you,

---

53. The fire pipe is an iron pipe used in the kitchen to blow on the fire.
54. It would appear that a self-introductory poem has dropped out of the text at this point.
55. The presence of this stage direction here suggests that the aria had been interrupted by a short dialogue or a line of inserted speech, perhaps as simple as, "And why did I do this?" See the usage of this stage direction in the aria *Hong xiuxie* later in this same act.
56. By quoting this proverb, Qin Gui's wife, it is said, convinced her husband of the need to kill Yue Fei once he had imprisoned him and made an enemy out of him.

So don't you laugh at me for my muttering,
I am far clearer than you!
You ask me for my background—
I disclose my background to you,
Let's see how you will answer!
What do you mean "I don't know why you're here"?
(*Ying xianke*)
I am fully aware of why you came,
I knew it before you could open your mouth.
I know how afraid you are!
You are having terrible dreams, and that's why
You come and bother our simple monastery,
To pray to gods and ghosts,
To join the congregation for worshipping, sutra reading, and confessions.
Forget about imploring our bodhisattva—
Isn't it said: "I pray for Guanyin's help"!
Waits until GRAND PRECEPTOR *has spoken.*
(*Shiliu hua*)
Grand Preceptor, you ask me for the truth in every detail,
Listen to me as I will explain cause and reason.
Didn't you at that time trust your worthy wife?
She urged you on and on—
How can you not know this yourself?
By the eastern window you did not grasp "the intention in coming from the west."[57]
I may be muddleheaded,
But you have no defense.
Just because
Slippery, treacherous, and cunningly obsequious you beclouded your own mind,
I know already in advance
Whatever thought you have.
(*Dou anchun*)
I know you collaborate with a foreign country—
How can that be "serving the nation, supporting the state"?
We have to carefully consider all our human actions
To avoid regretting them later.

57. The "intention in coming from the west" was the intention of the sixth-century Indian monk Bodhidharma in coming to China and preaching Chan. Here the expression more generally refers to the Buddhist notion of compassion.

Haven't you heard "Transparent clear Heaven cannot be deceived"?
Judging by the deeds you committed
You're here to scare the ghosts and fool the gods,
Playing [the turtle that] hides its head and shows its tail!

Speaks: Grand Preceptor, don't laugh at my fire pipe!

(*Hong xiuxie*)
It originally was a gentleman
But it wanted to grab power and rely on might;
As soon as you blow in it, it makes smoke disappear and ashes fly!
Because it grows branches beyond the nodes it makes people suffer.
So why don't I leave it in the kitchen
And carry it always with me in my hands?

This here is what I don't control: . . . *Sings*:

Daring to raise clouds of dust,
Ruining the altars of the state!
(*Shi'er yue*)
I laugh at you, a prime minister at court,
Who cares only about pestering this cleric.
Here I lay it out oh so clearly,
There he mulls it over oh so darkly.
It's not the case that this mad monk is just flapping his lips—
It's better than undeservedly eating palace food.
(*Yaomin ge*)
As long as you are seated you won't notice, but once you rise you'll feel hungry;
This is
Brought about by "white flour on both ends."[58]
Don't get alarmed when I eat yet another two,
For you've wrongly killed three—who are you going to blame it on?
Everyone under heaven clearly understands,
Clearly understands,
The motive at work.

The common people are just like a soured bun stuffing:

Everyone's belly is filled with gas![59]
(*Manting fang*)
You want only to ruin the dynasty and wreck the state.
When did you ever

---

58. A common saying that means that something is not what it appears to be, yet both people involved are still trying to use it to gain something or to gain favor; to put something over on someone.

59. Rage.

Wrest away a battle flag, overturn a battle drum,
Engage in a murderous fight?
You turn the merits of other people at the border into crimes:
Your only ability is changing right into wrong.
Even a divine prescription cannot remove that illness of yours;
Without a miraculous drug even I cannot cure you!
You had those heroes
All turned into ghosts by a blade of steel:
At Yunyang[60] blood soiled their clothes.
(*Kuaihuo san*)
Because of your crimes my storm[61] only increases,
And where the storm passes, the sun will shine.
Just because you
Grabbed the clouds and held them tight, no copious rain could fall.[62]
And should any rain fall,
It will be Heaven weeping for Yue Fei!
(*Baolao'er*)
That "head replacer" will catch up to you soon:[63]
Did you ever fear crossing the law with a senseless crime?
I recite no sutras, but that is so much better than you, cursed by all.
Please consider carefully the meaning of this eight-line poem.
Your heart I know —
Once one word has been spoken,
No four horses can chase it down!
The poem reads:

Long I've heard that a prime minister orders the cosmos;
Occupying the very first position among all officials.
All ministers he leads to bow at the imperial palace,
Offices are where he shows respect to elderly statesmen.
Having plans, he is able to make the barbarians retreat;
Having stopped treachery and heresy, he allows guards to be at ease.
Stalwart ministers will, with all their heart, loyally serve the state,
Road-traveling passers-by talk of Great Peace.[64]

60. A conventional name for the execution grounds.
61. The word *feng* has the meaning of both "storm" and "madness."
62. Dragons are in charge of rain and clouds. As the emperor is said to be a dragon, the line suggests that Qin Gui is abusing imperial power. The power of the emperor to enrich his people's lives is stopped.
63. The ghosts of those who have died before their time will be allowed to be reborn only once they have found a substitute, and so they are looking for victims. Here the suggestion is that Yue Fei will drag Qin Gui off to hell.
64. In the original, the opening words of these eight lines make up the sentence "For a long time you occupied the Executive Office and blocked advancement of worthy men."

The scenery here is really beautiful.

(*Shua hai'er*)

This monastery towers up grandly and beautifully as hills pile up their green;
At the lake's waterfall the haze is luminous, the water blue.

These mountains

Of a thousand layers and valleys by the myriad resemble cloth panels of a screen;
The clear expanse of the jade lake laps at the full length of Su's Dike.[65]
The green mountains can only grind down past and present,
But the verdant water can never wash away right and wrong.
To no avail you cultivate blessings:[66]

All it will achieve is

Your own death and your family's destruction,
Scattered like tiles, gone like stars.

(*Third from Coda*)

Now Yue Fei's merit in securing dynasty and nation is finished;
And Qin Gui's betrayal of the court is known to all:
The enmity between the two of you is like water from the eaves.[67]
Because this treacherous and sycophantic prime minister was vicious in a thousand ways,
He sent to his death a noble and heroic general whose might extended to the eight directions.
What you have done violates the principles of heaven.
Don't say the divinities will not repay you for that:
The only issue is whether that will happen early or late.

(*Second from Coda*)

Look, your bottle of sins is full;
Quickly now, so quickly the date of your death presses close,
And those three men will be waiting for you in the court of shades!

These words are right on:

"Before the Metal Wind[68] stirs, the cicada is already aware;
Secretly send off Impermanence,[69] you still don't know you are dead."
At that time you go off to the world at the springs,[70]

---

65. Su's Dike of West Lake was a causeway constructed by the famous statesman and poet Su Shi 蘇軾 (Dongpo 東坡, 1036–1101) when he served as prefect of Hangzhou.
66. Specifically by burning incense and distributing alms.
67. Water dripping from the roof always falls in the same spot.
68. The Metal Wind is the wind of autumn, since that season is associated with the element metal in the Five Phases theory.
69. Impermanence (Wuchang 無常) is the personification of death.
70. The "world at the springs" is the underworld, which is also known as Yellow Springs.

You will surely suffer the punishments for the Ten Abominations;
Don't think you can escape from retribution on the Six Paths![71]
(*Coda*)
I've explained it to you like a riddle for you to guess,
You should have doubts about it like some depressing affair in your heart.
One day you will understand what I meant by the affair of the eastern window exposed,
But I'm sure that you'll be beating your breast, for then you will be filled with regret.
Exits.

[WEDGE]

MALE LEAD, *costumed as* GUARD, *enters.—Speaks*: My surname is He; I'm He Zongli. I have been ordered by Grand Preceptor Qin to go and arrest that addled postulant in Lingyin Monastery in the Western Hills. Who would have imagined that he would have disappeared? He left behind one sheet of paper on which there is an eight-line poem. I'll have to show it to the grand preceptor.—*Acts out greeting* GRAND PRECEPTOR.—*Waits for* GRAND PRECEPTOR *to read the poem.—The poem reads*:

I've abandoned the cassock, taken leave of meditation;
I didn't come to the dusty world to live in this little temple of the mind.
I have no love for those two meals of vegetarian porridge;
Nor any greed for tiny profit or an empty name.
My nature resembles the white cloud just rising from a mountaintop;
My mind is like an orphaned moon sinking in a cold pool.
If the prime minister should ask, "Where did you go?"
Say, "I live on the Number One Mountain in the Southeast."

Grand Preceptor Qin orders me to go to Mountain Number One in the Southeast and arrest the addled postulant Ye Shouyi, so I will have to go.
Exits in a flash.[72]

Waits till SOOTHSAYER *has entered and finished speaking.*—MALE LEAD *enters quickly and speaks*:—Over there I see a soothsayer. First of all I'll ask him for the road to the Mountains of the Southeast, and secondly I'll buy a prediction.—*Waits until* SOOTHSAYER *has spoken and exits. Acts out gazing after him and bows.*

71. The Six Paths are the six stages of reincarnation: as a god, as a human being, as an animal, as a demon, as a hungry ghost, and as a denizen of hell.

72. Exits very quickly, unobtrusively.

([XIANLÜ MODE:] *Shanghua shi*)

Within the Six Lines[73] he can discern disaster and blessing;

He can guide the perplexed through the Eight Trigrams.[74]

Waits for HERDING BOY *to play his flute.—Acts out listening.*

I only hear

The sound of the flute slowly fade away.

At this time the sky is darkening, evening is falling:

This leads me straight to Ghost Gate Pass![75]

Exits in a flash.

Waits until KING KSITIGARBHA *enters and speaks.—After acting out greeting him.—Speaks*: Where didn't I look for you? But you were here! Grand Preceptor Qin issued a warrant for your arrest!

(*Reprise*)

Here

Is clearly written "Number One Mountain in the Southeast."

Waits until GRAND PRECEPTOR QIN *enters wearing a cangue and speaks.*

I see only demon runners and buffalo heads[76] in a somber mist;

I see the grand preceptor

Suppressing his tears to recount his sufferings.

He tells me to inform Her Ladyship:

"Only say, the Affair of the Eastern Window Is Exposed."

That will have to do as

"For both horse and man, report we are out of danger"![77]

Exits.

[ACT 3]

Waits until after EMPEROR *enters, speaks, stops, and falls asleep.—After* DOOR GODS *enter.*[78] MALE LEAD, *costumed as* HUN SOUL, *enters with* TWO GENERALS *and opens.—* After we were wrongfully murdered by Qin Gui, our predestined lifetime in the realm

73. The six broken (yin) and unbroken (yang) lines that make up each of the sixty-four hexagrams of the *Book of Changes.*

74. The Eight Trigrams are each made up of three broken or unbroken lines. The Eight Hexagrams combine in pairs to produce the sixty-four hexagrams of the *Book of Changes.*

75. The entry to the other world.

76. The huge staff of the underworld prisons includes horse-faced and buffalo-headed wardens and sbires.

77. In ironic use of the common phrase sent home to say one's travels are going well and that one is not in danger.

78. The door gods, depicted on the two panels of a gate, guard the house against the intrusion of ghosts. In this case, the ghost of Yue Fei will have to beg them to be allowed inside the palace.

of light was not yet finished and, having received a note from the heavenly Buddha and an edict from the Jade Emperor, the Sage Emperor of the Eastern Marchmount[79] has ordered us to appear in a dream to Gaozong, the retired emperor.

(YUEDIAO MODE: [*Dou anchun*])

Wherever we go clouds of resentment coldly obscure us
And mournful winds wildly howl.
We left the City of Those Who Wrongly Died,[80]
Made a quick turn and arrived at the backside of the Dark Mountains.
I failed to highlight my name in the green chronicles,[81]
All I achieved was
Losing my head to a blade of steel.
Each day
"Qin does not care, Wei will not take us."[82]
Eventually, for no rhyme or reason, we suffered execution,
But don't think I will just dumbly let it lie!
(*Zihua'er xu*)
Our three souls are cold and lonely;
Our seven spirits are resentful and full of grief;[83]
Our whole consciousness tumbles and drifts away.
I am no
Evil specter that brings down disaster;
I am
A liege lord who put out every effort.
You ask for the reasons?
I will clearly explain this bone-piercing enmity to our Sagely Lord,
And what I say will contain not a single lie or error.
Superior Gods,[84] I thank you for allowing these resentful ghosts who died unjustly
To enter these Phoenix Pavilions and Dragon Lofts.[85]
(*Xiaotao hong*)

---

79. Refers to the native Chinese god of Mount Tai in Shandong, who was in charge of the underworld and who is more commonly called Great Thearch of the Eastern Marchmount (Dongyue Dadi 東嶽大帝). He was one of the most widely venerated deities of China during the first half of the second millennium.
80. The City of Those Who Wrongly Died (Wangsicheng 枉死城) in the underworld houses the souls of those who died an unjust death.
81. Historical writings are referred to as "green chronicles" because before the invention of paper they were written on strips made of bamboo or wood.
82. A common phrase for a person no one wants to have anything to do with, or someone with no one to turn to.
83. Traditional Chinese concepts of the spirit of the body credit every human being with three souls and seven spirits that disperse upon his or her death.
84. The door gods.
85. The imperial palace.

I bow my body, fold my hands, and deeply lower my head;
I dare not knock on the dragon couch!
As I bow and dance and shout out thrice,[86] I am suffering in pain.
I see the emperor suddenly lift his head.
As he, alarmed, returns to the imperial bedchamber, so I address the Celestial Face.
In the shade of the candles I sincerely kowtow,
And as I speak, old memories wound my heart:
As before, my brows furrowed with sorrow for Temple and Hall.[87]
(*Gui santai*)
While still alive your servant suffered greatly,
As racing in armor and helmet
I was always the vanguard;
As your commander
Toward the sandy borderlands I pressed on my brave warriors.
As your servant
Says this, he is overcome by shame,
Recalling when my, your insignificant minister's,
Leading of men to take generals alive suddenly ended,
I ended up
Wearing a cangue, in shackles and chains, meeting the strictest incarceration.
Your servant had thought that
Leading the army, eternal spring would last forever,
And never imagined that
Halfway down the road of life he would draw a short straw.
(*Zihua'er xu*)
Your servant's life was
Worth no more than a dewdrop on a flowering branch,
Some willow floss tossed by the wind,
Or a floating bubble on the stream!
Leading the army your servant risked his life,
He was the opponent of the Fourth Great Prince,
And peacefully recovered the Four Capitals and Nine Prefectures.
I never imagined that
I could not serve my Lord and King to the very end—
When I raise this topic, my tears course down!

86. Officials approaching the throne bowed and "danced" (went through a prescribed series of ritual steps) and thrice shouted, "May the emperor live ten thousand years."
87. The Ancestral Temple of the reigning dynasty and the main palace hall stand metonymically for the state.

Just imagine how your servant's
Merits that capped the world
Are now all deleted with a single stroke!
The three of us have exhausted all our energy for the country!
(*Jin jiaoye*)
Your servant risked his life to fight on the battlefield;
Your servant has
Exhausted all his energy at the front and behind the lines.
Truly, I have been
Discarded on the execution field and no one cares.
Yet your servant's
Mind was always on the altars of state, its mountains and rivers, its universe!
(*Tiaoxiao ling*)
Your Majesty, you must get to the truth
And exact revenge for your humble servants!
As for your servant,
"One day of Impermanence, and everything is over."
I cannot
Wear a plaque or tie on a seal to receive my Lord's grace.
I wind up instead
Bound up and tied, trussed up and beaten, a victim of a hundred tortures!
How can you call that "a vassal for a thousand autumns"?
(*Tusi'er*)
Your servant hopes to be
Portrayed in an imperial pavilion, remembered for a thousand years;
Recorded in the green chronicles, leaving a name for ten thousand generations.
But your servant
Has become "a cake painted to dampen hunger,"[88] a candle in the wind.
This enmity,
This enmity,
How could I ever just let it go?
(*Sheng Yaowang*)
Your servant's
Writ of accusation
Never spelled out his crime.
You should have thought thrice before you pursued it.
Your servant
Recovered four hundred counties beyond the borders,

88. A common image for an illusion, a phantom.

Yet you turned Lingyan Gallery into a prison for officials,
So who in the future will agree to "share and so dispel the emperor's cares"?
(*Luosiniang*)
Your servant
Risked his life, exhausted his strength, and asked for coarse provisions to guard the borders;
Qin Gui lacked any merit, received emoluments, and undeservedly enjoyed palace food and imperial wine.
He wants to wipe away the mountains and rivers of the house of Song with a single stroke;
Out of love for gold and silk he collaborated with the Great Jin!
(*Miandaxu*)
Your servant
Avails himself of the mournful wind's soughing and sighing,
Of the sadness and pitifulness of enmity's ethers—
The Lord of Heaven pays no attention,
The dungeons of hell find it hard to take us in!
I abide with "wild grasses and idle flowers that fill the earth with sorrow,"[89]
I cannot
Be enfeoffed by imperial decree as marquis of ten thousand households.
I ponder the unfathomable nature of human affairs,
And lament that heroes flow away with the river!
(*Zhuolusu*)
Your servants want
To turn back away but do not turn
But crowd together where they were slain.
Qin Gui baited the hook,
And we fell into his trap—
How could we be saved?
At the beginning we saw only the bait and not the hook!
(*Reprise*)
Considering that your servant's ambition, alas, has not been requited:
Do away with Qin Gui so his life will be ended!
Your Majesty, pursue this matter,
Remember it well in your heart.
I have bitterly recalled the circumstances,
Clearly explained them to you.

89. This is a common line in Yuan drama, used in reference to, among other things, the sites of past glories of generals. Here, he means the memories of earlier days that the flowers and grass evoke in him.

Grab that beast,
Scrape the flesh from his bones
And publicly display his crimes—
Even so you cannot release the sorrow in my heart!
(*Coda*)
A loyal minister can never escape the schemes of an evil minister;
Your Majesty,
May you summon your civil and military officials for a discussion.
Have swords and axes execute Qin Gui in the marketplace,
Summon my unjustly slain and resentful soul and pour out a sacrificial cup of wine on my behalf.
[*Exits.*]

[ACT 4]

MALE LEAD, *costumed as* HE [ZONG]LI, *enters.—Opens*—Who could have imagined that I would be gone for so long when the grand preceptor dispatched me to the Number One Mountain of the Southeast to arrest that addled postulant Ye Shouyi?
([ZHENGGONG MODE:] *Duanzheng hao*)
Having received my order I dropped into the Fengdu Hell;
Saying good-bye to wife and children, I left my hometown.
But I am a capable runner,
And even in a warren of ghosts I can get by.
I've been gone for twenty years without any news.
(*Gun xiuqiu*)
On going, I was not yet forty;
On return, how many springtimes have passed?
Unaware that autumn frost has dyed my temples—
One turn of the head and a high tumulus with Qilin![90]
The changed days and months now are different;[91]
The reestablished altars of the state are secure.
Every old minister of merit is now worn-out from all his efforts;
Others now are high and prominent—this is a different world!

90. Referring to the death and burial of Qin Gui. The ceremonial path leading to a grave of a high official would be lined with stone statues of various real and mythical animals and bureaucrats. The *qilin* was a hoofed creature with the head of a dragon, tail of an ox, and shape of a horse or deer. Males had a single antler. It was a gentle animal that appeared during the reigns of true sages.

91. As a new emperor has ascended the throne and a new reign title has been adopted.

Indeed one may say:
"On the Long River the waves behind urge on the waves in front."
Today
"A new lord is enthroned, the old one is removed":
Years and months seem to rush!
(*Dai guduo*)
In front of the jade steps Your Majesty questions your servant,
Allow your servant to tell you the full story of the grand preceptor.
"On that day he returned from performing pious deeds,
And on the road he ran into a man:
That Shi Quan, with reckless courage, tried to kill him,
But Qin Gui's blessings were large so that none could get near.[92]
He had gone to Lingyin Monastery to pray for good fortune—
Who could have thought that on the way home he'd invite disaster!
(*Tang xiucai*)
The grand preceptor suddenly got it,
And he discussed the poem,
Saying, 'This addled postulant's good words set norms.'
Then he said, 'These eight characters
Hold all of heaven and earth by themselves and spell his own death!'
Because of this he dispatched me as a runner
To arrest and summon that monk;
Because of this
It was an urgent matter.
(*Gun xiuqiu*)
As I remember
Grand Preceptor Qin was by nature very fierce,
So I, He Zongli, had no choice but to hurry and leave.
As I was traveling a storm arose that shook the Gate of Heaven;
And in the shortest time it blew until the earth grew lifeless, heaven dark.
That storm left the mountains in a whirlwind of weird dust
And entered the mountains overturning failing clouds.
It almost blew so strongly that Mount Hua would collapse in a second;
It blew so strongly that it whistled by a Mount Kunlun that could scarce offer protection!
That storm toppled old trees of the Six Dynasties,[93] roots and all;

92. In the first month of 1150, Shi Quan 施全, a petty officer, unsuccessfully tried to assassinate Qin Gui, who was on his way to court.

93. The period of the fourth to six centuries, when Nanjing served as the capital of the so-called Southern Dynasties that ruled the Yangtze valley while northern China was ruled by a sequence of "barbarian" dynasties.

And stirred up frightening waves on the ten thousand mile Long River,[94]
No escape front or back!
(*Tang xiucai*)
Nowhere was there a distant village, its wide-spaced fence infringing on the ancient road,
But I saw a soothsayer hiding away in these deepest mountains;
His only neighbors
The wild grasses and idle flowers.
'If you want to know the road through the mountain,
You should ask the travelers on the road.'
. . .

When your servant went forward to question that soothsayer, that soothsayer said, 'Don't ask about . . .'
(*Daodao ling*)
As soon as I had finished asking,
Auspicious clouds and happy mists had appeared, carried by the breeze,
And I perceived the tune of a flute, [played by a herding boy on the back of his buffalo].[95]
I asked him for the road to the Mountains of the Southeast,
And when he pointed them out, that postulant of Lingyin Monastery became ever more distinct as closer he came.
That boy had already disappeared, oh yeah!
That boy had already disappeared, oh yeah!
So I stepped forward and grabbed that monk to question him!

Speaks: Your servant grabbed him and said, "The grand preceptor has issued a warrant for your arrest!" But that monk said, "There is no need to arrest me, because the grand preceptor is already here. If you don't believe me, have a look!"
(*Tang xiucai*)
He had just finished speaking when I saw the grand preceptor in [chains and a cangue],
And there sure were no jade maidens and golden lads to meet him and show him the way![96]

---

94. Following Zheng Qian's insertion of the three characters *hai lang ben* 駭浪奔; Zheng Qian 1962, 298. Ning 1988, 1:89, changes it to *guailang ben* 怪浪奔. The original text is heavily damaged here.

95. Zheng Qian leaves this line blank, with the notation, "Seven or eight characters are missing here." Ning 1988, 89, adds the words *jian yi mutong niubei* 見一牧童牛背, which would be a likely scene. But it remains a conjecture as to the exact wording.

96. When a virtuous person dies, he or she is escorted by a jade maiden and golden boy as he or she appears before the ten kings of hell.

There was only a gang of vicious buffalo heads and ghostly lictors.
Making Qin Gui
Come see your servant
And they pushed him tumbling out through the gates of hell.
(*Gun xiuqiu*)
The grand preceptor said, "I saw that addled postulant in the western hills write that text,
But never thought
That crime by the eastern window would be so important!"
We can say
His fate was fitting punishment for his desire to deceive his lord and king to build up his family fortune,
All because
He was matchless in past or present for abusing the common people and coveting gold and silk.
He should never have
[Stolen grain from] the state granaries,
Pilfered silver from the government vault.
His vicious mind in a thousand ways went way beyond his proper bounds;
He had usurped all military authority,
Wrongly slayed
Generals outside of the capital.
In the beginning, disaster struck Yue Fei,
But today disaster has hit him.
How could that be compared to
"Far away it will land on sons and grandsons, close at hand it will strike oneself."
Or to "scaring the ghosts and fooling the gods."
(*Tang xiucai*)
When Her Ladyship[97] heard me explain why he was in the world of shades,
Tears involuntarily coursed down her cheeks.
For she thought of "One night as husband and wife means loving thoughts for a hundred."
As I spoke, it made Her Ladyship truly sad and depressed
Because the grand preceptor suffered such misery.
But if she wants to meet with the grand preceptor,
She'll have to rely on her dream soul to cross those mountain passes!
(*Gun xiuqiu*)

97. Qin Gui's wife.

The instruments of torture in the world of shade are special,
More terrible than in government offices in the realm of light!
Who would have thought that he, depressingly bitter, would encounter danger and distress with such pain?
All because
Happily smiling he trapped the common folk, "washing away the grime to find their flaws"!
In exquisite pain, his skin and flesh were opened;
Gorily bloody, his flesh was separated from bone:
Wracked with pain—how could he endure the three deductions and six interrogations?
His jail keeps were all evil demons and ferocious gods.
If you want to escape the suffering of the grand preceptor's thousand kinds of cruel tortures—
You'll have to
Climb up some green mountain and transform your very body[98]
And demonstrate the ninefold loyalty and threefold chastity of a good wife.
(*Second from Coda*)
Yue Fei said Qin Gui was unwilling to learn from the story of Xiao He who pursued Han Xin
As far as Sandalwood Creek, and gave him such gifts that Han had to accept the seals of the Three Qi.[99]
He said that Your Majesty,
Ever since you left the capital fleeing on a clay horse—
Like the Exalted Ancestor of Han who got out of Yingyang[100]—
For nothing you had father and sons
Risk their lives and court their deaths
On bitter campaigns and in violent battles;
They stole battle flags and tipped over battle drums,
Nabbed generals and took their men;
Tossed the heads of men to roll on and on,
Gulped down their hot blood.

98. See chap. 3, n. 38.

99. See chap. 2, n. 38.

100. This is the posthumous title of Liu Bang, the founding emperor of the Han dynasty. When he was besieged by Xiang Yu in Yingyang and his situation was desperate, he could make his escape with a few men only because one of his generals sacrificed himself by dressing himself as Liu Bang and leaving through a different gate with the royal retinue, in this way creating a diversion. The decision to leave was first voiced by Xiao He. When Liu Bang left Yingyang, he retreated into the "area within the passes" (modern Shaanxi) and "soothed the fathers and sons outside the passes" with the idea that he would return.

You were utterly indebted to them for using their helmets as pillows—their cheeks imprinted by the moon[101]—
And for sleeping in their armor, the earth growing scales."
(*Coda*)
When a request is finally made to the Lord and King in his nine-layered Forbidden Palace and he authorizes it,
Have his decision burned and delivered to the divine Ksitigarbha who administers the vile Fengdu Hell.
Yue Fei, Yue Yun, and Zhang Xian all unjustly murdered,
Have already risen as immortals, three bodies made whole.
There is no need for a discussion about that murderous minister Qin Gui
For he lied to his emperor, deceived his lord,
And abused the black-haired people most cruelly!
Most recently there is the divine writ from the Eastern Marchmount[102]
That may replace Chen Shou's wordless stele of a thousand years ago,
A text from a thousand years ago that could not be used as evidence.[103]

[FINAL DEMI-ACT]

[MALE LEAD *enters costumed as god.*]
(*Houting hua*)
In one day I saw thirteen gold-lettered plaques;
Imperial emissaries were dispatched to open the summons.
Your servant was summoned to come to the capital as fast as fire,
And for this reason I left my stockade that very night;
Urging on my post horse I raced through the dust and crossed the Long River.
But how could I defend myself once I arrived at court?
I recall that Qin Gui had no grand strategy,
But he sent me off to the Court for Judicial Review for interrogation

101. The curved imprint of the helmet on their faces.

102. A revealed text, perhaps obtained by spirit writing, that detailed the punishments in hell of Qin Gui?

103. Chen Shou 陳壽 is the third-century author of the *Sanguo zhi* 三國志 (*Records of the Three Kingdoms*) and enjoyed a reputation as a fine historian. According to one account the stele at the grave of Qin Gui carried no inscription because his crimes were only too well-known. But this probably refers to the famous "wordless stele" at the Temple of the Jade Emperor on Mount Taishan, also the site of the Temple of the Thearch of the Eastern Marchmount, which carries no text (therefore a text that cannot be used as evidence) but was believed to be a "weight stone" under which precious documents of Taishan were kept. Here, the connection to Chen Shou is unclear since at the time this play was written, the stele was thought to have been erected by the First Emperor of the Qin. But it is clear that the writ reveals crimes so hideous that they cannot be kept silent.

And the name of "rebel against the court" was slapped on me.
Suffering such a wrong, tears of heroism filled my cheeks:
Your servant had fought your battles for more than ten years,
And now all his merits have been turned into crimes!
(*Liuye'er*)
Today this has all been thrown beyond the clouds of the ninth and highest heaven,
I will never "be one of the Three Dukes," "rise a thousand ranks in one day."
Destroy Qin Gui's three lineages and nine relatives:
Such is the enmity between these families!
May Qin Gui's coffin be split open and his corpse chopped to bits,
Because only in such a way
Will grace and revenge be clear to all!

Waits for KING KSITIGARBHA *and retinue to enter, and send off with a judgment.*

Title: Military Affairs Commissioner Yue removes threats on behalf
the of Song;
Grand Preceptor Qin secretly collaborates with rebellious traitors.
Name: He Zongli arrests the postulant of the Western Hills;
King Ksitigarbha Testifies to the Crime of the Eastern Window.

Newly Printed at the Great Capital, A Full Text with Complete Plot Prompts:
The Affair of the Eastern Window Exposed

7
Little Butcher Zhang Immolates His Child to Save His Mother

INTRODUCTION

Filial piety (*xiao* 孝) is one of the central virtues of Chinese traditional morality. As the first of the inborn moral qualities to be manifested in human relations, filial piety holds a unique and fundamental position in the growth of moral character. But, as an inescapable duty imposed on a person by virtue of birth, it held little attraction for early playwrights, unless the demands of filial piety resulted in extraordinary acts of self-sacrifice. Perhaps no act of self-sacrifice can be more extreme than the sacrifice of one's only child—in the Western tradition one only has to think of Abraham's sacrifice of Isaac or the Lord's sacrifice of his only-born Son.

Filial piety implied obedience to one's parents during their lifetime, care for them during their old age, appropriate mourning upon their death, and continual and proper sacrifices to their spirits. Its demands were total and unconditional. Few cultures can boast a written classical record that elaborated funerary ritual and ancestor worship with such meticulous care as ancient China. Filial piety was first of all an aristocratic virtue, and the earliest text exclusively devoted to filial piety, the *Classic of Filial Piety* (*Xiaojing* 孝經), stresses that filial sons make perfect bureaucrats.[1] From Tang times (618–906) we also have materials in the vernacular that set out to inculcate filial piety into more popular levels of society. These texts have a Buddhist provenance and especially stress the obligation the son incurs toward his parents for the care and pains they take in bringing him up, and they accentuate the sufferings of the mother during pregnancy, birth, and

1. Rosemont and Ames 2009. For the problematical origins of filial piety in Chinese culture, see Hsü 1971.

infancy of the child.[2] This emphasis is in line with traditional Chinese family structure—the father was expected to be stern and the mother indulgent, especially when marriages were arranged, so the emotional bond between mother and son often became the strongest of all relations.

In Song times (960–1279) and later, the teaching of filial piety was concretized in the *Twenty-four Cases of Filial Piety* (*Ershisi xiao* 二十四孝) that were depicted on temple walls and coffin sides and were printed as illustrated woodcuts with explanatory text.[3] Most of these cases deal with the devotion of sons to their living parent or parents. The acts of cheerful self-sacrifice and self-inflicted violence on behalf of often unreasonably demanding parents are many and varied. In some cases, the exemplary act of filial piety meant sacrificing one's child for the sake of the parent—one could always have other children but never a new parent. Such acts were of course, in the examples at least, always amply rewarded, occasionally by divine intervention. The names of many of these filial sons became household words.[4]

A number of these proverbial exemplars are mentioned by name in act 1 of the play translated here, *Newly Published in Old Hangzhou: Little Butcher Zhang Immolates His Child to Save His Mother* (*Gu Hang xinkan Xiao Zhangtu fen'er jiu mu* 古杭新刊小張屠焚兒救母). Zengzi 曾子, a disciple of Confucius's, was such a filial son that he felt a pain in his heart when his mother bit her finger. The filial son Guo Ju 郭巨, who lived during the Han, was so poor that he could not afford to feed both his mother and his baby son. Since his mother usually deprived herself to feed her grandchild, Guo Ju decided to bury his son. But, when he was digging the grave, at three feet into the ground, he discovered a pot of gold, inscribed with the legend "Heaven's gift to the filial son Guo Ju." Meng Zong 孟宗, an equally filial son, lived during the Jin dynasty (third and fourth centuries A.D.). His aged and ailing mother voiced a desire to eat bamboo shoots in winter. The tears he shed on the withered bamboo over the impossibility of satisfying her desire moved Heaven to sprout young bamboo. Wang Xiang 王祥, of the same era, served his evil stepmother in a most filial way. When she demanded fresh fish in the coldest month of winter, he lay down on the ice, hoping that the warmth of his body would melt the ice so he could fish. Before the ice melted, it broke open and two carp jumped out. Ding Lan 丁蘭, of Han times, lost his parents at a tender age and made a wooden statue of his mother that he served as if she were alive. When his wife pricked the statue's finger with a needle, he divorced her.

The theme of filial piety is linked in *Immolates His Child* with the veneration of the Great Thearch of the Eastern Marchmount (Dongyue Dadi 東嶽大帝). The Eastern Marchmount, or Taishan (in modern Shandong), has been venerated as a holy mountain

2. Cole 1998.

3. See Murray 2007, 65–72; Barnart 1993; and Knapp 2006.

4. Jordan 1986.

since the dawn of Chinese civilization. Since Han times at least, the Eastern Marchmount was seen as the location of the underworld (*diyu* 地獄, literally, "prison in the earth"), housing the souls of the dead. In later centuries, the Chinese came to view the realm of the dead as ruled by a huge and complicated judicial bureaucracy built on the model of its earthly counterparts. It included a host of subsidiary deities and clerks, runners, prison guards, and underlings. The Great Thearch of the Eastern Marchmount headed the central bureaucracy at Taishan. Here were kept registers of every person's predestined dates of birth and death and a full record of their deeds while alive. These files assured a speedy trial upon one's death. This central bureaucracy of Taishan had local counterparts of each level of the administration, housed throughout China in the temples of the city god (*chenghuang miao* 城隍廟). In the popular mind the underworld below the Eastern Marchmount became identified with the Buddhist notion of an underworld, headed by King Yama, in which the souls of the dead were judged in the Ten Courts of Hell, each with its own presiding judge-king.[5]

In Song times and later, the cult of the Great Thearch of the Eastern Marchmount spread widely. Its extensive bureaucracy allowed for the continuous incorporation of new deities. Our play mentions some of these—the Flaring Spirit (Bingling Gong 炳靈公), the Master of Fates (Siming Jun 司命君), and Prince Cui (Cui Fujun 崔府君). The Flaring Spirit was believed to be the third son of the Great Thearch of the Eastern Marchmount. The Master of Fates is Mao Ying 茅盈, the eldest of the three Mao brothers of Maoshan Taoist fame, who had his own temple hall at Tai'an in Eastern Peak Temple. He kept track of the good deeds and sins of each family and reported these yearly to the authorities concerned. Prince Cui had lived his mortal life during the seventh century, serving as magistrate in a number of districts. In the popular imagination, his probity as a judge on earth carried over into the underworld. Legend soon claimed supernatural powers for him during his life, and he was thought to render human justice during the day and pronounce his verdicts in the underworld at night. By the twelfth century he had become a widely venerated deity, whose yearly festival on the sixth day of the sixth month was one of the busiest festivals of the year in early twelfth century Kaifeng.

One of the specialized bureaus in the administration of the Eastern Marchmount, the Office for Speedy Retribution (Subao Si 速報司), in due time came to be headed by the incorruptible Judge Bao. The historical Judge Bao Zheng (999–1062) had established during his lifetime a reputation for perceptive investigatory powers and a fearless disregard of wealth and power. Tales soon started to circulate about his deeds and many *zaju* and *xiwen* dramatized his verdicts. Popular belief held that he had also been a judge in this world during daytime and a judge in the Court of Darkness at night.[6]

5. See Teiser 1993b.

6. See Idema 2010a for a history of the Judge Bao tradition. For a list of currently translated plays on Judge Bao, see West and Idema 2010b, 37–74, 237–82, and 462–63.

Many places erected temples to the Great Thearch of the Eastern Marchmount and his staff, which often sported detailed and grisly paintings or three-dimensional displays of all the underworld courts and all the punishments of hell, such as mountains of swords and forests of lances. The greatest temple was found, of course, in "the holy land" of Tai'an, the hometown of the Great Thearch of the Eastern Marchmount. This temple would appear to have been by far the most popular pilgrimage site in Song, Yuan, and early Ming China. A number of plays and other early vernacular texts make reference to a pilgrimage to Taishan. Pilgrims donated their votive gifts to the godhead by burning them in a pool of fire, the "scorching basin." For Yuan times, at least one actual case has been recorded of a father throwing his son into this pool of fire as a votive offering.[7] In the sixteenth century and later, the main object of devotion at Tai'an had become the Primal Princess of the Cyan Clouds (Bixia Yuanjun 碧霞元君), a female deity also known as Lady Taishan (Taishan Niangniang 泰山娘娘), first honored with a temple at Taishan between 1008 and 1016. By this later period, donations were simply cast into her temple, which was at the very top of Taishan, instead of into the fire pit, and were collected by the sensible authorities for public use.[8]

Many of the "Twenty-four Cases of Filial Piety" were adapted for the stage in Yuan times, but few have survived. *Immolates His Child* has been preserved only in a Yuan-dynasty printing; the title is not recorded in any of the early catalogues. It is a regular *zaju* consisting of four suites, preceded by a wedge. The songs are assigned to the leading male, who plays the part of Little Zhang the butcher in the wedge and acts 1, 2, and 4, and of the infernal runner Li Neng 李能 in act 3.[9] We believe that the second song in the fourth act was intended to be sung by the mother of Butcher Zhang. Among Yuan printings, the play is remarkable for the amount of prose dialogue, not only for the lead player but for ancillary characters as well.

The wedge opens with the self-introduction of the usurious merchant pawnbroker Wang. Little Zhang, whose mother has fallen ill, comes to his place in order to pawn a padded jacket. When, in act 1, Zhang returns home, he first lectures his wife on the importance of filial piety and wifely devotion and next invites a doctor to have a look at his mother. When the doctor prescribes cinnabar, Zhang goes out to purchase it from Wang, who sells him a fake substitute. Zhang's mother fails to improve after taking the medicine, so Zhang promises the Great Thearch of the Eastern Marchmount that he will give him his three-year-old son, Xisun 喜孫, as a votive offering, whereupon his mother miraculously recovers.

7. For Yuan descriptions of the pilgrimage to Taishan, see Idema 1997.

8. Dott 2004.

9. The text of the play suggests that the role of Li Neng is performed by an extra male. That would of course be very unusual but might not be impossible.

In act 2, Zhang, his wife, and their son travel to the main temple of the Great Thearch of the Eastern Marchmount at Tai'an. In a dream at night, Zhang witnesses a session of the infernal court: the runner Li Neng is ordered to take Zhang's son back to his grandmother and claim Wang's son in his place. The next morning Zhang throws his son into the pool of fire. At the same time, the son of Wang, who has also come to the temple to conduct his trade, also falls into the pool of fire.

In act 3, the infernal runner takes Zhang's little son back to his grandmother. He tells her that he is a friend of her son's, who had become too drunk to take care of the boy. At the same time, Wang's mother anxiously questions him about the fate of her grandson. In the final act, Zhang and his wife return home, worrying how they can explain the disappearance of her beloved grandchild to the grandmother. But when they get home, she soundly curses them for their presumed negligence. After the affair is sorted out, they all thank the deity for his miraculous intervention.

Modern Chinese critics all have been very negative in their verdict on this play, condemning it for its extreme traditional morality and its superstitious belief in cruel religious customs. This negative attitude toward the play fits in with the strident condemnations of filial piety and popular religions by reformers and revolutionaries throughout the twentieth century as two of the causes of China's "backwardness." However, while it cannot be denied that the play purports to teach the virtue of filial piety and to strengthen the belief in the efficacy and justice of the divine bureaucracy of the Great Thearch of the Eastern Marchmount, the play is at the same time a remarkable example of social criticism, providing lively and realistic details of contemporary practices. Moreover, tragedy turns into farce as divine justice turns the table on the sinners and as the virtuous couple gets only a sound scolding for all their anguish and suffering. Whoever the anonymous playwright of *Little Butcher Zhang Immolates His Child to Save His Mother* may have been, he could construct a tight and original plot and write convincing songs.

SUGGESTED READINGS

Baker 1925; Barnhart 1993; Chavannes 1910; Chen 1908; Cole 1998; Dott 2004; Dudbridge 1991, 1992; Ebrey and Gregory 1993; Fu 1995, 1999, 2008; Goodrich 1964; Hansen 1990; Idema 1997; Knapp 2006; Naquin and Yü 1992; Teiser 1993a, b; West and Idema 2010b; Wu 1992.

NEWLY PRINTED IN HANGZHOU: *LITTLE BUTCHER ZHANG IMMOLATES HIS CHILD TO SAVE HIS MOTHER*, A FOURTEENTH-CENTURY EDITION

DRAMATIS PERSONAE IN ORDER OF APPEARANCE

Role type	*Name and family, institutional, or social role*
EXTRA MALE/EXTRA	MAGNATE WANG
FEMALE, OLD WOMAN	BUTCHER ZHANG's mother
MALE LEAD/MALE	BUTCHER ZHANG (acts 1, 2, 4)
YOUNG FEMALE	BUTCHER ZHANG's wife
EXTRA MALE/GRAND PHYSICIAN	PHYSICIAN
EXTRA MALE/EXTRA	The god Flaring Spirit
MALE LEAD	LI NENG, fleetfoot (act 3)
EXTRA FEMALE	MAGNATE WANG's mother

✤ ✤ ✤

NEWLY PRINTED IN HANGZHOU: *LITTLE BUTCHER ZHANG IMMOLATES HIS CHILD TO SAVE HIS MOTHER*

[WEDGE]

EXTRA MALE *enters and opens*:—I am Magnate Wang, and I live in the Village of Hidden Worthies at the northwest corner of Bianliang. I'm worth ten thousand strings of cash. I have a child called Priceless,[10] and everyone in the family treats him like a divine pearl, a gem of jade! Against all principle, I sell paper images[11] already offered up to gods by someone else to others to offer up their vows. What I traffic in is denatured incense and watered-down wine. And so someone as crooked as me has made a success of himself. The only possible disaster that can befall me is death.

Exits.

10. Wanbaonu 萬寶奴 (literally, "Ten Thousand Treasures").

11. Literally, "paper horses," figures of gods intended to convey the prayers to the gods when they were burned.

FEMALE *enters and opens*: I am Butcher Zhang's mother. I am showing some signs of illness now and am on the verge of death—soon I will be gone. Call Butcher Zhang, I want some rice gruel to eat.—MALE LEAD *enters*: I am Butcher Zhang. All of the neighbors call me Little Butcher Zhang and my wife and I operate this meat stall. My mother has been widowed since twenty and now she is sixty-two. On our way back from viewing the lanterns on the fifteenth,[12] she suddenly got sick. It's taken a turn for the worse and now she wants some rice gruel to eat. Wife, we have no rice in the house. Bring out a padded jacket and pawn it at Magnate Wang's. YOUNG FEMALE *speaks*: This jacket is old and worth only two pints of rice. You take it there like it's a true pearl! Don't be taken advantage of.

Exits.

([XIANLÜ MODE:] *Duanzheng hao*)

I only want to amass hidden karma,
He only wants to covet things of value.
As for the two of us "like water and fire, two hearts' ambitions can't exist in one oven"—
He's never willing to donate any of his wealth to alleviate the sufferings of the poor,
And has not a single speck of compassion.

(*Reprise*)

Even if [you] had gold and silver piled up to the Dipper—what good is it?
In days gone by, Lu Zijing visited Zhou Yu,[13]
And now a Guo Yuanzhen calls upon a Yafu.[14]
Let me bring a new padded jacket
And you'll say that it's only old rags,
And two pints of rice
You treat like two bushels of pearls.
I can't help but be at wit's end,
At a loss about what to do—
It makes me so flustered I don't know what to say.

12. The first full moon of the new year (the night of the fifteenth day of the first lunar month) was celebrated by a display of lanterns. It was one of the liveliest festivals of the year as men and women thronged the streets, admiring the lanterns and other illuminations.

13. Lu Zijing 魯子敬 is Lu Su 魯肅 (172–217), who displayed great liberality toward Zhou Yu 周瑜 (175–210). Fragments have been preserved of a *zaju* titled *Zhou Yu Visits Lu Su*, but the inversion of this title here undoubtedly is intended as ironic. Lu Su and Zhou Yu both became major characters in the *Romance of the Three Kingdoms*.

14. Guo Yuanzhen 郭原真 (656–713) was renowned for his liberality. As a student in the National Academy he once donated the four hundred thousand cash he had just received from his parents as living allowance to a poor man in order to enable him to rebury his ancestors, without even bothering to ask for the man's name. Yafu 亞夫 is Fan Zeng 范曾, the leading adviser of Xiang Yu (232–202), who refused to grant his generals the rewards that he had promised them.

[ACT 1]

EXTRA MALE LEAD *arrives home carrying two pints of rice and goes in*: Wife, take this rice and pound it well and then brew up some gruel for my mother. Wife, why are you upset again? If Mother finds out, her symptoms will get worse. Let out a little more happiness, and Mother will be happy too. You know nothing about this business of filial piety!

([XIANLÜ] *Dian jiangchun*)

Mother's illness is deep in her body—
Your child looks up to heaven and full of grief beats [the earth],
Ever more distressed.
Mother suffered half a century as a lonely widow,
So why is there now no hope at all?
(*Hunjiang long*)
She has nothing else to rely on,
She suffered widowhood, sank into illness, suffered cold loneliness.
My mind is at wit's end,
My insides burning, my heart flustered.
She bore cold and hunger, but still took pity on the distress of her son:
How can I, despite my orphaned poverty, dare forget my mother?[15]
It's always been a hand-to-mouth existence—
Just a spoonful or two of dried grains.
Now she's on the verge of death,
Soon she will be gone.
And now we live through a season of no harvest,
A year of famine and starvation.
The tears from my mother's eyes fall nowhere but upon pillow and mat,
The sorrow in your child's heart is packed away on the tips of his brows.
In less than one hour, or even ten minutes,
I've thought of a hundred plans, a thousand cures.
(*Youhulu*)

Speak: Wife, imitate a few of the ancients!

Madame Meng was wise and virtuous, a model of propriety,
Her husband was surnamed Liang.[16]
Truly, in thorn hairpins and hempen jacket, she stayed by the cold window.
He, the husband, his literary art capped the world, his canonical learning was broad;

15. In China, children were called orphans upon the death of their father.

16. Meng Guang 孟光 was "fat, ugly, and dark-skinned" when she was married to Liang Hong 梁鴻 at thirty. He later became a famous recluse and scholar; she became the symbol of the devoted wife.

She, the wife, was filial and chaste, humane and proper, and her name is truly renowned.
When from time to time you report to Mother,
Ask ardently how she is doing.
And if you have a heart of devoted sincerity,
Not a speck of hypocrisy will appear.
It is always the case, "Wait upon her in the morning,
And cook her gruel in the evening."

Speak: Liang Hong was the husband and master of Meng Guang, but he would not speak to his wife. "If you want me to be happy, then it is a hempen jacket and thorn hairpins for you. Then we will be husband and wife." When she brought her husband and master his food, she bore it up high. This is what is meant by "Raising the tray to the level of the brows." My wife, do you really understand the business of "making their bed at dusk and inquiring of their well-being at dawn"?[17]

(*Tianxia le*)
Who doesn't want "to raise the tray to the level of their brow and imitate Meng Guang"?
Naturally I want to open up my shop,[18]
But where can I get even a pint or ladle of grain?
There's no problem working hard for others to make a living.
Of course I want to regularly slaughter a pig
And work hard at butchering a lamb,
To scrape together some copper cash and take good care of my mother.
(*Nezha ling*)
But we live in this isolated village, this small hamlet,
With no close relatives living with us.
If Mother dies,
O, heaven, who will take care of things?
My wife, pick up a little of that virtuous and filial heart,
And I will show some tolerant forgiveness.
Don't imitate those stubborn old bitches who,
(*Quetazhi*)
Wearing their head ornaments all decked out in gold,
Wearing their best clothes of fine silk,
Emerge in public to revile their elders in spades
And curse their neighbors one by one.

17. "Making their bed at dusk and inquiring after their well-being at dawn" are the duties of filial offspring toward their parents as prescribed in the Classics.

18. This aria seems to be sung in response to comments by his wife that he should make more money by working harder at his meat stall.

Imitate, instead, Beauty Cao or that Meng Jiang[nü], who wept by the Great Wall when she delivered winter clothes.[19]
Don't imitate that Jingniang, who shamelessly stole the fruit.[20]

MALE LEAD *speaks*: Wife, imitate the twenty-four filial people.

(*Jisheng cao*)
Although I've not read the *Analects* or *Mencius*,[21]
I've heard plenty about the passages on filial piety.
Zengzi was filial to his mother, and she was cared for by heaven,
Guo Ju buried his son, and heaven bestowed grace on him.
Meng Zong wept over the bamboo, and heaven revealed its signs,
Wang Xiang lay down on the ice
And is recorded with honor in the books of history.
Ding Lan carved a wooden likeness of his parents and depicted their portraits.

Act out inviting GRAND PHYSICIAN. EXTRA MALE, *a physician*, *speaks*: It'll be cured as soon as I use my Cinnabar Heart-Stabilizing Pill.

(*Zui fu gui*)
He makes a show of the alacrity of his fingertips,
The breadth of what he has read.
But it's really no more than *The Treatise on Displaying Alacrity*,
The Proven Prescriptions of the Hall of Auspicious Bamboo,[22]
"The Completely Divine Powder,"
"The Green Dragon Pills,"
And "The White Tiger Broth."
How in the world can this dose of medicine cost seven taels of silver?
Just consider that, in the morning, Butcher Zhang doesn't even have what he'll eat at night.
He can act only out of sincerity,
You can see his old mother confined by illness to her bed.

---

19. On Meng Jiangnü, see chap. 3, n. 37. Beauty Cao 曹娥 (Cao E), an exemplar of filial piety, lived during the Eastern Han (25–220). When she was fourteen years of age, her father drowned in a river. For seventeen days she walked by the side of the river, crying and weeping. Eventually she, too, jumped into the river and drowned, but after five days her body, clutching the corpse of her father in its arms, floated to the surface.

20. The story of "Jingniang, who stole the fruit" 盜果京娘 was adapted for the stage in Yuan times, but the play has not been preserved and we have no information on the plot.

21. The *Analects*, recording the sayings of Confucius and his discussions with his disciples, and the *Mencius*, recording the dialogues between Mencius and contemporary rulers and thinkers, both belong to *The Four Books*, the primer of Confucianism as defined by the neo-Confucian masters of the eleventh and twelfth centuries.

22. *The Essential Treatise on Displaying Alacrity* (*Jingyao xuanming lun* 精要宣明論) was written by the Jin-dynasty physician Liu Wansu 劉完素 (ca. 1140–1200); *The Proven Prescriptions of the Hall of Auspicious Bamboo* (*Ruizhutang jingyan fang* 瑞竹堂經驗方) was a medical treatise by the Uighur Sadumishi, known in Chinese texts as 薩德彌實 (fl. 1320–1360).

[FEMALE LEAD] *speaks*: The physician says that this prescription uses cinnabar as a catalyst. MALE *speaks*: The Honorable Magnate Wang has some, but he'll take only cash. He's not even human. FEMALE LEAD *speaks*: My husband, I have a pair[23] that my father gave me, go barter them for it. MALE *sees* EXTRA.—MAGNATE *gives him counterfeit cinnabar*—MALE *asks*: Is the cinnabar real? MAGNATE *explains*:[24] Let it kill her; I'm immune to any catastrophe except death.

(*Jinzhan'er*)

Cinnabar should have a deep luster,
But this stuff is faded and slightly yellowed.
There, he keeps on invoking "Heaven," swearing he's an honest man.
I regret that I cannot, with my own hands, snatch away the illness, raise her from her bed.[25]
If only my mother's three critical junctures would balance her lungs and stomach,
The five organs would enrich her liver and bowels.
Oh, this pitiful, unfilial son, me,
I will cause the death of my mother of seventy.

MALE *speaks*: Wife, Mother has vomited up this counterfeit cinnabar. The only way left to save her is for the two of us to go on pilgrimage to the Thearch of the Eastern Marchmount. We will take our three-year-old child along, and on the twenty-eighth day of the third month, throw him along with some devotional images into the pit of fire to substitute for one stick of incense. May the gods above show their miraculous power and divinity!

(*Houting hua*)

Here I face the direction of the Divine Thearch of the Eastern Marchmount
And pray to his spirit as I make this silent vow.
"Because the mother who bore me has a critical illness of the three junctures,
I promise my son Xisun[26] as a stick of incense."
Here I take tea to my mother
Hoping that all her pains will be alleviated.
Now she is bathed in a sweat as copious as the waters of the Yangtze,
And shivers as cold as ice.
Now with pleasant face, I show a happy radiance,
And wreathed in smiles, I personally ask after her.

(*Qingge'er*)

23. A pair of precious hairpins or other jewels.
24. This is an aside to the audience.
25. He has returned home, and, at the side of his mother's bed, he gives her the cinnabar.
26. Xisun, literally, "the grandson who brings happiness."

She is better now, just like her old self before,
The former presence that we knew.
Truly it is said, "A filial heart is a prescription from the immortals,"
Every day I told this to the neighbors
But no one was shamed.
So I raised my head and prayed to the azure vault,
And promised both bright incense:
My son as sacrificial lamb.
No one thought she would ever come back from death, return to life, rise from her sickbed—
This is a sure sign from heaven!
(*Zhuansha Coda*)

Speak: Mother! You've recovered from your illness. What a joy!

My mother's sickly body now is completely at ease,
Your son's joy rises ten thousand feet.
I've thrown away my only begotten son, this single chest full of warm blood.
Only when we have our own sons do we know how unfilial we are to our mothers.
You must have heard, "Alas! alas! my parents," that heartfelt emotion.[27]
Here I think it over carefully,
And break into happy laughter, forgetting my sorrow.
I will wipe away no more these tears of a broken heart.
I will burn my son in flaring flames, the whole brazier will burn brightly:
In this gruesome, cruel way his whole soul and body will be lost.
Giving up my little loved one,
I serve my mother with my whole heart.

[ACT 2]

Enters dressed as MALE LEAD, *opens, and speaks*: Mother, I want to tell you that the twenty-eighth of the third month is drawing near and I want to go with my wife and child to offer incense at the Temple of the Eastern Marchmount in the holy land of Tai'an. MOTHER *speaks*: Don't take Xisun with you when you go burn incense. MALE *speaks*: Your grandchild was part of the vow, and he has to go with us. MOTHER *speaks*: Don't the three of you drink too much, and hurry back.

([YUEDIAO MODE:] *Dou anchun*)

27. "Alas! alas! my parents, / [With what toil ye gave me birth!]" is a quote from the *Book of Odes*, one of the Classics and China's most ancient collection of poetry.

Clouds in the blue rise in a thousand layers,
Cover over ten thousand clusters of mountain peaks.[28]
Shimmeringly bright—the gold and blue glazed tiles,
Jutting up high—towers and terraces, halls and pavilions.
The jeweled horses and golden saddles of young dandies,
The perfumed chariots and gauzy silks of gentry girls.
And right now, when spring days are warm
And the beautiful sun is pleasant,
Curling in the spring winds, the green willows are like smoke,
Holding the nighttime rains, peach blossoms are as red as fire.

FEMALE *and* MALE *act out traveling on the road.* FEMALE *asks* MALE: How can we have traveled so long without reaching the holy land of Tai'an? [MALE *speaks:*] It's that high mountain there.

(*Zihua'er xu*)
Enlivening Clear and Bright,[29] songs of the oriole warble and coo;
Rustling the flowery stems, wings of the butterflies flutter and flap;
Dancing in the eastern wind, tails of the swallow wiggle and waggle.
Look at the dust from the carts and hooves of the horses,
The performing of plays, the banging of gongs,
The deafening pipes and songs—
There's never been a year so many people have come to the temple.
This is the most famous mountain of the whole world,
And it solemnly overlooks the ten thousand miles of the cosmos,
Forever dominating the mountains and rivers of the whole empire.

[EXTRA]MALE *costumed as* MAGNATE WANG *speaks*: I go every year on the twenty-eighth day of the third month to the holy land of Tai'an to do business. When I get there, the devotional images that have been sold to people—I take them after they have been used as offering for the spirits and resell them. I also have a child, called Priceless, and my whole family treats him like some divine pearl or jade. Those who do good deeds have neither money nor posterity; but a person as black hearted as me has both wealth and a son. I fear no disaster except death.—MAIN FEMALE *and* MALE *speak*: Here the three of us have arrived at the main gate. Let's rest overnight, get up early tomorrow, and repay the vow. EXTRA MALE *enters*: I am the Flaring Spirit and this Lord is the Master of Fates. This other gentleman is Officer of Speedy Retribution. We three divinities have determined that he is a filial son and not an immoral person. But there is now here a certain Magnate Wang, who is black at heart

28. These two lines are gibberish in the original edition, and modern editors have all filled in text that they feel would be suitable. We are following Ning 1988, 241n42.

29. The Clear and Bright festival was celebrated in spring, on the 105th day following the winter solstice. Here it seems more generally to refer to the third month of the year.

and does not abide by the way of the gods; vile misfortune is born from the gods. *Speaks* [*as a command*]: City God, obey our divine order. Order that runner Li Neng, sometime after midnight, to carry away in his arms Magnate Wang's son—that divine pearl, that person of jade—and tomorrow at noon throw him into the pool of fire to be burned to death. And let him take Xisun, son of the filial Butcher Zhang, and—while deceptively dressed as a mortal man—go on ahead and take him back to his grandmother. Don't let anyone find out he is not a mortal!

Exit.

[MALE LEAD *sings*:]

(*Jin jiaoye*)
Go outside the temple gate and hide away,
Go on over to the eastern gallery and don't come near me,
Just rest a while in the shade of the trees.
I'll go on in the temple and respectfully recite a few prayers.
(*Tiaoxiao ling*)
I have nothing else to offer up in celebration
To save my mother's life.
O, gods above, you have given Butcher Zhang no way out!
I must repay three years at my mother's breast, that great grace,
And the ten months in her womb, that rich love.
To immolate my child to save my mother leaves me no posterity,
But, as for my mother, I will "wrestle the tiger and ford the River."
(*Jin jiaoye*)
Who has been raised with such compassion as me?
My filial reputation will enwrap heaven and earth.
This pays off my mother's solicitous and tender care,
And her suffering and slaving for forty years.
(*Tiaoxiao ling*)
In order to cure my mother's illness,
I have promised him.
But how can I stand life without my son?
If only she hadn't recovered,
This would not be asked of me.
The ancients say, "One loves one's children best."
(*Xiaotao hong*)
It was some former life, her karmic sins of those years,
That accumulated six years of disaster
And in this life made her bear starvation and hunger,
Suffer poverty and want—
It was because her person [in that life] deceived the gods and committed evil as great as heaven.

It was something that person did in a former life,
That broke her down in this one,
And was the certain reason for a lifetime of poverty and grief.
(*Gui santai*)
I see the divinities sitting in midair,
Their ghostly attendants are the joined Six Ding spirits.[30]
The Flaring Spirit and Prince Lord are frightening in their divine might,
And the Officer of Speedy Retribution has white hair at his temples.
Many are the ranks of broad swords and long lances—
Those Yamas of the Ten Kings' Courts of Hell.
"O, gods, may your golden whips point the way for my child,
Stretch out your divine hands and protect him for me."
(*Sai'er ling*)
My heart is racing,
My expression, dumbstruck—
Who was it who suddenly startled me awake?
What I saw were divine images severe and frightening,
Ghostly attendants and their underlings,
All in ranks, shouting and clamoring.
The divine form clad in red bustled about,
The one in black meticulously evaluated the facts,
The one in green personally delivered the judgment—
Absolutely no difference from the light of day!
So, it turns out to have been only a dream at the Southern Branch![31]
(*Gui santai*)
Over there the sound of weeping is loud,[32]
But tomorrow, they'll only lack a source of disaster.
"Sons and daughters are but golden cangues and jade chains."
You say, "His grief is as it should be,
And tomorrow you will be just like him."
What was the name of the man who took your child?[33]
Can you recognize him in such a crowd?
If your child was wearing golden bracelets or silver rings,

30. The Six Ding spirits of the sexagenary cycle: Dingmao, Dingsi, Dingwei, Dingyou, Dinghai, and Dingchou. These are six yin spirits, envisioned as fearsome warriors who are dispatched by the heavenly thearch when summoned by Daoist talismans to dispel evil influences.

31. See chap. 3, n. 106.

32. Referring to the family of Magnate Wang as Priceless is kidnapped.

33. They appear here to go over to talk to the Wang family.

Then I'm afraid he'll never see home again, your divine pearl, your gem of jade.[34]
(*Tusi'er*)
Flames flaring up, blind anger and raging fire,
Dark and terrifying, the universe collapses together.
Son, here is where our duty and love are severed.
People mill and crowd about,
Shouting and clamoring,
Yet none of them can save you.
(*Shengyao wang*)
I've thought it over long enough,
"You can't avoid the fire when you face the stove"—
This single stick of incense is full of heart's prayers.
There his tears course down,
All he can do is tightly hang on to me.
To repay my mother's grace is no madness—
In the fire I bury this little monkey of mine.
(*Coda*)
Clear tears fall from his sparkling pupils,
The nine twists of my soft intestines are hacked by knives.
To throw away our little bundle of joy devastates her,
But to have preserved my honored mother fills me with joy.

[ACT 3]

EXTRA MALE[35] *enters dressed as* FLEETFOOT *and opens*: My name is Li Neng and I am from this area. When alive, I served His Excellency, Cui, from Cizhou. After His Excellency died, when he became a god, he chose me to be his ghostly fleetfoot. I've received the divine order today to take the son of the filial Butcher Zhang back to his home. Come to think of it, divine protection has resulted in the miraculous retribution of this affair. *Recites a poem*:

Keep to your lot, do not lust after ill-gotten gain,
What your fate says you should receive will come of itself.
If you strive after it using crafty schemes—
Heaven will send down disaster if people don't kill you off.

34. The first five lines of this song are addressed by Butcher Zhang to his own wife, the remaining four lines are addressed by him to Magnate Wang.

35. This would appear to be a mistake. However, it is also possible that the role of Li Neng was indeed played by a different actor than the leading male who plays the role of Butcher Zhang.

([ZHONGLÜ MODE:] *Fen die'er*)
Riches and poverty are the judgments of heaven and earth:
To employ devious schemes to lend out money and reap its interest
Angers the gods, stirs up calamity, and generates disaster.
Who is anyone to place himself over others?
All he wants is to collect interest above interest,
Never thinking this poison will kill.
Don't bring up "When bitter is exhausted, the sweet will come."
Or "On the field of profit and fame lie both victory and defeat."
(*Zui chunfeng*)
All he wants is to watch the capital that fills his eyes grow,
He could never imagine that, at the critical moment, heaven and earth will squeeze him dry.
Shimmeringly bright, the mountains of swords and forests of lances[36] are arranged all in a row.
Yet, no one will reform,
Reform,
Reform.
But let there be the eight troubles or three disasters,[37]
Then they fast and abstain with their whole heart,
But still keep the gods above highest heaven and beyond the clouds.

MALE *speaks*: By the order of the Flaring Spirit, I leave the divine land to take back the son of filial Butcher Zhang.
(*Ying xianke*)
I leave the crossroads of this divine land,
Descend the Soul-Snatching Terrace of the Eastern Marchmount,
And, bearing the order of the divine emperor, now arrive on this swift wind.
Those who accumulate goodness will encounter blessings and prosperity,
Those who practice evil engender affliction and harm.
That bastard who's crying, burning with anxiety, wipes the tears from his cheeks,
While Butcher Zhang, chuckling and smiling, finds in drunkenness a universe large.

EXTRA FEMALE *enters and opens*: I am the mother of Magnate Wang. I have this child, and every year on the twenty-eighth of the third month, my son travels to the divine land of Tai'an to do business. Someone came to tell me that my grandson, our divine gem, has disappeared. Well, it seems to me that the way Magnate Wang does business—completely against the way of the gods—has cost us the loss of my grandchild. Let me go see old lady Zhang to see if it is true.
Exits.

36. The mountains of swords and the forests of lances are often mentioned as punishments in hell.
37. The eight troubles and the three disasters here refer to all kinds of sudden disasters and unexpected adversities.

[MALE LEAD *sings*:]
(*Shiliu hua*)
Here I enter the hidden village and cross the main street,
With measured step I tread on fragrant paths and walk over deep green moss.
I see an old lady lower her head, cheeks covered with tears—
Isn't that Butcher Zhang's mother?
Say not? Her hair is speckled with white.[38]
Since that Magnate Wang, who aids the poor and uproots the rich,
Went to the Eastern Marchmount to extinguish his sins and dissolve his misfortunes—
Well, on the basis of his fair heart, such a good heart, such a magnanimous heart,
There's no need for you to burn incense or offer cash as a sacrifice.
(*Dou anchun*)
The basic nature of those who lust for cash cannot be moved,
Those who practice evil—mountains and rivers are more easily transformed.
This little guy here escaped from the jaws of death
And met goodness amid disaster.
Your child unearthed the Gate of Death,[39]
Encountered baneful Jupiter,
And ran into the Mourner.[40]
Woman, do not blame me.
This child—"A tooth that falls out is born anew,"
Your child—"A stone sinks into the great ocean."

EXTRA FEMALE *speaks*: Granny Zhang, Brother delivered this child, here. LEAD FEMALE *acts out receiving him*. [*Sings*:]
(*Shang xiaolou*)
I see a hunchback old woman over there,
She seems solicitous in receiving me.
Your own child is so drunk his eyes are spinning[41]—
Drunken ink splattered all about—
He passed out in the main street.
This little toddler I now bring back
So that your whole family may live in peace.
Now simply face Tai'an district, kowtow, and pay your respects.
(*Reprise*)

38. Following this line the old woman identifies herself to Li Neng as the mother of Magnate Wang.

39. He is speaking here to Madame Wang.

40. The Gate of Death, Jupiter, and the Mourner are three stars of baleful influence, causing misfortune, poverty, and epidemics.

41. Speaking now to Madame Zhang.

On the one hand it is a warning for men from the enlightened spirits,
On the other, the caring love of the lord of heaven.
Your child, by repaying his mother's grace,
Moved the sentient spirits—
He was distressed over his mother.
Your family wealth will now grow day by day,
Amass year after year,
There will be no disaster, no harm,
Your whole family, from the depth of destitution, will rise to prosperity.

EXTRA FEMALE *speaks*: Brother, how long have you been a friend of Butcher Zhang's?

(*Manting fang*)
We have been close acquaintances for many years,
Your Butcher Zhang has drunk so much that he teeters and totters back and forth,
Once you travel abroad, you take pity on all travelers,
So I could not turn my back on the deep feelings between brothers.
Mother, your child has saved you from disaster, as though plucking you from a sea of sickness,
I have saved his child, plucking him from a pit of fire.
She, there, quickly puts hands to her temples,
I am carrying gain and loss as great as the heavens,[42]
But it turns out that heaven and earth artfully arranged all this.

(*Putian le*)
If you ask of it all from the beginning,
It will increase your amazement and wonder.
He said that my head looks like a clump of earth,
And my body seems molded of clay.
I serve my duty watches in golden palaces,
And attend to cases inside the yamen,
On the plaque outside are written divine words to push along the offerings of incense.
Brushed by the western wind, my face is covered with dust and grime.
I am no Zhang Qian or Li Pai,[43]
Follow no district overseer or county magistrate—
On this mission, I'm just like a ghostly deputy or a divine messenger.

42. The image is of a carrying pole with gain on one end balanced by harm on the other.

43. Zhang Qian (Zhang Thousand) and Li Pai (Li the Tally) are conventional names in drama of servants of officials and yamen runners.

(*Kuaihuo san*)[44]
Outside the temple gate a great crowed amassed,
In the two corridors, a noisy clamor.
It was no matter of bad luck or failing times,
But all because he committed sins big enough to fill up heaven.
(*Chao tianzi*)
That bastard of yours is most evil
And capable only of loving money,
Since he thought foremost about being happy, King Yama punished him,
That bastard of yours hurt others to help himself,
And brought down calamity and disaster.

Speaks: Tell that Magnate Wang of yours,
Don't create any more debts to be repaid in future lives,
You may cry and wail until your gall is plucked and your heart gouged out,
But your grief and injury are to no avail.
He said, "I fear no disaster but death."
Well, the Flaring Spirit rendered a divine judgment,
The little Dragon King is a perverse character,
Who, in no time at all, will crush your skull to smithereens.
(*Shua hai'er*)[45]
Your child has great hidden merit because of his filial piety, purity, humaneness, and sense of duty.
That single stick of incense will spread his fame over the four seas.
To repay a mother with his loyal heart is a thing rare in the world,
His beautiful reputation will move the Secretariat and startle the Censorate.[46]
His filial and obedient name will be recorded in the eternal and everlasting biographies of the loyal and good.
For his wife will be erected an arch of ninefold ardor and threefold chastity,[47] a memorial to her virtue and filial piety.
A filial reputation is loved by all—
For those named Wang, disaster was reaped because of evil.
For those named Zhang, disaster has already been reborn [as blessings].
(*Two from Coda*)

44. Talking again to Madame Wang.
45. Now to Madame Zhang.
46. The Secretariat and the Censorate are among the highest organs of the central government, which will be moved to reward him.
47. "Ninefold ardor and threefold chastity" is an idiomatic expression for extreme chastity.

The family Zhang wanted only a reputation that was eternal and everlasting,
The family Wang wanted only a stash of cash that would by interest increase a hundredfold.
But now the ghosts and gods detest them, neighbors heap blame on them.
Sorrow and anxiety in the Ocean of Right and Wrong devastate the family Wang,
The family Zhang will be joyful indeed in the burrow of peace and happiness.
May I tell you this, you two mothers:
Granny Zhang, tell Butcher Zhang to drink less of this nameless wine,[48]
Granny Wang, tell Magnate Wang to lust no more for ill-gotten wealth.

LITTLE FEMALE[49] *acts out looking for child.* MALE *speaks*: Woman, there is a divine spirit. In life he was Rescriptor-in-Waiting Bao, upon his death, he became a god, the Officer of Speedy Retribution.

([*One from*] *Coda*)
That lordship over there once supported the security of the realm
And gave fullness to heaven and earth;
He wears a purple gauze gown,
Holds a white ivory tablet in his hands,
His waist is wrapped with a golden yellow sash.
That lordship opens wide his two weird eyes, black as raven clouds,
The silver strands on both his temples as white as snowy silk.
That lordship—his mighty air is complete, his miraculous powers great,
Making judgments in the Court of Darkness, he dispatches his ghostly attendants,
Pronouncing sentences in the Southern Yamen,[50] he does not covet the wealth of the people.

(*Coda*)
You can burn incense enough to fill a bucket,
You can have money enough to fill ten thousand bushels,
When you go home you'll "follow the fences and palisades."[51]
But when you call, nine of the ten vermilion gates[52] will not open.
Once you turn your back on the world of men,
You'll find nothing but mountains in front and ridges behind,
So don't amass a fortune to build great mansions.

---

48. While the text clearly writes *wuming* 無名 (nameless), it probably intends the completely homophonous expression *wuming* 無明 (lacking insight, stupidity, rage), The "nameless wine" would then mean the "wine of stupidity."

49. Magnate Wang's wife.

50. The Southern Yamen—as opposed to the imperial palace in the northern part of the capital—was the designation of the office of the prefect of the metropolitan prefecture Kaifeng during the Northern Song dynasty (960–1126). During his lifetime, Judge Bao served for a while as prefect of Kaifeng.

51. We take this to mean "you will beg from place to place."

52. Vermilion gates mark the mansions of the rich.

MALE *speaks*: Granny Zhang, I'm leaving this bundle behind with one word on it. Give it to Butcher Zhang and when he sees it, he'll recognize my name.

(*Final Coda*)

Try and find me, I'm nowhere to be found,
And when I come, you won't see me coming.
You might say there's nothing to prevent your hiding away this child,
But it's just as it says, "A child is as easily picked up as it is thrown down."

[ACT 4]

FEMALE *and* MALE *act out going home*—MALE *speaks*: Wife, what'll we say when we get back home and Mother asks about the child? FEMALE *speaks*: Just explain that he disappeared. *Act out leaving Tai'an district and descending the mountain.* [MALE LEAD *sings*:]

([SHUANGDIAO MODE] *Xinshui ling*)

Tears overflowing, hearts heavy and troubled, we go out the city gate,
I see clearly now [the meaning of] "You can have a home, but it's hard to find refuge there."
Raise my head to heaven, my eyes overflow with tears,
Lower my head, I wipe away the stains of weeping.
Reluctantly, I trod the red dust,
Wearily, I reach my mountain village.
Once inside the door,
What worries me is what Mother will ask.

FEMALE *and* MALE *act out arriving at home and calling out at the door.* MOTHER *asks*: Butcher Zhang, you two are back, but where's the child? FEMALE *and* MALE *act out kneeling down.*

(*Gu meijiu*) [MOTHER *sings*:]

You bow to your mother before the gate,
Still steeped in drunkenness.

Speaks: To hand the child over to your brother! Even my grandchild has disappeared! *Sings*:

You seem drunk, insensate, dazed from a dream,
From the first to last,
Tell me in detail everything that happened.

[(*Taipingling*) MALE LEAD *sings*:]

You, Mother, were bedridden and down with illness,
I, your child, burned with anxiety, had nowhere to find ease.
Facing the shrine of the gods of the Eastern Marchmount,

I gave up our child Xisun
And burned him in the fire
In the scorching basin.
This is the crime of your unfilial stupid son.

OLD WOMAN *speaks*: You two didn't have any idea of going on pilgrimage, you got drunk and lost the child. And now you lie in front of me and say that you burned him up! It's a good thing your brother Li Neng brought him back. And if you don't believe me, I'll call him out for you to see. Xisun, come here. FEMALE *and* MALE, *startled and frightened, kneel down.* [MALE LEAD *sings*:]

(*Yan'er luo*)
After I hear this, my soul is scared out of me.
Because of what she said, I am dumbstruck for a time.
My mother packs away the anxiety in my breast
And folds away the depression in my heart.
(*Desheng ling*)
I myself burned up the body of this Xisun in the fire,
Right at high noon, before it turned to dusk.[53]
This was all due to the strict virtue of your daughter-in-law,
And the demonstration of filial obedience by your undeserving child.[54]
I remember now, there was a divine spirit,
Who gave me good news last night in my dream.
This little one will later, when he has eventually grown-up,
Be a man of the Gallery Soaring Beyond the Mists.[55]

MOTHER *acts out giving the bundle to* BUTCHER ZHANG *to look at.* BUTCHER ZHANG *acts out recognizing it as the waist wrap of the divine fleetfoot,* LI NENG.—FEMALE *speaks*: So the divine spirit has already brought our child home. Let our whole family face his lordship of the Eastern Marchmount in the holy land of Tai'an, and bring out the incense table. MALE *calling to his* MOTHER, *speaks*: So, in this world every action good or bad has its appropriate reward. Let us all pay obeisance to the divine spirits.

(*Shuixianzi*)
Deceive not heaven and earth, deceive not the gods—
"As far away as your children and grandchildren, as close as your own soul"[56]—
Burning up a child to save a mother, I practice loyalty and trust
To repay the grace of my parents' nourishing and feeding us.
I spur on love between fathers and sons in the human world.
If fathers exercise loyalty and filial piety

---

53. That is, in clear daylight, clear to see.
54. That is, the reason that the child was rejected by the gods.
55. See chap. 5, n. 40.
56. That is, the workings of karmic retribution.

And sons exercise filial obedience,
An everlasting and enduring name can be handed down forever.

Title: The Flaring Spirit and Prince Cui exercise their divine anger,
The Officer of Speedy Retribution reveals his verdict in a dream.
Name: Magnate Wang loves money and covets riches,
Little Butcher Zhang Immolates His Child to Save His Mother.

Newly Printed in Hangzhou
Little Butcher Zhang Immolates His Child to Save His Mother.

WORKS CITED AND SUGGESTED READINGS

Akamatsu Norihiko 赤松紀彦, Inoue Taizan 井上泰山, Kin Bunkyō 金文京, Komatsu Ken 小松謙, Satō Haruhiko 佐藤晴彦, Takahashi Shigeki 高橋繁樹, Takahashi Bunji 高橋文治, Takenouchi Makoto 竹内誠, Tsuchiya Ikuko 土屋育子, and Matsuura Tsuneo 松浦恆雄, eds. 2007. *Genkan zatsugeki no kenkyū: Sandatsusaku, Ki Eifu, Seishokumu, Tantōkai* 元刊雜劇の研究:三奪槊、氣布英、西蜀夢、單刀會. Tokyo: Kyūko shoin.

——. 2011. *Genkan zatsugeki no kenkyū (II): Hen Yarō, Kaishisui* 元刊雜劇の研究II—貶夜郎、介子推. Tokyo: Kyūko shoin.

Andersen, Poul. 2008. "*Taiyi*: The Great One." In *The Encyclopedia of Taoism*, edited by Fabrizio Pregadio, 956–59. London: Routledge.

Anon. 無名氏. 1958a. *Liu Xuande zui zou Huanghe lou* 劉玄德醉走黃鶴樓. Palace ed. In Zhao Qimei 1958, 72:1a–47b.

——. 1958b. *Sima Xiangru tiqiao ji* 司馬相如題橋記. Palace ed., collated with Yu Xiaogu 于小穀 ed. In Zhao Qimei 1958, 45:1a–42b.

——. 1958c. *Yuankan zaju sanshizhong* 元刊雜劇三十種. Guben xiqu congkan 古本戲曲叢刊. Shanghai: Shanghai yinshuguan.

——. 1979. "Xinkan quanxiang Tang Xue Rengui kuahai zheng Liao gushi" 新刊全相唐薛仁貴跨海征遼故事. In *Ming Chenghua shuochang cihua congkan* 明成化說唱詞話叢刊. Shanghai: Shanghai bowuguan.

——. 1981. *Song Yuan pinghua wuzhong* 宋元平話五種. Taipei: Heluo chubanshe.

Aoki Masaru 青木正兒. 1941. *Yuanren zaju xushuo* 元人雜劇序說. Translated by Sui Shusen 隋樹森. Edited by Xu Tiaofu 徐調孚. Shanghai: Kaiming shudian.

Baker, Dwight Condo. 1925. *T'ai Shan: An Account of the Sacred Eastern Peak of China*. Shanghai: Commercial Press.

Baldrian-Hussein, Farzeen. 2008a. "*Lingbao bifa*: Complete Methods of the Numinous Treasure." In *The Encyclopedia of Taoism*, edited by Fabrizio Pregadio, 669–70. London: Routledge.

——. 2008b. "Zhong Lü: The Lineage of Zhongli Quan and Lü Dongbin." In *The Encyclopedia of Taoism*, edited by Fabrizio Pregadio, 1277–79. London: Routledge.

Bao Jianqiang 包建強 and Hu Chengxuan 胡成選. 2010. "*Yuankan zaju sanshizhong* de banben ji qi jiaokan" 《元刊雜劇三十種》的版本及其校勘. *Xibei shida xuebao* (*Shehui kexue ban*) 西北師大學報(社會科學版) 47.1:44–49.

Barnhart, Richard. 1993. *Li Kung-lin's Classic of Filial Piety*. New York: Metropolitan Museum of Art.

Burkus-Chasson, Anne. 2010. *Through a Forest of Chancellors: Fugitive Histories in Liu Yuan's "Lingyan ge," an Illustrated Book from Seventeenth-Century Suzhou*. Cambridge, Mass.: Harvard University Asia Center.

Bush, Susan. 1983. "Tsung Ping's Essay on Painting Landscape and the 'Landscape of Buddhism' of Mt. Lu." In Bush and Murck 1983, 105–31.

Bush, Susan, and Christian Murck, eds. 1983. *Theories of the Arts in China*. Princeton: Princeton University Press.

Cai Yi 蔡毅. 1989. *Zhongguo gudian xiqu xuba huibian* 中國古典戲曲序跋彙編. 4 vols. Jinan: Qi Lu shushe.

Chavannes, Édouard. 1910. *Le T'ai chan: Essai de monograhie d'un culte chinois. Appendice: Le dieu du sol dans la Chine antique*. Annales du Musée Guimet; Biblioteque d'études. Paris: Musée Guimet.

Chen, Fan Ben Li. 1992. "Yang Kuei-fei in *Tales from the T'ien-pao Era: A Chu-kung-tiao Narrative*." *Journal of Song Yuan Studies*, no. 22:1–22.

——. 2005–2006. "Translations from Wang Bocheng's *Tales of the Tianbao Era* (*Tianbao yishi*): Genre and Eroticism in the *Zhugongdiao*." *CHINOPERL* 26:149–70.

Chen Gongshui 陳公水, Xu Wenming 徐文明, and Zhang Yingji 張英基. 2011. *Qi Lu gudian xiqu quan ji* 齊魯古典戲曲全集. 5 vols. Beijing: Zhonghua shuju.

Chen, Ivan, trans. 1908. *The Book of Filial Duty: Translated from the Chinese of the Hsiao-ching by Ivan Chen; With Twenty-four Examples from the Chinese*. Wisdom of the East. London: Murray.

Chen Qiaoyi 陳橋驛 and Li Daoyuan 酈道元. 1999. *Shuijing zhu jiaoshi* 水經注校釋. Hangzhou: Hangzhou daxue chubanshe.

Ch'en, Shou-yi. 1936. "The Chinese Orphan: A Yüan Play and Its Influence on European Drama of the 18th Century." *T'ien Hsia Monthly* 3, no. 2:89–115.

Chen Zhongfan 陳中凡. 2003. "Lun Ji Junxiang *Zhaoshi gu'er* zaju" 論紀郡祥《趙氏孤兒》雜劇. In *Guanyuan wencun* 館員文存, edited by Zhou Xunchu 周勛初, 20–35. Nanjing: Jiangsu guji chubanshe.

Chida Daisuke 千田大介. 1991. "Setsu Jinki goji henkenkō" 薛仁貴故事變遷考. *Chūgoku bungaku kenkyū* 17:15–30.

Ch'ien, Chung-shu. 1935. "Tragedy in Old Chinese Drama." *T'ien Hsia Monthly* 1, no. 1:37–45.

Chu Renhuo 褚人穫. 2002. *Jianhu ji* 堅瓠集. In *Xuxiu Siku quanshu* 續修四庫全書, vol. 1260. Shanghai: Shanghai guji chubanshe.

Cole, Alan. 1998. *Mothers and Sons in Chinese Buddhism*. Stanford: Stanford University Press.

Crump, James I. Jr. 1972. "The Ch'ü and Its Critics." *Literature East and West* 16:961–72.

——. 1980. *Chinese Theater in the Days of Kublai Khan*. Tucson: University of Arizona Press.

——. 1994. "Ch'en Chi-ch'ing Mistakenly Boards the Bamboo Leaf Boat: Attributed to Fan K'ang (Tzu-an) fl. A.D. 1294." In *The Bamboo-Leaf Boat: The Magic of the Chinese Theatre*, edited by Dana Kalvodová, 11–65. Prague: Univerzita Karlova.

Crump, James I. Jr., and M. Dolezelová-Velingerová. 1971. *Ballad of the Hidden Dragon: Liu Chih-yüan chu-kung-tiao*. Oxford: Oxford University Press.

Degkwitz, Jochen. 1983. *Yue Fei und sein Mythos: Die Entwicklung der Yue-Fei-Saga bis zum "Shuo Yue quan zhuan."* Bochum: Brockmeyer.

Di Junhou 狄君厚. 1958. *Xinbian guanmu Jin Wengong huoshao Jie Zi Tui* 新編關目晉文公火燒介子推. In Anon 1958c, 20:1a–8b.

Dott, Brian R. 2004. *Identity Reflections: Pilgrimages to Mount Tai in Late Imperial China*. Cambridge, Mass.: Harvard University Asia Center.

Du Haijun 杜海軍. 2007. "Zhao Qimei jiaokan zaju ji qi dui xiqu wenxue fazhan de gongxian—jian lun Sun Kaidi shuo Zhao Qimei yu Maiwangguan zaju jiaokan wugong shuo" 趙琦美校勘雜劇及其對戲曲文學發展的貢獻–兼論孫楷弟說趙琦美於脈望館雜劇校勘無功說. *Xiqu yishu* 28, no. 4:48–54.

——. 2008. "Cong Yuan zaju Yuan Ming kanben zhi bijiao lun Mingdai xiqu de jinbu" 從元雜劇元明刊本之比較論明代戲曲的進步. *Yishu baijia*, no. 3:142–46.

——. 2009. "Cong Yuankan zaju chongxin shenshi Yuan zaju tizhi zhi yuanmao" 從元刊雜劇重新審視元雜劇體制之原貌. *Qiushi xuebao* 36, no. 4:107–11.

——. 2010. "*Yuankan zaju sanshizhong* de keben xingzhi ji xiqushi yiyi" 元刊雜劇三十種的刻本性質及戲曲史意義. *Yishu baijia*, no. 1:111–15.

Dudbridge, Glen. 1991. "A Pilgrimage in Seventeenth-Century Fiction: T'ai-shan and the *Hsing-shih yin-yüan chuan*." *T'oung Pao* 77:226–52.

——. 1992. "Women Pilgrims to T'ai Shan: Some Pages from a Seventeenth-Century Novel." In Naquin and Yü, *Pilgrims and Sacred Sites*, 39–64.

Ebrey, Patricia Buckley, and Maggie Bickford, eds. 2006. *Emperor Huizong and Late Northern Song China: The Politics of Culture and the Culture of Politics*. Cambridge, Mass.: Harvard University Asia Center.

Ebrey, Patricia Buckley, and Peter Gregory, eds. 1993. *Religion and Society in T'ang and Sung China*. Honolulu: University of Hawai`i Press.

Eskildsen, Stephen. 2004. *The Teachings and Practices of the Early Quanzhen Taoist Masters*. Albany: SUNY Press.

Espesset, Grégoire. 2008. "Bao Jing." In *The Encyclopedia of Taoism*, edited by Fabrizio Pregadio, 211–12. London: Routledge.

Esposito, Monica. 2008. "Xuanguan." In *The Encyclopedia of Taoism*, edited by Fabrizio Pregadio, 1131–32. London: Routledge.

Fan Kang 范康. 1958. *Xinkan guanmu Chen Jiqing wudao zhuyezhou* 新刊關目陳季卿悟道竹葉舟. In Anon 1958c, 27 :1a–8b.

——. 1998. *Chen Jiqing wushang zhuye zhou* 陳季卿悞上竹葉舟. In Zang 1998, 473–81.

Fan Xiheng 范希衡 and François-Marie Arouet [Voltaire]. 2010. *Zhaoshi gu'er yu Zhongguo gu'er* 《趙氏孤兒》與《中國孤兒》. Shanghai: Shanghai guji chubanshe.

Fei, Faye Chunfang. 2002. *Chinese Theories of Theater and Performance from Confucius to the Present*. Ann Arbor: University of Michigan Press.

Feng Menglong, comp. 2000a. "Humu Di Intones Poems and Visits the Underworld." In Feng, *Stories Old and New*, 557–771.

——, comp. 2000b. *Stories Old and New: A Ming Dynasty Collection*, translated by Shuhui Yang and Yunqin Yang. Seattle: University of Washington Press.

Fu Dixiu 伏滌修. 2008. "Yüe Fei ticai xiqu liubian kaoshu" 岳飛題材戲曲流變考述. *Zhejiang yishu zhiye xueyuan xuebao* 16, no. 3:39–44.

Fu, Hongchu. 1995. "Historicizing Chinese Drama: The Power and Politics of Yuan Zaju." Ph.D. diss., University of California, Los Angeles.

——. 1999. "The Cultural Fashioning of Filial Piety: A Reading of "Xiao Zhangtu" (Little Zhang the Butcher)." *Journal of Song Yuan Studies* 29:63–90.

——. 2008. "On the Authorship of Three Zaju Plays Commonly Attributed to Yang Zi." *Literary Heritage* 6:76–83.

Fu Xuanzong 傅璇琮. 1990. *Tang caizi zhuan jiaojian* 唐才子傳校箋. 4 vols. Beijing: Zhonghua shuju.

Gao Sixi 高禩熹. 1976. "Qingji cangshu dajia kao (3): Qiantang Dingshi Jiahui tang" 清季藏書大家考(3)錢塘丁氏嘉惠堂. *Jiaoyu ziliao kexue yuekan* 9, nos. 4–6:32–35.

Gao Wenxiu 高文秀. 1958a. *Haojiu Zhao Yuan yu Shanghuang* 新刊關目好酒趙元遇上皇. Palace ed. In Zhao Qimei 1958, 31:1a–27a.

——. 1958b. *Xinkan guanmu Haojiu Zhao Yuan yu Shanghuang* 新刊關目好酒趙元遇上皇. Guben xiqu congkan 古本戲曲叢刊, no. 5:1a–5b. Shanghai: Shanghai yinshuguan.

Gong Tianting 宮天庭 [Fei Tangchen 費唐臣]. 1958. *Shengsi jiao Fan Zhan ji shu* 生死交范張雞黍. Xijizi ed. In Zhao Qimei 1958, 12:1a–32b.

Goodrich, Anne Swann. 1964. *The Peking Temple of the Eastern Peak: The Tung-yüeh Miao in Peking and Its lore, with 20 plates*. Nagoya: Monumenta Serica.

Goossaert, Vincent. 2008a. "Quanzhen Taoism." In *The Encyclopedia of Taoism*, edited by Fabrizio Pregadio, 814–20. London: Routledge.

——. 2008b. "Taiyi jiao." In *The Encyclopedia of Taoism*, edited by Fabrizio Pregadio, 959–60. London: Routledge.

Graham, A. C. 1990. *The Book of Lieh Tzu*. New York: Columbia University Press.

Guan Hanqing 關漢卿. 1958. *Guan dawang du fu dandao hui* 關大王獨赴單刀會. Palace ed. In Zhao Qimei 1958, 15:1a–26b.

Hansen, Valerie. 1990. *Changing Gods in Medieval China, 1127–1276*. Princeton: Princeton University Press.

Harper, Donald. 1986. "The *Analects* Jade Candle: A Classic of T'ang Drinking Custom." *T'ang Studies* 4:69–91.

Hartman, Charles. 1998. "The Making of a Villain: Ch'in Kuei and Tao-hsüeh." *Harvard Journal of Asiatic Studies* 58, no. 1:59–146.

Hashimoto Yō 橋本堯. 1986. "*Xue Rengui*: Atarashii monogatari taipu no tanjō" 薛仁貴: 新らしい物語タイプの誕生. *Wakō daigaku jimbunkagakubu kiyō* 21:19–29.

Hawkes, David. 1985. *The Songs of the South: An Ancient Chinese Anthology of Poems by Qu Yuan and Other Poets*. New York: Penguin.

He Jinli 何金俐. 2006. "Wang Guowei *Song Yuan xiqu shi* zhongde wenyi meixue sixiang ji qi xiandai wudu" 王國維《宋元戲曲史》中的文藝美學思想及其現代誤讀. *Yishu baijia* 3, no. 89:112–17, 131.

He Yuming. 2007. "Wang Guowei and the Beginnings of Modern Chinese Drama Studies." *Late Imperial China* 28, no. 2:129–56.

Hennessey, William, trans. 1981. *Proclaiming Harmony*. Ann Arbor, Mich.: Center for Chinese Studies.

——. 1984. "Classical Sources and Vernacular Sources in *Xuanhe yishi*: The Presence of Priority and the Priority of Presence." *Chinese Literature: Essays, Articles, and Reviews* 6:33–52.

Hightower, Robert. 1970. *The Poetry of Tao Ch'ien*. Oxford: Clarendon Press.

Holzman, Donald. 1976. *Poetry and Politics: The Life and Works of Juan Chi (A.D. 210–263)*. Cambridge: Cambridge University Press.

Hsia, Adrian. 1988. "*The Orphan of the House of Zhao* in French, English, German, and Hong Kong Literature." *Comparative Literature Studies* 25, no. 4:335–51.

Hsia, C. T. 1974. "The Military Romance." In *Studies in Chinese Literary Genres*, edited by Cyril Birch, 339–90. Berkeley: University of California Press.

Hsu, Elizabeth. 2008. "*Huangdi neijing*." In *The Encyclopedia of Taoism*, edited by Fabrizio Pregadio, 506–7. London: Routledge.

Hsü, Francis L. K. 1971. "Filial Piety in Japan and China: Borrowing, Variation and Significance." *Journal of Comparative Family Studies* 2, no. 1:67–74.

Hu Ji 胡忌. 2008. *Song Jin zaju kao dingbu ben* 宋金雜劇考訂補本. Shanghai: Zhonghua shuju.

Huang Donglan. 2004–2005. "Shrines of Yue Fei: Spaces for Creation of Public Memory." Translated by William Crawford. *Chinese Sociology and Anthropology* 37, nos. 2–3:74–112.

Huang Pilie 黄丕烈. 1958. *Weijian shuzhai tilu* 未見書齋題錄. In Zhao Qimei 1958, 1:12a–17a.

Huang Shizhong 黄仕忠. 2009. "Cong Mori Kainan, Kōda Rohan, Sasakawa Rinbō dao Wang Guowei: Riben Meiji shiqi (1869–1912) de Zhongguo xiqu yanjiu kaocha" 從森槐南、幸田露伴、笹川臨風到王國維:日本明治時期(1869–1912)的中國戲曲研究考察. *Xiju yanjiu* 7:155–94.

Huang Tianji 黄天驥. 2001. "Yuan zaju de 'za' ji qi shenmei tezheng" 元雜劇的『雜』及其審美特徵. In *Zhongguo gudian xiqu yu gudai wenxue yanjiu lunji* 中國古典戲曲與古代文學研究論集. Beijing: Zhonghua shuju.

Huo Jianyu 霍建瑜. 2005. "Yuandai Xue Rengui huaben yu zaju" 元代薛仁貴話本與雜劇. *Yishu baijia* 1:54–57.

Idema, Wilt L. 1985. *The Dramatic Oeuvre of Chu Yu-tun (1379–1439)*. Sinica Leidensia. Leiden: Brill.

——. 1988. "The Orphan of Chao: Self-Sacrifice, Tragic Choice and Revenge, and the Confucianization of Mongol Drama at the Ming Court." *Cina* 21:162–89.

——. 1989. "The *Tza-jiu* of Yang Tz: An International Tycoon in Defense of Collaboration?" In *Di'erjie guoji Hanxue huiyi lunwen ji, Wenxue zu* 第二屆國際漢學會議論文集,文學組, 523–48. Taipei: Academia Sinica.

——. 1990a. "The Founding of the Han Dynasty in Early Drama: The Autocratic Suppression of Popular Debunking." In *Thought and Law in Qin and Han China*, edited by W. L. Idema and E. Zurcher, 183–207. Leiden: Brill.

——. 1990b. "The Remaking of an Unfilial Hero: Some Notes on the Earliest Dramatic Adaptations of 'The Story of Hsüeh Jen-kuei.'" In *As the Twig Is Bent . . . : Essays in Honour of Frits Vos*, edited by Erika de Poorter, 83–111. Amsterdam: Gieben.

——. 1993. "Some Aspects of *Pai-yüeh-t'ing*: Script and Performance." In *Proceedings of the International Conference on Kuang Han-ch'ing*, edited by Tseng Yong-yih [Zeng Yongyi], 3–23. Taipei: Xingzhengyuan wenhua jianshe weiyuanhui.

——. 1996. "Why You Never Have Read a Yuan Drama: The Transformation of *Zaju* at the Ming Court." In *Studi in onore di Lionello Lanciotti*, edited by S. M. Carletti et al., 765–91. Naples: Dipartimento di Studi Asiatici, Istituto Universitario Orientale.

——. 1997. "The Pilgrimage to Taishan in the Dramatic Literature of the Thirteenth and Fourteenth Centuries." *Chinese Literature: Essays, Articles, and Reviews* 19:23–57.

——. 2004. "Banished to Yelang: Li Taibai Putting on a Performance." *Minsu quyi* 145:5–38.

——. 2005. "Educational Frustration, Shape-Shifting Texts, and the Abiding Power of Anthologies: Three Versions of *Wang Can Ascends the Tower*." *Early Medieval China* 10-11, no. 2:145–83.

——. 2005–2006. "Li Kaixian's *Revised Plays by Yuan Masters* (*Gaiding Yuanxian chuanqi*) and the Textual Transmission of Yuan *Zaju* as Seen in Two Plays by Ma Zhiyuan." *CHINOPERL* 26:47–66.

——. 2007a. "Fighting in Korea: Two Early Narrative Treatments of the Story of Xue Rengui." In *Korea in the Middle—Korean Studies and Area Studies: Essays in Honour of Boudewijn Walraven*, edited by Remco E. Beuker, 341–58. Leiden: CNWS.

——. 2007b. "Madness on the Yuan Stage." *Hōrin: Vergleichende Studien zur japanischen Kultur* 14:65–85.

——. 2008. *Meng Jiangnü Brings Down the Great Wall: Ten Versions of a Chinese Legend.* With an Essay by Haiyan Lee. Seattle: University of Washington Press.

——. 2010a. *Judge Bao and the Rule of Law: Eight Ballad-Stories from the Period 1250–1450*. Singapore: World Scientific.

——. 2010b. "Prosimetric and Verse Narrative." In *The Cambridge History of Chinese Literature*, edited by Kang-i Sun Chang and Stephen Owen, 343–412. Cambridge: Cambridge University Press.

Idema, Wilt. L., and Stephen H. West. 1982. *Chinese Theater, 1100–1450: A Source Book.* Münchener ostasiatische Studien. Wiesbaden: Steiner.

——. 2012. *Battles, Betrayals, and Brotherhood: Early Chinese Plays on the Three Kingdoms*. Cambridge, Mass.: Hackett.

——. 2013. *The Generals of the Yang Family: Four Early Plays*. Singapore: World Scientific.

Iwaki Hideo 岩城秀夫. 1961. "Genkan kohon zatsugeki sanjūshū no denryū" 元刊古本雑劇三十種の伝流. *Chūgoku bungakuhō* 14:67–89.

Ji Junxiang 紀君祥. 1958. *Zhaoshi gu'er* 趙氏孤兒. In Anon 1958c, 13:1a–4b.

——. 1998. *Zhaoshi gu'er da baochou zaju*. In Zang 1998, 664–74.

——. 2010. *Zhaoshi gu'er*. Shanghai: Shanghai guji chubanshe.

Jiang Shaoyu 江少虞. 1981. *Songchao shishi leiyuan* 宋朝事實類苑. Shanghai: Shanghai guji chubanshe.

Jin Renjie 金人傑 [Kong Wenqing 孔文卿]. 1958. *Dadu xinkan guanmu diben Dongchuang shi fan* 大都新刊關目的本東窗事犯. In Anon. 1958c, 26:1a–8b.

Johnson, David. 1980. "The Wu Tzu-hsü *Pien-wen* and Its Sources: Parts I and II." *Harvard Journal of Asiatic Studies* 40, no. 1: 93–119; no. 2: 466–505.

——. 1985. "The City-God Cults of T'ang and Sung China." *Harvard Journal of Asiatic Studies* 45, no. 2:363–457.

Jordan, David K. 1986. "Folk Piety in Taiwan: *The Twenty-four Filial Exemplars*." In *The Psycho-Culture of the Confucian Family: Past and Present*, edited by Walter H. Slote, 47–106. Seoul: International Cultural Society of Korea.

Kang, Jinzhi. 1980. "Li K'uei Carries Thorns." In Crump 1980, 201–46.

Katz, Paul R. 1996. "Enlightened Alchemist or Immoral Immortal? The Growth of Lü Dongbin's Cult in Late Imperial China." In Shahar and Weller, *Unruly Gods*, 70–104.

——. 1999. *Images of the Immortal: The Cult of Lü Dongbin at the Palace of Eternal Joy*. Honolulu: University of Hawai'i Press.

Kim Bunkyō 金文京. 1983. "*Yuankan zaju sanshizhong* josetsu" 元人雜劇三十種序說, *Mimei* 3:46–75.

——. 1984. "*Yuankan zaju sanshizhong* josetsu hosei" 元人雜劇三十種序說補正. *Mimei* 4:64–67.

Kinney, Anne Behnke. 2014. *Exemplary Women of Early China: The "Lienü zhuan" of Liu Xiang*. New York: Columbia University Press.

Kirkland, Russell. 2008. "Sima Chengzhen." In *The Encyclopedia of Taoism*, edited by Fabrizio Pregadio, 911–13. London: Routledge.

Knapp, Keith N. 2006. *Selfless Offspring: Filial Children and Social Order in Medieval China*. Honolulu: University of Hawai'i Press.

Knechtges, David.1976. *The Han Rhapsody: A Study of the Fu of Yang Hsiung (53 B.C.–A.D. 18)*. Cambridge: Cambridge University Press.

——. 1982. *Wen Xuan, or Selections of Refined Literature, Volume I: Rhapsodies on Metropolises and Capitals*. Princeton: Princeton University Press.

——. 1987. *Wen Xuan, or Selections of Refined Literature, Volume II: Rhapsodies on Sacrifices, Hunting, Travel, Sightseeing, Palaces and Halls, Rivers and Seas*. Princeton: Princeton University Press.

——. 2006. "Jìngǔ and Lán Tíng: Two (or Three?) Jìn Dynasty Gardens." In *Studies in Chinese Language and Culture—Festschrift in Honour of Christoph Harbsmeier on the Occasion of His 60th Birthday*, edited by Christoph Anderl and Halvor Eifring, 395–406. Oslo: Hermes Academic.

——. 2008. *The Han Rhapsody: A Study of the "Fu" of Yang Hsiung, 53* B.C–A.D. *18*. Cambridge: Cambridge University Press.

Komatsu Ken 小松謙. 2001. *Chūgoku koten engeki kenkyū* 中国古典演劇研究. Tokyo: Kyūko shoin.

Komjathy, Louis. 2007. *Cultivating Perfection: Mysticism and Self-Transformation in Early Quanzhen Daoism*. Leiden: Brill.

Kong Wenqing 孔文卿. *See* Jin Renjie.

Lang Ying 郎瑛. 1959. *Qixiu leigao* 七修類稿. Beijing: Zhonghua shuju.

Lau, Joseph S. M. 1985. "Duty, Reputation, and Selfhood in Traditional Chinese Narratives." In *Expressions of Self in Chinese Literature*, edited by Robert E. Hegel and Richard C. Hessney. Studies in Oriental Culture. New York: Columbia University Press.

Lau, Joseph S. M., and John Minford. 2000. *Classical Chinese Literature: An Anthology of Translations*. Hong Kong: Chinese University Press.

Lee Haiyan. 2005. "Tears That Crumbled the Great Wall: The Archaeology of Feeling in the May Fourth Folklore Movement." *Journal of Asian Studies* 64, no. 1:35–65.

Leung, Cécile. 2002. *Étienne Fourmont (1683–1745): Oriental and Chinese Languages in Eighteenth-Century France*. Leuven Chinese Studies. Leuven: Leuven University Press.

Levine, Ari L. 2009. "The Reigns of Hui-tsung (1100–1126) and Ch'in-tsung (1126–1127) and the Fall of the Northern Song." In *The Cambridge History of Chinese History, Volume 5, Part 1: The Sung Dynasty and Its Precursors, 907–1279*, edited by Denis Twitchett and Paul Jakov Smith, 556–643. Cambridge: Cambridge University Press.

Li Fang 李昉, ed.1986. *Taiping guangji* 太平廣記. 10 vols. Beijing: Zhonghua shuju.

Li He 李賀. 1961. *Sanjia pingzhu Li Changji geshi* 三家評注李長吉歌詩. Beijing: Zhonghua shuju.

Li Kaixian 李開先. 1982. *Cinue* 詞謔. In *Zhongguo gudian xiqu lunzhu jicheng* 中國古典戲曲論著集成, 2nd ed., vol. 3:259–418. Beijing: Zhongguo xiju chubanshe.

——. 2004. *Li Kaixian quan ji* 李開先全集. 3 vols. Annotated and edited by Bu Jian 卜鍵. Beijing: Wenhua yishu chubanshe.

Li Lin 李琳 2004. "Song Yuan Ming 'fengsengxi' gushi liubian yanjiu" 宋元明瘋僧戲故事流變研究. *Shenyang shifan daxue xuebao* 28:52–54.

Li Xiusheng 李修生, Li Zhenyu 李真瑜, and Hou Guangfu 侯光復. 2003. *Yuanqu dacidian* 元曲大辭典. 1st rev. ed. Nanjing: Fenghuang chubanshe.

Little, Stephen, and Shawn Eichman. 2001. *Taoism and the Arts of China*. Chicago: Art Institute of Chicago; Berkeley: University of California Press.

Liu, James T. C. 1972. "Yüeh Fei and China's Heritage of Loyalty." *Journal of Asian Studies* 31, no. 2:291–97.

Liu, Wu-chi. 1953. "The Original Orphan of China." *Comparative Literature Studies* 5:193–212.

Liu Yiqing 劉一清. 1782. *Qiantang yishi* 錢塘遺事. *Siku quanshu* ed. Beijing: Wuying dian.

Liu Yiqing and Liu Jun. 2002. *A New Account of Tales of the World*. 2nd ed. Edited and translated by Richard Mather. Michigan Monographs in Chinese Studies. Ann Arbor: Center for Chinese Studies, University of Michigan.

Llamas, Regina. 2010. "Wang Guowei and the Establishment of Chinese Drama in the Modern Canon of Classical Literature." *T'oung Pao* 96, nos. 1–3:165–201.

Loewe, Michael. 1974. "The Fall of the House of Huo." In *Crisis and Conflict in Han China, 104 BC to AD 9*, edited by Michael Loewe, 113–53. London: Allen and Unwin.

Lü Weifen 呂薇芬 and Wu Gengshun 吳庚舜. 2000. *Quan Yuan sanqu guangxuan, xinzhu, jiping* 全元散曲廣選、新注、集評. 2 vols. Shenyang: Liaoning renmin chubanshe.

Lundbaek, Knud. 1991. *Joseph de Prémare, 1666–1736, S.J.: Chinese Philology and Figurism*. Acta Jutlandica. Aarhus: Aarhus University Press.

Luo Jintang 羅錦堂. 1977. *Jintang lunqu* 錦堂論曲. Taipei: Lianjing chubanshiye gongsi.

Lynn, Richard John. 1980. *Kuan Yün Shih*. Twayne's World Authors Series, TWAS 562: China. Boston: Twayne.

Ma Zhiyuan 馬致遠. 1958. *Lü Dongbin sanzui Yueyang lou* 呂洞賓三醉岳陽樓. Gu mingjia 古名家 ed. In Zhao Qimei 1958, 3:1a–23a.

McLaren, Anne. 1998. *Chinese Popular Culture and Ming Chantefables*. Leiden: Brill.

Meng Hanqing 孟漢卿. 1958a. *Xinkan guanmu Zhang Ding zhikan moheluo* 新刊關目張鼎智勘磨合羅. In Anon. 1958c, 43:1a–6a.

——. 1958b. *Zhang Ding zhikan moheluo* 張鼎智勘磨合羅. Gu mingjia 古名家 ed. In Zhao Qimei 1958, 43:1a–32b.

Miao Huaiming 苗懷明. 2004. "Ershi shiji *Yuankan zaju sanshizhong* de faxian, zhengli yu yanjiu" 二十世紀《元刊雜劇三十種》的發現、整理與研究. *Zhongguo xiqu xueyuan xuebao* 25, no. 1:15–17.

Miller, Amy Lynn. 2008. "Daluo tian." In *The Encyclopedia of Taoism*, edited by Fabrizio Pregadio, 299. London: Routledge.

Miura, Kunio. 2008. "Initiation." In *The Encyclopedia of Taoism*, edited by Fabrizio Pregadio, 16–17. London: Routledge.

Murray, Julia. 2007. *Mirror of Morality: Chinese Narrative Illustration and Confucian Ideology*. Honolulu: University of Hawai`i Press.

Naquin, Susan, and Chün-fang Yü, eds. 1992. *Pilgrims and Sacred Sites in China*. Berkeley: University of California Press.

Nienhauser, William, trans. 1978. "The World Inside a Pillow." In *Traditional Chinese Stories: Themes and Variations*, edited by Joseph S. M. Lau and Y. W. Ma, 435–48. New York: Columbia University Press.

Nienhauser, William H., Jr. 2010. *Tang Dynasty Tales: A Guided Reader*. Singapore: World Scientific.

Ning Xiyuan 寧希元. 1988. *Yuankan zaju sanshizhong xinjiao* 元刊雜劇三十種新校. 2 vols. Lanzhou: Lanzhou daxue chubanshe.

O'Hara, Albert R. 1945. "The Wife of Yang of Han and the Wife of Ho of Han." In *The Position of Woman in Early China According to the Lieh Nü Chuan, "The Biographies of Eminent Chinese Women,"* edited by Albert R. O'Hara, 222–25. Washington, D.C.: Catholic University Press.

Ouyang Xiu 歐陽修 and Song Qi 宋祁. 1975. *Xin Tangshu* 新唐書. 20 vols. Beijing: Zhonghua shuju.

Owen, Stephen. 1996. *An Anthology of Chinese Literature: Beginnings to 1911*. New York: Norton.

Pan, Ku [Ban Gu]. 1944. "Liu Ho's Brief Reign and Deposition," "The Selection of Emperor Shiun," "The Dangerous Intrigues and Downfall of the Ho Clan." In *The History of the Former Han Dynasty, Translation, Volume Two: First Division, Chapters VI–X*, edited and translated by Homer H. Dubs. 181–90. London: Kegan Paul, Trench, Trubner.

Penny, Benjamin. 2008a. "Guangchengzi." In *The Encyclopedia of Taoism*, edited by Fabrizio Pregadio, 457–58. London: Routledge.

——. 2008b. "Magu." In *The Encyclopedia of Taoism*, edited by Fabrizio Pregadio, 731–32. London: Routledge.

——. 2008c. "*Xu xianzhuan*: Sequel to Biographies of Immortals." In *The Encyclopedia of Taoism*, edited by Fabrizio Pregadio, 1123–24. London: Routledge.

Pregadio, Fabrizio. 2008a. "*Baopu zi*." In *The Encyclopedia of Taoism*, edited by Fabrizio Pregadio, 215–18. London: Routledge.

——. 2008b. "Ge Hong." In *The Encyclopedia of Taoism*, edited by Fabrizio Pregadio, 442–43. London: Routledge.

——. 2008c. "Huandan." In *The Encyclopedia of Taoism*, edited by Fabrizio Pregadio, 16–17. London: Routledge.

Qian, Cai. 1995. *General Yue Fei: A Novel*. Translated by T. L. Yang. Hong Kong: Joint Publishing.

Qian Zhongshu. *See* Ch'ien Chung-shu.

Raz, Gilbert. 2008. "Chisong zi." In *The Encyclopedia of Taoism*, edited by Fabrizio Pregadio, 271–72. London: Routledge.

Ren Zhongming 任中敏 and Ji Guoping 季國平. 1983. "Dui Wang Guowei xiqu lilun de jianping" 對王國維戲曲理論的簡評. *Yangzhou shiyuan xuebao (shehui kexue ban)* 1:33–37.

Robinet, Isabelle. 2008a. "*Daode jing*." In *The Encyclopedia of Taoism*, edited by Fabrizio Pregadio, 311–14. London: Routledge

——. 2008b. "*Han Wudi neizhuan*: Inner Biography of Emperor Wu of the Han." In *The Encyclopedia of Taoism*, edited by Fabrizio Pregadio, 472. London: Routledge

——. 2008c. "*Huangting jing*." In *The Encyclopedia of Taoism*, edited by Fabrizio Pregadio, 511–14. London: Routledge.

Rosemont, Henry Jr., and Roger T. Ames. 2009. *The Chinese Classic of Family Reverence: A Philosophical Translation of the Xiaojing*. Honolulu: University of Hawai`i Press.

Schipper, Kristofer. 1965. *L'Empereur Wou des Han dans la légende taoïste*. Publications de l'École française d'Extrême-Orient 58. Paris: École française d'Extrême-Orient.

Shahar, Meir, and Robert P. Weller, eds. 1996. *Unruly Gods: Divinity and Society in China*. Honolulu: University of Hawai`i Press.

Shao Zengqi 邵曾祺, ed. 1955. *Yuanren zaju* 元人雜劇. Shanghai: Chunming chubanshe.

Shi Junbao 石君寶. 1958. *Gu Hang xinkan diben guanmu Fengyue Ziyunting* 古杭新刊的本關目風月紫雲庭. In Anon. 1958c, 2:1a–7b.

Shih, Chung-wen. 1976. *The Golden Age of Chinese Drama: Yüan Tsa-chü*. Princeton: Princeton University Press.

Shu Dan 舒丹. 2008 "Yuan zaju *Xue Rengui yijin huanxiang* yu *Xue Rengui rong gui guli* zhi bijiao" 元雜劇《薛仁貴衣錦還鄉》與《薛仁貴榮歸故里》之比較. *Anhui wenxue (pinglun yanjiu)* 2:2–3.

Sima Qian 司馬遷. 1959. *Shiji* 史記. 10 vols. Beijing: Zhonghua shuju.

Slingerland, Edward G., trans. 2003. *Confucius Analects: With Selections from Traditional Commentaries*. Indianapolis: Hackett.

Smith, Thomas. 2008. "Wang Xianfu." In *The Encyclopedia of Taoism*, edited by Fabrizio Pregadio, 1008. London: Routledge.

Song Kefu 宋克夫 and Yu Ying 余瑩. 2003. "*Zhuye zhou* yuanben yu Zangben zhi bijiao" 《竹葉舟》元本與臧本之比較. *Hubei zhiye jishu xueyuan xuebao* 6, no. 2:43–48.

Ssu-ma Ch'ien. 1995a. *The Grand Scribe's Records: Volume I, The Basic Annals of Pre-Han China*. Edited by William H. Nienhauser Jr. Translated by Tsai-fa Cheng et al. Bloomington: Indiana University Press.

——. 1995b. *The Grand Scribe's Records: Volume VII, The Memoirs of Pre-Han China*. Edited by William H. Nienhauser Jr. Translated by Tsai-fa Cheng et al. Bloomington: Indiana University Press.

——. 2002. *The Grand Scribe's Records: Volume II, The Basic Annals of Han China*. Edited by William H. Nienhauser Jr. Translated by Weiguo Cao et al. Bloomington: Indiana University Press.

Stimson, Hugh M. 1966. *The Jongyuan In Yunn: A Guide to Old Mandarin Pronunciation*. Sinological Series. New Haven: Far Eastern Publications, Yale University.

Sun Kaidi 孫楷弟. 1953. *Yeshi yuan gujin zaju kao* 也是園古今雜劇考. Zhongguo xiqu lilun congshu 中國戲曲理論叢書. Shanghai: Shangza chubanshe.

Takahashi Bunji 高橋文治. 1988. "Genkanhon *Xue Rengui yijin huanxiang* geki o megutte" 元刊本薛仁貴衣錦還香劇をめぐって. *Tōhōgaku* 76:63–77.

Tan, Tian Yuan. 2008. "The Sovereign and the Theater: Reconsidering the Impact of Ming Taizu's Prohibitions." In *Long Live the Emperor! Uses of the Ming Founder across Six Centuries of East Asian History*, edited by Sarah Schneewind, 149–69. Minneapolis: Society for Ming Studies.

——. 2009. "Rethinking Li Kaixian's Editorship of Revised Plays by Yuan Masters: A Comparison with His *Banter about Lyrics*." In *Text, Performance, and Gender in Chinese Literature and Music: Essays in Honor of Wilt Idema*, Edited by Maghiel van Crevel, Tian Yuan Tan, and Michel Hockx, 139–52. Leiden: Brill.

——. 2010. *Songs of Contentment and Transgression: Discharged Officials and Literati Communities in Sixteenth-Century North China*. Harvard-Yenching Institute Monograph Series. Cambridge, Mass.: Harvard University Asia Center.

Tao, Jing-shen. 2009. "The Move to the South and the Reign of Kao-tsung (1127–62)." In *The Cambridge History of Chinese History, Volume 5, Part 1: The Sung Dynasty and Its Precursors, 907–1279*, edited by Denis Twitchett and Paul Jakov Smith, 664–709. Cambridge: Cambridge University Press.

Tao Zongyi 陶宗儀. 1959. *Nancun chuogeng lu* 南村輟耕錄. Beijing: Zhonghua shuju.

Teiser, Stephen F. 1993a. "The Growth of Purgatory." In *Religion and Society in T'ang and Sung China*, edited by Patricia Buckley Ebrey and Peter N. Gregory, 115–46. Honolulu: University of Hawai`i Press.

——. 1993b. *The Scripture on the Ten Kings and the Making of Purgatory in Medieval China*. Honolulu: University of Hawai`i Press.

Trauzettel, Rolf. 1975. "Sung Patriotism as a First Step toward Chinese Nationalism." In *Crisis and Prosperity in Sung China*, edited by John Winthrop Haeger, 199–213. Tucson: University of Arizona Press.

Tseng Yong-yih [Zeng Yongyi] 曾永義. 2009. *Xiqu zhi yasu, zhezi, liupai* 戲曲之雅俗、折子、流派. Guojia xiqu yanjiu congshu 國家戲曲研究叢書. Taipei: Guojia chubanshe.

Tuotuo 脫脫 et al. 1977. *Songshi* 宋史. Beijing: Zhonghua shuju.

Twitchett, Denis, ed. 1979. *The Cambridge History of China, Volume 3, Part 1: Sui and T'ang China, 589–906*. Cambridge: Cambridge University Press.

Wagner, Donald B. 1998. *A Classical Chinese Reader: The Han Shu Biography of Huo Kuang*. Richmond, Surrey, U.K.: Curzon Press.

Wang Bocheng 王伯成. 1958. "Gu Hang xinkan guanmu diben Li Taibo bian Yelang" 古杭新刊關目的本李太白貶夜郎. In Anon. 1958c, 18:1a–9b.

Wang Guowei 王國維. 1964. *Song Yuan xiqu shi* 宋元戲曲史. Hong Kong: Taiping shuju.

——. 1983. *Wang Guowei yishu* 王國維遺書. 16 vols. Shanghai: Shanghai guji shudian.

Wang Liqi 王利器. 1981. *Yuan Ming Qing sandai jinhui xiaoshuo xiqu shiliao* 元明清三代禁毀小說戲曲史料. Shanghai: Shanghai guji chubanshe.

Wang Meng'ou 王夢鷗. 1971. *Tangren xiaoshuo yanjiu—Zuanyi ji yu Chuanqi jiaoshi* 唐人小說研究:纂異記與傳奇校釋, vol. 1. Taipei: Yiwen yinshuguan.

Wang, Pi-twan. 1978. "The Revenge of the Orphan of Chao, by Chi Chün-hsiang." *Renditions* 9:103–31.

Wang Qi 王圻. 1959. *Ming Wanli Xu Wenxian tongkao* 明萬曆續文獻通考. In *Xu Wenxian tongkao erbaiwushisi juan* 續文獻通考二百五十四卷, vol. 11. Taipei: Wenhai chuban youxian gongsi.

——. 1988. *Sancai tuhui* 三才圖會. 3 vols. Shanghai: Shanghai guji chubanshe.

Wang Rutao 王汝濤. 1987. *Taiping guangji xuan* 太平廣記選. Jinan: Qi Lu shushe.

Wang Shipei 汪詩珮. 2008. "Wenrenhua yu zhezhonghua de gaibian: Cong 'Yuankanben' yu *Yuanqu xuan* de *Xue Rengui* shuoqi" 文人化與折衷化的改編:從元刊本與元曲選的薛仁貴說起. *Hanxue yanjiu / Chinese Studies* 26, no. 1:137–64.

Wang Shizhen 王世貞. 1982. *Quzao* 曲藻. In *Zhongguo gudian xiqu lunzhu jicheng* 中國古典戲曲論著集成, vol. 2:15–42. Beijing: Zhongguo xiju chubanshe.

Wang Xiaojia 王曉家. 2004. "Gao Wenxiu zaju kaolun" 高文秀雜劇考論. *Xiqu yanjiu* 65:87–97.

Wang Zhihan 王之涵. 2007. "*Yuankan zaju sanshizhong* biaoyan tishi yanjiu" 元刊雜劇三十種表演提示研究. *Chuzhou xueyuan xuebao* 9, no. 2:34–36.

Wang-Toutain, Françoise. 1998. *Le bodhisattva Ksitigarbha en Chine du Ve au XIIIe siècle*. Paris: Presses de l'École française d'Extrême-Orient.

Ward, Adrienne. 2010. *Pagodas in Play: China on the Eighteenth-Century Italian Opera Stage*. Lewisburg, Penn.: Bucknell University Press.

Watson, Burton. 1968. *The Complete Works of Chuang-tzu*. New York: Columbia University Press.

——. 1974a. "Accounts of the Families Related to the Emperor by Marriage (Excerpts)." In *Courtier and Commoner in Ancient China: Selections from the "History of the Former Han" by Pan Ku*, 247–78. New York: Columbia University Press.

——. 1974b. "The Biography of Huo Kuang and Chin Mi-ti." In *Courtier and Commoner in Ancient China: Selections from the "History of the Former Han" by Pan Ku*, 121–57. New York: Columbia University Press.

Weng Minhua 翁敏華. 2006. "Gudai jiusu yu Yuandai zaju *Haojiu Zhao Yuan yu Shanghuang*" 古代酒俗與元代雜劇《好酒趙元遇上皇》. *Shanghai shifan daxue xuebao* 35, no. 2:55–59.

West, Stephen H. 1997. "Playing with Food: Performance, Food, and the Aesthetics of Artificiality in the Sung and Yuan." *Harvard Journal of Asiatic Studies* 57, no. 1:67–106.

——. 2000. "The Emperor Sets the Pace: Court and Consumption in the Northern Song." In *Selected Essays on Court Culture in Cross-Cultural Perspective*, edited by Lin Yaofu, 25–50. Taipei: National Taiwan University Press.

——. 2002. "Huanghou, zangli, youbing yu zhu" 皇后、葬禮、油餅與豬. In *Wenxue, wenhua yu shibian* 文學、文化與世變, edited by Li Fengmao, 197–218. Taipei: Academia Sinica.

——. 2004. "Text and Ideology: Ming Editors and Northern Drama." In *The Song-Yuan-Ming Transition in Chinese History*, edited by Paul Jakov Smith and Richard von Glahn, 329–73. Cambridge, Mass.: Harvard University Asia Center.

——. 2005. "Meng Yuanlao, 'Recollections of the Northern Song Capital.'" In *Hawai'i Reader in Traditional Chinese Culture*, edited by Victor H. Mair, Nancy Shatzman Steinhardt, and Paul R. Goldin, 405–22. Honolulu: University of Hawai'i Press.

——. 2006. "Crossing Over: Huizong in the Afterglow, or the Deaths of a Troubling Emperor." In Ebrey and Bickford, *Emperor Huizong and Late Northern Song China*, 565–608.

——. 2008. "Shifting Spaces: Local Dialect in *A Playboy from a Noble House Opts for the Wrong Career*." *Journal of Theater Studies* 1, no. 1:83–108.

West, Stephen H., and Wilt L. Idema. 2010a. "Little Butcher Sun." In West and Idema, *Monks, Bandits*, 389–454.

——. 2010b. *Monks, Bandits, Lovers, and Immortals: Eleven Early Chinese Plays*. Indianapolis: Hackett.

Wilhelm, Helmut. 1962. "From Myth to Myth: The Case of Yüeh Fei's Biography." In *Confucian Personalities*, edited by Arthur F. Wright and Denis Twitchett, 146–61. Stanford: Stanford University Press.

Wong, Alan L., and Chün-hsiang Chi. 1973. *The Orphan of China: A Play of Five Acts and a Prologue*. London: Mitre Press.

Wu, Pei-yi. 1992. "An Ambivalent Pilgrim to T'ai Shan in the Seventeenth Century." In Naquin and Yü, *Pilgrims and Sacred Sites*, 65–88.

Xia Tingzhi 夏庭芝. 1996. *Qinglou ji jianzhu* 青樓集箋注. Edited by Sun Chongtao 孫崇濤 and Xu Hongtu 徐弘圖. Beijing: Guojia xiju chubanshe.

Xu Mengxin 徐夢莘. 1987. *Sanchao beimeng huibian* 三朝北盟會編. 4 vols. Shanghai: Shanghai guji chubanshe.

Xu Qinjun 徐沁君. 1980. *Xinjiao Yuan kan zaju sanshizhong* 新校元刊雜劇三十種. 2 vols. Beijing: Zhonghua shuju.

Xu Shuofang 徐朔方. 1956. *Xiqu zaji* 戲曲雜記. Shanghai: Shanghai gudian wenxue chubanshe.

——. 1993. "Zang Maoxun he tade *Yuanqu xuan*" 臧懋循和他的元曲選. In *Xu Shuofang ji* 徐朔方集, vol. 1:1–64. Hangzhou: Zhejiang guji chubanshe.

Xu Zheng 徐征 and Zhang Yuezhong 張月中. 1998. *Quan Yuan qu* 全元曲. 12 vols. Shijiazhuang: Hebei jiaoyu chubanshe.

Yang, Chi-ming. 2011. *Performing China: Virtue, Commerce, and Orientalism in Eighteenth-Century England, 1660–1760*. Baltimore: Johns Hopkins University.

Yang, Richard F. S. 1972. *Four Plays of the Yuan Drama*. Taipei: China Post

Yang Zi 楊梓. 1958. *Gu Hang xinkan guanmu Huo Guang guijian* 古杭新刊關目霍光鬼諫. In Anon. 1958c, 22 :1a–7b.

Yao Tongshou 姚桐壽. 1936. *Lejiao siyu* 樂郊私語. In *Xuehai leibian* 學海類編, edited by Cao Rong 曹溶, vol. 114. Shanghai: Hanfen lou.

Yen Yuan-shu. 1970. "Hsüeh Jen-kuei and Hsüeh Ting-shan: A Chinese Oedipal Conflict." *Tamkang Review* 1:223–32.

Yin Yun 殷芸. 1999. *Xiaoshuo* 小說. In *Han Wei Liuchao biji xiaoshuo daguan* 漢魏六朝筆記小說大觀. Shanghai: Shanghai guji chubanshe.

Yoshikawa, Tadao. 2008a. "*Baxian*: Eight Immortals." In *The Encyclopedia of Taoism*, edited by Fabrizio Pregadio, 220–22. London: Routledge.

——. 2008b. "Xiwang mu: Queen Mother of the West." In *The Encyclopedia of Taoism*, edited by Fabrizio Pregadio, 1119–20. London: Routledge.

——. 2008c. "Zhang Guolao." In *The Encyclopedia of Taoism*, edited by Fabrizio Pregadio, 1225–26. London: Routledge.

Yu Xuejian 于學劍. 2012. "Gao Wenxiu zaju: Tiegan yingzhi, panxuan duoci" 高文秀雜劇：鐵杆硬枝、槃旋多次. In *Xiju congkan* 喜劇叢刊, 1:33–40.

Yu, Shiao-ling. 2005–2006. "From Revenge to What? Seven Hundred Years of Transformations of *The Orphan of Zhao*." *CHINOPERL Papers* 26:129–48.

Zang Maoxun 臧懋循. 1998. *Yuanquxuan fu chatu* 元曲選附插圖. Hanfen Lou 1918 photolithograph of Ming edition of 1616. Hangzhou: Zhejiang guji chubanshe.

Zeng Zao 曾慥. 1982. *Leishuo* 類說. In *Beijing tushuguan guji zhenben congkan Zibu Zajia lei* 北京圖書館古籍珍本叢刊子部雜家類. Beijing: Shumu wenxian chubanshe. Original edition, Yue Zhongxiu 岳鍾秀, 1625.

Zhang Geng 張庚 and Guo Hancheng 郭漢城. 1980. *Zhongguo xiqu tongshi* 中國戲曲通史, vol. 1. Beijing: Zhongguo xiju chubanshe.

Zhang Guobin 張國賓. 1958. *Xinkan diben Xue Rengui yijin huanxiang* 新刊的本薛仁貴衣錦還鄉." In Anon. 1958c, 15:1a–5b.

——. 1998. *Xue Rengui rong gui guli zaju* 薛仁貴榮歸故里雜劇." In Zang 1998, 156–63.

Zhang Qingfa 張清發. 2008. "Qin Gui mingbao gushi de fazhan yu wenhua yihan" 秦檜冥報故事的演變與發展與文化意涵. *Guoli Gaoxiong haiyang keji daxue xuebao* 24:293–313.

Zhang Shaoduo 張紹鐸. 1981. *Zhaoshi gu'er zaju yanjiu* 趙氏孤兒雜劇研究. Taipei: Xuehai chubanshe.

Zhao Lingxia 趙玲霞. 2009. "Yi Quanzhenjiao ticai kan zongjiao ju zhong de 'dutuo' moshi" 以全真教題材看宗教劇中的『度脫』模式. *Nanchang gaodeng xuebao* 6:50–51, 56.

Zhao Qimei 趙琦美, ed. 1958. *Maiwangguan chaojiaoben gujin zaju* 脈望館抄校本古今雜劇. In Guben xiqu congkan siji 古本戲曲叢刊四集. Shanghai: Shanghai yinshuguan.

Zhao Wanli 趙萬里, ed. 1957. *Xue Rengui zheng Liao shilue* 薛仁貴征遼事略. Shanghai: Gudian wenxue chubanshe.

Zhao Youmin 趙幼民. 1975a. "Yuan zaju zhongde dutuo ju (1)" 元雜劇中的度脫劇(上). In *Wenxue pinglun* 文學評論, edited by Wenxue Pinglun Bianji Weiyuanhui 文學評論編輯委員會, 153–97. Taipei: Shuping shumu chubanshe.

——. 1975b. "Yuan zaju zhongde dutuo ju (2)" 元雜劇中的度脫劇(下). In *Wenxue pinglun* 文學評論, edited by Wenxue pinglun bianji weiyuanhui 文學評論編輯委員會, 169–217. Taipei: Shuping shumu chubanshe.

Zhen Weini 甄煒旎. 2008. "*Yuankan zaju sanshi zhong* yu Li Kaixian jiuzang zhi guanxi" 元刊雜劇三十種與李開先舊藏之關系. *Zhongguo dianji yu wenhua* 64:64–67.

Zheng Guangzu 鄭光祖. 1958. *Zuisixiang Wang Can denglou* 醉思想王粲登樓. Gu mingjia 古名家 ed. In Zhao Qimei 1958, 36:1a–21b.

Zheng Li 鄭莉. 2007. "*Maiwangguan chaojiaoben gujin zaju* zhong Ming gongting zaju kaozheng" 《脈望館抄校本古今雜劇》中明宮廷雜劇考證. *Dianying pingjie* 12, no. 9:98–100.

Zheng Qian 鄭騫. 1962. *Jiaoding Yuankan zaju sanshizhong* 校訂元刊雜劇三十種. Taipei: Shijie shuju.

——. 1972. *Jingwu congbian* 景午叢編. 2 vols. Taipei: Taiwan Zhonghua shuju.

Zheng Tingyu 鄭廷玉. 1958a. *Gu Hang xinkan guanmu fu Chengwang Zhougong shezheng* 古杭新刊關目輔成王周公攝政. In Anon. 1958c, 6:1a–8b.

——. 1958b. *Kancai nu mai yuanjia zhaizhu* 看財奴買冤家債主. *Xijizi* 息機子 ed. In Zhao Qimei 1958, 51 :1a–31a.

Zhong Sicheng 鐘嗣成. 1982. *Lugui bu* 錄鬼簿. In *Zhongguo gudian xiqu lunzhu jicheng* 中國古典戲曲論著集成, vol. 2:85–274. Beijing: Zhongguo xiju chubanshe.

Zhou Deqing. 2006. *Zhongyuan yinyun* 中原音韻. In *Lidai quhua huibian*: *Tang Song Yuan bian* 歷代曲話彙編唐宋元編, edited by Sun Rongrong 孫蓉蓉 and Yu Weimin 俞為民, vol. 2. Hefei: Huangshan shushe.

Zhou Shaoxian 周紹賢. 1983. *Liezi yaoyi* 列子要義. Taipei: Zhonghua shuju.

Zhou Yibai 周怡白. 1979. *Zhongguo xiqu fazhanshi gangyao* 中國戲曲發展史綱要. Shanghai: Shanghai guji chubanshe.

Zhu Quan 朱權. 2010. *Taihe zhengyin pu jianping* 太和正音譜箋評, annotated by Yao Pinwen 姚品文. Zhongguo wenxue yanjiu dianji congkan 中國文學研究典籍叢刊, edited by Luo Di 洛地. Beijing: Zhonghua shuju, 2010.

Zhu Xi 朱熹. 2010. *Zhuzi quanshu* 朱子全書. 27 vols. Shanghai: Shanghai guji chubanshe.

TRANSLATIONS FROM THE ASIAN CLASSICS

Major Plays of Chikamatsu, tr. Donald Keene 1961

Four Major Plays of Chikamatsu, tr. Donald Keene. Paperback ed. only. 1961; rev. ed. 1997

Records of the Grand Historian of China, translated from the Shih chi of Ssu-ma Ch'ien, tr. Burton Watson, 2 vols. 1961

Instructions for Practical Living and Other Neo-Confucian Writings by Wang Yang-ming, tr. Wing-tsit Chan 1963

Hsün Tzu: Basic Writings, tr. Burton Watson, paperback ed. only. 1963; rev. ed. 1996

Chuang Tzu: Basic Writings, tr. Burton Watson, paperback ed. only. 1964; rev. ed. 1996

The Mahābhārata, tr. Chakravarthi V. Narasimhan. Also in paperback ed. 1965; rev. ed. 1997

The Manyōshū, Nippon Gakujutsu Shinkōkai edition 1965

Su Tung-p'o: Selections from a Sung Dynasty Poet, tr. Burton Watson. Also in paperback ed. 1965

Bhartrihari: Poems, tr. Barbara Stoler Miller. Also in paperback ed. 1967

Basic Writings of Mo Tzu, Hsün Tzu, and Han Fei Tzu, tr. Burton Watson. Also in separate paperback eds. 1967

The Awakening of Faith, Attributed to Aśvaghosha, tr. Yoshito S. Hakeda. Also in paperback ed. 1967

Reflections on Things at Hand: The Neo-Confucian Anthology, comp. Chu Hsi and Lü Tsu-ch'ien, tr. Wing-tsit Chan 1967

The Platform Sutra of the Sixth Patriarch, tr. Philip B. Yampolsky. Also in paperback ed. 1967

Essays in Idleness: The Tsurezuregusa of Kenkō, tr. Donald Keene. Also in paperback ed. 1967

The Pillow Book of Sei Shōnagon, tr. Ivan Morris, 2 vols. 1967

Two Plays of Ancient India: The Little Clay Cart and the Minister's Seal, tr. J. A. B. van Buitenen 1968

The Complete Works of Chuang Tzu, tr. Burton Watson 1968

The Romance of the Western Chamber (Hsi Hsiang chi), tr. S. I. Hsiung. Also in paperback ed. 1968

The Manyōshū, Nippon Gakujutsu Shinkōkai edition. Paperback ed. only. 1969

Records of the Historian: Chapters from the Shih chi of Ssu-ma Ch'ien, tr. Burton Watson. Paperback ed. only. 1969

Cold Mountain: 100 Poems by the T'ang Poet Han-shan, tr. Burton Watson. Also in paperback ed. 1970

Twenty Plays of the Nō Theatre, ed. Donald Keene. Also in paperback ed. 1970

Chūshingura: The Treasury of Loyal Retainers, tr. Donald Keene. Also in paperback ed. 1971; rev. ed. 1997

The Zen Master Hakuin: Selected Writings, tr. Philip B. Yampolsky 1971

Chinese Rhyme-Prose: Poems in the Fu Form from the Han and Six Dynasties Periods, tr. Burton Watson. Also in paperback ed. 1971

Kūkai: Major Works, tr. Yoshito S. Hakeda. Also in paperback ed. 1972

The Old Man Who Does as He Pleases: Selections from the Poetry and Prose of Lu Yu, tr. Burton Watson 1973

The Lion's Roar of Queen Śrīmālā, tr. Alex and Hideko Wayman 1974

Courtier and Commoner in Ancient China: Selections from the History of the Former Han by Pan Ku, tr. Burton Watson. Also in paperback ed. 1974

Japanese Literature in Chinese, vol. 1: *Poetry and Prose in Chinese by Japanese Writers of the Early Period*, tr. Burton Watson 1975

Japanese Literature in Chinese, vol. 2: *Poetry and Prose in Chinese by Japanese Writers of the Later Period*, tr. Burton Watson 1976

Love Song of the Dark Lord: Jayadeva's Gītagovinda, tr. Barbara Stoler Miller. Also in paperback ed. Cloth ed. includes critical text of the Sanskrit. 1977; rev. ed. 1997

Ryōkan: Zen Monk-Poet of Japan, tr. Burton Watson 1977

Calming the Mind and Discerning the Real: From the Lam rim chen mo of Tsoṇ-kha-pa, tr. Alex Wayman 1978

The Hermit and the Love-Thief: Sanskrit Poems of Bhartrihari and Bilhaṇa, tr. Barbara Stoler Miller 1978

The Lute: Kao Ming's P'i-p'a chi, tr. Jean Mulligan. Also in paperback ed. 1980

A Chronicle of Gods and Sovereigns: Jinnō Shōtōki of Kitabatake Chikafusa, tr. H. Paul Varley 1980

Among the Flowers: The Hua-chien chi, tr. Lois Fusek 1982

Grass Hill: Poems and Prose by the Japanese Monk Gensei, tr. Burton Watson 1983

Doctors, Diviners, and Magicians of Ancient China: Biographies of Fang-shih, tr. Kenneth J. DeWoskin. Also in paperback ed. 1983

Theater of Memory: The Plays of Kālidāsa, ed. Barbara Stoler Miller. Also in paperback ed. 1984

The Columbia Book of Chinese Poetry: From Early Times to the Thirteenth Century, ed. and tr. Burton Watson. Also in paperback ed. 1984

Poems of Love and War: From the Eight Anthologies and the Ten Long Poems of Classical Tamil, tr. A. K. Ramanujan. Also in paperback ed. 1985

The Bhagavad Gita: Krishna's Counsel in Time of War, tr. Barbara Stoler Miller 1986

The Columbia Book of Later Chinese Poetry, ed. and tr. Jonathan Chaves. Also in paperback ed. 1986

The Tso Chuan: Selections from China's Oldest Narrative History, tr. Burton Watson 1989

Waiting for the Wind: Thirty-six Poets of Japan's Late Medieval Age, tr. Steven Carter 1989

Selected Writings of Nichiren, ed. Philip B. Yampolsky 1990

Saigyō, Poems of a Mountain Home, tr. Burton Watson 1990

The Book of Lieh Tzu: A Classic of the Tao, tr. A. C. Graham. Morningside ed. 1990

The Tale of an Anklet: An Epic of South India—The Cilappatikāram of Iḷaṅkō Aṭikaḷ, tr. R. Parthasarathy 1993

Waiting for the Dawn: A Plan for the Prince, tr. with introduction by Wm. Theodore de Bary 1993

Yoshitsune and the Thousand Cherry Trees: A Masterpiece of the Eighteenth-Century Japanese Puppet Theater, tr., annotated, and with introduction by Stanleigh H. Jones, Jr. 1993

The Lotus Sutra, tr. Burton Watson. Also in paperback ed. 1993

The Classic of Changes: A New Translation of the I Ching as Interpreted by Wang Bi, tr. Richard John Lynn 1994

Beyond Spring: Tz'u Poems of the Sung Dynasty, tr. Julie Landau 1994

The Columbia Anthology of Traditional Chinese Literature, ed. Victor H. Mair 1994

Scenes for Mandarins: The Elite Theater of the Ming, tr. Cyril Birch 1995

Letters of Nichiren, ed. Philip B. Yampolsky; tr. Burton Watson et al. 1996

Unforgotten Dreams: Poems by the Zen Monk Shōtetsu, tr. Steven D. Carter 1997

The Vimalakirti Sutra, tr. Burton Watson 1997

Japanese and Chinese Poems to Sing: The Wakan rōei shū, tr. J. Thomas Rimer and Jonathan Chaves 1997

Breeze Through Bamboo: Kanshi of Ema Saikō, tr. Hiroaki Sato 1998

A Tower for the Summer Heat, by Li Yu, tr. Patrick Hanan 1998

Traditional Japanese Theater: An Anthology of Plays, by Karen Brazell 1998

The Original Analects: Sayings of Confucius and His Successors (0479–0249), by E. Bruce Brooks and A. Taeko Brooks 1998

The Classic of the Way and Virtue: A New Translation of the Tao-te ching of Laozi as Interpreted by Wang Bi, tr. Richard John Lynn 1999

The Four Hundred Songs of War and Wisdom: An Anthology of Poems from Classical Tamil, The Puṟanāṉūṟu, ed. and tr. George L. Hart and Hank Heifetz 1999

Original Tao: Inward Training (Nei-yeh) *and the Foundations of Taoist Mysticism*, by Harold D. Roth 1999

Po Chü-i: Selected Poems, tr. Burton Watson 2000

Lao Tzu's Tao Te Ching: *A Translation of the Startling New Documents Found at Guodian*, by Robert G. Henricks 2000

The Shorter Columbia Anthology of Traditional Chinese Literature, ed. Victor H. Mair 2000

Mistress and Maid (Jiaohongji), by Meng Chengshun, tr. Cyril Birch 2001

Chikamatsu: Five Late Plays, tr. and ed. C. Andrew Gerstle 2001

The Essential Lotus: Selections from the Lotus Sutra, tr. Burton Watson 2002

Early Modern Japanese Literature: An Anthology, 1600–1900, ed. Haruo Shirane 2002; abridged 2008

The Columbia Anthology of Traditional Korean Poetry, ed. Peter H. Lee 2002

The Sound of the Kiss, or The Story That Must Never Be Told: Pingali Suranna's Kalapurnodayamu, tr. Vecheru Narayana Rao and David Shulman 2003

The Selected Poems of Du Fu, tr. Burton Watson 2003

Far Beyond the Field: Haiku by Japanese Women, tr. Makoto Ueda 2003

Just Living: Poems and Prose by the Japanese Monk Tonna, ed. and tr. Steven D. Carter 2003

Han Feizi: Basic Writings, tr. Burton Watson 2003

Mozi: Basic Writings, tr. Burton Watson 2003

Xunzi: Basic Writings, tr. Burton Watson 2003

Zhuangzi: Basic Writings, tr. Burton Watson 2003

The Awakening of Faith, Attributed to Aśvaghosha, tr. Yoshito S. Hakeda, introduction by Ryuichi Abe 2005

The Tales of the Heike, tr. Burton Watson, ed. Haruo Shirane 2006

Tales of Moonlight and Rain, by Ueda Akinari, tr. with introduction by Anthony H. Chambers 2007

Traditional Japanese Literature: An Anthology, Beginnings to 1600, ed. Haruo Shirane 2007

The Philosophy of Qi, by Kaibara Ekken, tr. Mary Evelyn Tucker 2007

The Analects of Confucius, tr. Burton Watson 2007

The Art of War: Sun Zi's Military Methods, tr. Victor Mair 2007

One Hundred Poets, One Poem Each: A Translation of the Ogura Hyakunin Isshu, tr. Peter McMillan 2008

Zeami: Performance Notes, tr. Tom Hare 2008

Zongmi on Chan, tr. Jeffrey Lyle Broughton 2009

Scripture of the Lotus Blossom of the Fine Dharma, rev. ed., tr. Leon Hurvitz, preface and introduction by Stephen R. Teiser 2009

Mencius, tr. Irene Bloom, ed. with an introduction by Philip J. Ivanhoe 2009

Clouds Thick, Whereabouts Unknown: Poems by Zen Monks of China, Charles Egan 2010

The Mozi: A Complete Translation, tr. Ian Johnston 2010

The Huainanzi: A Guide to the Theory and Practice of Government in Early Han China, by Liu An, tr. John S. Major, Sarah A. Queen, Andrew Seth Meyer, and Harold D. Roth, with Michael Puett and Judson Murray 2010

The Demon at Agi Bridge and Other Japanese Tales, tr. Burton Watson, ed. with introduction by Haruo Shirane 2011

Haiku Before Haiku: From the Renga Masters to Bashō, tr. with introduction by Steven D. Carter 2011

The Columbia Anthology of Chinese Folk and Popular Literature, ed. Victor H. Mair and Mark Bender 2011

Tamil Love Poetry: The Five Hundred Short Poems of the Aiṅkuṟunūṟu, tr. and ed. Martha Ann Selby 2011

The Teachings of Master Wuzhu: Zen and Religion of No-Religion, by Wendi L. Adamek 2011

The Essential Huainanzi, by Liu An, tr. John S. Major, Sarah A. Queen, Andrew Seth Meyer, and Harold D. Roth 2012

The Dao of the Military: Liu An's Art of War, tr. Andrew Seth Meyer 2012

Unearthing the Changes: Recently Discovered Manuscripts of the Yi Jing (I Ching) *and Related Texts*, Edward L. Shaughnessy 2013

Record of Miraculous Events in Japan: The Nihon ryōiki, tr. Burton Watson 2013

The Complete Works of Zhuangzi, tr. Burton Watson 2013

Lust, Commerce, and Corruption: An Account of What I Have Seen and Heard, *by an Edo Samurai*, tr. and ed. Mark Teeuwen and Kate Wildman Nakai with Miyazaki Fumiko, Anne Walthall, and John Breen 2014

Exemplary Women of Early China: The Lienü zhuan *of Liu Xiang*, tr. Anne Behnke Kinney 2014

The Columbia Anthology of Yuan Drama, ed. C. T. Hsia, Wai-yee Li, and George Kao 2014

The Resurrected Skeleton: From Zhuangzi to Lu Xun, by Wilt L. Idema 2014

The Sarashina Diary: *A Woman's Life in Eleventh-Century Japan*, by Sugawara no Takasue no Musume, tr. with introduction by Sonja Arntzen and Itō Moriyuki 2014

The Kojiki: *An Account of Ancient Matters*, by Ō no Yasumaro, tr. Gustav Heldt 2014

GPSR Authorized Representative: Easy Access System Europe, Mustamäe tee 50, 10621 Tallinn, Estonia, gpsr.requests@easproject.com

www.ingramcontent.com/pod-product-compliance
Lightning Source LLC
Chambersburg PA
CBHW081139300726
48982CB00006B/1013

* 9 7 8 0 2 3 1 1 6 8 5 4 0 *